Michael Twaddle
2007

The Intellectual Life of the British Working Classes

The Intellectual Life of the British Working Classes

Jonathan Rose

Yale University Press New Haven and London

"A Conservative Canon: Cultural Lag in British Working-Class Reading Habits," from *Libraries and Culture* 33:1, pp. 98–104. Copyright © by the University of Texas Press. All rights reserved.
"Willingly to School: The Working-Class Response to Elementary Education in Britain, 1875–1918," from *Journal of British Studies*, 32–2, pp. 114–38, published by The University of Chicago Press. © 1993 by the North American Conference on British Studies. All rights reserved.

For information about this and other Yale University Press publications, please contact:
U.S. Office: sales.press@yaleup.edu   www.yale.edu/yup
Europe Office: sales@yaleup.co.uk   www.yaleup.co.uk

Set in Adobe Garamond and News Gothic by Northern Phototypesetting Co. Ltd, Bolton
Printed in Great Britain by St Edmundsbury Press Ltd, Suffolk

Library on Congress Cataloging-in-Publication Data
Rose, Jonathan, 1952–
    The intellectual life of the British working classes/Jonathan Rose.
        p. cm.
    Includes bibliographical references and index.
    ISBN 0–300–08886–8
        1 Working class—Books and reading—Great Britain—History. 2. Working class—Great Britain—Intellectual life. 3. Books and reading—Great Britain—History. 4. Great Britain—Intellectual life. I. Title.
    Z1039.L3 R67 2001
    028'.9'0941—dc21   00–068562

A catalogue record for this book is available from the British Library.

10   9   8   7   6   5   4   3   2

Published with assistance from the Annie Burr Lewis Fund.

Contents

Tables

Acknowledgements

A small army of librarians, archivists, and public record office workers assisted me with my research. Special thanks are due to John Burnett, who generously gave me access to his collection of unpublished working-class autobiographies at Brunel University Library; and to the British Library, the New York Public Library, and the London office of the Workers' Educational Association, where most of my research was done. I owe a similar debt of gratitude to Paul Thompson and his coworkers at the Sociology Department of the University of Essex. They conducted the massive oral history project on family, work, and community life before 1918, which is the basis of Thompson's book *The Edwardians* (1975). My Chapter Five sifts, analyzes, and quantifies the interviews they collected, though my conclusions are not necessarily theirs.

Bill Bell, John Burnett, Sondra Miley Cooney, Anne Humpherys, Gerhard Joseph, Robert L. Patten, John Rodden, and David Vincent all slogged through the manuscript, and their comments did much to improve it. I must thank all my friends in the Society for the History of Authorship, Reading and Publishing, who together provided an education in the social history of literature. The National Endowment for the Humanities, the American Philosophical Society, the British Institute of the United States, the American Historical Association, and Drew University provided the time and the money needed to complete this project. Earlier versions of sections of this book were published in the *Journal of the History of Ideas, Libraries and Culture*, the *Journal of British Studies, Albion*, and *Biblion*, and I am grateful to their editors for allowing me to rework that material in this volume.

Permission to quote or cite unpublished documents was generously granted by the Bishopsgate Institute, the BBC Written Archives Centre, the British Library, the British Library of Political and Economic Science, the Brunel University Library, the Buckinghamshire County Record Office, the University of Edinburgh Library, the County Record Office Huntingdon, the Imperial War Museum, Keele University, Elizabeth Kirtland, Terence A. Lockett, the University of London Library, the Marx Memorial Library (London), the Mitchell Library, the National Library of Scotland, the Labour History Archive and Study Centre at the National Museum of Labour History, the Newcastle Central Library, the

Newport Central Library, the Wilson Library at the University of North Carolina at Chapel Hill, the Oxford University Archives (Bodleian Library), the Rotherham Central Library Archives and Local Studies Section, the Ruskin College Library, the Sheffield Local Studies Library, the South Wales Miners' Library, the Southwark Local Studies Library, the Suffolk Record Office (Ipswich), and the Waltham Forest Local Studies Library. A few of my attempts to contact copyright holders were unsuccessful, so I take this opportunity to thank them, wherever they may be.

Most of all, I thank my wife Gayle—for everything. This book is for her.

A Preface to a History of Audiences

This book addresses a question which, until recently, was considered un-answerable. It proposes to enter the minds of ordinary readers in history, to discover what they read and how they read it. It is relatively easy to recover the reading experiences of professional intellectuals: authors, literary critics, professors, and clergymen extensively documented their responses to books. But what record do we have of "common readers," such as freedmen after the American Civil War, or immigrants in Australia, or the British working classes?

Not long ago David Perkins concluded that "for most times and places, we lack the sources, such as accounts of reading experiences, from which a history of reception could be written."[1] According to Jeffrey Richards, "It is pointless to ask for the first-hand accounts of ordinary people about how their reading or leisure has affected them. For such evidence cannot exist. The nature of popular culture and of its consumers provides no means of articulating such a conscious verbal response."[2] Historians, as Robert Darnton observed in 1980, "want to penetrate the mental world of ordinary persons as well as philosophers, but they keep running into the vast silence that has swallowed up most of mankind's thinking."[3]

Just six years later, however, Darnton had become more optimistic. "It should be possible to develop a history as well as a theory of reader response," he now suggested. "Possible, but not easy ...."[4] In fact, in the 1980s and 1990s, scholars in the emerging discipline of "book history" invented the research methods and tapped the archival resources that allowed them to penetrate this mystery.[5] Common readers disclosed their experiences in memoirs and diaries,[6] school records,[7] social surveys,[8] oral interviews,[9] library registers,[10] letters to newspaper editors (published or, more revealingly, unpublished),[11] fan mail,[12] and even in the proceedings of the Inquisition.[13]

Of these sources, the most useful are the autobiographies of ordinary people. Richard Altick well appreciated their value when he wrote the pioneering work in the field, *The English Common Reader*, back in 1957. He was handicapped by the fact few such memoirs were known to scholars at the time ("If only we had the autobiography of [a] pork butcher...!").[14] By 1981, however, David Vincent had assembled 142 memoirs by early nineteenth-century British workers, and in *Bread, Knowledge and Freedom* he showed how they could be used to reconstruct a detailed history of reading response.[15] In 1989 Vincent, together with John Burnett and David Mayall, completed *The Autobiography of the Working Class*, a bibliography listing nearly two thousand documents, published and unpublished, from nineteenth- and twentieth-century Britain.[16] My book, based as it is on a reading of most of those memoirs, would have been impossible without their groundwork.

Like any other historical source, autobiography contains certain inherent distortions and biases. Memoirists are not entirely representative of their class, whatever that class may be, if only because they are unusually articulate. Autobiographies were produced in every stratum of the British working classes, ranging down to tramps and petty criminals, but a disproportionate number were written by skilled workers. Women account for only about 5 percent of the memoirists born before 1870, rising to about 15 percent for the 1870–89 cohort and about 30 percent for the 1890–1929 cohort. Of course, some autobiographical manuscripts were bowdlerized or rejected by bourgeois publishers, but that is not so great a problem as one might suppose. The majority of these surviving memoirs are unpublished, or were self-published, or were published by local or radical presses. Agitators usually managed to record their lives in some form, with the result that our whole sample is actually skewed to the political left: the Burnett–Vincent–Mayall bibliography lists many more Communists than Conservatives.

As one washerwoman's son warned us, the autobiographer "may helplessly, perhaps even thoughtlessly, but more probably designedly, select, omit, minimize, exaggerate, in fact lie as wholeheartedly" as the novelist.[17] None of this disqualifies the memoir as a historical document: after all, similar uncertainties are built into everything we find in archives and published records. We can minimize those uncertainties if we use these sources with some awareness of their limitations, and if we check them against other kinds of documents. Historians have descended into archives to verify two classic proletarian memoirs (William Lovett's *Life and Struggles* [1876] and Flora Thompson's *Lark Rise* [1939]) and both proved reasonably (if not perfectly) accurate.[18] This book uses oral history, educational records, library records, sociological surveys, and opinion polls to confirm what memoirists tell us, and they usually (though not always) point to similar conclusions. They also make possible the double focus of this book: while autobiographies tell us a great deal about the vital minority of self-improving workers, other sources offer a more representative portrait of the working class as a whole.

The great strength of these memoirs is that they represent an effort by working people to write their own history. All historians must use data selectively, but here, in the first instance, within some limits, the working classes decided what to include. Tellingly, they wrote at length about their reading, as if they were pointing the way for future historians. An entire chapter on the subject is not unusual, and some autobiographies, such as Thomas Carter's *Memoirs of a*

Working Man (1845), are predominantly accounts of a lifetime of reading.[19] Robert Collyer (b. 1823), who rose to become a celebrated Unitarian minister, deliberately chose to dwell upon the moment when, as a child laborer in a Fewston linen factory, he bought his first book, *The History of Whittington and His Cat:*

> Does some reader say, Why should you touch this incident? And I answer, I have a library now of about three thousand volumes ...; but in that first purchase lay the spark of a fire which has not yet gone down to white ashes, the passion which grew with my growth to read all the books in the early years I could lay my hands on, and in this wise prepare me in some fashion for the work I must do in the ministry. ... I see myself in the far-away time and cottage reading, as I may truly say in my case, for dear life.[20]

Significantly, these memoirists devoted far more space to reading than later generations of labor historians. Though the "new social historians" of the past few decades have produced important and innovative work, they have harbored a prejudice against literary history, perhaps because it seems "elitist" and lacking in social scientific rigor. They have focused instead on the grittier or material aspects of working-class life—diet, housing, workplace culture, trade unionism, radical politics, crime, and family structure. All this has filled in large gaps in our knowledge, but it has left unwritten a critical chapter in the history of what were once called "the inarticulate masses"—who, it turns out, had a great deal to say.

Their reminiscences make possible a broader kind of reading history, which could be called a history of audiences. Put simply, a history of audiences reverses the traditional perspective of intellectual history, focusing on readers and students rather than authors and teachers. It first defines a mass audience, then determines its cultural diet, and describes the response of that audience not only to literature, but also to education, religion, art, and any other cultural activity. For reading is not limited to books. We also "read"—that is, we absorb, interpret, and respond to—classroom lessons, concerts, radio broadcasts, films, in fact all varieties of human experience. Broadly, an audience history asks how people read their culture, how they experienced education in the widest sense. This book tracks working-class responses to classic literature (Chapter One), informal education (Chapter Two), fiction and nonfiction (Chapter Three), dead authors (Chapter Four), primary education (Chapter Five), adult education (Chapter Eight), Marxism and Marxists (Chapter Nine), school stories (Chapter Ten), popular culture (Chapter Eleven), and the avant-garde (Chapter Thirteen). It uses social surveys to measure cultural literacy, the stock of knowledge acquired through reading, which in turn determines reading comprehension (Chapter Six); and it uses library records to quantify reading habits (Chapter Seven). It chronicles the first generation of common readers who became professional writers, ascending to careers in clerkdom and popular journalism, where they often encountered striking hostility and jealousy on the part of more affluent intellectuals, as illustrated in Chapter Twelve.

A history of audiences can of course address the impact of literature on political consciousness. The question of whether Dickens, Conrad, or penny dreadfuls reinforced or subverted patriarchy, imperialism, or class hierarchies has become an obsession in academic literature departments and cultural studies programs. Although literary criticism has been narrowed and impoverished by this fixation, the question is a legitimate one, and it is addressed (alongside other issues) in this book. The failure of political criticism, as it is actually practiced, is methodological: with some exceptions, it ignores actual readers.[21] In this terrain, critics repeatedly commit what might be called the receptive fallacy: they try to discern the messages a text transmits to an audience by examining the text rather than the audience. This blind spot is not easy to excuse or even explain, given that over the past two decades we have become used to the notion that readers make meaning: they may enjoy wide latitude in interpreting what they read. We can discover how an Edwardian housemaid read *Tess of the d'Urbervilles*, but only if we do some serious scholarly retooling.

That kind of history could cast a sharper light on provocative issues such as canon formation. Do the "great books" embody universal moral values, psychological insights, and aesthetic standards? Or, as Janice Radway (and a large cadre of contemporary cultural critics) would put it, is it "the dominant class who define and maintain the value of high culture"?[22] The second theory suggests that if the job of literary criticism were handed to readers farther down the social scale—say, colliers and millgirls—they would produce a different canon. But without a history of audiences, how do we know? What if the same books recommended by intellectual elites brought aesthetic joy, political emancipation, and philosophical excitement to these ordinary readers? If the dominant class defines high culture, then how do we explain the passionate pursuit of knowledge by proletarian autodidacts, not to mention the pervasive philistinism of the British aristocracy? A past president of the Modern Language Association, Barbara Herrnstein Smith (to take a representative of our own dominant cultural class) authoritatively states, as something too obvious to require any evidence, that classic literature is always irrelevant to people who have not received an orthodox Western education. It is an undeniable "fact that Homer, Dante, and Shakespeare do not figure significantly in the personal economies of these people, do not perform individual or social functions that gratify their interests, *do not have value for them.*" It is an equally self-evident "fact that other verbal artifacts (not necessarily 'works of literature' or even 'texts') and other objects and events (not necessarily 'works of art' or even artifacts) have performed and do perform for them the various functions that Homer, Dante, and Shakespeare perform for us."[23]

This theory has no visible means of support. If classic authors have no "transcultural or universal value," as Smith alleges, they would never be translated into other languages. And how can Smith explain Will Crooks, Labour MP? Growing up in extreme poverty in East London, Crooks spent 2d. on a secondhand *Iliad*, and was dazzled: "What a revelation it was to me! Pictures of romance and beauty I had never dreamed of suddenly opened up before my eyes. I was transported from the East End to an enchanted land. It was a rare luxury for a working lad like me just home from work to find myself suddenly among the heroes and nymphs of ancient Greece."[24]

Smith claims that we respond to a great book only because it tends to "*shape and create* the culture in which its value is produced and transmitted and, for that reason, to perpetuate the conditions of its own flourishing."[25] But how did the *Iliad* create the culture of the East End? Again and again we find classic literature embraced by working people who thoroughly lacked literary education. Though Smith dismisses the notion of "cultural deprivation" as mere condescension, it was painfully real to those who were denied her educational privileges. Bryan Forbes (b. 1926) grew up in a nearly bookless home: "I never saw my mother read a book until she was in her eighties when, like somebody coming off a starvation diet, she consumed three or four novels a week."[26] Nancy Sharman (b. 1925) recalled that her mother, a Southampton charwoman, had no time to read until during her last illness, at age fifty-four. Then she devoured the complete works of Shakespeare, and "mentioned pointedly to me that if anything should happen to her, she wished to donate the cornea of her eyes to enable some other unfortunate to read."[27] Margaret Perry (b. 1922) wrote of her mother, a Nottingham dressmaker: "The public library was her salvation. She read four or five books a week all her life but had no one to discuss them with. She had read all the classics several times over in her youth and again in later years, and the library had a job to keep her supplied with current publications. Married to a different man, she could have been an intelligent and interesting woman."[28]

One finds similar blind spots in the scholarly handling of popular culture. T. J. Jackson Lears takes a fairly typical approach to the subject when he analyzes a 1930 radio scenario: after a tired housewife tells her fatherly doctor her troubles, the program segues into a commercial, which assures women that a good night's sleep on a Beautyrest mattress will preserve their good looks and their husbands' affections. Lears then poses a leading question—"Consider the constructions of gender and power at work in this passage"—and answers it himself. A history of audiences, however, would first consider the questions that Lears (and most other practitioners of cultural studies) fail to ask. Even if this advertisement seems to endorse "female dependency" on male authority figures, how do we know that any listener consciously or subliminally absorbed that message? Assuming that women were paying attention when it was broadcast (a risky presumption), they might well have treated it as just another sales pitch. Possibly some listeners put a feminist construction on it: an overworked housewife may have concluded that, after years of sacrificing for her family, it was high time to purchase something for her own comfort. Or perhaps an immigrant learned that in America a doctor was not an unapproachable shaman, but a neighbor who could help him negotiate a strange culture. My point is that there is as much hard evidence for any of these readings as there is for Lears's, which is to say, none at all; and we will get no closer to answering these questions unless we shift our attention from the text to the audience. After all, why focus selectively on this particular advertisement, when others may have projected a very different image: for example, patriotic women performing men's jobs in the Second World War? In fact, why devote so much analysis to something that flashed by the audience in a few minutes? Of all the radio programs, books, magazines, newspaper articles, and school lessons that a Depression era housewife absorbed over a lifetime, how do we know which ones significantly shaped her attitudes and opinions?

Perhaps we should ask her. She may not be able to tell us the whole story, but we must begin with her. She might have left behind a document telling us which books and radio programs were important to her, and why. Lears claims that neither he nor other practitioners of cultural studies "would deny consumers a place alongside producers in the process of constructing cultural meanings," but most of them have failed to redirect their research toward those consumers.[29] Even historical studies that promise to tell us something about the "impact" and "influence" of the press usually do not focus directly on audience response.[30] When we do address those issues, we will discover what Roger Chartier calls "appropriation": the power of an audience to transform received messages and render them "less than totally efficacious and radically acculturating."[31]

This book describes how people at the bottom of the economic pyramid appropriated the Bible, *Jude the Obscure*, the *Girl's Own Paper*, Beethoven, the BBC, *Marines of Guadalcanal*, adult education courses, elementary school lessons, even the disciplinary thrashings administered by schoolmasters. All of these experiences required interpretation. In every case, the "reader" had to ask what sociologist Erving Goffman treated as the most basic question of human existence, the question we ask when we first become aware of an external universe, and continue to ask up to the moment of death: "What is it that's going on here?" How do we interpret not only books, but all the raw sensory data that is constantly showering on us? Goffman developed the useful concept of the "frame," meaning "the organization of experience," our ground rules for processing information, "the basic frameworks of understanding available in our society for making sense out of events."[32] The frame does for the human mind what a program does for a computer. It determines how we read a given text or situation: whether we treat *Alice's Adventures in Wonderland* as a bedtime story or a Freudian fable, *Finnegans Wake* as densely meaningful or gobbledygook, the morning newspaper as biased to the left or the right, Bible stories as truth, lies, or parables. Every political ideology, psychological theory, religious doctrine, scientific method, literary genre, and school of literary criticism is a distinct frame. Thus the frame is an essential tool for historians of reading: it explains why Robert Darnton was right to treat print, rather than economics, as the prime cause of the French Revolution.[33] To say that revolutions are caused by economic crises begs the question: in the mind of the politically active public, who or what causes such crises? The king? Aristocrats? Economic overregulation? Bankers? Capitalism?

The inevitable vissicitudes of the free market? An act of God? Foreign investors? Greedy workers? The Jews? Different frames will lead individuals to different "readings" of the situation, with radically different political results.

Goffman's approach can help resolve that long and increasingly sterile literary debate over whether meaning is inherent in the text or created by the reader. One might as well ask whether a computer printout is produced by the program or the data: obviously, it is a matter of one working on the other. Readers do play an active role in making meaning, but they cannot capriciously or randomly assign meanings to texts without destroying the usefulness of language as a communication tool. They generally follow certain rules of interpretation (frames), though these rules vary from reader to reader and from situation to situation. Readers can adopt any frame they choose, provided it produces some kind of meaningful reading, and provided the readers have learned the rules laid down by the frame. One cannot read *Pilgrim's Progress* as an allegory unless one knows what an allegory is.

Of course, an excellent way to learn the nature of allegory is to read Bunyan. Since every literary work frames reality in a particular way, we can build up a repertoire of interpretive strategies simply by reading widely. The authentic value of a liberal education lies not so much in acquiring facts or absorbing "eternal truths," but in discovering new ways to interpret the world. We read Homer and Shakespeare and Milton primarily to learn how they saw things, and thus to enhance our own powers of sight. That, fundamentally, is why autodidacts like Will Crooks pursued knowledge under difficulties. The British class system had always drawn a sharp distinction between workers and thinkers: it was the prerogative of the latter to interpret religion, economics, society, and literature for the former. The founders of the Labour Party and other self-educated radicals realized that no disenfranchised people could be emancipated unless they created an autonomous intellectual life. Working people would have to develop their own ways of framing the world, their own political goals, their own strategies for achieving those goals. Locked out of Christminster, Jude Fawley would chalk that political program on the college walls: "I have understanding as well as you; I am not inferior to you …" (Job 12:3).[34]

The whole canon of world literature—not just literature with an explicit political message—could help them develop those powers of understanding. In fact, when autodidacts were asked which books made all the difference to them, they usually pointed to the same canon of "great books" derided by contemporary critics such as Barbara Herrnstein Smith. They knew that Homer would liberate the workers. If the classics offered artistic excellence, psychological insights, and penetrating philosophy to the governing classes—if, in fact, this kind of education equipped them to rule—then the politics of equality must begin by redistributing this knowledge to the governed classes. Anyone growing up in an industrial or rural slum would be predisposed to take the existing social order for granted: the vision of a long-dead author could come as a salutary shock, creating new discontents and suggesting radical possibilities. The epiphany that struck Will Crooks is one of the most persistent themes of working-class autobiography.

As for noncanonical literature, by and large it did not perform the same function for proletarian readers. Joseph McAleer has documented working people who freely testified that they resorted to popular fiction as an escapist narcotic. "As the Cockney said: 'Getting drunk is the nearest way out of London,' so reading is the quickest way out of Glasgow," quipped a Scottish postman in 1944.[35] This is not to say that all romance novels, school stories, and tough-guy detective fiction were pernicious: some of them, as we will see, had a certain educational value for common readers. But they usually did not do what the *Iliad* did. To explain why, one would have to explain why some books enter the canon and some do not, an intimidatingly complicated question. Certainly, the tendency of popular fiction genres to follow stereotyped formulas limits their value: they cease to offer much after one has read a few volumes. Authors are far more likely to inspire generations of readers, disciples, critics, and commentators if they produce novel, distinctive, provocative, even subversive ways of interpreting reality. That is exactly what autodidacts, struggling to make sense of it all, found in Shakespeare, Bunyan, Defoe, Carlyle, Dickens, and Ruskin. They embraced Sir John Lubbock's "Hundred Best Books" list, that much ridiculed quick guide to the classics, because it offered a hundred ways of understanding the world, and a hundred plans for changing it. Probably more than a hundred: classics appeal to diverse populations of readers because they are usually capable of diverse readings. *Pilgrim's Progress*, as we will see, was not always read through the frame of religious allegory.

One alternative to this versatility is to view the world through a single tunnel: what in common usage is called "ideology." Putting it in Goffman's terms—terms consonant with Edward Shils's definition of the word[36]—an ideology is a particularly rigid frame. Of course, we cannot think without using some kind of frame, no more than a computer can work without a program. But we can be more or less flexible in our choice of strategies for determining truth, more or less willing to revise the frame in the light of new knowledge. We can (and most of us do) use a variety of frames in different situations: one in church, another in the laboratory, a third in an art gallery, a fourth in the polling booth, a fifth in courts of law, a sixth when we sit down with a novel. But we can also become stuck in a frame and judge everything by it, as in the old joke about the psychoanalyst who wonders what his doorman really meant when he said "Good morning." If we cleave to Marxism, feminism, Christianity, Islam, liberalism, the traditional British class structure, or any other intellectual system to the point where we can no longer step outside it and assume another frame, then we are in the cage of ideology.

Generations of liberal critics, from Matthew Arnold to Lionel Trilling, recognized that literature, by suggesting a wealth of alternative perspectives on the world, would inevitably subvert ideology. As Arnold phrased it, culture can liberate us from "system-makers and systems" by "turning a stream of fresh and free thought upon our stock notions and habits."[37] Today Arnold's vision is less than popular among academic literary critics, who (as a glance at the *MLA International Bibliography* will reveal) tend to see literature as freighted with ideological baggage that may insidiously indoctrinate the unsuspecting reader. This school of criticism tells us more about the preoccupations of critics than the experiences of common readers in history, which, frankly, Arnold understood much better. Far from reinscribing traditional ideologies, canonical literature tended to ignite insurrections in the minds of the workers, exactly as *Culture and Anarchy* predicted.

This book is a history of that revolution in thought, a revolution represented in the intellectual lives of Elizabeth Ashby and her descendants. She was a War-wickshire cottager's daughter, who lived her entire life within a sixteen-mile radius of the village of Tysoe. In 1859 she bore a son out of wedlock. Recovering from childbirth, she read the book that most people in her station started with—a vast family Bible. But no consistent ideology was communicated by Scripture: it was capable of multiple readings, even by the same reader. For Elizabeth Ashby, it could be a powerful tract for equality as well as a font of spiritual truth. When the vicar once made her take communion after a prosperous farmer's wife, she defiantly quoted at him "Thou shalt not even secretly favour persons" and "No respect of persons with God, no distinction between Jew and Greek; the same Lord is Lord of all that call upon Him." "It was the first time that in all the centuries of Tysoe's church's existence a woman's voice had been clearly raised in it to utter words of her own choosing, audible to many," wrote her granddaughter, a professional historian. On other occasions Elizabeth treated the Bible simply as a collection of wonderful yarns, reading Chronicles to her children as bedtime stories.

She later married and had two more children. When her husband died after five years, she relied on the charity of the parish for 6s. to 7s. a week. Even at that level of poverty, the family began to expand its range of reading. Her son Joseph learned some Shakespeare at a National School. Though he left school before his eleventh birthday to become a farm laborer, his mother still gave him a few shillings to buy books. In any town it was possible to find a bookstall in the market square, where old volumes could be had for pennies. In Banbury Joseph bought something by John Wesley for his mother, a geometry text, and a 1759 edition of Samuel Johnson's *Rasselas*. One could hardly avoid treating the Bible as absolute truth if one had read nothing else, but exposure to other books might set off a debate in the mind, each volume offering another perspective, opening up a limitless cycle of readings and questionings. Joseph and mother perhaps alluded to that open-endedness with a passage from *Rasselas* which they liked to quote: "There are many conclusions in which nothing is concluded."

By age nineteen Joseph had become a preacher for the Wesleyan Methodists: he was too eager for a broad range of secular knowledge to join the more anti-intellectual Primitive Methodists. Rigid dogmas were more attractive to those with deeper scars. One of Joseph's intellectual companions, an orphan raised in hard poverty, concentrated his reading more narrowly on increasingly radical schemes for political salvation. He began with Mill's *On Liberty*, turned to the progressive income tax Tom Paine proposed in *The Rights of Man*, then embraced the single tax of Henry George's *Progress and Poverty*. By the late 1940s he was a lockstep Stalinist, the sole village Marxist. Joseph remained the kind of liberal whose ideology amounted to a rejection of ideology. *On Liberty* "suited him down to the ground," his daughter recalled, "but there was nothing doctrinaire or monopolistic about that." The other villagers found their political vision not in Marx, but in the humane radicalism of Charles Dickens, who was probably the most popular author in the community.

The village children had to struggle with ponderous Victorian textbooks, and their reading was constantly interrupted by chores. Nevertheless, they managed to extract from these volumes something relevant to their individual lives. Joseph's daughter described it as a process of appropriation: "What they heard and read was brought so immediately into contact with events and with work" that they developed a remarkable knack "for discerning unsuspected aspects of a topic and expounding them in terms of their own."

In 1872 farm workers at the nearby village of Wellbourne went on strike, backed by Joseph Arch's union. Local laborers were sympathetic but never expected the stoppage to succeed: the *Banbury Guardian* was given over mainly to hostile letters from farmers and clergymen. But when the *Daily News* took up the issue, Tysoe laborers chipped in to buy it—this was their first exposure to a London paper. Working-class readers throughout the country were gradually shifting from the local to the national press, which could offer a dramatically different perspective on events. The *Daily News* coverage of the strike was not only far more balanced, it was placed in the context of national issues. Now the men of Tysoe saw themselves as part of a larger struggle to win the right to vote and organize trade unions. The range of discussion in village shops grew to embrace the entire range of politics, even *Progress and Poverty*.

For workingmen, the expanding culture of print opened up opportunities to write and act in the public sphere. Joseph Ashby contributed notes on village affairs and politics to newspapers in Leamington and Warwick. He became a Liberal Party agent and a travelling agitator for the Land Restoration League. The quest for education carried his son Arthur to Ruskin College, an educational center for workingmen, and ultimately to the directorship of the Agricultural Economics Research Institute at Oxford University. Women of Joseph's generation could not take advantage of the new ferment to the same extent. His daughter recalled that her mother

would never greatly develop her literary taste or any other intellectual quality, for it seemed her duty to be perpetually poised for swift service—to husband, child, animal, neighbour and the chapel. Her delicate senses and vivid emotions were under the severest control—no job too hard or dirty, once its necessity was seen; the most innocent tastes were permitted no indulgence; no strong feeling was allowed to break through her resignation to heaven, husband, and fate. And so, naturally, she passes into the background of her husband's and children's lives, not often to emerge.

Yet Joseph taught his wife to enjoy Walter Scott and George Eliot, and would not permit her to waste time with the *Girl's Own Paper*. He sincerely believed in the importance of education for the next generation of girls, according to his daughter, who became principal of the Hillcroft Residential College for Working Women.[38]

The roots of that autodidact culture go back as far as the late middle ages. It surged in the nineteenth century, particularly in Joseph Ashby's late Victorian generation, and crested with the Labour Party landslide of 1945, the climax of this history. Thereafter, the working-class movement for self-education swiftly declined, for a number of converging reasons. This is, then, a success story with a downbeat ending.

Chapter One **A Desire for Singularity**

Plenty of people will try to give the masses, as they call them, an intellectual food prepared and adapted in the way they think proper for the actual condition of the masses. The ordinary popular literature is an example of this way of working on the masses. Plenty of people will try to indoctrinate the masses with the set of ideas and judgments constituting the creed of their own profession or party. Our religious and political organisations give an example of this way of working on the masses. I condemn neither way; but culture works differently. It does not try to teach down to the level of inferior classes; it does not try to win them for this or that sect of its own, with ready-made judgments and watchwords. It seeks to do away with classes; to make the best that has been known and thought in the world current everywhere; to make all men live in an atmosphere of sweetness and light, where they may use ideas, as it uses them itself, freely,—nourished, and not bound by them.

This is the *social idea*; and the men of culture are the true apostles of equality. The great men of culture are those who have had a passion for diffusing, for making prevail, for carrying from one end of society to the other, the best knowledge, the best ideas of their time; who have laboured to divest knowledge of all that was harsh, uncouth, difficult, abstract, professional, exclusive; to humanise it, to make it efficient outside the clique of the cultivated and learned, yet still remaining the *best* knowledge and thought of the time, and a true source, therefore, of sweetness and light.[1]

—Matthew Arnold,
Culture and Anarchy

The masses, as they call them: Arnold sensed that the word erased personality. And he was right to suspect that individuals within that class were pursuing, in the face of intimidating obstacles, a liberal self-education much as Arnold would have understood the term. Their motives were various, but their primary objective was intellectual independence. For centuries autodidacts had struggled to assume direction of their own intellectual lives, to become individual agents in framing an understanding of the world. They resisted ideologies imposed from above in order to discover for themselves the word of God, standards of beauty, philosophical truth, the definition of a just society. There is nothing distinctively "bourgeois" in this desire for intellectual freedom. If anything, it may have been strongest in people who had spent their lives following orders and wanted to change that. More than a few members of the educated classes supported this movement, but many others treated it as a serious threat to their own social position—which, in an important sense, it was.

This may have been the most crucial arena of the class struggle, and it can be traced all the way back to the Lollards. The reaction against Lollardry was so intense because a vernacular Bible threatened to break a clerical monopoly on knowledge, and throw scriptural interpretation open to artisans. Men of this class dominated underground Lollard reading parties in the fifteenth and early sixteenth centuries, and they openly demanded a share of the "hidden buried treasure" hoarded in monastic libraries. Priests warned that they would be made redundant if, as one of them put it, "every lewde man is becomen a clerke and talkys in his termys." Then, complained Bishop Reginald Pecock, common readers "would fetch and learn their faith at the Bible of holy scripture, in a manner as it shall hap them to understand it." There was a clear and fearful recognition that a vernacular Bible would allow room for any number of individual interpretations of Scripture. Centuries before Jacques Derrida, Thomas à Kempis wrote in *The Imitation of Christ*: "The voice of books informs not all alike."[2]

Henry VIII would try to suppress Scripture reading before the Reformation, and even after the Bible had been legally published in English. A 1539 proclamation limited discussion and reading of Scripture to graduates of Oxford and Cambridge universities, and the 1543 Act for the Advancement of True Religion dictated that "No women nor artificers, 'prentices, journeymen, servingmen of the degrees of yeomen or under, husbandmen nor labourers" were permitted to read the English Bible. Thomas Cranmer proposed to confiscate heretical texts and prosecute Bible readers, and at least twenty people were burned for discussing heresy between 1539 and 1546.[3]

But artisans were soon entering spiritual debates from all points on the theological compass. Polemics were published by the orthodox Protestant weaver John Careless of Coventry, by the separatist Henry Hart, and on the Catholic side by the London hosier Miles Hogarde. The emergence of individualism in this period, writes J. W. Martin, has been found "in such varied manifestations of a slowly changing upper class sensibility as the rising interest in portrait painting, in mirrors, in sequences of love sonnets, in a greater provision for privacy in country house architecture." But the emergence of these artisan controversialists indicates that "There may be plebeian parallels also. It may be little more than a coincidence that this insistence on airing their personal religious views, differing as those views were, should appear at almost the same time in three Englishmen of the artisan class. But the coincidence still suggests that the century's growing interest in individual identity may be found on levels lower than where we have been accustomed to look."[4]

Henry Hart led a group of about sixty dissidents who believed that the educated class had misinterpreted Scripture, and were determined to read it for themselves. In East Anglia the carpenter Christopher Vitel was promoting a similar movement among itinerant weavers, basketmakers, musicians, and bottlemakers—the gospel of Familism as preached in the works of Hendrik Niclaes. Niclaes's *Terra Pacis* emphasized literacy as the road to salvation. His significantly-titled *A Publishing of the Peace Upon Earth* outlined a utopia based on intellectual liberty and free will. Niclaes, who felt the learned classes were arrogantly enforcing a literal reading of the Bible, looked instead to the untutored common reader (he was perhaps the only writer of the period who addressed them directly) and welcomed the new fashion for silent individual reading. That individualism particularly irked one of Vitel's opponents: he "could never lyke of any publicke doctrine which was taught but had always a desire for singularitye."

T. Wilson Hayes makes the point that elites feared the Familists not simply because they were heretical. More threatening than the content of their theology was the fact that they were discussing it outside of official channels, bypassing the clergy entirely. "The priests and lawyers who ran the royal bureaucracy ... were willing to tolerate dissent within the framework of established institutions where traditional rules of debate were observed," Hayes notes, "but they were not willing to give up the power those institutions wielded or to seriously alter their modes of operation." Monitored by the Privy Council, the Familists were singled out for suppression in a royal proclamation of 1580, which pointed out their real crime: the fact that "privy assemblies of divers simple unlearned people" were engaging in a "monstrous new kind of speech."[5] The Familists were, of course, a small sect, but when Margaret Spufford studied popular reading in post-Reformation England, she was "startled" to find that this style of plebeian disputation was becoming increasingly common: "the laity ... were far from being the docile material which their ministers no doubt desired." A Jesuit reported on a Puritan meeting in the late 1580s: "Each of them had his own Bible, and sedulously turned the pages and looked up the texts cited by the preachers, discussing the passages among themselves to see whether they had quoted them to the point, and accurately, and in harmony with their tenets. Also they would start arguing among themselves about the meaning of passages from the Scriptures—men, women, boys, girls, rustics, labourers and idiots .... "[6]

Did this provide the ideological kindling for the Puritan Revolution of the 1640s? There is no question that English Bibles and Testaments were reaching a mass audience: we estimate that more than a million of them were printed between 1534 and 1640. But in his study of the role of Scripture in the English Revolution, Christopher Hill ran up against the fact that "the Bible produced no agreed new political philosophy: it came to be used as a rag-bag of quotations which could justify whatever a given individual or group wanted to do." It could be a weapon against tyranny and economic inequality, and no revolutionary message was too extreme to be read into Scripture. If it was sinful to worship graven images, some radicals leapt from that premise to condemn equally the "idolatry" of wealth, the nobility, the king, Parliament, and even the Bible itself. Yet it was just as easily cited in defense of colonialism, war, the subjection of women, and religious intolerance. Sixteenth-century conservatives had correctly predicted that the publication of a vernacular Bible would be a subversive and equalitarian act, but not because Scripture was an unambiguously revolutionary text. The danger was that ordinary people would enter into theological debates once reserved for an elite. As Hill explains, the end of press censorship after 1640 released an explosion of pamphleteering, much of it produced by

> authors who were "illiterate" in the eyes of academics. They knew as little Latin or Greek as Shakespeare. So in the interregnum discussions there was no longer a shared background of classical scholarship; the rules of logic which structured academic controversy were ignored. University scholars treated the newcomers with contempt, and this in turn fuelled opposition to the universities as such. The whole classical curriculum and the conventions of academic argument were called into question. Indeed, were universities of any use at all?

Armed with the Bible, radical autodidacts like Gerrard Winstanley "could beat academics at their own games …. So in the forties uneducated men and women read back into the Bible themselves and their problems, and the problems of their communities, and found Biblical answers there, which they could discuss with others who shared the same problems." What they would not find therein was an authoritative consensus ideology. Thus, Hill concludes, after 1660 "the Bible ultimately contributed to pragmatism, lack of theory, the rise of empiricism." Most importantly, it left a legacy of intellectual freedom that extended to all literate people:

> The seeds of all heresies are to be found in the Bible, and most of them were cultivated and flowered during the Revolution. The glory of that Revolution, as Milton grasped, was the discussion, the ferment: truth may have more shapes than one—the principle of dissent, the contempt for established authority shown by those ordinary people who could not, in Bunyan's immortal phrase, with Pontius Pilate speak Hebrew, Greek and Latin. Failure to prevent continuing discussion by the middling and lower classes, to which the survival of dissent testified, was perhaps as important in preparing the intellectual climate for the Industrial Revolution as the political changes and liberation of the revolutionary decades.[7]

It is meaningless, then, to speak of the "ideological work" performed by Scripture or any other text. Texts do nothing by themselves. The work is performed by the reader, using the text as a tool. What is significant here is that the Bible alone offered plebeian readers enormous latitude for individual interpretation and social criticism, even when they had access to very few other texts. As the range of books and periodicals available to the laboring classes expanded over the next three centuries, the scope for interpretive freedom would increase apace.

Scottish Overture I

In the eighteenth century, autodidact culture flourished especially in Scotland, particularly among weavers. By then one of the highest literacy levels in the world had been attained in a belt across Lowlands Scotland and the far north of England. (Literacy was far lower in the Gaelic-speaking Highlands, in part because few books in Gaelic had been published.) And weavers as a class had long been legendary readers. Between 1580 and 1700 about half of the weavers in rural England had been literate; in London and Middlesex the proportion may have been two-thirds.[8] Scottish weavers accounted for 38.1 percent of the identifiable subscribers to Isaac Ambrose's *Prima Media* (1757), and 43.7 percent for a 1759 edition of Thomas Watson's *A Book of Practical Divinity*.[9]

In 1742 there was a well-documented explosion of religious revivalism at Cambuslang, with a revealing sociological profile. More than two out of three converts interviewed by William McCulloch, the Cambuslang pastor, were of the artisan class. Of them, half belonged to weaving families, and the majority of weaving-community converts were unmarried women. Although McCulloch's preaching began the revival, the clergy soon lost control to lay leaders, nearly all of them weavers, who urged converts to rely on their own individual interpretations of the Bible rather than the guidance of ministers. These converts often felt a sense of sin not because they were deviating from clerical orthodoxy, but because they had not done enough to read and speak for themselves: they expressed shame at their illiteracy, their lack of serious reading, their inability to voice their theological feelings in public. The Presbyterian clergy had closely monitored the theological views of their parishioners, enforcing orthodoxy through relentless preaching and catechizing. But, observes Ned Landsman, "even in such an environment ministers and hearers could come to hold ... sharply diverging views of the religious experience, and ... converts could create ... lay-centered understandings of conversion. The laity possessed a rather remarkable capacity to integrate seemingly disparate beliefs and actively forge their own understandings of the delivered message and create their own religious symbols."[10]

"There seems to have been a subtle association between weaving and Radicalism in Scotland," noted Clydeside militant David Kirkwood (b. 1872), citing his own great-grandfather as an example. "It may be that these men and women, weaving patterns of cloth, wove at the same time patterns of life. Or it may be that the work, although intricate, became automatic and allowed the mind to browse in the meadows of thought. Did not David Livingstone learn Latin from a text-book propped up in front of him as he wove the cloth?"[11] In all parts of the kingdom, weavers were legendary for their habit of reading at the loom. "For hours together I have done this, without making bad work," boasted Joseph Livesey (b. 1794). "The book was laid on the breast-beam, with a cord slipped on to keep the leaves from rising. Head, hands, and feet, all busy at the same time!" Livesey would be involved in no less than eight unsuccessful attempts to set up mechanics' institutes and reading rooms in Preston.[12] In the large factories of Aberdeen, weavers would discuss literature after work:

> The Wizard of Waverley had roused the world to wonders, and we wondered too. Byron was flinging around the terrible and beautiful [words?] of a distracted greatness. Moore was doing all he could for love-sick boys and girls,–yet they had never enough! Nearer and dearer to hearts like ours was the Ettrick Shepherd, then in his full tide of song and story; but nearer and dearer still than he, or any living songster—to us dearer—was our ill-fated fellow-craftsman, Tannahill, who had just then taken himself from a neglecting world. … Oh! how they did ring above the rattling of a hundred shuttles! Let me again proclaim the debt we owe those Song Spirits, as they walked in melody from loom to loom.[13]

The Statistical Account of Scotland, a sociological survey of the 1790s, found that communities of engaged plebeian readers were no longer limited to weavers:

> *Auchterderran, Fife*: In common with the rest of Scotland, the vulgar are, for their station, literate, perhaps, beyond all other nations. Puritanic and abstruse divinity come in for a sufficient share in their little stock of books; and it is perhaps peculiar to them, as a people, that they endeavour to form opinions, by reading, as well as by frequent conversation, on some very metaphysical points connected with religion, and on the deeper doctrines of Christianity. They likewise read, occasionally, a variety of other books unconnected with such subjects. … Although the parish consists wholly of the poorer ranks of society, newspapers are very generally read and attended to.[14]

> *Kirkpatrick-Juxta, Dumfries*: Several of the farmers read history, magazines and newspapers. The vulgar read almost nothing but books on religious subjects. Many of them are too fond of controversial divinity; a taste which the Dissenters are very diligent in promoting, and which the few books they are acquainted with, are rather calculated to confirm.[15]

> *Wigtown*: Servility of mind, the natural consequence of poverty and oppression, has lost much of its hold here. … An attention to publick affairs, a thing formerly unknown among the lower ranks, pretty generally prevails now. Not only the farmers, but many of the tradesmen, read the newspapers, and take an interest in the measures of government.[16]

In Dunscore, Dumfries a squire had set up a parish library for his tenants and neighboring farmers, with Robert Burns serving as librarian.[17] It was also observed that shepherds, in their isolation, were often great readers.[18] John Christie (b. 1712), the "literary shepherd" of Clackmannan, built up a library of about 370 volumes, including complete sets of the *Spectator*, *Tatler*, and *Rambler*.[19]

The Milkmaid's Iliad

Until the late nineteenth century, autodidact culture was an overwhelmingly male territory. Few working women would participate in adult education or commit their life stories to paper. The owner of a mid-Victorian London bookstall told Henry Mayhew that women only occasionally bought from him: "Sometimes an odd novel, in one volume, when it's cheap, such as *The Pilot*, or *The Spy*, or *The Farmer of Inglewood Forest*, or *The Monk*."[20]

Some feminist academics have argued that these women were practically silenced because nearly all the literature available to them was written by men and loaded with misogynist ideology. One critic has insisted that reading a traditional male literary canon may cause "grave psychic damage" and even "schizophrenia" among unsuspecting females, though she produced no evidence of anyone actually diagnosed with that disorder.[21] In fact, that canon seems to have had precisely the opposite effect. John Milton and Alexander Pope may well have been male supremacists, but Joseph Wittreich and Claudia Thomas have respectively shown that they nevertheless provided profoundly emancipating reading experiences for eighteenth-century women. In his translations of Homer, Pope directly addressed the female reader, inviting her into what had hitherto been an exclusively masculine cultural realm. Women made up 8 percent of the subscribers to his *Iliad* and 13 percent for his *Odyssey*, impressive proportions for the period, certainly large enough to disturb some male authors. In their *Homerides* (1715) Thomas Burnet and George Duckett warned that, thanks to Pope, "every Country Milkmaid may understand the *Iliad* as well as you or I." Claudia Thomas confirms that female poets of all classes—including milk-maid Ann Yearsley and nurseryman's daughter Mary Leapor—found Pope inspirational. He was no feminist, but his work was a useful foil to these women, who could appropriate it to their own purposes.[22]

Donna Landry likewise notes that the literary models for plebeian women poets of the eighteenth century were the standard male authors—Pope, Dryden, Virgil, Ovid, Homer, Milton, Swift, Thomson, Young, and Johnson. Yet they used these sources to produce "a far from servile discourse, … potentially more culturally critical in its implications than many later, more 'authentic,' working-class self-representations. … To take these plebeian poets at their word, acquaintance with the pleasures of high literary texts enables them to take pleasure in their own intellectual powers, representing a form of critical empowerment rather than cultural acquiescence." That kind of literature strengthened Ann Yearsley's resolve to resist the control of the woman who patronized her in every sense of the term, Hannah More. An evangelical author, More favored teaching the poor to read, but only to indoctrinate them in Christian morality and obedience: they were not to be taught to write. She tried to present Yearsley to the world as a simple untutored folk poet, but was repeatedly startled when the milkmaid drew on classical sources for her work. "How I stared!" More exclaimed, "besides the choice was so *professional*."[23] The emphasis is telling. As an amateur poet, Yearsley could be treated with condescension, but More saw that she was breaking into a literary sphere reserved for the educated class. The two women fell out over control of a trust fund, though for Yearsley it was an issue of intellectual as well as financial independence. "She tells everybody my envy of her makes me miserable, and that I cannot bear her superiority," More complained, while Yearsley protested that her patroness ruined her poetry with corrections and insulted her by consigning her to the role of a poor milkwoman: "You tax me with ingratitude, for why? You found me poor yet proud. ... You helped to place me in the public Eye; my success you think beyond my abilities, and purely arising from your protection. ... I cannot think it ingratitude to disown as obligation a proceeding which must render me and my children your poor dependents for ever."[24]

Yearsley was asserting the kind of artistic individualism that we have come to associate with the Romantic poets. She knew that Hannah More would treat that as a threat: "A fear of being singular, which claims/A fortitude of mind you ne'er could boast."[25] Plebeian poets of both sexes were confined by their betters to the ghetto of folk poetry.[26] (Lord Byron would direct withering ridicule toward the pretensions of shoemaker-poet Joseph Blacket.) Ann Yearsley would have encountered no difficulty if she had been content to remain a representative of the faceless masses, but she could only find her independent voice by mastering classical literature, which she appropriated as the collective property of all classes. With extraordinary nerve, she staked that claim in "Addressed to Ignorance, Occasioned by a Gentleman's desiring the Author never to assume a Knowledge of the Ancients." This poem, a high-wire burlesque, transforms the great Greeks and Romans into Hogarthian lowlife. Zeno and Socrates are starving Grub Street hacks, Lycurgus a thief to be hanged at Tyburn, Horace a streetsweeper, Penelope a sluttish tramp, Ajax a butcher, Clytemnestra a Billingsgate fishwife, while Helen sells laces and pins at Charing Cross. Yearsley's levelling message is uncompromising: this is my culture as well.

Here's Trojan, Athenian, Greek, Frenchman and I,
    Heav'n knows what I was long ago;
No matter, thus shielded, this age I defy,
    And the next cannot wound me, I know.[27]

Female autodidacts were held back not by the standard male authors, but by the scarcity of other female autodidacts as models. There were hardly any women in G. L. Craik's popular tract, *The Pursuit of Knowledge under Difficulties* (1830–31), though in 1847 he issued a companion volume trumpeting the achievements of self-educated women.[28] In 1842 Mary Ann Ashford, a London domestic servant, saw an advertisement for *Susan Hopley, or the Life of a Maid Servant*. She was intrigued, since she so rarely saw such women in print, except for the occasional newspaper crime story. "And," she added, "in penny tracts, now and then, a 'Mary Smith,' or 'Susan Jones,' is introduced, in the last stage of consumption, or some other lingering disease, of which they die, in a heavenly frame of mind, and are duly interred." Disappointingly, *Susan Hopley* turned out to be fiction, but at least it spurred Mary Ashford to publish her own life.[29]

As Ann Yearsley discovered, women as well as men looked askance at the female plebeian intellectual. For Janet Hamilton (b. 1795)—the Langloan weaver, poet, and essayist—self-education was an imperative for workingmen, but not quite so important for their wives:

> Education of the mind, when adapted to sex and circumstances, is both useful and becoming in a working-woman; and a well-informed and intelligent woman is a most interesting and pleasing object, but the seat of her strength is not in her head—it is in the heart. What would man be, what would the world be, were it not for the full fountains of true and tender love, sweet and holy affections, gushing sympathies, kindly feeling, and the warm and active charities which are ever overflowing from the cultured heart and affections of true womanhood?[30]

Ellen Johnston (b. 1830s), who achieved some fame around Glasgow as the "Factory Girl" poet, found that she was "courted for my conversation and company by the most intelligent of the factory workers, who talked to me about poets and poetry." That aroused suspicion from another quarter: "The girls around me did not understand, consequently they wondered, became jealous, and told falsehoods of me. ... I was a living martyr, and suffered all their insults."[31]

Knowledge and Power

The contest of wills between Ann Yearsley and Hannah More illustrates an enduring aspect of the class struggle in Britain. Educated people commonly (though by no means universally) found something profoundly menacing in the efforts of working people to educate themselves and write for themselves. As Arnold predicted, culture was a force for equality and was destructive of ideology, including the ideology supporting the British class structure. That hierarchy rested on the presumption that the lower orders lacked the moral and mental equipment necessary to play a governing role in society. By discrediting that assumption, autodidacts demolished justifications of privilege. That they presumed to write about their own lives provoked a Tory growl from John Gibson Lockhart of the *Quarterly Review* in 1826:

The classics of the *papier mâché* age of our drama have taken up the salutary belief that England expects every driveller to do his Memorabilia. Modern primer-makers must needs leave *confessions* behind them, as if they were so many Rousseaus. Our weakest mob-orators think it a hard case if they cannot spout to posterity. Cabin boys and drummers are busy with their commentaries *de bello Gallico*; the John Gilpins of "the nineteenth century" are the historians of their own *anabases*, and, thanks to the "march of intellect", we are already rich in the autobiography of pickpockets.[32]

During the Napoleonic Wars, Scottish cotton-spinner Charles Campbell (b. 1793) earned 8s. to 10s. a week, but set aside a few pennies for a subscription library, where he read history, travels, and the English classics. He joined a club of twelve men, mainly artisans and mechanics, who met weekly to discuss literary topics. He admitted that, without much education or guidance, they had to grope their way towards knowledge, "like way-fairers storm-steaded," yet one of their number went on to become a philosophy lecturer and editor of a medical journal. Their aim, however, was not to get on in the world, but the disinterested pursuit of knowledge:

The lover of learning, however straitened his circumstances, or rugged his condition, has yet a source of enjoyment within himself that the world never dreams of. … Perhaps he is solving a problem of Euclid, or soaring with Newton amidst the planetary world, and endeavouring to discover the nature and properties of that invisible attraction by which the Almighty mind has subjected inanimate matter to laws that resemble the operations of intelligence; or descending from the harmony of the spheres, he contemplates the principle of animal life, and explores the intricate labyrinths of physiological phenomena. … Pursuing the footsteps of Locke and of Reid, he traces the origin of his own ideas, feelings, and passions: or … he unbends the wing of his imagination, and solaces his weary mind in the delightful gardens of the classic muse [of] poetry and music.

These sentiments, it would seem, were the uncontroversial commonplaces of the late Scottish Enlightenment. The club barred any discussion of political and religious topics, and yet, "being the only thing of the kind that was ever instituted in the village, it experienced a good deal of opposition at its first outset." The fact that laboring men were engaged in cultural pursuits that involved no monetary reward provoked intense suspicion: "These honest people branded us with the designation of atheists, poets, and play-actors; and their officious gossiping was to me the sources of many a domestic lecture. No poor devil was ever more tortured, or persecuted, for his attachment to books than I was. Every cross accident—every misfortune, that chequered my early life, was ascribed to my love of books, and the influence of our club." Campbell grasped the nature of these fears when, as a sailor, he visited Jamaica and noted that the slaves were denied education by their masters: "A West Indian slave is every whit as rational a creature as a Scots peasant or mechanic, and tinged with less vulgarity. I have conversed with slaves who could reason on right and wrong with as much, and sometimes more good sense than some philosophers—slaves who were conscious of the birth-right of human nature, and eyed their own degradation with just but silent indignation."[33]

The stonemason-geologist Hugh Miller (b. 1802) encountered a more genteel expression of that hostility when he sought to publish his poems, and approached a clergyman who had some influence with the *Inverness Courier*. After waiting in an anteroom with the charity cases (the minister only received supplicants from the poorer classes between eleven and noon) he presented his verses. "Pretty well, I dare say," the clergyman granted. "You, however, use a word that is not English—'Thy winding *marge* along.' Marge!—What is marge?" Miller pointed out that the word was in Johnson's dictionary, and had been used by poets from Edmund Spenser to Henry Kirke White. Rattled, the minister professed no acquaintance with the editor of the *Courier* and ushered Miller out.[34] In 1812 radical tailor Francis Place learned the same lesson more painfully, when one of his oldest customers discovered that he had built up a personal library of 1,000 volumes:

> He expressed much surprize at the number of books, the fitting up, and the library table though there was nothing in the least expensive but it was all neat and in keeping. His remarks were sarcastic and he was evidently displeased. I waited upon him in a few days when some trifling omission being discovered, he told me, he supposed I was thinking more about my books, than about his orders.

The realization that his tailor had intellectual interests was intolerable to the gentleman, and his reaction was vindictive:

> He could not bear to think of me, my presence was excessively obnoxious to him, he took away his custom, and thus ridded himself of much of the annoyance, but he could not forget me his pride was hurt, and his meanness could only be satiated by doing me injury, and he took away some of the best customers I had. Other somewhat similar instances occurred as some of my customers learned from time to time, that I was a "bookish man", and had made acquaintance with other "bookish men". Had these persons been told that I had never read a book, that I was ignorant of every thing but my business, that

I sotted in a public house, they would not have made the least objection to me. I should have been a "fellow" beneath them, and they would have patronized me; but,–to accumulate books and to be supposed to know something of their contents, to seek for friends, too, among literary and scientific men, was putting myself on an equality with themselves, if not indeed assuming a superiority; was an abominable offence in a tailor, if not a crime, which deserved punishment, had it been known to all my customers in the few years from 1810 to 1817— that I had accumulated a considerable library in which I spent all the leisure time I could spare, ... half of them at the least would have left me, and these too by far the most valuable customers individually.

Years later, the scars from that incident produced an almost Freudian nightmare. Place dreamt

that I went along the passage to my library and into it, every thing was disarranged and there was no carpet on the floor, stooping down to pick up a book, I could not rise again, something pressed me down and kept my face near the floor. I soon ascertained that it was an immense hand which covered the back of my head and shoulders, the fingers spread over me and I endeavoured to grasp the thumb but could not move. The oppression was dreadful and I have no doubt that if it could continue for a few minutes I must die.[35]

It is sometimes argued that the working-class pursuit of education was an accommodation to middle-class values, a capitulation to bourgeois cultural hegemony. Actually, it represented the return of the repressed. "Knowledge is Power" may strike us as a naive Victorian slogan, but it was embraced passionately by generations of working-class radicals who were denied both. Artisan Christopher Thomson (b. 1799) wrote,

Let the horny-handed labourer, by inadvertence, drop the two short words "I think," and every "Jack in office," by virtue of his one step upward, is in a fever. Yes! he fears the contagion engendered by the march of intellect will kill his occupation. The tyrant whipper reminds the luckless wight who prates of thinking, "He has no right to think; let those think who are paid for thinking". ...

[So] he was forbidden to think! Why? Oh, the free exercise of thought would have taught him to scan the war-debt ... would have taught him to calculate taxes on food, and the blessings flowing from the rights of commerce, property taxes, pensions, high-priced legislation, the debasing system of place-making—to assert his right of citizenship—his duty to control the law-makers who contrive the statutes that are to feed or starve, reward or punish him— would have taught him self-dependence and moral elevation, instead of serfish cringing crumb-picking.

Economic inequality rested on inequality of education: hence, monopolies on knowledge had to be broken by any means necessary. Toward that end Thomson organized an artisans' library in Edwinstowe, set up an adult school for both sexes, and (he claimed) subscribed to every issue of the *Penny Magazine* from first to last.[36] If George Howell (b. 1833), the bricklayers' MP, was forever compiling long and difficult reading lists for workingmen, it was because he remembered that farmers and squires had tried to cut short his own early schooling: "What do the working classes want with education? They have only to work." Howell remembered that "The wealthier and employing classes thought that education would foment discontent," and took them at their word.[37]

Such attitudes survived well into the twentieth century. Jean Rennie (b. 1906), a Scottish kitchenmaid, recalled that her employer bristled when she confided that she had once aspired to attend a university and become a French teacher. When the lady was assured that these plans had come to nothing for lack of money, her smile returned. (Her son was equally stunned when Rennie, who had attended high school, spoke to him in fluent French and Latin.) "Not a word about my dreams of academic brilliance," Rennie recalled bitterly, "not a word about the sorrow of my mother, who struggled and saved to give me a chance— not a word about whether I'd wanted to do anything else. ... No, she'd got a cheap scullerymaid, and if my dreams were thrown in the dustbin, then it was the 'station in life to which–'." Once she protested to the cook, "I want a private life—I have a soul," only to meet the acidic response, "You are not allowed a private life, or soul, in service, and once you're in, you'll never get out." Ultimately she found some release in classical concerts and writing. Once she astonished herself when she entered a love story competition in a Scottish weekly and earned four guineas, but the pursuit of a literary career entailed risks for a servant: one employer gave her an uncomplimentary reference because she spent too much time "scribbling."[38]

Dorothy Burnham (b. 1915), who grew up in an overcrowded home ("circumstances that would have affronted the dignity of a guinea pig") and, after her family disintegrated, a Catholic hostel, found her private life in Keats, Tennyson, and Arnold:

> Communication between these poets and myself was instantaneous. I saw with delighted amazement that all poetry had been written specially for me. Although I spoke—in my back street urchin accents—of La Belly Dame Sans Murky, yet in Keats's chill little poem I seemed to sense some essence of the eternal ritual of romantic love. And Tennyson's "Morte D'Arthur" bowled me over. I read it again and again until I fairly lived in a world of "armies that clash by night" and stately weeping Queens. So the poets helped me escape the demands of communal living which now, at thirteen, were beginning to be intolerable to me.

As a servant girl she took an evening class in English and stood breathless before a Fragonard at Kenwood House, though employers hardly approved of her intellectual pursuits. When an older sister considered taking an evening class, her mistress immediately crushed the idea: "What! And what do the likes of you want with learning? As well teach a monkey to type as try to educate the lower orders!" Remarkably, Dorothy recalled, her sister related this incident with "an odd mixture of pride and a sort of defiant admiration as if she dared me to contradict Ma Arnold. *She* at least, her attitude seemed to say, had an employer who would not stand for any nonsense."[39]

As late as 1935 a Liverpool journalist reported that, according to letters from his readers, some employers were still trying to control their servants' reading—for example, banning newspapers with the wrong political slant.[40] This was never a universal practice: one could produce many counterexamples of employers who gave servants theater tickets and allowed them the run of their libraries.[41] But even the most liberal-minded could be nonplussed by a literary housemaid. Margaret Powell (b. 1907) once worked for an aristocratic couple in Chelsea, who were considerate and gracious in every other respect, until she asked the lady of the house

> if I could borrow a book from her library to read, and I can now see the surprised look on her face. She said, "Yes, of course, certainly you can, Margaret," adding "but I didn't know you read." They knew that you breathed and you slept and you worked, but they didn't know that you *read.* Such a thing was beyond comprehension. They thought that in your spare time you sat and gazed into space, or looked at *Peg's Paper* or the *Crimson Circle.* You could almost see them reporting you to their friends. "Margaret's a good cook, but unfortunately she reads. Books, you know."[42]

Having read *Remembrance of Things Past* three times through, she could be touchy on that point, especially when her allusions to Dickens and Conrad scared away boys.[43]

All this tends to support Marshall McLuhan's conclusion: "Print carries the individuating power of the phonetic alphabet much further than manuscript culture could ever do. Print is the technology of individualism."[44] Walter Ong contended that print accelerated the disintegration of feudalism when it "created the isolated thinker, the man with the book, and downgraded the network of personal loyalties which oral cultures favor as matrices of communication and as principles of social unity."[45] The benefits of print have been questioned by those who uphold the value of "rich oral traditions" (no one ever seems to have a poor oral tradition) but plebeian observers who witnessed that change had no doubt that it represented progress. Popular almanacs of the Stuart period commonly cited the invention of printing as one of the blessings of technology.[46] From Thomas Hardy of the London Corresponding Society (b. 1752)[47] to the first

Labour MPs, working-class agitators were acutely conscious of the power of print, because they saw it work. The political awakening of J. R. Clynes (b. 1869) came when three old blind men paid him 3d. a week to read the newspapers to them:

> Reading aloud was a new joy to me. Some of the articles I read from the local Oldham papers of the time must have been pretty poor stuff I suppose, but they went to my head like wine. ... Then I began to feel the power of words; that strange magic which can excite multitudes to glory, sacrifice or shame. As blindly as my blind hearers, I began to conceive that these words that I loved were more than pretty playthings: they were mighty levers whereby the power of the whole world could be more evenly and fairly distributed for the benefit of my kind.

If Clynes needed a second lesson in the subversive power of print, it came when his foreman nearly sacked him for sneaking a look at *Paradise Lost* during a work break at the mill.[48]

William Johnson (b. 1849) left school at age twelve, and then spent a lifetime pursuing further education via night classes and essay competitions sponsored by workingmen's clubs. The breadth of his studies was astonishing: geology, agriculture, chemistry, physiology, English history, political economy, the cooperative movement, literature, and a reading knowledge of French and German. When Johnson said "Knowledge is Power," he meant specifically the power to turn a fresh stream of ideas on our stock notions and habits: "This wide range of study and reading broadened my mind and gave me that capacity for looking at both sides of a question, which is invaluable to a man in public life."[49] His fellow MP Charles Duncan invested his spare cash in books, promoted the creation of public libraries, and urged workers to read the ancient classics, because otherwise they would be at the mercy of the educated classes: "The unread man has a narrow outlook, and easily goes astray; he is the sport of political tricksters and the tool for all knaves." Granted, some of their parliamentary colleagues, like collier Thomas Glover, asserted (somewhat defensively) that they had been educated by experience rather than books. But he too recognized the political imperative of an enlightened working class, if only because the capitalists' "main object has always been to keep the working man as much in the dark as they can."[50]

When Richard Hoggart extolled the unlettered "oral tradition," Robert Roberts pointed out that Edwardian autodidacts "showed impatience with the many stale saws and clichés that peppered working-class talk. ... These expressions, in fact, brilliant at birth, had been worn to vacuity through over-use and met condign ridicule from the more intelligent." After the First World War, Salford workers would become markedly less deferential, more articulate, readier to debate politics and question the existing order—and that ferment was directly linked to print:

Many more books, periodicals, newspapers were to be seen in ordinary homes. My mother recalled the plaint of our burial club collector. "Some of 'em are reading mad!" he grumbled. "They buy paper after paper, but won't pay the weekly penny these days, to bury their dead!" The *Daily Herald*, a powerful left-wing voice now, had reached a circulation of nearly 300,000. Certainly our two newsagents' shops, poor strugglers before the war, flourished now, dealing with printed words in a quantity and variety unprecedented; though let it be admitted that the racing novels of Nat Gould and the exploits of Sexton Blake and Nelson Lee stood easily first in popular taste.[51]

George Bourne, the Edwardian chronicler of country life, reminds us not to romanticize the oral culture that Sexton Blake superseded. Rural people were not idiots,

But the concentration of their faculties on their rural doings left them childish and inefficient in the use of their brains for other purposes. ... Fatalism is too respectable a name for that mere absence of speculative thought which was characteristic of the peasant kind of people I have known. The interest of their daily pursuits kept their minds busy upon matters obvious to the senses, while attention to opinions and ideas was discouraged.

For men and boys, there was not much to do in the evenings except stand around outside the pub "and try to be witty at one another's expense, or at the expense of any passers-by—especially of women—who might be considered safe game." Around 1900 Bourne helped organize a village "Entertainment Club," which offered fortnightly shows run entirely by working people. It carried on with great enthusiasm for a few years, but the performers quickly exhausted their folk repertoire. Then the club had to fall back on those members with some drawing room culture, and their piano recitals had an air of social superiority that drove away the audience.

I entertained a shadowy hope of finding amongst the illiterate villagers some fragment or other of primitive art. It is almost superfluous to say that nothing of the sort was found. My neighbours had no arts of their own. For any refreshment of that kind they were dependent on the crumbs that fell from the rich man's table, or on such cheap refuse as had come into the village from London music-halls or from the canteens at Aldershot. Street pianos in the neighbouring town supplied them with popular airs, which they reproduced— it may be judged with what amazing effect—on flute and accordion; but the repertory of songs was filled chiefly from the sources just mentioned. The young men—the shyest creatures in the country, and the most sensitive to ridicule— found safety in comic songs which ... dealt with somebody's misfortunes or discomforts, in a humorous, practical-joking spirit, and so came nearer, probably, to the expression of a genuine village sentiment than anything else that was done. But for all that they were an imported product. Instead of an indigenous folk-art, with its roots in the traditional village life, I found nothing but worthless forms of modern art which left the people's taste quite unfed.

"The breaking up of the traditional life of the village [has] failed to supply the [villager] either with the language or with the mental habits necessary for living successfully under the new conditions," Bourne argued. A literate laborer might read newspapers aloud to his fellows, but only with painful difficulty:

> He goes too slowly to get the sense; the end of a paragraph is too far off from the beginning of it; the thread of the argument is lost sight of. An allusion, a metaphor, a parenthesis, may easily make nonsense of the whole thing to a reader who has never heard of the subject alluded to, or of the images called up by the metaphor, and whose mind is unaccustomed to those actions of pausing circumspection which a parenthesis demands.

It was pointless to talk about preserving a traditional rural culture, because the rural laborer was no longer part of a self-sufficient economic or cultural community: "He is entangled in a network of economic forces as wide as the nation; and yet, to hold his own in this new environment, he has no new guidance. ... For making our modern arrangements a standard English language is so necessary that those who are unfamiliar with it can neither manage their own affairs efficiently nor take their proper share in the national life." For precisely that reason, some men were having their children teach them what they learned in school. "Certainly the old contempt for 'book-learning' is dying out," Bourne noted, and there was a growing realization of the need to understand political affairs. "Thanks to the cheap press"—even if it was the gutter press—"ideas and information about the whole world are finding their way into the cottages of the valley; and at the present stage it is not greatly important that the information is less trustworthy than it might be. The main thing is that the village mind should stretch itself, and look beyond the village; and this is certainly happening. The mere material of thought, the quantity of subjects in which curiosity may take an interest, is immeasurably greater than it was even twenty years ago." Coal-heavers could now be surprisingly knowledgeable about working conditions, wages, royalties, transport, and trade unionism in the mining industry.

> Shackleton and the South Pole are probably household words in most of the cottages; it may be taken for granted that the wonders of flying machines are eagerly watched; it must not be taken for granted at all that the villagers are ignorant about disease germs, and the causes of consumption, and the spreading of plague by rats. Long after the King's visit to India, ideas of Indian scenes will linger in the valley. ... The newspapers, besides giving information,

encourage an acceptance of non-parochial views. The reader of them is taken into the public confidence. Instead of a narrow village tradition, national opinions are at his disposal, and he is helped to see, as it were from the outside, the general aspect of questions which, but for the papers, he would only know by his individual experience from the inside. To give one illustration: the labourer out of work understands now more than his own particular misfortunes from that cause. He is discovering that unemployment is a world-wide evil, which spreads like an infectious disease, and may be treated accordingly. It is no small change to note, for in such ways, all unawares, the people fall into the momentous habit of thinking about abstract ideas which would have been beyond the range of their forefathers' intellectual power.

These issues had shaken the rural poor out of their fatalism, and mobilized them in the 1906 election. "Men who had never before in their lives tried to follow a logical argument began at last to store up in their memory reasons and figures in support of the fascinating doctrine [of tariff reform], and if they were puzzle-headed over it, they were not more so than their leaders."[52]

Literature and Dogma

Though autodidact culture was nurtured by the evangelical revival, it also presented a challenge to evangelical ideology. Many of the earliest working-class memoirs were published by evangelicals as conversion narratives, and as such were strictly orthodox, formulaic, and deferential: otherwise they would have hardly passed the editors. But autobiographies that were not written for publication, or were published by the author, reveal a real individual effort to grapple with political and religious controversies. The outcome of these mental struggles was, quite commonly, a critical attitude toward not only evangelicalism, but all received ideologies, including those of the militant left.

Joseph Mayett (b. 1783), a Buckinghamshire laborer, usually respected his betters, yet was not inclined to put up with obvious injustice, and he resented that he "was deprived of a liberal education." The son of a Methodist farm worker, he studied Bunyan's *Pilgrim's Progress* and *The Two Covenants*, but did not limit himself to religion. As a soldier in the Napoleonic Wars he had access to his captain's library, where he studied politics. He was a critical reader who recognized and struggled with the internal inconsistencies in Scripture. Proselytized by a follower of the mystic Joanna Southcott, he read some of his propaganda but "found Some things that did not Correspond with the bible and also that it was a trick to get money so I declined his religion and bid him adue." He was no less discerning about the tracts printed in the millions by evangelicals:

Their Contents were Chiefly to perswade poor people to be satisfied in their situation and not to murmur at the dispensations of providence for we had not so much punishment as our sins deserved and in fact there was but little else to be heard from the pulpit or the press and those kinds of books were often put into my hands in a dictatorial way in order to Convince me of my errors for instance there was [Hannah More's] the Shepherd of Salisbury Plain ... the Farmers fireside and the discontented Pendulum and many others which drove me almost into despair for I could see their design.

In that frame of mind, he was receptive to the radical anticlericalism of William Cobbett, T. J. Wooler, and Richard Carlile, given

the perplexities and trials I met with under oppression[,] the Sophistry and deceit of those who gloried in appearance and not in heart and the general Conduct of many who professed to be Christians. ... These books seemed to be founded upon Scripture and Condemned all the sins of oppression in all those that had supremacy over the lower order of people and when I Compared this with the preceptive part of the word of God I began to Conclude that most if not all professors of religion did it only for a Cloake to draw money out of the pockets of the Credulous in order to Spare their own and no wonder for I had experienced Something of this myself.

Mayett was on the brink of becoming an atheist or deist, but when one of his radical friends denounced Jesus as a fraud, he recoiled in shock and returned to his Bible. He hoped, like Bunyan, to find a conclusion to his spiritual pilgrimage, but he never completely worked out the contradictions of Christianity. What did remain was an unsectarian faith in education. When his fellow Methodists set up a Sunday school, he warned that their children would be better educated at the existing Anglican National School, but nevertheless supported the Methodist school by teaching there himself.[53]

Uriah Plant (b. 1786), a wheelwright's son, affirmed that "My uncertainty about the truth of religion not only increased my sense of its importance ... but gave me a habit of thinking, a love of reading, and a desire after knowledge." As an office boy and bookkeeper in Leicester he organized a discussion group devoted to religion and, over six years, spent "only" £21 10s. 9d. on books, mostly second-hand. He fearlessly read across the spectrum of theological opinion, including *The Age of Reason*, and opposed the suppression of antireligious literature. Later he joined the Wesleyan Methodists without completely accepting their dogma, noting that Wesley in "The Witness of the Spirit" was rather more liberal than some of his followers.[54]

At age thirteen John Clare was shown *The Seasons* by a Methodist weaver, and though he had no real experience of poetry, he was immediately enthralled by Thomson's evocation of spring. The weaver laughed and assured him that Wesley's hymns were far superior. "I said nothing but thought (whatever his religion might be) the taste of him and his friends was worth little notice. I have seen plenty of these fanatics to strengthen my first opinion, as some of them will not read a book that has not the words Lord and God in it." Clare came to loathe all ideological extremes: a pamphlet on the execution of Louis XVI destroyed any sympathy he might have had for the French Revolution.[55] For him the target of John Foxe's *Book of Martyrs* was not just Catholic persecutions, but every kind of religious fanaticism: "Tyranny & Cruelty appear to be the inseparable companions of Religious Power & the aphorism is not far from truth that says: 'All priests are the same.'"[56] Growing up in a village where he was sneered at for his bookish interests, literature became for Clare a means of affirming his individuality. "Self-identity is one of the finest principles in everybody's life & fills up the outline of honest truth in the decision of character," he proclaimed, "a person who denies himself must either be a madman or a coward."[57]

Opposition to secular literature ran wide and deep among Nonconformists and Anglican evangelicals in the first half of the nineteenth century, though the virulence varied among denominations. Those with predominantly working-class congregations, such as the Baptists and Primitive Methodists, tended to be the most hostile.[58] The mother of Joseph Wright, the millworker-philologist, did not learn to read until age forty-eight, and then apparently never ventured beyond the New Testament, *Pilgrim's Progress*, and a translation of Klopstock's *Messiah*. As a Primitive Methodist she considered the theater sinful: when her son brought home a volume of Shakespeare she literally threw it out of the house.[59]

On this much Mrs. Wright was entirely correct: literature posed a real threat to the more dogmatic varieties of Wesleyanism. Christopher Thomson was a "zealous" Methodist until he discovered Shakespeare, Milton, Sterne, and Dr. Johnson at a circulating library. When his absence from Sunday chapel was noticed

> I was called to account for it; by way of defence, I pleaded my desire for, and indulgence in, reading. This appeared rather to aggravate than serve my cause. It was evidently their opinion, that all books, except such as they deemed religious ones, ought not to be read by young men. I ventured somewhat timidly to hint, that it was possible for a young man to read novels, and other works of fiction, and still keep his mind free from irreligion and vice. ... The senior [class leader], with a sternness that reminded me of some of the bigots in those famous councils written in Foxe's *Book of Martyrs*, declared, that "if I did not at once, and unconditionally, renounce all books, except such as they should approve of, I was for ever lost!" At that sentence I paused, and wept; the iron mandate was driven into my soul, and after a long self-struggle, I renounced my connection with all bodies who would prescribe the free range of thought in matters of such vital importance. Although I lingered with them some time after, from the very moment of that unchristian sentence I belonged to myself and God.[60]

Circuit preacher Joseph Barker (b. 1806) found that theology simply could not compete with Shakespeare:

> What pleased me most was the simplicity and beauty of his style. He had always a meaning in what he said, and you could easily see his meaning. He never talked at random, or lost himself in a mist. I had at this time been so accustomed to meet with dull, mysterious, and unmeaning stuff in many religious books as they are called, that I felt quite delighted to read something that was rational, plain, stirring, and straightforward.

Shakespeare incited his appetite for poetry: Cowper, Pope, Dryden, Goldsmith, Thomson, Byron. Not only were they more interesting than the fifty volumes of Wesley's Christian Library: eventually Barker realized "that the reason why I could not understand them was, that there was nothing to be understood,—that the books were made up of words, and commonplace errors, and mystical and nonsensical expressions, and that there was no light or truth in them." When his superintendent searched his lodgings and found Shakespeare and Byron there, Barker was hauled before a disciplinary committee. "They talked to me about the danger of such books, and told me that *my* business was to be a Methodist preacher, and that I had nothing to do with any other books than those that would qualify me for teaching, inculcating, and defending Methodistical doctrines, and for exercising Methodistical discipline in the societies." Barker refused to back down, and in retrospect he admitted that he was already veering away from New Connexion Methodism. Byron had intoxicated him "with the freedom of his style of writing, with the fervour or passionateness of his feelings, and with the dark and terrible pictures which he seemed to take pleasure in painting." The general effect of reading Milton, Hobbes, Locke, and Newton had been

> to make me resolve to be free. I saw that it was impossible for the soul of man to answer the end for which it was created, while trammelled by human authority, or fettered with human creeds. I saw clearly that if I was to do justice to truth, to God, or to my own soul, I must break loose from all the creeds and laws of men's devising, and live in full and unrestricted liberty. And this I resolved to do. That measure of bondage in which I saw myself placed in the New Connexion began to be exceedingly irksome to me, and I felt strongly inclined to throw off the yoke and to assert my liberty.[61]

The special bugbear of early Victorian evangelicals, within and outside the established church, was the theater, if only because it threatened to draw away audiences. With alarming frankness, J. H. Pratt explained that "The sermon is the essence of dulness after a play: this shews the evil of the play-house."[62] Though one former ploughboy extolled Shakespeare for possessing "a deep sense of the pure morality of the Gospel," and quoted him on most of the 440 pages of his autobiography, he was anxious to insist that "Shakespeare can be far more appreciated and better understood in the closet, than in a public theatre." Surely, he added, the Bard would have agreed: his lines "The instruments of darkness … win us with honest trifles, to betray us in deepest consequence" clearly alluded to the seductions of the playhouse.[63] As a Lancashire weaver's son recalled, in the last decades of the nineteenth century some Methodist Sunday school teachers still asked their pupils to consider the condition of their souls if they died while attending a theater. It took some persuading to bring him to his first play, *Julius Caesar.* "Actors were considered no better than they ought to be," he explained. "A girl who left home to go on the stage was a girl who had gone to the bad. I dare say the poor quality of the stuff produced in the wretched local theatres and the types of performers who came to act there in those days were, in part, responsible for this poor opinion."[64]

These attitudes changed dramatically toward the end of the century, thanks to several influences. Undenominational Board schools proliferated after the Education Act of 1870. English literature became their most widely taught subject, especially after 1882, when readings from Shakespeare, Milton, Defoe, and other "standard authors" were mandated for the higher grades. In response, publishers churned out numerous school editions of Scott, Goldsmith, Cowper, Bacon, Pope, Byron, Lamb, and Gray.[65] Thomas Jones, born in the year of the Education Act, was brought up in a Welsh Nonconformist home where there were few books beyond a Bible, a hymnal, *The Christian Instructor,* and *Pilgrim's Progress* (all in Welsh), as well as the usual penny dreadfuls. Farell Lee Bevan's *Peep of Day* (759,000 copies in print by 1888) supplied him with the frame of a totalistic religious ideology:

> It was from these pages that I got my first ideas of the moral foundations of the universe, was handed the first key with which to unlock the mysteries of the world in which I found myself. These little books served the purpose of an index or filing system; a framework of iron dogma, if you like, providing an orderly arrangement of the world and its history for the young mind, under two main categories, Good and Evil.

But Jones also attended a Board school, where he found "salvation" in an old cupboard of books presented by the local MP. They were mainly volumes of voyages and natural history, "which took a Rhymney boy away into the realms of wonder over the seas to the Malay Archipelago, to Abyssinia, to the sources of the Nile and the Albert Nyanza, to the curiosities of natural history, piloted by James Bruce, Samuel Baker, and Frank Buckland." His father blamed the Board schools for undermining children's respect for their elders, and of course he was right. While he read little but the Bible and religious periodicals, his son was soon working his way through the Rhymney Workmen's Institute Library and Cassell's National Library of 3d. paperbacks. Macaulay's essays, Goldsmith's *History of*

England, Far From the Madding Crowd, Self-Help, Josephus, Plutarch, Shakespeare, Pepys, Johnson's *Lives of the Poets,* and *The Sorrows of Young Werther* were among the books Jones read, often on his employer's time. (He hid them under the ledger at the Rhymney Iron Works, where he worked a thirteen-hour day as a timekeeper for 9s. a week.)[66]

Whatever their attitudes toward Goethe, all Nonconformist sects encouraged the habits of close reading, interpretive analysis, and intellectual self-improvement. Those talents, exercised on Scripture and sermons, could be carried over to any kind of secular literature. The Primitive Methodists may have been the most anti-intellectual of the Wesleyans, yet miners' MP John Johnson (b. 1850) "found their teaching the strongest possible incentive to trying to improve myself, not only morally, but mentally, and towards the latter end I took to serious and systematic study." He read deeply in history and philosophy, as well as such this-worldly tracts as *The Wealth of Nations,* John Stuart Mill's *Principles of Political Economy,* and Alfred Marshall's *Principles of Economics.*[67]

The Labour Party was founded by such half-lapsed Methodists. As Beatrice Webb wrote, a major impetus behind the late Victorian socialist revival was "the flight of emotion away from the service of God to the service of man." In the same generation there was a parallel shift among Nonconformist readers, a transference of reverence from the Good Book to the Great Books. From 1886 William Robertson Nicoll, a Free Church minister, recommended classic and contemporary authors in the columns of the *British Weekly,* reassuring his vast audience (circulation 100,000+) that there was no necessary conflict between proper piety and belles-lettres. "I thought that much more might be done in the way of uniting religion with literature," he wrote, "believing that Nonconformists had too long behaved as exiles from the world of culture."[68] Another popular paper, *Great Thoughts* (founded 1884), made the same impression on Edwin Muir while he was working as a Glasgow clerk:

> It was filled with a high but vague nonconformity, and tried to combine the ideals of revivalist Christianity and great literature. There were articles on "aspects" of Ruskin, Carlyle, Browning, and other uplifting Victorians, and a great number of quotations, mainly "thoughts," from their works and the writings of Marcus Aurelius and Epictetus. For some time this paper coloured my attitude to literature; I acquired a passion for "thoughts" and "thinkers," and demanded from literature a moral inspiration which would improve my character: there were many "thoughts" bearing on character, particularly in its aspect of "self-culture," in which the reader was encouraged to strike a balance between the precepts of Christ and Samuel Smiles.[69]

Emblematic of the change was the President of the Methodist Conference, Richard Pyke (b. 1879). He remembered only a handful of books in his parents' home in rural Devon: the family Bible, *Pilgrim's Progress,* Baxter's *Saints'*

Everlasting Rest, Jessica's First Prayer, A Peep Behind the Scenes, and Foxe's *Book of Martyrs*. His theological training at Shebbear College was "slender and inadequate," but there he studied with an inspiring and progressive headmaster, Thomas Ruddle: "While the custodians of the true faith spoke of evolution as 'the gospel of dirt', he would exalt Darwin almost to the level of a Hebrew prophet." As a circuit preacher Pyke introduced farm people to Milton, Carlyle, Ruskin, and Tolstoy. His own reading ranged from Shakespeare and Boswell to Shelley's poems and George Henry Lewes's *History of Philosophy*. He was even prepared to acknowledge the "genius" of *Jude the Obscure*, though he would have preferred a happy ending.[70]

Over the course of the nineteenth century, a similar transformation had worked itself out at the other end of the ideological spectrum. In his investigation of early radical periodicals, Paul Thomas Murphy found that they scarcely mentioned *Pilgrim's Progress* or *Robinson Crusoe*, which probably had more working-class readers than any book except the Bible. Regarding literature, radical editors like William Cobbett and Richard Carlile were as blinkered as the most philistine Methodist. They too "feared the imaginative in literature and especially in fiction. By these standards a work that was personally liberating for many could be seen as socially dangerous and hardly 'useful'." Carlile might publish Byron and Shelley, but for their politics, not their poetry. He dismissed Walter Scott as Tory propaganda, while Cobbett discounted Shakespeare, Milton, and Johnson. The Co-operative journals of the 1820s and 1830s likewise avoided imaginative literature in favor of fables and didactic verse, though they would publish excerpts from great authors if they had some political relevance.[71]

Evangelicals, utilitarians, and radical journalists of the early nineteenth century equally distrusted literature, and for much the same reason. Each of these sects was trying to convert the masses to their own ideology, and struggling to control the flow of information to the working classes. Their audience, however, was increasingly distracted by the growing availability of imaginative literature, which could not be contained in any ideological system. In Carlile's case the ideology was atheism (he did more than anyone to popularize Paine through the publication of cheap editions) and his approach to education was dismally utilitarian. He insisted that schools teach only science—not dead languages, history, or anything "metaphysical." He denounced poetry and drama (*Macbeth*, for example) as unrealistic and amoral, favored the suppression of carnivals, and generally loathed the hard-drinking "nonrespectable" poor. Because most literate working people had broader tastes in books and beer, he dismissed them as "human cattle," save only a few enlightened souls who shared his opinions. Ultimately, Carlile descended into what a sympathetic biographer called "messianic gibberish."[72] He would not be the last crusader on the left to end in that particular cul-de-sac.

Thomas Wooler was different, however. His *Black Dwarf,* a popular radical periodical, reviewed Edmund Kean's *Othello* and Philip Massinger's *A New Way to Pay Old Debts*, though they contained no apparent political message. Wooler's own writings drew heavily on Pope for inspiration, and he published extracts from great authors following no consistent ideological pattern—Aristotle, Erasmus, Machiavelli, Thomas More, Holinshed, Shakespeare, Bacon, Marvell, Milton, Locke, Pope, Cowper, Goldsmith, Swift, Lord Chesterfield, Johnson, Sterne, Franklin, Burns, Hazlitt, Coleridge, Byron. Wooler was able to recognize the autonomous worth of literature because he was less interested in lecturing his readers and more willing to allow them to find their own salvation. He appreciated that literature was a means of expanding human freedom, and that freedom was intrinsically valuable: "By excursions into the fields of Anecdote and Poetry ... we hope to produce some proof, that a sense of Liberty is not a thing begotten on the poverty of yesterday, by yesterday's oppression; that Liberty is not the trimming shifting ignis-fatuus, which the servile world would have us believe, but a real entity, unchangeable, eternal, and one of the chief blessings of social existence."[73]

Some of the Chartist papers that flourished in the late 1830s and 1840s explicitly subordinated literature to politics. The *Labourer* proclaimed that it "had one great goal before our eyes—the redemption of the Working classes from their thraldom—and to this object we have made the purpose of each article subservient. ... We have placed poetry and romance side by side with politics and history."[74] But this resistance to imaginative literature was beginning to weaken. By now established critics, who had once disdained the novel, were coming around to recognizing it as a legitimate art form, and radical journalists followed suit. Dickens was difficult to ignore: not only was he a genius and spectacularly popular, but he also called attention to the same social issues that the Chartists had raised. Moreover, though radical journals were now more free to publish, they were also in danger of losing their audience if they remained dryly political. Cobbett's 2d. *Political Register* could sell as many as 200,000 copies in 1816, in part because he had few competitors for working-class readers. In contrast, the average annual circulation of the Chartist *Northern Star* peaked at 36,000 in 1839; it usually sold half that number or less.[75] The proliferation of cheap mass circulation general interest periodicals, starting with *Chambers's Edinburgh Journal* and the *Penny Magazine* in 1832, forced the Chartist papers to leaven their editorial mix with imaginative literature. The *Northern Star* published Captain Marryat, Fenimore Cooper, and Charlotte Brontë. W. J. Linton's *National* excerpted Chaucer, Shelley, Keats, Spenser, Confucius, Robert Herrick, Izaak Walton, Socrates, and Milton. Some Chartist reviewers tried to introduce their readers to an international selection of writers—George Sand, Eugène Sue, Victor Hugo, Whittier, and Pushkin. And one could argue (as the *Chartist Circular* did in 1840) that Homer, Aesop, Socrates, Shakespeare, Milton, Defoe, and Dr. Johnson were all sons of the proletariat.

Meanwhile, "Knowledge Chartists" such as William Lovett made intellectual freedom their first political priority, calling for adult education programs and public libraries governed by the workers themselves.[76] Though Lovett had once been attracted to Robert Owen's materialist socialism, he came to question what human beings may become when the *individualism* in their nature is checked by education, and endeavoured to be crushed out of them by the mandate of a majority—and, it may be, that majority not always a reasonable and enlightened one. ... What even may become of the best portion of man's nature (of his industrial, skilful, persevering, saving energies), when some aspiring, hopeful individual, resolving to labour and to save while youth and vigour favour him, in hopes of realizing leisure and independence, or to procure some cherished object of his heart, is constrained to abandon his resolution, to conform to the routine of the majority, and to make their aspirations the standard of his own? Of what advantage the splendour and enjoyment of all art and nature *if man has no choice of enjoyment?* And what to him would be spacious halls, and luxurious apartments, and all the promised blessings of a community, if he must rise, work, dress, occupy, and enjoy, not as he himself desires, *but as the fiat of the majority wills it?* Surely the poorest labourer, bowed down with toil and poverty, would have reason to bless the *individualism* that gave him some freedom of choice, and a chance of improving his lot, compared with a fellowship that so bound him in bondage.[77]

All that contributed to a growing sense within the Chartist movement that literature was compatible with and necessary to political liberation. As Julian Harney put it in the *Red Republican*, the workers needed the "Charter and something more."[78] The propaganda of Robert Owen alone did not convert printer Thomas Frost (b. c. 1821) to socialism: "The poetry of Coleridge and Shelley was stirring within me, and making me 'a Chartist, and something more.'"[79] Frost had been an omnivorous reader since childhood, when he read his grandmother's volumes of the *Spectator* and *The Persian Letters*. Most subversive of all were the letters of the second Lord Lyttelton: "The attraction which this book had for me consisted, I believe, in the tinge of scepticism to be found in several of the letters, and in the metaphysical questions argued, lightly and cleverly, in others. I was beginning to assert for myself freedom of thought, and to rebel against custom and convention; and there was naturally much in common between the writer and the reader."[80]

Similarly indiscriminate reading brought the same kind of liberation to Chartist Robert Lowery (b. 1809). A prolonged illness gave him the opportunity to work through a bookseller's entire circulating library, and much else besides. Most autodidacts shared his habit of devouring any book that came to hand, and this indiscipline made it the best method of liberal education. Where a prescribed reading list might have reflected the biases of the compiler, improvisational reading offered him a broad "general knowledge of history, ... poetry and imaginative literature." The very fact that "I read without any order or method" forced his mind to exercise "a ready power of arranging the information this desultory reading presented." It inspired him to write poetry and fiction. After seeing his first play, *As You Like It*, he even attempted a drama, "a very long one about some romantic adventure of some Highlanders in Spain during the middle ages." Though he went nowhere as a creative writer, he did learn to frame the world in his own terms: "I would take a passage or an idea suggested from some author and endeavour to enlarge upon it. I found this enabled me to trace ideas in their connections, gave me a wider view of subjects, and a facility of expression in writing."

That exercised imagination left Lowery skeptical of all ideological systems. Though not unsympathetic to Owenite socialism, he was alienated by Owen's environmental determinism and his grandiose promises of human perfectibility. Lowery could also see the limits of another ideology—temperance. He agitated against pubs, yet was willing to tell the readers of a Quaker temperance weekly that the vital autodidact culture of early nineteenth-century Newcastle had been based largely in taverns, a symposium in the original sense of the term:

> A fondness for company, and a passion for speculative inquiry and discussion, prevailed along with much intemperance. Thus, while the intelligence of the people was strong and they had their literary and philosophical institutions and a number of public libraries, and every week public lectures on various subjects, the old tavern system still prevailed. All classes met there to compare notes and to hear individual remarks and criticisms on what occupied public attention. ... Every branch of knowledge had its public-house where its disciples met. ... There was a house where the singers and musicians met—a house where the speculative and free thinking met—a house where the literate met—a house where the artists and painters met—also one where those who were men of science met.[81]

One finds a strikingly modern taste for many-sidedness in the shoemaker-poet Thomas Cooper (b. 1805). He veered away from the Primitive Methodists when they condemned his love of secular literature.[82] As a Chartist he worshipped Homer, Shakespeare, Swift, and Dickens for reasons that transcended any particular dogma. "The power of fiction to instruct, the sources of the charm it exercises over the human mind," he wrote, cannot be explained by any one-dimensional political, utilitarian, or scientific calculus. "Perhaps, the secret of the charm of fictitious writing lies in the fact that it appeals to *all* the powers of the mind"—imagination, memory, reason, morality. A great book is defined as a book that astonishes the reader on many levels:

> What matchless beauty, what deep truth, what life-like pictures of humanity, what opulence of moral, in that transcendent *Iliad*—and yet it enthrones the bad passion for war; and if one anecdote be credible, that Alexander read it every day, and slept with it under his pillow by night—we owe the record of his ambitions, his ravages, and slaughterous conquests, to his reading of Homer! I do not mention this to induce any one to commit so great a folly as

to throw Homer away: if he will do so, be it remembered that he must throw the older part of another old book after it, as even more pernicious—because it teaches war and slaughter under still higher sanctions.[83]

As a Manchester warehouse porter, Samuel Bamford (b. 1788) found the same richness in Milton: "His 'L'Allegro' and 'Il Penseroso' were but the expressions of thoughts and feelings which my romantic imagination had not unfrequently led me to indulge, but which, until now, I had deemed beyond all human utterance." In "Il Penseroso" the provocative ambiguities in the line "Call him up that left half told"

set my imaginative curiosity to work—What him? who was "him"? when did he live? where did he reside? and how happened it that he "left half told/The story of Cambuscan bold"? What a strangely interesting subject for thoughtful conjecture was his "story half told," with its Cambuscan, and Algarsife, and Canace, who, whether or not she was ever wived at all, was a mystery impenetrable to me.

There was a direct connection between that reading experience and Bamford's subsequent turn to radical agitation, and not because he had read any overtly political message into "Il Penseroso." Milton established a habit of serious reading, which brought Bamford to Homer, Virgil, Shakespeare, the great poets, classic histories and voyages, and, ultimately, William Cobbett's *Political Register*. More importantly, "Il Penseroso" taught Bamford to ask questions and voice his thoughts—a revolutionary transformation. Of all poets, "none has so fully spoken out the whole feelings of my heart—the whole scope of my imaginings," and that, Bamford concluded, is what made Milton so "fascinating and dangerous."[84]

Conservative Authors and Radical Readers

Even literature that appeared to be safely conservative was potentially explosive in the minds of readers. This may seem counterintuitive: in the recent "canon wars," the Left and Right agreed that a traditional canon of books would reinforce conservative values (the Right arguing that this was a good thing). But both sides in this debate made the mistake of believing each other's propaganda. Contrary to all the intentions of the authors, classic conservative texts could make plebeian readers militant and articulate. Rooted in the New York Jewish autodidact culture, Irving Howe gratefully acknowledged his debts to Edmund Burke, whose oratory was equally inspirational to Edward Milne (b. 1915), an ILP[85] organizer and an unsuccessful applicant for conscientious objector status during the Second World War. In his later parliamentary career Milne particularly liked to quote *Thoughts on the Present Discontents*: "A strenuous resistance to every appearance of lawless power; a spirit of independence carried to some degree of enthusiasm; an inquisitive character to discover, and a bold one to display, every corruption and every error of government; these are the qualities which recommend a man to a seat in the House of Commons."[86]

The most famous example of a menial laborer emancipated by an arrogantly elitist author was Catherine McMullen (b. 1906), the daughter of a washerwoman who had served time in a workhouse. In 1926 she was herself a workhouse laundress, struggling to improve her mind by reading *T. P. and Cassell's Weekly*. The magazine was full of literary gossip that made her aspire to be a writer, but she had no idea which books to read until she came across Elinor Glyn's *The Career of Catherine Bush*. In this story of a romance between a duke and a secretary, the secretary is advised to read the *Letters of Lord Chesterfield to His Son*. Catherine McMullen then visited a public library for the first time in her life and borrowed the book: "And here began my education. With Lord Chesterfield I read my first mythology. I learned my first real history and geography. With Lord Chesterfield I went travelling the world. I would fall asleep reading the letters and awake around three o'clock in the morning my mind deep in the fascination of this new world, where people conversed, not just talked. Where the brilliance of words made your heart beat faster. ... Lord Chesterfield became very real to me": after all, his letters were addressed to a boy who, like Catherine, had been born illegitimate. He launched her into a lifetime course of reading, beginning with Chaucer in Middle English, moving on to Erasmus, Donne, *The Decline and Fall of the Roman Empire*, and even *Finnegans Wake*. Ultimately, as Catherine Cookson, she became one of the best-selling authors of all time, producing more than ninety novels with total sales of more than 100 million copies, at one point responsible for one-third of all the books loaned by Britain's public libraries. "Dear, dear, Lord Chesterfield," she sighed. "Snob or not I owe him so much."[87]

Radical papers of the early nineteenth century had often assailed Walter Scott's conservatism, but their readers did not necessarily concur. In 1832 a writer in the Edinburgh *Schoolmaster* ventured that Scott could be read as an anti-Tory, whose lower-class characters were more attractive than his aristocrats. One scholar of Chartist journals finds this reading "incredibly far-fetched,"[88] yet Ramsay MacDonald claimed that the Waverley novels "opened out the great world of national life for me and led me on to politics."[89] For one grocer's boy (b. 1860), Scott's works (in the 3d. Dicks editions) were studies in social history, and he came away feeling that Rebecca, not Rowena, was the right girl for Ivanhoe.[90] Socialist agitator Walter Hampson (b. c. 1866) agreed: he suggested that Scott used Rebecca to voice a satire on chivalry, no less devastating than Sancho Panza's.[91] T. A. Jackson (b. 1879), the most brilliant proletarian intellectual to come out of the British Communist Party, did not dispute that Scott "was a shocking old Tory, and a reactionary," but saw the same subversive streak in the Waverley novels: "He thought kings, lords, and gentlemen, had 'rights' which it was folly and worse to question; but he thought also, they had 'duties' which it was scandalous and worse in them to evade. No radical could be more unsparing than he of the mere 'aristocrat.'"[92] By 1945 another Communist was calling Scott a great friend of the Russian people, indeed one of their favorite authors, and pointing out that Marx considered *Old Mortality* a "masterpiece."[93]

Jackson's response to Scott offers a fine illustration of intertextuality: the fact that our understanding of a text is shaped by everything else we have read. (To put it another way, while the frame controls how we interpret information, that new information is constantly modifying the frame.) Jackson first encountered *Ivanhoe* before he became a socialist, and at that point he absorbed completely its conservative romanticism. Later he came back to it after having read Robert Blatchford's socialist fable *Merrie England*, and in that context *Ivanhoe* became something quite different: a denunciation of economic rapacity. John Ruskin, William Morris, and Blatchford had all embraced an anti-industrial socialism that owed a great deal to Scott's medievalism, so it was not a great stretch to read *Ivanhoe* in those terms. Jackson recognized that Scott was no socialist, but at least in his feudal England the people belonged to the land and the land belonged to the people:

> For me capitalism had been revealed as equivalent to the castle of Torquilstone, manned by the brutal Front de Boeuf, the unscrupulous and faithless Bois Guilbert, the mercenary adventurer de Bracy and their brutal, hireling followers. Against them all the forces of the true English spirit were united in revolt—the gallantry and efficiency of Robin Hood, and his outlaws, the sturdy courage of the Saxons, and jolly Friar Tuck, the intrepid valour, strength and chivalry of Coeur de Lion, all that was English and opposite to sordid money-greedy meanness, treachery and brutality were in perennial revolt against this common enemy and destroyer of all that makes life noble, dignified and worth living.
>
> *Ivanhoe* had headed me off from Socialism once—now it led me right straight to its heart.[94]

When the first large cohort of Labour MPs was elected in 1906, the *Review of Reviews* asked them to name the books and authors that had most deeply influenced them. Of the forty-five who responded, eleven cited Walter Scott (Table 1.1, p. 42).[95]

Note that thirteen respondents mentioned Thomas Carlyle, a writer whose ideological legacy is even more ambiguous. Autobiographical evidence confirms that he had a huge following among autodidacts. There was nothing extraordinary about the Newlyn fisherman who owned his complete works and could discuss them knowledgeably.[96] Carlyle's ability to attract disciples from all points on the political spectrum, from Communists to Nazis, marks him as an author who might be turned to many purposes. *Sartor Resartus* could support one workingman struggling to break with religious orthodoxy,[97] while another might read it as a guide to romantic love.[98] It provided a gospel to self-improvers like Sir

Table 1.1: Favorite Authors of Early Labour MPs, 1906

John Ruskin	17	Robert Burns	8	Adam Smith	4
Charles Dickens	16	John Bunyan	8	William Cobbett	4
The Bible	14	Lord Tennyson	6	W. M. Thackeray	4
Thomas Carlyle	13	Giuseppe Mazzini	6	J. R. Green	4
Henry George	12	Charles Kingsley	5	Charles Darwin	4
Walter Scott	11	T. B. Macaulay	5	Henry Drummond	4
John Stuart Mill	10	James Russell Lowell	5		
William Shakespeare	9	Sidney/Beatrice Webb	4		

Henry Jones (b. 1852), who began his rise from a shoemaker's bench to a professorship of philosophy when a well-to-do lady warned him away from Carlyle, of whom he had never heard. When he read *Sartor Resartus*, "It was a case of love at first sight."[99] The same book was an effective aid to self-expression for Fred Gresswell (b. early 1890s), a farm laborer's son and 25s.-a-week insurance agent. When he first encountered it he was baffled, his literary education having been limited to penny novelettes. But later, in the midst of a speech for a YMCA debating society, "I found myself quoting from *Sartor Resartus*. This surprised everybody, including myself. Although I had read the book without much understanding, I could remember whole passages, word for word. On the strength of this supposed knowledge of the classics I was made editor of the YMCA magazine."[100] An obscure railway stationmaster could justify publishing his autobiography simply by quoting "On History": "In a certain sense all men are historians. Is not every memory written quite full with Annals, wherein joy and mourning, conquest and loss manifoldly alternate; and, with or without philosophy, the whole fortunes of one little inward Kingdom, and all its politics, foreign and domestic, stand ineffaceably recorded? ... The rudest peasant has his complete set of Annual Registers legibly printed in his brain."[101]

For those who were struggling to rise out of "the masses" and establish an identity, Carlyle was irresistible. An Edwardian slumdweller spoke for many readers when he wrote "I fancied myself a Teufelsdrockh."[102] Despising his job in a Birmingham factory, V. W. Garratt (b. 1892) surrounded his workbench with a barricade of boxes, set up a small mirror to provide early warning of the foreman's approach, and studied the Everyman's Library *Sartor Resartus* when he was being paid to solder gas-meter fittings. In retrospect he admitted that he probably "deserved the sack," but Carlyle made him feel justified in taking advantage of his employer: "I was virtuously trying to overcome circumstance and to live up to the individualist's doctrine of forcing a way in life without too much moral scruple." He felt much the same contempt for his workmates:

> I found little evidence to convince me that individuality flourished in the close contact of factory life or that generally speaking anything better emerged than a stubborn domination of the group mind over the individual worker. To be

oneself courageously and unashamed in matters of dress, talk, and action, meant running the gauntlet of ridicule and tribal opposition. Much easier was it to fall into the rut and become moulded to mediocrity. The preparation for this attitude was in the elementary schools. After mass education in which the absorption of historical absurdities was more important than mental development, boys passed into the factories with minds ill-equipped to withstand a new environment. ... Growing up in an atmosphere of constraint in which individual thought and action stubbornly follow the groove of class prejudice, there eventually emerges the "sound, solid British working-man."

Garratt escaped to an evening course in English literature, where he felt "like a child that becomes ecstatic with a fireworks display." Keats, Shelley, and Tennyson "swamped the trivialities of life and gave my ego a fulness and strength in the lustre of which noble conceptions were born and flourished." He spent his free evenings in Birmingham's Central Free Library reading Homer, Epictetus, Longinus, and Plato's *Dialogues*, a classical education which further undermined his confidence in the status quo: "I began to wonder in what way we had advanced from the ancient civilizations of Greece and Rome." In the First World War, he took Palgrave's *Golden Treasury* with him to France and wrote his own verses in the trenches. Later he became a journalist: his reading of the great books made it intolerable to continue as a cog in the industrial machine. Carlyle helped him break out from the factory, which he loathed not only for the dirt and poisonous fumes and low wages. What he resented most was the managing director parading "through the shops as if the workers never existed." In *Sartor Resartus* and other Everyman's Library volumes he found what he called "helps toward self-realization."[103]

For everyone who read Carlyle as an early Victorian Nietzsche, there were others, such as Labour MP G. J. Wardle (b. 1865), who admired him for a more conventional kind of moralizing: "Do the duty nearest to you."[104] For the pre-1914 generation of labor activists, however, he was preeminently a political prophet. Bookbinder Frederick Rogers (b. 1846) called him a "stern ... preacher of social righteousness" in the tradition of William Langland.[105] As a seaman in the mid-1870s, Ben Tillett had not yet been exposed to revolutionary literature, "But I discovered Thomas Carlyle and was held spellbound by the dark fury of his spirit, and the strange contortions of his style."[106] As a young South Wales miner, Edmund Stonelake (b. 1873), who had never heard of the French Revolution, asked a bookseller for something on the subject and was sold Carlyle. At first it was hard reading, but eventually he extracted an entire political education from its pages:

I learned the causes which fomented the minds of the people and gave rise to the Revolution, how ferociously it was conducted, and how the proclaimed hero of today was carted away tomorrow in the tumbrils to a place where his noble head fell under the merciless guillotine. I could visualise the Foreign Legion swooping down upon a vast unsuspecting concourse of quiet people slashing all around them with swords and sabres, leaving the dead and the dying whilst they dispersed and pursued the remainder who were fleeing in terror. I learned also of the great and lasting influence the Revolution had on peoples and countries struggling to establish democratic principles in Government in various parts of the world.[107]

Keir Hardie remembered that a "real turning point" of his life was his discovery of *Sartor Resartus* at age sixteen or seventeen. He had to read it through three times before he understood it: "I felt I was in the presence of some great power, the meaning of which I could only dimly guess at." Fifty years later he was more aware of Carlyle's flaws, but there was still plenty to admire. One could draw a pacifist lesson from his fable of the sixty French and English soldiers who massacred each other over a trivial territorial dispute. Carlyle's hero-worship made him appear a proto-fascist in the eyes of many readers (including Joseph Goebbels) but it inspired Hardie to embrace the role of the Hero as Proletarian.[108]

From Carlyle, as one agitator proclaimed, the working classes "learnt to hate shams." He exposed the ideological facades of the class system, preached independence of mind, and offered a vision of economic justice.[109] Having taken "Good strong doses of individualistic teaching" from Carlyle and Emerson, George Lansbury (unlike some other Labour MPs) refused to wear evening dress or court dress.[110] And Carlyle was a powerful influence in yet more radical circles. Helen Crawfurd (b. 1877), a baker's daughter from the slums of Glasgow, married a clergyman and trained for missionary work, until her evangelism took a sharp left turn. Joining the militant suffragettes of the Women's Social and Political Union (WSPU), she smashed the minister of education's windows and spent time in Holloway Gaol, where she staged a hunger strike. Later she would serve on the executive committee of the Communist Party of Great Britain. She attributed her political awakening to *Sartor Resartus, Heroes and Hero-Worship, Past and Present,* and *The French Revolution,* as well as Froude's biographical studies of both Carlyles. Everything she later read in Marx she discovered first in Thomas Carlyle:

He stripped naked the Law, the Church and many of the fraudulent shams of his day. I was deeply impressed by his denunciation of quackery masquerading as Truth, his honour of honest work, his exposure of war, his gift of stripping people of all the vestures designed to overawe the simple—the bombazine gown, the horsehair wig of the judge, the Crown and Sceptre of the Kings and Queens; the cheap snobbery of "Gigmanism" [sic]—his "everlasting nay" and his "everlasting yea." He revealed the sham world, where honest men could not breathe, the mockery of the Church, and told of the starving Irish widow, having to sink down in an Edinburgh slum and die of typhoid after appealing to every charitable organisation for help, and infecting the whole people with typhoid, in order to prove to them "that she was bone of their bone and flesh of their flesh." Then there was his picture of the men of the village of Drundrudge in France and Britain, slaughtering each other at the behest of their masters; his admiration for the worker, whose hands performed such wonders, his love for his family. With Carlyle I had fellowship, and was greatly helped in feeling that I was not alone in my experiences or in my awakening scepticism of existing traditions and customs. ... I could weep for the African and American slaves. ... Like Carlyle's Irish widow, I saw them "bone of each other's bone, flesh of each other's flesh."[111]

If there could be a socialist Walter Scott, some working-class women found a feminist in Carlyle. Mary Smith (b. 1822) was a shoemaker's daughter whose love of books was discouraged at every turn. At a Methodist school she was taught ladylike manners, embroidery, and little else. "For long years Englishwomen's souls were almost as sorely crippled and cramped by the devices of the school room, as the Chinese women's feet by their shoes," she later protested. She found emancipation in Shakespeare, Dryden, Goldsmith, and other standard male authors, whom she extolled for their universality:

These authors wrote from their hearts for humanity, and I could follow them fully and with delight, though but a child. They awakened my young nature, and I found for the first time that my pondering heart was akin to that of the whole human race. And when I read the famous essays of Steele and Addison, I could realize much of their truth and beauty of expression. ... Pope's stanzas, which I read at school as an eight year old child, showed me how far I felt and shared the sentiment that he wrote, when he says,

Thus let me live unseen, unknown,
    Thus unlamented let me die;
Steal from the world, and not a stone
    Tell where I lie.

By age twenty she had read and understood George Payne's *Elements of Mental and Moral Science*, Thomas Brown's *Moral Philosophy*, and Richard Whateley's *Logic*. But two authors in particular offered magnificent revelations. First, there was Emerson on Nature; and later, as a governess for a Scotby leatherworks owner, she discovered Thomas Carlyle:

Emerson and he thenceforth became my two great masters of thought for the rest of my life. Carlyle's gospel of Work and exposure of Shams, and his universal onslaught on the nothings and appearances of society, gave strength and life to my vague but true enthusiasm. They proved a new Bible of blessedness to my eager soul, as they did thousands beside, who had become weary of much of the vapid literature of the time.

Carlylean hero-worship may strike us as rampantly masculine, but as Mary Smith wrote, "A woman without friends in the world, as I was, must harden herself to dare and endure much." Carlyle bolstered her mental independence, gave her the confidence to think and speak and write. When her employer warned her that Carlyle might be a dangerous skeptic, she brushed him aside and boldly discussed her literary interests with his wife, proclaiming "Intellect knows no rank." She wrote poems, publishing them in the *People's Journal* and *Cassell's*. Like the great man himself, she studied Fichte, Schiller, and Goethe. And when Robert Chambers's *Vestiges of the Natural History of Creation* anticipated Darwinian evolution, she struggled through the same crisis of faith: "Like Thomas Carlyle, my own early life owed its best and brightest influences to the devout Calvinism under which it was reared." For a time she corresponded with both Mr. and Mrs. Carlyle: "The young woman has something in her," he conceded. Later she campaigned for women's suffrage and the Married Woman's Property Bill, agitated against the Contagious Diseases Acts, and wrote on politics for local newspapers.[112]

At age fourteen Elizabeth Bryson (b. 1880) read *Sartor Resartus*, a favorite book of her father, an impoverished Dundee bookkeeper. There she encountered "the exciting experience of being kindled to the point of explosion by the fire of words," words that expressed what she had always been trying to say:

It seems that from our earliest days we are striving to become articulate, struggling to clothe in words our vague perceptions and questionings. Suddenly, blazing from the printed page, there *are* the words, the true resounding words that we couldn't find. It is an exciting moment. ... "Who am I? The thing that can say I. Who am I, what is this ME?" I had been groping to know that since I was three.

She consumed *Heroes and Hero-Worship*, *The French Revolution*, and *Sartor Resartus* with the same intoxication. All of them resonated powerfully with that Victorian working-class ethic of self-education, which her father embraced thoroughly. Seven of his nine children won university degrees, including Elizabeth, who became a distinguished New Zealand physician and president of the Wellington chapter of the International Federation of University Women. She was not a feminist as such, and disliked androgyny: what drove her career was a Carlylean imperative to do the work that must be done. "I didn't care for short hair, and I was never worried about the vote," she wrote, "but I *did* want my hospital position."[113]

Not all working people viewed Carlyle as a man of the left. Sam Shaw (b. 1884), a Welsh farm laborer and coal miner, was driven into the ranks of the Conservative Party by *The French Revolution*, which made him suspect that socialist street orators were really "out for their own financial and political aggrandisement."[114] Chartist W. J. Linton (b. 1812) condemned Carlyle's hostility to the 1789 Revolution and his support of Governor Eyre, while applauding him for offering a humane alternative to laissez-faire liberalism and materialist socialism.[115] Secularist G. J. Holyoake (b. 1817) denounced him as a racist and "the greatest ruffian in literature since the days of Dr. Johnson," but admitted that "he had, like the doctor, the redeeming virtues of honesty and heroic love of truth." He admired the Carlyle who defended Mazzini, the Carlyle whose gospel of work gave dignity to the worker.[116] Labour Party pioneer F. W. Jowett (b. 1864), reading *Heroes and Hero-Worship* as a young millworker, was attracted by its vision of a new society but repelled by its authoritarianism:

> There must have been something in me that could not respond to his powerful and eloquent glorification of the supermen—including the captains of industry who would organise production not for profit but for use—for in all things else he made a deep impression on my young mind. What could it be? What other experience had woven itself into me? The more I read of Carlyle's heroes, the less attraction they had. I did not like his Luther, his Frederick the Great, nor his Cromwell. In some way, at some time, I must have imbibed a repugnance to personal domination which rests on force. I had in me the feeling that the common people should not be driven, and the more Carlyle crowned and canonised a ruling class, the more I felt I was on the side of the common people.[117]

Robert Blatchford (b. 1851) felt the same shudder. He found *Sartor Resartus* intimidating: "After reading the famous meditation on the sleeping city, I threw the book across the room. I felt I should never be able to write like that."[118] It was just as well: Blatchford's true voice, far more friendly than Carlyle's jeremiads, won an enormous audience for the *Clarion*, his popular socialist weekly. It was Blatchford's populism that turned him against *Heroes and Hero-Worship*, which had profoundly affected him as a young man:

> Heroes accomplish much brilliant butchery; they are great dust-raisers and provokers of tumult; they find employment for the players on brazen instruments, and the perpetrators of heroic verse; but there are precious few of them in history who do not fill places that would have been better filled if they had left them vacant. ... Music, and the arts, and the richest treasures of tradition, romance and fairy lore, as well as most of the handicrafts, and much of the useful kind of learning, are less due to the labours of the heroes than to the slow accumulation of the added mites of long generations of Nobodies. ... Who does all the loading and firing, the charging and cheering, on the battle-field? The Nobodies! Who defended the pass at Thermopylae, and the biscuit-box breastwork at Rorke's Drift? The Nobodies! Who invented needles, and files, and umbrellas, and meerschaum pipes, and soap, and blotting pads, and beefsteak puddings, and the Greek mythology, and warming pans, and double stout, and lucifer matches, and the Norse Edda, and kippered herrings, and

kissing, and divided skirts, and the Union Jack of Old England, and *The Clarion*? The Nobodies!

Who wrote Shakespeare's plays–! ... Of what stuff do our novelists, poets, orators, and painters weave their spells? Of the loves and trials, the smiles and tears, the follies and the heroisms of the Nobodies.[119]

The Craftsman's Tools

With that easygoing style, Blatchford was able to reach a larger readership than any other socialist journalist of his day. The *Clarion* built up a circulation of 60,000. He claimed that his tract *Merrie England* (1893) sold a million copies in Britain alone, and a census at one north country Labour Club found that it had converted forty-nine of its fifty members to socialism. The *Clarion* succeeded because it was not all socialist propaganda: there were also large helpings of literary criticism, and many readers were more interested in that part of the magazine.[120] The son of an impoverished dressmaker, Blatchford had grown up with *Robinson Crusoe*, the Brontës, and *The Old Curiosity Shop*, while he dreamt of writing novels that sold better than *David Copperfield*. As a soldier he had engaged in sharp barrack-room debates over the relative virtues of Dickens and Thackeray; and discussed music, painters, and poetry with a sergeant who could recite *Alastor*.[121] That background convinced Blatchford that the working classes could be politically awakened by the great authors. According to one of his converts, millworker-suffragette Annie Kenney, he was entirely right: "His writings on Nature, Poetry, Philosophy, Life, were my great weekly treat. Thousands of men and women in the Lancashire factories owe their education to Robert Blatchford. He was our literary father and mother. He it was who introduced us to Walt Whitman, William Morris, Edward Carpenter, Ruskin, *Omar Khayyam*, the Early English Poets, Emerson, Lamb. Robert Blatchford has always kept Labour clean, fresh, upright, virile."[122]

Blatchford realized that the emerging Labour Party had no single statement of ideology. Its doctrinal texts were nothing less than the whole canon of classic literature. When, in 1906, the *Review of Reviews* asked Labour MPs to define their program, they gestured broadly to a kind of Everyman's Library compendium of great books. (In fact the Everyman series, launched in the same year, would eventually publish all the authors in Table 1.1 except the Webbs and Henry Drummond.) ILP leader J. Bruce Glasier proclaimed that Bunyan, Burns, Shelley, Byron, Aeschylus, Dante, Schiller, and *Les Misérables* "all helped to rouse and nourish in me a passionate hatred of oppression and an exalting hope of the coming of a new era."[123] There Blatchford found the stuff that made socialists. When critics hailed Arthur Morrison's novel *A Child of the Jago* (1896) as a brutally realistic slice of slum life, Blatchford pointed out that it contained nothing one could not find in the standard English classics:

Let any admirer of Mr. Morrison's ... read the gambling scene in *Catherine*, the chapter in *Vanity Fair* wherein Rawdon Crawley finds the Marquis of Steyne with his wife; the drawing of lots in the Lantern Yard Chapel in *Silas Marner*; the account of Jane Eyre's childhood, or the school scenes in *Villette*; the military scenes in *Barry Lyndon*; the rape, the murder, or the basket-making in *Tess*; and the tavern scenes in *Janet's Repentance*, and I think he will admit that *A Child of the Jago* has no more right to pose as the greatest piece of realistic fiction since Defoe than Rudyard Kipling's *Seven Seas* has to be called the noblest poems since Milton. ... Has Mr. Morrison discovered the London slums? What about Douglas Jerrold, Charles Dickens, Henry Kingsley, Walter Besant, Rudyard Kipling, and George Gissing? Have you never read *Oliver Twist, The Nether World, Ravenshoe,* or *The Record of Badalia Herodsfoot*?[124]

Burns, *Sartor Resartus*, and *Unto This Last* were the formative influences on Keir Hardie. In his early years he read almost nothing specifically on economics or politics, and nothing by Marx or other socialists.[125] Most of his fellow Labour MPs shared his faith in the emancipatory power of literature. "I have a library of over 700 volumes," boasted John Ward (b. 1866),

the majority of which represents ten hours' work a day at 5d. an hour; sometimes even less—4½d. was the rate when I helped to make the Manchester Ship Canal.

Reading, then, changed the whole course of my life, for, let me tell you, twenty years ago British navvies were intellectually the lowest, as they were physically the finest, class in the country. They took absolutely no interest in public affairs; in the mess hut or the canteen you never heard a word of discussion on political or social matters, and so it was books and books alone that directed my thoughts towards progress and reform. ... There has since been a remarkable change in this respect. To-day navvies are amongst the keenest and most intelligent critics of political and social questions, and I am proud to think that my work amongst them has helped to awaken them from the mental torpor in which they were plunged.[126]

Philip Inman (b. 1892) conveyed a more specific sense of the uses of literacy for an early Labour MP. The son of a widowed charwoman, he bought up all the cheap reprints he could afford and kept notes on fifty-eight of them, all purchased for less than £5. There were Emerson's essays, Ruskin's *Sesame and Lilies*, Holmes's *Autocrat of the Breakfast Table*, Lamb's *Essays of Elia*, classic biographies (Boswell on Johnson, Lockhart on Scott, Carlyle on Sterling), several Waverley novels, *Wuthering Heights, Don Quixote, Robinson Crusoe, Pilgrim's Progress, The Imitation of Christ*, Shakespeare's sonnets, Tennyson, Browning, William Morris, and Palgrave's *Golden Treasury*. He loved everything by Charlotte Brontë, partly for what she had to say about the class system: "Characters like Jane Eyre and Lucy

Snowe were humble individuals in the eyes of the world, with only their dogged determination and lack of 'frills' as weapons against the dash and arrogance of those haughty and wealthy rivals among whom their lot was cast." Yet he admired Jane Austen for an equal but opposite reason: "The world of which she wrote, in which elegant gentlemen of fortune courted gentle, punctilliously correct ladies in refined drawing-rooms, was a remote fairy-tale country to me. Some day, I thought, perhaps I would get to know a world in which voices were always soft and modulated and in which lively and witty conversation was more important than 'brass'." Perhaps Brontë and Austen together taught him how to straddle the working and ruling classes, an indispensable skill for a nascent Labour politician: he eventually became chairman of the BBC and Lord Privy Seal under Attlee.[127]

One might also argue, of course, that Austen's roseate country-house sketches were subtle Tory propaganda indoctrinating the most literate workers—especially those few who would ultimately be coopted into the highest governing circles. Workingmen of this period, however, observed a direct correlation between literary taste and political radicalism. "The intellectual awakening of the work-shop came with the spread of Socialism," wrote London bookbinder Frederick Rogers. Before then, "The average workman, as I knew him, was not capable of sustained reading."[128] Robert Roberts likewise noted that the most literate workers—"readers of Ruskin, Dickens, Kingsley, Carlyle and Scott"—were likely to be socialists: those who read only the racing papers tended to vote Tory.[129] James Murray found the same link between culture and socialism in his Glasgow woodcarving shop: "Art, Philosophy, Politics, and Religion were all tossed around indiscriminately. Most [workmates] had Socialistic leanings and I was not long in observing those with the keenest minds were rabid Socialists."[130] As J. R. Clynes argued, it was the mass circulation press that was doping the workers with trivia and distractions. Shakespeare, Balzac, William Morris, and Bernard Shaw "would be no cure for labour unrest. Labour unrest would be increased, though better expressed and more scientifically directed if workmen used to a greater extent the intellectual levers of Ruskin, Dickens, Meredith, and Masefield—to throw in only a few uneven names."[131]

The mainstream of the labor movement agreed that great art and literature had eternal value, and ought to be disseminated among the workers out of a disinterested concern for truth, beauty, and a higher morality. Whether or not these works had any explicit political message, they would produce a deeper political consciousness and a more fervent desire to transform society. Of course *The Decline and Fall of the Roman Empire* might have a corrosive effect on religious belief, and *Les Misérables* was not likely to increase public confidence in the police.[132] The encouragement Dickens gave to the labor movement cannot be exaggerated: agitators were particularly fond of quoting Oliver Twist on the subject of asking for more.[133] It was also generally recognized that a knowledge of Shakespeare and Milton could make workers more aware and articulate in the political arena. But except on the more dogmatic Marxist fringes, literature was not judged solely or even primarily for its propaganda value. When asked how books had shaped him, Labour MP F. W. Jowett ranged widely: *Ivanhoe* made him want to read, *Unto This Last* made him a socialist, *Past and Present* made him think, *Vanity Fair* and *Les Misérables* taught him human sympathy, and *Wuthering Heights* taught him respect for man and nature.[134]

There were Marxists, like housepainter James Clunie (b. 1889), who claimed to value literature solely "in support of the cause of Labour and Peace," but in practice almost any book could be used for that purpose, "the same way as a craftsman uses his tools." It was "the stimulating anarchism of Walt Whitman and the prophetic works of Robert Burns" that made him rebel against the factory system. Clunie even saw his childhood games of Robinson Crusoe, when he constructed and sailed his own raft, as "a suitable prelude to … my search for the Voice of Labour," a preparation and inspiration for a life of political adventure. As Labour MP for Dunfermline in the 1950s, he still felt a thrill gazing at the bookshelves in the House of Commons library.[135] "Books to me became symbols of social revolution," not just because they preached the right kind of left politics, but because they allowed working people to control their own minds. "In my rediscovered social philosophy the miner was no longer the 'hewer of wood and the drawer of water' but became the worker-student, public administrator, a leader in his own right, advocate, writer, the equal of men."[136]

Percy Wall (b. 1893), jailed for defying draft notices in the First World War, was inspired in part by a copy of *Queen Mab* owned by his father, a Marxist railway worker. But neither father nor son applied ideological tests to literature. In the prison library—with some guidance from a fellow conscientious objector who happened to be an important publishing executive—Percy discovered Emerson, Macaulay, Bacon, Shakespeare, and Lamb. It was their style rather than their politics that he found liberating: from them "I learned self-expression and acquired or strengthened standards of literature."[137] Emrys Daniel Hughes (b. 1894), another imprisoned CO and son of a Tonypandy miner, learned that the authorities were not unaware of the subversive potential of great literature. Following a Home Office directive to examine prisoners' books, the chaplain confiscated a volume of Shelley, though not before Hughes had a chance to read and discuss it. The padre also apparently removed *Tristram Shandy* from the prison library: Hughes found it while cleaning the chaplain's room and had read it on the sly. "That's what does all the mischief. Books!" a warder shouted at another working-class CO. "If I had my way I'd burn them all."[138] He had a point: prison libraries could not be cleansed of politically questionable books without pulping the entire corpus of English literature. When Hughes found the grave of a hanged woman in the prison cemetery, he could not help but think of *Tess of the d'Urbervilles*. In More's *Utopia* he discovered a radical rethinking of crime and punishment. *The World Set Free*, in which H. G. Wells predicted the devastation of nuclear warfare, naturally spoke to his antiwar activism, and he was greatly impressed by the Quaker idealism in George Fox's journal, a biography of William

Penn, and Walt Whitman's poems. He read the social history of Macaulay, Froude, and J. R. Green; Thorold Rogers's *Six Centuries of Work and Wages* particularly appealed to him because it offered "not the history of kings and queens, but of the way ordinary people had struggled to live throughout the centuries. It gave me confidence that the war was a passing episode in history and that when it ended great changes in society would come." Hughes was one of those agitators who found a virtual Marxism in Thomas Carlyle. *The French Revolution* inspired the hope that a popular revolt somewhere would end the war. (He never expected it to happen in Russia, where he assumed all the revolutionaries were in jail or Siberia.) Hughes was convinced that Carlyle, the apostle of German philosophy, would have been antiwar: "He would have certainly seen through all the sham patriotism and the hypocrisy of the Governments and the war propaganda." He particularly admired the Carlyle who wrote, "We must all either work or steal, whatsoever we call our stealing." After all, Hughes noted, "most of the prisoners had really stolen far less than some of the people who were sending them to prison."[139]

By age fourteen, Durham collier Jack Lawson (b. 1881) would find the same kind of emancipation at the Boldon Miners' Institute,

> which was then nothing more than two pit-houses knocked into one. And didn't I follow the literary trail, once I found it! Like a Fenimore Cooper Indian, I was tireless and silent once I started. Scott; Charles Reade; George Eliot; the Brontës; later on, Hardy; Hugo; Dumas, and scores of others. Then came Shakespeare; the Bible; Milton and the line of poets generally. I was hardly sixteen when I picked up James Thomson's *Seasons*, in Stead's "Penny Poets". ... I wept for the shepherd who died in the snow.

The historical classics "came as a revelation"—Macaulay, J. R. Green, Gibbon, Motley's *Dutch Republic*, Prescott on Peru and Mexico, and *The French Revolution*. Academic critics today might discern ideologies in all of the above, but that was not Lawson's reading of them. "Of politics I knew nothing and cared less," he recalled, yet his purely literary readings had helped him form

> some very definite opinions on the right and wrong of things social. ... My strange ideas are the accepted general ideas of millions of Labour supporters today [1932], though I had no idea at the time [1900] that many others were thinking as I did and that a great movement embodying these opinions was on the horizon. ... But there was growing up in me at that time something which springs from the very roots of my being and waxes stronger as the years come and go, something which is not in political or economic programmes, for it goes so deep down to the soul of a man that it seems a dream, a thing of the imagination, hard to apprehend, difficult to hold, and impossible to interpret. ... I had actually arrived at the conclusion that if there was any good life, and

freedom from insecurity, and beauty, and knowledge, or leisure, then the men who did the world's dirty, sweaty, toilsome, risky work, and the women who shared the life with them, ought to be the first entitled to these things. ... I held that no man needs knowledge more than he who is subject to those who have knowledge—and because they have knowledge. That if there is one man in the world who needs knowledge, it is he who does the world's most needful work and gets least return because he lacks knowledge.

Though Lawson began reading politics and economics when he joined the ILP in 1904, his political ideas still came largely from literary sources: otherworldly Thomas à Kempis offered as much inspiration as this-worldly Thomas Carlyle. At Ruskin College he was exposed to Marx, but he found a more compelling utopian prophet when he read Lewis Carroll to his daughters: "Then one could look at life and affairs from the proper angle, for was not all our work to this end—that little children should live in their Wonderland, and mothers and fathers be heartful of the good of life because they were."[140]

Liberal education proved more effective than straight indoctrination in making radicals because, frankly, it was more thrilling, more likely to generate the enthusiasm that mobilized students to change the world. For Alice Foley (b. 1891) the pursuit of culture was an act of rebellion against both her strict Catholic upbringing and the working conditions at her Bolton cotton mill. It was not only the monotonous labor, the wretched factory lavatories, the constant threat of automation and reduced wages: "Most resented of all was the lack of human dignity accorded to our status as 'hands' with appropriate check numbers," a system that reduced workers to "a cowed and passive community. ... But these subservient days were occasionally shot through with moments of magic when the spirit of freedom and joy broke through." For 8d. there was Gilbert and Sullivan at the Theatre Royal, as well as grand opera staged by the Moody Manners and Carl Rosa companies. Nearby Manchester offered inexpensive seats at the Hallé Orchestra, as well as Annie Horniman's experimental repertory company at the Gaiety Theatre:

As a member of a group of young socialists I hoarded my scanty pocket-money, amounting at that time to one penny in the shilling of factory earnings, so that I could afford with them the luxury of a monthly matinée. With a cheap seat in pit or gallery we saw most of the early Shaw and Galsworthy plays, followed by tea in the Clarion café in Market Street, where I remember there was a fine William Morris fireplace. If the café was crowded, we hived off to the Art Gallery and over tea, brown bread, peaches and cream we animatedly argued and discussed the philosophy, art or satire of the productions. The whole outing cost about five shillings each, but we returned home like exultant young gods, tingling and athirst with the naive faith that if only sufficient human beings could witness good drama and comedy it might change the world. ...

Two world wars had not yet shattered or devastated man's moral and spiritual heritage. Life was ever meaningful, even if something of a battlefield, and we had an abiding faith in the ultimate achievement of the human race.

Alice Foley's achievements were considerable: she became a trade union leader, a justice of the peace, and an activist for the Workers' Educational Association (WEA). She read some Morris and less Marx, but for her, a liberal education for the proletariat was not merely a means of achieving socialism: it was socialism in fact, the ultimate goal of politics. At night school she staged a personal revolution by writing a paper on *Romeo and Juliet* and thrilling to the "new romantic world" of *Jane Eyre*. She joined a Socialist Sunday School, where "Hiawatha" was recited for its "prophetic idealism," and a foundry hammerman intoned Keats's "Eve of St. Agnes" and "Ode on a Grecian Urn." Handel's songs were taught by an operatic carpenter, "a wholly self-taught musician who passionately believed that 'the people' endowed and stimulated by 'sounds that delight and hurt not' could, and should, sing their way into a new millennium." There was also a former croft worker who saw the brave new world through a telescope:

He hated the industrial system and had found liberation by operating a market-garden on the edge of the moors where he had the use of a powerful telescope erected on his land. Indoors he gave us magic-lantern shows of the heavens and their constellations, and on clear evenings at the dark of year we were invited to view the rings round Saturn, the beauty of the Milky Way or the craters and valleys of the Moon. After carefully sighting the objects he turned to us saying solemnly, "Sithee, lasses, isn't that a marvellous seet; a stupendous universe, yet we fritter our lives away i' wars and petty spites!" As youngsters we gazed, inclined to giggle; then came a moment of silent awe as the awareness of "night clad in the beauty of a thousand inauspicious stars— the vast of night and its void"—seeped into consciousness. To recapture these moments of rare experience is to realise the debt owed to these humble, self-taught men who, uninvited, prodded a corner of my being in those far off impressionable years.

Her first WEA summer school, at the end of the First World War, was "a new and undreamt-of experience. ... We argued over Wilson's Fourteen Points and in literary sessions read and explored Browning's poems. It was a strange joy to browse over the niceties of *Bishop Blougram's Apology* or to delve into the intricacies of *The Ring and the Book*. ... It was a month of almost complete happiness; a pinnacle of joy never to be quite reached again." It was specifically the joy of breaking the chains of ideology: "In its complete rejection of what then seemed to be religious shackles the new-born idealism was healthy and intoxicating. It released youthful, buoyant energy and hope." That was what Alice learned from Emily Brontë:

Vain are the thousand creeds
That move men's hearts, unutterably vain,
Worthless as withered weeds
Or idlest froth amid the boundless main.[141]

In London's Jewish East End, the liberating power of literature was most effectively mobilized by the anarchists and their intellectual leader, Rudolf Rocker. Though he was not Jewish, Rocker taught himself enough of the language to edit the Yiddish anarchist paper *Arbeter Fraint* (peak circulation 5,000), as well as a more literary journal, *Germinal* (peak circulation 2,500). Jewish laborers were in awe of this German gentile who introduced them to the writings of I. L. Peretz, Sholem Aleichem, and Sholem Asch. "He was one of those who stood at the cradle of modern Yiddish literature," gushed one garment worker. Rocker also published Yiddish translations of Molière, Herbert Spencer, Strindberg, Tolstoy, Ibsen, Chekhov, Gorky, Andreiev, Hauptmann, Anatole France, Maeterlinck, Knut Hamsun, Wilde, Zangwill, and Kropotkin. In 1906 an Arbeter Fraint Club and Institute opened in Jubilee Street, with an 800-seat hall, a free library, adult courses, lectures, concerts, and theatricals, including a Yiddish *Ghosts*. Rocker himself taught history, sociology, *Hamlet*, *Gulliver's Travels*, and Beethoven's Ninth Symphony. On Sundays he took his classes round to the British Museum. For Rocker all ideologies, even anarchism itself,

> were subordinate to the great idea of educating people to be free and to think and work freely, … [making] it possible for the individual to develop his natural capacities unrestrained by hard and fast rules and dogmas. My innermost conviction was that Anarchism was not to be conceived as a definite closed system, nor as a future millennium, but only as a particular trend in the historic development towards freedom in all fields of human thought and action, and that no strict and unalterable lines could therefore be laid down for it.
>
> Freedom is never attained; it must always be striven for. Consequently its claims have no limit, and can neither be enclosed in a programme nor prescribed as a definite rule for the future. Each generation must face its own problems, which cannot be forestalled or provided for in advance. The worst tyranny is that of ideas which have been handed down to us, allowing no development in ourselves, and trying to steamroller everything to one flat universal level.

Rocker reversed the Marxian theory that culture is economically determined, arguing that all economic systems are culturally determined. Modern industrial society, for example, had been created by modern scientific culture, not vice versa. Culture was not, then, constructed by a particular class, but was "the creation of countless generations of people of all social classes," and "cannot be judged from the point of view of class or of economic conditions." Therefore, the injustices of capitalism would be abolished not by scrapping the Western cultural heritage, but by redistributing it to the workers: "What the human spirit has created in science, art and literature, in every branch of philosophic thought and aesthetic feeling is and must remain the common cultural possession of our own and of all the coming generations. This is the starting-point, this is the bridge to all further social development."[142]

Immersion in Western literary culture could be tremendously emancipating for the children of immigrants. Though Chaim Lewis (b. 1911) attended a Jewish school in Soho, it was his English teacher "who jolted me out of my intellectual torpor. ... He traded with words: he blew the wind of rhythm into them, he caressed them to mean more than they said and made them sing as I had never heard them sing before." It did not matter that Lewis "had read precious little till then and could only obscurely guess at the meaning of much of what he read to us. ... Such knowledge was to come later." That stands as a caveat to educationalists who tailor school readers to fit the cultural backgrounds of their pupils: the books that do most to stretch children's minds are those they do not fully understand. Lewis enthusiastically embraced the literature of an alien culture—"the daffodils of Herrick and Wordsworth ... the whimsey of Lamb and the stirring rhythmic tales of the Ballads" and, yes, "the wry eloquence of Shylock." Even before he discovered the English novelists, he was introduced to Tolstoy, Dostoevsky, Turgenev, and Pushkin by a Russian revolutionary rag merchant, who studied Dickens in the Whitechapel Public Library and read aloud from *Man and Superman*. Another friend—the son of a widowed mother, who left school at fourteen—exposed him to Egyptology, Greek architecture, Scott, Smollett, the British Museum, and Prescott's *History of the Conquest of Peru*.

How did the assimilation of English culture and European literatures affect Lewis? They certainly did nothing to dampen his socialism: the *Daily Herald* was gospel in his home. Nor did he become an imperialist: the roster of kings and conquests that made up his history classes did not interest him, for as a Jew he was inclined to sympathize with history's losers. His reading of classic writers clearly ignited his authorial ambitions, but did not make him devalue his Yiddish literary heritage: the same rag merchant who acquainted him with Pushkin and took him to free Beethoven concerts at Queen's Hall also introduced him to Sholem Aleichem. This synergy may appear paradoxical today, when partisans of ethnic and mainstream literature seem locked in trench warfare. But for those who are not narrow academic specialists, reading in one literature can stimulate reading in another. Lewis's training in English and Russian authors provided models of taste, cultural standards, and intellectual challenges which then led him back to find similar virtues in Yiddish writers. Before his literary education, Lewis recalled, "we were inclined to write off the past of our parents as something inexcusably alien and not worth remembering." He discovered later that "Yiddish had a grammar, a dictionary and writers of genius to rank with the great names of European literature"— something he could only appreciate after he had mastered those great Europeans.

This pattern would be common enough among the post-1945 generation of New York Jewish intellectuals. Yet for them, as for Lewis, absorbing a cacophony of literary cultures could be disorienting. Rapid assimilation inevitably left him wondering which side he was on. "At one moment I saw myself as no different from others—a like among likes," Lewis recalled, "at another, I struck out for my own singularity." Yet the same promiscuous reading that brought on this crisis of identity also gave him a means of dealing with it. Reading made him a writer, and in writing he found that most basic of intellectual moorings, the power of naming: "I must be the identifier, never the identified: it was I who established order, each separateness in the world but a living fragment of my own being." He was deeply affected by the Jewish legend that the elect who know the name of God possess great power, and had sustained the Jewish nation through centuries of exile. He was equally struck by Adam's power to name all the birds and beasts, a power that made him in one respect a creator above the angels and on a level with God: "Life only becomes conscious of itself when it is translated into word, for only in the word is reality discovered."[143]

That was the autodidacts' mission statement: to be more than passive consumers of literature, to be active thinkers and writers. Those who proclaimed that "knowledge is power" meant that the only true education is self-education, and they often regarded the expansion of formal educational opportunities with suspicion. That was a point made by Thomas Thompson (b. 1880), who rose out of the Lancashire mills via Co-operative society classes. In a Sunday school library set up by a cotton mill fire-beater, he read Dickens, Thackeray, Oliver Wendell Holmes, and Marcus Aurelius. He joined a workingmen's naturalist society, frequented also by a housepainter who had built his own observatory. By 1940 he had acquired some contempt for a generation that took educational opportunity for granted: "Learning is so cheap that people do not even stop to pick it up. We had to fight for what bit we got." He conceded that

> It was pathetic to see the faith in education as a cure for all ills. But then it is as pathetic now. So-called education can be used to produce slaves, soldiers, and snobs, as well as gentlemen. ... You can Bolshevize people by education, or you can make them into the perfect Nazi. Unless the intended victim has trained himself to think for himself.[144]

To preserve that independence, working people had to create their own network of informal self-schooling programs. This they accomplished by improvising a vast grass-roots movement, which had no central organization, but was a presence in hundreds of chapels and millions of kitchens. It touched more students than all organized adult educational institutions combined. It never had a formal title, but was generally known as "mutual improvement."

Chapter Two **Mutual Improvement**

A Coventry millworker once proclaimed that "The Labour movement grew out of Mutual Improvement Societies."[1] We need to be reminded of that, for these institutions are scarcely mentioned in studies of labor history. Richard Altick and E. P. Thompson appreciated the critical role they played in adult education, but could locate very little information about them.[2] Though they were ubiquitous in Victorian and Edwardian Britain, they left few surviving records. In most cases, they can only be reconstructed through the memoirs of their members.

The mutual improvement society was a venture in cooperative education. In its classic form, it consisted of a half dozen to a hundred men from both the working and lower-middle classes who met periodically, sometimes in their own homes but commonly under the auspices of a church or chapel. Typically, at each meeting one member would deliver a paper on any imaginable subject—politics, literature, religion, ethics, "useful knowledge"—and then the topic would be thrown open to general discussion. The aim was to develop the verbal and intellectual skills of people who had never been encouraged to speak or think. There was complete freedom of expression, the teacher-pupil hierarchy was abolished, and costs were minimal: about 2s. per member per year in the case of a Gallatown society in 1912.[3] In addition to the mutual improvement societies *per se*, the working classes organized innumerable adult schools, libraries, reading circles, dramatic societies, and musical groups. They all belonged to the mutual improvement tradition, in that they relied on working-class initiative rather than state provision or middle-class philanthropy.

In turn, these collaborative cultural activities were but one branch of a vast popular movement of voluntary collectivism. Nineteenth-century workingmen organized an array of friendly societies, clubbing together to offer basic health and unemployment benefits, savings banks, job referral services, and burial plans. Perhaps a quarter of all male workers belonged to some kind of friendly society by 1830, 75 to 80 percent by 1880.[4] A mutual improvement society could be defined simply as a friendly society devoted to education.

Scottish Overture II

David Vincent found that the term "mutual improvement" had been used in a working-class context as far back as 1731, when the the plebeian poet Stephen Duck met regularly with a servant to discuss literature and arithmetic.[5] The phrase had been adopted even earlier by the Easy Club, which Allan Ramsay founded in 1712, and it became a commonplace among the societies of the Edinburgh Enlightenment.[6] Unsurprisingly, mutual improvement was Scottish in origin. Perhaps the earliest recorded group discussed literature, history, and philosophy at the home of Kinnesswood weaver Alexander Bruce (b. 1710), father of the poet Michael Bruce.[7] But at first, Scottish mutual improvement expressed itself chiefly in libraries.

John Crawford has located fifty-one Scottish working-class libraries founded by 1822, which charged annual subscriptions of 6s. or less, and were governed democratically, mostly without interference by the middle classes. Few such libraries existed in England at the time. All of these Scottish libraries were in towns with a population of less than 10,000, and all were in the Lowlands, with a large concentration in the southwest. The Leadhills Reading Society (founded 1741 and in use until about 1940), the Wanlockhead Miners' Library (founded 1756), and the Westerkirk Library (founded 1792) were the first working-class libraries in Britain, and all incorporated mutual improvement principles in their rulebooks.[8]

Craftsmen in Lowlands Scotland enjoyed particularly high literacy rates between 1640 and 1770: 74 percent for weavers (compared with 52 percent in northern England) and an amazing 94 percent for wrights. These groups patronized one of the first true public libraries in the world, the Innerpeffray Library in Perthshire near Crieff. Of 287 borrowers with identifiable trades between 1747 and 1800, twenty-six were weavers, compared with only twenty-two teachers. (By the end of the century, there were only ninety-two weaver heads of households in Crieff.) In the decade 1747–57 the library was used by seven wrights, out of perhaps ten in the area.[9]

Weavers and lead miners were well-paid and had short work hours: six hours a day for miners, four days a week for weavers. Weavers had to be literate for their work, and mining companies wanted an educated work force. Both trades had a history of friendly society activity and self-education. Scottish miners—like the South Wales colliers who would set up their own network of libraries more than a century later—lived in isolated villages with stable populations, and upheld strong traditions of working-class independence.[10]

In 1796–97 the *Scots Chronicle* reported the existence of thirty-five reading societies, mostly in and around Glasgow and Paisley, many of them based in weaving communities. They usually had thirty to forty members and assessed a monthly subscription (typically 6d. or 9d.). Acquisitions were decided democratically and some book collections approached 1,000 volumes. They generally stocked the standard histories and travels, along with the *Spectator* and other periodicals, but not much poetry, fiction, science, or religion.[11]

There was also a large measure of working-class participation in the East Lothian Itinerating Libraries. Founded in 1817 by merchant Samuel Brown, this service rotated boxes of fifty books through a circuit of villages: mostly moral and religious volumes, but also some dealing with popular science, travels, agriculture, and the mechanical arts.[12] In 1825 the twenty volunteer librarians managing the system included six teachers, two shoemakers, two smiths, two wrights, two sadlers, a weaver, a draper, a collier, a tailor, and a laborer.[13]

To all this must be added countless informal networks for sharing reading matter. In the first years of the nineteenth century, shepherds in the Cheviot Hills maintained a kind of circulating library, leaving books they had read in designated crannies in boundary walls. The next shepherd who came that way could borrow it and leave another in its place, so that each volume was gradually carried through a circuit of 30 to 40 miles, on which the shepherds only occasionally met.[14] The Lochend poet Alexander Bethune (b. 1804) and his brother John could afford few books, but Alexander remembered that "After it became known that we were readers, the whole of our acquaintances, far and near, and even some people whom we could hardly number as such, appeared eager to lend us books."[15]

Even in that hospitable atmosphere, the pursuit of literature could be a struggle for a man like John Bethune. A laborer whose annual earnings rarely exceeded £19, he hoped to write his way out of poverty like Robert Burns. His *Tales and Sketches of the Scottish Peasantry* was published in 1838, but as his brother Alexander recalled, the writing of it

> had been prosecuted as stealthily as if it had been a crime punishable by law. There being but one apartment in the house, it was his custom to write by the fire, with an old copy-book, upon which his paper lay, resting on his knee, and this, through life, was his only writing-desk. On the table, which was within reach, an old newspaper was kept constantly lying, and as soon as the footsteps of any one were heard approaching the door, copy-book, paper, pens, and inkstand, were thrust under this covering, and before the visitor came in, he had in general a book in his hand, and appeared to have been reading.

Mutual improvement was useful for acquiring and sharing general knowledge, but it could not provide the privacy necessary for writing and serious study. The Bethune brothers actually went to the trouble of building a room for John, to no avail: the day after it was finished, work called him away to another town.[16]

Mutual improvement continued to gain momentum in Scotland through the nineteenth century. In the rural northeast region around Aberdeen, Ian

Carter found nineteen such societies in 1851, and between thirty-five and fifty by 1897, many of which maintained their own libraries. In an otherwise conservative region, they were a backbone of radical Liberalism, closely linked with the Free Church of Scotland (founded 1843) and the temperance movement. Their members were drawn from the lower middle and upper working classes. A society organized in Rhynie in 1846 typically included five farmers, two merchants, a baker, a soldier, a contractor, a miller, a traveling salesman, three estate workers, and five students. Notably missing were itinerant agricultural workers: mutual improvement societies were the domain of settled tenant farmers, craftsmen, and tradesmen.

Though committed to the pursuit of knowledge for its own sake, their members commonly rose in the world, often into the ranks of journalism.[17] William Donaldson has shown how the culture of mutual improvement in Victorian Scotland nurtured an impressive cadre of editors, among them weaver William Scott of the *Montrose Review*, shoemaker W. H. Murray of the *Falkirk Herald*, railwayman James Bridges of the *Perthshire Advertiser*, engineer Henry Alexander of the *Aberdeen Free Press*, James Macdonnell of the *Times*, and Alexander Allardyce of *Blackwood's*. Mutual improvement was also incarnated in reader-written periodicals, such as the remarkably interactive *Dundee, Perth, and Forfar People's Journal*. Its working-class subscribers contributed letters, reports of meetings, notes on Scottish folklore and history, and commissioned articles, as well as thousands of entries to fiction and poetry competitions, for prizes of 10s. to 50s. In turn, the "To Correspondents" column advised contributors on the weaknesses and strengths of rejected articles. The editor, William Latto, was an archetypal autodidact: a Chartist weaver who read from books propped against his handloom, and learned Latin from a Free Kirk minister. Founded in 1858, the *People's Journal* was selling more than 100,000 copies by 1866, a quarter million by 1914. That represented the largest circulation of any weekly outside London, and a higher level of penetration in the remote areas of northern Scotland than any other periodical.[18]

This was the culture that produced J. Ramsay MacDonald, who won a prize of £10 for a humorous dialect story sent to the *People's Journal*.[19] He served as secretary to the Lossiemouth Mutual Improvement Association, which in 1884 debated questions such as "Ought Members of Parliament to be Paid?", "Is Temperance Better than Total Abstinence?", "Is Emigration the best remedy for the existing distress among the Highland crofters?", "Ought Capital Punishment to be Abolished?", "Is Competition injurious to the Community?", and "Is Novel-Reading Beneficial?"[20] Educated first in the Scottish rigor of a parish school, inspired by Hugh Miller's *My Schools and Schoolmasters*, he grew up in a milieu saturated with mutual education. A tubercular watchmaker introduced him to Shakespeare, Burns, and *The Pickwick Papers*. Then there was the ragman who kept a book propped open against his barrow, and presented it to MacDonald when he showed an interest. It was a translation of Thucydides.[21]

Self-Culture

The mutual improvement societies often took the form of a more advanced level of Sunday school. Most nineteenth-century Sunday schools were indigenous working-class self-help institutions: even the Chartist *Northern Star* extolled them for creating a literate proletariat. According to radical weaver Samuel Bamford, the surge of political agitation after 1815 owed much to "the Sunday Schools of the preceding thirty years, [which] had produced many working men of sufficient talent to become readers, writers, and speakers in the village meetings for parliamentary reform."[22] As early as 1834, one in every five Sunday schools offered a library. The organizers and teachers were largely drawn from the working class, where the Sunday school experience was nearly universal: 91.8 percent of workers in twelve Manchester cotton mills in 1852 had attended at least for a time. By 1881 no less than 19 percent of the entire population of Great Britain—and more than 70 percent of young people aged five to twenty in Keighley—were currently enrolled.[23]

Mutual improvement was not necessarily political: the early Scottish working-class libraries generally avoided political books. But as Francis Place described it, the London Corresponding Society—the first laboring class political organization—was organized on the mutual improvement model. It purchased books and loaned them to members, and devoted its weekly meetings to readings and general discussion. One week the chairman (a rotating position) would read a chapter from a book; the following week it would be reread and thrown open to discussion. No one could speak a second time until all who wished had spoken once. Place also organized a French class with four other LCS workmen, reading a French grammar propped up before him at work and reading three hours or more each night from Helvetius, Rousseau, and Voltaire. The "moral effects" of this regimen of study, he concluded,

> were considerable. It induced men to read books, instead of wasting their time in public houses, it taught them to respect themselves, and to desire to educate their children. It elevated them in their own opinions. It taught them the great moral lesson "to bear and forbear." The discussions in the divisions, in the Sunday evening readings, and in the small debating meetings, opened to them views which they had never before taken. They were compelled by these discussions to find reasons for their opinions, and to tolerate others. It gave a new stimulus to an immense number of men who had been but in too many instances incapable of any but the grossest pursuits, and in seeking nothing beyond mere sensual enjoyments. It elevated them in society.

As proof of that last point, Place recalled an 1822 dinner to commemorate the anniversary of the acquittal of Thomas Hardy, who had been arrested for high treason in 1794. There Place met twenty-four LCS veterans from the 1790s, when most of them were journeymen or shopmen: now they were all prosperous businessmen. Place was a fervent apostle of working-class respectability, and he was prone to exaggerate the role of the LCS as "a great moral cause of the improvement which has since taken place among the *People*."[24] But contemporary social observers agreed that there had been a dramatic "reformation of manners" among the lower classes between the Gordon Riots of 1780 and the Great Exhibition of 1851. And this was not simply or even primarily a matter of aping the middle classes: it was a product of a grass-roots working-class struggle for mutual improvement, of which the LCS was certainly a part.

In the early nineteenth century, the middle classes often associated mutual improvement with political radicalism, not without reason. An Uxbridge carpenter recalled that, as the campaign for the First Reform Bill approached its climax,

An agitation was raised by a few of the leading artisans for a mechanics' institute. A room was taken over the market-place and opened three evenings a week. Books of all kinds were presented, most of them of a religious and disputative kind. The *Penny Magazine*, the *Penny Cyclopaedia*, the *Mirror*, also *Dispatch*, and *Examiner* were taken in. Most of the mechanics in the town joined, beside a few shopkeepers and innkeepers. Scientific and literary lectures were occasionally given by itinerant lecturers. The genteel people would not attend lectures at a mechanics' institute, and they started a literary and scientific institution. It was a bad time for educational work. Bread was dear, trade was bad, and the country was passing through the throes of a political convulsion which was fast ripening into a revolution. The mechanics' institute gradually degenerated into a violent revolutionary club. The door was locked, the passages watched, the most inflammatory and seditious things were read and discussed, and most of the men took an oath and swore if there was a general rising they were to march at once on the local bank. Collections were frequent to meet the expenses of trials which were taking place all over the country. One of these meetings had been held far into the night. The following morning found all the shops closed and the militia on the pavement.[25]

Thomas Cooper and other Knowledge Chartists evangelized for the organization of mutual improvement societies.[26] William Lovett (b. 1800) conveys a sense of what they were struggling against and what they aimed to accomplish. Lovett served his apprenticeship as a rope-maker in Newlyn, where there was no bookshop, a few hopeless dame schools, and "scarcely a newspaper taken in, unless among the few gentry. ... With the exception of Bibles and Prayer Books, spelling-books, and a few religious works, the only books in circulation for the masses were a few story-books and romances, filled with absurdities about giants, spirits, goblins, and supernatural horrors." These were all he read until he moved to London and joined (around 1825) "The Liberals," a group of workingmen who paid a small subscription to support a library, and met two evenings a week to discuss literary, political, and philosophical topics. Lovett's first meeting was a revelation: "It was the first time I had ever heard impromptu speaking out of the pulpit—my notions then being that such speaking was a kind of inspiration from God .... My mind seemed to be awakened to a new mental existence; new feelings, hopes, and aspirations sprang up within me, and every spare moment was devoted to the acquisition of some kind of useful knowledge." He read William Paley and other theologians in their library, plunged into religious and political controversies, attended coffee-house debating societies, went without food to build up a small personal library, petitioned for the Sunday opening of the British Museum and other cultural institutions. Later, as a Chartist, he would agitate for free access to education up to the universities, including adult schools and public libraries. As he vociferated in an 1837 speech: "Unhappily, though the time has gone by for the selfish and bigoted possessors of wealth to confine the blessings of knowledge wholly within their own narrow circle, and by every despotic artifice to block up each cranny through which intellectual light might break out upon the multitude, yet still, so much of the selfishness of *caste* is exhibited in their fetters on the Press, in their Colleges of restriction and privilege, and in their dress and badge-proclaiming charity schools, as to convince us that they still consider education as their own prerogative, or *a boon to be sparingly conferred upon the multitude*, instead of a universal instrument for advancing the dignity of man, and for gladdening his existence."[27]

The Northumberland Chartist Robert Lowery (b. 1809) claimed that in his mutual improvement society of twenty men, mostly workers, half went on to become authors or public speakers.[28] J. B. Leno (b. 1826), who identified profoundly with Alton Locke, edited a manuscript newspaper for an Uxbridge mutual improvement society, out of which grew the Chartist journal *Spirit of Freedom*.[29] With little formal education, William Farish (b. 1818) acquired basic literacy and political knowledge by reading newspapers to Newtown weavers. (Their favorite was the tri-weekly *Evening Mail*, a condensation of the *Times*.) With a self-help philosophy drawn from Thomas Cooper, William Cobbett, and the autobiography of Benjamin Franklin, Farish joined a workingmen's school in Carlisle around 1840:

Hiring a six-loom weaving shop in the Blue Anchor Lane, we fitted it up ourselves with desks and seats, rude enough, doubtless, but we could not very well complain of our own handiwork, and there was nobody else to please. The [Carlisle] Mechanics' Institution, although well managed and liberally supported, had failed somewhat in its mission, mainly, as was thought, through the reluctance of the weaver in his clogs and fustian jacket to meet in the same room with the better clad, and possibly better mannered, shop assistants and clerks of the city. So these new places were made purely democratic, having no master, and not permitting even any in the management but such as lived by weekly wages. Those who could read taught those who could not, and those who could cypher did the same for those less advanced.

Farish himself learned much from an uneducated Irishman who had somehow picked up a broad knowledge of English etymology, and a Cockermouth weaver "who was an adept in algebra, and yet could scarcely either read or write." The school could not break even on its 1d.-a-week subscription, but contributions were accepted. Some gentlemen supplied free subscriptions to respectable journals, while the school itself paid for radical papers, which were usually less expensive.[30]

Farish's experience was entirely typical of Carlisle, where at least twenty-four reading rooms were founded between 1836 and 1854, with a combined total of almost 1,400 members and 4,000 volumes. The town (population 25,000) was a center for handloom weavers, who were often the prime movers behind these enterprises. Many reading rooms also offered classes in reading, writing, and math, taught cooperatively by the members themselves or by professional teachers who volunteered their services. These schools undoubtedly boosted literacy before the 1870 Education Act: in one working-class parish the proportion of those who could sign the marriage register jumped from 70.36 percent in 1841 to 92.69 percent in 1871.

Reading rooms and adult schools were organized largely as an alternative to the mechanics' institutes, founded and governed by paternalistic middle-class reformers, where religious and political controversy was usually barred and the premises could be uncomfortably genteel. In 1843 workingmen petitioned a Croydon institute to form a discussion class and to drop the rule barring controversial political and religious works from the library (a rule not strictly enforced against conservative literature). The gentry and clergy on the governing committee rejected the plea and, on top of that, increased user fees, thus driving out so many working-class members that the institute virtually shut down. A few years later, radical journalist Thomas Frost helped organize a more democratic society, which sponsored lectures, musical performances, and debates on such contentious issues as Owenite cooperation. This forum attracted such a large following that it was eventually able to rent the premises of the now-defunct institute. "The causes of the failure in the one case, and of success in the other, do not lie very deep," Frost observed. "Working men do not like to be treated like children, to have the books they shall read chosen for them; and they naturally resent any attempt to set up barriers between themselves and other classes, when all are associated on the same footing for a common object."[31]

Since mutual improvement schools and reading rooms relied on the support of workingmen, they were liable to be short-lived, vulnerable to economic downturns and internal squabbles over the acquisition of radical literature. Volunteer teachers could be unreliable or incapable. Many students attended simply to acquire basic literacy and once they reached that goal, they abandoned the school and allowed it to collapse. Yet if these institutions had accepted middle-class help, they might have lost their independence and, with it, their working-class followers. The Lord Street Working Men's Reading Room in Carlisle fell victim to this dilemma. It began when fifty men, anxious to read about the

European revolutions of 1848, clubbed together to buy newspapers. A year later, with 300 members and 500 books, it had far outgrown its premises, a borrowed schoolroom. A new Elizabethan-style building was constructed and opened in 1851, with congratulatory messages from Charles Dickens and Thomas Carlyle. Governed by a committee of workingmen, it charged a subscription of only 1d. a week, and even that was waived for the unemployed.

It all looked like a triumph of working-class self-help, yet nothing on that scale (the construction cost £393) could have been accomplished without generous middle-class assistance. There were contributions of books, money, and low-interest loans; the architect donated his services; a solicitor rented the land for a 1s. a year. However well intentioned, it all bore the taint of bourgeois patronage, especially when the rule was adopted "that party politics and controversial religion are shut out from all meetings of the institution." At first Lord Street attracted crowds to its library and classes, but as it assumed the trappings of a conventional mechanics' institute, it was deserted by the working classes. By 1863 it was nearly moribund: only the possession of its own physical plant kept it going.[32]

Though mutual improvement societies tended to be ephemeral, they were fairly easy to set up and answered a need for remedial education. Fustian cutter Joseph Greenwood was one of a dozen men who founded an institute in Hebden Bridge at the end of 1854. Renting an empty cottage with absolutely no furniture, "we met and stood in a circle, one holding the candle while we deliberated, and another wrote out the resolutions on loose paper." The entrance fee was 1s.6d., plus weekly dues of 2d. By May 1856 they had 131 working- and middle-class members and had outgrown their premises. Interest in the Crimean War attracted newspaper readers to their reading room, which subscribed to the *Daily News*, the *Manchester Examiner*, and the *Athenaeum*. There was also a library of 230 volumes, most of them loaned by a silk-dresser. The institute offered classes, starting with basic arithmetic, grammar, and writing, then adding courses in drawing and higher mathematics, taught by two paid and three voulnteer teachers.[33] In 1860 another such institute, Culloden College, was launched on a tiny investment:

We rented a garret, for which we paid (I think) 25s. a year, bought a few second-hand forms and desks, borrowed a few chairs from the people in the house, bought a shilling's worth of coals, had the gas (which was already in the house) laid on at the cost of a few shillings, and started our College. We did not advertise it in the newspapers or on the streets, for we could not afford to do that, but we invited all our friends and acquaintances to join us, and in a few days we had about twenty members. ... We had no men of position or education connected with us, and I believe we were better without them, but several of the students who had made special study of some particular subject were appointed teachers, so that the teacher of one class might be a pupil in another.

Except for a grammar school boy who taught Latin, the teachers were all printers, tailors, shoemakers, and shopmen, who offered classes in English, drawing, Euclid, and arithmetic. The members gave Friday evening lectures, and ventured out together on summer rambles to collect zoological, botanical, and geological specimens. Culloden College was in every respect a learning collective: "The belongings of the students were considered public property. We had no library, but we lent and borrowed the books belonging to each other." Like most mutual improvement groups, Culloden College depended on the organizing energy of a few enthusiasts, and it collapsed when they migrated elsewhere or lost interest. But four of its students, including two shoemakers and one printer's apprentice, went on to obtain MA degrees.[34] And some of these societies did become permanent. The imposing mechanics' institutes at Bradford, Keighley, Halifax, and Stalybridge all began as small mutual improvement societies.[35] The Huddersfield Mechanics' Institute was founded in 1840 with only one room and one teacher: in less than twenty years it was offering ninety-one classes to 800 students.[36]

The workingmen who created these schools earned not only an education, but tremendous pride and independence. "Never was more delightful work engaged in than in the earlier struggles of [our] Society," boasted Ben Brierley (b. 1825), the Lancashire millworker-poet. "Like newly-married people who look forward to important events we made our cradle before the child was born—we shelved a corner to accommodate what we had the presumption to call a library" when they had no books as yet. "It afterwards became a labour of love to cover the bindings, which we did with stout nankeen, so as to make them last for ever. This work accomplished we had a show night for friends, who, while they encouraged us in our undertaking, did not think we could have achieved so much in so short a time."[37] "These institutions in England's educational barrenness were as oases in the desert," proclaimed Tunstall potter Charles Shaw. Organized around 1850, his society instilled, if anything, too much self-confidence in its members:

We met to discuss and criticise all things in heaven and earth, and sometimes even a far deeper province of the universe. This habit was not born of our conceit—it was the pure birth of our simplicity. We could expatiate about the universe when an examination in the geography of England would have confounded us. We could discuss astronomy (imaginatively) when a sum in decimals would have plucked us from our soaring heights into an abyss of perplexity. We could discuss the policies of governments and nations, and the creeds and constitutions of churches, while we would have been puzzled to give a bare outline of our country's history.

By the 1890s, Shaw noted, the Board schools were providing that kind of basic knowledge, making education less of an adventure and more a matter of examinations. "But we had the freedom of the universe, and such lesser matters as nations and churches, policies and creeds, statesmen and preachers, came easily under our purview." If they lacked a clear sense of direction, they acquired impressive assurance: "No members of the 'Imperial Parliament' ever go with a prouder joy to their great 'House' than we went on Saturday nights to our meetings. There was a hum, a bustle and an interest when we first met, as if the fate of the nation depended on that night's debate." And perhaps it did: several alumni later took up public service at home and throughout the Empire, as far as Canada and Australia. "Without knowing it, our poor little society was preparing to help in empire-building," Shaw boasted, though he was quick to add that "Our contributions never became the elements of reckless and unscrupulous aggression."[38]

The chief ideologist of mutual improvement was Samuel Smiles. His *Self-Help* (1859) sold a quarter million copies by the end of the century and was translated into all the major European and Asian languages. The volume grew out of lectures delivered to a Leeds mutual improvement society in 1845, and drew inspiration from a whole subgenre of self-improving literature: G. L. Craik's *The Pursuit of Knowledge under Difficulties* (1830–31), Thomas Dick's *Improvement of Society by the Diffusion of Knowledge* (1833), Timothy Claxton's *Hints to Mechanics on Self-Education and Mutual Instruction* (1839), and William Robinson's *Self-Education*, as well as the endless stream of popular education articles from the *Penny Magazine* and *Chambers's Edinburgh Journal*. The secularist whitesmith G. J. Holyoake had published *Self-Help by the People*, a history of the Rochdale Pioneers, just two years before Smiles. By then the Sunday schools had indoctrinated an entire generation in the self-help ethic.[39]

The Smiles philosophy was more than a crude success ethic. He was a radical who favored universal suffrage, had some sympathy with Chartism and the ten-hour workday, and strongly supported the Co-operative movement and adult education. He condemned class-bound standards of respectability and denounced pure economic individualism as empty and selfish. In his vision, the working class would raise its educational and economic standards through its own cooperative efforts. Autodidacts like Samuel Bamford, William Lovett, and Thomas Cooper were local heroes in Yorkshire's West Riding: they were also Smiles's models. He preferred to write about workingmen whose achievements were intellectual rather than commercial, though he ruefully noted that his business success stories sold much better.[40]

A labor leader once warned Robert Blatchford away from *Self-Help*: "It's a brutal book; it ought to be burnt by the common hangman. Smiles was the arch-Philistine, and his book the apotheosis of respectability, gigmanity, and selfish grab." It is difficult to imagine who actually spoke those words, because most pre-1914 labor leaders who commented on *Self-Help* admired it. Certainly Blatchford, once he read it carefully, found it "one of the most delightful and invigorating books it has been my happy fortune to meet with," and seriously suggested it should be required reading in schools. He conceded that no socialist could feel entirely comfortable with Smiles's individualism, but *Self-Help* also denounced the worship of power, wealth, success, and keeping up appearances. And, he noted, Smiles himself had second thoughts about the title: he wished he had done more to encourage altruism as well as self-reliance.[41]

Smiles's fans included Labour MPs William Johnson and Thomas Summerbell.[42] Ramsay MacDonald enjoyed his biographies of working-class naturalists. Even A. J. Cook, who became a Communist miners' leader, started out with *Self-Help*.[43] At the turn of the century, Smiles was the most popular author in the 20,000-volume prison library at Wormwood Scrubs.[44] (Benjamin Franklin's autobiography, which conveyed a similar philosophy, was equally inspirational to autodidacts.)[45] Not until the great disillusionment following the First World War would misgivings about Smiles surface in workers' memoirs.[46]

George Gregory (b. 1888) offers a case study in the importance of *Self-Help*. His father was an illiterate Somerset miner, his mother a servant who read nothing but the Bible. "There was a feeling in the home that books were not intended for people like us, and were not actually necessary," he recalled. Gregory only had a few school prizes—*Jack and the Ostrich*, a children's story; *The Crucifixion of Philip Strong*, a gripping tale of labor unrest; and the verses of Cornish poet John Harries—and the family read a weekly serial, *Strongdold the Gladiator*. Having left school at twelve to work in the mines, Gregory had no access to serious reading matter until mid-adolescence, when a clerk introduced him to *Self-Help*. That book, he recalled in old age,

> has lived with me, and in me, for more than sixty years. ... The reference may raise a smile among some moderns for they have no liking for the industrial context that made the volume so popular in the Victorian Era. Nevertheless, I was impressed by its quality for I had never touched such a book of high quality; and the impression deepened and became vivid as I took it home, read the stories of men who had helped themselves, struggled against enormous difficulties, suffered painful privations, became destitute, and overwhelmed by conditions. Many of them reached the lowest levels of depression, but went on to rise phoenix-like from the ruins of their plans and collapse of their expectations to find a way to success. Such information stirred dormant powers in me. I began to see myself as an individual, and how I may be able to make a break from the general situation of which I had regarded myself as an inseparable part. I realised that my lack of education was not decisive of what I might become, so I commenced to reach out into the future.

In his isolated rural community, Gregory never imagined that he might aspire to a higher profession. Now he returned to his old school for evening classes in chemistry, arithmetic, and mining engineering, where he won a prize book of world history and was introduced to Charles Lyell's *Principles of Geology*. These two volumes taught him to think in evolutionary terms, and he began to read widely on the historicity of religion and the development of capitalism. "My mind underwent an expansion," as did his personal library, "and ambition began to stir." Gregory won a diploma in Mining Engineering and Surveying but, fearful that he might rise out of his class and become a Tory, he returned to work as an ordinary miner. He became a socialist, a trade union organizer, a Co-operative society manager, an antiwar activist, a branch secretary for the Workers' Educational Association and for the League of Nations Union, a Congregational minister, and the owner of more than a thousand books.[47] That is what *Self-Help* set in motion.

Proletarian Science

Samuel Smiles's favorite working-class heroes were amateur scientists, who did real research with no money or training. They were remarkable for their ability to work in isolation. Thomas Edward, the shoemaker-naturalist (b. 1814), had an income of 9s. 6d. a week, little formal education, no books on natural history, and no community of autodidacts with whom he could discuss his research. Learning from the *Penny Magazine* and from observation, he eventually discovered twenty-six new species of crustacea in the Moray Firth; contributed to the *Naturalist*, the *Zoologist*, *Ibis*, and the *Linnaean Journal*; was elected an associate of the Linnaean Society in 1866; and won a Civil List pension of £50 a year.[48] There was also railway porter John Robertson, who made drawings of sunspots and published notices in scientific journals; and John Jones, who loaded slate at the Bangor docks and constructed a telescope powerful enough to observe the icecaps of Mars.[49]

Yet in one important respect these success stories are unrepresentative: proletarian science was a predominantly collective endeavor. Well before Lord Brougham and George Birkbeck established the "first" mechanics' institute in 1824, the working classes were organizing their own. Arguably, the first mutual improvement group was the Spitalfields Mathematical Society, founded in 1717. It met weekly on Saturday evenings to explore the natural sciences, at first at local taverns, later at its own premises. In the mid-1740s about half its members were weavers, the rest a variety of other tradesmen, including braziers, bakers, and bricklayers. By 1784 it had sixty-four members, an impressive library, globes, air pumps, and microscopes.[50] In 1817 whitesmith Timothy Claxton founded a "Mechanical Institution" in London, which sponsored weekly lectures and discussions on the arts and on science. Lacking affluent supporters, it could not acquire its own library, and folded after three years.[51] At about the same time, institutes at Hulme and Salford were set up by fustian cutter Rowland Detrosier, one of several artisan radicals who used scientific lectures as propaganda for Tom Paine's materialism. As Gwyn Williams observed, their faith in education and respectability was so thorough "that they, no less than the evangelicals, can claim the title of prototype Victorians," precursors of Samuel Smiles.

That impulse gave rise to a network of plebeian circles devoted to natural history, predominantly in northern England. In 1829 some botanical workingmen, discontent with the middle-class tone of the Manchester Mechanics' Institution, founded the Banksian Society (after Sir Joseph Banks) and elected Rowland Detrosier its first president.[52] With not more than fifty members, the society had a well-used library of fifty-four books, acquired a microscope and some cabinets of plants and insects, and met monthly to examine specimens. Within a few years, deaths and retirements had broken the group's momentum, and in 1836 it was absorbed back into the Manchester Mechanics' Institution.[53] One of the organizers of the Banksian Society was handloom weaver John Horsefield, who headed two other similar groups, the Prestwich Botanical Society and the General Botanical Meetings.

The plebeian botanists built on a long tradition of popular herbalism and floriculture. Nicholas Culpeper's classic *Herbal* (1652) and John Wesley's *Primitive Physic* (1747) continued to be reprinted well into the nineteenth century and were widely distributed in working-class communities. Artisan botanists of the north country not only exchanged information among themselves: they were also important sources for gentleman naturalists, with whom they traded specimens and discoveries. William Withering's *A Systematic Arrangement of British Plants* owed much to contributions from artisan correspondents. Before science was professionalized at the end of the nineteenth century, working-class naturalist societies were active participants in scientific research.

Following the Methodist model, they organized themselves into local groups of eight to forty members, and came together for larger area meetings (70 to 250 participants) on Sundays. The local societies were commonly based in pubs, which offered meeting rooms and housed specimens and libraries in return for a certain minimum purchase of refreshment. The pub setting, combined with high rates of female illiteracy, insured that these meetings were, with some exceptions, exclusively male. There was commonly a membership fee of 6d. a month, which was spent on drink and books. The Prestwich Botanical Society, for example, purchased 131 volumes between 1820 and 1850.[54]

Chartist Robert Lowery found among the miners of Northumberland and Durham

many superior mathematicians, and the booksellers of Newcastle were known to sell, chiefly among the workmen of the north, a larger number of works on that science than were sold in any other similar district of the country. Some of these men were excellent horticulturalists and florists .... I was acquainted with one: ... as he walked among his flower beds he would sound their scientific names in his provincial tones, intermingling his conversation with remarks on the philosophy of Locke, or quoting passages from Milton, Byron, Shelley, or Burns.[55]

Followers of Robert Owen saw revolutionary potential in those worker-scientists. In the mid-1840s Allen Davenport—shoemaker, poet, and former president of the Tower Street Mutual Instruction Society—estimated that there were nearly fifty groups in and around London where working men and women were studying

> chemistry, geology, mathematics, and astronomy, with all the gravity, deliberation, and confidence, of old and experienced professors. And will the government and legislature of this country still look on and remain stationary, while every thing is changing around them? Will they stand still and see the intellectual struggle that is being made by the working classes, to acquire a thorough knowledge of every branch of useful science—such as the agricultural, manufacturing, and commercial systems—the principles and powers of the production and distribution of wealth—the science of government— and the best means of establishing and extending through every grade of the community, a free, and untrammelled education! Will they be the last in the race of improvement, and cling to the old worn-out laws and institutions? while inventive genius, with steam and mechanical powers, is revolutionizing every nation, and changing the political, the commercial, and the manufacturing systems of the world! Are they so blind, or so infatuated, that they neither see, nor will be persuaded of the approaching storm—the moral earthquake, which will shake the world, and convulse Europe from its centre to its circumference—from the Baltic to the Mediterranean, and from the Bay of Biscay to the Bosphorus; unless an universal change in the political and social system of nations takes place, and a more equal distribution of human subsistence shall be conceded.[56]

Perhaps more typical, however, were eight apolitical Kettering velvet-weavers, who in the 1830s hung a map of the world in their workroom, placed entomological specimens in the window-sills, and pooled money to buy books. Five of those eight would rise out of the artisan class. A sixth (who became a poet) explained that weaving was

> very favourable to self-culture—almost infinitely more so than the business of the trading classes; and if there is one study to which mechanical employment is particularly favourable, it is that of metaphysics .... No costly laboratory or apparatus is required; but the topic can at all times be followed up, without anything to interfere with the thinker, and without extraneous aid.

He could ponder philosophical questions while at work, jotting his conclusions in a notebook kept by the loom, sometimes discussing Locke and Reid with a philosophical woolcomber.[57] As late as 1900 such societies were still quite common in Lancashire.[58] But the tradition of proletarian naturalists did not last long into the twentieth century, when scientific research became the preserve of university-trained specialists.

How They Got On

Mutual improvement, then, was an evolving movement that changed in several directions over two centuries. Workingmen developed their own libraries until the late nineteenth-century expansion of public libraries made their efforts redundant. In areas where public library services were slow to penetrate, notably the coal valleys of South Wales, miners made exceptional efforts to support their own libraries up to the mid-twentieth century. Political controversy found a home in mutual improvement societies until around 1850, faded out in the mid-Victorian years, then revived in the 1880s. Women were mostly excluded from mutual improvement activities before the late nineteenth century. And mutual improvement societies were important providers of adult remedial schooling until the 1870 Education Act and the achievement of near universal literacy, when they could turn to exploring politics and literature on a more sophisticated plane.

One can trace some of these trends in the Gallatown Mutual Improvement Association (founded 1863), one of the very few that has left any historical record. The members came from a range of social ranks—miners, handloom weavers, and potters as well as teachers and manufacturers—but they had in common a lack of basic education. In its early years, therefore, the society concentrated on teaching grammar and history. The first essays presented focused on elementary topics: Art, The Sheep, Coal, Good Habits, Paper, Water, The Power of Steam, The Eagle, The Seasons, Countries, Domestic Animals, The Late Flood at Sheffield, War, Gravitation, Strong Drink, The Bible, Safe Company, Indolence and Industry. Equally light subjects were selected for debate, such as The Eye and the Ear—Which Affords the Most Pleasure? Within a decade, however, more controversial papers appeared on the agenda: Stability of Society, Primeval Man, Strikes, The Drinking Traffic, The Relation between Science and Scripture, Equality. The first generation of members had held to the theology of their fathers; now biblical criticism and Darwin were having an impact. In 1875 there was a debate on republicanism vs. monarchism, with the royalists winning by a single vote. The first paper on socialism appeared on the roster for 1887, and within a few years the members were discussing Home Rule for Ireland and women's suffrage. By 1891 there were presentations on the French Revolution and the Oppression of the Masses. In 1895, the all-male club voted twenty-six to fifteen to support a resolution for women's equality. At the turn of the century they were discussing the Dreyfus Affair and anarchism, and they voted down (eleven to twenty-two) a motion to support the war in South Africa.[59] (One historian has observed a similar shift to controversial issues in a Unitarian mutual improvement society in Keighley).[60]

The autobiography of miner Chester Armstrong (b. 1868) densely chronicles the role of mutual improvement in transforming working-class intellectual life. He grew up in a Cumberland village where there were few books other than the Bible, *Pilgrim's Progress*, Baxter's *Saints' Rest*, and some devotional volumes. All the same, mid-Victorian rural Nonconformity provided a real foundation for cultural growth. His family often had preachers and elders over for tea: the discussions focused on detailed critiques of sermons and ministers, and close readings of Scripture and spiritual experiences. "I always listened intently, and in doing so was unconsciously cultivating the habit of analysis which has become all the more intense as I have advanced in years," he recalled. Simultaneously, his political consciousness was awakened when his father, a self-help Radical, read aloud the weekly paper, which brought home the horrors of the Afghan and Zulu wars.

Armstrong relocated to Ashington, another mining town, where the mechanics' institute was the only cultural resource. But in its library he discovered "a new world" and "a larger environment" in Defoe, Marryat, Fenimore Cooper, Dickens, and Jules Verne. As the population of Ashington grew, other cultural institutions blossomed: a Co-operative society hall that featured political speakers, a Harmonic Society concert hall and orchestra, a Miners' Association hall, a new library, several new churches, and Gilchrist Lectures on the sciences that attracted large and rapt audiences. In 1898 Armstrong organized the Ashington Debating and Literary Improvement Society, and his reading broadened out to Shakespeare, Burns, Shelley, Keats, Tennyson, Byron, Whitman, Wordsworth, Scott, Robert Browning, Darwin, and T. H. Huxley. Robertson Nicoll's *British Weekly* had introduced him to a more liberal Nonconformity that was hospitable to contemporary literature. The difficulty was that the traditional Nonconformist commitment to freedom of conscience was propelling him beyond the confines of Primitive Methodism, as far as Unitarianism, the Rationalist Press Association, and the Independent Labour Party. His tastes in literature evolved apace: Ibsen, Zola, Meredith, and Wilde by the 1890s; then on to Shaw, Wells, and Bennett; and ultimately Marxist economics and *Brave New World.* Meanwhile, his conception of the function of literature changed as well. Great books were "the common property of mankind," transcending time and provinciality, but they were not scriptures containing absolute truths. In his immaturity he had worshipped particular authors,

> each on his separate pedestal, to whom I bowed in grave humility. We talked of our household gods in authors. In heated dispute we quoted our respective gods by way of clinching the argument, just as in religion Biblical authority is used. … It now seems to me obvious that to lean on authority is to acknowledge the philosophy of crutches, which is fatal to culture and to companionship in literature. … I have good reasons to know the spell which canonized writers and others yet cast over the minds of mankind—a spell yet fatal to free initiative and self-reliance in culture.
>
> It was not until I made the discovery that all writers who ever penned a document, whether they were included among the saints or not, belonged to one common humanity and were therefore capable of error, that a free avenue was opened for my approach to them. And now [1938] when I know how

widely the great ones differ—even among the saints—in their own special departments, I think there is no need to fear if I should have to differ from all of them. I now feel assured that to make an idol of an author or a fetish of a book is tantamount to slavery in one of its many forms. I still retain, however, my household gods; only that halo round their heads has vanished, and my worship has given place to a more matured respect born of the knowledge of their fallibility and therefore of the success of their achievements. I now feel that I can, so to speak, walk arm in arm with them and so converse on familiar terms.

This, I think, suggests the right relationship between author and reader … .

In other words, "Book culture is distinctly a matter of mutuality," just as it had always been in the Ashington Debating and Literary Improvement Society.[61] For people accustomed to accepting dogmas handed down by churches, chapels, teachers, politicians, and employers, mutual improvement provided invaluable training in forming and expressing opinions. Exercising that atrophied muscle was painful for David Willox (b. 1845), a Parkhead handloom weaver and iron-puddler. "I was a silent member for a long time," he admitted, "but latterly began to offer a few trembling remarks, principally of an enquiring kind. It was long before I ventured into the ocean of controversy. I was like a child learning to skate or slide upon ice. I kept pottering away about the margin of the lake to see how the ice was bearing before I would trust myself on the open sheet."[62] These miniature parliaments did much to build the confidence of future Labour politicians. In 1910, on the floor of the Malton Mutual Improvement Society, chemist's apprentice Philip Inman called for the abolition of the House of Lords. Thirty-six years later he was sitting in it.[63]

For F. H. Spencer (b. 1872), a Swindon factory worker's son, mutual improvement provided all the intellectual stimulation he did not receive in teacher training. "The education of a pupil teacher in the eighteen eighties … was designed to enable a mediocre head master to prepare an unintelligent pupil teacher for a very easy examination. Any lad or girl of energy and intelligence could have passed the fourth-year examination before the end of the first year," he protested. "In history we just learned facts out of a date-book. And I got some background out of Scott. Geography was a thing of names, meaningless, wearisome names, and our instructor was dull, stupid and conscientious beyond words." It was a Young Men's Friendly Society that "liberalised and awakened such mind as I had." Members debated capitalism and socialism, performed scenes from *The Merchant of Venice* and *The Pickwick Papers*. A mix of students, workers, and lower professionals encouraged Spencer to read broadly and trained him in public speaking. (There were some women in the group, but they were not yet bold enough to contribute to the debates.) He could also use the celebrated GWR Mechanics' Institute Library, which, with more than 20,000 volumes, was "as good as that of any London club": "The son of a duke could have been little better off in the matter of access to English books." Spencer went through a phase of regretting the lack of a university education, but he came to realize that mutual improvement had brought him into contact with a much broader section of humanity, and had prepared him to rise to the rank of Chief School Inspector for the London Education Committee.[64]

Mutual improvement drives home the lesson that no autodidact is entirely self-educated. He or she must rely on a network of friends and workmates for guidance, discussion, and reading material. Exclusion from those networks (together with lower rates of literacy) largely accounts for the scarcity of female proletarian intellectuals and autobiographers in the nineteenth century. Only as working women became more active in corporate bodies such as the Labour Party, the Co-operative movement, trade unions, and mutual improvement societies did they begin to produce memoirs in large numbers.

In the early Scottish workingmen's libraries studied by John Crawford, between zero and 10 percent of members were women, and they had no role in governance. Wanlockhead barred women until 1812, Leadhills until 1881, though they might have read books borrowed by male family members.[65] Later, some mechanics' institutes were open to women in a limited way, and a few institutions specifically for women were founded at Bradford, Huddersfield, and Keighley. The 1851 census reported that only 9.4 percent of all mechanics' institute students were female, many of them middle-class. In 1857 one hundred associated mechanics' institutes and mutual improvement societies in Lancashire and Cheshire had a total of 19,880 male members and only 2,150 female members, with 8,050 men and 500 women attending evening classes.[66]

Where workingmen had access to education and women did not, communication between the two was likely to break down. One wife complained that when her husband brought home fellow students from the Working Men's College,

> These people would come, bow to us, say "How do you do?" when they came, and "Good night" when they went; all the rest of the time would be spent talking about things we did not understand. If we asked questions, we heard about Algebra, Shakespeare, or Red Sandstone. What these things were we had no idea; nor did our lords and masters seem to know enough about them to be able to explain them in simple words that we could understand … . All that *we* learned from the conversation of the learned Collegians on Sundays was, that all the teachers of some sort of classes (I think they called them Mathematical) wore double-breasted waistcoats and Albert watchguards of the same pattern. We women felt, naturally, not quite satisfied with this.

When she had the chance to attend college classes, even for a few months, she learned just enough to establish an intellectual rapport with her husband.[67] But there was no united female front on this issue: another student's wife affirmed that women belonged in the domestic sphere, and doubted that further education would be helpful there.[68] And workingmen of the early nineteenth century rarely acknowledged women as intellectual equals or companions. Like Felix Holt, they were liable to regard females as a distraction for men in pursuit of the truth.[69] In early Victorian Carlisle, women had very limited access to workingmen's reading rooms. In 1852 some men seceded from their reading room in protest against the admission of too many women. By the 1860s and 1870s, however, there was at least serious discussion of extending adult education to women in Carlisle.[70] As late as 1893 women were admitted to only one of Keighley's numerous mutual improvement societies, which was connected with the Unitarian Church.[71] In fact, workingmen in northern England were more hostile to female education than their brothers in the south: by the late 1870s, twenty out of twenty-seven Methodist mutual improvement associations in the London area admitted both sexes.[72] At this time women were generally more literate than men south of the Wash–Severn line but less literate north of it.[73] And in the Co-operative movement, between 1897 and 1915, women were far more likely to be elected to educational committees in southern England than in Lancashire and the West Riding.[74]

Autobiographical evidence suggests that provincial groups were finally opening up by the turn of the century,[75] but the women who joined them could still encounter some suspicion. Alice Foley recalled that her older sister Cissy— a suffragette, Labour Church member, and textile workers' union officer—found a circle of girlfriends in Bolton who met to discuss "politics, men, votes for women and culture." Together they took an Oxford extension course on Robert Browning, and talked of William Morris and Karl Marx. Their mother dismissed them as "fuss-pots" indulging in "long-curtain" talk. "To replace short by long curtains was a sign of moving up in the social scale," Alice explained, and in fact Cissy's intellectual friends were mostly shopclerks and office workers rather than factory girls.[76]

The Women's Co-operative Guild (founded 1883) was a female mutual improvement association with a feminist agenda, peaking at 88,000 members in 1938. But it too faced opposition among northern miners,[77] as D. H. Lawrence observed in Sons and Lovers. Though Mrs. Morel finds stimulation reading papers before her local chapter, and wins "the deepest respect" of her children, many men treated such activities as a threat: "From off the basis of the guild, the women could look at their homes, at the conditions of their own lives, and find fault. So, the colliers found their women had a new standard of their own, rather disconcerting."[78]

The Guild certainly had revolutionary consequences for Deborah Smith (b. 1858), a Nelson weaver. She was raised by parents who were poor, illiterate, and not inclined to encourage education. Having had only a brief interval of half-time schooling she was, as Secretary of the Nelson Women's Co-operative Guild, initially embarrassed by her inability to write and spell. Nevertheless the Guild, with its meetings and lectures, "opened up a new life to me .... I got new ideas, a wider view of life. It taught me to think for myself on all questions." She began reading poetry and, at age fifty-one, discovered her own spiritual longings in Tennyson:

> Break, break on thy cold grey stones, oh sea,
> Oh would that my tongue could utter
> The thoughts that arise in me!

She had always hesitated to write about her own life, because she did not know "if anyone had an experience like mine." The revelation that classic authors shared her thoughts liberated her latent powers of self-expression. "I began to realise the experience of the poets who had written such poetry, and I felt like getting in touch with them," she explained. "We find that Art and Literature and Beauty are stored in our own souls once that creative power gives them life." Though raised as an Independent Methodist, she now found that class meetings did not welcome her questioning spirit: "Sometimes I gave them poetry, but one of our women said, we must have nothing but the Bible." It was in reading circles that she found "The questions, the friendly discussions, the exchange of opinions about many things [that] all teach us to be tolerant."[79]

Working-class women had less opportunity to practice public speaking than their men, and here again mutual improvement proved invaluable. When Elizabeth Andrews (b. 1882), a Welsh miner's daughter, prepared a paper for the Wesley Guild, the prospect of reading it made her physically ill, and the minister had to present it for her. Though she eventually became a suffragist and Labour Party organizer, the experience taught her "to be very patient and understanding when training women to take part in public work for the first time."[80]

Since most mutual improvement societies are beyond the reach of historical detection, estimating their total membership is next to impossible. Nevertheless, studies focusing on small geographical areas have found impressively high levels of participation. The 1851 census reported that something less than 1 percent of the total population belonged to mechanics' institutes, but as Ian Inkster notes, the census-takers probably missed most of the smaller informal societies. Adult education appealed mainly to workingmen aged twenty to thirty-nine, and may have reached as much as 15 percent of that target population in the Huddersfield area.[81] In rural districts, where there were few other distractions, institutes could attract an even larger proportion. In 1850 the village of Ripley had only 300 inhabitants, of which fifty-seven belonged to its own little institute, based in a hayloft.[82] By 1881 nearly every church and chapel in Keighley sponsored mutual improvement societies, with an estimated total membership of nearly 1,000, or about 6 percent of the male population.[83] Impressionistic evidence offered by autobiographers suggests the same level of saturation in Newcastle[84] and North Wales.[85]

Although the Working Men's Club and Institute Union was primarily a social organization, it also made a contribution to mutual education. In 1874 it comprised 312 clubs: of those that filed reports, 21 percent held classes in the arts and sciences,

33 percent sponsored lectures, 64 percent held "musical and elocutionary entertainments," and nearly all had lending libraries.[86] By 1903 there were about 900 clubs with 321,000 members. Five hundred of those clubs had libraries with a total of 187,000 volumes, though mostly fiction was in demand. Some clubs staged theatrical productions, usually melodramas but occasionally Shakespeare.[87]

Similarly, the Co-operative societies were authorized to spend up to 2.5 percent of their profits on education. Most spent nothing at all, but some developed impressive programs. In the 1870 and 1880s there were actually more Co-operative libraries than public libraries nationwide.[88] The Royal Arsenal Co-operative Society in Woolwich was devoting nearly £1,000 to education in 1901, up to £18,792 in 1937 for its 362,000 members or about 1s. per member. It opened a library in 1879, twenty-two years before any municipal library service began. By the 1930s it had 10,000 volumes, mostly light fiction, but also economics, social science, and philosophy. In 1928 the society fielded 280 dramatic and musical groups, staging Shakespeare, Ibsen, Galsworthy, and Shaw. The London area Co-operative societies together could mobilize armies of performers for mass musical events. Eight hundred choristers plus orchestras offered a concert version of *Carmen* at the Albert Hall in 1927. John Allen of the Unity Theatre massed 400 singers from fifteen Co-operative society choirs for Handel's *Belshazzar* in May 1938, when the fall of Babylon and the liberation of the Jews had a clear anti-Nazi message.[89]

Chekhov in Canning Town

By their very nature, amateur theatricals were an exercise in mutual education, the Board of Education noted in a 1926 report. As one participant put it, drama at once encouraged community and individuality: it demanded not the regimentation of the shop floor, but a more creative kind of collective action. The actor "takes his place in the team, and passes on to self-expression, self-discipline and conscious co-operation with others. He finds perhaps for the first time, that he is doing something, is giving out rather than merely receiving impressions from others." Townspeople bitterly opposed to each other in religion and politics could work together on a common project, and producing foreign plays broke through the provincialism of industrial towns. Those who were intimidated by a university-level extra-mural course might be more receptive to practical drama. Onstage, working people could enjoy an opportunity that they rarely had in life— to assume another role and express themselves to an audience. If they were not ready for that, they could always make costumes and build sets.

Recognizing this, settlement houses sponsored fringe theaters for local amateurs. The Mary Ward Settlement in London was home to the St. Pancras People's Theatre, with seats priced from 6d. to 2s. 6d., as well as the Working Class Dramatic Club, which staged prize-winning productions of *Arms and the*

Man and Gilbert Murray's *Andromache*. The first season of the Mansfield House Players in Canning Town featured Galsworthy's *Strife*, *The Merry Wives of Windsor*, *Pygmalion*, Tolstoy's *Michael*, Chekhov's *The Proposal*, and Anatole France's *The Dumb Wife*, attracting audiences of up to 800. Between 1919 and 1945, the Little Theatre at the Sheffield Educational Settlement produced Aeschylus (*The Oresteia*), Sophocles (*Oedipus Rex, Antigone*), Euripides (*The Trojan Women*), Aristophanes (*The Frogs*), Marlowe (*Dr. Faustus*), Shakespeare (*Twelfth Night, Hamlet, King Lear, Macbeth, Othello, Romeo and Juliet*), Milton (*Comus, Samson Agonistes*), Goethe (both parts of *Faust*), Schiller (*The Maid of Orleans*), Pushkin (*Boris Godunov, Mozart and Salieri*), Ibsen (*A Doll's House, Emperor and Galilean*), Tolstoy (*Where God Is, Love Is*), Wilde (*A Woman of No Importance*), Shaw (*The Devil's Disciple, Arms and the Man, The Man of Destiny, Major Barbara*), Yeats (*Cathleen-ni-Houlihan*), Synge (*The Playboy of the Western World*), and Ernst Toller (*Masses and Men*).

Strictly speaking, settlement houses were not mutual improvement societies, they were university-sponsored institutions staffed by educated men and women. But the literary, musical, and dramatic groups they hosted offered the same kind of collaborative working-class education. In 1938 Alexander Hartog, an apprentice tailor, found in Toynbee Hall the creative community that affluent intellectuals might hope to find in a university or bohemian quarter:

> I fitted in there like a very happy bug in a well-known and well-loved rug ....
> Brilliantly gifted people of the many shades of Art were there—ballet dancers,
> actors, musicians, singers, painters, sculptors .... It was a common meeting-
> ground of people who had some artistic bent. One person gave forth to
> another, and the other received it and gave out something of his own to others.
> The atmosphere was truly magical. It hit me then and, even now as
> I look back, I still think, "That was the first time in my life I felt I was
> really where I belonged." I was surrounded by people who were like myself.
> They were searching, they were participating. In an atmosphere almost of
> gaiety people were talking about their art and their pleasure and their
> activities.[90]

With the same goal in mind, the YMCA, London County Council Evening Institutes, and the WEA sponsored dramatic activities. Beginning in 1912, the Oxford and Bermondsey Shakespeare Society staged annual productions performed entirely by boys from one of London's roughest districts. The producer admitted that "About 5 per cent or less of our boy actors learn to appreciate the language of Shakespeare, but very few of them read, and hardly one writes decent English." Their passion for drama, he concluded,

> lies in their keen enjoyment of the acting as a form of expression and legitimate
> self-display, and the intensely valuable training of the team spirit necessitated

by everyone merging his own wishes and convenience in the requirements of the whole cast—punctuality for rehearsals, thoroughness at dull spade work, striving for corporate effect rather than individual brilliance, etc. In fact, the value of our yearly production (which I am certain is very great) is much the same as the value of a good football team—only it appeals to a rather different type of boy who would probably not be interested much in football.

Even prison educators found that Shakespearean tragedy could reduce convicts to tears and provoke profound moral self-examination. The Board of Education reported "it was a common experience of one of the teachers to meet members of his class at Shakespeare performances after their release." One instructor found that Shakespeare dissolved the teacher-student hierarchy, even when the audience was literally captive:

If I took a class in economics, I should always be in the position of a teacher, by whatever title I chose to call myself. I would have the advantage of a trained mind, and an accumulation of facts far greater than that of anyone in my class. But in the study of the drama my education has left me little, if at all, in advance of any of my class, because the points which come up for discussion are questions of life and character where their knowledge and experience are as great, and probably greater, than my own. It seems to me that we find in the plays, and particularly in the Shakespeare plays, a basis of common experience and common humanity which destroys any barrier erected by social conventions and differences in educational opportunities.

To break down the barriers separating different levels of employees, drama societies were sponsored by a number of progressive corporations, such as Lyons Teashops and the cocoa manufacturers Rowntree and Cadbury. One large London office found that company athletic clubs rarely appealed to more than a single grade of workers, but a drama society attracted more than 400 employees of every rank. Shakespeare was selected for the first production, and an outside director brought in to ensure impartiality. Two executives were cast as artisans, two messengers played courtiers, and the society's chairman gave orders to players who far outranked him in the office.

Shakespeare dominated the repertory of amateur dramatic groups partly because his plays were labor intensive. Where most modern plays had small casts, Elizabethan drama offered roles to battalions of actors, musicians, dancers, dressmakers, and set builders. That was a vital consideration when 400 people, with much enthusiasm but very mixed talents, showed up at an organizational meeting. Greek tragedy was also remarkably popular, thanks largely to the translations of Gilbert Murray, which put a premium on accessibility and stageworthiness. At a competition for amateur groups sponsored by the British Drama League, an educational official was stunned by two of the finalists:

The Merchant of Venice had been produced by a boys' club in one of the worst parts of the East End, and the Shylock who had so thrilled me was a boy of 16. The *Andromache* had been given by a working girls' club in a very poor neighbourhood. And I thought of these boys and girls taking into their poor homes the beauty and splendour of two of the world's greatest masterpieces, and of all that it must mean in the enrichment of their lives. If I had any doubt as to the power of the drama as an instrument of education in its highest sense, it was resolved that evening.

Though the drama was always a disciplined group activity, it offered the kind of intellectual freedom that had always been the prime objective of autodidacts. J. R. Gregson, a cotton mill worker turned factory clerk, wrote, produced, and performed in plays for the Stockport Garrick Society, the Huddersfield Thespians, the Leeds Art Theatre, the Leeds Industrial Theatre, and the York Everyman Theatre. For him, the theater was a repudiation of the "insane ideal of standardisation" imposed by his old Board school, where "variety in boyhood was a vice, apparently, to be exorcised at whatever cost (to the boy!)." He found "a freer, more human, discursive and conversational method of tuition" in adult drama classes. "No digression was too long, no bypath too tortuous to be explored in company with, not ahead of, us. We were encouraged to think for ourselves and to follow our individual bent." That experience convinced him that knowledge is only valuable when

acquired as a bye-product of one's own originality and special turn of mind .... Only in the drama did I find the fullest scope for this vital activity and in the service of the drama I have acquired, as a bye-product, what real knowledge I possess and what real mental ability I exercise .... I know what modern industry means in terms of monotonous routine tasks. I know what a working-class home-life means, with few outlets for emotional "release" save the "pub" and the "chapel." I know the mental apathy and the crippled spirit they engender. I have spent my life fighting against this state of mind and temper, both in myself and in my fellows. The working-man's first instinct is to distrust beauty when he is made to see it. Talk to him of what life means to you, and he will confide to his neighbour—behind your back—that you are a bit funny sometimes!

The drama, he was convinced, offered working people a true "release" for the individual spirit:

This is not theory or hearsay. ... I have proved it myself and seen and helped others to prove it. I believe that the most valuable result of the work at the Industrial Theatre was that it allowed, nay demanded, that the workpeople-players should break their shells and "come out of themselves." This, to me, is the first and all-sufficient justification of the drama. Before a player can be anything but a stick he must try, at the cost of violence to his timid reserve, to become someone else. He must conquer his inbred repression, rouse his dormant spirit, practise insight and a sympathetic understanding of the "other fellow," and the pleasure of this, the freedom and relief it brings in train, will result in the practice of the imaginative faculty off the stage as well as on. As one workman put it, "It's no use trying to be somebody else unless you try to feel what he feels." Another description of this sensation of release is most pithy. Said one of my actors in *The Merchant of Venice*, "Eh, I've been miles away from myself tonight, and I feel pounds lighter for it."[91]

A Common Culture?

Especially in the late nineteenth and early twentieth centuries, after the achievement of mass literacy but before radio and television, working-class culture was saturated by the spirit of mutual education. Every day, information and ideas were exchanged in literally millions of commonplace settings—parlors and kitchens, workplaces and shops. One has to multiply thousands of times over the self-educated Leeds shoe repairer whose customers (including the local vicar and policeman) would congregate at his shop to debate religion, politics, and economics. Though his young son (b. 1887) could not entirely follow the discussions, he went on to become secretary of a Methodist Young Men's Class.[92]

Everywhere informal groups of militant workingmen, even from the London police force, came together for intellectual discourse. C. H. Rolph remembered the "Turneymen," a circle of radical intellectual constables led by Bob Turney, that flourished between the world wars. They clubbed together to buy used BBC classical records from a Shaftesbury Avenue shop. They circulated among themselves copies of the *New Statesman* and a collective season ticket to the Promenade Concerts at Queen's Hall.

> They read Proust and Spengler, Macaulay and Gibbon, Tom Paine and Cobbett, Hume and Herbert Spencer. They never missed a Harold Laski public lecture. They went in a solid phalanx to hear Shaw, Belloc and Chesterton debate at Kingsway Hall. And they formed an archaeological group to look for relics of Norman and Roman London whenever they happened to have freshly excavated building sites on their beats.[93]

The tailoring factories of the Jewish East End offered the same kind of radical ferment. In the sweatshop Hymie Fagan was pleased to call "my university," the shop steward introduced him to Jack London's *The Call of the Wild* and *The Iron Heel*, Upton Sinclair's *The Jungle*, and *The Ragged Trousered Philanthropists*. There were passionate and sophisticated shopfloor debates about Tolstoy, Gorky,

Pushkin, Zola, Anatole France, Zangwill, Sholem Aleichem, religion, Zionism, and the recent (and much welcomed) Russian Revolution. Workers would re-enact Morris Moscovitch performing a Yiddish Hamlet in the style of Henry Irving, or Chaliapin singing *Boris Godunov*.[94]

Meanwhile, the second generation was making good use of the Whitechapel Public Library. It has acquired legendary status as a haven where Jewish slum kids could escape overcrowded flats and plunge into books, but there also study was a social activity. "It was not only a place where one could just about get an hour's homework done in four hours, but a meeting place for boys and girls," recalled one habitué. "It was something like a drugstore without the coloured drinks. The girls of many different schools sat there and the boys of other schools helped them with their homework." There was much conversation and some rowdiness, in spite of a stern librarian.[95]

By far the most pervasive form of mutual education was, quite simply, reading aloud. In pubs and on street corners, at Chartist meetings and in Methodist circles, the communal reading of newspapers multiplied their audience far beyond their circulation figures. In workshops, one laborer commonly read aloud while the others divided his share of the work. In an oral history investigation of social life between 1870 and 1918, half of all working-class interviewees indicated that reading aloud (including Bible reading and parents reading to children) was practiced in the homes where they were raised.[96] Even the illiterate, the sight-impaired, and eternally busy housewives could share to some extent the world of print.

Oral reading was institutionalized in the form of the penny reading. Its inventor, Samuel Taylor, was a clayworker who became secretary of the Hanley Mechanics' Institute and part-proprietor of the *Staffordshire Sentinel.* A passionate Liberal apostle of a "free, cheap, enlightened press," Taylor began in 1854 to read Russell's Crimean War dispatches for the *Times* from a terrace in Hanley's market square. The first "war readings" attracted 8,000 to 10,000 people. The authorities welcomed them as a means of keeping the lower orders out of pubs and music halls, so they offered Taylor the free use of the town hall for other readings. In September 1856 he began his "Literary and Musical Entertainments for the People," consisting of readings of selections from popular writers along with some vocal and instrumental music, topped off by the national anthem. At first the events were free, but soon attendance was so great that 1d. admission had to be charged. Within months other towns in the Potteries had adopted them, and a report in the *Times* broadcast the movement over the entire country.[97] Between October 1857 and April 1858 nine Staffordshire towns were staging penny readings for overflow crowds, with a total admission of 60,000 to 70,000—this in a district with a population of 100,000.[98]

All these influences combined to produce a shared literary culture in which books were practically treated as public property, before public libraries reached most of the country. It was a culture that extended even to Flora Thompson's rural

Oxfordshire. "Modern writers who speak of the booklessness of the poor at that time must mean books as possessions," she wrote; "there were always books to borrow." At home, besides the Bible and *Pilgrim's Progress*, there were volumes that some neighbors had discarded when they left town: *Gulliver's Travels*, Grimm's fairy tales, *The Daisy Chain*, and Mrs. Molesworth's *Cuckoo Clock* and *Carrots*. The women exchanged penny novelettes, the men weekly newspapers. One could borrow *Pamela* and the Waverley novels from a neighbor, *Christie's Old Organ* from the Sunday school library. Her uncle, a shoemaker, had once carted home from a country-house auction a large collection of old books that no one would buy: novels, poetry, sermons, histories, dictionaries. She read him *Cranford* while he worked in his shop, where he would discuss politics, science, and religion with the locals. Later, she could borrow from her employer (the village postmistress) Shakespeare and Byron's *Don Juan*, as well as Jane Austen, Dickens, and Trollope from the Mechanics' Institute library. The women held parties where they sewed clothing for the poor while one of them read aloud. The penny reading, dying out in most parts of the country by the 1890s, was still popular in these rural villages, though the material was fairly standard. Poetic selections were usually on the level of "Excelsior," "The Village Blacksmith," "The Wreck of the Hesperus." An attempt to read episodes from *The Heart of Midlothian* and *Vanity Fair* brought no visible response from the audience. Of course, Dickens made them laugh, cry, and demand encores, but they rarely borrowed his works from the parish library. Urban readers were more active, but as Flora Thompson noted, these country people "were waiting, a public ready-made, for the wireless and the cinema." In fact, a conspicuously precocious reader was likely to arouse resentment among the neighbors:

> None of their children had learned to read before they went to school, and then only under compulsion, and they thought that Laura, by doing so, had stolen a march on them. So they attacked her mother about it, her father conveniently being away. "He'd no business to teach the child himself," they said. "Schools be the places for teaching, and you'll likely get wrong for him doing it when governess finds out". ...
>
> There was a good deal of jealousy and unkindness among the parents over the ... one annual prize for Scripture. Those whose children had not done well in examinations would never believe that the success of others was due to merit. The successful ones were spoken of as "favourites" and disliked. "You ain't a-goin' to tell me that young So-and-So did any better n'r our Jim," some disappointed mother would say. "Stands to reason that what he could do our Jimmy could do, *and* better, too." The parents of those who had passed were almost apologetic. "'Tis all luck," they would say. "Our Tize happened to hit it this time; next year it'll be your Alice's turn." They showed no pleasure in any small success their own children might have. Indeed, it is doubtful if they felt any, except in the case of a boy who, having passed the fourth standard, could

leave school and start work. Their ideal for themselves and their children was to keep to the level of the normal. To them outstanding ability was no better than outstanding stupidity.[99]

The great virtue of mutual improvement was a general sharing of knowledge; its great drawback was a corollary distrust of private study, which was regarded as selfish and unneighborly. The mother of Ruth Johnson (b. 1912) made it clear that reading was not only a distraction from housework, but unsociable as well. As a Lancashire millhand she "had become so habituated to the continuous clamour of the machines that, for her, silence had become almost an unnatural and unfriendly state .... Silence should be devoted to speech, and not frittered away in a still deeper and uncommunicating void of book-reading."[100] The mineworker and novelist J. G. Glenwright (b. early 1900s) aroused resentment among his workmates because he devoted mealtimes to reading rather than conversation.[101] Communing with nature in search of poetic inspiration could generate even greater hostility. As one sympathetic observer recalled, Alfred Williams, the poet of the Swindon railway works,

was considered mad by those villagers to whom animals were just animals, either of value or pests according to their type. Said one "I see'd Alfie Williams t'other night walkin' down 'Poor Meadow' wi' 'is 'ands behind 'n an' gawkin' up at the sky for all the world like a b———— lunatic." By most of his workmates in the forge he was not appreciated. His omission to join them in small talk while waiting between "heats"—preferring to spend the time in studious meditation—was construed by them as snobbishness.[102]

Any kind of serious writing involved prolonged solitude and rumination, and that ran against the grain of working-class culture, as Margaret Thomson Davis (b. 1926) discovered when she began her career as a novelist:

Writers were a different breed from us. They lived in a different world. Indeed it was hard to imagine that such creatures existed in flesh and blood at all. They were so far removed from the tenement flat in the middle of Glasgow in which we lived. For anyone in such an environment to have writing pretensions was treated with the utmost suspicion. More than that, it aroused in one's friends, neighbours and relations acute embarrassment, shame, discomfort and downright hostility.

"There's a lot more important things you could be doing than sitting there scribbling," her mother scolded. "Give that floor a good scrub, for instance." Her father complained of the cost of keeping the light burning at night, and was outraged when he found her using the typewriter he had on loan from his union for his work as branch secretary. When she announced her first acceptance from a publisher, her family responded with embarrassed silence, then resumed talking about the weather. "I felt terribly ashamed," she recalled. "The unspoken belief had been confirmed, that there always had been something odd about me." It was worse for one of her friends, an uneducated Irish laborer. When he shut himself in a bedroom to write, his anxious family held a conference and did everything to dissuade him. "There's something far wrong with a man who writes letters to himself!" his brother exploded. "If you'd just been a pouf the priest could have talked to you or one of us could have battered it out of you. But what the hell can anybody do about a writer?" When he received his first check for a short story, his mother was convinced that he had committed some kind of fraud and insisted that he return it. And when a television play of his was reviewed "his mother was shocked and said that theirs had been a respectable family until then; never once had any of their names been in the paper."[103]

Reading was acceptable provided it was a collective activity, as it commonly was in working-class homes. In turn-of-the-century Bolton, Alice Foley was delegated to borrow books from the public library for her entire family. (After a long trek in clattering clogs, she had to confront enormous catalogues and equally intimidating librarians.) At home the books were doled out to her several brothers and sisters. To her mother, however, a roomful of children reading quietly was practically an insult: "Well, I met as weel goo eaut, for this place is nowt but a deaf an dumb schoo'." Her attitude was understandable: she was illiterate, and silent reading cut her off from literature. It was entirely different when her husband read aloud from Dickens and George Eliot, or when Alice offered to read *Alice in Wonderland*: "To my surprise, mother entered quite briskly into the activities of the rabbit hole. From that time onwards I became mother's official reader and almost every day when I returned from school she would say coaxingly 'Let's have a chapthur.'"[104]

This tradition of collective reading pervasively reinforced the importance of literature and education, even in the many working-class families that were indifferent or even hostile to culture. "It would be easy to summarize my memories of home in one word—quarrels," wrote Harry M. Burton, in his memoir of a bleak London street before the First World War. "When I remember the childhood of other autobiographers—the Boston and Quincy of Henry Adams, the border-country of John Buchan, the Cornwall of Mr. Rowse, even the mining valleys of those teeming literary children of South Wales—I am depressed at the complete absence of any inspiring quality in our little suburban lives. … We never bought a book, never went to an art-gallery, a concert or a theatre (except to the pantomime)." His father, an irregularly employed housepainter, liked a "stirring novel" but nothing more challenging than Conan Doyle: "He had no use whatever for anything remotely approaching the spiritual in art, literature or music, and he seldom took the trouble to conceal his contempt." And yet the whole family read and, on some level, took pleasure in sharing and discussing their reading. His mother recited serials from the *Family Reader* and analyzed them at length with grandma over a cup of tea. Every few minutes his father would offer up a snippet from the *Daily Chronicle* or *Lloyd's Weekly News*. The children were not discouraged from reading aloud, perhaps from Jules Verne: "I can smell to this day the *Journey to the Centre of the Earth*," Burton recalled. The whole family made use of the public library and enjoyed together children's magazines like *Chips* and the *Butterfly*. It was this atmosphere, perhaps, that propelled Burton up the scholarship ladder to the faculty of Cambridge University.[105]

When mutual improvement alumni graduated to the ancient universities, they were likely to be disillusioned. "I had been used to the informal learning situations provided by the Mutual Improvement Society and the WEA class, with the ample opportunities they provided for questions and discussion," explained ex-fitter and Oxford adult student John Allaway (b. 1902), "and I was amazed at the formality of the university lecture system, the aloofness of the university teacher from his students, the perfunctoriness of much of the teaching and the evident reluctance of many university teachers to answer questions or to allow themselves to be drawn into discussion."[106] When Derek Davies attended Oxford after the Second World War, the "elderly dons ... and their Edwardian attitudes consorted ill with the Brave New World I was looking for." He achieved "emancipation" later, in the living rooms of his fellow schoolteachers. "There I found, often without being able to analyse consciously the components, a style of living which rapidly became my ideal. There was talk and argument, and books and music, and pictures on the wall that clearly did something more than merely fill up a space."[107]

The universities did provide the privacy necessary for intensive study, which was in short supply in working-class homes. "Homework was a bit of a problem because our house was hardly ever quiet, and no one sat still for long," recalled scholarship girl Elizabeth Flint (b. c. 1905), whose father worked a vegetable barrow in the East End. "Certainly no one would alter their ways for the sake of homework. If they thought about it at all, which is doubtful, they would have regarded it as a mild lunacy on my part." She usually had to study in a stifling bedroom or at a neighbor's house. As for the kitchen table, that

was always crammed with such a miscellany of things that I would be lucky if I could find space enough for one book alone. On our table there would be cups and mugs, a bag of sugar, like as not Dad's cap would be there, and perhaps a clothes peg or a pile of roughly dried clothes, waiting for whoever would bother to iron them. At home, if you tried to tidy things up a bit, everyone would grumble. "If your old school wants this house to be put upside down for your old books," Mum had said more than once, "then you'd better leave the place."[108]

As late as 1949, Jack Lawson could write: "A library for a workman means a corner in the kitchen or the sitting-room. It is a triumph when he gets a real bookcase or presentable bookshelves in a room apart from workaday affairs. ... Every student workman knows the stages and the progress from no books to books, from books in the kitchen to books in a separate room. These stages are the milestones of his life."[109]

Even when parents cleared the kitchen table and gave their children every encouragement, cramming for examinations could be an alienating experience. Dennis Marsden (b. 1933) came from a solidly respectable, library-using family. His father owned an Esperanto dictionary, lectured on Malthus before a mutual improvement society, enjoyed Shakespeare, Jane Austen, the Brontës, Dickens, Hardy, Conrad, Galsworthy, and Palgrave's *Golden Treasury*. He had been an exceptional essay-writer in school before leaving at thirteen to work in the mills for 5s. a week, and he found a bittersweet satisfaction in the successes of the next generation. Of his fifteen children, nieces, and nephews, all but one passed scholarship examinations, most attended grammar school, five took university degrees, three others attended teacher training colleges, one became a doctor, another a senior civil servant, and yet another a regional child care officer. Dennis went all the way to Cambridge University, but at a price: "More than sheer loneliness, I knew what a mountaineer feels on an exposed climb." His three best friends went to inferior schools, fell back into the ranks of manual workers, and lost contact with him. There was no caning at Marsden's grammar school, but there was relentless cramming. The fact that his parents sacrificed enormously for his education added to the psychological pressures, for they aimed at nothing less than Oxford or Cambridge ("You show 'em, Dennis lad"). "This was a family effort, yet the divide between us was growing," Marsden recalled. "My father began to make jokes about taking me for a walk to get to know me better." When his brother only won a scholarship to Leeds University ("an occasion for tears, recriminations and bad temper") his parents complained that he had spent too much time with his youth club, "a very powerful object lesson for me had any been needed." Marsden shut down his social activities and lived almost in

> suspended animation, a kind of monastic novitiate. Only one of my close friends had any sort of relationship with girls. For the rest of us sex was confined to fantasy or lone visits to American musicals, which involved me very painfully at times. … I was emotionally frozen, and sex came to have two aspects for me. It was a danger to academic work. And more than that it was lower-class. [A] friend who knew girls lived in a notorious council estate, and central-school boys whom I met at the town swimming-club also had girl friends. They seemed more confident and complete; yet all the time I felt I was Grammar-School and my day would come.[110]

For anyone who had spoken before a mutual improvement society, attended a WEA class, or read aloud bits from the evening paper in the kitchen, education was a social activity, not essentially different from the fellowship of the pub, chapel, or trade union. Knowledge was something to be shared around. The scholarship student, in contrast, had to withdraw into a shell and hoard as much information as possible:

> This immediately produced difficulties. Should the wireless be on or off? Could the younger children play noisily? Could the father stretch his legs and tell the day's tales? To ask for silence here was to offend the life of the family, was to go against it in its natural moments of coming together, of relaxation. So many learned the early habit of working with the wireless on and the family talking, of building a cone of silence around themselves. To a certain extent this worked well, but … the family was not always untroubled at this, for the private concentration could produce an abstraction, a forgetfulness, an off-handedness that also gave offence …. These long homework hours, even more than "accent", cut into the vital centres of family life, dislocated the whole household's living. It could generate hostility, misunderstanding, irritation, jealousy; and many mothers had to make a special effort to take it under their protection, to create a new rhythm around it.[111]

Ironically, the conflicts worsened as educational opportunities opened up for working-class children. Mutual improvement societies enabled some of their alumni to rise out of their class, but they could at least feel that they had all helped each other in the disinterested pursuit of knowledge. By the mid-twentieth century, the proliferation of scholarships pressured bright students to abandon the ideal of cooperative liberal education for intense academic competition. Jeremy Seabrook (b. 1939) was painfully sensitive to the change. His mother, who had worked in a boot and shoe factory, cherished her old editions of Dickens, Tennyson, George Eliot, Keats, Shelley, and Browning:

> My mother's school prizes were her most sacred possessions, and, in the hope that I would follow her example, she gave them to me when I was far too young, with the result that I scribbled in them or tore open the binding to see how they were held together; and the works of Tennyson and the *Gems of George Eliot* and the improving fiction with embossed covers and pages edged with gold fell apart in a disorder of dried gum and loose thread. She attributed to education a magical power that was far removed from the pedestrian and dispiriting experience I was subjected to. For her, education represented the chance for working-class people to think for themselves and take control of their own destiny; by the time I came to be educated it had become a process elaborated specifically to avoid this.
>
> We went to the school she had attended thirty years earlier, but it was no longer a place where being clever was consoled with gold-embossed books. Cleverness had become something to be isolated and fostered, like a culture of bacteria, in a vessel free from contamination.

Exceptional students were now set apart in a classroom where "we underwent a programme of social rather than academic training. We were treated like postulants to a closed order." Seabrook won his scholarship, but by then the glittering prizes were meaningless. When his teacher rewarded him with Lamb's *Tales from Shakespeare*, "I told her that I really didn't like Shakespeare, but we needed a teapot stand."[112]

Chapter Three The Difference Between Fact and Fiction

My point of departure is a question posed by Roger Chartier. Discussing the roguery tales of the *Bibliothèque bleue*, he wondered how these popular chapbooks of the seventeenth and eighteenth centuries were actually read. The only evidence of reader response here is textual: these stories combined elements of documentary and parody. That, Chartier concluded, suggests that they were read simultaneously as fiction and nonfiction:

> Belief in what is read is thus accompanied by a laugh that gives it the lie; the readers' acceptance is solicited, but a certain distance shows literature for what it is. There is a subtle equilibrium between the fable presented as such and realistic effects. This delicate balance permits multiple readings that fluctuate between a persuasion by literal interpretation and an awareness of and amusement at the parody. Is it impossible to read with both belief and disbelief? To accept the veracity of the narrative and still refuse to be duped into thinking it authentic? And can we not characterize as "popular" this relation with texts that ask to be taken as real even as they show themselves to be illusory? This was perhaps the most fundamental expectation of the readers of the "blue" volumes. It is also the reason for the success of the literature of roguery, which gave written expression to fragments of social experience even as it parodically denied them. Thus the reader could simultaneously know and forget that fiction was fiction.[1]

This is an ingenious theory, but one could just as easily argue the opposite, and David Hall does: for him the *Bibliothèque bleue* and romances of that genre represent "a paradigm of the literature of escapism" in which "there is nothing of everyday reality."[2] So how were they read: as fact, fiction, or both? More importantly, how can these hypotheses be tested? This chapter does not directly address the reading experiences of seventeenth-century French peasants. Rather, it points toward a method of answering such questions by examining British plebeian readers since the eighteenth century.

Cinderella as Documentary

Hanoverian Britain had its counterpart of the *Bibliothèque bleue*—chapbooks offering romances, fairy tales, and other fantastic stories.[3] And a few of their readers, in memoirs, helpfully explained how they read them. As a boy, the poet John Clare (b. 1793) consumed 6d. romances of Cinderella and Jack and the Beanstalk, "and great was the pleasure, pain, or surprise increased by allowing them authenticity, for I firmly believed every page I read and considered I possessed in these the chief learning and literature of the country."[4] He also had a neighbor who

> believes every thing that he sees in print as true and has a cupboard full of penny books the king and the cobler Seven Sleepers accounts of People being buried so many days and then dug up alive Of bells in churches ringing in the middle of the night Of spirits warning men when they was to die etc each of the relations attested to by the overseers churchwardens etc of the parish where the strange relations happened always a century back where none lives to contradict it such things as these have had personal existences with his memory on as firm footings as the bible history itself.[5]

As he wrote in his poem, "St. Martin's Eve," peasants implicitly accepted the tale of Bluebeard as fact:

> Yet simple souls their faith it knows no stint
> Things least to be believed are most preferred
> All counterfeits as from truth's sacred mint
> Are readily believed if once set down in print.[6]

Why were even the most fantastic chapbooks commonly read as true? Consider the factor of intertextuality. If readers' responses to one text are shaped by other texts, then the second question any historian of reading must ask is: What else were they reading? In this case, three books in particular stand out: the Bible of course, *Pilgrim's Progress*, and *Robinson Crusoe*. In the memoirs of common readers they are frequently discussed together, and men from humble backgrounds, such as miners' MP Thomas Burt (b. 1837), remembered reading *Pilgrim's Progress* or *Robinson Crusoe* as literal truth.[7]

By way of explanation, it is sometimes suggested that the credibility of a story can be enhanced simply by setting it in print. One old illiterate carter, listening to a reading of reports from the *Banbury Guardian* on Joseph Arch's efforts to organize an agricultural laborers' union, certainly felt that print had more truth value than oral communication:

The best things be in books, Joe. Look at the letters you rades me out o' the *Banbury Guardian.* Who'd think there was any sense in Jeff Southerton to hear him talk? But when he writes a letter to *Guardian* about the waages or the schoolin' he has somewh't to say. He's wrong, but there's a pinch o' sense in it. And they lines you says to me, nobody couldn't *talk* like that. It's the pen, you see.[8]

But if print inherently enhances credibility, why do more educated readers read it more skeptically? Something else is at work here. Fiction is a frame, a fairly sophisticated literary convention that must be learned. We are not born with this strategy of reading. In their first encounters with literature, the initial assumption of uneducated readers is that the stories must be true. That is the frame we all start with. A joiner's son in an early nineteenth-century Scottish village recalled that phenomenon when he read his first novel, David Moir's *The Life of Mansie Wauch* (1828):

I literally devoured it. ... A new world seemed to dawn upon me, and Mansie and the other characters in the book have always been historical characters with me, just as real as Caius Julius Caesar, Oliver Cromwell, or Napoleon Buonaparte. ... So innocent, so unsophisticated—I may as well say so green— was I, that I believed every word it contained. I never saw a novel before. I did not know the meaning of the word fiction. My little mind was in a state of unhesitating receptivity, and so deep an impression did this work of Dr. Moir make upon its fresh incipient tablet that even now I can hardly divest myself of that impression. It is with an effort that I can realise these characters are airy, mythical creations of his exuberant fancy.[9]

It requires some training to distinguish fact from fiction, and still more training to distinguish fiction from lies. (A failure to draw the latter distinction accounts for much of the early evangelical hostility to the novel.)[10] But if all readers start with the assumption that all stories are true, how do they learn that some stories are not? That happens when one encounters two texts that cannot both be true. If there is a fundamental incompatibility between (say) Genesis and *The Origin of Species, Uncle Tom's Cabin* and *Native Son,* what your parents say and what the television says, then you must select one of the two as more "realistic." But if a reader is exposed only to a limited range of texts, which basically agree with each other, then there is no basis for concluding that any of them are fiction. And the best-sellers of Hanoverian Britain—chapbook romances, the Bible, *Pilgrim's Progress,* and *Robinson Crusoe*—all told essentially the same story. They were all thrilling tales of adventure, about amazing journeys and terrific struggles, and memorable heroes who, with the help of God, miraculously prevail. The similarities should hardly surprise us. Bunyan, Defoe, and the chapbook tales all drew heavily on biblical themes and imagery. Though Bunyan denounced chapbooks as a sinful distraction, the fact that he freely borrowed their age-old formulas contributed to the astonishing popularity of *Pilgrim's Progress. Robinson Crusoe* was frequently reprinted as a chapbook, abridged to as few as eight pages, and illustrated with the same kind of crude woodcuts.[11]

Common readers could therefore read all these texts in the same way: as ripping yarns, but also as gospel truth. As a boy, stonemason Hugh Miller (b. 1802) first learned to appreciate the pleasures of literature in the "most delightful of all narratives—the story of Joseph. Was there ever such a discovery made before! I actually found out for myself, that the art of reading is the art of finding stories in books, and from that moment reading became one of the most delightful of my amusements." Once Miller had learned to read Scripture as a story, he soon found similar and equally gripping tales in chapbooks of Jack the Giant Killer, Sinbad the Sailor, Beauty and the Beast, and Aladdin. And then, he recalled, from fairy tales "I passed on, without being conscious of break or line of division, to books on which the learned are content to write commentaries and dissertations, but which I found to be quite as nice children's books as any of the others": Pope's *Iliad* and *Odyssey*. "With what power, and at how early an age, true genius impresses!" Miller exclaimed, yet he recognized that Homer's genius had certain clear affinities with penny dreadfuls: "I saw, even at this immature period, that no other writer could cast a javelin with half the force of Homer. The missiles went whizzing athwart his pages, and I could see the momentary gleam of the steel, ere it buried itself deep in brass and bull-hide," he recalled. "I next succeeded in discovering for myself a child's book, of not less interest than even the *Iliad*." It was *Pilgrim's Progress*, with wonderful woodcut illustrations. And from there it was a short step to *Robinson Crusoe* and *Gulliver's Travels*.[12]

When radical weaver Samuel Bamford (b. 1788) first discovered *Pilgrim's Progress*, it impressed him as a thrilling illustrated romance: woodcuts of Christian's fight with Apollyon and his escape from Giant Despair encouraged "the exercise of my feeling and my imagination." Then the New Testament became "my story book, and I read it all through and through, but more for the interest the marvellous passages excited, than from any religious impression which they created." At a bookshop he picked up stories about witches, Robin Hood, Jack the Giant Killer, St. George and the Dragon, and the *History of the Seven Champions*, all with the same kind of deliciously garish woodcuts he had found in Bunyan. Since these stories followed the same narrative conventions, there was no reason to doubt them. "For my part I implicitly believed them all, and when told by my father or others that they were 'trash' and 'nonsense,' and 'could not be true,' I, innocently enough, contrasted their probability with that of other wondrous things which I had read in books that 'it were a sin to disbelieve.'"[13]

Soldier's son Joseph Barker (b. 1806) likewise first read the Bible "chiefly as a work of history, and was very greatly delighted with many of its stories. ... One effect was to lead me to regard miracles as nothing improbable." Consequently, his response to *Pilgrim's Progress* was exactly the same: "My impression was, that the whole was literal and true—that there was, somewhere in the world, a real city of destruction and a new Jerusalem, and that from the one to the other there was a path through some part of the country, just such a path-way as that which Bunyan represents his pilgrim as treading." Ghost stories, highwayman stories, fairy tales, *Paradise Lost*, and Daniel Defoe were all equally credible. "I was naturally a firm believer in all that was gravely spoken or printed," he recalled. "I doubted nothing that I found in books. ... I had no idea at the time I read *Robinson Crusoe*, that there were such things as novels, works of fiction, in existence."[14] Another reader of Bunyan and Defoe claimed that we "believed every fact we read as readily as if there had not been such a thing as fiction in the world: and for anything which we knew there was not; for we had never heard of people making books which were not true." "Tell a boy in his teens that [*Pilgrim's Progress*] is a fiction, and he will not readily believe you,"[15] testified one Chartist weaver. "The great allegory is a great fact."[16] Another called it "*The* book of my boyhood. ... [I] could not but believe the pilgrimage to be a real one, and often wished my mother to set out, with me and my sister, upon the journey."[17]

The notion that there can be different versions of one story—suggesting that no version is absolutely true—is again an acquired literary convention. Growing up in Colchester with access to few books besides an illustrated Bible and some children's chapbooks, laborer's son Thomas Carter (b. 1792) had no opportunity to learn that. Therefore, he not only read Revelations literally: he assumed that the books of Kings and Chronicles were

> unconnected narratives of two distinct series of events; and also, that the four Gospels were consecutive portions of the history of Jesus Christ, so that I supposed there had been four crucifixions, four resurrections, and the like. I was, indeed, sometimes perplexed by the apparently repeated occurrence of events so nearly resembling each other; nor could I perceive the exact design or bearing of these events; but I knew no one of whom I could ask for the needed explanations.

Later, apprenticed to a woollen-draper, he was allowed the run of his master's library and discovered Thomson's *Seasons*, which he read more closely than any other book except the Bible: "I did not then know that the poet's business is rather to present pictures of what ought to be than of what really is; and therefore I regarded Thomson's beautiful and impressive descriptions of rural life and manners as being strictly in accordance with existing realities."[18]

Those who only had access to a limited range of books, all of which offered the same view of reality, had no reason to doubt any of them. Welsh scholar Robert Roberts, born to a Denbighshire tenant farmer in 1834, recalled that his father had a substantial library, mainly of religious books. Except for a Latin dictionary, all were in Welsh. They included some poetry, a couple of history books, and a geography text; but the only fiction Roberts read as a boy was an abridged Welsh-language

Robinson Crusoe. The family took in a couple of Welsh magazines, but because there were no newspapers published in that part of North Wales, his neighbors never discussed politics. "None of them knew much of the Reform Bill, or who the Prime Minister was," though they intensely analyzed clergymen's sermons. And what they read unambiguously reinforced their belief in the miraculous:

> Methodist books of that date swarmed with marvels; supernatural appearances, warnings, singing in the air, sudden judgments on rulers and persecutors; God's miracles and the devil's miracles abounded everywhere. The *Lives of the Saints* is not more full of such wonders than the *Mirror of the Times*, the Methodist Church History. And for people who read the Old Testament histories so much, what more natural than to expect miracles everywhere? ... To disbelieve supernaturalism was then thought utter infidelity; it was flying in the face of Providence—an obstinate hardening of the mind against all evidence.[19]

Flora Thompson recalled that, in the 1880s, the older generation in her Oxfordshire village still "looked upon 'the Word' as their one unfailing guide in life's difficulties. It was their story book, their treasury of words and sayings, and, for those who could appreciate it, their one book of poetry." But now, for the first time, weekly newspapers were offering a competing source of information, and younger people who read these were inclined to question the Bible. It would be too simple, however, to say that they had become more critical and discerning readers: rather, there had been a transference of credulity from the word of God to the word of journalists. Many villagers were prepared to admit that the "tale of Jonah and the whale, for instance, took a good deal of swallowing. But the newspaper everybody believed in. 'I seed it in the paper, so it must be true' was a saying calculated to clinch any argument."[20] When a reader first encountered something that did not square with Scripture, he might embrace it as a surrogate Bible rather than treat both texts skeptically. That was the response of some working-class radicals to Darwin and, later, Marx. V. S. Pritchett had an uncle, an atheist cabinetmaker, who taught himself to read from *The Anatomy of Melancholy*, even acquiring a few Latin and Greek words from the notes. "Look it up in Burton, lad," became his inevitable response to any question. "Burton was Uncle Arthur's emancipation," wrote Pritchett, "it set him free of the tyranny of the Bible in chapel-going circles." Whenever his pious relatives quoted Scripture at each other, he could trump them with something from *The Anatomy of Melancholy*.[21]

Even into the early twentieth century, many older working people had not learned a different method of reading. Thomas Jones (b. 1870) recalled that his mother, a Rhymney straw-hat maker, "was fifty before she read a novel and to her dying day she had not completely grasped the nature of fiction or of drama." When she read *Tom Jones* "She believed every word of it and could not conceive how a man could sit down and invent the story of Squire Allworthy and Sophia and Tom out of his head."[22] The Yorkshire villagers Fred Kitchen (b. 1891) lived and worked with, especially the less literate, attached the same kind of sanctity to all standard literature:

> The most remarkable thing was the number of books each family possessed. There was not a cottage in the village but had a row of books on the dresser, well-bound books in embossed covers, many of them wearing the tissue-paper in which they left the shop. Though these were mostly school prizes, they were held in great reverence by the parents, and no one was allowed to open a book with unwashed hands. Perhaps they carried their regard for books to an extreme, but it was a fact that the less able they were to read a book themselves the greater was their desire to know of its contents. Thus it was that the "good reader" child read aloud to the family, not once but often, and it would be useless to tell them that these stories were fiction. To them Tom and Maggie Tulliver became real flesh and blood people, and so were Silas Marner and Harriet Beecher Stowe's Uncle Tom.[23]

Classic literature assumed an air of reality for Kitchen as well, perhaps because so much of it echoed his experience as a farm laborer. "Life has been made rich because when ploughing up a nest of field-mice I could recite Robert Burns's *Ode to a Field-mouse*," he wrote. Unearthing a cow's skull, "I was immediately transported to the churchyard scene in *Hamlet*." At the workmen's Christmas ball at the great house, "In my childish fancy I likened it to the courtyard at Torquilstone in *Ivanhoe*." Omar Khayyam spoke directly to his station in life—"Unable to piece life together into any satisfactory shape, [I] intend henceforth 'to make jest of that which makes as much of me.'" He "enjoyed the company of Tom and Maggie Tulliver on the corn-bin. ... Having no distractions such as football results, horse-racing, wars, and politics to drive them away, they just dug themselves in, and now I couldn't turn them out if I tried."[24]

Audience Participation

Of course, as common readers read more widely, they generally learned to read more critically. If John Clare's neighbors believed everything in print, eventually John Clare knew better. Yet when he was confronted with a new medium of expression, Clare could revert to an amazing credulity. Attending a performance of *The Merchant of Venice*, he was so gripped by Portia's judgment that he leapt from the box and assaulted Shylock.[25] That was a common reaction among working-class audiences as late as 1900, when farmworker William Miles did a stint with a traveling theater company. When the melodrama *Grip of Iron* called for him to be strangled on stage, "Pandemonium broke out at times, as the audience was (for the moment) convinced that I was being cruelly murdered. They became so perturbed and restless that, on occasion, the progress of the play had to stop to allow the hostile feelings to die down."[26] In one Pirandellian performance a local amateur, playing the villain in a melodrama, resisted furiously when arrested by a stage policeman, precipitating an actual brawl that was warmly encourged by the audience and had to be broken up by genuine policemen.[27] "Well, it was all real life to me, y'know," remembered a devotee of melodramas at the Britannia in Hoxton Street, where fans would accost actors after the show and make no distinction between the player and the part:

I've seen 'em offer 'em a drink, you know—"Have a drink, my dear, do you good after all that hard work—bloody scoundrel, knocking you about like he did." They would talk as if it had actually happened. "Oh, I'm so glad you're alive. I thought you was dead." And the men used to say to the villain, you know: "Why didn't you 'it 'im on the head with a 'ammer?"[28]

In the theater as well, fiction is a convention that must be learned. By 1900, thanks to compulsory education and cheap reading matter, even relatively unsophisticated readers knew not to believe everything they saw in print. Their grandparents read Jack and the Beanstalk and *Pilgrim's Progress* as documentaries not because print is inherently credible, but because there is something powerfully compelling in a new and unfamiliar medium of communication. Its dazzling and novel capacities for transmitting information may so impress an audience that they must learn all over again how it can be manipulated. The stage was a new medium for many Victorian working people: those who had migrated from rural areas, where there were no theaters, and those who grew up in Nonconformist households, where plays were regarded as sinful. The audience had to learn, first, that the theater is make-believe, but even when they gave their intellectual assent to that proposition, they might still view the drama through the same frame that they viewed real life, and respond accordingly. They had yet to master the very different frame that governed the theater—the prohibition against talking during performances, the stricter prohibition against audience participation, the fiction of the "fourth wall," and so forth.[29] In 1815, Methodist artisan Christopher Thomson prevailed upon his fearful mother to permit him to see *King John* in Hull's Theatre Royal:

It was an event to be remembered; the mass of gorgeous decorations— the myriads of iris-tinted rays, glancing their diamond fires from the costly chandeliers—the spirit-stirring strains from the orchestra—the piles of human faces, each as comfortable as smiles and laughter could make them—that babel of noises from the "gods" overhead, their bawling for the "Downfall of Paris," "Rule Britannia," "Play up, Nosey," "The Bay of Biscay O"—their whistles, stamping, barking, and mewing, were all commingled—such a scene I had never before witnessed; yet so absorbing as to render suspense a stranger.

When the curtain went up on John and his court, Thomson was astounded, completely unprepared for the conventions of the theater. What he then experienced was part political rally, part religious rapture, part time travel, and thoroughly real:

> So enwrapped was I in the business that, at the fall of "the drop" at the end of the first act I felt bewildered, and almost doubted my existence, I was so struck "By the very cunning of the scene." I had read of the chivalric daring of bold knights, and of the subduing charms of "fair ladies" with their loves; but now I was in company with them. It might be a dream, but what if it was? it was a waking one! the only fear was, would it be as "Baseless, as the fabric of a vision," and so throw me back again upon the every-day world? I had read of "Magna Charta," without knowing its importance, but still believing it to be a something worth the fighting for—now I was in sight of that very Runny-meade, and moving with "A braver choice of dauntless spirits" ready to grapple with the pale heart, and wring from him anew that deathless germ of liberty. ... As the scene moved onward, I was every thing by turns; now ready to "hang a calf-skin" over the recreant Austria, or rave with Constance for her "absent child." By the time the fourth act came on, all my fear of the play ending was gone. I thought of nothing but the story. ... I sat absorbed in that new mode of visiting the inner-soul by such strange realities. Let those, who swim upon the surface stream of life, echo the purist's cry of the irreligious play-house if they choose; it would be sheer hypocrisy were I to join the puritanic shout. Many a time have I felt my soul light up with pure and holy fire at the altar of our Shakespeare.

Reading that, one can understand why so many radicals were convinced that Shakespeare would emancipate the working classes—and why the early Methodists feared that drama would subvert religious orthodoxy.[30] It also helps to explain the rowdy audience participation in Victorian lower-class theaters. On one occasion, when an actor died an elaborately melodramatic death, his proletarian fans loudly chanted "Die again!" (He did.)[31] The spectators at a turn-of-the-century *Richard III* in Shoreditch brought to the climactic battle scene the same frame that they would bring to a prize fight ("Go it, Harry!" "Go it, Dick!").[32]

After 1900, at least some working-class theatergoers had learned to see through the clanking stage machinery of melodrama. One Glasgow mason "could never take seriously" *East Lynne*: "I seemed to see only the humorous side of the proceedings, and instead of joining with the audience in shedding tears over the sufferings of the heroine I would notice, perhaps, that the heavy villain entering the drawing room of the mansion had forgotten to remove his silk hat."[33] A London observer noted the gradual and uneven transformation of the audience:

> "Look out!" an overwrought galleryite would shout, "'e's going to stab yer with a knife." Or when the poisoned cup was offered to the handsome hero, the

action of the play would be delayed by voices anxiously bidding him not to drink it. "Shut up, Fathead!" some grumpy old chap would say to the nearest possessor of one of those voices; "'ow can the play go on if he don't get drugged? Besides, the 'ero's bahnd to win in the end, ain't he?"[34]

By then, however, a still newer medium had arrested the popular imagination. In the cinema, working-class audiences commonly engaged in a running dialogue with the characters on the screen, carrying over the habit from theatrical melodrama. Silent movie titles would be read aloud (and, in the Jewish East End, translated) by a chorus of children's voices, an effective lesson in literacy for their elders.[35] "Only the screen was silent," wrote one immigrant's son.[36] Viewers would vocally warn Tom Mix about the machinations of baddies and alert Pearl White to the approach of runaway locomotives.[37] As the proletarian novelist Jack Common noted, "Films were still far too real for anybody to be cynical about them. It was the utterly convincing reality of these scenes which compelled us to behave as though we were at the point of joining in upon them."[38] Stoker's son Emlyn Williams (b. 1905) found the images on the screen more authentic than his neighbors in Connah's Quay, Flintshire:

It occupied the foreground of my life, vibrant and clear, while fuzzy in the background was the Quay; moreover, while the phantoms were all the more real for being mute, reality was sterile with sound. Avidly, stone-deafly, I watched the quick gay exchanges between Mabel Normand and Wallace Reid, the staccato protests of Anna Q. Nilsson; their vocal inaccessibility, combined with their physical nearness, was perfection. The magic was rendered invincible for me, too, by my indifference to machinery: I heard the whirring and felt the rays play on the screen, but never consciously knew that I was under the spell of photographs off a spool. And when [my brother] told me he had been inside the station and seen a metal box which a porter assured him contained "the pictures from the Hip", I did not believe him: Norma Talmadge, Milton Sills, Dorothy Gish, William Farnum all in the Quay lying about in tins? ... Shutting my eyes I thought, I am about to watch people *who are going to be there*, in strange rooms, strange clothes, and I pledge myself to watch every ornament on every wall and every earring and necklace, because each will *prove* that this is a reality which will last me till Saturday and then start again. And when I moped along High Street to collect the margarine from the Maypole, all the faces were grey compared to the shadows I had watched; they looked like prisoners of war.

Since 1913 films had opened with the censor's certificate, and one might assume that this would signal to any audience that what they were about to see was less than the unvarnished truth. But again, only the relatively sophisticated will be sensitive to these clues. As Williams recalled, "I never wondered what a censor was, it was merely a fatherly message: 'Yes, your film is here, enjoy it.'"[39]

This pattern would repeat itself as new media followed in succession. In America under the New Deal, opinion polls revealed that radio enjoyed a much higher level of public confidence than the newspaper press. Compare the enormous prestige of Edward R. Murrow with the manipulative, lying print journalists of *The Front Page* and *Citizen Kane*, and consider the national panic ignited by Orson Welles's *War of the Worlds* radio hoax of 1938.[40] That, at any rate, is a media theory offered by someone who had to be told not to believe everything on television, and who now must warn his students that the Internet is not an impeccable source.

Blood, Iron, and Scripture

Of course, the same processes of textual interpretation could work in the opposite direction. Readers might at first assume that everything should be read as fact, but once they mastered the concept of fiction, they could apply that frame to books that were supposed to be read as truth. Thomas Thompson (b. 1880), from a family of Lancashire weavers, grew up with tales of Robin Hood and the Black Hole of Calcutta, as well as an abridged *Faerie Queene* and *Pilgrim's Progress*. So when a clergyman asked him why he read the Bible, he innocently replied "that I liked the battle stories." That answer got him in serious trouble,[41] but any good Sunday school teacher knew that the action heroes of the Old Testament could be as rousing as Charles Kingsley.[42] In school, farm laborer Richard Hillyer (b. c. 1900) enjoyed Scripture in the same spirit as *Black Beauty*, *Treasure Island*, *The Pickwick Papers*, and *Masterman Ready*.

> If you liked books at all the Bible was as exciting as any, it was so full of turbulence and strangeness. You could feel the heat of the desert, and hear the camel bells, as the caravans passed over the wild roads to ancient cities. And the people were so much larger than the people in other books, filled with more urgent desires, so grand and yet so simple. There was Abraham, wandering with his tent, and flocks and herds, through the timeless past in search of the future. David and Jonathan, bound in that deathless friendship. Saul, mad and broken, leaning on his spear and waiting for the welcome stroke that would end his shame. Above all there was David, old and tired, sick of kingship and its troubles, hearing of the death of the evil son he loved so greatly, and turning to seek a hiding place for the grief he could not contain, "O my son Absolom, my son, my son Absolom! Would God I had died for thee, O Absolom, my son, my son!" Words like that did things to me. It seemed as if my heart would break with David's.[43]

John Paton (b. 1886) was raised in the Aberdeen slums on a diet of penny dreadfuls ("good healthy stuff for an imaginative boy") and he found similar thrills in the Bible, at least in the earlier episodes. "I revelled in the same way in the bloodier scenes of the Old Testament while the moralities of the New made no contact in my mind," he remembered. "In this I was typical of most of my mates. We throve on a diet of blood and iron."[44] One shop boy in Victorian London bought an illustrated Bible at a stall for 3d. and then skipped the dull parts to "pick out chapters here and there that told of wonderful and magical things, like there are in the *Arabian Nights* and just as hard to believe in."[45] Memoirs of Bible reading frequently focus on the gaudy illustrations,[46] which suggest that it could be read as a dime novel. As children, miller James Saunders (b. 1844) and his sister enjoyed an old family *History of the Bible*, though "our attention was more taken by the pictures than the actual text. They may have been crude and original, but they were impressive, and we took our ideas accordingly." They particularly wondered how the whale managed to swallow Jonah, who was "dressed in suitable English costume."[47] Jack Common recalled that his grandmother once gave him an illustrated Bible, implying that he was in need of spiritual improvement, and that he astonished his family

when I actually read the thing, right through, cover to cover, as if it was *Chips* or *Hereward the Wake* …. They all looked upon the clever little horror with some distaste and askance …. Yet it was no stunt I was guilty of …. Here on a wet Saturday morning was this handsome volume, leather-bound, of clear bold type and frequent illustrations—I'd look at the pictures. They were gaudy and full of action, quite a lot of them. Look at the priests of Dagon with their blood-splashed knives; Jael creeping into the tent of Sisera; Egyptian chariots overwhelmed by the Red Sea; Judas gloating over his pieces of silver like a carroty-headed Quilp; the stars grouping themselves in the sky for St. John on his flat roof at Patmos. You simply had to read all of these matters; and if the narrative didn't always come up to the quality of the illustrations, when it did, you had a story which stayed in your imagination and gave it something to glow with.

It was some time before Common realized that the real hero of the story was Jesus, not one of the kings or warriors.[48] For compositor's son T. A. Jackson, illustrations by Gustave Doré and Felix Philippoteaux elicited a penny-dreadful *frisson*:

Especially the battle-pictures and those of storm and wreck. There was one of Joshua's army storming a hill-fortress—with the great iron-studded door crashing down before the onrush of mighty men with huge-headed axes—that never failed to thrill. There was Ahab slain in his chariot by the man who "drew a bow at venture," and Jezebel hurled down from her window to the avenging

Jehu—who "drove furiously"—and his hungry hounds. There was Ehud the left-hander who slew Eglon in his summer-parlour. That always struck me as very nice work. I liked the fine realist detail that Eglon was so bulged in the belly that his fat "closed over the haft of the knife" as Ehud drove it in.

Jesus, in contrast, looked crashingly dull: "He was always so stiff, starched, and perfectly proper. I could imagine myself as David slinging stones at Goliath, or Samson tearing a lion into strips as I might tear an old rag, or Peter cutting off the ear of the 'servant of the high priest'. … These were all living men; but Jesus? No! He never came to life for me, and never has."[49]

Even an unillustrated Bible could be read in a highly visual, cinematic fashion, as if it had been written with Cecil B. DeMille in mind. What fascinated was not the tedious ceremonials of Leviticus, but the special effects of Ezekial's vision or the Apocalypse.[50] Robert Story, an early nineteenth-century shepherd-poet, described the experience:

The unconsumed bush burned before me—the successive plagues that visited Egypt were present in all their horror and blood—I saw the Red Sea divide and "stand on an heap," while the favoured race "passed through on dry ground"— I saw the leading cloud darken before them, the "flame of fire" by night crimson the sand of the desert—and I heard the Law from Mount Sinai

"Mid thunder dint, and flashing levin,
And shadows, clouds, and darkness, given!"[51]

When young, Frederick Rogers read not only the Bible as a thriller ("the men and women of the sacred books were as familiar to me as the men and women of Alexander Dumas") but also *Pilgrim's Progress*: "There is a dark street yet in East London along which I have run with beating heart lest I should meet any of the evil things Bunyan so vividly described."[52] As a child William Heaton (b. 1805), the Yorkshire weaver-poet, "rambled with Christian from his home in the wilderness to the Celestial City; mused over his hair-breadth escapes, and his conflict with giant Despair," enjoying it exactly as he enjoyed *Robinson Crusoe* and *Roderick Random*.[53] "I made no distinction between Thackeray's *Barry Lyndon* and Orczy's *Scarlet Pimpernel*—or between *Pilgrim's Progress* and *Sexton Blake*," recalled upholsterer's son Herbert Hodge (b. 1901). "All four were simply exciting stories."[54] In homes where fiction was banned, Bunyan could unintentionally offer the wonderful revelation that literature could appeal to the imagination.[55] Elizabeth Rignall (b. 1894), a London painter's daughter, was not permitted to read anything else on Sundays, so she treated *Pilgrim's Progress* as a horror comic. Irresistibly drawn to the lurid color illustration of the horned Apollyon, "and stretched out at full length on the sofa with the book open before me I would proceed, week after week, to frighten the life out of myself."[56] At age ten Harry

West (b. 1880), the son of a circus escape artist, read *Pilgrim's Progress* merely as "a great heroic adventure." Only later did he appreciate it as a religious allegory, and still later—after his exposure to Freud and Jung—he came to "discover it as one of the greatest, most potent works on practical psychology extant."[57]

Pilgrim's Progress was by far the most widely stocked work of fiction in mid-nineteenth century prison libraries (followed by *Robinson Crusoe*) and one of the most frequently requested by prisoners.[58] Though Bunyan was disseminated by the governing classes to make the working classes more deferential, he often had exactly the opposite effect, inspiring radicals like Samuel Bamford.[59] There was even a Chartist *Political Pilgrim's Progress* (1839), serialized in the *Northern Liberator*, in which the hero journeys from the City of Plunder to the City of Reform.[60] Chartist John James Bezer preferred to read it in the original, as a political fable:

> My own dear Bunyan! if it hadn't been for you, I should have gone mad, I think, before I was ten years old! Even as it was, the other books and teaching I was bored with [in Sunday school], had such a terrible influence on me, that somehow or other, I was always nourishing the idea that "Giant Despair" had got hold of me, and that I should never get out of his "Doubting Castle." Yet I read, ay, and *fed* with such delight as I cannot *now* describe—though I think I could *then*. Glorious Bunyan, you too were a "Rebel," and I love you *doubly* for *that*. I read you in Newgate,—so I could, I understand, if I had been taken care of in Bedford jail,—your books are in the library of even your Bedford jail. Hurrah for progress![61]

Emrys Daniel Hughes, son of a Welsh miner, first treated *Pilgrim's Progress* as an illustrated adventure story. When he was jailed during the First World War for refusing conscription, he reread it, and discovered a very different book:

> Lord Hategood could easily have been in the Government. I had talked with Mr. Worldly Wiseman and had been in the Slough of Despond and knew all the jurymen who had been on the jury at the trial of Hopeful at Vanity Fair. And Vanity Fair would of course have been all for the War. Bunyan's *Pilgrim's Progress* was one of the great books that showed great understanding of the life of man, of his setting out on a long and dangerous journey, his meeting with all sorts of difficulties and temptations on the way and his spirit in keeping on and the winning through ultimately to final victory and to the end of the quest.[62]

For the founding fathers of the Labour Party, it was a revolutionary manifesto "to create a new heaven and a new earth," to quote G. H. Roberts.[63] Robert Blatchford, who had practically memorized *Pilgrim's Progress* by age ten, always found its political message supremely relevant: "Mr. Pliable we all know; he still votes for the old Parties. Mr. Worldly Wiseman writes books and articles against

Socialism. Mr. Facing-both-ways is never absent from the House, and I think Mr. By-ends is become the guiding spirit of the British Press."[64]

In much the same way, Scripture supplied a fund of imagery, allusions, parables, and quotations for the first generation of Labour Party orators—and for agitators further to the left. "My first impressions of Labour came from Genesis; my idea of morality from the 'Sermon on the Mount,' and my spiritual leadership from Jesus" proclaimed Marxist James Clunie (b. 1889), son of a Plymouth Brethren lay preacher.[65] Jailed for suffragette disruptions, millworker Annie Kenney (b. 1879) rediscovered the Bible, "and I interpreted it quite differently in prison to the way I had interpreted it outside. It is a beautiful book, full of hope; the poetry of it is charming, and the wisdom and philosophy truly helpful to the struggling soul."[66] Her brother Rowland and Robert Blatchford were both militant secularists who enjoyed Scripture as belles-lettres. "My hunger for word-music found satisfaction in many passages the sense of which I ruthlessly denounced," Rowland recalled, "but as time went on I began to enjoy the sensuousness of the language and to smile at the meaning."[67]

Despite the disapproval of her comrade Palme Dutt, Helen Crawfurd (b. 1877) found Communist propaganda in Scripture, which was certainly more palatable than Marx to the Scottish working women she addressed. According to her un-authorized version, "The Lamb dumb before her shearers, represented the uncritical exploited working class." In the Book of Esther, Queen Vashti, who would not parade before her king, was "my first suffragette." For the Book of Revelation she read Revolution, and the Children of Israel who danced before the Golden Calf were obviously the running dogs of the capitalists. She modeled herself on Isaiah, and took her favorite Biblical text from St. John: "The man that says he loves God, whom he hath not seen, and loveth not his brother whom he hath seen, *the same is a liar and the truth is not in him.*" And when she had studied the Psalms long enough, she somehow discerned there the materialist conception of history: "I saw the Psalmist David as a shepherd on the hills, making his poems from the material things surrounding him, such as 'the green pastures, the still waters.'"[68]

New Crusoes

The Bible and Bunyan, then, were both read through the same set of inter-changeable frames: literal, fictional, allegorical, spiritual, political. Much the same was true of the one book that could match their readership. When adolescent schoolboys (mostly middle-class) were asked to name their favorite books in an 1888 survey, *Robinson Crusoe* was the clear winner, with its derivative *Swiss Family Robinson* in second place.[69] One bibliographer has located 974 English-language editions of *Crusoe* published through 1919.[70] That does not include all the desert island tales that were variations on the same theme, such as *Swiss Family Robinson* and R. M. Ballantyne's *Coral Island*: at least 505 of them appeared between 1788 and 1910.[71]

How was Defoe's documentary fiction actually read? "Now we are bound to see it as profoundly imperialist, both in Robinson's relations to Friday, and in the stimulus it gave young Englishmen to go out and join in the adventure of the British Empire," asserts Martin Green, expressing the current critical consensus. Nevertheless, he admits it was first received as a denunciation of Spanish imperialism. Though it may appear indisputably racist today, "Yet it has been read with enthusiasm by non-Englishmen. It was translated into every language, from Ashanti to Zulu, and we hear more of the inspiration it gave coloured readers than of their revolt against it." Crusoe's story "was for 150 years a charter of freedom, freeing men from the constraints of social and vocational tradition, from feudalism and hierarchy. ... As baker, builder, tanner, etc., he plays every social role. He carries further the breakdown of the apprentice-dominated society we label 'feudal'. Crusoe's island is 'open to the talents'; it is the opposite of immemorial village culture; it breaks the spell of ancestor-worship."[72]

An even more equalitarian reading of the book is possible. Crusoe presumes to own and trade human beings, though he knows from experience the life of a slave. For that sin he is banished to an island where division of labor has been completely abolished, where he receives exactly the value of his own work—a punishment that exactly fits the crime, and an ideal form of rehabilitation. The shipwreck teaches him that money is worthless, that usefulness is the only measure of value. Victorians often cited the suppression of cannibalism as a pretext for imperialism; but Crusoe, though disgusted by the practice, assumes an attitude of cultural relativism: "It is certain these People either do not commit this as a Crime; it is not against their own Consciences reproving, or their Light reproaching them." Far worse, he argues, was the genocide carried out by the Spanish Empire against American natives.[73] His attempts to convert Friday to Christianity backfire when the native poses the kind of innocent questions ("Why God no kill the Devil?") that expose the contradictions in Western theology, and force Crusoe to recognize that heathens are often more moral than Christians.[74]

One more critical warning is in order. A scholar today who sits down with the "definitive" edition of a literary work, and tries to discern how past readers responded to it, must take into account that those readers may not have had anything like the complete text. In the eighteenth century *Robinson Crusoe* (along with *Moll Flanders*, *Pilgrim's Progress*, and *Gulliver's Travels*) was widely distributed in the form of greatly condensed chapbooks. The first abridgement of *Crusoe* appeared within weeks of its 1719 debut, and a total of 151 chapbook versions would be published over the next century, compared with only fifty-seven complete editions. Two-thirds of the chapbooks were issued by provincial publishers, indicating a broad national distribution.[75]

Clearly, most lower-class eighteenth-century readers could only afford a fraction of *Robinson Crusoe*. (One mid-century chapbook was a mere eight pages, with Friday appearing only in the final paragraph.) By comparing the abridgements, and seeking out the common denominators, Pat Rogers has isolated what were apparently considered the indispensable elements of the story. Nearly all the chapbooks have an illustration of Crusoe in goatskin, armed, with a wrecked ship in the background. Significantly, he is alone: Friday and the cannibals were evidently regarded as peripheral, but Crusoe's individualism was essential. Rogers concludes that early readers

> responded to the book as a story of survival, as an epic of mastery over the hostile environment, as a parable of conquest over fear, isolation and despair. These messages seem to have come through, however the book was truncated or travestied. It was above all the shipwreck and the early part of Crusoe's sojourn on the island that drew attention to these aspects of the myth, and this is a part of the narrative that is never sacrificed, however abbreviated the text. Crusoe's "readability" for a mass audience was variously negotiable, but the *sine qua non* can be firmly located in this crucial episode.[76]

For Thomas Spence and his followers, *Robinson Crusoe* had a radically egalitarian message. A Newcastle netmaker and schoolteacher, Spence argued that all land should be owned collectively by the parishes and leased out, with the rental income used to support social services. Defoe's novel offered him a site on which to construct his utopia. In Spence's *A Supplement to the History of Robinson Crusoe* (1782), Europeans have peacefully settled (not conquered) Crusoe's island, established friendly relations with the natives, and intermarried with them. They call themselves Crusonians: the neighboring continent, in the spirit of racial equality, has been named Fridinea. There are few laws, no lawyers, and complete religious freedom. In each parish, public land underwrites the cost of a free public school, a public theater, and a public library stocked with "copies and translations of all the best books in the world."[77]

Robinson Crusoe made innumerable plebeian readers discontented with their station in life and eager to explore. For John Clare, it "was the first book of any merit I got hold of after I could read," and it set in motion an early ferment: "New ideas from the perusal of this book was now up in arms, new Crusoes and new Islands of Solitude was continually muttered over in my Journeys to and from school."[78] Ebenezer Elliott, the foundryman and future "Corn-Law Rhymer," yearned to leave the Tory England of the 1790s for America, inspired in part by "Crusoe-notions of self-dependence and isolation."[79]

Joseph Greenwood (b. c. 1833), the son of domestic handloom weavers, with very little formal schooling, went on to found a mechanics' institute, the Hebden Bridge Fustian Manufacturing Co-operative Society, the Burnley Self-Help Society, the Bradford Cabinet Makers' Society, the Leicester Hosiery Society, and his own fustian and dyeing firm, as well as becoming a local councillor and justice of the peace. As for his motivation, the book that figured most importantly in his memoirs was a cheap edition of *Robinson Crusoe*. "To me Daniel Defoe's book was a wonderful thing, it opened up a world of adventure, new countries and peoples, full of brightness and change; an unlimited expanse."[80] At age twelve, recalled ploughboy John Ward (b. 1866), "I devoured—*not read*, that's too tame an expression—*Robinson Crusoe*, and that book gave me all my spirit of adventure, which has made me strike *new ideas* before the old ones became antiquated, and landed me into many troubles, travels, and difficulties." These included agitating against British intervention in the Sudan, organizing a navvies' trade union, becoming a Labour MP, and building up a personal library of more than 700 volumes.[81]

Some landlubbers recalled that it made them want to run away to sea.[82] In the 1930s one old seaman claimed that nearly all English sailors used to read *Robinson Crusoe*: "I consider that Defoe sent more boys to sea than any other person who ever lived."[83] It was Thomas Jordan's (b. 1892) favorite book, read through in one sitting at age eleven. The promise of "faraway places fired my imagination" and ultimately inspired him, the son of an illiterate miner, to leave the pits of his Durham mining village and join the Army. From there he went on to diligent reading on his own and studying with the Workers' Educational Association.[84]

The language of *Crusoe* might not be easy for children, but far from being intimidated, they often used it to expand their language skills. "I found it fascinating but difficult," remembered one handicapped boy (b. 1923). "The descriptions of the first storm at sea impressed me considerably. ... I found the relentless detail of Crusoe's life on the island at once compulsive and maddening, and his constant references to God rather embarrassing. The Friday episodes I found strange and curiously haunting. No doubt I was too young really to appreciate the book, nevertheless even at that age I think I dimly sensed its greatness."[85] "The words I didn't understand I just skipped over, yet managed to get a good idea of what the story was about," wrote James Murray (b. c. 1894), the son of a Scottish shoemaker. "By the time I was ten or eleven years old I did not need to skip any words in any book because by then I had a good grounding in roots and derivations." *Crusoe* so aroused his appetite for literature that, when his schoolteacher asked the class to list all the books they had read, Murray rattled off titles by Ballantyne, Kingston, and Dickens until "I realised the eyes of everyone in the room were on me. Some of the boys and girls had only written one book down, some had written down two, a few had not read any books and were completely stuck."[86]

Robinson Crusoe, it has been argued, appealed to a new middle-class reading public. Freed from manual labor, they found thrills and some nostalgia in the story of a man who could provide for all his survival needs with his own hands.[87] That may be true, but laborers also identified with the story—because they were still doing that kind of work. The son of a Welsh blacksmith, Michael Gareth Llewelyn (b. 1888) understood the "appeal in the story which describes the fashioning of a home out of a primitive environment."[88] In 1951 postal worker Spike Mays was studying English literature at Newbattle Abbey College with Edwin Muir, who criticized Defoe for going on at such length about carpentry. Himself a good handyman, Mays felt bound to go to Defoe's defence, saying it was all very well for Edwin to condemn a man who could use tools and write about men who could use them; that it would be more convincing if Edwin could use them. To my certain knowledge he could not knock a wire nail into a hunk of balsa wood without bending the nail, hammering his finger-nails, and splintering almost unsplinterable wood. Moreover, when he as a writer made some mistake, he had but to reach for an eraser and could then start again from scratch. Not so the chiseller. I invited Edwin's attention to the fireplace. Carved from one great tree was a massive grape vine, twelve feet wide and four feet high, bearing fruit and leaves. I asked Edwin to examine its detail, to note the curling fronds, the minute veins of the leaves and the beauty of the nodal joints. I reminded him that the Neapolitan carver had no eraser. One scratch, and his work was ruined. Edwin came and put his arm around me, ... took ... me to his study, and poured us sherry.[89]

At the close of the nineteenth century, on a farm in the Derbyshire Peak District, *Robinson Crusoe* was read aloud every winter, and never palled on the audience. As Alison Uttley remembered, it was even more popular than *Pilgrim's Progress*:

Christian on his journey met giants and evil men, but Robinson Crusoe fought against the elements, the wind and rain, lightning and tempest, droughts and floods. He lived a life they could understand, catching the food he ate, sowing and reaping corn, making bread, taming beasts, planting and fencing, and each one translated the tale into terms of his own experiences on the farm, and each shared that life of loneliness they knew. ... The family shared the life of Robinson Crusoe, hoping and fearing with him, experiencing his sorrows, his repentance, his setbacks, rejoicing when he found a set of tools in the ship's cabin, troubled when he built the boat that he couldn't move. They were thankful about the cask of rum, for it was their own remedy for colds and chills. ... The deep religious feeling was their own simple belief. He read the Bible as they read it, seeking solace and help in times of trial. It was their own life, translated to another island, but still an island like their own farmland, enclosed by the woods, a self-contained community, a sanctuary.

For those who had missed the chance to emigrate to America or Australia, *Crusoe* offered a vicarious escape. Laborers could buy cocoanuts at the village fair, or dream of venturing out each morning to shoot game with a fowling piece, as Crusoe did. Uttley herself concocted new stories around Defoe's novel, until she leapt effortlessly over the boundaries of sex and "became Robinson Crusoe himself, and acted his life and adventures unceasingly, so that she was ... a shipwrecked man on a desert island alone in a vast ocean. ... Crusoe was there, living his life on her own."

In a hierarchical and conformist society that offered little freedom for the laboring classes, *Crusoe* was read as a fable of individualism. It showed what one workingman could do without landlords, clergymen, or capitalists. According to Uttley, Crusoe's reflections on the worthlessness of gold on a desert island spoke with particular force to an audience of rural laborers: "That was a powerful thought! That was Bible truth!" The impact of the parable lay in this: it collapsed all social distinctions into one person. Crusoe, as Uttley put it, is "a romantic mixture of poacher and gamekeeper and farmer."[90]

Pickwickian Realism

Only one other author ever matched the steady and overwhelming popularity of Defoe and Bunyan. Shortly after its opening in 1888, the Belfast Public Library reported that *The Pickwick Papers* and *David Copperfield* were among its four most requested books.[91] Dickens's own public readings attracted mobs of working people—at least those who could afford the shilling seats.[92] And at the Loveclough Printworks Library, Dickens accounted for 10 percent of all loans in 1892–93.[93]

It has been argued that the sensational novelist G. W. M. Reynolds (1814–79) outsold Dickens in his day, but his books had no staying power. By the early twentieth century, when Dickens was the most widely stocked novelist in twenty Welsh miners' libraries, only one of those collections had anything by Reynolds on the shelves.[94] Their relative impact on readers is apparent in working-class memoirs, where Dickens is a dominating presence and Reynolds is scarcely mentioned. A typical paean was offered by a London leather-bag maker (b. 1880): "Two names were held in great respect in our home, and were familiar in our mouths as household words, namely, Charles Dickens, and William Ewart Gladstone."[95] George Acorn, growing up in extreme poverty in London's East End, scraped together 3½d. to buy a used copy of *David Copperfield*. His parents punished him when they learned he had wasted so much money on a book, but later he read it to them:

> And how we all loved it, and eventually, when we got to "Little Em'ly," how we all cried together at poor old Peggotty's distress! The tears united us, deep in misery as we were ourselves. Dickens was a fairy musician to us, filling our minds with a sweeter strain than the constant cry of hunger, or the howling wind which often, taking advantage of the empty grate, penetrated into the room.[96]

True, autobiographers may unconsciously fictionalize, rewriting memories to create an engaging story. Acorn's account does sound suspiciously Dickensian, and if he was enthralled by *David Copperfield*, he may well have recast his own life in the same melodramatic mode. But for the historian of reading, it does not really matter if Acorn embellished his biography. The question here is Dickens's influence on working-class readers. If Acorn thought *David Copperfield* important enough to place at the center of his memoir, if he used it as a literary model, if he adopted a Dickensian frame in reading and then used the same rules for interpreting experience when he wrote his reminiscences, then that influence was very great and deep.

When a memoirist uses fiction as a model, he is not necessarily drifting farther from the truth—not if the novelist he follows captures reality better than the historian. Most working people had to struggle with the art of recording their lives, and they cited Dickens, more than anyone else, as the man who got it right. They attended a school out of *Nicholas Nickleby*,[97] or one like Dr. Blimber's Academy.[98] The fate of Mr. Wopsle, they confirmed, accurately illustrated the treatment of inferior actors by the patrons of cheap theaters.[99] Their first employer was Wackford Squeers ("Dickens did not exaggerate").[100] They worked alongside Micawber in the mines ("I knew men like him in the pit").[101] They honored the "many Sydney Cartons in the Great War."[102] They might shudder to recall a Catholic orphanage refectory "as though Mr. Bumble himself had placed his ghostly, icy hands on me."[103] "I went through all Oliver's trials with him," wrote Grace Foakes, whose father was a docker in Edwardian London. "I cried over him and loved him, for in those early days we lived in such conditions and it was easy for me to identify myself with him. I knew the threat of the workhouse, the threat of prison and bread-and-water. If we misbehaved, all these threats were held against us and we were fearful of being sent there."[104] As a boy, V. S. Pritchett (b. 1900) read *Oliver Twist*

> in a state of hot horror. It seized me because it was about London and the fears of the London streets. There were big boys at school who could grow up to be the Artful Dodger; many of us could have been Oliver; but the decisive thing must have been that Dickens had the excited mind, the terrors, the comic sense of a boy and one who can never have grown emotionally older than a boy is at the age of ten. One saw people going about the streets of London who could have been any of his characters.

Pritchett read Thackeray for escape, a taste of "the gentler life of better-off people," but in Dickens "I saw myself and my life in London."[105] For the same reason, Percy Wall (b. 1893) loved to hear his father, a railway worker and construction laborer, read to the family from Charles Dickens and Mark Twain: "It seemed that the world they portrayed was more real than the world around us. Here was compensation for the things we missed, if you can be said to miss things of whose existence you are but faintly aware." The fact that his father had actually seen Dickens on the streets (not unusual for a London workingman of that generation) only reinforced the authenticity of what he read.[106] At age sixteen, Neville Cardus (whose parents were launderers in turn-of-the-century Manchester) read in the *Athenaeum* that no one was reading Dickens anymore: he then trudged from one public library to another, only to be told that every copy of his novels had been loaned out. His discovery of Dickens in shilling Harmsworth editions did more than erase the boundary between fiction and life: "It was scarcely a case of reading at all; it was almost an experience of a world more alive and dimensional than this world, heightened and set free in every impulse of nature; not subtle and abnormal impulses but such as even a more or less illiterate youth could at once share." Critics who saw only caricatures in Dickens's people had thoroughly missed the point: "He simply let me see them more than life-size. David Copperfield so often behaved and thought as I behaved and thought that I frequently lost my own sense of identity in him."[107]

Cumberland tailor's son Norman Nicholson (b. 1914) had the same answer when asked why he liked Dickens: "Because he's so real." He and his schoolmates had no time for the sentimentality of *The Old Curiosity Shop*, but they were gripped when a scholarship class introduced them to "the darker Dickens": *Great Expectations* in the 1s. 6d. Nelson's Classics edition. While the first wave of modernist critics was dismissing Dickens as a melodramatic caricaturist, working people were reading his novels as documentaries, employing the same frame that their grandparents had applied to Bunyan. Nicholson saw an almost photographic realism in the Phiz illustration in *Dombey and Son*

which shows old Mrs. Pipchin, in her widow's weeds, sitting beside little Paul Dombey, and staring into the fire. I had never seen widow's weeds, of course, but everything else in that illustration, drawn in the 1840s, was as familiar to me, eighty years later, as the flags of my own back yard. The little, high, wooden chair, with rails like the rungs of a ladder, is the chair I sat in at meal-times when I was Paul Dombey's age. The fireplace itself, the bars across the grate, the kettle on the coals, the bellows hanging at the side, the brass shovel on the curb, the mirrored over-mantel, the mat, the table swathed in plush, the aspidistra on the wall-bracket—all these I had seen many times in my own house, or Grandpa Sobey's, or Grandma Nicholson's or Uncle Jim's. On a winter tea-time, before the gas was lit, the fitful firelight populated the room with fantasies as weird as any in Dickens. I would pick up my book sometimes and try to read by the glow from the coals, and the world I entered seemed not far removed from the world I had left. It was no more than walking from one room into the next.[108]

These readers were not prisoners of the text, uncritically adopting a Dickensian frame of mind. They were more sophisticated than the devotees of chapbooks and *Pilgrim's Progress* a century earlier, and when Dickens contradicted their own experience, they were not reluctant to say so. One East End tough doubted that anyone as naive as Oliver Twist could have survived a moment in those mean streets.[109] A circus performer found a laughable ignorance of circus life in *Hard Times*.[110] A laborer's son, growing up in Camberwell in the early twentieth century, recognized that the local crooks "were far removed from the 'Bill Sykes' image created by Dickens, for the most part they were good-looking, smartly dressed men, intelligent conversationalists and witty raconteurs, they regarded prisons as no more than industrial hazards, to be avoided of course if possible, but philosophically accepted as part of the game."[111] In the depressed steelworks town of Merthyr Tydfil between the world wars, schoolboys were baffled by *A Christmas Carol*: "For one thing, we never could understand why it was considered that Bob Cratchit was hard done by—a good job, we all thought he had. And the description of the Christmas party ... didn't sound bad at all—great, it must have been in Dickens' day!"[112]

As a general rule, however, Dickens's universe was solid enough and familiar enough to provide a common frame of reality for all social classes. In the late Victorian Warwickshire village where M. K. Ashby's father was a farm laborer, Dickens was so often recited that even

> People who were not at all literary, who had not read Fielding or Scott, needed no introduction to Dickens other than the infectious laughter and smiles of his readers. His books were the favourites at the penny readings, and passages from them were read and recited in the "public" and on religious platforms. So all sorts of folk became Dickensians in their degree: the hopeful young like Joseph, farmers, magistrates on the bench, the clergy, all read at least three or four of Dickens's novels. Even the children read them. Not to have your mind touched by Dickens was to remain a relic of the early nineteenth century, or maybe the eighteenth, as after all quite a number were. Dickens exercised the muscles of laughter and practised the imagination. If the Vicar preached one of his pre-Christian sermons, or a lay preacher's language was unequal to his message, or a mean mistress locked every cupboard although there was next to nothing in them, or a shopkeeper watched his scales over-sharply, or his local lordship was unbearably patronising, the risable muscles stirred before the frowns. All the tyrants and fools could be transmogrified into Dickens characters, and once you had smiled at your enemy you could think the better how to deal with him. The best of it was that everybody benefited. Lord Willoughby de Broke found a Dickens name for everyone he thought tiresome as easily as did Joseph. Thus Dickens affected the community life. The New Testament taught the principle of forbearance and Dickens supplied the technique of it.[113]

Perhaps Dickens's most important gift to the working classes was the role he played in making them articulate. He provided a fund of allusions, characters, tropes, and situations that could be drawn upon by people who were not trained to express themselves on paper. When the *People's Journal*, with its huge circulation among Scottish workers, sponsored Christmas story competitions it was deluged with submissions (about one for every hundred subscribers in 1869) and many of them clearly reflected the influence of Dickens.[114] As rules for organizing experience, frames are essential tools for writing stories as well as reading them. For people who had never been taught how to tell their own histories, Dickens supplied the necessary lessons. Lancashire dialect poet Ben Brierley (b. 1825) began his literary career when the manager at his cotton mill sent him to pick up the monthly installments of *The Pickwick Papers* from the stationers: "I gathered fresh life from his admirable writings," he recalled, "and even then began to look into the distant future with the hope that at sometime I might be able to track his footsteps, however far I might be behind."[115] How would the daughter of a shoe repairer, or a seaman's son, or a textile worker know how to begin a memoir? They could all follow David Copperfield and write simply, "I am born."[116] And if one were struggling to describe a Welsh mining town as it actually was, the opening lines of *A Tale of Two Cities* would be precisely right.[117]

Chapter Four A Conservative Canon

Alf Garnett and his American cousin, Archie Bunker, may be caricatures, but working-class cultural conservatism is a real phenomenon in industrial societies. Some of its manifestations can even be quantified. In France, Pierre Bourdieu has plotted taste and class on Cartesian coordinates and found a distinct correlation between conventionality and manual labor.[1] In Britain one can detect a similar and remarkably persistent pattern throughout the industrial era. Literary canons may change over time; but at any given point, the reading tastes of the British working classes consistently lagged a generation behind those of the educated middle classes, a cultural conservatism that often coexisted with political radicalism.

This tendency can be traced back to eighteenth-century Scotland, where the first working-class libraries in the British Isles were founded. In this period, a preference for religious books reflected conservative tastes; the avant-garde was represented by the growing acceptance of fiction as a legitimate literary genre. Table 4.1 (p. 117), based on statistics compiled by John Crawford, reveals a striking difference in library collections serving different social classes. The first line is a benchmark drawn from William Bent's *London Catalogue of Books*, which listed new titles published in London between 1700 and 1773. The second line analyzes a catalogue from around 1786 for James Sibbald's circulating library in Edinburgh's Parliament Square, which served a middle-class clientele. The next set of figures represents averages of the holdings of four other middle-class libraries in smaller Scottish towns (Greenock, Hawick, Forfar, Duns) compiled from catalogues published between 1789 and 1795. The last two lines reflect the stock of two libraries run by and for lead miners, in Wanlockhead (1790) and Leadhills (1800).

These statistics suggest that in the golden afternoon of the Scottish Enlightenment, reading tastes among the affluent were quite up-to-date in the provinces as well as in the heart of the Caledonian metropolis. Leadhills, in contrast, was much slower to shift its collection from religion to fiction; at Wanlockhead, fiction would not overtake theology until the early twentieth century. Some other Scottish working-class libraries banned fiction altogether, at least until the success of Sir Walter Scott forced them to change or die. The Dunfermline Tradesmen's Library (founded 1808) made the transition when it found that weavers were clubbing together to buy the Waverley novels: by 1823, eighty-five out of 290

Table 4.1: Holdings in Eighteenth-Century Scottish Libraries (in percent)

	Religion	Fiction
Bent's *Catalogue* (1700–73)	19	8
Sibbald's Library (c. 1786)	8	20
Four proprietary libraries (1789–95)	3.1	14.1
Wanlockhead library (1790)	23.6	14.2
Leadhills library (1800)	24.6	8.5

volumes in its collection were fiction, and as a result membership and usage increased dramatically. These libraries also avoided controversial politics. In 1837 miners at Leadhills and Wanlockhead refused to accept George Combe's *Constitution of Man* because they considered it hostile to revealed religion.[2] Combe was in fact a radical, dismissive of classical literature, and a vocal advocate of phrenology, scientific reason, shorter work hours, and female education. His Edinburgh lectures, as Lord Cockburn reported, attracted "hundreds of clerks and shopkeepers, with their wives and daughters, nibbling at the teats of science," but not manual workers, in part because they were disinclined to pay 6d. per lecture.[3]

Janet Hamilton grew up among Scottish weavers who read newspapers together and discussed parliamentary politics, but whose reading was otherwise almost entirely theological. Most homes in her village of Langloan had *Pilgrim's Progress* and Watts's hymns. Some religious periodicals circulated, but no secular magazines. When local workingmen, farmers, and schoolteachers set up a sub-scription library, half the books they voted to acquire were religious: "then biography, travels, voyages, and several sets of the *British Essayist*, a fair proportion of history and geography; no poetry, nothing of the drama, and but one novel"—Henry Brooke's *The Fool of Quality* (1766), in five volumes. Consequently, Janet had a heavy literary diet as a child—history by Rollin and Plutarch, *Ancient Universal History*, Pitscottie's *Chronicles of Scotland*, as well as the *Spectator* and *Rambler*. She could borrow books by Burns, Robert Fergusson, and other poets from neighbors, and at age eight she found, "to my great joy, on the loom of an intellectual weaver," *Paradise Lost* and Allan Ramsay's poems. But during the radical agitation of 1819–20, the common people of the village would have nothing to do with the *Black Dwarf*:

A small, mean-looking sheet, overflowing with scurrilous epithets and venomous invectives against the Government, and utterly subversive of all lawful authority and social order, and interlarded with scepticism and blasphemy. … [We] felt a strong desire to see what we would at other times have deprecated—parties of soldiers among us, to protect property and insure social order. … Long after the terror had passed away mothers would frighten their wayward children into submission by telling them that the radicals would catch them.[4]

This attachment to religious literature held up the development of inexpensive secular magazines. According to farm laborer Alexander Somerville, George Miller's 4d. *Cheap Magazine* (published 1813–14) failed partly because potential readers found it insufficiently pious.[5] It took a generation of political activism—as well as the popularity of Burns, Wordsworth, Byron, and Scott—to prepare the working classes for *Chambers's Edinburgh Journal* and the *Penny Magazine*. Before then, they could only glean that kind of "useful knowledge" from old volumes of middle-class magazines. As a boy Thomas Carter was baffled by adult books like *Paradise Lost*, but his schoolmaster loaned him volumes of the *Arminian Magazine* and the *Gentleman's Magazine*, whose miscellaneous contents were far more digestible. Later, as an apprentice, he found in his master's kitchen an odd volume of the *Spectator*, wherein Addison helpfully explained what *Paradise Lost* was all about. Carter read so much about London in the *Spectator* and *Rambler* that in 1810 he moved to the metropolis, half expecting to join the coffeehouse intelligentsia.[6]

The only books John Clare repeatedly read were *Paradise Lost*, Thomson's *Seasons*, *Robinson Crusoe*, *Tom Jones*, and *The Vicar of Wakefield*: he had no desire to read Scott or any other contemporary novelist.[7] As the great Romantics were not yet available in cheap editions, worker-poets had to look to the eighteenth century and earlier for their models, even if the styles were antiquated and inappropriate to a new industrial world. "Every poet must at first be an imitator," admitted the Northumberland shepherd poet Robert Story (b. 1795). With little formal education, he knew that untutored genius could not find expression "unless a medium is found through which it may dart its irradiations. That medium is the language of our country's *approved* bards," and only by studying and borrowing from them could any aspiring poet find his own voice. Pope happened to be first English poet that Story discovered, so he provided the template from which the herd-boy minted pastorals "delightfully free from everything connected with real life or rural manners; and wrote descriptions that were descriptive of nothing." Story soon hungered for "a freer or less measured style of composition," but in the wilds of Northumberland he had no way of knowing that the Romantic movement in literature was in full swing:

> At the very time when I was lamenting the lack of poets in the nineteenth century, and almost fancying that I should myself be the *oasis* in the desert— Wordsworth had produced his "Lyrical Ballads," Rogers his "Pleasures of Memory," and Campbell his "Pleasures of Hope;" the strains of Scott were still in all their freshness; Byron had just wrapped himself in the mantle of "Childe Harold;" Moore had displayed—or was displaying—the riches of oriental imagery; and Southey, by tale upon tale, each more brilliant than the last, was continuing a climax that was to terminate in "Roderick!"—It might be poetically said, that the gales of Britain were *alive* with harmony; but the sound was turned aside by the mountains that sheltered my cottage; and it rolled away into distance—unheard and unenjoyed!

When he was finally exposed to Scott's *Lay of the Last Minstrel,* he reeled from the shock of the new. Pope may have been too refined, but this, Story insisted, was "uncontrolled barbarism," poetic anarchy, "harsh, puerile, and fantastic."[8] Robert White, another pastoral poet born just seven years after Story, had somewhat more progressive tastes, which extended to Shelley, Keats, *Childe Harold,* and *The Lady of the Lake.* But his reading stopped short at the Romantics. In 1873 he confessed that he could not stomach avant-garde poets like Tennyson. "As for our modern novel-writers—Dickens, Thackeray and others I do not care to read them, since Smollett, Fielding and Scott especially are all I desire."[9]

Perhaps the most popular proletarian author of the century was Hugh Miller (b. 1802), a Scottish stonemason who achieved great celebrity as a geological writer. His *The Old Red Sandstone* (1841), *First Impressions of England* (1847), and *Footprints of the Creator* (1849), as well as his memoir *My Schools and Schoolmasters* (1854) each sold more than 50,000 copies by 1900.[10] But Miller was still trying to reconcile modern geological science with Genesis, a paradigm already rendered obsolete by the evolutionary theory advanced in Charles Lyell's *Principles of Geology* (1830–33). Even Miller's literary style was out of date: in 1834 he alluded to "my having kept company with the older English writers,—the Addisons, Popes, and Robertsons of the last century at a time when I had no opportunity of becoming acquainted with the authors of the present time."[11] Growing up in Cromarty, Miller had access to the substantial personal libraries of a carpenter and a retired clerk, as well as his father (sixty volumes), his uncles (150 volumes), and a cabinetmaker-poet (upwards of 100 volumes). These collections offered a broad selection of English essayists and poets—of the Queen Anne period.[12]

Miller's continuing popularity may be an indicator of persistent working-class resistance to Darwin. When Jim Bullock (b. 1903) wrote an examination essay on coal formation, his father (a Yorkshire miner and Baptist fundamentalist) tossed the paper in the fire, appalled that his son's treatment of geology so clearly contradicted Scripture.[13] Of course, urban working-class militants like T. A. Jackson (b. 1879) had been promoting Darwinism as a weapon against evangelical religion—only to discover that they too were behind intellectual fashion. "The Darwinian battle ... had not only been fought and won for middle and upper class culture," Jackson observed, "the ultra-Left, as in the case of Erewhon Butler were stirring beyond Darwin into neo-Lamarckism. In proletarian circles the fight still had to be won." As an apprentice, Jackson relied upon secondhand bookshops and cheap out-of-copyright reprints for his reading: "There was thus a perceptible time-lag between the culture of the reading section of the proletariat and that of the middle and upper classes."[14]

Before the First World War, elderly Lanarkshire miners were known as "fourpenny professors," because they had attended village schools at 4d. a week and were solidly grounded in theology. But they rarely read daily newspapers or contemporary authors. Patrick Dollan, who organized an informal library service for them, found that they preferred Byron, Carlyle, Ruskin, Oliver Wendell

Holmes, James Russell Lowell, Thomas Hardy, Hall Caine, George Meredith, Ouida, Zola, Dumas, Jules Verne, Hawthorne, Harrison Ainsworth, Mark Twain, and Bret Harte, while Shelley was a favorite for quoting at ILP meetings. Shaw, Wells, Galsworthy, and Bennett were completely unknown to them: Dollan himself only discovered them when he visited Manchester and attended Miss Horniman's Gaiety Theatre.[15] And there were still a few ancient mechanics' institute veterans who had never accepted fiction as "improving literature." One of them was appalled to find his grandson reading a novel from a public library: "What are you doing with this trash? Read proper books, young man—*proper* books." (The novel was *Anna Karenina*.)[16]

A General Theory of Rubbish

The high cost of new books and literary periodicals was an obstacle to the working-class reader, but not an insurmountable one. Every industrial town of any size had at least one secondhand bookstall in the market square. In the mid-nineteenth century, journalist Henry Mayhew found that the prime customers of London bookstalls were workingmen. When he asked what sold particularly well, the answers fell into a clear pattern: *Rasselas, The Vicar of Wakefield, Peregrine Pickle, Tom Jones*, Goldsmith's histories, *A Sentimental Journey, Pilgrim's Progress, Robinson Crusoe, Philip Quarll, Telemachus, Gil Blas*, the letters of Junius, Shakespeare, Pope, James Thomson, William Cowper, Burns, Byron, and Scott. For the most part, they were the standard classics of the long eighteenth century. Bound volumes of almost any periodical from the same period (e.g., *Spectator, Tatler, Guardian, Rambler*) sold briskly for 1s. 6d. to 3s. 6d. a volume. Equally revealing was a list of what was *not* generally available for sale. The supply of old black-letter editions was far less than it once had been, since they were now snapped up by second-hand dealers for resale to affluent collectors. It could be equally difficult to find popular nineteenth-century poets like Shelley, Coleridge, Wordsworth, Thomas Moore, and Thomas Hood, because they were still in demand. "They haven't become cheap enough yet for the streets," said one stall-owner, but "they would come to it in time."[17]

That stall-owner recognized a market phenomenon familiar to any dealer in "collectables." More than a century later, Michael Thompson would explain it in terms of "Rubbish Theory." Almost any cultural product—from Melville novels to Elvis Presley lunchboxes to cast-iron storefront facades in lower Manhattan—seems to follow a three-phase life cycle. At first everyone must have one simply because it is novel and confers a certain distinction on the owner. That distinction is lost when ownership becomes so common that the market is saturated. At that point the artifact becomes "banal," and its value plummets to the level of "rubbish." Production ceases, and the thing is gradually junked—until it becomes so scarce that it acquires an antique cachet. In this final phase its value rises once again, often quite dramatically.[18]

The literary marketplace is governed by the same laws. First editions of books in nineteenth-century Britain could be very expensive, but eventually they would pass out of vogue and end up in the 2d. bookstalls. A generation or two later they would become collectors' items, and bibliophiles would bid up their price. Only in the intervening window of unfashionability would they be affordable for the working-class autodidact, whose reading would therefore always be a certain distance behind the times. By the mid-nineteenth century, as Charles Knight observed, *Tom Jones, Roderick Random,* and *Tristram Shandy* had "utterly gone out of the popular view."[19] Therefore, they were widely available. In the 1920s Janet Hitchman acquired her literary education among the derelict bookshelves of an orphanage, which included a huge collection of "drunken-father-death-bed-conversion" stories (*Christie's Old Organ,* 'The Little Match Girl', *A Peep Behind the Scenes*), as well as everything by Dickens, old volumes of *Punch* and the *Spectator,* and *The Life of Ruskin.* "My undigested reading made me look at the world with mid-Victorian eyes," she recalled. "Much as present-day [1960] Russians are supposed to do, I thought there were still little boys in London who swept crossings to support their ailing mammas, and that if I ever ran away I could always earn my bread by cleaning doorsteps. I also believed that you had a baby if you allowed a man to kiss you, for this was always the sequence of events in the books."[20]

As late as 1940, Mass Observation found that while 55 percent of working-class adults read books, 66 percent never bought books, another 10 percent once bought them but no longer did, 19 percent bought books only occasionally, and only 5 percent had bought a book within the past two to three weeks. Sixty-eight percent never patronized any kind of library and only 16 percent used the public library: the remainder resorted to subscription and 2d. libraries.[21] In working-class communities books were usually acquired second-hand or as gifts (notably the ubiquitous Sunday school prizes), borrowed, inherited, or scavenged. From rubbish heaps and used-book stalls, labor activist Manny Shinwell (b. 1884) was able to build up a library of 250 volumes, including Dickens, Meredith, Hardy, Keats, Burns, Darwin, Huxley, Kant, and Spinoza.[22] Autodidacts could afford reprints such as John Dicks's English Classics and Everyman's Library, but they were generally out of copyright.

Thus Welsh collier Joseph Keating (b. 1871) was able to immerse himself in Swift, Pope, Fielding, Richardson, Smollett, Goldsmith, Sheridan, Keats, Byron, Shelley, Dickens, and Greek philosophy, as well as the John Dicks edition of *Vanity Fair* in weekly installments. The common denominator among these authors was that they were all dead. "Volumes by living authors were too high-priced for me," Keating explained. "Our school-books never mentioned living writers; and the impression in my mind was that an author, to be a living author, must be dead; and that his work was all the better if he died of neglect and starvation." His initiation into modern literature came when his brother introduced him to

Jerome K. Jerome's *Three Men in a Boat*: "I had thought that only Smollett and Dickens could make a reader laugh; and I was surprised to find that a man who was actually living could write in such a genuinely humourous way."[23] In the early 1870s bookbinder Frederick Rogers wanted to read Tennyson and Browning, but a half-crown Tennyson was not available until 1879, and no cheap Browning appeared until the year of his death (1889). Rogers was able to enjoy Browning's "Paracelsus" in the Guildhall Library, but beyond that its collection was fairly antiquated.[24]

The People's Bard

Nineteenth-century popular culture was dominated by one dead author in particular, and Victorian "Bardolatry" was driven largely by working-class demand. In mid-century London newsboys spent their odd 6d. on *Hamlet* and *Macbeth*.[25] Drama critics reported on Shakespeare productions where the boxes and stalls were half-sold, while the pit and gallery were filled with enthusiastic audiences who loudly commented on the performance and even prompted the actors. Between the 1840s and 1870s, popular demand drove Birmingham's Theatre Royal to boost the proportion of Shakespeare and other classic drama from about 15 to 30 percent of its repertoire, while melodrama fell from a half to a quarter. In 1862 a theater manager provoked something approaching a riot when he attempted to substitute a modern comedy for an announced production of *Othello*. A London reporter described the proletarian audience for an 1872 production of *The Winter's Tale*: "Without knowing anything of poetry they felt the wondrous power of the poet's genius, and their flushed faces and brightened eyes betokened the thrill which some of the magnificent passages sent among them." As a Birmingham reviewer noted in 1885,

> The pit has had a dramatic education …, and the pit knows at once what is good, bad or indifferent. The criticism of the pit … if rough and ready, is formed on a sound basis. Listen between the acts to the remarks passed around you on a new exponent of a celebrated part, and you will hear comparisons drawn between the present performance and all the great ones who have trod the boards.[26]

Before the cinema, caravans of barnstorming actors brought Shakespeare to Durham mining villages, often using local talent for the lesser roles.[27] "I knew several men who could recite long passages from Shakespeare's plays impromptu at any time," recalled Bradford millworker F. W. Jowett (b. 1864). "One man, a workmate of mine who could neither read nor write, never missed seeing a good play and could appraise the actors with sound judgment."[28]

These enthusiasts were not crowding into the theaters out of deference to middle-class tastes. For many of them, Shakespeare was a proletarian hero who spoke directly to working people. One weaver's son made that point by translating *The Merchant of Venice* into Lancashire dialect.[29] In Leicester Thomas Cooper founded his Shakespearean Chartist Association in 1841, quickly attracting 3,000 members. The Leicester Working Men's College (founded 1862), the Working Men's Club (founded 1866), and the local Independent Labour Party (from the early 1900s) sponsored regular Shakespeare readings. The Leicester Domestic Mission men's class attracted up to a thousand to its annual Shakespeare recitals, among them a worker-poet who opened the 1866 program with these lines:

I have a right, a kindred right I claim,
Though rank nor titles gild my humble name,
'Tis from his class, the class the proud discard,
For Shakespeare was himself the people's bard.[30]

One ex-ploughboy proclaimed, "It was Shakespeare who taught me to say, 'I am a true labourer: I earn what I eat, get what I wear, owe no man's hate, envy no man's happiness, glad of other men's good.'"[31]

The plays also provided a language of radical political mobilization. As E. P. Thompson noticed, radicals and Chartists habitually quoted Shakespeare in their polemics.[32] So did the confrontational secularists associated with G. J. Holyoake: for them, the plays became a surrogate "Bible of Humanity."[33] When John Dougherty attempted to ally all trade unions in a National Association for the Protection of Labour, his 1830 manifesto began with militant words from *Julius Caesar*.[34] Jailed for incitement to riot in 1919, Manny Shinwell kept his spirits up by reading the plays and taking notes on them. On his release, his notebook was taken away and returned only after most of the pages had been removed: "Shakespearean quotations, together with my reflections on man's inhumanity to man, were doubtless regarded as dangerous material by the prison authorities."[35]

Shakespeare provided a political script for J. R. Clynes, the son of an Irish farm laborer, who rose from the textile mills of Oldham to become deputy leader of the House of Commons. In his youth he drew inspiration from the "strange truth" he discovered in *Twelfth Night*: "Be not afraid of greatness." ("What a creed! How it would upset the world if men lived up to it, I thought.") Urged on by a Co-operative society librarian, he worked through the plays and discovered they were about people who "had died for their beliefs. Wat Tyler and Jack Cade seemed heroes." Reading *Julius Caesar*, "the realisation came suddenly to me that it was a mighty political drama" about the class struggle, "not just an entertainment." According to his comrade Will Thorne, Clynes was "the only man who ever settled a trade dispute by citing Shakespeare." (Evidently, he overawed a stubborn employer by reciting an entire scene from *Julius Caesar*.) Elected to Parliament in 1906, he read *A Midsummer Night's Dream* while awaiting the returns.[36]

Robert Smillie, president of the Scottish Miners' Federation, felt that his lack of education hampered his trade union work, until Shakespeare exercised his powers of thought and expression: "It was a new and enchanting world. Those tragedies and comedies, to an ardent young mind which had hitherto been 'cribbed, cabin'd, and confin'd,' caught and held in the iron clutch of the industrial machine, were a sheer revelation. ... Outside of the boards of the Bible I know of no greater mental stimulus than Shakespeare."[37] Then there was Alice Foley who had to endure home performances by her father, a Bolton millhand:

> I can remember the agony of having to be Desdemona. You see, he knew all the tragedies of Shakespeare and he would enact them, you see, half drunk he would enact them. And he used to go stalking round the house ... he was a majestic man ... giving us Hamlet's soliloquies and all these long speeches and if he took Othello he would fling me suddenly into either an armchair or on the old horsehair sofa and smother me with a cushion, you know. I can remember to this day the stuffy old cushion that he used to put over my mouth. And then just as suddenly he would fall back in his chair and he would say, "The pity of it, Iago, the pity of it." And it was his own soliloquy. It was the pity of it, you see, that he could do that kind of thing so magnificently, and yet ....[38]

If Shakespeare still had a proletarian following in the nineteenth century, it melted away in the twentieth. By the 1880s, popular demand for his plays was already beginning to slacken. In 1910 the *Leicester Pioneer* noted the trend, and placed the blame squarely on the mass media and public education: working people had been "*Daily Mailed*" and "School Boarded into preferring Mr. Hall Caine before the late William Shakespeare."[39] Here were the outlines of what would become a common leftist critique of modern culture: while the popular media distracted the masses from serious literature, a bureaucratized system of compulsory education reduced Shakespeare to tedious classroom drill. It was certainly hard for classic drama to compete with popular fiction, the music hall, and the cinema. At the same time, it seems unfair to blame the 1870 Education Act for the decline of the people's bard. In school memoirs, some of the most rhapsodic passages harken back to Shakespeare recitals in class. *The Merchant of Venice* was "unforgettable," something that "brought into our very classroom the human passions of the outside world, its scheming hatred, scorn, avarice and injustice"—this from a Lancashire girl (b. 1912) who "simply did not know what drama was," since she and her classmates had never seen a play performed.[40]

Another factor may have been involved here. The same workers who read a radical political message into Shakespeare had hopelessly conservative tastes in stagecraft. Even Victorian critics complained about the stodginess of plebeian audiences. They "preferred their Hamlet acted in a mannered, dated way," observes Jeremy Crump, and reserved their greatest applause for warhorse soliloquies delivered with predictable grandiosity.[41] As a Glasgow power-loom tenter admitted, "I suppose it was the melodramatic element in them that made *Julius Caesar* and *Hamlet* such a draw" among the same audiences that were spellbound by *East*

Lynne.[42] Frederick Rogers found that no one else in his London bookbinder's shop would tolerate Henry Irving's new psychological treatment of Shakespeare in the 1870s. "He was making a revolution in dramatic art," Rogers recalled, "and the workshop wanted no revolution there. It held certain stereotyped ideas as to Shakespeare's conceptions of his own characters, and these ideas were represented by the men and women it was used to—or it thought they were—and Irving's wonderful psychological studies of passion or crime were things it could not understand, and would not accept." In *Hamlet* the line "Look here upon this picture, and on this … " traditionally called for gestures toward two actual paintings, but with Irving the portraits were only suggested: "The workshop rose in furious revolt at this innovation."[43] As melodrama and stage literalism went out of fashion (at least among middle-class sophisticates), working-class audiences would be left far behind. If they found Irving too avant-garde, how would they respond to the still more innovative Edwardian productions staged by Harley Granville Barker, which experimented with nonrepresentational sets?

Perhaps they turned to the pages of Robert Blatchford's *Clarion*, where they could find a more familiar mix of socialism and literary conservatism. "I sometimes wish our people would give less time to modern and more to ancient English literature," Blatchford once sighed. Emerson, Ruskin, and George Eliot were fair enough, but Blatchford directed his readers to *The Faerie Queene*, More's *Utopia*, Sir Philip Sidney, and Shakespeare.[44] Contemporary literature had even less appeal for W. E. Adams, a compositor and editor who began his political career as a Chartist and a republican. By 1903 he was fulminating against "the loathesome suggestiveness of the problem play," in which "harlots and strumpets have been made the heroines of dramas." He condemned publishers who brought out translations of Zola, and he vilified modern English novelists who seemed to be suggesting "that the father of a woman's child was no more anybody's concern than the cut or fashion of her under-garments." Adams's tastes had been formed in the 1850s by a literature course at the London Working Men's College, taught by the philologist F. J. Furnivall, who concentrated on Chaucer and the Elizabethans. Adams was prepared to concede that, even in the wholesome Victorian era, there was a huge audience for the novels of G. W. M. Reynolds—sensational trash, verging on pornography, modeled after Eugène Sue. But, he protested, back then everyone *knew* it was trash: "With the taste for sensation and salacious details which the modern novelist and modern dramatist have cultivated, it is not at all unlikely that [Reynolds] would, if he had flourished at the end of the century, have been admitted to the hierarchy of fiction."[45]

The Hundred Best Books

That comment was a remarkably far-sighted anticipation of today's postmodern literary standards, and it points to a cultural gap that was opening up between the classes. Artist Frank Steel (b. early 1860s) was not inclined to sentimentalize the Victorian era: at his workhouse school he had been force-fed moralizing tales designed to "induce in the plastic minds of dependent children a habit of cringing humility that, however proper some may deem it to their 'station in life,' is the greatest curse of the poor." Yet when the Stracheyite reaction against Victorianism set in, Steel was disgusted: "I am prone to impatience with … the antics of certain new schools or circles of pseudo-criticism which affect to despise, or at best to patronize condescendingly and 'damn with faint praise,' anything bearing the stamp of nineteenth-century British refinement. As if true-to-type Victorian literature (and art) did not fill its place and period, and fulfil its mission as worthily as that of any other epoch!"[46]

At the dawn of the twentieth century, when literary modernism was emerging, the self-educated had only just mastered the great English classics. By the time the masses caught up with post-Victorian writers, literary elites had moved on to still more advanced authors. It was not until 1929 that Norman Nicholson, a Cumberland tailor's son, discovered modern literature in Bernard Shaw and H. G. Wells. These two eminent Edwardians already had all their great works behind them, and were considered obsolete in avant-garde circles: five years earlier, Virginia Woolf had dismissed their entire generation in her essay "Mr. Bennett and Mrs. Brown." But for a working-class boy from a provincial town in the far north, they represented the last word in subversive literature. Shaw, who was not yet available at the Millom public library, opened Nicholson's eyes to unemployment, made him an angry socialist, and taught him what he had never appreciated before—"that the Victorian age was over and gone."

He could not have learned that lesson in the classroom, though he attended a good grammar school. His sixth form English teacher was an exceptionally brilliant woman, who taught him to love Chaucer, Shakespeare, Milton, Sheridan, Lamb, Coleridge, Byron, Shelley, Keats, Wordsworth, and Scott. Yet even she could not venture beyond the Victorians. "She once drew on the blackboard a graph of the progress of English poetry, as she saw it," Nicholson recalled, as if she were charting the stock exchange index:

First, Chaucer jutted up, like a cliff, out of sheer nothingness; then, after a gap, came the towering Everest of Shakespeare, the lesser peak of Milton, and a whole century and a half of fen-land flatness, until the Romantics soared up, nearly as high as Shakespeare, followed by the lower rolling ranges of the Victorians. Of Eliot, Pound and Joyce, I doubt if she even knew the names, and if she'd heard of Lawrence, it was only in the pages of the Sunday newspapers. [John] Drinkwater was her idea of a modern poet, Galsworthy, of a modern dramatist, and when I managed to persuade her to include *St. Joan* in our syllabus, I fancy she saw herself as being quite daringly contemporary.[47]

She was in fact a progressive teacher, and Nicholson a fortunate student. At that time the literary education of most working-class pupils stopped in the mid-nineteenth century or even, in some cases, the eighteenth century.[48] Yet for those at the bottom of the social scale, the most old-fashioned literary canons could be terrifically liberating. What was dismally familiar to professional intellectuals was amazingly new to them. For Richard Hillyer (b. c. 1900) the revelation struck when he came across the words "Poet Laureate" in *Lloyd's Weekly News*, and asked his teacher what it meant:

So, for ten minutes, he let himself go on it, and education began for me. There was Ben Jonson, the butt of canary wine, birthday odes and all the rest of it. I was fascinated. My mind was being broken out of its shell. Here were wonderful things to know. Things that went beyond the small utilities of our lives, which was all that school had seemed to concern itself with until then. Knowledge of this sort could make all times, and places, your own. You could be anybody, and everybody, and still be yourself all the time.

For a cowman's son in a Northamptonshire village it was a revolutionary insight. From a classroom library of perhaps two dozen volumes he borrowed one by Tennyson, simply because it had "Poet Laureate" printed on the title page:

The coloured words flashed out and entranced my fancy. They drew pictures in the mind. Words became magical, incantations, abracadabra which called up spirits. My dormant imagination opened like a flower in the sun. Life at home was drab, and colourless, with nothing to light up the dull monotony of the unchanging days. Here in books was a limitless world that I could have for my own. It was like coming up from the bottom of the ocean and seeing the universe for the first time.

Later, at a second-hand stall, he bought a four-volume *Half Hours with Best Authors*. One could dismiss it as a potted Anglocentric collection of arbitrary snippets by dead writers, but as Hillyer explained:

The all important thing was that within the battered covers were bits and pieces from a vast range of literature, people I had always wanted to read, and others I had never heard of, but standing in the full tradition and waiting to be discovered. It is easy to talk of epochs in a life, events which are permanent, and far-reaching, enough to be called that are rare, but this was one. The dilapidated old book opened to me the sweep and grandeur of English literature better than most professional teachers would have done. It was literature itself, not talk about literature. It made its own impact, spread the goods out in front of me, and let me make my choice. Nobody told me what I ought to like, it was just there for me to like, if I wanted to. All the great people were there, from Chaucer to Tennyson, in passages which were supposed to take a half hour to read; and there was one for every day of the year, with a gossipy little introduction to each which gave all that was needed to be in the picture. From them I learned that behind the English writers lay others, belonging to far off times and places, in the old days of Greece and Rome; and that was a fact that I had never heard of before, but something to go into, if ever the chance came along.[49]

Racing to make up educational deficits, autodidacts often resorted to prepackaged collections of classics. Any number of them testified to the inspiration of Palgrave's *Golden Treasury*.[50] "Hot with the hunter's passion, I began to chase everything labelled 'standard,'" recalled orphanage boy Thomas Burke (b. 1886), who devoured books until "my mind became a lumber-room." Inevitably, "Criticism was beyond me; the hungry man has no time for the fastidiousness of the epicure. I was hypnotised by the word Poet. A poem by Keats (some trifle never meant for print) was a poem by Keats. Pope and Cowper and Kirke White and Mrs. Hemans and Samuel Rogers were Poets. That was enough."[51]

C. H. Rolph (b. 1901) recalled that his father, a London policeman, invested the same unquestioning faith in middlebrow reference works. *Nuttall's Standard Dictionary* was the last word in lexicography, *Pitman's Shorthand Dictionary* the absolute standard for pronunciation, while Meiklejohn's English Grammar "occupied in our household a position usually accorded at that time to the Bible." With that kind of deference to intellectual authority, his father read diligently through a list of the "Hundred Best Books" compiled in 1886 by Sir John Lubbock. "It included nearly all of the books that one didn't want to read, or gave up if one tried," Rolph recalled: "Aristotle's *Ethics*, *The Koran*, Xenophon's *Memorabilia*, *The Nibelungenlied*, Schiller's *William Tell*; and it ended with 'Dickens's *Pickwick* and *David Copperfield*' (only) but 'Scott's novels' (apparently the lot). For the most part they were the books which, it seemed, you should expect to find in every intelligent man's private library; with, in most such libraries, their leaves uncut."

Matthew Arnold and Henry James were equally dismissive of the Hundred Best list, and everyone has a right to argue with Lubbock's choices. But no one who has ever handed students a syllabus of required readings can in good faith object to the principle of a best books list. Though canons can be changed, canonization is inevitable, given that we must choose among the millions of books available to us. And Sir John Lubbock had earned the right to publish his own selection: he was a committed adult educator, president of the Working Men's College, and a best-selling popular science writer. As an MP, he sponsored a Bank Holidays Act and early closing legislation to allow working people more time for cultural pursuits. If you already know your way around the literary canon, it is easy to sneer at Lubbock's list; but it was enormously popular among readers like

Rolph's father, who was eager to make up for an education that had been denied him, and was not ashamed to ask for a roadmap.[52] Without it, he would never have gone beyond the authors popular in his family circle: Edgar Wallace, Silas and Joseph Hocking, Stanley Weyman, Anthony Hope, W. J. Locke, Jeffery Farnol, Emma Worboise, Mrs. Henry Wood ("I cried in bed over *The Channings*"), and Mrs. Humphry Ward. "Marie Corelli was more revered in our home than Thomas à Kempis himself. Their books went through our household like a benignly infectious plague," writes Rolph, but there was "a marked absence of authors such as Jane Austen, the Brontës, and Mrs. Gaskell." For all his limitations, Sir John Lubbock was pointing the way to *Pride and Prejudice*.[53]

One would expect Lubbock to be a sitting duck for contemporary critics of the "Great Books" tradition. "No longer the 'undulating and diverse' relation to knowledge which Matthew Arnold prescribed, the 'hundred best books' has an attainable completeness, a finality of its own, existing precisely as a fetish which may be owned," wrote academic Marxist N. N. Feltes.[54] Yet for working-class Marxist T. A. Jackson, Lubbock's list was exactly the opposite. It was conservative only in the sense that it included no living authors. Its impact on the minds of readers like Jackson was profoundly radical, inspiring them to range far beyond the limits of the "hundred best."

Compositor, full-time lecturer and educator for the Communist Party, author of sophisticated studies on dialectical materialism and Charles Dickens, T. A. Jackson was the beau idéal of the proletarian philosopher. A fellow street orator hailed him as "the intellectual head of the communist movement in this country; so much so that if he dropped out of the movement the intelligence which remained would not be discernible without the aid of a powerful microscope."[55] According to Harold Heslop, the miner-novelist, "his immense intellectual ability" was equalled only by his scruffiness: "He was the spiritual father of all the hippies of this day [1971]. ... He strode all the pavements of London with the intentness of George Gissing, often unwashed, always undignified, curiously unaware of his forlorn appearance." Yet he could successfully debate Trotsky, argue down George Lukács on the virtues of Walter Scott, and do it all in language "almost as magnificent as that of Edmund Burke."[56] Jackson himself affirmed that he owed his intellectual gifts largely to Sir John Lubbock. "Expensively educated comrades" laughed at him for saying so, but the act of reading through nearly all of those one hundred books set in motion an intellectual odyssey that eventually brought Jackson to Marxism, though Marx was certainly not on the list:

It rescued me from the notion that the only books properly to be called "good" were prose fiction, and such history and biography as could be read as if it were prose fiction—which, alas, it all too often, is. It drove me into reading translations of the Greek and Roman classic authors I would never have faced otherwise. It started me off upon an intensive study of English poetry and, thereafter upon a similar study of Romance and Saga literature. It taught me there were other branches of literature than prose fiction, and other dramatic writers than Shakespeare. It taught me Shakespeare was something much more than an old bore invented to plague the lives of schoolboys. It drove me back upon a wider grasp of history—since I found in practice that there were other literatures than English—literatures of at least equal merit. I found too that all could be understood only in their historical sequence. In the end it led me to philosophy and Marxism and thereby to the revolutionising of my whole life. … Whether he desired it or not, he gave me the urge which sent me adventuring with courage and confidence until I had found them all for myself.

Jackson's tastes had been formed by the old books in his parents' home: "A fine set of Pope, an odd volume or two of the *Spectator*, a *Robinson Crusoe*, Pope's translation of Homer, and a copy of *Paradise Lost*." He read them all "for the simple reason that there was nothing else to read." Hence his talent for preaching Marxism in Burkean prose: "Mentally speaking I date from the early 18th century. And, after all, one could date from worse periods than that."[57]

Besides, many of these older authors offered anticipations of Marxism. "Incongruous though it may seem," Jackson wrote, "it was Macaulay as much as anybody who gave me a push-off on the road from the conventional conception of history as a superficial chronicle-narrative to the wider philosophical conception of history as an all-embracing world-process as understood by Marx."[58] Jailed for incitement to mutiny, Communist J. T. Murphy (b. 1888) was amused to find that the prison library barred subversive literature but permitted Macaulay's essay on Milton—"a most powerful justification of the Cromwellian Revolution," he noted. "It is only necessary to transpose 'bourgeois revolution' to 'proletarian revolution' and you can soon think you are reading an essay by Trotsky, whose style of writing is not unlike Macaulay's, on the Russian Revolution."[59] Working-class readers continued to enjoy Macaulay's drama and accessibility long after professional historians had declared him obsolete. Kathleen Woodward (b. 1896) read Gibbon's *Decline and Fall* and Macaulay's *History of England* twice through over factory work, with such absorption that she once injured a finger, leaving an "honourable scar." "I derived great pleasure from these histories, which, as I grew up, I heard slighted, maligned. The colour and movement of Macaulay, the onward swing from Parliament to Parliament and from King to King daily transported me; nor was my pleasure spoiled by any awareness of his prejudices or inaccuracies."[60] Even when social and economic history came into vogue in the late 1930s, miner's son Alan Gibson was bored by it, preferring Macaulay and Carlyle to J. H. Clapham. "When Macaulay published his *History of England* he received a letter from a working-men's club thanking him for writing a history which working men could read," he noted. "It remains true that if working men cannot read a history book it is not history at all (it might be antiquarianism or archaeology or something like that, but it is not history)."[61] Note that the reading preferences of the first Labour MPs listed in Table 1.1 (p. 42) included Macaulay but no living authors other than Beatrice and Sidney Webb.

Everyman's Library

In addition to reading from lists like Lubbock's, autodidacts could resort to inexpensive editions of the world's great books. J. M. Dent's Everyman's Library, begun in 1906, would be the largest, most handsome, and most coherently edited series of cheap classics, though it was certainly not the first. When the House of Lords issued its landmark decision in *Donaldson v. Beckett* (1774), ending perpetual copyright, it opened the way for publishing uniform editions of works in the public domain. In 1776 John Bell began his Poets of Great Britain, 109 volumes for 18d. each. John Cooke followed with 6d. numbers of British poets and dramatists, much admired by John Clare and Thomas Carter.[62] Richard Altick counted upwards of a hundred such series commenced between 1830 and 1906. By 1863 there was Charles Knight's Library of Classics, Bentley's Standard Novels, Bohn's Standard Library and British Classics, W. and R. Chambers's People's Editions, Chapman and Hall's Standard Editions of Popular Authors, Murray's British Classics, Routledge's British Poets and Standard Novels. Most of these editions were not so cheap, selling for between 3s. 6d. and 5s., but eventually a growing demand for school editions made possible economies of scale, and fierce competition among publishers drove down prices. John Dicks offered the Waverley novels for 3d. each, a huge illustrated Byron for 7d., and Shakespeare at 1d. for two plays or 1s. for the complete works. Henry Morley edited two rival series: Routledge's Universal Library (from 1883) selling at 1s. a volume and Cassell's National Library (from 1885) at 3d. paper, 6d. cloth.[63] Prices hit rock bottom in May 1895, with the inauguration of W. T. Stead's Penny Poets. In January 1896 there followed the Penny Novels which, anticipating the *Reader's Digest*, were condensations of 30,000 to 40,000 words. Stead proved that the demand for cheap classic reprints was enormous: by October 1897 there were sixty volumes of Penny Poets with 5,276,000 copies in print, and about 9 million copies of ninety Penny Novels.[64]

An important immediate precursor of Dent was Walter Scott—not the Waverley novelist, but an unrelated Newcastle publisher. He was an uneducated self-made entrepreneur in the construction trade who acquired a near-bankrupt publishing firm in 1882 and appointed David Gordon, a bookbinder, to manage it. Gordon put the business in the black with several series of inexpensive classics, reprinting Dickens, Smollett, and the other Walter Scott. In 1884 he launched the 1s. Canterbury Poets, edited by the collier-poet Joseph Skipsey. There followed a profitable and popular Contemporary Science Series, overseen by Havelock Ellis. The Scott firm was instrumental in introducing English readers to the works of Tolstoy and Ibsen, publishing some of their first English translations. There was also the Camelot Classics, prose reprints edited by Ernest Rhys, who would later apply that experience to Everyman's Library.[65]

J. M. Dent was yet another product of the working-class autodidact tradition. Born in 1849 to a Darlington housepainter with musical interests, he was raised along strict Nonconformist lines and attended a good Wesleyan school. At age fifteen he joined a chapel-based mutual improvement society and agreed to present a paper on Samuel Johnson. He knew nothing about the man except the dictionary on his father's bookshelves. Boswell's biography and Macaulay's essay were at first hard to decipher, unfamiliar as he was with the larger constellation of eighteenth-century literary men, but he was absolutely

> amazed that these greater men, as they seemed to me, should bow down before this old Juggernaut and allow him to walk over them, insult them, blaze out at them and treat them as if they were his inferiors—men like Edmund Burke, Sir Joshua Reynolds and Oliver Goldsmith, with a host of others. At last it dawned upon me that it was not the ponderous, clumsy, dirty old man that they worshipped, but the scholarship for which he stood. ... I quickly learnt to worship at the same altar, and I bless the day that brought me in touch with Boswell's *Life*. I got up from the book feeling there was nothing worth living for so much as literature, otherwise how could this uncouth man rule over such a company? To write a book seemed to me to be the only way to gain Olympus, and I am very much of the same opinion to-day, but it must be *literature*.[66]

(He always pronounced it "litterchah", according to employee Frank Swinnerton.)[67] Dent's literary tastes were naive, old-fashioned, petit bourgeois, and blindly worshipful; but he recognized early on that the great books were an engine for equality, a body of knowledge that anyone could acquire, given basic literacy and cheap editions. Naturally, his reading was marked by the autodidact's characteristic enthusiasm and spottiness. He knew *Pilgrim's Progress*, Milton, Cowper, Thomson's *Seasons*, and Young's *Night Thoughts*; but even Dickens was not widely available in a provincial mid-Victorian town, and he did not read Shakespeare seriously until he was nearly thirty.[68]

His cultural contacts broadened when he became an apprentice bookbinder in London, discovering the work of William Morris, Cobden-Sanderson, and the Arts and Crafts movement. Increasingly unhappy with dogmatic Nonconformity, he found a more liberal community of minds in Toynbee Hall's Shakespeare Society, where he also discovered a potential mass market for inexpensive quality books. "It was amusing to see the texts brought to our readings" in the Toynbee Shakespeare Society, he recalled, "second-hand editions, quartos, Bowdlerized school editions—no two being the same and all without proper machinery for elucidating difficulties. Neither types nor pages gave proper help to reading aloud." He filled that gap with the forty volumes of the Temple Shakespeare (1894–96), edited by Israel Gollancz. Printed on fine paper, with act and scene headings on each page, lines numbered for ready reference, and title pages designed by Walter Crane, it was priced at 1s. For a time the series sold a quarter of a million copies annually—"the largest sale made in Shakespeare since the plays were written," Dent boasted. It was followed by the Temple Classics, of which 300 were published by 1918, including Chapman's Homer, *The Romance of the Rose*, Plutarch in ten volumes, Boswell's Johnson in six, William Caxton's *The Golden Legend*, all four Brontës, *The Mahabharata*, and an annotated Dante in English and Italian on facing pages.[69]

In 1904 Dent began to think seriously about a still grander venture in cheap classics. He was familiar with the earlier series issued by Bohn, Morley, and Stead, as well as the French "Bibliothèque nationale" and the "Réclam" series of Leipzig. But they represented fairly random selections of titles, unattractively produced and poorly edited. Dent envisioned nothing less than a uniform edition of standard English and world literature in 1,000 volumes. Priced at 1s., the break-even point would be at least 10,000 copies, for some volumes 20,000 or 30,000. But the moment seemed right: the copyrights of the great Victorians were expiring, and he had £10,000 in liquid capital.[70]

The same general idea had occurred independently to Ernest Rhys, who would edit Everyman's Library from its inception until his death in 1946. Like Dent, Rhys had some experience in bringing literature to the masses. As an apprentice mining engineer in a Durham coal town, he had set up a small library (which included works by Plato and Shelley) and a book discussion group for the colliers. As editor for Walter Scott's Camelot Classics, Rhys coined the phrase "the suffrages of the democratic shilling," later appropriated by Dent.[71] And it was Rhys who hit upon the name Everyman's Library, borrowed from the medieval mystery play. Launched in February 1906 with (of course) *The Life of Samuel Johnson*, Everyman's Library sold so well that Dent soon had to begin construction of a costly new plant at Letchworth Garden City.

Modern and postmodern critics would be less enchanted with Everyman's Library specifically and, more generally, the entire species of "Five-Foot Shelf" packaged classics. Their creators stand accused of neglecting authors who were female, non-Western, subversive, avant-garde, or otherwise "marginalized" (Zora Neale Hurston is often cited as an example here).

The truth is the House of Dent was innocent on every count. This is not to defend all of Rhys's choices. Hugh Kenner, for one, laughed heartily over the inclusion of Adelaide A. Procter (1906), an early Victorian poet remembered today only for "The Lost Chord."[72] The backbone of Everyman's Library was the standard roster of English literature, from *The Anglo-Saxon Chronicle* to sixteen volumes of John Ruskin, along with the predictable Greek, Latin, American, and Western European authors.[73] In a way, it was impressive that Dent was willing to invest in so many lengthy and intimidating classics: George Grote's *History of Greece* in twelve volumes, Richard Hakluyt's *Voyages* (introduced by John Masefield) in eight, J. A. Froude's *History of England* in ten, fifteen volumes of

Balzac, and six of Ibsen. But even as Rhys pressed ahead with the project, the canon was shifting under his feet. When Everyman's Library finally reached Volume 1,000 (Aristotle's *Metaphysics*) in 1956, Dent's editorial director was forced to concede that many of their Victorian novelists, historians, and materialist philosophers were obsolete: "Already during the fifty years of the Library's existence it has been perfectly clear that the standards of 'immortality' have been changing."[74]

Still, it is unfair to criticize Rhys for failing to anticipate the literary fashions of the late twentieth century. Compared with all the earlier series of cheap classics, his represented the most deliberate and inclusive effort to assemble a library of world literature. It was very much an open canon, frequently venturing beyond the safe and familiar. Rhys was willing to take chances on what he judged to be forgotten masterpieces, such as Richard Ford's *Gatherings from Spain* and Robert Paltock's fantasy *Peter Wilkins and the Flying Indians*. (Both ended up on Dent's "worst-sellers" list.) He included not only Tolstoy, Dostoevsky, Turgenev, Gogol, and Pushkin, but also other Russians who were scarcely known in Britain: Ivan Goncharov's *Oblomov* (1932) and Shchedrin's *The Golovlyov Family* (1934) were each issued just three years after their first complete English translations. When few English readers had heard of Herman Melville, and he had yet to be revived in the United States, Everyman's Library issued *Moby Dick* (1907), *Typee* (1907), and *Omoo* (1908). And these decisions were not necessarily market-driven: Dent complained that he could not make Russian or American literature sell in Britain.[75]

As a radical liberal, Dent was happy to publish Tom Paine, William Cobbett, Giuseppe Mazzini, and Henry George. He even toyed with the idea of a Lenin anthology,[76] though neither Robert Owen nor *Capital* would appear in Everyman's Library until after his death in 1926. Dent was a puritan who personally vetoed the inclusion of Smollett and *Moll Flanders*: "There is no reason why we should try to perpetuate the uncleanness of a very unpleasant age."[77] Only after control of the firm had passed to his sons would they publish *Roderick Random*, *Madame Bovary*, Rabelais, *The Decameron*, and Rousseau's *Confessions*.

By its very nature, the Everyman canon had to be conservative. While America's Modern Library emphasized modern literature, Everyman usually drew its texts from the public domain. The Copyright Act of 1911, which extended protection to fifty years after the author's death, held up the publication of *Middlemarch* until 1930 and some of Robert Browning until 1940. The series included nothing from the twentieth century until a translation of Henri Barbusse's First World War novel *Le Feu* (1916) was published as *Under Fire* in 1926. Yet Dent clearly wanted more contemporary literature: specifically *Lord Jim*, *The Old Wives' Tale*, Wells, Galsworthy, and Henry James,[78] all of which were admitted to Everyman's Library in 1935. They were soon followed by the great modernists: Aldous Huxley (1937), Virginia Woolf's *To the Lighthouse* (1938), Thomas Mann (1940), J. M. Synge (1941), and E. M. Forster's *A Passage to India* (1942). In 1936 the company was eager to issue a Sigmund Freud anthology, only to be blocked by Leonard Woolf, who controlled the rights for the Hogarth Press.[79] Outside of Everyman's Library, the Dent list would feature a number of avant-garde authors, among them Luigi Pirandello, Henry Green, and Dylan Thomas. Before the nineteen-year-old artist had made his reputation, Dent recognized in Aubrey Beardsley "a new breath of life in English black-and-white drawing," and commissioned him to illustrate *Morte d'Arthur.*

Everyman's Library made at least some effort to include Eastern literature: *The Ramayana, The Mahabharata, Shakuntala, Hindu Scriptures* introduced by Rabindranath Tagore, as well as the Koran. Apparently Dent consulted a Japanese scholar about adding East Asian literature, but the First World War put an end to those plans.[80] As for women writers, Dent published all the Brontë sisters, Jane Austen, George Eliot, Christina Rossetti, and personally introduced Elizabeth Gaskell's *Cranford,* one of his favorite novels. Here again he went beyond the great names: several of the forgotten female authors that feminist scholars have lately tried to resuscitate (and some they have yet to rediscover) were in Everyman's canon, among them Dorothy Osborne, Aphra Behn, Lady Mary Wortley Montagu, Ann Radcliffe, Maria Edgeworth, Susan Ferrier, Mary Russell Mitford, Dinah Mulock Craik, Charlotte Yonge, Margaret Oliphant, and Mrs. Henry Wood. Mary Wollstonecraft's *A Vindication of the Rights of Woman* was included, as was the autobiography of Elizabeth Blackwell, the trailblazing female physician.

With that record, it was only natural that the House of Dent became Zora Neale Hurston's English publisher.[81] The company built up a strong list of proletarian writers, including basketweaver Thomas Okey, collier-novelists F. C. Boden and Roger Dataller, farm laborer Fred Kitchen, journalist Rowland Kenney, and Labour Party politicians James Griffiths and Harry Snell. For the Dent firm, publishing new books by disenfranchised authors and publishing old books for disenfranchised readers were all part of the same egalitarian project. A later generation of literary theorists might argue that there is an irrepressible conflict between "canonical" and "nontraditional" literature, that the great books somehow "marginalize" or "silence" oppressed peoples; but to Dent and Rhys that would have been absurd, contrary to everything they knew about working-class readers. "Canon wars" are purely a campus phenomenon, the result of an academic economy of scarcity. If an English faculty is allowed only one new hire, they may have to decide between a Miltonist and a Caribbeanist; and they can only add Zora Neale Hurston to a survey course by bumping someone else, in which case Dr. Johnson may seem a tempting target. But this is an internal professional controversy, irrelevant (if not slightly comic) to general readers, who have time for both Johnson and Hurston.

By 1975 more than 60 million copies of 1,239 Everyman volumes had been sold worldwide, but we only guess how many of them were bought by British working people. Their memoirs are not much help here: while they are quite forthcoming about books and authors read, they only occasionally mention specific editions. Everyman books did become a standby of Workers' Educational Association syllabuses[82]: as one student said, you could easily afford them if you went without smokes.[83] Some indirect evidence of readership comes from *Everyman*, a cheap literary weekly launched by Dent in 1912.[84] *Everyman* sponsored literary competitions, and it is revealing that in 1913 it received 360 essays on the topic "The Life of a Teacher," compared with more than a hundred from miners on colliery life.[85] An occupational breakdown of entrants to a January 1932 *Everyman* competition produced comparable results: only 13 percent were operatives, the rest mainly clerical workers (20 percent), teachers (10 percent), tradesmen (10 percent), journalists and artists (7 percent), civil servants, professionals, students, and performers of "home duties" (5 percent each).[86] A file of surviving letters to the editor from 1912–14 shows they were written mainly by middle-class readers, though there were also some appreciative notes from workingmen.[87] The working-class readership was probably somewhat larger than these proportions suggest, assuming that the average laborer was more reticent about putting pen to paper than a schoolmaster or businessman. The safest surmise is that the working classes bought a substantial fraction of Everyman's print run, amounting to several million volumes.

James Murray (b. c. 1894), a Glasgow woodcarver, represented the kind of reader Dent and Rhys were trying to reach. He credited *Everyman* magazine with "opening up an entirely new set of ideas to which I had previously been a stranger. I became familiar with the names and works of all the truly great authors and poets, and was now thoroughly convinced I had been misplaced in my life's work." His reading ranged from *Rasselas* to *Looking Backward*. He began writing poems, stories, and essays; and tried (without success) to get his work published in *Everyman* and other periodicals. Murray was handicapped as a writer because he could not afford to have his work typed, but he did take classes in French and German, enough for a reading knowledge of both. In the First World War he was one of those soldiers, noted by Paul Fussell, who marched to the front with a volume of poetry in his kit. Remarkably, considering the men he was fighting, it was Goethe in the original.[88] Both publishers and readers had invested an enormous liberal faith in the cheap classics, which might somehow abolish classes and establish universal peace. One world war was not enough to destroy that vision. In 1940 Ernest Rhys was still convinced that if the Nazis had only read Plato's *Republic*, Carlyle's *French Revolution*, John Locke, Abraham Lincoln, *War and Peace*, and *The Federalist Papers*, there would have been no war, and Germany would be a democracy in a united Europe.[89]

Catching Up

Proletarian cultural conservatism was also transmitted and reinforced by the first generation of schoolteachers called into existence by the Education Act of 1870. They themselves were often from working-class backgrounds, and what training they received was seriously obsolete. Philip Ballard, the son of a Welsh tinplate worker, was taught geology entirely out of a book—no one thought to visit the coal mines or the quarry in the area. The one geography textbook in use at his training college, James Cornwell's *School Geography* (1847), was about forty years old. Lectures on Old Testament history were plagiarized from Dean Milman's *History of the Jews* (1830). The school library was a bookcase kept locked except one evening a week, so Ballard could only pick up some knowledge of literature from fellow students and from visits to the Guildhall Library. Even then he had no exposure to contemporary writers until the 1890s: "I gained a nodding acquaintance with the life and letters of Ancient Greece and Rome, and … I had read most of Dickens, much of Thackeray, and some of Scott; but I had never read a line of Henry James, of Meredith, or of Hardy. And Browning I only knew as the man who had written 'How They Brought the Good News from Ghent to Aix.'"

But Ballard was able to catch up very quickly, thanks in part to the popular press. By the end of the nineteenth century mass circulation newspapers were offering an outlet to innovative authors, thus making the literary avant-garde more accessible to general readers. In the *Star* Ballard read the music criticism of Bernard Shaw, and Richard Le Gallienne on books: the latter kindly sent him a lengthy letter when he asked for advice about modern literature. He pressed on to Meredith and Walter Pater. In 1910 he attended that revolutionary event in English culture, the First Post-Impressionist Exhibition. Two artist friends who accompanied him were stunned: they considered Sargent avant-garde, and were in no way prepared for Gauguin, Van Gogh, or Matisse. By then Ballard, who had attended an "Independents" show in Paris, was actually more familiar with and receptive to modern art.[90]

An overdose of modernism, however, was likely to alienate the worker-intellectual from his own class. Welsh collier D. R. Davies (b. 1889) had been raised to regard the stage as sinful, and it was with some guilt that he attended his first play, at Miss Horniman's theater in Manchester. Immediately he was hooked on Shaw, Galsworthy, Masefield, and Ibsen. But when he had to return to the mines of South Wales, his exposure to new cultural opportunities only served "to intensify my egotism and inflate my pride. Its net effect was to isolate me from my fellows. … I now disliked and despised the people among whom necessity had placed me. A better education had made me less sociable." His resentments turned him toward revolutionary socialism, and he escaped the mines to become, in 1917, a Congregationalist minister in Ravensthorpe. But the modernist social gospel he preached was only a means (generally successful) of keeping his own congregants at arm's length:

> Inevitably, I was inwardly isolated from my people, and except for one or two, drifted away from them all. I lived in a world of my own—an abstract, intellectual world. My gospel was nothing but a system of ideas to which the rank-and-file of my church did not respond. Beyond these ideas, I had nothing to say. I became more and more a misfit. What was once said of a celebrated

Anglican could probably have been said of me, that during the week I was invisible and on Sundays I was incomprehensible.

Through a Bradford art dealer he met prominent modern artists: Jacob Kraemer and Jacob Epstein. Once he posted a photo of Epstein's Christ in the vestibule of his church and praised it in a sermon, "to the great disgust of some members of my congregation, but to the indifference of the majority." These contacts clearly broadened his enjoyment of art and architecture: he devoted holiday time to exploring the Tate and the Louvre, and became friends with Walter Gropius and Erwin Gutkind of the Bauhaus. Yet as he described it, his pursuit of the modern was in part a deliberate effort to alienate himself from the masses, which soon led him to quit the ministry:

I acquired the silly delusion of possessing the "artistic temperament." What that meant I never discovered, but it seemed to carry with it licence to disown responsibilities. In practice it put a premium on subjectivism. You did a thing only if you felt like it, and if you felt it: that was its justification. The effect upon me was altogether bad. It gave me the excuse I needed for alienation from my church and people. Moreover, it fostered my pride. It made me feel superior to kindly, decent people who, whatever their narrowness and provincialism, fulfilled their obligations in life, which was more than I was doing, and more than most of the artists I met were doing.[91]

Modernism did not have much of an audience in northern England, even among the worker-intellectuals of the WEA. In 1932 a Yorkshire instructor, Roger Dataller, noticed that the feminist message of *The Man of Property* was not getting through to his female students:

While the figure of Irene may have been all the "concretion of disturbing beauty" that the author intended, it is a conception not quite concrete enough for the working women of south Yorkshire. I find them totally unmoved by Irene. They cannot conceive an abstract beauty apart from the companionable, living presence. They conceive it impossible that this woman should have no capacity for mirth, for even a little graciousness towards her husband, for affability, or for general exuberance. Frankly, Galsworthy's conception does not come off, and the general compassion of these women is for Soames, poor fellow, linked with so insufferable a creature.[92]

Likewise, "The women in one of my classes were not in the least impressed by Mrs. Ramsay in *To the Lighthouse*. That she should allow her mind to wander while trying on the stocking that she was knitting for her little son, seemed inept, and their sympathy was for the little boy with so introspective a mother!"[93] Another WEA class on "The Modern Novel" totally baffled N. B. Dolan, a Scarborough trade unionist:

After two hours of hearing a lecturer who took for granted that each member of the class was well versed in Virginia Woolf, Aldous Huxley, and D. H. Lawrence I left the room dazed. Vague references to Freud and Behaviourism ran riot in my brain in bewildering confusion. The revelation of my colossal ignorance so stunned me that I did not even know how or where to begin. Moreover, the discussion afterwards gave me such a feeling of humiliation that I daren't even ask the lecturer for advice.

He could not in good conscience invite others to join the WEA, because "I do not want to choke them by bringing them into an environment of the middle class." In fact Dolan's experience was not typical: WEA courses usually avoided avant-garde authors. Yet it is revealing that, in his eyes, Freud, Woolf, Huxley, and Lawrence constituted bourgeois culture.[94] One Nottinghamshire collier (b. 1906?), a devotee of Gray, Goldsmith, Tennyson, and Keats, found in Lawrence's poetry only meaninglessness punctuated by obscenity. He rather enjoyed earthiness in a "classic" like Rabelais, but the "smut" that modern writers turned out was quite another matter.[95] A secondhand bookdealer noted that Huxley and even Bennett could not sell in Camberwell in 1931, while Marie Corelli and Mrs. Henry Wood were among his strongest sellers as late as 1948.[96]

In 1932 Q. D. Leavis asserted that the books considered avant-garde before the War, such as *Tono-Bungay* and *Ann Veronica*, were only now beginning to reach the masses.[97] Four years later WEA tutorial class students in the London area were asked to "Name one or more fiction writers whose novels you read frequently and enjoy": the results are listed in Table 4.2 below.

Compared to the northern WEA students cited above, these Londoners had relatively advanced tastes. Eight of their twelve favorite novelists were actually living, and their favorite nonfiction authors were Bernard Shaw, Wells (again),

Table 4.2: Favorite Novelists of London WEA Students, 1936 (in percent)

	All	*Men*	*Women*
John Galsworthy	20.2	9.5	29.2
H. G. Wells	13.8	16.5	11.4
D. H. Lawrence	10.6	10.0	11.0
Hugh Walpole	9.2	3.0	14.4
Aldous Huxley	8.9	12.5	5.9
Charles Dickens	8.9	8.0	9.7
Sinclair Lewis	8.7	8.5	8.9
Upton Sinclair	6.9	9.5	4.7
Thomas Hardy	6.7	6.0	7.2
J. B. Priestley	6.0	6.5	5.5
A. J. Cronin	5.7	6.6	5.1
Philip Gibbs	5.5	2.5	8.1

A. S. Neill, and Freud. Still, such high modernists as Virginia Woolf (1.4 percent), E. M. Forster (0.7 percent), and Marcel Proust (0.2 percent) ranked at the very bottom of the poll. These readers preferred the more accessible and (frankly) sexier modernists, Lawrence and Huxley. And they were unrepresentative of the working-class average: nearly half of them were clerks, and all were metropolitans, more aware of modern literature than provincial readers. (In 1944 hardly anyone borrowed Forster, Huxley, Woolf, Lawrence, Robert Graves, or Hemingway from the Bristol public libraries, where Hugh Walpole, Dickens, Hardy, Jane Austen, and Wells were the most popular novelists.)[98]

More significantly, the London students read book reviews. Fully a third of all the magazines they mentioned were literary and political reviews such as the *New Statesman, John o' London's*, and the *Highway* (the WEA organ). When asked which parts of the newspapers they read, book reviews were identified as a prime interest by 36.0 percent of the men (compared with 15.5 percent for sports) and 47.9 percent of the women (compared with 23.7 percent for the women's page).[99] That habit was strikingly uncharacteristic of the working class as a whole. During the Second World War, Mass Observation asked readers how they selected books, and some marked class differences emerged:

Table 4.3: Guides to Book Selection, 1944 (in percent)

	Middle Class	Upper Working Class	Lower Working Class
Author	20	31	37
Subject, title	22	21	27
Recommendation	23	18	19
Library	11	22	7
Reviews	28	11	7
Haphazard	8	8	5
Bibliography, catalogues	14	0	2
Bookseller	6	3	3
Other	19	17	27
Don't know	0	3	0

The middle classes were more likely to rely on reviews, reading lists, and catalogues: that is, guides to new or unfamiliar books. The working classes most often selected books by author: that is, authors they had already read.[100] In 1945, a lack of book reviews (not to mention bookshops) was still an obstacle to publicizing new books in rural counties like Norfolk.[101] A half-century earlier, closed-stack public libraries had been a serious barrier to adventurous reading, as Jack Common noted: "The system tended to canalize our curiosity about books into a safe and time-saving pursuit of a few popular authors: the whole of Henty was ever before us."[102] Even where librarians encouraged broader reading, they often met resistance. One who worked in the Lever company town of Port Sunlight between the wars remembered a girl who invariably requested "a book about a Duchess or a Countess." Then there was the elderly lady who would only read Annie Swan. When she had ploughed through her oeuvre a dozen times over, the librarian suggested she might try David Lyall, pointing out that David Lyall was a pen name used by Annie Swan. The woman reluctantly accepted a volume, only to return it the following day: "This one can't write; give me one by Annie Swan."[103]

Scholars on the left have again and again tried to recover lost plebeian writers, only to find them disappointingly old-fashioned. Brian Maidment notes that, in spite of its occasional political radicalism, Victorian working-class poetry was stylistically antiquated and generally expressed "conservative ideologies of temperance, stoicism, domesticity, religious devotion, and quietism."[104] If the Great Proletarian Author was never found, it was not because there were no candidates for the role. The difficulty was that leftist intellectuals were looking for a modernist in overalls, and that combination was almost impossible to find. A more typical working-class writer was Alexander Baron (b. 1917), whose *From the City, From the Plough* (1948) was a best-seller. "My masters are Balzac, Dickens and Hardy," he affirmed, "and I find it hard to admit that any fiction of importance has been written in the English language since 1914."[105]

While working in the great railway factory at Swindon, Alfred Williams taught himself enough Greek and Latin to translate Ovid, Pindar, Sappho, Plato, Menander, and Horace. He mastered the Greek alphabet by chalking it up on machinery, and faced down a resentful supervisor who tried to make him erase it. In 1900 he began a Ruskin College correspondence course in English literature, beginning with Bede and ending with Wordsworth. It was an astonishing feat of self-education—and it left out the whole Victorian era. Even a reviewer for the WEA magazine, trying hard to be positive, advised him to write less anachronistic verses: "Poems where shepherds and shepherdesses are of Arcadia and not of Wiltshire, and rhymed translations of the classics, are part of a literary output which is necessarily and frankly imitative."[106] But Williams stubbornly resisted the new. As he put it, W. B. Yeats, Robert Bridges, Thomas Hardy, Richard Le Gallienne all "produced in me a veritable disgust of modern '*tack*.' FORTY LINES OF DRYDEN CONTAIN MORE POETRY THAN TWELVE LARGE VOLUMES OF THE MODERN MUDDLE. I cannot help it one bit, but I can get more pleasure out of a page of Ovid than out of a bundle of our moderns."[107]

The tramp-poet W. H. Davies (b. 1871) did not read contemporary authors, though several of them (Bernard Shaw, Edward Thomas, Walter de la Mare, W. H. Hudson, Edward Garnett, Arnold Bennett) befriended and promoted him. That made for some awkwardness when they met, "for the simple reason that they knew my work and I did not know theirs," but he could only afford to buy classics at secondhand stalls.[108] As a result, Shaw noted, "His work was not in the least strenuous or modern: there was in it no sign that he had ever read anything later than Cowper or Crabbe, not even Byron, Shelley or Keats, much less Morris,

Swinburne, Tennyson, or Henley and Kipling. There was indeed no sign of his ever having read anything otherwise than as a child reads."[109]

Peter Donnelly (b. 1914), the Barrow steelworker-poet, tried to find inspiration in contemporary sensibilities:

> In extracts from the notebooks of some modern writer I read that he had had no success, that he had not sold a story until he cast away all the books and memories of books which made his mind a lumber room. Since I was a writer steadily collecting rejection slips and unable to discuss my work with anyone or to seek advice, I decided to emulate him. I wanted to make poems, and this writer advised me to forget all the poetry with which I was acquainted, and study the moderns. I wanted to write prose, and he said to turn my back upon any prose writer who had been dubbed classical.
>
> So I began to read modern poetry in magazines and anthologies in order to acquire a modern outlook, to find some clue that would make my verses tingle with the life of my own time. But ... all the modern poetry was barren stuff with never an echo from the thunder, the sound and sweet airs which I had always associated with poetry and could not forget; never the little shock that raises the mind and heart like a prayer.

Donnelly found himself "insensibly leaving the moderns, proceeding back and back as though I had missed the road somewhere and must retrace my steps to pick it up again. I discovered that my affinities were with those who had started writing before the 1914 war, and from them it was natural to go farther back, for it seemed that they derived from those who had gone before them."[110] Whoever it was who recommended reading only the moderns (Donnelly never names him) the advice was senseless. What work of modernist literature was not constructed largely from the lumber of classical literature? This strategy would have failed any writer, but especially for someone like Donnelly—with little education and no literary connections—casting aside the old meant throwing away his only store of literary capital.

Conversely, as scholarship children assimilated a more modern outlook, they found themselves alienated from the conservative working-class culture that had nurtured them. Kathleen Betterton, the daughter of a lift operator for the London Underground, was born (1913) into a family that placed a high value on a thoroughly outdated style of education. In the parlor was that monument to working-class respectability, a glass-fronted bookcase, which contained an odd collection of literary hand-me-downs. There were morality tales that her father had won as school prizes, *Little Lord Fauntleroy*, Bulwer Lytton, *Little Women*, *Christie's Old Organ*, and *The Wide Wide World*. Her school library consisted of another small cupboard stocked with "dehydrated versions of the classics for the most part—*Silas Marner*, *The Mill on the Floss*, *Westward Ho!*" Because this literary diet was as digestible as it was banal, it could be quite inspiring to a nine-year-old girl: when her mother read Longfellow to her, Kathleen recited his verses at length and then composed her own, to general applause. But as she later recognized, "We were gathering up the fag-ends of middle-class Victorian culture."

As a scholarship girl she flourished at Christ's Hospital in Hertford, because the curriculum there was equally anachronistic. She studied Latin and Greek, memorized Shakespeare, and took classes in English history that stopped cold in 1715. There were no courses in biology ("that would have brought us up against the dangerous subject of sex") so when she saw a production of *The Beggar's Opera*, she was far too innocent to understand it. In the school library, books touching even remotely on love—including the works of Thomas Hardy—were jacketed in red calico, and she was not permitted to borrow these until she reached the Sixth Form.

Consequently, when she entered Somerville College Oxford on another scholarship, she found herself academically prepared but culturally backward. One of her classmates was the intimidatingly brilliant Mary Fisher, a cousin of Virginia Woolf, whose work Kathleen could not even discuss. Befriended by a daughter of Fabians, she discovered that even her socialism was outmoded: she was still a follower of William Morris when Marx was becoming fashionable at Oxford. Eventually she learned to appreciate W. H. Auden and Stephen Spender, but as she caught up with her university friends, she grew ever more remote from her parents. Her father always had a taste for sentimental Victorian paintings, with titles like "To the Rescue," and he could not have been happy when she replaced them with reproductions of Turner and Vermeer. On her visits home she was shocked to discover that

I hated more than ever the ugly working-class district to which I belonged, and I even began to hate the people in it—the women with hair in curlers and bulging string bags, the stall-holders shouting raucously in the street-market, the grubby babies left to howl in their prams outside the pub. After Oxford, everything was so *ugly*. I was incapable of fusing my disparate existences; the gap between them left me bewildered and resentful. …

Every time I returned home I experienced the same confusion of feeling. It was good to see my parents again, good to be back in a homely atmosphere, good to be kindly welcomed in the street by neighbours who had known me from babyhood … but before a week was out I would feel depressed with Fulham and out of touch with almost everyone with whom I came in contact.

With every term I seemed to grow yet further away from the class to which I belonged. I had always been frank among my friends about my home and circumstances, but in the setting of Oxford they seemed unreal even while I spoke of them. Unconsciously I had assumed the outlook, the manners, the speech of those among whom I spent half the year, and I should probably have been taken anywhere as one of them, if I had been able to imitate their easy assurance. An American friend who thought he understood the English had assumed that I was the daughter of a country parson. At home, my tastes, my interests, even my voice, cut me off from the people about me. It was saddening and filled me with a vague sense of guilt, as though in some undefined way I had rejected my own class.

That guilt propelled her into leftist politics, but the ambivalence remained. She joined the Oxford Labour Club, ostensibly to reaffirm her loyalty to the working class, but on a less conscious level she was doing exactly the reverse: distancing herself from the Fulham Labour Party, where her parents joined in whist drives. That represented the plebeian culture she now found so backward. Even Ruskin College students now struck her as too serious and too proletarian. She preferred "the fluency, the superficial glitter" of Oxford undergraduates. When she chanted the "Internationale" with them, it was not simply a gesture of solidarity with the workers, "it was also a reaction against the correctness of my upbringing."[111]

A generation later, Jane Mitchell (b. 1934) would experience the same dissonance. Her father (a Glasgow lorry-driver) and mother encouraged education, turned down the radio when it was time to do homework, and filled their home with old books: *Robinson Crusoe, Oliver Twist, The Wide Wide World, John Halifax, Gentleman*, Greek and Roman legends. The last of these were particularly inspiring: she eventually became a university lecturer in classics. But as she moved from one scholastic triumph to another, her classmates seemed increasingly resentful and distant. When she entered Oxford on a scholarship she felt no sense of social, economic, or academic inferiority: "However, I began to feel myself at a considerable disadvantage because of the narrowness of my interests and experience." She fell in with leftist students, where she "was at first completely at sea, and felt abysmally ignorant. ... [I] followed up references to unfamiliar authors and pondered on unfamiliar value-judgments." Her formal education had done nothing to prepare her for Suez, Hungary, jazz, or the *New Left Review*. She quickly made up for lost time ("an intellectual explosion was taking place in me") but joining the left wing of the Labour Party created friction with her Tory parents. For her mother in particular, political discussion consisted in repeating what she had read in Conservative newspapers. "At the same time," her daughter recalled, "she found in my Socialism a source of pride, since it was for her a symbol of my having entered a society of intellectuals."[112]

If one did not come from a home environment where education was valued, the climb up the scholarship ladder could be even more disorienting. Ronald Goldman (b. 1922) was the son of a Manchester hatmaker and a narrowly religious woman who hardly ever engaged in conversation. "I never recall anyone reading a book, nor there being a book in the house apart from a dusty Bible and a medical dictionary of almost equal ancient vintage." He acquired an insatiable appetite for reading from his senior school, the public library, evening classes, and WEA courses, and found his intellectual home matriculating at Manchester University. But

[i]t soon became evident to me that I was growing away from my home, despite the fact that I was militantly working-class and politically active in left-wing politics. My time at home made me increasingly irritable since no one seemed to perceive why I wanted to read. When I attempted discussion my open questioning of every convention was simply not understood as an exploration of ideas, but was received by my mother with shocked outrage. The small talk, the three times weekly visits to the local Odeon …, the evenings spent card playing were a crushing bore to me and there was no quiet place to read in the house, other than going to my unheated bedroom. … Being at home was like a slow death to me and leaving home felt like moving into a free world of light and rationality.[113]

These generational skirmishes were part of a broad transformation of the left, which began early in the twentieth century and is only now reaching completion. Within the Labour Party, the shift from a working-class self-educated leadership to a middle-class university-educated leadership brought with it a shift from economic protest to cultural protest. By now the right has won the battle for privatization, lower taxation, and a hospitable climate for business; while multiculturalism, feminism, gay rights, and government support for the "creative industries" have become potent issues for the left. This change began with these scholarship children, whose anger was directed primarily against a hopelessly bourgeois working-class culture. No doubt they sincerely desired an end to poverty and fair shares for all, but Kathleen Betterton admitted that she had other priorities. What she really wanted was a socialism that would abolish "lace curtains and aspidistras."

Chapter Five **Willingly to School**

The schools that served British working-class children in the late nineteenth and early twentieth centuries have been almost universally condemned by historians. They are consistently depicted as places of brutal discipline and rote learning, where children were taught only the basics and trained to become obedient cogs in an industrial machine. This dismal portrait is, however, based almost entirely on information and impressions culled from official sources—from educational bureaucrats rather than their pupils. That is why this history is in need of revision. Administrative directives do not tell us what teachers actually did in the class-room, and government reports cast no light on the attitudes of the children. School inspector Edmund Holmes is often cited as a witness to the oppressiveness of Victorian schools,[1] but no inspector could know intimately the thousands of schoolchildren he was charged with assessing. "Under this regime neither the teacher nor the inspector could get into living touch with the child, or make any serious attempt to understand his character or take the measure of his capacity," Holmes protested. "The mind, the heart, the whole personality of the child, was an unknown land which we were forbidden to explore. ... I took little or no interest in my examinees either as individuals or as human beings, and never tried to explore their hidden depths."[2]

If we want to discover how late Victorian and Edwardian working-class children actually experienced school, we must consult them directly. Historians have assumed that the sources for such an investigation simply do not exist.[3] In fact, we can draw upon two rich mines of first-hand information. In the late 1960s Paul Thompson and Thea Vigne conducted a University of Essex oral history project which compiled a quota sample representative of the British population in 1911 in terms of sex, social class, regional distribution, and urban–rural balance. The 444 interviewees, all born between 1870 and 1908, belonged to the first generation of schoolchildren to feel the full impact of the 1870 Education Act. The respondents were classified according to their current political affiliations (Table 5.1, p. 147), the religions they were raised in (Table 5.2, p. 147), and their fathers' class status (Table 5.3, p. 147). This chapter also draws on the autobiographies of working people, most of them belonging to the same 1870–1908 cohort. One valid objection to using memoirs as a source for educational history is that they

Table 5.1: Party Affiliation

	N	Percent	Percent Less Unspecified
Conservative	78	17.6	21.5
Liberal	72	16.2	19.8
Labour/Socialist	96	21.6	26.4
Apolitical	116	26.1	32.0
Welsh Nationalist	1	.2	.3
Unspecified	81	18.2	–
Total	444	100.0	100.0

Table 5.2: Religion in Which Respondent Was Raised

		N	Percent Less Unspecified
Anglican		172	39.1
Nonconformist *of which*		220	50.0
Methodist	60		13.6
Presbyterian	34		7.8
Baptist	20		4.5
Congregationalist	15		3.4
Salvation Army	3		.7
Unitarian	1		.2
Unspecified Nonconformist	87		19.7
Catholic		40	9.1
Jewish		3	.7
Atheist		3	.7
None		2	.5
Unspecified		4	–
Total		444	100.0

Note—"Nonconformist" includes Methodist, Presbyterian, Baptist, Congregationalist, Salvation Army, Unitarian, and unspecified Nonconformist.

Table 5.3: Father's Class

	N	Percent
A: professionals	15	3.4
B: employers and managers	74	16.7
C: clerks and foremen	36	8.1
D: skilled manual workers	147	33.1
E: semiskilled manual workers	117	26.4
F: unskilled manual workers	52	11.7
G: unclassified	3	.7
Total	444	100.0

overrepresent the winners: those children whom the system failed were much less likely to record their lives on paper. For any statistical measure of attitudes toward schooling, we must rely on the more representative Thompson–Vigne sample. Autobiographical sources, which do offer more detailed accounts of school experiences, are used here to flesh out the harder data.

As Thompson and Vigne asked their subjects a set of questions about their schooling, it is possible to reconstruct a kind of "poll" assessing the quality of primary education in turn-of-the-century Britain. Drawing on their 444 interviews, I generated all the tables in this chapter except Table 5.10. It should be stressed that this "poll" is not unimpeachably scientific. The interviewees were not all asked the same questions in precisely the same language. They were not asked to check boxes rating their schools as good, bad, or middling. Instead, they had to describe their experiences in their own words; it was then up to me to classify those responses as positive, negative, or mixed.[4] Rough as it may be, this quantitative method can help us avoid the selective use of evidence—and the evidence used previously to construct our grim image of working-class schools has often been highly selective.[5]

These schools certainly were dismal places in the early nineteenth century. The Anglican National Society (founded 1811) and the Nonconformist British and Foreign School Society (founded 1807) created networks of voluntary schools, which began to receive government aid in 1833. Large numbers of children could be taught the basics through the "monitorial system", under which each teacher recruited several monitors from among the older pupils, trained them in some very basic lessons, and had them transmit what they had learned to the rest of the class. Of course the quality of instruction was poor, and schools became the kind of educational factories satirized in *Hard Times*. The church schools naturally emphasized reading and religious indoctrination. Writing, or any other form of self-expression, was not encouraged.

There were, however, definite improvements as the century progressed. The 1870 Education Act supplemented the church schools (which had never served the entire population) with state schools governed by elected school boards. From 1846 there were better facilities for training teachers: brighter students could be apprenticed to schoolmasters as pupil-teachers for five years, their salaries paid by the government. They could then take an examination for the Queen's Scholarship, which entitled them to formal training at a teachers' college. Having completed that course they became "certificated teachers," who received a higher salary and could (for extra fees) train their own pupil-teachers. Sons and daughters of the working classes could now step up into one of the lower professions. By the late nineteenth century, then, working-class children were often taught by teachers from the same social background, who enjoyed some professional respect, and who understood well the obstacles their pupils faced.

In 1862 a "payment by results" scheme was instituted, under which government school subsidies were partly tied to test results. Educational reformers, such as school inspector Matthew Arnold, protested that the system would force teachers to cram pupils narrowly for their examinations. In 1871 the effects of "payment by results" were mitigated by a new set of grants for passes in specific subjects such as history, geography, science, algebra, geometry, and grammar, which tended to expand the curriculum beyond the three Rs. From the 1850s attempts were made to introduce literature into the curriculum, in the form of *Pilgrim's Progress*, *Robinson Crusoe*, and *Swiss Family Robinson*. From 1882 students in Standard VI were required to "Read a passage from one of Shakespeare's historical plays or from some other standard author, or from a history of England." In 1880 only 12 percent of inspected schools in England and Wales had their own libraries, but by 1900 the proportion was up to 40 percent, with an average of 221 volumes per school.[6]

"Payment by results" was abolished by 1897, but some scholars have claimed that its stultifying effects were felt well into the twentieth century.[7] Educational historian H. C. Dent himself attended three public elementary schools between 1900 and 1904, and he remembered the classroom as "a place of hatred":

> I can testify from personal experience that the spirit inculcated by that Code was still very much in evidence in the attitudes and actions of both teachers and pupils. With relatively rare exceptions—I was most fortunate in one school—teachers and taught were sworn enemies. The latter resisted by every means known to them (and some of these means were extremely unpleasant) the dessicated diet of irrelevant facts the former insisted in pressing upon them; teachers retaliated with incessant applications of corporal punishment, impartially inflicted for crime, misdemeanour or mistake.[8]

Yet if we turn to the Thompson–Vigne interviews, a very different picture emerges. Literally hundreds of Dent's contemporaries testify from *their* personal experience that school was a far happier place. Tables 5.4 (p. 150) and 5.5 (p. 151) group together the middle and upper classes (ABC) and the working classes (DEF). Only those respondents who unambiguously enjoyed or disliked their schools or their teachers were classified "positive" or "negative": everyone else who gave a response was placed in the "mixed" category. Two-thirds of all working people who expressed an opinion remembered school as a positive experience, a slightly higher proportion than their more affluent contemporaries, and only one out of seven had unhappy memories. In each social class, few respondents regarded teachers as their enemies, and seven out of ten working people rated them positively. About 90 percent of working people who gave a response said they had derived some benefit from their schooling, compared with 95 percent of the upper and middle classes. More than two-thirds of those who attended Board schools or Anglican schools rated them positively. The low negative score for private schools suggests that those classic horror stories of prep school life, George Orwell's "Such, Such Were the Joys" and Cyril Connolly's

Enemies of Promise, do not speak for most privately educated pupils.[9] Catholic and Nonconformist schools appear to have been less well loved, though the samples are quite small.

Table 5.4: School Experience: Did the Respondent Enjoy School? (in Percent)

	Positive	Negative	Mixed	N
All	66.2	14.7	19.1	429
Sex:				
Male	59.7	17.1	23.2	211
Female	72.5	12.4	15.1	218
Class:				
ABC	62.8	14.9	22.3	121
DEF	67.5	14.4	18.0	305
A	85.7	.0	14.3	14
B	56.3	21.1	22.5	71
C	66.7	8.3	25.0	36
D	69.2	12.6	18.2	143
E	70.3	15.3	14.4	111
F	56.9	17.6	25.5	51
Party:				
Conservative	68.8	13.0	18.2	77
Liberal	75.0	11.8	13.2	68
Labour/Socialist	61.7	12.4	25.5	94
Apolitical	61.1	15.0	23.9	113
Religion:				
Anglican	63.9	12.7	23.5	166
Nonconformist	69.3	14.6	16.0	212
Catholic	57.5	22.5	20.0	40
Religion and class:				
Anglican ABC	52.3	18.2	29.5	44
Anglican DEF	67.8	10.7	21.5	121
Nonconformist ABC	67.2	14.9	17.9	67
Nonconformist DEF	70.8	13.9	15.3	144
Catholic ABC	75.0	.0	25.0	8
Catholic DEF	53.1	28.1	18.8	32
Schools:				
All schools	69.4	13.2	17.4	402
Board schools	68.8	15.1	16.1	199
Anglican schools	72.0	11.4	16.7	132
Catholic schools	58.3	20.8	20.8	24
Dissenting schools	57.1	21.4	21.4	14
Private schools	66.7	9.1	24.2	33
Dame schools	100.0	.0	.0	3

Note—*N* excludes respondents who did not address the question.

Table 5.5: Rating Teachers: Did the Respondent Like the Teachers? (in Percent)

	Positive	*Negative*	*Mixed*	*N*
All	66.5	6.8	26.8	385
Sex:				
Male	58.7	8.2	33.2	184
Female	73.6	5.5	20.9	201
Class:				
ABC	58.5	2.8	38.7	106
DEF	69.6	8.0	22.5	276
A	66.7	.0	33.3	12
B	60.3	3.2	36.5	63
C	51.6	3.2	45.2	31
D	69.8	4.7	25.6	129
E	70.7	9.1	20.2	99
F	66.7	14.6	18.8	48
Party:				
Conservative	67.6	5.9	26.5	68
Liberal	60.9	3.1	35.9	64
Labour/Socialist	66.7	10.7	22.6	84
Apolitical	68.6	5.7	25.7	105
Religion:				
Anglican	62.3	7.5	30.1	166
Nonconformist	72.0	5.2	22.8	193
Catholic	61.1	7.5	30.1	36
Religion and class:				
Anglican ABC	43.2	5.4	51.4	37
Anglican DEF	68.5	8.3	23.1	108
Nonconformist ABC	66.1	1.7	32.2	59
Nonconformist DEF	74.4	6.3	18.8	133
Catholic ABC	75.0	.0	25.0	8
Catholic DEF	57.1	7.1	35.7	28

Note—*N* excludes respondents who did not address the question.

A Better-Than-Nothing Institute

Only three respondents attended dame schools, so here we must rely on the assessments of autobiographers. "Dame school" is a generic term applied to any working-class private school. Not all of them were conducted by women: often they were a last resort for workingmen whom accident, illness, or old age had rendered otherwise unemployable. Until the late nineteenth century, anyone could set up as a schoolmaster in his or her own home and take in paying pupils, though inspectors protested that such schools were good for little more than child-minding. Once universal compulsory education was introduced in 1880, schools that did not meet government standards could be shut down, and dame schools were swiftly harried out of existence.

Phil Gardner and other educational historians have attempted to rehabilitate the dame school. They argue that it offered a less rigid, more "progressive" style of schooling, free of evangelical propaganda, where each child could learn at his own pace. Parents were willing to pay extra for such schools, where they exercised consumer sovereignty over their children's education, and could pull them out of class whenever they were needed for work or chores. The fact that educational bureaucrats decried such schools only reflected their own middle-class prejudices, as well as a fear of competition.[10]

Yet the inadequacies of dame schools are undeniable. An 1838 survey of sixty-three such schools in Westminster found that, though 425 of their 721 pupils were over five years old, nearly half were taught nothing more than spelling. Only twenty-one were learning arithmetic, only twenty-five grammar. None of the schools had maps or globes, and many had only one book.[11] There is no question that many working-class parents voted with their weekly pennies to send their children to dame schools, for whatever reason. But schools do not exist to serve parents: they must ultimately be judged by their students, looking back across a lifetime of experience. And the verdict of working-class memoirists is not far short of unanimous: they did not mourn the passing of dame schools.[12]

A typical (and vivid) account was offered by Wellingborough shoemaker and sanitary inspector John Askham (b. 1825). He warned the reader not to imagine "an airy and commodious room, such as those of the infant schools of the present day [1893]. ... Our schoolroom was the one and only down-stairs room of the dwelling (excepting a coal-hole, of which more anon,) and not only served for parlour, kitchen, and hall, but for schoolroom and all." It was cluttered with a fantastic collection of ancient furniture, and as for the dame:

> Her mode of teaching would scarcely do for this age; it consisted chiefly of oral instruction, and I am afraid her spelling and pronunciation were sadly wide of the mark—hymns, I remember, she called humes, and bishops bushops—the number 6 she spelled s-i-c-k-s, and so on. But learning was a secondary consideration; to be kept out of harm's way and from troubling our parents were the main considerations. Her chief occupation was knitting stockings; that seemed to be her special mission upon earth. She used to sit with a perfect armoury of long steel needles projecting from her side as if they sprang from her body, and a large ball of worsted, knitting for ever and ever. She was an epitome of old errors, a repository of recipes, a cyclopaedia of superstition. ... Her chief reading was Foxe's *Book of Martyrs*, of which she possessed an old dog-eared copy, with wood-cuts of the early Christians hung up with hooks in their flesh, or being boiled in cauldrons, burnt at the stake, or being cooked before cheerful fires.

She also punished her charges with threats, a dunce's cap, and, as an ultimate deterrant, confinement in that coal-hole. That may help to explain why Askham, after the 1870 Education Act, became one of the first members of the Wellingborough School Board.[13]

Such stories can be reproduced indefinitely. Robert Collyer (b. 1823) was yanked out of one school when his mother learned that he had been set to work scraping potatoes.[14] William Gifford (b. 1756) and Francis Place (b. 1771) were taught nothing but a spelling book.[15] W. J. Hocking, son of a Cornish carpenter, could only read the simplest sentences after two years of instruction.[16] "The only thing I remember learning there was to hold skeins of wool for Miss Annie or Miss Hettie to wind into balls," wrote a Southend printer (b. 1848), who regretted that he had come of age before the advent of the Board school.[17] William Cameron (b. c. 1785), son of a mashman at a Scottish distillery, had a full nine years of virtually worthless schooling:

> The teacher was an old decrepit man, who had tried to be a nailer, but at that employment he could not earn his bread. He then attempted to teach a few children, but for this undertaking he was quite unfit; writing and arithmetic were to him secrets as dark as death, and as for English, he was short-sighted, and a word of more than two or three syllables was either passed over, or it got a term of his own making. At this school I continued four years, and was not four months advanced in learning, although I was as far advanced as my teacher.

He then wasted five more years at another school, where an equally incompetent teacher crammed the children's heads with various catechisms "till our little judgements were so mixed up, that, in a few years, I could not answer a question in any of them. All this time was lost, the scholar robbed of his learning, and the parents of their money, through the teacher being ashamed to say 'he could go no further.'" With that intellectual training, Cameron spent much of his adult life as a beggar and died in the Glasgow Poorhouse, though he himself worked for a time as a schoolmaster.[18]

One Slaithwaite boy characterized his 1d.-a-week school as "A better-than-nothing institute." It was conducted by an old woman ("when they could do nothing else they could keep a school") out of her married son's house. She had a leather lash tied to a walking stick and sometimes used it. Nothing much was taught beyond the alphabet, and the pupils often slipped away when she dozed off. "We began, continued, and ended in Standard 0," but he liked the old woman, and was sorry that she had to go into the workhouse when she could no longer teach. He went on to the stricter discipline of a National school: though he described it as something out of *Nicholas Nickleby*, he had to admit that he learned much more there. In 1926, having worked as a school visitor, he could vouch that "The contrast of present day order, obedience, and mutual respect between teacher and taught, and the high standard of mental attainment contrasting with past time rumpus and slow progress is as daylight to twilight, if not as daylight to darkness."[19]

Shoemaker's son Allan Jobson attended two of the last surviving dame schools, in London around the turn of the century. At one, the schoolmistress "was like Queen Victoria in a play, always off-stage. She had one or two pupil teachers who did the work, which was but a pretence at teaching, and I was given small sums to do yet never instructed as to how they might produce an answer." At a second school he was read to from an old magazine ("I think the tale was *Queechy*"), as painless as it was valueless.[20]

Probably the greatest social service performed by such schools was that they provided work for the otherwise unemployable. John Harris (b. 1820), son of a Cornish smallholder, learned his letters from a crippled miner with a wooden stump for a leg:

> In those days any shattered being wrecked in the mill or the mine, if he could read John Bunyan, count fifty backwards, and scribble the squire's name, was considered good enough for a pedagogue; and when he could do nothing else, was established behind a low desk in a school. I do not think John Robert's acquirements extended far beyond reading, writing, and arithmetic; and I doubt if he knew what the word geography meant.

Still, he taught Harris the basics—enough to become a preacher, a Sunday school superintendent, and a published poet.[21]

It has also been suggested that dame schools were at least adequate to the job of providing day care for very young children. In fact they failed even at that for Joseph Burgess (b. 1853), a founding member of the Labour Party:

> In my mind's eye, I can see her now, making her porritch, and repeating to us The Lord's Prayer, while she stirred them over the fire. Near the hearthstone, she had a long rod, which would reach across the house, and it was a custom of hers to break off in the middle of the prayer, and use the rod vigorously on any boy who was not paying attention to the prayer. After laying the rod about some unruly boy, she would pick up with the prayer exactly where she had broken off.[22]

Another difficulty with that argument is that dame schools often catered to older children, for whom they were a complete waste. One Staffordshire workhouse boy (b. 1860) at age nine was taught (or rather, minded) by a woman who attended to her washing while he studied on his own. He did some complicated sums but had no way of checking them, because neither his teacher nor her son (a night worker at a colliery) could do them. His father decided that was not worth 4d. a week, and sent him to work on a farm for £2 a year.[23]

Radical artisan Christopher Thomson (b. 1799) became a passionate activist for working-class education partly because he did not get much instruction from his schoolmistress. "This ancient had the reputation of 'keeping a good school,'" he noted, "which goodness consisted mainly in having a large number of pupils— so large, that the 'letter learning' was all she could afford time for, except drilling into the young mind a goodly array of ghost stories."[24] Frederick Rogers, a dame school boy, made his first foray into politics agitating for the 1870 Education Act, which he considered necessary euthanasia for inferior private schools.[25] He was only one of many Victorian workingmen who regretted that Board schools had not existed when they were children. "I now see Board schools almost equalling the colleges of some of the older universities," proclaimed a Tunstall potter in the 1890s. "Even poor children now receive a better education than what I heard 'Tom Hughes' once say he received when a boy at much greater cost."[26] Walter Freer (b. 1846), a Glasgow power-loom tenter, could not understand why Lord Shaftesbury opposed free education: "For me education consisted of three months' tuition at a penny school. Every Monday morning the school-master collected our pennies, then left us to do whatever we wanted, while he went out to get tipsy. I left school, unable to write, and able to read only the simplest words."[27] George Lansbury (b. 1859) was not so hard on his old teachers, who apparently did convey the basics of writing and arithmetic, but he did not regret the extinction of dame schools:

Children of to-day, no matter where they live or to what class they belong, ought to bless the memory of W. E. Forster who introduced compulsory education. School is now [1928] a place, not for learning and discipline only, but for individual development. The teaching profession, taken as a whole, is one of which we are all proud. The enormous amount of voluntary work given by teachers in working-class districts teaching music, games, and sports of all kinds to both boys and girls, is beyond all praise.[28]

"Schools have changed considerably from my childhood, and totally for the better" remarked miller James Saunders (b. 1844). "Sometimes now [after 1888] when I see the opportunities children have I feel a little jealous."[29] Elizabeth Flint's mother had hated her dame school, where the cane was wielded freely and she hardly learned to read, but Elizabeth herself was "enthralled" by the East End school she attended during the First World War: "If you listened a whole new world could open out before you in the classroom."[30] In 1895 a Suffolk farm laborer gave thanks that education had improved vastly since 1850, when even church schools

were very little better than dame schools. Many of them were held in cottages which had been adapted for the purpose, but the rooms were gloomy and unfit to accommodate a number of children. The teachers had to make all sorts of shifts, owing to the absence of suitable apparatus. ... The Bible was the general reading book. Maps were in some cases hung on the walls, apparently by way of ornament, as there were teachers who did not know how to use them.

The parish had 900 inhabitants and property assessed at £5,000 a year, with a benefice worth about £900, but the rector, squire, and parish each contributed only £5 annually to the school. The teachers were mostly untrained females paid 5s. to 10s. a week; the schoolmaster earned only a little more than that. "The farmers as a class were dead-set against the school. They often said, 'We don't want to have children educated above their station'; though there was but little chance of that with a schoolmaster at 12s. a week." That schoolmaster estimated that most boys had only two years of formal education, and two-thirds of them left school without knowing how to read or write properly.[31]

Possibilities of Infinitude

In contrast, the 1870 Education Act produced a school building boom. Twentieth-century architects and historians would denounce them as ugly run-down brick cubes, but for late Victorian children they were brand new and marvelously equipped. Engraver Frank Galton (b. 1867) first attended a parish school in St. Pancras, where all boys' classes were in one large room. The teachers were incompetent and miserably paid, and one of them could only maintain discipline "by sheer brute strength." At age ten he transferred to a mint condition Board school, where he enjoyed professionally trained teachers, orderly classrooms, and French lessons.[32] His contemporaries offered equally loving testimonials:

... a wonder building, sumptuous and indeed palatial beyond belief, with its large classrooms, brand-new equipment so different from the mouldy patchwork of the [old] school, the desks with lids.[33]

We all thought it marvellous, judging by the standards of those days. It was a fine building ...: it had flushed toilets, heated water pipes in the class-rooms, and a playground, asphalt of course, but, alas, no playing-field with soft green grass.[34]

... the smell of copal oak varnish as the big windows, desks, partitions and fittings were of pitch-pine well and truly varnished, even today if I get a whiff of oak varnish I remember the new school. Two other features of the school of which we were justifiably proud was that it was the first school in Bolton to be lit by this new electricity, the other feature is that it was the first in central heating with radiators and a constant supply of hot water for domestic purpose.[35]

Even when the physical plant was dingy, the curriculum could be innovative and exciting. The daughter of a Sheffield flatware stamper (b. 1911) described her first classroom as

sunless and gloomy because it overlooked a prison-like quadrangle surrounded by high buildings. But we did not need the sunshine, for we made our own. School was sheer bliss, and I could not wait to get there. By some miracle, the teachers had achieved a balance between formal and informal methods, a technique which could not be improved upon today [1984], and we learned quickly.[36]

A London gasfitter's son (b. 1884) recalled that his Higher Grade School offered "an unceasing panorama of knowledge … a harvest of kindly instruction coming little short of a college education. At ten we were doing what secondary children do at 14."[37] Another boy was taught to love music by the future operatic star Frank Mullings.[38] In an advanced class (age thirteen) at a London County Council school in the Surrey Docks district, John Edmonds (b. 1911) had a teacher who gave students copies of textbooks to take home, taught them how to do research in a library, and brought in newspapers for information on current affairs. Edmonds was also taken to the National Gallery, the Tate, and the Victoria and Albert—the beginning of a lifelong love affair with museums.[39] Frank Goss (b. 1896), the son of a pianomaker and dressmaker, loved his teachers in spite of excessive corporal punishment. Among poor children, he explained,

teachers were thought to belong to a higher social order than their pupils. Their private lives away from school, to the extent that we ever thought of them, were conceived to be on a higher plane than our "bread and margarine" lives; a world of gaiety and fashion, an educated cultured world such as we might read about in the best Victorian literature, this was the life we thought to be theirs. We had nothing but gratitude for their patronage in bearing with us over the long days and weeks of our tutelage.

He had reason to be grateful: his teacher took some pupils to see the unknown wonderland of the City of London, treating each child to a bun and a cup of tea.[40]

English literature was the subject most often singled out for praise.[41] One Essex headmaster, who read aloud from *Macbeth*, *The Pickwick Papers*, and *The Water Babies*, so profoundly inspired an ironmoulder's son that he spent the next forty-seven years studying with the WEA "to try to catch up" (Interview 12). Historians usually describe rural education in this period as hopelessly inadequate, but every day Spike Mays (b. 1907) ran to his East Anglia school, where he studied *Robinson Crusoe*, *Gulliver's Travels*, and *Tales From Shakespeare*. His headmaster, was "a kindly, cultured gentleman whose mind was well-stocked with classics."[42] "Thinking back, I am amazed at the amount of English literature we absorbed in those four years," recalled Ethel Clark (b. 1909), a Gloucestershire railway worker's daughter, "and I pay tribute to the man who made it possible. … Scott, Thackeray, Shakespeare, Longfellow, Dickens, Matthew Arnold, Harriet Beecher Stowe and Rudyard Kipling were but a few authors we had at our finger-tips. How he made the people live again for us!"[43] H. M. Tomlinson (b. 1872/73), a successful author and dockworker's son, credited his East End Board school with encouraging free expression in composition classes and giving him a solid literary footing in the Bible, Shakespeare, and Scott. "In my childhood, I never met another youngster who could not read," he recalled. "Some of them could be so excited by the printed page that they passed on the fun they had found, and thus … I was introduced to Mayne Reid, and again to Harrison Ainsworth, with *The Headless Horseman* and *Rookwood*."[44]

Even schools that did nothing else well usually managed to instill a passion for literature. Edgar Wallace (b. 1875), the adopted son of a Billingsgate fish porter, remembered attending

A big yellow barracks of a place, built (or rumour lied) on an old rubbish-pit into which the building was gradually sinking. … I was a fairly intelligent boy, and I am trying to remember now just what I *did* learn. At geography, roughly the shape of England; nothing about the United States, nothing about the railway systems of Europe. I learnt China had two great rivers, the Yangtse-kiang and Hoangho, but which is which I can't remember. I knew the shape of Africa and that it was an easy map to draw. I knew nothing about France except that Paris was on the Seine. I knew the shape of Italy was like a top-booted leg, and that India was in the shape of a pear; but except that there had been a mutiny in that country, it was *terra incognita* to me.

History: The ancient Britons smeared themselves with woad and paddled round in basket-shaped boats. William the Conqueror came to England in 1066. Henry VIII had seven—or was it eight?—wives. King Charles was executed for some obscure reason, and at a vague period of English history there was a War of the Roses.

Chemistry: If you put a piece of heated wire in oxygen—or was it hydrogen? —it glowed very brightly. If you blow through a straw into lime water, the water becomes cloudy.

And so on through religion ("No more than I learnt at Sunday school"), drawing ("Hours of hard work in an attempt to acquire proficiency in an art for which I had no aptitude"), and arithmetic ("the ability to tot columns of figures with great rapidity"). But in the midst of this wasteland was an electric moment, when the teacher read aloud *The Arabian Nights*. "The colour and beauty of the East stole through the foggy windows of Reddin's Road School. Here was a magic carpet indeed that transported forty none too cleanly little boys into the palace of the Caliphs, through the spicy bazaars of Bagdad, hand in hand with the king of kings." And every so often

There were golden days—poetry days. We learnt the "Inchcape Rock," of that Sir Ralph the Rover who sailed away
  "And scoured the seas for many a day.
  At last grown rich with plunder's store,
  He steered his course for Scotland's shore."

And Casabianca, and Brave Horatius, and so by degrees to the Master. I learnt whole scenes of *Macbeth* and *Julius Caesar* and *Hamlet*, and could—and did—recite them with gusto on every and any excuse.

Wallace's grounding in literature "was of the greatest service in after life," when he became a staggeringly popular novelist.[45]

Educational histories tend to assume that official curricula were actually carried out in the classroom, but students recall imaginative teachers who improvised. John Allaway (b. 1902), who went on to become a journeyman fitter and WEA leader, had a teacher who disregarded the timetable that prescribed one hour each for history, geography, and English. Long before the word "interdisciplinary" had been invented, he taught them all together as one subject: "Although I never heard him mention the unity of knowledge, [he] vividly brought it home to us in his classroom teaching. ... As we worked he moved round among us asking questions and giving advice and encouragement." He introduced the class to *Huckleberry Finn*, *Tom Sawyer*, and *The Call of the Wild*

> for their own sake and as models to follow in creative writing, which he set us to do. Gathered round him we would listen to readings from these books and discuss key passages. Once in Art session he dropped an old boot on my desk and said, "Make a pen and ink sketch of this." It seemed an odd request, since the only Art I had previously done in school consisted of copying pictures from instructional cards.[46]

Mark Grossek (b. 1888), son of a Jewish immigrant tailor, concluded that his Board school in dismal Southwark was in many respects superior to the genteel grammar schools he later attended on scholarship. While public school boys struggled with Latin, he was treated to Byron, Shakespeare, clay modelling, basketweaving, woodwork, tonic sol-fa singing lessons, and a science class with all kinds of interesting apparatus and explosions.[47] George Hitchin (b. c. 1912), raised by an impoverished Durham miner, affirmed that his teachers accomplished great things, though they had no free time or staff-room for classroom preparation:

> With few exceptions the teachers were capable and imaginative. They worked hard, for they were expected to teach all the subjects in the curriculum with the minimum amount of equipment and in the meanest accommodation to an uncooperative class of forty or so urchins. Not one of our teachers had any academic distinctions—one or two, I believe, were even unqualified; but each knew his job, namely, how to impart knowledge, in as interesting a way as possible, to his pupils. If they were not always successful, this was due more to the attitude of the boys than to any fault in teaching methods.[48]

Alfred Green (b. 1910), who rose from poverty to become a Sheffield councillor and justice of the peace, recalled that

Whilst the schools were sadly overcrowded, with classes at a minimum of 50 scholars, and the equipment poor and insufficient, at least the teachers did their best for us. ... Here and there were men and women of character and vision, who in spite of all the difficulties they had to contend with, gave intelligent and devoted service in the teaching and care of their charges. ... School was not all boredom and discouragement; this there was in plenty, but there were other things too. ... Some of the teachers, quite frankly, were simply inadequate, probably reflecting the paucity of their own education and the training they had received, as well as the difficult circumstances in which they had to work: a few, if not actual sadists, were tyrants; and others—these to my mind worst of all—were severe because they were toadies to the system and the times. ... However, many of the teachers ... brought to their work a cheerfulness and sense of humour and kindliness that bore witness to their devotion to humanity.

There was also the headmaster who assigned him to write an essay on "My Ambition." In "a white-hot enthusiasm," Green described his dream of becoming a Labour prime minister, in "an amazing miscellany of fact and fancy, of glowing hopes and clumsy expression, of insight and sheer ignorance." The paper was handed back drenched in red ink ("like a bloody battlefield") with the comment: "This is certainly the most interesting essay I have received for some time, but your English and spelling are simply appalling." Green's self-esteem was not even dented: "I was so accustomed to adverse comment on my work, that this did not greatly trouble me, but the praise he gave to the ideas independent of the form of expression, sent my spirits soaring into a seventh heaven!" Another teacher, with artistic talents, dazzled the students with colored chalk pictures on a blackboard strip that encircled the classroom. One head teacher awed his students into wide-eyed attention with his upright manner, his bamboo cane ("rarely used"), and an intolerance of laziness ("Come, Green lad, this won't do. The workers will need the best leaders they can get for the future"). He also had a genius for shock tactics:

He made a great impression on me one day, when he strode into the classroom carrying a copy of *Pears Encyclopaedia* in his hand, demanding that we ask him any question of fact, to which he promised to give us the answer from this book. Our minds immediately became alert, and most of us were sufficiently crafty to choose answers likely to be answerable from such a book. So the questions flowed thick and fast: what was the capital of such a country, or what was such a river's length, or who was Prime Minister in a certain year, or on what date did the war end—the usual run of questions that could be summoned at short notice. The pages of the book were quickly turned and the answers given with speed and accuracy—a veritable virtuosity of performance! At length he snapped the book closed, and held it up in triumph: "There you are, lads," he said, "worth its weight in gold, isn't it?" Dazed and fascinated, we obediently chanted, "Yes, Sir." "Right," he said, thrusting the book into the hands of a startled lad in the front row, "Here is the book, now give me its weight in gold!" A deadly silence fell on us all. A critical person might regard this as cheap humour at the expense of defenceless children. We did not see it that way: we knew that we had fallen into a trap, but we knew too that there was something to be learned from it. What he had done within the compass of a few minutes was illustrate that knowledge is to hand if only we will take the trouble to use it, and at the same time he had warned us that every statement or thing was not to be taken at its face value. In a vivid way he illustrated what was meant by an enquiring mind, and a critical spirit; not bad going in an elementary school of the twenties![49]

T. A. Jackson credited his Board school teachers with starting him on his career as a Marxist philosopher. They introduced him to Greek mythology, "which in time brought me to Frazer and the immensities and infinitudes of *The Golden Bough*, and all that that implies." Of course,

> They gave me no notion at the time of any such thing as a revolutionary philosophy. Rather the reverse since they left only the conservative impression that the universe was so structured that it could not by any contrivance be altered. But indirectly they fed my appetite for wonders insofar as they enabled me to see possibilities of an infinitude of happenings and combinations hidden beneath the exterior aspect of even the most ordinary things. So far this fed my romanticism—my liking for things unusual and extraordinary, for things as they had been, and might still be in places remote and all but inaccessible.[50]

In rural areas, where education had been particularly inadequate before 1870, the new generation of teachers could have a revolutionary impact. Fred Gresswell attended a Lincolnshire village school where no real education was accomplished until a dynamic new schoolmaster took over around 1900. On his first day the pupils were so disruptive that he spent all morning marching them in and out of the classroom to teach basic discipline. With only one female assistant, he was able to give each child individual attention, helping some to win scholarships and encouraging others to emigrate. The students were soon performing concerts and a scene from *The Merchant of Venice*, though Shakespeare was unknown to most of the villagers. In the evenings, the schoolmaster conducted adult literacy classes for farm laborers, including Gresswell's father. One school manager, a prosperous farmer, predictably complained that the children were being overeducated—and his fears were not groundless. Though it was a Church of England school, wrote Gresswell,

> Elementary education weakened the hold of evangelism over children of my generation. Though we had been "converted," we soon found that not only did this form of worship mean nothing to us, but that we were no worse if we did

without it. In other words, day school teaching gave us a code of conduct which superseded the purely emotional influence of the chapel. Moreover, the local preachers were on the whole uneducated, and they had no power of reasoning which could appeal to children who had had some systematic instruction.[51]

Ironmoulder's son Joseph Stamper left his Lancashire school in 1899, just as "a new kind of teacher was coming along," more inclined to entertain pupils than to cane them. One schoolmaster won a lifetime of gratitude by presenting Stamper (a future novelist) with a dictionary. It was, as he later appreciated, a "silent revolution."[52] Arthur Goffin (b. 1879), a compositor's son, concluded that his Board school education "was remarkably good" compared with the fact-grubbing that children were offered in 1933:

> In my time and day we learnt facts too—limited, granted, but in addition to learning them we were taught how to assimilate and make use of the knowledge thus gained. We were taught direction and guidance. We were taught to use sense and application, and acquired the soundness, contentment, control and stability which most middle-aged people possess today. ... [One teacher] had always something beyond the textbook for us, and he drove his lessons home by unforgettable—at least to me—anecdotes and stories. ... The other teachers, too, were splendid and we grew to love and respect them. ... I can recall so many things they said which I realized in later life have helped me in different ways.[53]

Many alumni felt that the Board schools, with all their limitations, provided a solid foundation for lifetime education. They taught basic learning skills, introduced the best in English literature, then set their pupils free at adolescence to read on their own. "One advantage of leaving school at an early age is that one can study subjects of your own choice," wrote Frank Argent (b. 1899), son of a Camberwell laborer. Taking advantage of the public library and early Penguins, he ranged all over the intellectual landscape: Freudian psychology, industrial administration, English literature, political history, Blake, Goethe, Mill, Nietzsche, the Webbs, Bertrand Russell's *Essays in Scepticism*, and Spengler's *Decline of the West*. It all prepared him for multiple careers as a trade unionist, a factory inspector, and a writer for taxi industry journals.[54] Lancashire weaver Elizabeth Blackburn (b. 1902) conceded that

> By present [1977] standards our horizons were very limited and our education, linked up as it was to our economic conditions, provided little room for the cultivation of leisure pursuits. But I left school at thirteen with a sound grounding in the basic arts of communication, reading and writing, and I could "reckon up" sufficiently to cope with shopping and domestic accounts and calculate my cotton wages. ... I had gained some knowledge of the Bible,

a lively interest in literature and, most important, some impetus to learn. To a State school and its devoted teachers I owe a great debt, and I look back on it with much affection.

She proceeded to an evening institute course in English literature, and by the rhythm of the looms she memorized all of *The Rime of the Ancient Mariner*, Shelley's "Ode to the West Wind," Milton's "Lycidas," and Gray's *Elegy*. She discovered the ancient Greeks in the home of a neighbor, a self-educated classicist with six children, and a Sunday School teacher introduced her to the plays of Bernard Shaw.[55] While attending her looms she silently analyzed the character of Jane Eyre's Mr. Rochester, "sometimes to the detriment of my weaving!"[56] She studied commercial arithmetic at a technical college, classical music with the WEA, and Esperanto at an Adult School; she also pursued residential courses at Woodbrooke College and at Manchester's Cooperative College. And she accomplished all that well before her thirtieth birthday.[57]

Board school alumni could indulge their intellectual passions with far more freedom than the typical graduate student today. Once Richard Hoggart (b. 1918) began studying English at the University of Leeds, he had to suppress his natural enthusiasm for the subject. "I could jump the fences as required and give a passable imitation of understanding," enough to get a First Class Degree, but he never really grasped Shakespeare until he found *Macbeth* in a North African army barracks in 1942:

> It was as though, to get through to the point at university at which you sat those eight or nine papers on different periods and genres, you could not allow the force of the works to flood into you; you might have been pushed off course. Or as though someone writing about many varieties of physical love had suffered powerful but temporary inhibitions in the practice of it. You did not for those three years dare to release yourself to the power of the works; you controlled your responses to them, almost unconsciously.[58]

Of course, even students who praised their schools overall often admitted that certain subjects got short shrift. Autobiographical evidence suggests that the same schools that so splendidly introduced children to the English classics usually reduced geography to the memorization of place names. History rarely dealt with modern times or, indeed, anything other than English kings and queens. "Scratch us, even now, and we'll break out into a rash of Browning, Wordsworth, Shelley, Milton; and, of course, the Bard," wrote Amy Gomm (b. 1899), daughter of an Oxfordshire electrician. But "Geography was a fairly sketchy affair. History was a matter of battles and kings, and trying to remember their dates. We'd hear, in passing, of certain villains who 'rose up in revolt.' It was years before we realized that they might have had a point of view. We didn't learn real history."[59] In the early 1920s one south London school was still using a history text published around 1900, which included no pictures except monarchial portraits and stopped short at George IV.[60] C. H. Rolph complained that

> never once, in my twelve years of schooling in various parts of London, did I come across a teacher or a textbook able (or perhaps permitted) to convey the fascination and excitement of those twin subjects, history and geography. They were twin bores: heavy-hearted subjects, dull, stripped of nearly all the magic and the human interest to be discovered years later in "adult education." The history lessons were, it seemed, judged to be sufficiently human if they were larded with fancy legends like Alfred and the Cakes, Bruce and the Spider, Canute and the Tide, and Turnagain Whittington. … What history I ever learned I was to get, in due course (a euphemism for middle age), from Gibbon, Froude, Macaulay, Wells, Toynbee and the marvellous teams of scholars who compiled the Oxford and Cambridge Modern Histories.[61]

Without that historical background, literature could be hard to decipher. Jack Common recalled that his mother once bought him a secondhand and severely abridged *Life of Johnson* for 1d., and he had to read it several times before he even partially absorbed it. He did adopt the great man as his hero and model, introducing Johnsonian flourishes into his school essays, but

> the world of Doctor Johnson was so unknown to me, I couldn't really see what he was trying to do. He wrote a dictionary—yes, well, you'd only to look at a dictionary to appreciate that that was an heroic job all right. He knew all the words, give him that. And he always won his arguments. But what were they about? Why were they so important to all these gladiators of the verbal arena? Our history lessons, you see, had nowhere near reached the eighteenth century. We were still bogged among the Plantagenets, and by the same method of slow torture employed in the issue of books for class-reading, it was all too likely that next term would find us starting the Plantagenets all over again. In fact it might easily take us as long to get down the centuries as it did the folks who originally made the trip, except that in one class or another we were bound to encounter a teacher who dropped us quickly down a ladder of dates into an era he had been reading up on.[62]

There certainly were some pupils who found the classroom stifling, especially the endless lessons in copperplate.[63] Edna Bold (b. 1904) felt "incarcerated" in her Manchester Board school:

> Not for long could the creature withstand such confinement and the dust-laden atmosphere of the place. … Visually, aurally, mentally stultified, the days passed, featureless and painless. Dry as dust knowledge was literally poured into colander-like craniums, and any wretched, under-par child was expected to absorb that

which refused to be contained. Its self-respect, its confidence, its love of life was eroded. To love life, to live life was not the prime function of EDUCATION.[64]

Given the very large classes common in such schools, mass memorization was often the only workable teaching strategy. Jack Lanigan (b. 1890) recalled that his overcrowded classroom accommodated five grades: "Under such conditions each individual scholar had to learn how to concentrate on his own class and lesson, and shut his eyes and ears to what was taking place in the other classes." Yet Lanigan concluded that the system, within its limits, worked: "I must admit I did not know of any children of my age who could not read or write, do arithmetic and know something about history and geography."[65] Another memoirist dismissed his Catholic school as "totally inadequate" but conceded that "although there were many ragged and neglected children in the poorer parts of large cities and towns [in 1915], there were not many illiterates among the younger generations."[66] After 1950, old-age pensioners commonly insisted that they had actually received a better education than their grandchildren. "We were taught the three Rs, which is more than they are today [1956]" is a typical growl.[67] In 1978 one Catholic school graduate recalled that she was not fond of her spinster teachers but admitted "they did their job most conscientiously, and I consider that even though most children left school at 12–14, we were far better educated than the present day children."[68] In 1972 a former workhouse boy, who flourished under the semi-military discipline at his Poor Law school, dismissed modern education as "balderdash ... the principal reason why a very large percentage of young people are almost completely illiterate when they leave school and another large percentage semi-literate. ... The education the boys received at this Poor Law school was sound and prepared a boy for a fair start in life. The three Rs were properly dinned into the minds of all."[69]

Not all working-class children disliked rote learning. For many, it was both easy and fun; some even enjoyed the endless practice of penmanship. "Did we find it drudgery? Not so," one woman (b. 1890) asserts. "There was pride in achievement, and we all worked to get the word of praise that would follow our 'best work.'"[70] "There was much repetition," admitted a Bermondsey tanner's son (b. 1883), "but we didn't notice the drudgery of it all. Children, young children particularly, love habit formation and they like what would be regarded as drudgery by those older. They love to follow, adults love to lead."[71] "The continuous chanting of so many facts was a hopeless mumbo jumbo to me at first," recalled the son (b. 1878) of a Suffolk factory foreman, "but gradually light dawned and I began to see what it was all about and enjoyed finding out more. The chief aim seemed to be to give children sufficient education to carry on the life of the village, which was at that time a self-contained unit."[72] "To some modern theorists the chanting of [mathematical] tables is shocking," wrote the son (b. c. 1911) of a Cornish fisherman, "but we enjoyed it—and learned the tables. ... Pendlebury's Arithmetic books were old and fusty in appearance, but we worked enormous numbers of examples," and when some pupils went on to secondary school they were already doing math at School Certificate level.[73] The son (b. c. 1930) of a Devon farmhand wrote:

> There was a time when I thought there was little value in … the alphabetic chanting about cats and mats, … but the circumstances were so different in those days. There were not the books and other aids that tend to clutter up today's [1983] classrooms. There was no TV, and just the beginnings of radio. I never saw any advisers, or remedial teachers, or other supporting staff, and there could not have been much in the way of encouragement or refreshment for the workers at the "chalkface". So [our teachers] found themselves *invested* with numbers of country children, a good proportion of whom were not bright. On a restricted site, with few props, such teachers had to ring the changes to keep us occupied and educated. They did this; and more. The drills I once thought tiresome, if not useless, were conditioning us into a work routine which we were going to need. I often feel that such discipline ought to be more in evidence today.[74]

The example of Jane Mitchell (b. 1934), a lorry driver's daughter who became a lecturer in classics at the University of Reading, demonstrates that even an unusually creative and ambitious student could thrive on the rote method:

> I enjoyed the mental drill and exercise I was put through, even the memorizing from our geography book of the principal rivers and promontories of the British Isles, going round the coasts clockwise, and the principal towns, with the products appropriate to each. Arithmetic I enjoyed as an agreeable game, and made it a point of honour to do as much as possible of it mentally. For a year or two, I had what was almost a tic—I would go round compulsively factorizing and multiplying numbers in my head—dates, bus-ticket numbers, anything. … It never occurred to me to question the purposes or methods of what we were made to do at school. The stuff was there to be learned, and I enjoyed mopping it up.[75]

In the same spirit, a Devonshire girl (b. c. 1919) memorized most of the poems in Palgrave's *Golden Treasury*

> even when not required to do so, and I can recite them to this day. Educationists would think this was a terrible way to teach poetry; for me, it was pure magic, pure enchantment. I loved the poets' tone of calm authority; they suggested nothing, they stated, not aggressively but with conviction. It was like listening to an argument that had already been won, to a debating motion that had already been carried, to a recorded programme where nothing could go wrong.[76]

Memorization was not incompatible with creativity, an insight put into practice by Bert Linn, one of the most respected and innovative teachers at London's Paragon school in the 1930s. He taught poetry by giving each boy one line of verse to learn by heart, and then calling on them to recite in order. "His methods might be frowned upon today" [1977], one of his admiring pupils conceded. "Yet they were extremely effective instilling into so many of us boys from the grimy back streets of South London a love of poetry and fine writing which has enriched a lifetime." In fact, he brought close reading to the slums:

Bert would dissect a poem line by line, phrase by phrase and even word by word. There are those today who say that you shouldn't do that; that the work should be appreciated as a symmetrical whole. Had Bert attempted this, we would have quickly become bored with words and idioms we simply couldn't understand. As it was, we were able to eventually appreciate not only the final structure but all of the fine detail which went to build it. By working in this way he added enormously to our knowledge of our own great language.[77]

Of course many teachers did not range far beyond the three Rs, but not always for want of trying. Robert Hayward (b. 1907), son of a Wiltshire farm laborer, recalled that his old headmaster honestly attempted to teach a broad curriculum, but was forced back on the basic skills his students would need to find work. His attempts at music instruction were frustrated by the pupils themselves:

It must be confessed that we were an untalented lot (with just one or two exceptions) and trying to teach us to sing melodiously offered as much prospect of success as trying to teach the subject to a flock of geese. ... Even now, over 60 years after, I feel sad for him when I think of the daunting prospect confronting him each Monday morning; rows of unwilling, untidy, unruly, grubby ignorant kids facing him with a surly expression, hating the prospect of five days of confinement; a prospect to deter any but the most dedicated. And to his eternal credit he achieved some success. ... He taught us to become good citizens by precept and example. I never knew, or heard of, any pupil or ex-pupil of his who in any way disgraced the school or the village; neither have I ever known any who did not grow up to be a credit to the school and the village, with a keen sense of social responsibility.[78]

Newcastle Labour politician T. Dan Smith (b. 1915), explained why a strictly disciplined and inadequately equipped classroom could seem attractive to a slum child: "School, even though a sterile place as compared with today [1970], was still an oasis in a grim social situation."[79] The Board schools offered what many poor households did not: a structured learning environment, recognition for academic achievements, and (often) sympathetic adults, not to mention proper heating, lighting, and plumbing. For Nancy Day (b. 1912), an orphan who had difficulty winning acceptance from her stepfather, school was a place where "I could be myself. ... I became something of a teacher's pet, which compensated for having to be 'seen & not heard' at home." The headmaster "taught me not to be afraid of men, & perhaps became a father figure to me. ... His approval made me feel more confident & secure, & as I grew older, & made myself useful at home, I was accepted by Dad & was much happier."[80] Lottie Barker (b. 1899) worshipped her teachers because

> They were always so kind to me. ... I know they appreciated the fact that I tried very hard, for one or the other would at times praise me. This I loved for at home I was always considered bad tempered, and try as I might I always seemed to get blamed for any mishap that occurred. ... No one at home encouraged me except perhaps in my cookery.[81]

For the daughter of an unemployed painter, growing up in Derby between the wars, school was a haven from life on the dole:

> I enjoyed the order and the routine of school days and hated weekends and holidays. They meant a repeat of the domestic rows that plagued our household and I was handed the responsibility for the care of the younger children. The headmistress ... was very strict, but her heart was in the right place. All the children went hungry at times but I must have looked more hungry than the rest, being thin as a beanpole and tall for my age. She would often call me into her office on the pretext that there was punishment ahead and then demand that I sit down and eat the sandwiches she had placed on her desk.[82]

Strict but Just

If we have painted too harsh a portrait of these schools and teachers, we have also been too sweeping in our indictments of corporal punishment. G. A. N. Lowndes and Brian Simon asserted that "in boys' schools every sum wrong, every spelling mistake, every blot, every question which could not be answered as the fateful day of examination drew near, was liable to be visited by a stroke of the cane."[83] Paul Thompson writes that "Caning in school was ubiquitous,"[84] and Standish Meacham claims that turn-of-the-century teachers were uniformly brutal: "All of them punished a lapse from the expected standard with the cane."[85]

What, all of them? The Thompson–Vigne interviews (quantified in Table 5.6, p. 169) do not entirely support that conclusion. True, hardly any boys completely escaped corporal punishment in school, but at least a quarter of working-class children, a third of other children, and 42 percent of all girls suffered little or no such punishment. About a quarter of both social classes reported that there was corporal punishment without offering any opinion on it. One out of six working

Table 5.6: Respondents Reporting Corporal Punishment (in Percent)

	None	Little	Punishment, No Comment	Strict But Just	Too Severe	N
All	11.9	17.3	25.4	14.7	30.6	421
Sex:						
Male	5.3	10.2	32.5	18.4	33.5	206
Female	18.1	24.2	18.6	11.2	27.9	215
Class:						
ABC	19.3	15.1	24.4	10.1	33.1	119
DEF	8.7	18.4	25.8	16.4	30.8	299
A	50.0	0.0	14.3	14.3	21.4	14
B	17.1	12.9	27.1	11.4	31.4	70
C	11.4	25.7	22.9	5.7	34.3	35
D	9.3	18.6	28.6	16.4	27.1	140
E	8.9	17.9	23.2	17.9	32.1	112
F	6.4	19.1	23.4	12.8	38.3	47
Party:						
Conservative	13.3	20.0	24.0	18.7	24.0	75
Liberal	17.9	14.9	29.9	13.4	23.9	67
Labour/Socialist	7.5	14.0	28.0	16.1	34.4	93
Apolitical	10.4	19.1	26.1	12.2	32.2	115
Religion:						
Anglican	12.9	19.6	23.3	18.4	25.8	163
Nonconformist	11.6	16.4	28.0	13.0	30.9	207
Catholic	10.5	15.8	23.7	7.9	42.1	38
Religion and class:						
Anglican ABC	19.0	16.7	26.2	9.5	28.6	42
Anglican DEF	10.8	20.8	22.5	20.8	25.0	120
Nonconformist ABC	21.2	13.6	21.2	10.6	33.3	66
Nonconformist DEF	7.1	17.9	30.7	14.3	30.0	140
Catholic ABC	12.5	25.0	37.5	0.0	25.0	8
Catholic DEF	10.0	13.3	20.0	10.0	46.7	30

Note—N excludes respondents who did not address the question.

people said that corporal punishment was fair and necessary, compared with only one in ten middle-class respondents. The phrase "strict but just," or words to that effect, is a commonplace in workers' memoirs.[86]

In working-class communities there was a consensus in favor of corporal punishment in the schools. A 1949 Gallup Poll found that only 31 percent of adults were completely opposed to it, while 45 percent favored it for both boys and girls.[87] There would be outrage if the innocent were punished, of course, but few objected in principle. Though some of the boys at one Birmingham school went on to become professional boxers and footballers, none of them dared to retaliate against their teachers. "There was that inborn fear of rebellion against authority," as one of them (b. 1902) put it. "Because these lads knew, if the lads went home and reported to their parents that a teacher had thrashed you, you booked yourself for another thrashing at home."[88] "We found nothing wrong with the strap," asserted William Campbell (b. 1910). "To be confined to school after class to write hundreds of lines was a much worse punishment." His mother backed a campaign by the Communist Party Women's Committee to abolish corporal punishment in the schools, and ordered her reluctant son to mobilize his classmates, though at home she had a strap on the wall. Campbell organized fifty boys into a schoolyard demonstration, confronted the headmaster, and "piped something about the strap being a tool of World Imperialism." He was promptly nabbed by the ear and hustled off to his punishment, abandoned by his timorous followers.[89] Even pupils supported the system, if the alternative was *Lord of the Flies*. "We knew we deserved it and there were no hard feelings," remembered one Battersea boy (b. c. 1900). One day a teacher,

> impelled by I know not what feelings, ... told us that henceforward he would dispense with the use of canes and would trust us to behave ourselves. In furtherance of this good resolve, which even then we didn't feel we could take the chance of applauding, he ceremonially took his several canes from his desk drawer, broke them over his knee and threw the pieces into the wastepaper basket. Whether this gesture was but an experiment in better living we never knew, but it didn't work with our high-spirited crowd for more than a day or two. Candidly no one knew just where they were .... The only way out was for him to get fresh canes: then we settled down in mutual comfort again, like Paradise Regained.[90]

Children might interpret an unwillingness to use the cane as a sign of weakness, to be exploited ruthlessly. Flora Thompson recalled a young Oxfordshire teacher of the 1880s who completely lost control of her pupils on her very first day, when she made the fatal error of telling them "I want us all to be friends."[91] These memoirists tend to confirm the common-sense notion that corporal punishment is traumatic only when it is sadistic and arbitrary, not when it is administered solely for violating a clear and reasonable set of disciplinary rules. One Board school alumnus (b. 1911) drew that distinction when he denounced a schoolmaster who caned him every day. "As a result of his treatment I have a thorough appreciation of what constitutes victimization and injustice," he wrote, adding that "subsequent masters also caned me but with just cause and never for trivialities."[92]

There may have been some correlation between unfair canings and political ideology in later life. Conservatives and Liberals were less likely to complain of severe corporal punishment and more likely to rate their schools well than those who embraced the left or apathy. Punished for an offense he did not commit, C. H. Rolph never forgave or forgot: "It's more than sixty years ago and I remember the whole thing with total clarity. ... From that time onwards I never had any faith in 'justice';

and am quite certain that I acquired a kind of qualified contempt for 'law and order' at the hands of one fatheaded and probably distracted schoolmaster." That came from a man who made a career as a London policeman.[93] Though her parents were caretakers at a Yorkshire Conservative Club, and she herself belonged to the Tory Primrose League, Gladys Teal (b. 1913) rebelled when she was caned on the hands for simple mistakes in arithmetic: "All my life I have been unable to tolerate injustice, perhaps because the seed was sown then."[94] Militant socialist Rowland Kenney (b. 1883) claimed that unfair corporal punishment transformed him into a political rebel and destroyed the prestige of adults in his eyes:

> "Grown-ups," those incredible and unpredictable creatures, ... were reviewed and presented to me in a new light. Previously I had believed in grown-ups. In the realm of knowledge, in spite of the plain evidence of my acute childish senses, I had accepted as a fact their assumption that they *knew*. They must know. Until that moment my little world would have seemed impossible had I consciously thought that they did not know. Had I thought of it at all, I should have assumed that their difficult and apparently wrong answers to simple questions, their foolish contradictions and obvious avoidance of certain points, were due to the fact that I was neither old nor sensible enough to understand. Whereas now I knew that they did not know; this teacher did not know; these lessons of hers were mostly mere chatter. She was a poor, ignorant creature pretending to be all-wise, and she was afraid of something—of our questions perhaps—and she hid her fear under a mask of sternness and acts of cruelty. She was merely a fool. I began to feel sorry for her. I had seen through her and beyond her and I knew so much more about her now than she knew about herself.

After he lost faith in his teacher and adults in general, God was the next domino to fall: "Now, in this big all-seeing, all-knowing, all-denouncing, all-threatening bully there was no substance at all. ... And with this realisation was linked up the idea of a general falsity, in which all grown-ups—parents, teachers and elders—were included."[95]

On the other hand, among those who did not object to corporal punishment, it may have had the opposite effect, reinforcing and internalizing a set of conservative social values. One Leytonstone carman (b. 1899) affirmed that caning "taught us to respect those in charge and get on with the job and must have helped to turn out some fine craftsmen." It taught him as well the basic literacy and self-discipline that enabled him to write his memoirs, "what I term an achievement, especially when I hear of children today [1979] when the school leaving age is sixteen, unable to read and write."[96] Luton welder Aubrey Darby (b. 1905) loathed his school for its corporal punishment and its "sparse and insipid" curriculum, but his bitterness did not make him a radical. On the contrary, toward the end of his life he railed against an intelligentsia obsessed with a need for stimulation, taking in its stride drugs, sexual abnormality and neurotic criminal tendencies. Meditation, sit-ins, protest and banner carrying, painting a picture called self expression, psycho-analysis, raping the mind, delving back to the mother's womb, the parents getting the blame.

Could it be that our environment of ignorance, made for a more contented and stable society?[97]

Lest we fall into the error of overcorrection, this point needs emphasis: a large minority of pupils suffered abuses of school discipline. Paul Thompson suggests that "a good quarter of Edwardian children left school to harbour resentments against their teachers for the rest of their lives."[98] My own estimate is actually somewhat higher: 30.8 percent for the working class, slightly more for affluent pupils. (I placed in the "too severe" column anyone who made any complaint at all about school discipline, even if they could recall only one incident of unjust punishment.) Nevertheless, in both social classes, the resentful were outnumbered by those who reported that corporal punishment was invariably fair, or infrequent, or simply not done.

Parental Support

The statistics suggest that several other assumptions concerning working-class schooling should be modified or discarded entirely. According to Standish Meacham, neither parents nor children were much interested in further education: "Family and friends expected them to work as soon as the law allowed, and they themselves looked forward eagerly to doing so."[99] That was true in the majority of cases, but as Table 5.7 (p. 173) indicates, 36.6 percent of working people recalled that they were unhappy to leave school, compared with 39.0 percent of middle- and upper-class respondents. J. S. Hurt was still farther off the mark when he concluded that "For the bulk of working-class children attending school firm [parental] support was lacking."[100] Although parental interest in education did decline with class status, no less than 71.3 percent of working people described their parents as interested in their schooling, compared with 82.3 percent in other classes (Table 5.8, p. 174).

Table 5.9 (p. 175) confirms what appears to be a universal truth in educational research: that parental involvement strongly influences a child's attitude toward school. Among those who reported that their parents were interested in their education, 70.9 percent found school a positive experience and only 10.9 percent found it a negative experience, compared with 51.6 percent positive and 24.2 percent negative for those with uninterested parents. Among children with interested parents, 44.2 percent were unhappy to leave school and 53.6 percent

Table 5.7: Feelings on Leaving School (in Percent)

	Happy	Unhappy	Unsure	N
All	60.0	37.2	2.8	325
Sex:				
Male	65.8	31.7	2.5	161
Female	54.3	42.7	3.0	164
Class:				
ABC	58.5	39.0	2.4	82
DEF	60.5	36.6	2.9	243
A	50.0	50.0	.0	8
B	63.0	34.8	2.2	46
C	53.6	42.9	3.6	28
D	58.8	39.5	1.8	114
E	63.5	31.8	4.7	85
F	59.1	38.6	2.3	44
Party:				
Conservative	57.1	35.5	5.4	56
Liberal	55.1	42.9	2.0	49
Labour/Socialist	59.0	39.7	1.3	78
Apolitical	60.2	37.6	2.2	93
Religion:				
Anglican	59.8	36.2	3.9	127
Nonconformist	59.2	38.2	2.5	157
Catholic	68.8	31.3	.0	32
Religion and class:				
Anglican ABC	58.6	37.9	3.4	29
Anglican DEF	60.2	35.7	4.1	98
Nonconformist ABC	62.2	35.6	2.2	45
Nonconformist DEF	58.0	39.3	2.7	112
Catholic ABC	33.3	66.7	.0	6
Catholic DEF	76.9	23.1	.0	26

Note—N excludes respondents who did not address the question.

were happy to leave, compared with 20.5 percent and 76.9 percent of those with uninterested parents.

It is remarkable that half of all children who received no parental encouragement nevertheless enjoyed school. That discrepancy could reflect the fact that the schools were doing too good a job, educating young people far beyond their parents' understanding. For scholarship girl Elizabeth Flint, school was a place where "we were allowed to think for ourselves and to discuss things. Great long discussions we had about practically every topic under the sun. Each day the world opened out a little more, and again a little more." But her East End family

Table 5.8: Respondents Reporting Parental Interest in Their Education

	Interested	Uninterested	N
All	74.4	25.6	390
Sex:			
Male	68.4	31.6	196
Female	80.4	19.6	194
Class:			
ABC	82.3	17.7	113
DEF	71.3	28.7	275
A	92.3	7.7	13
B	81.5	18.5	65
C	80.0	20.0	35
D	73.2	26.8	127
E	69.6	30.4	102
F	69.6	30.4	46
Party:			
Conservative	82.8	17.2	64
Liberal	77.8	22.2	63
Labour/Socialist	69.7	30.3	89
Apolitical	72.1	27.9	104
Religion:			
Anglican	74.0	26.0	146
Nonconformist	75.6	24.4	197
Catholic	69.7	30.3	33
Religion and class:			
Anglican ABC	86.1	13.9	36
Anglican DEF	70.0	30.0	110
Nonconformist ABC	80.0	20.0	65
Nonconformist DEF	73.3	26.7	131
Catholic ABC	87.5	12.5	8
Catholic DEF	64.0	36.0	25

Note—*N* excludes respondents who did not address the question.

saw no value in books, would not set aside study space at the kitchen table, and could not understand the school play she performed in. Her mother promised to see her perform on Speech Day, but then lost heart at the door: "I didn't go in, Liz. I meant to, honest I did. I meant to go in all right, I did, but it was too grand for me, it was. ... It was them other mothers, Liz, that's what. Why, some of them came in cabs, they did, right up to the door. I couldn't go in with them, I couldn't."[101] Even if they wanted scholastic success for their children, working people of that generation sometimes felt constrained to express any encouragement. A construction worker (b. 1888) recalled that attitude in his grandfather, a Cornish farmer who was very much a man of the Victorian era: "Dear old man!

Table 5.9: Cross-tabulating Parental Interest (in Percent)

A. With Respondent's Regrets

	Regret Schooling	No Regrets	N
Interested	42.6	45.6	208
Uninterested	39.5	50.0	68
N	131	146	...

B. With School Experience

	Positive Experience	Negative Experience	N
Interested	70.9	10.9	233
Uninterested	51.6	24.2	72
N	251	54	...

C. With Feelings on Leaving School

	Happy to Leave	Unhappy to Leave	N
Interested	53.6	44.2	219
Uninterested	76.9	20.5	76
N	180	115	...

Note—The totals for these tables do not add up to 100.0 percent because the percentages for some responses have been eliminated: "unspecified regrets" and "own effort" have been eliminated from pt. A; "mixed" has been eliminated from pt. B; and "unsure" has been eliminated from pt. C. Also, N excludes respondents who did not address the question.

He did love us ... [but] he was not a demonstrative man and would flatter nobody and he rarely gave us a word of praise. We 'were never very clever' and were 'never going to be.'" Once, when the schoolmaster came to visit,

I happened to have a book in front of me and Master asked what I was reading. Before I could reply Grandpa began: "They are no great readers!" "Oh well, they won't be much," said Master. "No, no, they won't be much," agreed Gramp, yet in his heart he thought the world of us. He was always interested in our work at school and as we got older he would enquire about our respective jobs until he died.[102]

That post-Victorian generation would be more interested in and more outspoken on the quality of schooling, at least through the Second World War. A 1944 poll in London revealed deep discontent with the existing educational

Table 5.10: Attitudes toward Education, 1944 (in percent)[103]

	Middle Class	Upper Working Class	Lower Working Class
"What do you feel about the way education was run in the country before the war?"			
Adequate	19	17	32
Inadequate	47	45	22
Bad	23	26	34
No opinion	11	11	12
"Do you think there are any changes which ought to be made after the war?"			
Yes	90	85	79
No	7	4	16
Don't know	3	11	10
"If yes, what changes?"			
Equal and greater opportunity	35	39	48
"What do you feel about the school leaving age being raised?"			
Approve	61	72	50
Qualified approval	21	24	32
Disapprove	14	4	16
No opinion	4	0	2
"What do you think about education carrying on after leaving school?"			
Approve	41	43	32
Qualified approval	43	41	48
Disapprove	13	13	12
No opinion	3	3	8

system. In the upper working class 84 percent favored adult education, and hardly anyone was opposed to raising the school leaving age (Table 5.10).

That passion for education had, however, largely burned out just a few years later, when a WEA poll of 414 parents of Stockport schoolchildren found that 81 percent wanted the schools to put more emphasis on vocational training. Only a minority (42 percent) felt their children should do homework. A majority (56 percent) regretted that the school leaving age had been raised to fifteen in 1947, and most (84 percent) opposed raising it to sixteen.[104] By the early 1960s, a survey of affluent working-class parents (corresponding to Class D in Table 5.8, p. 174) would find that only 40 percent of them regularly discussed their children's education. Fifty-four percent felt they could help their children with schoolwork, only 37 percent wanted them to pursue academic rather than vocational subjects, and a mere 27 percent had talked with teachers about their educational hopes for their children.[105] Social commentators who lamented the decline of the old working-class respect for education were not entirely the victims of false nostalgia.

Unmanly Education

When the Thompson–Vigne survey is broken down by sex, the results are even more striking and surprising. Girls were more likely than boys to find school a positive experience, more likely to praise their teachers, and less likely to have regrets concerning their education—perhaps because they were considerably less likely to suffer corporal punishment. More women (10.4 percent) than men (6.8 percent) felt they reaped no benefit from their education, but the proportion was small in both cases. Girls were more often unhappy to leave school than boys were, a fact that can be construed two ways: either girls enjoyed school more than boys, or they missed the opportunities that boys had for further education. The latter conclusion seems unlikely, for several reasons. First, Elizabeth Roberts's study of Lancashire working women found that boys were not much more likely than girls to go on to grammar school.[106] In Wales, boys and girls were attending secondary schools in equal proportions in 1901, and the girls were slightly ahead by 1914.[107] Of course, there were fewer places for women at universities, but that was an unimaginable goal for slum children of either sex. This point is confirmed by the third column of Table 5.11 (p. 183), which gives the percentages of respondents who regretted that they did not receive more education. There is hardly any difference between the results for men and women—or, for that matter, between the working classes and the upper and middle classes.

It is usually taken for granted that "Parents and teachers colluded in believing that girls' academic education mattered less than boys,"[108] but Table 5.8 (p. 174) reveals that 80.4 percent of the women interviewed felt their parents had taken an interest in their education, compared with 68.4 percent of the men. M. K. Ashby noted that though her Victorian paterfamilias was opposed to female suffrage, "he thought that fathers ought to provide for their daughters and to give a better schooling to girls than to boys."[109] Girl pupils could find models for emulation in their female teachers, many of whom came from similar working-class backgrounds. "The teaching profession was greatly admired by all the people I knew," recalled the daughter (b. c. 1912) of a London commercial traveller, who tremendously respected "the dedication of these single women, all devoting their lives to the education and training of children other than their own."[110]

Obviously, girls in this period were trained to conform to a Victorian ideal of womanhood, and for many feminist historians it necessarily follows that these girls felt oppressed and confined by that style of schooling.[111] If one looks to the memoirs of emancipated women, such as minister of education Ellen Wilkinson,[112] one can certainly find protests against the limitations of girls' schooling. But these autobiographies are hardly representative: they were mostly produced by a tiny minority of emancipated women, rarely by those who were contented with (or at least never questioned) their social roles. When Elizabeth Roberts resorted to oral interviews to get at these invisible women, she was compelled to abandon one working assumption: "As a feminist, in the face of the empirical evidence, I have been forced to conclude that it is not sufficient to indict the injustices of the past, nor allow one's concern for women's causes of today to obstruct the understanding of women's roles and status yesterday." Roberts found "that there was little feeling among the majority of women interviewed that they or their mothers had been particularly exploited by men": they were much more likely to feel exploited by their employers. Nearly all of the women she interviewed disliked domestic science classes in school, but not because they rejected traditional domestic roles: they simply preferred to learn housewifely skills from their mothers.[113]

Other evidence suggests that Roberts may have underestimated the popularity of these classes. In a 1949 Gallup poll, 15 percent of all respondents identified domestic science as the most useful subject they had taken at school. Assuming that very few of them were men, they probably represented 30 percent of the women. A year later, 71 percent of housewives told Gallup they derived satisfaction from housework, while only 16 percent said they did not.[114] Joanna Bourke reminds us that married working-class women in the early twentieth century valued domesticity and the opportunity to stay home. Only 14 percent of married women were employed outside the home in 1901, 1911, and 1921, partly because the jobs available to them were unattractive, but also because women enjoyed authority in the domestic sphere and found fulfillment in creating a comfortable home.[115] Even a working-class feminist like Elizabeth Andrews affirmed that, while all professions should be open to both sexes, "Nevertheless to the majority of women, homemaking will still remain their chief and noblest contribution in life, for home is not only a place to eat and sleep in, it is the abiding place of the family where the character of our future citizens is made or marred."[116] As a scholarship girl at Christ's Hospital in the 1920s, Kathleen Betterton was a trifle disappointed that the school disdained domestic science on feminist principles:

> Though it was obvious that many of us would marry and have children, we were not supposed to think of this. The idea of any practical preparation for marriage would have seemed almost indelicate .... To have gained a degree, to be launched on a career—these were high achievements .... If any of us, when questioned in the choice of a career, had answered, "I just want to be an ordinary mother," they would have felt that this was letting down the side.

We tend to assume that sex discrimination was to blame if a boy enjoyed further education while his sister did not, but often the situation was reversed. Kathleen Betterton ascended all the way to Oxford University via the scholarship ladder, while her brother, whom she considered brighter, only receieved an inferior secondary education at a Central school, owing to "the chanciness of the system."[117]

Of course, slum girls were frequently ordered to get their noses out of books and attend to their chores. Adeline Hodges (b. 1899), a Durham stonemason's daughter, loved *The Last of the Mohicans* and her other Sunday school prizes, "but Mother wasn't keen on reading 'trash.' All books were 'trash.' She thought one's time was better spent on mending, darning, knitting, etc."[118] But as Robert Roberts noted, the lower working classes discouraged reading among children of both sexes: "'Put that book down!' a mother would command her child, even in his free time, 'and do something useful.'" If reading distracted girls from housework, in boys it was regarded as effeminate: "Among ignorant men any interest in music, books or the arts in general, learning or even courtesy and intelligence could make one suspect." Roberts identified D. H. Lawrence as a victim of "this linking of homosexuality with culture": his Eastwood neighbors "would have smiled to think that such a youth in later life could have set himself up as an expert on sex virility in the working classes."[119] Lawrence did accuse the Board schools of emasculating slum boys. "Everybody is educated: and what is education? A sort of *unmanliness*," he sputtered, sounding very much like a scholarship boy impersonating a street tough. "Pitch them overboard, teach the three Rs, and then proceed with a certain amount of technical instruction, in preparation for the coming job."[120] Vernon Scannell and his brother had to endure the same kind of sneers ("Head always stuck in a book, just like a girl. No wonder you've got spots!") from their father in the 1930s:

"Put that book down and get outside. Go and chop some trees down!" This exhortation to deforest the landscape was issued quite frequently and after our first mild perplexity, since he must have known there were no trees in Kingsbury Square and we possessed neither the skills nor the tools of lumberjacks, we assumed the command was some kind of metaphor or simply further evidence of his doubtful sanity.[121]

It was a prejudice spoofed in *A Hard Day's Night* (1964):

PAUL'S GRANDFATHER: Would you look at 'im! Sittin' there with his hooter scrapin' away at that *book!* ...
RINGO: You can learn from books.
PAUL'S GRANDFATHER: You can, can ye? Bah! Sheepsheads! You can learn more by gettin' out there and livin'! ... But not her little Richard, oh no. ... Yer tormentin' your eyes with that rubbish!
RINGO: Books are good ....
PAUL'S GRANDFATHER: When was the last time you gave a girl a pink-edged daisy? When did you last embarrass a Sheila with your cool appraisin' stare? ...
RINGO: Ah, stop pickin' on me, you're as bad as the rest of 'em.
PAUL'S GRANDFATHER: Ah, so you *are* a man after all!
RINGO: What's that mean?
PAUL'S GRANDFATHER: Do you think I haven't noticed? ... And what's it all come to in the end? ... A *book!*

RINGO [*converted*]: Yeah, a bloomin' book!

PAUL'S GRANDFATHER: When you could be out there betrayin' a rich American widder, or sippin' palm wine in Tahiti before you're too old like me.

As a construction worker, Rowland Kenney (b. 1883) feared that his love of poetry might mark him as "effeminate," until he heard his foreman reciting Tennyson's "The Lotos-Eaters" "in a powerful voice with a Lancashire accent, breaking the rhythm of the lines now and then with a long gurgling suck at an old clay pipe. The effect was tremendous. I hugged myself with delight. … If a fighting, drinking, you-go-to-Hell man like [him] could openly mouth poetry, so could I." Thenceforth the two of them recited *Omar Khayyam* to each other on the job.[122] Sid Chaplin had to be more circumspect when he broke into literature by writing essays on poets for local papers: John Greenleaf Whittier for a half crown. "It was very exciting," he remembered, but "I never thought in terms of becoming a professional writer. In the first place it was somehow feminine, that's why it had to be a secret occupation for me." He wrote under pseudonyms for the next three years, "so nobody ever knew excepting the immediate family." One might think that there was no need for Chaplin, a colliery blacksmith, to feel anxious about his masculinity, but "That was the feeling you got in a [Durham] mining village, a man found his place through his muscular strength and ability, or agility. Same whether it was the big hewer, or a good footballer, or a breeder of pigeons, or a leekman. These were masculine things, and writing was very effeminate, so I said nothing about it."[123]

For the same reason, merchant seaman Lennox Kerr (b. c. 1899) ditched overboard his early experiments in authorship:

If my shipmates had found them and read how I described them as having bodies like Greek gods they would have laughed me out of the ship. Because writing isn't for a working man. It sets him apart. Makes him lonely among his own people. It is an extravagance a working man cannot afford. He isn't such a good toiler if he knows too much or does things like writing. Even reading Shakespeare and the Bible and my *Cobbett's Grammar* put me under suspicion. … I had to take up every challenge as soon as it showed: had to swipe a chap's face when I did not want to, or boast about my splicing—just to prove that reading books was not making me any less a good sailor.

But underneath this philistinism, Kerr perceived a suppressed literary impulse among his shipmates. In groups they would conform to a rough anti-intellectualism, yet when they were alone on lookout the subconscious would start talking out loud:

The secret desires in men come out as they feel themselves alone and free from the screen of cynicism men don in public. That deep, creative wish to be more than merely an obedient worker appears, and men are romantic, noble, courageous, poetic in the secrecy of darkness. I have heard a man announce in dramatic tones: "Silas Blackadder, touch that maiden and I shall choke the life out of your foul body." I heard a man, the most foul-tongued on our ship, reciting the Song of Solomon to the darkness and the rustle of the sea breaking against the ship's forefoot. Alone, man becomes what he would be if he were not forced to a mould by the system he lives in.[124]

By the early twentieth century, it was not unusual to find working-class families where the women were better read than the men. The son (b. 1890) of a barely literate Derbyshire collier recalled a sister, a worker in a hosiery factory, who was steeped in the poetry of Byron, Shelley, Keats, and D. H. Lawrence. Their mother's reading "would astonish the modern candidate for honours in English at any university," he claimed. "Tolstoy, Dostoevsky, Turgeniev, Dumas, Hugo, Thackeray, Meredith, Scott, Dickens, all the classics, poetry, etc., all these gave her immense joy. What she would have thought of today's trivia I do not know."[125] In contrast to workingmen of an earlier generation, Labour MP John T. Macpherson (b. 1872) was not ashamed to acknowledge that his mother-in-law had helped him make up his lack of schooling: "Well-educated herself, she was never too weary or tired to help me, and she opened up many avenues along which I trod, and continue to tread to-day."[126]

For all these reasons, it is hardly surprising that girls were often more reluctant than boys to leave the warm world of the classroom for a lifetime of manual labor. "I cried my eyes up at the idea of having to leave school," recalled a houseservant (b. 1871) who had to begin work after only four years of schooling. "They were the happiest days I think I ever had, that was the freest time I have ever had in my life."[127] Having failed the entrance examination for secondary school, gardener's daughter Anita Hughes (b. 1892) had to become a cotton mill worker at 5s. a week: "I could never forget my last day at school—I was heartbroken and just sobbed."[128]

Some boys shared her feelings. Charles Shaw (b. 1832), in a memoir appropriated by Arnold Bennett for *Clayhanger*, remembered leaving school at age seven to work in a Staffordshire pot works, and his sharp resentment at seeing a man who could afford "reading of his own free will. … I felt a sudden, strange sense of wretchedness. There was a blighting consciousness that my lot was harsher than his and that of others. … I went back to my mould-running and hot stove with my first anguish in my heart."[129] But for others, the first day of work was a rite of passage into manhood, a graduation into the ranks of wage earners, a liberation from schoolroom disciplines. This was particularly true in the mining districts of South Wales, where boys sang

Down the pit we want to go
Away from school with all its woe,
Working hard as a collier's butty
Make us all so very happy![130]

Wil John Edwards (b. 1888) hated the "unsurpassed monotony" of school, where "the only time I felt myself identified as an individual was when I was caned. … I cannot help recalling the sense of exciting adventure I felt when, at the age of twelve, I was able to abandon school to work in the pit in the friendly, helpful, comradely environment of underground life." There he discovered the intense intellectual debates so common in the mineshafts of South Wales: "a paradox if you like: because it was only when I began to work in the darkness of the pit that the true light of learning shone."[131] Though Bernard Taylor (b. 1895) loved his Mansfield school, he was equally happy to begin work in the mines: "This was an occasion, a red-letter day, an important milestone in life's journey, a new venture; the routine of the past years at school was ended, the prospect of going out into the world was not unattractive, and the opportunity of bringing a little grist to the domestic mill was welcomed."[132] As another colliery boy (b. 1866) put it:

> What on earth did *I* want with any more schooling? Couldn't I read any other boy off his feet and gabble the newspaper over to my short-sighted elders! Couldn't I, didn't I, read everything that came within reach! And what more could any boy be supposed to do? Hadn't I heard time and again that reading and experience were the great turnpike-road to knowledge? And wasn't I travelling that way?—with the one always in my pocket and the other harvested by a perversity to be ever on the move.[133]

Yet they may have changed their minds after a few years at work. "I was full of enthusiasm at the thought of going into the mill, and earning money," recalled Thomas Thompson, who disliked his Lancashire school. But "the very first week I knew I had been led into a trap. … I loathed it, and the recollection of my mother and sister having to work in that noisy, steaming, smelly weaving shed when they were hardly fit to stand has shorn me of any enthusiasm for the success of factory life." He made a desperate escape by taking Co-operative society classes, reading through the Sunday school library, joining a workingmen's naturalist society, and even studying French Impressionism with an art teacher.[134]

Regrets and Discontents

Table 5.11 (p. 183) quantifies such discontents as expressed in the Thompson–Vigne interviews. Unspecified regrets are tabulated in column 1, regrets concerning the poor quality of schooling in column 2, and regrets over the lack of opportunities for further education in column 3. Column 4 numbers those who regretted a personal failure to take advantage of available opportunities, such as a soapworks foreman born to an East End construction laborer: "That's always up to the individual that is. If you can't learn you can't learn. And if you can learn you pick it up" (Interview 124). Those who explicitly said they had no regrets (not counting those who did not address the question) are in column 5.

The results reinforce the conclusion that most children of this generation enjoyed their schooling, as far as it went. Respondents in all classes were far less likely to complain about the quality of their schools than the fact that they had to leave at such an early age. Of course, the totals of columns 2 and 3 show that a large proportion expressed some kind of grievance against the educational system: 43.7 percent of the working classes and 41.5 percent of other classes.

Table 5.11: Respondents Expressing Regrets Concerning Education (in Percent)

	Unspecified Regrets (1)	Poor Quality of Schooling (2)	Regrets on School Leaving (3)	Lack of Personal Effort (4)	None (5)	N (6)
All	1.8	9.8	33.2	9.2	46.0	337
Sex:						
Male	2.5	11.7	34.0	9.9	42.0	162
Female	1.1	8.5	32.4	8.5	49.4	176
Class:						
ABC	1.1	6.7	34.8	18.0	39.3	89
DEF	2.0	11.3	32.4	6.1	48.2	247
A	.0	.0	33.3	33.3	33.3	9
B	1.9	9.4	34.0	15.1	39.6	53
C	.0	3.7	37.0	18.5	40.7	27
D	.0	10.3	37.1	3.4	49.1	116
E	3.4	14.9	27.6	9.2	44.8	87
F	4.5	6.8	29.5	6.8	52.3	44
Party:						
Conservative	.0	1.7	45.0	10.0	43.3	60
Liberal	.0	7.7	32.7	15.4	44.2	52
Labour/Socialist	3.8	11.4	30.4	8.9	45.6	79
Apolitical	1.0	14.4	30.9	8.2	45.4	97
Religion:						
Anglican	1.6	8.0	34.4	9.6	46.4	125
Nonconformist	1.7	8.1	35.3	8.7	46.2	173
Catholic	3.0	27.3	18.2	9.1	42.4	33
Religion and class:						
Anglican ABC	.0	6.5	29.0	12.9	51.6	31
Anglican DEF	2.2	8.6	35.5	8.6	45.2	93
Nonconformist ABC	2.0	8.0	38.0	22.0	30.0	50
Nonconformist DEF	1.6	8.2	34.4	3.3	52.5	122
Catholic ABC	.0	.0	50.0	.0	50.0	6
Catholic DEF	3.7	33.3	11.1	11.1	40.7	27

Note—*N* excludes respondents who did not address the question.

"They didn't care much about the child," recalled an Islington carpenter's son, "it was very elementary rudiments they taught you, and there wasn't a great interest in your future" (Interview 245). "I feel that I was wasted from a social point of view in that I had the capacities that were not used, because [the] opportunity to develop them was not there," complained the son of a Lancashire packer. "But I don't feel sore about it or anything like that. I don't feel any aggrieved. It's just because it's the way society [was]. There's a lot of others the same as myself," he noted, adding that he tried to catch up by studying with the WEA and the Marxist National Council of Labour Colleges (Interview 108).

At the same time, in every one of the six class strata, the discontented were outnumbered by those who either had no complaints or were sorry only that they had not invested more effort in their own education. Granted, some of these people regretted nothing only in the sense that Edith Piaf regretted nothing: they accepted a rough schooling as part and parcel of a hard life, because they neither knew nor expected anything better. The daughter of a Durham joiner could feel no bitterness about her limited schooling because "nobody seemed to go in for education in those days" (Interview 281). Some compensated by educating themselves: "I've managed without it," said a Lancashire ironfitter's son who hated his Catholic school, "I've been a great reader" (Interview 55).

On the other hand, many expressed regrets precisely because they enjoyed their schooling and were sorry that they did not enjoy more of it: "I think it's one of the finest things out, education" (Interview 177); "The best years of your life, if you did but know it" (Interview 168); "I think it's the happiest time we ever had …. I mean a good sporting teacher and you're at home" (Interview 356). The son of an Essex silk mill laborer praised his headmaster as "a very, very artistic cultured gentleman" who whetted his appetite for a true liberal education. He never had an opportunity to continue in school, but "I'd always been very much interested in … well, what little smattering you got at an elementary school … of cultural things, you know"—meaning poetry and ancient Greek history (Interview 14). In a backhanded way, the stepson of an East End crane driver acknowledged his intellectual debt to the Board school teacher who told him, "'You'll have to do some homework, young man, there's some good in you.' And I never forgot those words. I thought to myself, well, that's the first time any teacher ever said that to me" (Interview 417).

Working-class Catholics stand out as more critical of their schooling than Anglicans or Dissenters. They gave their schools and teachers a much lower positive rating, were much more likely to complain about corporal punishment, reported lower parental interest in education, were less likely to see any benefit in their education, were far more prone to regret the quality of their schooling, and were much happier to leave school. Alice Foley would eventually find an outlet for her frustrated intellectual energies in the WEA, after a "perfunctory and uninspiring" Catholic schooling:

History, that might have been exciting, began with the Roman Conquest and seemed to end mysteriously with the Reformation. Frequently I ... tried to sort out the strange doings of early English Kings and Queens, so remote from everyday existence. Dictation and composition were more to my liking, especially poetry readings, but our young minds and spirits were rarely ever stirred or fertilised by the wonder and splendour of our great literary inheritance.[135]

Growing up in a Catholic crofting family in the Grampians, Anne Kynoch (b. 1913) attended first a non-Catholic school and then a Catholic school. She clearly preferred the former for its intellectual freedom, incarnated in a homely piece of furniture:

Nothing has ever given me a greater thrill than the old school bookcase did. From the first day I was its slave. Even now I cannot think of it as a glass-fronted cupboard in a country school, some half-dozen shelves stacked with an odd collection of volumes, many bearing a record of fingerprints unwittingly left by generations of careless scholars. To me it was The Library, a silver fountain, a source of wonder from which indescribable satisfactions poured, the gateway to a kingdom of unending pageantry.

After that, however, Catholic school was "a prison and hell for me." She felt insulted by the low academic standards, the history lessons grossly slanted in favor of Mary Stuart ("the blackmail of hate"), the time wasted on saints' lives and catechism, her teacher's sadistic bouts of caning ("which gave her great sensual pleasure"), and above all the restrictions on library privileges:

How I longed for the old bookcase! ... Children are not a homogeneous mass equal in background, intelligence, or spiritual leanings but individuals, and thoughtless, unwarranted trespass on young minds is evil. ... Despite being reverent and submissive there was still an intense longing to select my own reading, a longing that could not be quenched or denied. A deep-rooted love of freedom early implanted, for ever stirred. Something inside me called "freedom" and it attracted me.[136]

Ultimately, how reliable are these recollections of experiences long past? Robert Roberts once warned oral historians that pensioners, interviewed in the 1960s, were liable to see "the Edwardian era through a golden haze."[137] One could, however, just as legitimately argue that memories can grow sour with age: biographers have discovered that Cyril Connolly and George Orwell greatly exaggerated the evils of their old school.[138] Against both those objections, Paul Thompson cites a test that revealed that, when Americans were asked to recall school experiences that particularly interested them, there was no loss of accuracy over fifty years. Oral history, as Thompson notes, is much better at recording attitudes than "facts," and here we are concerned chiefly with attitudes.[139]

True, attitudes toward education can change over a lifetime. One way of taking that into account is to do what Thompson and Vigne did: ask some questions about childhood responses to school (Tables 5.4, p. 150, 5.5, p. 151, and 5.7, p. 173) and some about present-day opinions (Table 5.11, p. 183). The interviewees generally seem to have appreciated that distinction, since they gave very different answers to each set of questions. While many working people regretted (as adults) their lack of educational opportunities, fewer recalled that (as children) they disliked their schools or their teachers. Far from growing nostalgic with age, the interviewees seem to have become more aware and critical of their disadvantages. A slum child in 1910 would probably accept the existing social order since he knew nothing else, but by the end of his life, having witnessed the creation of the welfare state and the scholarship ladder, he was more likely to see the inadequacies of his own education. Many interviewees who were happy to leave school at thirteen or fourteen later came to regret it. "I would now ... like to have been a bit better educated," said a London servant woman, "but as it was in those days one had to take it as it came. One was satisfied" (Interview 53).

I would not argue with those who say that these people should have been dissatisfied with their education—but the fact remains that most of them were not. One may well wonder whether children living in poverty today, in Britain or the United States, would give their schools such high marks. Most late Victorian and Edwardian schools did a fair job of teaching the basics, and often something more than the basics. They succeeded in maintaining discipline, albeit via the cane. Granted, most of us would have felt stifled in an old Board school classroom, but we should avoid projecting our own needs and demands on past generations. My intention is not to suggest that these schools provided a wholly adequate education. It is to break our habit of viewing them through the dark glass of *Hard Times*.

Chapter Six **Cultural Literacy in the Classic Slum**

When German autodidact Carl Moritz visited England in 1782, he was impressed by one especially striking contrast between the two cultures. At home German authors were rarely read outside the educated classes, but "It is plain beyond all comparison that ... the common people of England read their English authors!" His landlady, a tailor's widow, enjoyed Milton: her late husband fell in love with her because she read him aloud so well. "This single example would mean nothing by itself," wrote Moritz, "but I have spoken with more of the common people, all of whom know their English authors and have read some of their works. This improves the lower classes and brings them nearer the higher, so that there are few subjects of general conversation among the latter on which the workers are not able to form an opinion." The laboring classes took advantage of the British Museum and the broad availability of cheap literature. Secondhand dealers sold *The Vicar of Wakefield* for 6d. and Shakespeare for 1d. or ½d. Circulating libraries advertised all the standard English authors, as well as translations of French, Spanish, Italian, and German novels. Consequently, "The commonest man expresses himself in the proper phrases and anyone who writes a book at least writes correctly, even if the matter is poor." As Moritz concluded with some astonishment, "Good style seems to have spread all over England."[1]

From the beginnings of industrialization, the British working class enjoyed a reputation for self-education. That demand made for the success of *Chambers's Edinburgh Journal,* a compendium of "useful knowledge": what we now call "cultural literacy." It offered (for instance) some remarkably sophisticated literary discussions, turning to Homer, Herodotus, Livy, Tacitus, Petrarch, Boccaccio, Ariosto, Tasso, Chaucer, and Defoe. The first issue (4 February 1832) sold 25,000 copies, all in Scotland; nationwide circulation would peak at 87,000 in 1844.[2] *Chambers's Journal* was followed by several successful series of cheap educational texts: Chambers's Information for the People (begun 1833), Chambers's Educational Course (1835), and the twenty-volume Chambers's Miscellany of Useful and Entertaining Tracts. Robert Chambers's *History of the English Language and Literature* and his *Cyclopaedia of English Literature* (1844) were, respectively, the first history and annotated anthology of English literature aimed at a popular audience. *Chambers's Encyclopaedia* (ten volumes, completed 1868) was the crowning achievement, offering more and shorter entries than earlier encyclopedias and at a cheaper price.

While it is difficult to generate a socioeconomic profile of the readers of *Chambers's Journal*, scattered evidence suggests that they were largely working-class. In its early years a bookseller reported its popularity among country milk-boys. The editors claimed that they sold eighty-four copies weekly to a cotton mill near Glasgow, and mentioned letters received from "a mechanician, assistant draper, bootmaker, tailor, coal miner, farmer, weaver, millhand."[3] In the 1870s it was still among the most frequently borrowed magazines at a Newcastle workingmen's club.[4] In 1836 a Banff clergyman had noted that the journal was often bought by local farm laborers and artisans, and perceptively explained why that audience was at last ready for it. The advance of capitalism and technology "makes every profession more difficult of acquisition, furnishes new occupation for ingenuity, new aims for mental activity, new subjects of emulation." All that had called into existence "new desires, new ideas, new sources of excitement," and an unprecedented popular demand for information: "Newspapers are circulated as long as the texture of the paper holds together, or its colour can be distinguished from that of the printer's ink." Banff, a town of less than 4,000 inhabitants, could therefore support at least four church and chapel libraries as well as a tradesmen's library, all open to the working classes for free or a nominal subscription. Recent political controversies over the Reform Act, the New Poor Law, and labor unrest had excited public interest not only in politics, but in all kinds of practical knowledge, "there being few political questions that do not, at least indirectly, excite a curiosity, and lead to enquiries, touching a variety of extrinsic subjects in history, geography, statistics, arts, commerce, &c. A man who sets up for a politician finds occasion to learn a great many things besides politics." Full participation in the political and social life of a modern society was impossible without the "useful knowledge" served up by *Chambers's Journal*.[5]

Well into the twentieth century, radicals (Thomas Cooper, Alexander Bethune, W. E. Adams, G. J. Holyoake) and self-improvers testified to the value of the *Journal* and other Chambers publications.[6] Chartists and Owenite socialists relied on *Chambers'* for scientific information.[7] As late as the First World War, a Manchester boy could find an epiphany in an old volume of the *Journal* rescued from a rubbish bin: "It was dog-eared and pages were missing but never before had I seen and held such a volume of reading matter and it provided months of utmost delight and interest. It was my introduction to life through the written word. The sciences, philosophy, religions, politics, literature, poetry, much of it far beyond my understanding."[8]

John Cassell, a Manchester millworker and carpenter's apprentice turned entrepreneur, matched the Chambers brothers' achievement with his *Popular Educator*, published in penny weekly parts from 1852 to 1854. Early Labour politicians (Keir Hardie,[9] Ramsay MacDonald,[10] John Wilson,[11] Robert Smillie[12]) and countless other workingmen[13] used it to teach themselves mathematics, science, English literature, modern languages, Greek, and Latin. Cassell's students included two eminent proletarian lexicographers, Joseph Wright and James Murray, who respectively became editors of *The English Dialect Dictionary* and *The Oxford English Dictionary*.[14]

All the impressionistic evidence suggests that, fertilized by such publications, autodidact culture flourished in the years leading up to the First World War. Frank Goss (b. 1896) remembered that time as a golden era for men like his father, a pianomaker and activist for the Marxist Social Democratic Federation. The proliferation of public libraries, the high tide of the Victorian ethic of mutual improvement, and the lack of other distractions (the cinema, radio, television) were all contributing factors; but two other developments in particular made

> reading for the masses an exciting interest probably to a greater degree than it had ever been before or is likely to be in the future. One was the tremendous increase in literacy arising from the various Education Acts of that period, and the publication of cheaper books and pamphlets about every subject under the sun; and the second was the bursting out of scientific thinking on subjects which previously had been accepted as inexplicable mysteries. Future history may record this period and the early years of the twentieth century as the age of reading for pleasure and enlightenment. Later on reading was to become an escape from monotony or an occupation undertaken to acquire specialised knowledge which might prove useful to one's business or career. There was little thought, by most of these readers of my father's time, that the knowledge acquired would qualify them to get a better job, more money, or a higher social status; like a child's discovery of the new and exciting world which being able to read opens up, these new literates discovered a world of infinite depth and scope beyond their dreams, a world where, previously, talking had been the only medium of exchanging ideas.
>
> My father read everything he could lay his hands on: history, geography, science, economics, poetry, fiction, drama, and enjoyed his hobby purely from the mental excitement he gathered in the assimilation of knowledge, perhaps sometimes confused, sometimes not adequately digested but always broadening his outlook and developing his personality.[15]

In 1906 *Pearson's Weekly* published "How I Got On," a series of mini-autobiographies by twenty-six new Labour MPs. Their prime emphasis was not on economic or professional advancement: rather, all twenty-six discussed their education and/or their reading experiences. They too hailed "the cheapening of good and useful literature" in their lifetimes, and described a lifelong effort to read "everything I could lay my hands on."[16]

Sheffield 1918

But how typical were such working people, and how much did they know? What of the overwhelming majority who never wrote memoirs, never engaged in any serious political agitation, never became a government or trade union official? Unfortunately, we cannot assess levels of cultural literacy with any precision before the First World War. The testimony we have from Moritz and others is sketchy and subjective. We have only a rough sense of Victorian levels of participation in adult education. We have statistics of literacy, but none for the actual readership or name recognition of particular authors. We can say something about the reading of "working-class intellectuals," but even if we could define such a slippery term, we could not know how many intellectuals there were in the working class. In fact we can say very little about working-class cultural literacy until 1918, when a remarkable survey was carried out in Sheffield. The city had a long tradition of independent working-class education. The Sheffield People's College, founded in 1842, was governed democratically by its students: in 1849 the president was a shoemaker. The College taught geography, history, modern languages, Latin, Greek, science, and philosophy, and students were encouraged to discuss politics.[17] Thanks to the People's College, observed one radical artisan, "There is a peculiarity in the town of Sheffield above all others that I have noticed: in that town, all classes of labourers dare to speak out the truth that is within them, ay, and labour while they think."[18]

The 1918 survey was organized by Arnold Freeman, son of a tobacco importer, warden and founder of the Sheffield Educational Settlement. His investigators interviewed and assessed 816 adult manual workers, a random sample representative in terms of sex, age, and income strata within the working class. They were asked to identify local government officials, landmarks in English history such as the Battle of Hastings and the Industrial Revolution, and a long list of important artists, writers, and scientists from the past and present. This survey gives us a sense of what working people read and (equally important for a history of audiences) what they knew.

Based on the answers received, the investigators sorted their subjects into three categories: 20 to 26 percent were judged intellectually "well-equipped," 67 to 73 percent were "inadequately-equipped," 5 to 8 percent were "mal-equipped." Freeman was trying to separate out the working-class intelligentsia, the more-or-less respectable but unphilosophical masses, and what would today be called the "underclass." (We will simply designate them Intellectuals, Respectables, and Underclass.) As might be expected, his attempts to define these three species were subjective and sometimes hilarious. The "mal-equipped" were "unemployable," "rotters," "wastrels," "Yahoos," and in some cases "not all there." The whole survey might be written off as bourgeois prejudices masquerading as social science, but when it turns to the "well-equipped," the definitions become more helpful. Investigators were instructed that "A worker in this class would read good literature; have an active and well-informed interest in politics; be keen on Trade Union, Co-operative Society, Church or Socialist Club; live in a really pleasant home; understand the value of education; show signs of aesthetic sense; have elevated 'root desires'; make a good Tutorial Class Student or WEA worker."[19] Though most of the 816 completed questionnaires have been lost, fifty-six were reproduced and another 190 summarized in Freeman's published report. They convey a more specific sense of cultural activities and levels of knowledge among Sheffield working people, without demanding that we accept Freeman's arbitrary classifications. The following sums up eight men from the Intellectual group:

1. Private in an infantry regiment, formerly a skilled painter, age eighteen. Spends evenings painting, reading, working on model airplanes, attending public lectures at the university. Has attended art school, visits Mappin Art Gallery frequently and Ruskin Museum sometimes, particularly admires Turner. Has almost never visited any other town, but knows Sheffield local politics fairly well. Enjoys orchestral and choral concerts. Patronizes Free Library. Has read *The Pickwick Papers, The Old Curiosity Shop, David Copperfield,* Bulwer Lytton, Ballantyne, Henty, *Robinson Crusoe, Quentin Durward, Ivanhoe, Waverley, Kidnapped, Treasure Island,* and *Two Years Before the Mast,* as well as the travels of David Livingstone, Fridtjof Nansen, Matthew Peary, and Scott of the Antarctic.

2. Skilled engineer, age twenty-two. Takes singing lessons, performs individually and in a choir, frequent concertgoer. Occasionally visits art galleries and museums. Knows Bible well, but has only rarely seen Shakespeare performed. Has read some Dickens and lesser writers, borrows light literature from library.

3. Engine tenter, age twenty-seven. Broad knowledge of local politics and recent economic history but knows little about other towns. Supports Labour Party, active in National Union of General Workers and Co-operative movement. Often attends operas (*Tales of Hoffmann, Madame Butterfly, Carmen, Il Trovatore,* Gilbert and Sullivan) and concerts. Visits museums and art galleries about twice a year. Methodically building up a personal library following the guidelines of Arnold Bennett's *Literary Taste.* Has read the Bible, Shakespeare (*The Merchant of Venice, Julius Caesar, The Tempest, Much Ado About Nothing*), Pope, Tennyson, Masefield, *Dr. Jekyll and Mr. Hyde,* Emerson, William Morris, most of Ruskin, Dickens (*Nicholas Nickleby, David Copperfield, Oliver Twist, A Tale of Two Cities, The Old Curiosity Shop, A Christmas Carol*), *The Cloister and the Hearth,* G. K. Chesterton, Bernard Shaw (*Major Barbara, John Bull's Other Island, The Doctor's Dilemma, Man and Superman, The Shewing Up of Blanco Posnet, The Devil's Disciple, You Never Can Tell, Socialism and Superior Brains, Fabian Essays, An Unsocial Socialist, The Irrational Knot*), John Galsworthy, about a dozen books by H. G. Wells and perhaps twenty by Bennett, Sidney and Beatrice Webb's *Industrial Democracy* and other books on trade unionism, Sir Oliver Lodge, Edward Carpenter's *Towards Democracy* and *The Intermediate Sex,* J. A. Hobson

and Alfred Marshall on economics, and Plato's *Republic*. Attends WEA Tutorial Class and university lectures, and has taken classes in theology, logic, and botany.

4. Munitions worker and ex-porter, age twenty-eight. Thoroughly respectable but has read little beyond a few Dickens novels and the newspaper.
5. Grinder, age thirty-three. Attends opera and concerts at every opportunity, superb amateur pianist. Sometimes goes to museums, galleries, and the theater. Has read a few Shakespeare plays.
6. Fitter, age thirty-five. Seems to have read little but the Bible and few novels: he enjoyed *Ivanhoe* and Ouida's *Under Two Flags*.
7. Gasworks engineer, age forty-five. Interested in local politics, good knowledge of history. Has read some Shakespeare, Dickens, Ruskin, and Stevenson as well as the Bible, but little else in the way of serious literature. Occasionally visits the theater.
8. Gas stoker, age sixty. Thorough knowledge of local politics and fair knowledge of history. Owns only a Bible and a few other books, occasionally borrows from the public library a volume on social issues or history.

Of the fourteen women in the Intellectual group, perhaps five had serious intellectual interests:

1. Munitions worker, age eighteen. Attends WEA lectures and a settlement house social study circle. Has read Seebohm Rowntree's *Poverty* and a basic economics textbook as well as *Little Women*. Enjoys opera, visited the Weston Park Museum, but never uses the public library.
2. Machinist in a shell factory, age twenty-four. Attended a WEA tutorial class in economics, active in the Co-operative movement. Often visits art galleries, loves concerts and sacred music. Has read Shakespeare, Burns, Keats, Scott, Tennyson, Dickens, *Vanity Fair*, *The Rubiyat of Omar Khayyam*, Ella Wheeler Wilcox, biography, and history.
3. Machine file cutter, age twenty-five. Occasionally goes to art galleries, the theater, and the opera. Attended a Girls' Club study circle on economics. Has read *The Old Curiosity Shop*, *Innocents Abroad*, *The Scarlet Pimpernel*, and the Bible.
4. Housewife, age twenty-eight. Occasionally visits an art gallery or the public library. Has read *David Copperfield*, *The Old Curiosity Shop*, *Lorna Doone*, Louisa May Alcott, and the travels of Livingstone and Darwin.
5. Cutlery worker, age seventy-two. Knows history and local politics well, active in trade unions, sang in chapel choirs. Fond of Longfellow, Stevenson, Ruskin, William Morris, and Charles Dickens.

The nine other women in this category seem to have read almost nothing above the level of Gene Stratton Porter.[20] The investigators apparently counted as "well-equipped" some respondents who were respectable and moral but devoid of any intellectual interests. These full questionnaires, along with the larger number of summarized questionnaires, suggest that about one-fifth of the men and two-fifths of the women that Freeman judged "well-equipped" really belonged in the "inadequately-equipped" category. That adjustment leaves roughly one out of six workers—one in five men and one in eight women—in the working-class intelligentsia, with cultural backgrounds and interests similar to those listed above.

A few years earlier Florence Bell had conducted her own investigation of working-class reading in Middlesbrough, and arrived at similar conclusions. More than 25 percent of workingmen read books and newspapers, almost half only the papers, a quarter nothing at all. As in Sheffield, women tended to read less than men.[21] In fact, Lady Bell was surprised to find so many women above age fifty (and some who were younger) who not only could not read, but were almost glad to have never learned. "Nearly all women of the working-classes have a feeling that it is wrong to sit down with a book."[22]

The Sheffield survey also asked a series of identification questions. Table 6.1 (p. 194) counts correct answers in the surviving questionnaires: eight male and fourteen female Intellectuals, nine male and twelve female Respectables, seven men and six women in the Underclass.

The survey revealed a striking ignorance of working-class history. Only two respondents correctly identified Robert Owen, two the Chartists, none at all Francis Place, though seven (all Intellectuals) knew of Sidney Webb. By 1918 the working classes were evidently losing their Victorian passion for Shakespeare: his totals include anyone who could name one of his plays. (Only three respondents could name as many as six.) Anyone who identified Edison as an inventor was counted correct, though several mistakenly credited the telephone to him. The fact that the Ruskin Museum and Edward Carpenter were two of Sheffield's leading cultural institutions undoubtedly contributed to their high scores. But Ruskin also clearly had a national following; and at a Norwich bookshop with a working-class clientele, Carpenter's *Civilisation: Its Cause and Cure* was one of the most frequently requested books.[23] Of course, not everyone who recognized the name of an author had read him, but six or seven of the eight Intellectual men had read Dickens.

The name of Darwin was widely recognized, even by two of seven men in the Underclass. How well his work was understood is another matter. For one collier among the Respectables, he was vaguely associated with "the missing link."[24] Flora Thompson wrote that the postmistress was the only inhabitant of her Oxfordshire village who had read *The Origin of Species*, but the locals seem to have appreciated a Negro Minstrel number that assumed at least a superficial familiarity with evolutionary theory:

A friend of Darwin's came to me,
A million years ago said he
You had a tail and no great toe.
I answered him, "That may be so,
But I've one now, I'll let you know—
G-r-r-r-r-r out!"[25]

Table 6.1: Name Recognition in Working-Class Sheffield, 1918

	Intellectuals		Respectables		Underclass	
	8 Men	14 Women	9 Men	12 Women	7 Men	6 Women
Battle of Hastings	3	3	2	1	1	1
Magna Carta	5	3	3	1	0	1
French Revolution	5	4	2	0	0	0
Industrial Revolution	8	3	0	0	1	1
1832 Reform Act	5	2	1	0	1	0
Evolution	7	2	2	1	0	0
Aristotle	5	3	3	0	1	0
Beethoven	5	3	2	1	0	0
Arnold Bennett	3	2	0	0	0	0
Edward Carpenter	6	3	1	1	0	0
G. K. Chesterton	6	1	2	0	0	0
Columbus	8	5	4	1	1	2
Oliver Cromwell	7	4	4	0	0	0
Dante	1	0	1	0	0	0
Darwin	7	3	5	1	2	0
Dickens	7	9	4	4	1	2
Edison	8	4	6	1	3	1
Gladstone	5	5	4	1	2	0
Goethe	4	0	1	0	0	0
Haeckel	3	1	1	0	0	0
Huxley	5	2	2	0	0	0
Sir Oliver Lodge	6	1	3	0	0	0
Maeterlinck	2	0	0	0	0	0
Milton	7	5	2	2	1	1
William Morris	4	3	0	1	0	0
Napoleon	6	4	3	2	1	1
Sir Isaac Newton	6	2	2	0	1	0
Plato	3	1	2	0	0	0
Raphael	2	3	1	0	0	0
Ruskin	7	5	1	1	1	0
Bernard Shaw	6	2	3	1	0	0
Shakespeare	7	6	4	2	0	0
Herbert Spencer	3	0	1	0	0	0
R. L. Stevenson	5	2	1	1	1	0
Sir Arthur Sullivan	4	4	3	1	1	0
Tolstoy	5	2	2	1	0	0
Turner	3	1	1	0	0	0
Virgil	1	0	0	0	0	0
Watt	6	3	2	0	1	1
H. G. Wells	6	2	2	1	0	0
Wolsey	7	3	2	1	0	0

Wilfred Wellock (b. 1879) claimed that many of his fellow Lancashire millworkers could discuss *The Origin of Species*.[26] Whether they had actually read it is unclear. One memoir recalled a Lancashire ironmoulder of the 1890s who attempted to explain the origin of language in Darwinian terms, as a set of linguistic conventions agreed upon by groups of monkeys:

> Terrific arguments used to spring up among working people at the mention of Darwin's name. Nobody had read any of his books, nobody knew anything about the origin of species. But that was all the better. If you only have a small amount of exact knowledge, and if you are a truthful sort of person, your knowledge limits your arguments. But when you know nothing at all you can argue north, south, east, and west, just as your fancy takes you.[27]

The high level of recognition for John Milton might have been matched by other standard poets, which the Board schools had taught to a generation of children by 1918. The labor movement had also done much to popularize poetry. Chris Waters found that in nine socialist songbooks published between 1888 and 1912, 15 percent of the songs were by canonical poets such as Whitman, Blake, Burns, Lowell, and Shelley. Lowell's "True Freedom" appeared in all nine, Shelley's "Men of England" in six.[28] In 1955 Manny Shinwell—who read all of Palgrave's *Golden Treasury* to his children, and had consoled himself in prison with Keats and Tennyson—regretted that that poetic heritage had been surrendered to the cinema and radio: "In the early days of the [socialist] movement it was a common practice of speakers to recite poetry. Some of our well-known propagandists like W. C. Anderson, Dick Wallhead, Russell Williams and even the severely practical Philip Snowden rarely wound up a speech without some snatches of poetry. I remember a number of popular speakers whose orations consisted entirely of poetic excerpts which their audiences loved."[29]

Wilfred Pickles (b. 1904), a bricklayer turned radio announcer, proved that poetry could find a mass audience. While Harold Acton was declaiming *The Waste Land* through a megaphone from his Oxford balcony, Pickles—with as much éclat and perhaps a more receptive audience—was reciting *A Shropshire Lad* to laborers working on a sewer fifteen feet underground. Though BBC staff warned him it would never play on the Light Programme, in 1949 Pickles began broadcasting poetry on his show *The Pleasure's Mine*, which won a huge response from "managers, mechanics, miners and housewives. ... We gave them Shakespeare, Milton, Kipling, Chesterton, Wordsworth, Yeats, Hardy, Francis Thompson," as well the proletarian poets of Lancashire, Ammon Wrigley and Samuel Laycock. Its success "convinced me that the BBC had made a big mistake in making poetry the preserve of the 'arty' clique who dwell in a never-never world sealed off from everyone else."[30] Actually, the show's high ratings undoubtedly owed a lot to Pickles's own stupendous popularity. In 1941 only 15.4 percent of working-class listeners felt "Enthusiastic" or "Favourable" toward poetry broadcasts, compared with 28.2 percent of the middle classes and 30.9 percent of the well-to-do. Still, those figures translated into a potential audience of 2 million poetry fans, half of them working-class.[31]

Wagner and Hoot Gibson

The relatively high recognition of Beethoven is hardly surprising. Sheffield steelworkers participated widely in choirs and orchestras, many of them supported by their company directors.[32] A working-class culture of classical music had long flourished in the same regions and trades where the autodidact tradition was strong, notably among Welsh miners and Lancashire weavers. James Leach, a weaver born near Rochdale in 1762, became a notable (though untrained) composer of hymns. Weaver-poets like Joseph Hodgson (b. 1783) published their songs as broadsides.[33] William Millington, a millwright-bassoonist, compiled a collective biography of minor Lancashire musical celebrities from the late eighteenth and early nineteenth centuries, including thirty-four handloom weavers, eight colliers, seven carpenters, five powerloom weavers, five metalworkers, four shoemakers, four engineers, three spinners, three warpers, two coopers, two crofters, a butcher, pavior, tailor, gardener, coal carter, turner, laundryman, boatbuilder, blacksmith, printer, and gravestone letterer.[34]

For most working people, only the Sunday schools offered opportunities for serious musical education, performance, and composition, via hymns and oratorios.[35] Poverty virtually barred John Shinn (b. 1837) from formal schooling, but his father, a London cabinetmaker, somehow acquired a violin and was given an old piano to store. John bought cheap instruction manuals and taught himself to play both. Starting at age ten he had to work with his father six days a week from 7 a.m. to 8 p.m., yet he found time to practice in the workshop after hours by candlelight. He received his first formal musical education in a singing class at Sunday school, where he was allowed to practice once a week on a small organ with only four stops. Eventually he was invited to play at evening services. His instructor, the chapel organist, introduced him to the London Sacred Harmonic Society at Exeter Hall: there, and later with the Polyhymnion Choir, he received his first really rigorous vocal training. At twenty-six he was appointed church organist at St. Jude's Whitechapel at £25 a year, and began to consider abandoning the cabinet trade. He supplemented his earnings by taking on pupils, opening a small and eventually profitable music shop on Holloway Road, and composing music for Sunday schools, which sold quite well. At fifty-two he passed the examinations for a Mus. Bac. from Cambridge University. In his eighties he began writing a Lent Cantata, until failing eyesight forced him to give it up.[36]

Light classical music was also widely broadcast by thousands of string and brass bands. German string bands of twelve to fourteen players strolled from town to town playing Strauss, Offenbach, and Gilbert and Sullivan. One Suffolk village boy recalled that he memorized their tunes and played them on his father's organ: he went on to become a church organist himself.[37] Military bands did not play with much expression or imagination, as one performer admitted, but the repertoire could be impressive: *Lohengrin, Aida,* the *Peer Gynt Suite,* Suppé, Rossini, Berlioz, Mozart, Mendelssohn, Beethoven, Brahms, Weber, Chopin's "Polonaise," the *William Tell* Overture, the Soldiers' Chorus from *Faust,* and the *1812 Overture.*[38]

One of the most vital expressions of working-class culture was the brass band movement. Originating in the early nineteenth century, it was organized mainly by workingmen, though many bands were sponsored by employers. In 1913 the *British Bandsman* reported on 230 bands in Yorkshire and ninety in Durham in the early twentieth century: extrapolating those figures yields a minimum of 2,600 bands throughout Britain, or one band for every 15,500 people. Concentrated in the smaller industrial towns and coalmining regions, they performed in parks, at seaside resorts, and at massively attended competitions. At first the repertoire drew heavily on Italian opera, giving way to more classical and romantic symphony pieces in the twentieth century, with a leavening of musical comedy and Gilbert and Sullivan.[39]

The Thompson–Vigne interviews reveal that, around the turn of the century, there was some kind of family musical activity in 86 percent of all working-class homes: Sunday singalongs, playing a violin or accordion, banging away at a piano or harmonium (with or without lessons), playing gramphones, singing in a choir, attending the opera or a band concert. "We larked about and sang in the kitchen because we had no other way in which to express ourselves, and we seemed always to quarrel unless we sang," recalled boilermaker's daughter Marjory Todd (b. 1906). She had one brother who learned soprano solos from the *Messiah* before his voice broke, another who took piano lessons from a cinema accompanist. The family's musical library was typical:

> *Item:* a Star Folio volume of operatic overtures arranged for the piano, including *Tannhäuser, Zampa, Martha, Faust, The Bohemian Girl* and so on.
> *Item:* some volumes of music issued in fortnightly parts by Newnes, including waltzes by Waldteufel, *Songs Without Words* by Mendelssohn, a sentimental ballad or two "as sung by Dame Clara Butt", *Whisper and I Shall Hear* and *Ora pro Nobis* and arias from *I Pagliacci* and *Cavalleria Rusticana.*
> *Item:* The full score of *The Mikado,* which we knew by heart.
> *Item:* a copy of the *Pink Lady Waltz,* a favourite of 1917–18, bought by my father when he was drunk.

Marjory Todd offered that list as evidence of cultural impoverishment, but its breadth is fairly impressive. She never attended a concert until she went to London and heard Moiseiwitsch perform sonatas by Beethoven: "I felt as though I had been drugged. I walked all the way back to the East End, and I am only surprised that I was not run over." Just possibly, singing in the kitchen prepared her for that experience.[40]

From the later nineteenth century, philanthropic efforts would bring music to the masses. In 1878 the South Place Ethical Society began its series of free Sunday evening concerts, supported by voluntary contributions. At about the same time Jesse Collings launched the Birmingham Musical Association, and the Working Men's Concerts were inaugurated in Manchester, with most seats selling for 4d. and an average audience of 3,400. Later, J. M. Dent would persuade Toynbee Hall to sponsor a successful series of Sunday afternoon concerts.[41] While most of these programs were based in cities, E. V. Schuster of New College mobilized his Oxford University Musical Club to offer penny concerts in North Oxfordshire villages. The programs were uncompromising: Purcell, Beethoven, Gluck, Haydn, Mozart, Schumann, Mendelssohn, Strauss, Scarlatti, Lully, John Blow, as well as more contemporary work by Dvořák, Stanford, and Saint-Saëns. Schubert appealed the most to these audiences, particularly his Trio in B Flat for Piano, Violin, and Violoncello. Even in small villages the performances would attract fifty to 150 concertgoers, mostly working people, more from the artisan classes than tenant farmers or poor laborers. As a WEA class leader reported in 1909,

> out of a few cottage doors there float in the evening, when work is done, strains by Handel or Bach—so well indeed as a harmonium or an old piano and fingers not yet perfect in the art can send them forth. Horses have been groomed to a whistled rendering of Schubert's "Who is Sylvia?" Best of all, it is quite certain that the audience is getting more and more able to enjoy difficult music. Brahms, at first unintelligible, is getting to be liked, if not yet altogether understood.[42]

The Welsh working class, of course, boasted the strongest tradition of popular music, as well as the foundryman-composer Joseph Parry. Miners commonly named their children after classical composers, explained Walter Haydn Davies (b. 1903): "In fact, in one family there was a Handel, Haydn, Elgar, Verdi, Joseph Parry, Caradog, Mendy (short for Mendelssohn) and an unforgettable Billy Bach, together with an only daughter Rossini (called Rosie for short)."[43] The Second World War forced the suspension of many of these activities, but even at the end of the conflict, Wales still had 104 choral societies, sixty-five music clubs, twelve gramophone societies, thirty-five school music festivals, four professional and ten amateur chamber music groups, three major orchestras, four theater orchestras, forty-eight semi-professional and amateur orchestras, and eighty-three brass bands.[44]

Perhaps it was in the nature of mining communities to develop great musical traditions, and not only in South Wales. While Jennie Lee (b. 1904) practiced *Tannhäuser, Il Trovatore*, and *Aida*, her father and other colliers always attended the D'Oyly Carte and Carl Rosa companies when they passed through Cowdenbeath. "Whether it was Gilbert and Sullivan or Verdi, Mozart or Puccini, the companies that came to our mining town to play to mining audiences could depend on a full house."[45] Walk through any North Staffordshire coal town on any evening, wrote Harold Brown (b. 1906), and "You will not pass many houses before you hear a piano being played, someone practising singing exercises, others working hard at some brass instrument preparing for contest day." The churches and chapels would be lit up, rehearsing for Sunday services or some musical competition. Down in the pits, a collier-cellist explained that "It makes it possible for one to express finer feelings and I think that the cello is a beautiful instrument for one to display these inner, intimate feelings. ... When you are doubled up here for seven hours a day with nothing but darkness and nasty smells, you can go home, get out your instrument, close your eyes and enter another world with music." For miners, wrote Brown, music "is their only means of balance. Without ... some means of expression..., they would go mad working as they do under such pressure and under such horrible conditions." And perhaps they found a political message in classical music as well. After the failure of the 1921 strike, one miner-choirman quoted from Handel's *Israel in Egypt*: "They oppressed them with burdens and made them serve with rigour."[46]

Great music as much as great literature could stir up unrest among the working classes, even when it conveyed no overt political message. Millworker James Whittaker (b. 1906) was the son of a cooper and washerwoman, and an activist in the Labour League of Youth. He traced his ideals and his discontents to the days when he would dodge school to attend organ recitals at Liverpool's St. George's Hall:

> After most recitals I came away with my head in a whirl, and my emotions and feelings in a state of tumultuous rebellion. The music used to get hold of me and carry me away and away into a realm which defies description: it was a realm of pure feeling, not of sights or sounds. ...
>
> My soul clamoured for solid brightness, enduring, uplifting, edifying, real and splendid. I went down, engulfed completely, before music that had strength in it, and I liked to feel myself upborne, on an oceanic surge, leaving all the beastly sordidness and muck of the life I knew far behind.

He thrilled to Bach and Beethoven, but Grieg especially spoke to him

> for, under all his music, I constantly felt a weird note running that struck an answering chord in the lostness and desolation within myself. ... Going home from these recitals, up the narrow, squalid length of poverty-ridden Scotland Road and Byrom Street, I used to shiver and feel miserable. The beauty of the hours I had just spent only accentuated the dirt, misery, poverty and cruelty about me.

> Folk who know me to-day ... cannot understand, nor can I make them understand, just what real music, by the masters, meant to a ragged slum kid. I was empty in body and soul when I went to listen to those wonderful compositions, and that music did for me all the things food, comfort, security and beauty would have done had I had them. I was starving in more ways than one at the time.[47]

While many autodidacts looked to Everyman's Library to emancipate themselves, for others music was the high road to a better world.[48] To emphasize "that Socialists were interested in the higher things of life," the Glasgow ILP organized a small orchestra to play classical interludes before its lectures, including a talk by Charles Manners (of the Moody-Manners Opera Company) which attracted an overflow crowd of 7,000.[49] For a Nottingham hosiery worker (b. c. 1910) the people's music proved that

> The working class did have the capacity to be creative. ... They had the ability to enjoy some of the good things of life; I don't mean having culture rammed down their throats, but we loved nothing so much when I was a kid as going to my auntie's and listening to her records ... the *Messiah*, the Nuns' Chorus, the Triumphal March from *Aida*, *Trovatore*. And a lot of people had read Shaw, the pamphlets and the plays, Robert Blatchford, H.G. Wells, Dickens, Thackeray. Ordinary working people, some of them who'd left school at thirteen or fourteen. Above all, they weren't afraid of ideas. We went to see travelling performances of operas; we saw *Carmen* I remember. We had to queue for hours to get a seat in the gallery. There was this hunger for something that was better, you could feel it, it flowed like blood through the people. Now [1978], well, I know all those things still exist, only it's somehow harder for the working class to find them, they're offered so much that's superficial and empty.[50]

Classical music was not always easy to find a half-century earlier. Other than Handel's ubiquitous *Messiah*, hardly anything else was available in the depressed shipyard town of Jarrow after the First World War, only a school excursion to a symphony concert in Newcastle City Hall. Arthur Barton doubted that his Standard Five classmates would take to it, but he was wrong:

> These weren't at all like the plaintive strains that drifted from the Sunday bandstand or the undifferentiated racket Uncle Jim's gramophone made. This was music, adding a new dimension to our poor little street-circumscribed lives. Suddenly it was over, and as we clapped I looked round at the audience, and noticed that except for us they were all posh people—"Done up like ninepenny rabbits" as sharp-eyed Herbert was observing at that very moment. Was such music only for them? I wondered rather uncomfortably, as the doom-laden opening of Beethoven's Fifth silenced us once more.
>
> I searched the faces of my friends. There was at least no boredom anywhere. Their faces were alight and alive and on one—Alf's—a rapture that even a child like me could recognize. Alf, backward reader, potential street sweeper, butt of so many masters' easy sarcasms had escaped us all and entered into his kingdom.

Twenty years later, during the Second World War, Arthur ran into one of those classmates and discovered that they were both on the way to hear Barbirolli conduct.[51]

Manchester, in contrast, offered a thriving musical culture that cut clean across class lines. Walter Greenwood remembered a young man from a Pennine village just twenty miles away who deeply envied him on that count: "Eight theatres in three streets, all number one dates—all on your doorstep. I don't think you realize just what you've got." In fact he did: Greenwood loved Hallé Orchestra concerts and borrowed *The Perfect Wagnerite* from an engineering worker. His father received free opera tickets for displaying playbills in his barber shop, and his mother (a former charwoman and waitress) was a fan of Sir Thomas Beecham ("If I ever came into a fortune I'd give it to Tommy Beecham for all the pleasure I've had").[52]

This was a city where Neville Cardus, whose parents took in washing, could become music critic for the *Guardian*. He could lecture on the songs of Hugo Wolf in a small depressed factory town to a roomful of millworkers: "I have never since spoken to an audience so quick of apprehension, and so absorbed and moved at times." Cardus's training consisted of tonic sol-fa lessons, reading the music reviews of Ernest Newman and James Agate in the *Guardian*, and gorging on all the concerts and operas that the city could offer:

> I cannot imagine that any young man today [1950] will be equal to grasping the astonishing mixed state of excitement and of reverence which young men of those years felt when they knew that Elgar and Strauss and Richter were each and all actually present in their city's midst, and likely to be seen with one's own eyes any day going here or there between the Midland Hotel and Peter Street.[53]

In an important sense Cardus was educated for his career, for opera permeated even the slums of Manchester. There was no piano at home, but his mother sang him to sleep with tunes from *Norma*. Arrangers cannibalized Bellini, Donizetti, and Wagner for the background music to Christmas pantomimes, one of which concluded with the company singing the Hunting Chorus from *Der Freischütz*. "The point," said Cardus, "is that producers of this, the lowest nineteenth-century form of public entertainment, thought the public liked it all, and they did."[54]

By the early twentieth century a taste for classical music could spring from the most barren environments. As an ironworks clerk A. E. Coppard (b. 1878) found "several men in that shop who were music enthusiasts and it was astonishing to me, and deeply moving too, to hear them one day chanting above the uproar of the machinery, of all things the Pilgrims' Chorus from *Tannhäuser*."[55] In the mills of Blackburn weavers rehearsed the *Messiah* and *Elijah* over the roar of the looms.[56] In the worst streets of Sunderland, tough kids heard and appreciated classical records played by the local pawnbroker.[57] Derbyshire millgirl Elsie Gadsby (b. 1912) recalled that her mother, who had "arms like a navvy and a vocabulary to match," bought a Victor gramophone through 1s.-a-week instalments and an astonishing selection of records:

Now up to this time there was never any music in the house, apart from our singing. … Her choice amazed me at first. Strauss's "Blue Danube," "Peer Gynt Suite," "Poet and Peasant Overture," and some of Gilbert and Sullivan's music. No bawdy pub songs, or anything like that.

She would sit there at the side of the table turning the gramophone handle. Then the music would start and a dreamy, wrapt expression would come over her face, and she'd be in another world.[58]

There was nothing extraordinary in a gasworker hearing *Tales of Hoffmann* sung in a proletarian pub on a Saturday night.[59] In 1924, as deputy leader of the House of Commons, former textile worker J. R. Clynes wanted to secure a government subsidy for opera, knowing that it had a following among his constituents.[60]

Given all those influences, it is hardly surprising that someone like C. H. Rolph should end up with an impressive fund of musical knowledge. His father was a solo flautist in the City of London Police Band. The family owned two big volumes of *Star Folios* containing the standard classical pieces: "The names at the page-tops were truly exciting—*Masaniello, Crown Diamonds, Fra Diavolo, Poet and Peasant, Rosamunde, L'Italiana in Algeri, The Caliph of Baghdad, La Gazza Ladra, The Barber of Seville, The Magic Flute, Oberon.*" On the gramophone they could play Caruso, Tetrazzini, *Zampa, William Tell,* and *The Merry Wives of Windsor.* "Never since, among the superb reproductions of modern hi-fi technology or even in any concert hall, have I been so excited and engulfed by the power of music." When his older brother was ditched by a girlfriend, he spent the money he had been saving for marriage on records of all nine Beethoven symphonies.

True, not everyone in working-class communities owned a gramophone, but classical music was literally in the air. Rolph recalls that the milkman would whistle (flawlessly) the entire waltz from Delibes's *Naïla.* Lift operators and street boys whistled tunes from *Carmen*: they had seen Cecil B. DeMille's film of the opera and bought the records.[61] One of the greatest thrills of Rolph's childhood was supplied by the four-piece "orchestra" that accompanied Charlie Chaplin and Westerns at the Putney Bridge Cinema. "The sound of that little ensemble tuning-up when it was about to begin the Overture to *Raymond* or the *William Tell* ballet music has lodged in my memory as more exciting than any music ever written, an ecstasy of anticipation which no performance in the world could have surpassed," he remembered. They "would go straight through the *Rosamunde* Overture, Luigini's *Ballet Egyptien,* or Allan Macbeth's *Love in Idleness* whether it matched the picture or not, with results that were sometimes comic to everyone but me."[62]

"I learnt to whistle the classics" at the cinema was a common refrain in plebeian memoirs.[63] "We got a good knowledge of Beethoven during the cowboy pictures of Tom Mix and W. S. Hart," wrote a London butler's son, who also recalled hearing selections from Elgar, *Carmen,* and *Aida* Sunday evenings at the Regents Park bandstand.[64] As a boy, colliery worker Sid Chaplin was bombarded by classical music every Sunday morning. First he heard cinema accompanists appropriate Wagner (who seemed to serve Emil Jannings and Hoot Gibson equally well), then he walked through the streets of his Durham mining town:

> Each walk was a musical education. All the folk would be sitting outside on crackets or rocking chairs, and the big horns of the gramophones inside would be belting out everything, from Caruso, John McCormack and the great Chaliapin in opera to Dame Clara Butt in Handel's *Messiah* or, along with the grand old songs of the English music hall and such commercial syncopation as Yes, We Have No Bananas and Ain't Gonna Rain No More, snatches of the purest jazz. ... For years I listened to the best without knowing it.[65]

Once the movies acquired soundtracks, studios began churning out biopics for the great composers. In 1945 surveys, many working-class moviegoers reported that they had acquired a new taste for "serious" music from *A Song to Remember* (Chopin), *The Great Mr. Handel*, *Battle for Music* (London Philharmonic Orchestra), and *Song of Russia* (Tchaikovsky), as well as the "Warsaw Concerto" in *Dangerous Moonlight*.[66] Some were introduced to the classics through what we would now dismiss as laughable kitsch. Michael Stapleton, son of an Irish navvy, grew up during the Great Depression in Clapton. The only books at home were some "dull looking old volumes, gathered from goodness knows where," one of which was *Pictures from the World's Great Music*.

> I opened it in the middle, and there was a wonderful picture of a horse, galloping madly across a desolate plain with a naked man tied to its back. Great dark clouds glowered in the distance and steam issued from the horse's nostrils. Under the picture was just one word, *Mazeppa*. This struck me as being a funny name for a horse, even if it was a strange sort of horse. I puzzled over it for a moment, trying to understand why he was running off with that poor man tied to his back without any clothes. I gave it up and turned the page. The next picture I saw was of a man and woman leaning against each other in a dungeon. An Egyptian dungeon, it must be, because it showed you outside the dungeon as well and the buildings were just like the things I saw in the British Museum when I saw the mummified body. The dungeon had a flat roof and there was a woman kneeling on it, wearing Egyptian clothes. The people in the dungeon were wearing nightdresses. The words under the picture made no sense at all. *O Terra, Addio!* What did it mean?

There was no wireless or gramophone at home: "Music was little more to us than hymns, popular songs that other people sang, and the band on Hackney Downs." But there was the public library, where benevolent librarians broke the rules to allow Stapleton into the adult reference room, in spite of his ratty clothes.

The Oxford Companion to Music was brought out, and "I spent the rest of the summer holidays exploring this wonderful new world."[67]

Thus, when the wireless arrived in working-class communities between the wars, it built on an existing familiarity with popular classics. Percy Edwards, a Suffolk ploughmaker who later became a broadcaster himself, described its impact: "The day after the BBC broadcast *The Magic Flute* from Covent Garden in 1923 you'd have thought the Martians had landed there was such excitement."[68] Though some criticized BBC classical programming as elitist, it was lavishly praised in the memoirs of all sorts and conditions of working people. "When I heard the works of Beethoven, Mozart and Tchaikovsky for the first time, I was transported to a realm I had never entered before," recalled a Kimbolton tailor, "and I regretted the wasted years without the 'inarticulate, unfathomable speech' of music."[69] Growing up in Shadwell, Louis Heren regularly listened in to the "Foundations of Music" series. "Later I was taken aback by the sneers at Lord Reith's crusade to improve the quality of listening, and of life itself. No sneers were heard in our house …. I can remember doing homework to Bach and Mozart…, and the first time I was emotionally overwhelmed by Beethoven's Fifth."[70] Music hall star "Wee" Georgie Wood, though barely educated, was a dedicated fan of Beethoven, Mozart, Chopin, and Schubert; and he hailed the BBC for bringing "first-class music, played by great orchestras" to the masses. "They have been given a taste for good music, and have learnt that music which is good is not of necessity music which is 'highbrow' and beyond the comprehension of any but those minds which have been musically educated."[71]

By the outbreak of the Second World War, radio reached 79.1 percent of all homes: 97.4 percent in the upper middle class (where the chief breadwinner earned £10 or more weekly), 92.4 percent in the lower middle class (£4–£10), 84.4 percent in the upper working class (£2 10d.–£4), and a majority of 57.7 percent even in the lower working class (under £2 10d.).[72] A July 1938 survey, which asked listeners what kinds of program they liked, found that working-class demand for classical music, while less than the middle-class, was still considerable (Table 6.2, p. 205). Given that working people outnumbered the middle classes among listeners by about two to one, the respective audiences for grand opera and recitals were roughly equal in absolute numbers. Remarkably, half of all working-class listeners tuned into orchestral music. When the Committee for the Encouragement of Music and the Arts offered its popular factory concerts during the Second World War, it was catering to an audience that already existed. CEMA was so successful that it aroused bureaucratic jealousies in the Entertainments National Service Association (ENSA), which offered lowbrow programs of popular songs and vulgar humor.[74] In 1944 more than 1.5 million people attended a total of 6,140 CEMA concerts, and the majority were held for working-class audiences, including 3,169 at factories, 371 at war-workers' hostels, and forty at camp construction sites.[75] In 1946 the Gallup Poll found 52 percent of the public favored continued government funding of the arts, with only 27 percent opposed.[76]

Table 6.2: Expressed Interest in Radio Programs, 1938 (in percent)[73]

	Middle Class	*Working Class*
Variety	88	97
Theatre or Cinema Organs	74	91
Military Bands	65	77
Musical Comedies	62	77
Dance Music	59	78
Plays	70	69
Light Music	73	61
Brass Bands	43	63
Orchestral Music	62	49
Talks	61	45
Discussions	53	45
Running Commentaries on Cricket	49	48
Serial Plays	32	52
Light Opera and Operetta	47	30
Recitals — Singers	32	29
Running Commentaries on Tennis	34	19
Recitals — Piano	28	14
Grand Opera	27	15
Recitals — Violin	24	12
Serial Readings	12	11
Chamber Music	11	4

Table 6.3: Cultural Interests of Newspaper Readers, 1948 (in percent)

	Daily Herald readers	*All newspaper readers*
Interested in classical music	17	26
Interested in books	40	50
Read books	54	61

Electrician Frank Chapple, who picked up a taste for classical music from his barber's adopted son, militantly defended that perk. Called up for army service in 1943, he religiously attended recitals near his base in Croydon. One evening he was outraged to learn that the concert had been replaced with a "brains trust" featuring the Bishop of Croydon, and he "gave the poor old Bishop a particular grilling over how much he got paid for doing his job."[77]

In 1946 a Mass Observation survey found a 97 percent recognition of the name of Beethoven, even if he was only vaguely associated with music, a level equal with Sherlock Holmes. Allowing for the fact that this sampling was more representative of the whole population, it still represents a dramatic improvement over the 1918 Sheffield survey. (By comparison, about 90 percent knew Bernard Shaw, an impressive three-quarters recognized John Gielgud, and less than half were familiar with Cecil B. DeMille.)[78] A sampling of the audience at a cheap classical concert at Central Hall, Westminster in 1948, featuring Haydn and Mozart on the program, turned up eighteen middle-class and forty-five working-class enthusiasts.[79] That year a survey of *Daily Herald* readers (nearly all manual or clerical workers) produced commensurate results (Table 6.3, p. 205).[80]

These figures suggest that, while there was a substantial working-class audience for Beethoven, British autodidact culture was more literary than musical. That was partly a matter of availability: secondhand bookstalls and Sunday school prizes could be found in the smallest and remotest communities, unlike symphony orchestras. Choir groups commonly used tonic sol-fa musical notation, which had the virtue of simplicity for untrained singers but seriously narrowed the repertory of available sheet music. There was also the hangover of a Puritan tradition which exalted the printed word and frowned upon secular music and art. For Stan Dickens, raised by strict Nonconformists, hearing Sir Henry Wood conduct at Queen's Hall was terrifically stressful. He was told to follow the theme and tried his best, "but it always gave me the slip. On one occasion the strain was such that I had to go to the toilets and be sick." As he put it, he never developed a taste for fine music for the same reason that he never learned to like caviar: "To someone reared on Moody and Sankey, songs from the classic operas and music from Bach and Beethoven were, at the time, unappreciated."[81] This was a culture that produced men like George Tomlinson, Lancashire weaver and minister of education under Attlee. He studied *Hamlet* over his looms, but confessed that he completed his first visit to the National Gallery in five minutes: "I should have done it in three only the floor was slippery." He attributed his insensitivity to his years at the Rishton Wesleyan School, which had only one picture in the building, *The Landing of the Danes*. He also liked to tell the story of two gentlemen who hailed a taxi and said they had a pressing engagement to play chamber music at the BBC. "Well," replied the driver, "walk."[82]

Working-class cultural conservatism also manifested itself in total resistance to modern music, which never enjoyed a place in the brass band repertory. During the Second World War, the Army Educational Corps discovered that lectures on *L'Après-midi d'un faune* wasted everyone's time ("Seen any phones lately?" "What the hell do they look like, these phones?" "Are there any girl phones about?").[83] Instructor Sidney Harrison—concert pianist, composer, and tailor's son—was genuinely eager to make the subject accessible, but even he was hard put to explain serial music to Welsh soldiers trained in tonic sol-fa.[84]

Aristotle and Dr. Stopes

It is significant that twelve respondents to the Sheffield survey (about 20 percent of the total) recognized the name of Aristotle, of which five (including a 72-year-old female trade unionist) identified him as the author of a sex manual. When Roy Porter and Lesley Hall chronicled "the creation of sexual knowledge in Britain," they had difficulty answering a related question: How much of that knowledge was transmitted to a mass audience? What did the working classes know about sex, and where did they read about it?

Popular almanacs of the sixteenth through eighteenth centuries contained advice (or, more often, warnings) about sexual profligacy, abortifacients, aphrodisiacs, and anti-aphrodisiacs.[85] The same kind of information could be found in *Aristotle's Masterpiece*, a handbook of folk gynecology and obstetrics by an unknown author (certainly not Aristotle). Several versions were frequently reprinted through the eighteenth and nineteenth centuries. Porter and Hall conclude that "The profile of the readership is largely guesswork," but the book was fairly inexpensive,[86] and evidence supplied by the Sheffield survey and autobiographers (when they are willing to discuss such matters) suggests that *Aristotle's Masterpiece* had a large working-class audience. It pops up incongruously in a list of dissenting tracts read by an eighteenth-century apprentice shoemaker.[87] In the late nineteenth century it was circulating surreptitiously even among Welsh Nonconformists.[88] V. S. Pritchett's parents kept it behind the bedroom chamberpot.[89] In the early twentieth century, it was something you might purchase at secondhand bookstalls,[90] pass around your workmates,[91] or send to an open-minded girlfriend.[92] Since his sex education was limited to warnings that "there were certain habits cultivated by sinful boys that must be avoided at all costs lest I end a physical or mental wreck," Stan Dickens clubbed together with other children to buy under-the-counter volumes in brown paper covers from a bookstall in Nunningford market. "Judged by modern [1975] standards the books were innocuous and no doubt similar books are being presented as Sunday School prizes today," he granted, but "There was one book that we all thought was sensational"—*Aristotle's Masterpiece*. "At last we understood what was meant when, during Scripture lessons, reference was made to 'the mother's womb.'"[93]

Whether the book provided much enlightenment beyond that is another question. "It was all about curing warts, worms, ringworm, delivering babies, and symptoms of pregnancy," recalled Edith Hinson (b. 1910), a Stockport mill girl who found it under her mother's mattress. "I didn't understand a word."[94] Mary Bertenshaw (b. 1904) had been told nothing about sex except the vague horrors of venereal disease, which only left her terrified of the local Manchester VD clinic. The girls at the hat and cap factory where she worked would huddle round at dinner to read *Aristotle's Masterpiece* over general giggles: "It contained explicit pictures of the development of a foetus; in turn, we read out passages. This went on until our boss Abe interrupted us. We felt so ashamed and from then on kept even further away from the VD clinic and became very dubious about the male sex."[95]

It may be simplistic to write off the Victorian era as one of sexual repression, but the circulation of sexual information in print was certainly constricted. On that point the evidence supports Porter and Hall and contradicts Michel Foucault. In the nineteenth century, *Aristotle's Masterpiece* was bowdlerized.[96] Even so, allusions to the book, not uncommon in pre-Victorian and post-Victorian autobiographies, disappeared in the intervening period. As David Vincent found, workingmen's memoirs of the early nineteenth century were so reticent that no useful information about sexuality could be gleaned from them.[97] Sexual references that appeared in the 1855 edition of J. D. Burn's *The Autobiography of a Beggar Boy* were cut from the 1882 version.[98] Similar deletions were made from William Cameron's *Autobiography of a Gangrel*, written in the 1840s but not published until 1888.[99] Michael Mason has described a sexual puritanism among Victorian workers that developed independently of middle-class influences. Any suggestion that Owenite socialism involved an advocacy of sexual freedom deeply alienated working-class women from the movement. And when Charles Bradlaugh disseminated birth control information he was frequently attacked by workingmen, who associated contraception with the dismal demographics of the Rev. Thomas Malthus.[100]

In contrast, Francis Place (b. 1771), an early birth control advocate, recalled that he was "pretty well acquainted with what relates to the union of the sexes" by age thirteen. Looking back on the 1780s from the second quarter of the nineteenth century, he noted that "Conversation on these matters was much less reserved than it is now, books relating to the subject were much more within the reach of boys and girls than they are now, and I had little to learn on any part of the subject." Obscene penny prints were commonly sold to laboring people, and Place read *Aristotle's Masterpiece*: as a result, he could not accept the Gospels' account of the conception of Jesus. He felt a near-erotic thrill when his school-master showed him an anatomy textbook, "which strongly excited me, and made me desirous of information on the subject." He would often ferret out and read surgical texts at bookstalls until the owner chased him away.[101]

The atmosphere was more repressive for Joseph Barker, a solider's son born thirty-five years later. At about age fifteen he found an old folio on anatomy and surgery by Helkiah Crooke (physician to James I) and was delighted by "certain parts of the work which treated on subjects which are generally wrapt in mystery by people, and which my [Yorkshire Methodist] parents would have been least disposed for me to think about or understand." When he indiscreetly shared his knowledge with some friends, there was a general uproar and even death threats. His angry parents confiscated the book, then returned it "on condition that I would *paste up* two particular parts of it. But I soon took the liberty to break loose the sealed-up parts, and read them again."[102] James Bonwick (b. 1817) recalled that, at Southwark's Borough Road School, "a stray book of a lascivious order occasionally came into our play hour, but was not lent about as in later and more cultured school days."[103]

One sex manual was universally available even to the most pious Victorians. Thomas Okey (b. 1852) remembered that girls and boys would relieve the tedium of Methodist services by passing around the Bible opened to passages "which do not form part of the lessons in school or of the church services." They were introduced to "wores" (as they pronounced it) and "the wicked Mrs. Potiphar, [who] victimized the good Joseph because he would not tell a lie with her."[104] For that reason, nineteenth-century Bibles were often edited for children: adultery was erased from the story of David and Bathsheba, and if Mrs. Potiphar did not disappear entirely, her agenda was left unclear.[105] James Bonwick's Scripture lessons "contained no doubtful references to a more ancient, darker, lower age, as we never handled the *whole* Bible."[106] But the edition that V. W. Garratt (b. 1892) studied at St. James Church School in Birmingham was wonderfully explicit: "Fascinating as the Old Testament was in the graphic descriptions of battles, murders, and floods, the sex lore of Leviticus was our chief attraction, for it inspired earnest inquiry into the full meaning of adultery, fornication, and childbirth, the information being communicated to each other by gestures and whisperings that cleared up some of the mysteries that puzzled our inquisitive minds." Other points were clarified by scribbled marginal notes, which were "anything but decent."[107]

Abroad, in Indian bazaars, where there were no Ten Commandments, soldiers could buy the semi-pornographic Paul de Kock and *Droll Stories of Balzac*. "As for the *Decameron of Boccaccio*, in my time every soldier of the British Forces in India who could read had read this volume from cover to cover," according to an enlisted man stationed there from 1901 to 1909. "It was considered very hot stuff; but the Prayer-wallah used to say that in this respect it did not come within shouting distance of certain passages in the Old Testament, once you got the hang of the Biblical language."[108] For a boy as young as seven, they could offer a syllabus of dirty words.[109] Atheist propagandists made wicked use of such passages in their tract *101 Obscenities in the Bible*, for example Ezekiel 23:20: "And she doted upon their Egyptian paramours, whose members are as big as donkeys' and who come with the abundance of stallions."[110] For Tom Barclay (b. 1852), son of a Catholic rag-and-bone collector, the erotic episodes in the Douay Bible "aroused my curiosity as to sexual matters." He found some answers in secondhand schooltexts of Ovid, Juvenal, and Catullus: though he knew no Latin beyond the Mass, the English notes offered plenty of background on the "filthy loves of gods and goddesses."[111]

The erotic information available in the Bible and other sources was, however, fragmentary and often inaccurate. Working-class children growing up in the late nineteenth and early twentieth centuries suffered from notoriously low levels of sexual literacy, a fact confirmed both by oral history[112] and by autobiographies. For the daughter (b. 1890) of a London compositor, "Sex was a well-kept secret. Any visitor or neighbour who got anywhere near the subject in conversation was silenced by sign language by my Mother. We didn't discuss things with our parents. We were told what to do, or not to do, and were not allowed to answer back."[113] Kathleen Woodward was the daughter of a puritanical washerwoman who would tell her nothing about sex. She learned a little from the women she worked with at a shirt-collar factory, from the couples lurching from pubs at closing time, and, "as a child, prowling down the canal bank in the dark—furtive, sly, silent, wrapped in an inexpressible and fearful ugliness from which I by early training shrank and covered my face. ... Passionately, obscurely, sex came to mean for me all that was horrible and revolting, all that was inexpressibly ugly; and only a little less strong than my horror was my curiosity."[114] In Jim Bullock's (b. 1903) Yorkshire mining village, "One thing the children talked about a great deal was sex, and what they did not know, they imagined." They endlessly and ignorantly debated how babies were made, and engaged in some childish sex play, but the subject was never discussed at home.[115] When Herbert Hodge (b. 1901) asked about it, his father (an upholsterer) reluctantly and "haltingly described the motions. Just like that. No word of desire, delight, attraction, or repulsion. No word of any life. Merely the motions. It sounded duller than the excretory motions—and without even their urge."[116]

At that level of ignorance, it could be difficult to decipher sexually suggestive literature. Allen Clarke (b. 1863), the son of Bolton textile workers, found physiology books in the public library incomprehensible. A newspaper reference to Rabelais motivated him to borrow *Gargantua and Pantagruel*, which was no more helpful: "Love passages in the tales were meaningless and boring and I skipped them."[117] Harry Dorrell (b. 1903) read his brother's copy of George Moore's *A Mummer's Wife*, but "I could not understand why the lady who was undressed said to the man 'Bite me' and also got into bed with no clothes on. Mother always wore a nightdress in bed."[118] Mary Bentley's father, who worked in a soap factory, at first took *Jude the Obscure* away from her, but relented when an uncle advised him that she would only read it under the sheets. "It didn't do me any harm because"—even at age fourteen—"most of it I didn't understand and I didn't like it anyhow. I didn't cry over it as I did over Tess when she christened her baby."[119] Margaret Wharton's parents were highly literate, and with their encouragement she entered a teaching training college in 1936, but they taught her nothing about sex:

> Though we read books like *Tess of the d'Urbervilles* and *Hatter's Castle* both dealing with the defloration of innocence and an ultimate baby, we drew no parallels and made no application to ourselves. I even read Radclyffe Hall's classic story of lesbianism, *The Well of Loneliness*, without having the faintest idea of what it was about. At the age of nineteen in college, in common with my contemporaries, we anxiously awaited a much touted lecture by the college doctor on the facts of life. While she gave a graphic description of the birth process, she made no mention of the part the father played in how the baby got there and I remember the disappointment in which most of us seemed to share.[120]

The sexual themes in these novels may seem obvious, but without the appropriate frame, the reader will not know how to decode the allusions. Norman Nicholson recalled that a friend, who had been instructed by a girl cousin,…informed me fairly accurately of the basic method and anatomy of sex, but, though I was immensely curious, I scarcely associated this with girls at all. The beautiful and disturbing feminine shapes which I sometimes saw in the photograph section of *The Sketch* and *The Tatler*, turning over the pages furtively in the Public Library, did not immediately strike me as being what might lie beneath a gymslip. I still thought of sex mainly as a process married people had to go through to get children, and I felt, on the whole, that it was rather hard on them.

Nicholson had no sex education except a puritanical pamphlet handed out by the vicar, which "struck me as being just silly. … It was not until several years later that I discovered, to my immense surprise, that the Gay 'Twenties were supposed to have been a period of new sexual liberation." In his mind love was almost entirely divorced from sex:

"Love" was something I had learned about from *David Copperfield* and *Under the Greenwood Tree* and from the stories in *The Woman's Weekly*, which my mother occasionally bought. And, of course, from the poetry I was just beginning to enjoy. I was naively oblivious to the sexual innuendoes of Keats and Tennyson but their romantic raptures set me trembling like a tuning fork. "Come into the garden, Maud" roused nothing of the derision, or even downright ribaldry, that it would surely rouse in a boy of today [1975]. I thought it said just what I would have felt in the circumstances. And put it very nicely too.[121]

In his essay "Boys' Weeklies," George Orwell ridiculed the *Magnet* and *Gem* for ignoring sex, but as one reader remembered, "The total absence of sex as a story ingredient was never even noticed."[122] "I doubt whether the fact that Harry Wharton and his merry band were denied any sexual contact with either boy or girl confused or troubled his innocent readers," wrote charwoman's son Bryan Forbes. "Certainly I never detected any sense of sexual deprivation within my own circle of friends, avid followers of the stories like myself. We had all the normal urges and curiosities but there were few outlets for practical field studies in those halcyon pre-war days, for we did not grow up in an age sated with sex."[123] Leslie Paul (b. 1905) reminds us that boys of his generation actually did talk like Frank Richards characters ("You must believe in God, you must, you rotter"). Thus "it was possible to grow up in a curiously sexless world in that age so unlike our own, and to prove incapable of reading the plain signs under one's nose, like the twelve-year-old Leo in L. P. Hartley's *The Go-Between*. … I read about love in the romantic novels I pored over—I would read anything—without ever suspecting it had anything to do with sex." He remembered a preacher lecturing on the dangers of masturbation, but his warnings were so vague that the boys could only guess (incorrectly) what he was alluding to.[124]

That ignorance could produce fear, loathing, and trauma. Sex was never discussed when Edna Bold (b. 1904), a baker's daughter, was growing up in

Manchester. Yet on a barely conscious level, an unmistakable message was sent by the four layers of skirts and petticoats she was dressed in, starting with "an unmentionable undergarment that never went on display on the washing line, but was hung on a rack near the ceiling amongst other articles of washing. Vaguely, slowly, haphazardly I sensed the layers of petticoats that hung down like drawn blinds had a significance I did not yet comprehend." The shock of discovery came one summer day when, on her way to school, she was accosted by another child who, quite unbidden, told her where babies came from. That "torrent of obscenity" created a "fear and revulsion of 'Seks'" which was only aggravated by her reading. When they were alone at home, she and her cousin Dorothy extracted from the kitchen bookcase and read, side by side, a medical book and Foxe's *Book of Martyrs*. The intertextuality was profoundly scarring: "Childbirth and martyrdom were synonymous. We suffered the torments of the damned. Neither my cousin Dorothy nor myself ever underwent such physical torture as we discovered in those two hideous books. We never 'reproduced.' On this score she went unrepentant to the grave as I shall go to mine."[125] Sexual ignorance made Edith Evans (b. 1910), a seaman's daughter, "terrified of the opposite sex. I had no desire for a boy friend, in fact I made sure I was never alone with one. I was a very romantic minded girl and enjoyed reading love stories, and hoped to marry one day and have children. I loved babies, but the thought of how one was conceived made me decide to remain childless," and she did until age thirty-eight, some years after she had married.[126]

It was different for rural children, like East Anglia farm boy Spike Mays (b. 1907). He inevitably learned a great deal observing farm animals, spying on spooning couples, passing around lewd sketches, and playing doctor:

> As far as we were concerned old Sigmund Freud was not far out when he postulated that experience relating to sex enters into a child's life from infancy. … Many local girls had practical experience before puberty … sometimes with schoolboys, but more often with uncles and cousins. Nor were they in the least ashamed. Some even bragged about personal experiences, considering it their duty to inform the virginal minority who had preserved that intact and immaculate state thus far to the ripe old age of twelve years. … Despite their advanced knowledge, some of the bigger boys would ask questions specifically designed to embarrass our headmaster …. "Now, Donald," said Mr. Tuck, putting on his angry voice. "You know perfectly well where babies come from. Any more of this and I will have you out in front to lecture about it."[127]

In Oxfordshire fieldhands exchanged traditional bawdy tales: "A kind of rustic *Decameron*, which seemed to have been in existence for centuries and increased like a snowball as it rolled down the generations," recalled Flora Thompson. She could not offer any details, since these stories were not repeated in front of females, but overheard snippets suggested that "they consisted chiefly of 'he said' and 'she said', together with a lavish enumeration of those parts of the human body then known as 'the unmentionables.'" In any case, they would have hardly shocked her: as a young girl she had once come across a bull "justifying its existence" and walked on "without so much as a kink in her subconscious."[128]

Britain was a mainly urban society, however, and soon an expanding range of sexual literature became available in the cities. Mark Grossek (b. 1888), the son of a Jewish immigrant tailor in Southwark, acquired his knowledge from grafitti, scandalous stories in the local press, *Lloyd's Weekly News, Measure for Measure*, the Song of Solomon, some old plays a fellow student had dug out of his father's library, General Booth's *In Darkest England*, Tobias Smollett, Quain's *Dictionary of Medicine*, as well as Leviticus ("For myself, the most subtle aura of enticement was wafted from the verb '*begat*' and the noun '*concubine*'"). There was also Ovid, but unfortunately the popular translation published by Bohn "had left all the tasty chunks in Latin."[129]

One could consult popular textbooks, such as *Dr. Foote's Plain Home Talk and Cyclopaedia*. "This book made a great impression on me," wrote Glasgow foundryworker Thomas Bell (b. 1882), "and I handed it round my workmates until it was as black as coal, and the batters torn."[130] Elsie Gadsby and her mother secretly studied a similar book on pregnancy and women's health, which some neighbors had left behind when they moved away.[131] Joseph Stamper (b. 1886), an ironmoulder's son, picked up quite a lot about obstetrics from an anatomy text.[132] The pro-chastity Alliance of Honour taught hygiene and sex education via two volumes by Dr. Sylvanus Stall, *What a Young Man Ought to Know* and *What a Young Woman Ought to Know*, though readers' responses were mixed: some found them helpful,[133] while others thought they only purveyed myths and fears.[134]

The beginning of the twentieth century is generally treated as an era of erotic liberation, driven by the socialist and feminist movements, the pioneering sexual studies of Edward Carpenter and Havelock Ellis, the return of the repressed in modern literature, and (a bit later) the popularization of Sigmund Freud and birth controller Marie Stopes. Some emancipated working-class women were caught up in these movements. In her Bolton Socialist Sunday School, Alice Foley heard a phrenologist offer "uninhibited talks on sex, with never the blinds down; we seemed to take the problems in our stride and were not unduly bothered with emotional upsets."[135] Yet these currents of liberation reached only a tiny fraction of the proletariat. A 1912 survey located only 108 Socialist Sunday schools with a total of 12,656 pupils, half of them adults.[136] Even the most intellectually active working women confronted mountains of sexual ignorance and anxiety. Margaret Bondfield (b. 1873), a shop assistant who became Britain's first female cabinet minister, was raised by a radical mother and a father (a foreman lacemaker) who had taken evening courses in science and classical literature. Nevertheless, she was terrified by the onset of menstruation: "All I knew of sex was the shaming gossip of schoolgirls. I felt hot all over if I saw a pregnant woman, because one was not supposed to know anything about a baby until or unless it appeared—*and* as a result of marriage." Later in life she was delighted to see the Woolwich Women's Co-operative Guild offer classes in physiology: "We haven't any words to tell our children about birth," the students told her.[137]

Ethel Mannin (b. 1900) was an exceptionally liberated letter-sorter's daughter, an early reader of Freud who made something of a career championing sexual freedom in the popular press. But when she approached the subject as a girl, she was far more fearful than informed:

> At the board-school all the girls were morbidly interested in parturition, menstruation, and procreation. The older girls talked of little else. We raked the Bible for information, and those of us who came from homes in which there were books made endless research, looking up in encylopaedias and home medical works, such words as "confinement," "miscarriage," "after-birth," "puberty," "menses," "life, change of." We were both fascinated and horrified. At the age of twelve I ploughed through a long and difficult book on embryology. My brother did likewise at the same age. God knows what either of us got as a result of our search for knowledge. ... Apart from the purely scientific aspect, which was beyond our comprehension, everything was "all along a dirtiness, all along a mess ... all along of finding out, rather more or less."

She copied passages from the Song of Songs into her commonplace book, but was disgusted when she came across the phrase "Esau came forth from his mother's belly":

> It seemed unspeakably dreadful, conjured up visions of sanguinary major operations. I was very miserable .... After that ... I looked at every woman who passed us in the street to see if she was going to have a baby. ... I was unhappy for a long time about the whole thing, and not until I was fifteen did I know how parturition took place, and horror was heaped on horror's head. Menstruation was another shock. It all seemed dreadful. One took refuge more and more in one's secret self .... For a long time I refused to believe that the father had anything to do with the creation of a baby—in spite of all the funny little indecent rhymes and the assertions of the girls who had it on good authority from home medical books and older brothers and sisters.[138]

As Harry McShane explained, early working-class Marxists had thoroughly bourgeois sexual mores:

> Although the average socialist looked forward to some vague equality in the new socialist society, on the whole they seemed to think that the family would continue. Its abolition never occurred to them, although some did read Engels's *Origin of the Family, Private Property and the State* and Morgan's *Ancient Society* on which it was based. It seems that when they read these books they were more

interested in tracing the origins of society from savagery onward, and the other argument passed them by. Marx mentioned the family in *The Communist Manifesto* but, again, most socialists didn't grasp all that was in it. The ideas they got out of it were about class struggle and international solidarity.[139]

Radical politics were not incompatible with strict sexual puritanism. At age thirteen or fourteen John Edmonds (b. 1911), who was reading *The Cloister and the Hearth* with a lower-middle-class girlfriend, asked her how Margaret had become pregnant. (He assumed that pregnancy followed automatically from marriage and cohabitation). She laughed, told him he was silly, and offered a "surprisingly accurate" explanation. He now understood why his father (a staunch socialist and *Daily Herald* reader) had angrily thrown out a jam jar in which he was raising a few beetles ("I'll not have you watching those things breed!") and demanded the return of a school library book with illustrations of classical sculpture. "He expressed a mixture of horror and indignation when some years later he learned from me that my school's curriculum had included lectures illustrated with lantern slides, dealing with human anatomy and physiology."[140]

Even those who read widely about sex often learned very little. In the 1920s Jennie Lee won a psychology degree from the University of Edinburgh, where she learned about abortion methods in forensic medicine classes. She went beyond the syllabus to read Ellis and Freud. While her collier father could not quite bring himself to discuss the subject, he was progressive enough to leave a book by Marie Stopes where she was likely to find it. All the same, Jennie was still capable of chatting with a prostitute on Princes Street without realizing what was going on. Stopes on sex "was all a bit remote and unattractive," she found. "Some of us at that time went in for a great deal of poetry to carry us through our adolescent phase, what was then called sublimation." She might talk a good game with a girlfriend ("provided my inclinations were sufficiently aroused, I cannot see myself running away from life. ... Please God, lead me into temptation") but He had other plans for her, and for a while she remained virginal in every sense of the term.[141] At nineteen Marjory Todd (b. 1906) liked discussing birth control with her WEA and ILP friends, until "one evening I was suddenly afraid that it would be discovered that I had not the faintest idea how such control was achieved." Nor did she entirely understand why it was necessary: "Did you know—I didn't, that men kiss you on the *mouth?*" she asked her sister, who confessed that she had only recently discovered that herself.[142]

These women had achieved, not sexual freedom, but some freedom to talk about sex, with a mixture of fervor and confusion, audacity and fear, sophistication and bluffing. The most remarkable records of that working-class sexual discourse are the letters and diaries of Ruth Slate (1884–1953), a packer who worked her way up to clerkdom, and Eva Slawson (1882–1917), a domestic servant who became a typist. Ruth was raised a Methodist, but in her first diary entry, at age thirteen, she frankly writes "I am rather fond of taking notice of boys (most of my companions do it)," and discusses their attractions in some detail. She organized a mutual improvement society, vigorously debated political and social issues with fellow salesgirls at a London grocer's, and embarked on a voracious course of reading, with a special passion for George Eliot.[143]

Both women recognized in Charlotte Brontë their own ambivalence between two rival passions: marriage and motherhood versus the intellectual freedom that had long been the lodestar of male autodidacts. They felt trapped between the social conservatism of their own class and the arrogance of middle-class feminists. Ruth explained to Eva

> how from my earliest years I have longed to study and learn, how it has been my fairy dream often, and occasionally such dreadful moods overcome me, that I feel fit for no one's company. I want to read and study, and yet at the same time to be helpful at home, and spare Mother all the work I possibly can, and between the two feelings I am often sorely vexed.[144]

On the other hand she felt intimidated by educated women who flaunted their "college connections by calling one person a 'fool', and speaking cynically of mankind as a whole." She quarrelled with a boyfriend over women's suffrage: "I told him that I could not go on as I have been doing, for I felt the best in me was being starved. I want to live." Years of reading had made her tired of the squabbling between competing religious sects, and it was Tolstoy's *Resurrection* that finally gave her the courage to plow her own furrow: "I *must* be different, or the best in me will die! This is no idle rhapsody—I would 'Live'!" When she embraced the modernist "New Theology" of R. J. Campbell, her family nearly "ostracised" her. She astonished her parents (and herself) when she "declared with vehemence that what the revival people had been praying for had come, though not in the way they expected."[145]

With an evangelical zeal freed from the moorings of dogma, Ruth plunged into the post-Victorian "sex question." She heard lectures on eugenics and women's diseases and read Auguste Forel's *Sexual Ethics*, though she could scarcely bear to glance through *The Great Scourge*, where Christabel Pankhurst insisted that the vast majority of men were infected with venereal disease. She was intrigued when a woman argued in the avant-garde *New Age* that the temple prostitutes of the East were a much better arrangement than the "unsanitary" way of ordering these things in the West. She gravitated to Françoise Lafitte and the *Freewoman* magazine, which agitated for the sexual emancipation of women.[146]

Meanwhile, *Jude the Obscure*, Edward Carpenter's *Love's Coming of Age*, Grant Allen's *The Woman Who Did*, H. G. Wells's *The New Machiavelli* and *Ann Veronica*, as well as the examples of Mary Wollstonecraft and George Eliot all made Eva think furiously about free love, wavering between acceptance and apprehension. Carpenter's manifestos for homosexuality plunged the two women into an earnestly muddled discussion: "We wondered whether the great teachers

Christ and Buddha belonged to this category, having in themselves the experiences and nature of either sex—then we talked of the procreation of children by the intermediate sex either naturally or by thought and ended in a confusion of ideas, having lost the thread of our discussion." They had once talked about exploring London disguised as men, and they both experienced a polymorphous erotic fascination with dancers, male and female. Ruth loved Isadora Duncan as a revolutionary. Eva was infatuated with an Indian girl dancer ("Here was dancing expressive of body, mind and soul—my idea of 'redemption' exemplified—harmony is unity!") and fascinated by a performance of *Hiawatha* where the war dancers appeared to be men, but in fact were "fine athletic women." She was equally enthralled by an amateur production of *The White Boys*: "The vigour and activity of the men appealed to me in a most curious way as they fought and leapt—I felt (I think almost for the first time in my life) distinctly attracted by the male body with its squareness, sinew, muscle and vitality. Following upon this came the old heart sickness—the longing for one love and the bearing of children."[147]

In 1909 *Peter Pan* had an almost Freudian impact on the women's collective subconscious. "Confused images haunted our dreams," Ruth noted, "the lissom"—not to mention transvestite—"form of Peter Pan, the crocodile, the pirates and all kinds of things."[148] In 1913 Eva records her belief in an unconscious childhood sexuality,[149] and a year later Ruth was telling her about the "Origin and Meaning of Taboo."[150] Possibly they had picked up some of the early reports of Freud's work to reach England, or perhaps they absorbed these ideas from Havelock Ellis and his circle. The larger point is that a few working women were swept up in the post-Victorian cultural revolution, with all its fervent and unfocused notions about sexuality, and this rush of new ideas was bound up with the kind of passionate individualism that had always driven male autodidacts. "I have felt lately something like a traveller on a voyage of discovery—books have lately been opening up to me new worlds," Eva told Ruth in 1907. "I believe our hearts and minds are so formed for the *infinite* that things *finite* cannot possibly satisfy us."[151] For all her social conscience, Ruth felt that intellectual freedom was more important to the working classes than welfare legislation: "The aim of progress is to make self-realisation—fullness of life—possible to *all*. ... The fundamental thing I believe to be knowledge and education, and until these are open in equal measure to all, as part of humanity's natural heritage, I believe social legislation to be prejudicial to the individual."[152] Ruth and Eva could enjoy that kind of emancipation because their educational opportunities, though still limited, were distinctly better than those available to their parents' generation. They both took evening classes and later attended the Woodbrooke Settlement, a Quaker adult education center near Birmingham. There Ruth studied social philosophy, economics, industrial legislation, comparative religion, education, and anthropology with a feminist spin ("the prevalence of the 'witch' in fairy tales is probably a relic of the Matriarchate period").[153]

Ruth and Eva were still exceptional, but after the First World War there would be a wider working-class audience for sexual science. Marie Stopes's *Married Love*, published in 1918, sold more than half a million copies by 1925.[154] Her works, according to Robert Roberts, were beginning to appear in the rubber shops "snuggling between the works of Paul de Kock and Balzac's *Droll Tales*." True, for most workingmen her name "was always good for a mindless guffaw. Yet we had the few journeymen, too, and the odd woman in the mill and sewing shop, who would quietly lend out their own copy of *Married Love* or *Wise Parenthood* to anyone genuinely seeking enlightenment."[155] Gladys Teal's parents never discussed sex (after all, they were caretakers at a Harrogate Conservative Club) but when Gladys took a job at a draper's shop around 1930, a female assistant gave her a Marie Stopes book on birth control, which she gratefully read.[156] Houseservant Margaret Powell (b. 1907) was unusually daring: she left Marie Stopes, along with the *Kama Sutra* and Havelock Ellis, on the bedside table for her husband. (Eventually she was forced to conclude that the books went unread, or at least unheeded.)[157]

Dr. Stopes clearly had a large working-class following. Although *Married Love* and her other books were expensive, she also published articles in *John Bull* and other popular papers. Literally thousands of readers wrote in response, asking for advice on birth control. Claire Davey has sorted the letters (mostly from 1919–27) into those who responded to Stopes's books (mainly middle-class) and those who responded to her articles (mainly working-class), and the differences between the two are striking. The book readers were far more likely to use birth control methods that required some education in contraception, such as caps and pessaries, sheaths, and douches. The article readers relied more on traditional and unsophisticated methods: abstinence, abortion, breastfeeding, or no method at all.

The latter group protested that the medical profession was largely responsible for this relative ignorance. When doctors warned working-class women that pregnancy could be dangerous, they usually declined to explain how it could be prevented. (With middle-class patients they were far more forthcoming.) Moreover, article-readers accounted for only 30 percent of Stopes's correspondents, far less than the proportion of working people in the general population.[158] The working classes, then, not only knew less about contraception: they were more reluctant to ask, and far less likely to receive a straight answer. It was this inequality of information that Stopes's correspondents resented, even more than economic poverty. One man who could not afford books on contraception wrote, "I don't begrudge wealth but I do its value of knowledge." A compositor's wife, who lived in a lodge on a country estate, feared that the lady of the "big house" might intercept Stopes's reply: "The rich seem to think a working woman has no right to know anything, at least that has been my own experience." One desperate mother of three ("My Doctor has warned me that if I have any more he will not be answerable for me, but even he does not tell me what to do") put it in these terms: the birth control movement was a "fight for common knowledge."[159]

At the same time, there was much hostility to contraception within the working classes. It was one thing to read Dr. Stopes surreptitiously, but it took some courage to walk into the free clinic she opened in Holloway in 1921. The decor was warm and unintimidating, the staff entirely female: nevertheless, an average of only three women a day used it during its first year of operation. When the Malthusian League set up its own clinic later that year near the Elephant and Castle, local people pelted the building with stones and rotten eggs, smashed windows, and defaced the walls with obscene graffiti.[160] "At that time birth control was not a subject of discussion, the women would pass this shop almost with their head lowered in case anyone would think they were interested," recalled one Camberwell resident.[161] "Husbands on learning of their wives visiting Dr. Stopes would in many cases punish their wife with blows, how dare she show him up with his pals, they would taunt him about his virility."[162]

An emancipated working woman like Elizabeth Ring was free to read the works of Freud, Havelock Ellis, and Bertrand Russell in the late 1920s, but she was familiar with those books only because her schoolteachers had her exchange them at the Finsbury Public Library. And she was clearly an unusual case, the only woman in her office who knew the meaning of the word "orgasm."[163] That fact should be borne in mind when we consider the results of early sex surveys. In a 1943–46 study of 100 working-class wives, mostly from London and under age forty, forty-nine reported having orgasms always or frequently, thirty-six infrequently, five never, and ten supplied no information. But as the investigators conceded, many of these women may not have understood the question.[164]

Still, some real progress toward mass sexual literacy had been accomplished by the end of the Second World War. That same survey found that contraception had become almost universal among younger working-class couples in London, excepting those who were infertile or planning pregnancies. True, *coitus interruptus* was still the most popular method, followed by the condom. Yet the investigators felt justified in sounding a note of triumph: "Enlightenment has filtered down to the masses, at any rate in a sophisticated urban area, through the pioneer work of Marie Stopes, through improved education, and—more recently—through public discussion of population problems."[165]

A 1949 national sex survey conducted by Mass Observation confirmed that attitudes had become more liberal in all social strata. It was significant, first of all, that nearly everyone questioned was happy to cooperate. Only 9 percent of the middle class and 17 percent of the working class now completely disapproved of sex education.[166] Yet only 6 percent of the whole sample had learned about sex primarily from schoolteachers, and only 18 percent had received any formal sex education at all: the proportion was lower among the less educated and those over age forty-five. Seventy-one percent now knew the meaning of "birth control," though only 55 percent of those with an elementary education approved of it, as opposed to 70 percent of those with higher education. The less educated were also somewhat more opposed to divorce, while the middle classes and the highly educated were less likely to think that moral standards were declining. In sex as in literature, the working classes still tended to be conservative. Girls were actually more likely to be told "the facts of life" than boys, perhaps because they had to be warned about menstruation and pregnancy, and it was assumed that boys would pick it up. In fact, "picking it up" was still the main source of sexual knowledge for one out of four respondents. Thirteen percent were taught by other children, 11 percent by mothers, 6 percent each by fathers and workmates, 5 percent "when I got married," 4 percent in the army. Only 8 percent learned primarily from reading (including the Bible), while for another 12 percent it just "came naturally."[167] Though this section has focused on sex in print, one should not forget that working people always relied far more on friends, parents, and the street for answers to their questions.

Current Affairs

The low level of working-class sexual literacy is hardly surprising. What may be more remarkable is the lack of knowledge of current affairs, even in a century when the daily newspaper habit became almost universal. C. H. Rolph was in retrospect amazed by the dimness of political consciousness in his family, though they were all great readers. His happiest memories were of the "countless evenings on which five or six of us would be thus absorbed, each with his own book, for two or three hours at a time." Yet even in that unusually literate working-class parlor, the degree of ignorance was stunning. Only his grandmother had any awareness of politics, and what she knew "seemed mainly to have been absorbed, and was exclusively expressed, in the kind of clichés and catch-phrases with which the Northcliffe Press was newly nourishing a readership that could be satisfied or fobbed off with outlines and jeering witticisms. Mr. Asquith, to my Grandma Hewitt, was 'Old Wait-and-See.'" In the months leading up to the First World War, Rolph learned shorthand by taking dictation as his father read from the *Daily Telegraph*, *The Times*, the *Referee*, and *John Bull*. That exercise drilled into his head words like the Schlieffen Plan, Entente Cordiale, the Balkans, Triple Alliance, Mesopotamia, Little Englanders, women's suffrage, tariff reform, passive resistance, Sarajevo, mobilization. Yet there were all meaningless to him and to other boys his age (twelve) because they were scarcely mentioned or explained in school. Instead, Rolph and his family swallowed whole the bumptious politics of Horatio Bottomley's *John Bull*:

> I knew about the assassination at Sarajevo on 28 June, I knew that the shots were fired by a Serbian student (I even knew his name), I knew that the dead man was called Archduke Franz Ferdinand of Austria-Hungary and that he was soon to be an Emperor of somewhere. ... The newspaper articles and the *John Bull* rhetoric I was regularly committing to Pitman's shorthand at the back-parlour

table made it seem that the Kaiser and the Austrian Emperor were sub-human monsters intent on either dominating or destroying Europe, while Britain was blessed with far-sighted statesmen who could see the horrors that would attend any great war in the twentieth century and were determined to find "peaceful solutions." But the idea of a solution suggested that there must be a problem, and I could never understand what problems they were trying to find peaceful solutions to. If the problem was really one of "naked aggression" (I can see the Pitman's outline for that now), I didn't see how that could be peacefully solved. And I didn't know anyone to ask.[168]

In Camberwell the newspaper more commonly served as a tablecloth. "The information on its pages was seldom read," according to a bus conductor's son, "most parents could not read, and the general news meant nothing to those who had nothing, even the paper was not of course bought, it was found."[169] Aubrey Hicks (b. 1900) offers an illustration of how little world news reached even the best-informed workers. His father, a painter on the Rothschild estate at Tring, had attended night school and read widely, and unlike most of his neighbors he took in a quality newspaper, the *Daily Chronicle*. Young Aubrey read it avidly, and took advantage of the reading room Lord Rothschild provided for his employees. Of course he was most interested in cricket scores. The Wright Brothers' first flight, the 1910 London–Paris air race, the *Titanic*, Dr. Crippen, Lloyd George's National Health Insurance Scheme, the assassination of the Portuguese royal family, the tragic death of suffragette Emily Wilding Davison—all these made some impression. But in the midst of those sensational events, he only had the vaguest recollection of reading something about Sir Edward Grey's diplomacy.[170]

And Hicks was far more knowledgeable than the average rural reader. Labour politician Harry Snell (b. 1865) recalled that, as a young farm laborer in a Nottinghamshire village, he never saw a book and "never heard any one mention the names of Lincoln, Wilberforce, or Lloyd Garrison."[171] In Surrey George Bourne's gardener, who never read books or newspapers, first heard of the American Civil War some thirty years after Appomattox, when he learned that a relative was collecting a widow's pension for her husband, who had fought and died in the conflict.[172] Even in 1900, the Suffolk village of Langham only received one newspaper per week: the owner would read it on a street corner to his neighbors before Sunday dinner, and that one copy would supply conversation for the rest of the week.[173] The diary of one Cornish farmer, typically, is concerned mostly with religious reading and activities between 1892 and 1912. Only occasionally did he notice current events: the Boer War and the Russo-Japanese conflict, the 1912 coal strike and a hard winter for the poor in London, a local lecture on Irish Home Rule, the death of Queen Victoria and the *Titanic* disaster.[174] "I don't remember ever seeing or reading a newspaper during my school days," wrote W. J. Paddock (b. 1898), who was raised by a Hampshire sawmill worker. "It must have been two weeks before I heard of the sinking of the *Titanic*.

Our teacher, Miss Jerrett, would bring the monthly illustrated magazine to school and that's how we got the news. I remember seeing pictures and reading about the Balkan War and I thought what funny hats they wore."[175]

As late as 1937 Roger Dataller, ex-collier and WEA tutor in South Yorkshire, reported that

> it is possible to converse with alarming numbers of working people without ever hearing the slightest mention of Hitler, Mussolini, or Stalin. Some years ago, when European affairs had reached a stage of great economic tension, I made the practical experiment of noting during a given term of days such comment as was made in the course of general conversation. It was negligible, and it confirmed the feeling that the "masses" (like sailors) simply do not care.[176]

Yet even as Dataller wrote, the impending world crisis was beginning to break through that barrier of inattention. In January 1938 the BBC found that 60 percent of working-class listeners regularly tuned into the 6 p.m. newscast, compared with 54 percent of middle-class listeners.[177] In March 1942 Mass Observation reported that at least the upper working classes did not lag too far behind the middle class in their ability to name government ministers:

Table 6.4: Ability to Identify Cabinet Members, 1942 (in percent)[178]

	Middle	Upper Working	Lower Working
Chancellor of the Exchequer (Kingsley Wood)	60	40	22
First Lord of the Admiralty	59	50	33
Minister of War	32	13	14
Lord Privy Seal	36	13	14
Minister of Labour (Ernest Bevin)	86	73	66
Minister of Food	89	82	72
Minister of Information	41	29	16

During the Second World War, the Army Bureau of Current Affairs was set up to correct these deficits, offering the troops lectures and discussion on political issues. Early reports in 1941 found much boredom, ignorance, lazy cynicism, and resistance in the ranks to ABCA activities. While most armed forces units had libraries, they consisted mainly of thrillers and Westerns, and very little serious reading was accomplished.[179] One Royal Tank Corps officer who organized a discussion circle in his unit found "Men who were vague about the whereabouts of Poland (this is no exaggeration), who did not know the difference between Dominion and Colonial status, who had never heard of the Low Countries, who were uninstructed in the elementary workings of Parliament and who were wholly ignorant of the meaning of Local Government." As the war progressed, however, soldiers became more receptive. Surveys in 1943 and 1944 found that ABCA activities were being carried on regularly in at least 60 percent of home units, irregularly in another 10 to 24 percent; among North African units the figures were 30 percent and 45 percent. Though soldiers rarely mentioned educational activities in letters, when they did the comments were nearly always positive. One survey of 8,500 service men and women found 78 percent interested in the discussions, with 17 percent indifferent and only 5 percent bored. Of another 5,000 soliders in transit camps and convalescent depots, fully 83 percent said they would still attend ABCA sessions if they were voluntary.[180]

The Right to Language

The ABCA and BBC newscasts made political discourse intelligible to the undereducated, something that "quality" newspapers, weekly reviews, and most statesmen had failed to do. Even Herbert Morrison, the populist Labour politician and former shop-assistant, was liable to talk over the heads of his listeners without realizing it. After he delivered a speech in Lancashire in 1939, an audience survey found that it contained more than fifty words not generally understood by those who had left school at fourteen. In fact, of every hundred words spoken, three were unintelligible and seven ambiguous. One local Labour Party activist was baffled by "conceive", "demeaning", "emancipation", "issues", "lineal", "deflected", "evolution", "integral", "pliant", "suppliant", and "fundamental".[181]

Had these words been spoken by a Conservative, they would have aroused much more resentment. Vocabulary was a class barrier, and this particular form of cultural illiteracy effectively cut off the less educated from the political arena. For as long as writing has existed, the literate classes have attempted to preserve a closed shop through exclusionary languages. In ancient Mesopotamia scribes were a privileged and exclusive caste, and they commonly concluded cuneiform tablets with the epigram "Let the wise instruct the wise, for the ignorant may not see."[182] Granted, not all sophisticated vocabularies represent conspiracies of the learned. Some concepts simply cannot be adequately framed in basic English, a point driven home by George Orwell's Newspeak, and the example of Herbert Morrison shows that even a loyal son of the proletariat could inadvertently talk above his audience. Nevertheless, Latin tags, professional vocabularies, and postmodernist jargon have all been used in turn as forms of encryption, permitting communication among elites while shutting out everyone else.

Since the Lollards, the working classes had seen through this game. The seventeenth-century waterman-poet John Taylor had read More's *Utopia*, Plato's *Republic*, Montaigne, and Cervantes in translation, but he never mastered a foreign language and he relentlessly satirized latinate prose:

I ne'er used Accidence so much as now,
Nor all these Latin words here interlaced,

> I do not know if they with sense are placed,
> I in the book did find them.

Taylor once offered to give lessons in a concocted "Utopian" language, and he spoofed the pretensions of scholarly apparatus by interlarding his work with bogus references, fake bibliographies, and citations from "Books which I never read." The value of any commodity can be inflated by creating an artificial scarcity, and Taylor recognized that jargon could enhance the prestige of literature by rendering it less accessible to a mass audience:

> Yet I with Non-sense could contingerate,
> And catophiscoes terragrophiocate,
> And make myself admired immediately,
> Of such as understand no more than I.[183]

Henry Mayhew found that Victorian costermongers reacted negatively to any use of foreign words—even a reference in one of Edward Lloyd's papers to *noblesse*.[184] When Leicester Chartist Thomas Cooper set out to master Greek he aroused intense suspicion among his neighbors. Even his shift from the Lincolnshire dialect to standard educated English made them uneasy: "To hear a youth in mean clothing, sitting at the shoemaker's stall, pursuing one of the lowliest callings, speak in what seemed to some of them almost a foreign dialect, raised positive anger and scorn in some, and amazement in others. Who was I, that I should sit on the cobbler's stall, and 'talk fine'! They could not understand it."[185]

In the nineteenth century, working-class participation in botanical research had been made possible by the Linnaean system of classification, which was relatively easy to master. In place of a confusing welter of local names for plants, it offered a common language for gentlemen and artisan botanists. Gardener James Lee had published a cheap guide to the system as early as 1760, and that knowledge was constantly expanded and reinforced at the meetings of local botanical societies, where specimens were brought in and identified. William Withering's *Botanical Arrangement* (1776) and William Jackson Hooker's *Muscologia Britannica* (1818) were written in accessible English, because the authors depended so heavily on the contributions of plebeian naturalists. Even when experts conceded that Antoine Laurent de Jussieu had developed a better mode of classification, they often stuck to the Linnaean system for that reason. As Hooker protested in 1846, to change the vernacular of botany would only "increase the difficulty ... & you cannot render the study *popular*." Linnaeus had created a "universal language," proclaimed Edward Forbes, professor of botany at King's College London, in 1843. An "easy means of acquiring and arranging information is a great help to the workmen of science, and no department has gained more thereby than botany."[186]

By the twentieth century, university-trained professionals had taken over the business of science. In their laboratories and their private scientific languages, there was no place for either genteel or proletarian amateurs. In adult education, science became increasingly difficult to "popularize": a zoology lecturer in the 1920s advised against the use of Greek and Latin in botany courses.[187] The same stumbling block could arise in the pursuit of philosophy. One Kimbolton tailor dedicated himself to studying Plato, Spinoza, and Kant, but could not understand why they resorted to indecipherable words like "idea," "essence," and "categorical imperative."[188] Adult educators in rural areas had to be even more careful with language. In 1931 a couple who had taught in Devonshire warned that

> the very nature of modern life tends to create forms of expression uncongenial to the countrymen's rhythm of thought. The extent and complexity of modern expert knowledge forces the objective thinker to modify, qualify, relate this to that idea to avoid dogmatic assertion; subjectively, the artist's style is often allusive, staccato, built up, like the kindred modern arts, out of new rhythmic clashes, and disharmonies. Much modern expression of modern ideas is as incomprehensible to the countryman as D. H. Lawrence might be to Sir Thomas Malory.

One had to avoid the vocabulary and issues surrounding modern industrialism, which dominated urban WEA courses. Though rural counties certainly had their share of substandard housing, the word "slum" was meaningless here. Unfamiliar with the conventions of modern drama, country people responded well to amateur productions of medieval miracle plays, Shakespeare, Beaumont and Fletcher, even *Riders to the Sea*, "but to attempt Sheridan or Shaw or Coward would be disastrous from the outset because these write in an idiom which is entirely foreign to their mode of thinking. Verbal wit, abstract idea, symbolize an idiom of thought that expresses itself in an entirely different key from their own."[189]

For generations, self-taught authors had resorted to William Cobbett's *Grammar of the English Language*, which laid down rules for writing basic, crystalline English. Anticipating Orwell's "Politics and the English Language," Cobbett warned his readers away from classical allusions or quotations, arguing that "what are called the *learned* languages, operate as a bar to the acquirement of real learning."[190] He was admired for just that reason by a host of proletarian authors and politicians, from John Clare to J. R. Clynes.[191] "If any don has beaten that book as an exposition of English I have yet to see his work," testified best-selling novelist Howard Spring.[192] In his own style guide, Robert Blatchford advised readers to buy a 2s. Cobbett and to model their prose on English literature that stuck closest to "the plainest Saxon": the Bible, the Book of Common Prayer, Shakespeare, Milton, and William Morris.[193]

Blatchford's accessibility made him, of all the socialist propagandists, the most successful in reaching a mass working-class audience. If T. A. Jackson was more engaging than most Marxist critics, it was partly because he modeled his style on Blatchford.[194] "Blatchford was no orator," wrote Labour MP Manny Shinwell, "but his language was simple, clear-cut, easily understood and for a person like myself, with limited education, more likely to be of value in forming ideas than the writings and speeches of some of the Labour politicians of the period." This was a testimonial from one of the most accomplished autodidacts of the twentieth century. In the public library he doggedly tackled volumes "whose contents I usually failed to understand": Paley's *Evidences of Christianity*, Haeckel's *Riddle of the Universe*, Herbert Spencer's *Sociology*, the *Meditations* of Marcus Aurelius. Shinwell's whole intellectual career was an exciting but laborious exercise in decoding. All his life he used a dictionary to correct his pronunciation. The future Minister of Fuel and Power even faulted plain-spoken Keir Hardie for his "somewhat prosy, economic jargon." From the moment he entered Parliament in 1922, Shinwell was painfully conscious of this language barrier. It was not a matter of being intimidated by Eton and Harrow men:

> Having seen and heard them I was consoled, at any rate for a time, for my lack of education. Yet it must be made clear that the lack of a sound education, the struggle to acquire knowledge, the need to be able to understand the meaning of every paragraph one reads in a book or periodical, created an inhibition which I suffer even to this day [at age ninety-six]. Two years of schooling in London, nine months in South Shields, a year and a half in Glasgow and leaving school before the age of twelve, and then what? Reading, much of which I failed to understand, without guidance or advice, maybe unconscious of ignorance; just forcing one's way through the jungle, the hustle, bustle and rivalry of political life, yet throughout it all seeking to retain the characteristic to which I attach most importance, that of being independent—all of these impediments could have been avoided.[195]

Which of the early Labour MPs did not feel that sting? Those Latin quotations sprinkled through parliamentary debates sent J. H. Thomas to the House of Commons Library to look them up. "It was a tremendous handicap," one that impressed him with "the supreme value of education. Critics, cartoonists and others have made much capital of my shortcomings in this respect; although I have accepted it all with philosophy, the hurt has been there all the same."[196] Will Crooks was a passionate fan of Homer in translation, but when Arthur Balfour used a Latin tag on the floor of the House of Commons (as prime ministers are wont to do) Crooks sharply reminded him that some of those present had not had the privilege of a classical education.[197]

Farm boy Richard Hillyer (b. c. 1900) was a rare example of a classical autodidact, who acquired some Latin from old textbooks found in a junkshop. It helped that the previous owner had scribbled translations between the lines, and an abridged Roman history text provided enough context to make the pursuit interesting. But the real motive was a desire to break the code, to gain access to privileged information:

> There was the satisfaction of solving a puzzle, as meaning began to emerge from the chaos of unknown words. But there was more than that. Latin gave me self respect. Plodding my way through this noble old language, feeling that I was breaking into a secret which brought distinction to those who possessed it; and that I was doing this without the help or even knowledge of others, kindled a pride that was very good for me just then. Where it would lead to, or if it would lead anywhere, I could not tell. What earthly use Latin would be to a farm labourer it was impossible to see ....

In fact it led to a scholarship at Durham University.[198] On the other hand, as Marjory Todd noted, the mastery of any foreign language marked the point when a scholarship pupil would irreversibly leave his parents behind:

> ... soon after he went to his grammar school he was "showing off" at the table. He said that sugar and bread in French would be masculine things but others might be feminine. His father, who up to this point had been his absolute authority on everything, told him this was nonsense, and he felt for the first time that they would henceforth drift apart. His French teacher he knew was right; his father disagreed with his teacher; *both* could not be right.[199]

Language did not prove to be a difficult barrier for the children of Jewish immigrants who escaped the Czarist empire between 1881 and 1914. The gentile manager of three predominantly Jewish East London elementary schools reported that "The keenness of those Hebrew parents for the education of their offspring was astounding. No Jewish child ever gave our attendance officer any trouble; none made any demand on our local organization for the feeding and supplying of boots and warm clothing to East End school-children."[200] The immigrants, mainly skilled and semiskilled urban workers, already enjoyed high levels of literacy in Yiddish and/or other Eastern European languages. Many of them were socialist or anarchist intellectuals, eager to wean Jewish workers away from their rabbis and educate them into a common secular culture shared by the international proletariat.[201]

By the 1920s, the Jewish East End was an intellectual hotbed. Harry Blacker (b. 1910), the son of a Russian immigrant cabinetmaker, admitted that artistic tastes generally ran to Edwin Landseer on the milkman's calendar and sentimental Pre-Raphaelite reproductions, but some ghetto children became artists, thanks to classes available at local institutes. A number won university scholarships, not surprising in an environment where education was encouraged, teachers were highly respected, and the kitchen table was cleared for homework. Blacker had access to a good local reference library and "a wonderful selection of books and magazines" owned by his uncle, a printer. Landsmen's clubs offered political speakers as well as lectures on Yiddish poetry and *A Midsummer Night's Dream*. While immigrants attended the raucous and sentimental Yiddish theater, their children, who had been exposed to the great English dramatists in school, ventured out to the West End to see Shakespeare, Shaw, O'Neill, and O'Casey. Blacker discovered Bach, Mozart, Beethoven, Brahms, and Schubert at Workers' Circle concerts. Once his family acquired a radio, "Great international pianists became household words and my father called Heifetz by his first name."[202]

The parents of playwright Arnold Wesker (b. 1932) were both immigrants, tailor's machinists, Communists, and culturally Jewish atheists. Wesker admitted he was "a very bad student," but his parents provided an environment of

> constant ideological discussion at home, argument and disputation all the time. ... All this affected my parents' attitude to study. It wasn't ever a question of, "Now you must study," and "Education is a good thing because it is necessary to be a lawyer and get on," but it was the common currency of day-to-day living that ideas were discussed around the table, and it was taken for granted that there were books in the house and that we would read.

The books mostly had a leftward political slant (Tolstoy, Gorky, Jack London, Sinclair Lewis) but Wesker soon reached out to Balzac, Maupassant, and a broader range of literature.[203]

That second generation assimilated with breathtaking speed and thoroughness: Harold Laski, Selig Brodetsky, Lewis Namier, and Jacob Epstein were among the many immigrants' children who moved into the mainstream of British intellectual life. While his widowed mother (who had studied medicine in Russia) worked a market stall, Ralph Finn (b. 1912) scrambled up the scholarship ladder to Oxford University. He credited his success largely to his English master at the Davenant Foundation School: "When I was an East End boy searching for beauty, hardly knowing what I was searching for, fighting against all sorts of bad beginnings and unrewarding examples, he more than anyone taught me to love our tremendous heritage of English language and literature." And Finn never doubted that it was *his* heritage: "My friends and companions, Tennyson, Browning, Keats, Shakespeare, Francis Thompson, Donne, Housman, the Rossettis. All as alive to me as though they had been members of my family." After all, as he was surprised and proud to discover, F. T. Palgrave (whose *Golden Treasury* he knew thoroughly) was part-Jewish.[204]

Language and cultural barriers could be more difficult for another group of immigrants, though they were born within the United Kingdom and generally spoke English. Bill Naughton (b. 1910), who created the proletarian unhero *Alfie* (1966), grew up in Lancashire among Irish colliers, whose attitude toward education was very different from East End Jews. "Ambition of any kind was suspect amongst my boyhood street-corner pals: the thing was, you knew what you were, and you left it at that, so that folk knew where they were with you," he remembered. "You didn't welcome anybody who began chopping and changing, or who wanted to improve himself; others were made to feel even worse by such capers." When he repeatedly scored at the top of the class in examinations, his mother uneasily suggested that he allow someone else to take first place next time. There was

> an almost inborn impression of belonging to the ignorant, the poor, and the uneducated—the ones who had nothing to give to the world but the labour of their two hands, and the best thing to do was not to expose yourself to ridicule by writing, but to conceal yourself and your thoughts—keep your mouth shut, stick to your job, and leave writing and the running of the world to your superiors and those in authority above you.

When it became known that Naughton had literary aspirations, an old coalbagger warned him "tha'll never make a writer as long as tha has a hole in thy arse," pausing for the words to take effect. "I'm afraid tha'rt like us all, tha's never been eddicated to it or to usin' thy mind. That's where they have the workin' man beat. There's no harm in having a try, I suppose, but I understand that them as has had a university eddication have a job to master the art of writing. If I were thee, lad, I'd keep to coal."

Naughton concealed his literary work as best he could. He went to bed immediately after coming home from work and got up at 11:30 p.m. to begin writing. Without a room of one's own, "it wasn't easy," he recalled. "There is almost no privacy in working-class life, and any change in routine arouses suspicion." Under those pressures, he found writing far more stressful and exhausting than manual labor. "The sight of the rows of little lettered keys on the typewriter tended to make me feel dizzy or at times faintly sick. Just as I enjoyed the familiar feel of the big coal shovel ... so I disliked the sight of those keys. ... I often thought, thank God none of my mates can see me." Naughton had a circle of intellectual friends, all unemployed workers,

> But we couldn't discuss much. It was difficult for us to formulate in our own words the ideas we had understood. I remember one youth ... who used to console himself after losing a game of billiards by quoting Bishop Berkeley. He used to prove in words that the game had been all imaginary, that billiard balls as such did not exist, and that even the money he was paying out was not what we thought it was.

If they did acquire the necessary language, the educated classes were likely to be unappreciative. When Naughton applied for conscientious objector status during the Second World War, the tribunal chairman found him suspiciously literate: "Where did you pick up that word 'background'? ... That word ... is not one a lorry driver would use." "I couldn't help feeling hurt," Naughton recalled, "that they should deny one the right to use the English language." That hit both ethnic and class nerves: he had been born in County Mayo, of peasant stock. At any rate, he was using the language to read Locke, Nietzsche, Thoreau, Schopenhauer, Marx, and *The Faerie Queene*. They were not easy to decipher at first, but as he pieced together an understanding of what he was reading, he became more critical and less deferential, more inclined to see individuals where others saw only "the masses":

> After reading some few hundred pages of anthropology, and being supposed to have some comprehensive picture of a strange tribe among whom the author had lived for a couple of years, I would think: "Curious, he seems to know everything about these people, but if I write about these people I have always lived among I find they are almost every one different. And even as a whole, I don't actually know very much about them. Each single home I visit is unlike the rest. Even my wife, whom I have known, slept beside, eaten and lived with, watched and wondered about, I dare not speak of her with as much authority as he speaks of these whole peoples." I'm afraid this took some time—realising that writers and philosophers were ordinary people.

Once he had grasped that, however, he could see that the literary anthropologists who went snooping around his own community were equally fallible. "Almost every portrayal of working-class life and people that I read was a travesty. No wonder the different classes had such absurd notions of how one another lived. I felt it was my personal obligation to rectify this disparity, so far as possible."[205]

The Most Unlikely People Buy Books Now

Once public libraries and cheap classics were widely available, motivated working people were able to narrow the cultural gap separating them from the educated classes, at least in the realm of literature. By the 1930s and 1940s, a large personal library was no longer a rarity in the slums. Rose Gamble, the daughter of a cleaning woman and an irregularly employed seaman, remembered that her sister acquired and read secondhand penny volumes of Conrad, Wodehouse, Eric Linklater, Jeffery Farnol, Edgar Wallace, Jane Austen, Thomas Hardy, Mark Twain, Arnold Bennett, R. L. Stevenson, and John Buchan.[206] The family of one Soho dustman had, by 1930, accumulated 750 volumes, largely from a secondhand stall beneath their window.[207] A 1932–33 survey of a mainly working-class London neighborhood within a one-mile radius of the Mary Ward Settlement found that only 6 percent of households possessed fewer than six books, while 23 percent had more than a hundred.[208] (A century earlier, in the poor sections of Bristol, only 57 percent of families had Bibles or prayer books, and 27 percent had no books at all.)[209] A 1944 survey found that nearly two-thirds of skilled workers and almost half of all unskilled workers grew up in homes with substantial libraries, and that many working-class parents of the previous generation had encouraged reading:

Table 6.5A: Reading in Parents' Home, 1944 (in percent)[210]

	Middle Class	Upper Working Class	Lower Working Class
How many books were in your parents' home?			
Many	87	63	42
Few	12	35	54
Other and vague	1	2	4
Did your parents encourage reading?			
Yes	63	48	38
No	31	45	58
Other and vague	6	7	4

Only a fifth of the current generation of parents in the lower working class (and none in the middle class) said they discouraged reading. The time spent reading books clearly declined with income, but was still fairly substantial even in the lower working class, and there was little class difference in the time devoted to newspapers and magazines:

Table 6.5B: Average Hours Per Week Spent Reading, 1944

	Middle Class	Upper Working Class	Lower Working Class
Books	8.7	5.0	3.1
Newspapers	4.3	4.0	3.8
Magazines	1.1	1.0	0.9

To get a sense of which books were being read, one can turn to a 1940 survey of pupils (634 boys, 611 girls) at what were called Senior, Central, Intermediate, Modern, or Area schools, where education terminated at age fourteen. This cohort, represented something less than the working-class average: the best pupils had already been skimmed off and sent to grammar schools on scholarship.[211] The remaining students were asked which books they had read over the past month, excluding those required at school. These figures, then, must be multiplied by twelve to arrive at the number of readers over the past year. Of course, if the pupils had been asked whether they had *ever* read these titles, the numbers would have been larger still. Though there was a large demand for Edgar Wallace and Edgar Rice Burroughs, some of the most popular books were classics:

Table 6.6: Books Read by Senior School Pupils, 1940

		Boys (N = 634)	*Girls (N = 611)*
	Arabian Nights	10	11
	The Bible	2	19
Blackmore	*Lorna Doone*	9	12
Brontë, C.	*Jane Eyre*	0	11
Bunyan	*Pilgrim's Progress*	7	7
Carroll	*Alice in Wonderland*	6	23
Defoe	*Robinson Crusoe*	33	11
Dickens	*A Christmas Carol*	28	31
	David Copperfield	18	29
	Nicholas Nickleby	4	5
	The Old Curiosity Shop	2	31
	Oliver Twist	22	45
	The Pickwick Papers	5	7
	A Tale of Two Cities	11	19
Eliot	*The Mill on the Floss*	0	8
Grahame	*The Wind in the Willows*	1	10
Hughes	*Tom Brown's School Days*	27	12
Kingsley	*The Water Babies*	5	25
	Westward Ho!	7	1
Stevenson	*Kidnapped*	4	6
	Treasure Island	62	18
Stowe	*Uncle Tom's Cabin*	1	22
Swift	*Gulliver's Travels*	13	27
Twain	*Tom Sawyer*	10	5

Even in this below-average group, 62 percent of boys and 84 percent of girls read at least some poetry outside of school: some favorites were Kipling, Longfellow, Masefield, and Newbolt among the boys, Blake, Browning, de la Mare, Longfellow, Masefield, Tennyson and Wordsworth among the girls.[212] Sixty-seven percent of girls and 31 percent of boys read plays outside of school, with Shakespeare accounting for 23 percent of the plays mentioned by girls and 32 percent of the boys' choices.[213] Out of school and in schooltime private reading periods, boys read about six books per month and girls just over seven.[214]

In 1940 light fiction was still the staple at the public library in working-class Fulham, but the men were also borrowing Huxley's *Antic Hay*, Zola's *The Downfall*, Kipling's *Limits and Renewals*, and *Les Misérables*; the women, *Sense and Sensibility* and *The Story of an African Farm*.[215] By 1944 Dickens, Hardy, and Jane Austen were the second, third, and fourth most popular novelists at the Bristol public libraries.[216] In February 1940 a Gallup poll found that 62 percent of adults were currently reading a book, settling back to 51 percent a year later and 45 percent in 1946–47.

A wartime surge in working-class demand was reported to Mass Observation by London librarians and booksellers in 1943–44:

There are a great many more of the younger working class people to be seen now, taking an interest in books. I notice them everywhere I go. But a lot of them want the classics, and nearly everything is out of print. I think there never was a time when there was so much obvious hunger for books, and so few books to satisfy it. (British Museum Reading Room)

There's quite a new interest in books on the part of the less educated section of the community,—factory hands and so on. I suppose it must be the blackout that has made them take to reading. We certainly get a lot of young people in, that you can see are quite unused to bookshops and feel rather awkward at first. We've had dozens of new customers among young people earning good wages in factories and so on, who come in regularly and do a suprising amount of buying. (Victoria bookshop)

I should say that there have been big changes in the trade since the war .... There are two quite new classes who are buying books; the people who have been making money out of the war and who are really quite ignorant about books, and the factory workers. We get a lot of mechanics in here, constantly buying books. It's partly that they don't cost [ration] coupons. But I think there's a genuine desire for what one might call culture, on the part of these mechanics. They don't buy technical books only, by any means. Some of them buy poetry, some of them buy the classics when they can get them, and quite a number buy books on painting and on different painters. Books on Cézanne or Gauguin or other painters that aren't too modern,—these mechanics buy all those. That's one reason for the book shortage, these new types of people all buying books. (SW1 bookshop)

The factory workers up there are all going mad on buying books, and there's the ARP and the demolition squads quite near, and they buy books too. (SW3)

Quite a different type of person is buying books now from the ones that bought books before the war. They still do, of course, but the big extension is among people who aren't used to buying books. You can tell that from all the letters and enquiries we get from people in the provinces. Some of them are factory workers, some of them have obviously made money during the war, and you can tell from the style of their letters that they don't know much about buying books, it's quite new to them. I can't give you figures, of course, but I can assure you that we're selling large numbers of books to people who before the war would have been the non-book buying public. (Bloomsbury bookshop)

The most unlikely people buy books now .... We've extended sales tremendously among the working classes. Just to give you a typical example: there's a parcel here, we're sending off to a factory hand in the Midlands. He used to write and ask for a book occasionally. Now he sends us a pound a week, regularly, and we send him books. Most of them are technical books, but not all. That's fifty-two pounds a year on books; we like people like that. I should say that the skilled worker has been buying more books since the war than he ever saw in all his life before. (WC1 bookshop)

As to people reading more, well, I should say that large numbers of people who hardly read at all before the war are reading regularly now. It's partly the black-out and the fact that they have to make their own amusements. But it's a direct result of the war, too. People's curiosity has been awakened,—they want to read and find out a few facts for themselves,—they want to understand the world better, and so they've started to read. (Chief librarian, SW)

When Mass Observation asked why they read, practically the same proportion in all classes (38 or 39 percent) said "knowledge," though among the working classes it was still usually young men who gave this answer, not often women.[217] Big employers like the International Chemical Company responded to the wartime culture boom by offering its workers lecture series on company time. Coping with severe labor shortages, the corporation felt that these perks helped to recruit and retain good employees.[218] Meanwhile, CEMA was bringing classic theater to the proletariat. "Never had we heard such music in the human voice," one Durham miner's daughter recalled.

Miners and their wives sat entranced, with little smiles on their listening faces, while the Shakespearean cadences whispered and roared over them. It was a unanimous verdict that the experience was better than the pictures. Even the older miners, who had in their youth walked miles to attend the live theatre to see real actors in melodramas like *Murder in the Red Barn*, and therefore had standards of comparison other than those of us who had been fed on celluloid pap, added the weight of their approval to the general verdict.[219]

In the words of P. C. Vigor, a worker at Vauxhall Motors, that was "How Culture Nearly Came to the Masses." This surge of artistic ferment gained impetus from the general optimism created by the 1942 Beveridge Report and the 1945 Labour landslide. "More than this promised security, there seemed an under-current of something more: a fuller life based on the practise of and the appreciation of Further Education and ART in all its forms," Vigor wrote. After the war many companies sponsored cultural programs designed to make their employees "rounded citizens who were interested in other subjects than sex, strong drink, cowboys and football." You may detect a dash of lemon in that last sentence:

as a WEA student, Vigor was amused by the presumption that workers enjoyed no higher pursuits and had to be spoon-fed culture. All the same, he admitted,

> One of my friends at the time often affirmed that, although his job consisted of throwing white hot rivets to a rivetter working on a truck chassis, his intellectual field widened at the opportunity of being able to listen free to such speakers as Dr. Joad, Lord Lucas and the educationalist Dr. Livingstone, in the works canteen.
>
> He joined the theatrical section of the recreation club, the debating section and the art section. At an exhibition one of his pictures was accepted. It hung in the works canteen and showed blue grass, mauve trees and purple sheep and cows under a pinkish sky. It was commended by the eminent *Sunday Times* critic, Mr. Eric Newton ....
>
> At one period nearly everybody went on a course of some sort or other. I ... enjoyed week-ends in colleges at Cambridge, Oxford, Nottingham and in other cities and boast to acquaintances of my experiences at "my" university. ... There was talk of hanging copies of masterpieces on the [factory] walls, but although this became a feature in many offices as a counterblast to the usual pin-ups of Betty Grable and thrilling calendars, it never took off.

Even if it did not displace calendar girls, the "Art for the People" movement clearly "sprang from the grass roots," Vigor asserted: "Ordinary folk wanted it." The Vauxhall canteen was decorated with murals and hosted concerts. "For one shilling to hear the London Philharmonic Symphony Orchestra under Sir Adrian Boult or Basil Cameron and other international conductors was wonderful." The experience transformed Vigor from a self-described "philistine, and musical pariah" into a music lover who helped organize local concerts in Luton.[220]

In his postwar sociological surveys, Ferdynand Zweig estimated that 20 to 25 percent of workingmen could be considered self-educated, much the same proportion that Arnold Freeman arrived at thirty years earlier. His case studies included a blacksmith who enjoyed H. G. Wells, travel books, and films like *Caesar and Cleopatra* and *Jane Eyre*; two sailors who were fans of Joseph Conrad; a gasfitter who bought 5s. seats for the Albert Hall, and particularly liked Strauss, Beethoven, Bach, Mozart, and *La Bohème*; a fitter and turner who read biographies, autobiographies, and philosophers like Marcus Aurelius; a retired electrician who almost daily attended lectures at the South Kensington Science Museum; a public park sweeper who read Dumas, Dickens, and Jack London. In a pub Zweig overheard two hotel kitchen workers debate whether religious faith and morals are innate or socially conditioned, and why God permits human suffering. When Zweig asked his subjects "What in your view is the greatest factor in workers' progress and betterment?" the answer "invariably" was "Education," though different respondents variously emphasized vocational, liberal, political, or moral education.[221]

Thanks largely to the postwar expansion of secondary and higher education, cultural literacy continued to improve. When Zweig returned in the late 1950s to survey workingmen, he found roughly 40 percent recognition of Marx and Einstein, 35 percent for Darwin, 25 percent for Tolstoy, 17 percent for Freud, and more than 90 percent for Dickens, Shaw, and Wells. (Working-class women still scored much lower.) Surely the BBC deserves some credit for the fact that practically all the men recognized Mozart and Chopin.[222] A 1975 poll found that Shakespeare was correctly identified by 92 percent, Beethoven 91 percent, Columbus 87 percent, Napoleon 86 percent, Karl Marx 59 percent, Rubens 56 percent, Freud 54 percent, Tolstoy 45 percent, Raphael 41 percent, Whistler 35 percent, Aristotle 33 percent, and 68 percent for the date 1066.[223] The contrast with Sheffield in 1918 is striking, even allowing for the fact that the 1975 survey was not limited to the working classes. In current debates over cultural literacy, it would be a serious error to look for any golden age in the past. The WEA and Everyman's Library did noble work, but only for a motivated minority: Britain really is better off with the Open University and Penguins in every airport bookstall. The question that still confronts us is whether this vast cultural wealth is fairly shared among all, in inner city schools as well as those that serve the affluent. In that sense, E. D. Hirsch is entirely right to criticize the maldistribution of knowledge in contemporary America. When he argues that democracy and equality are impossible without mass cultural literacy, he is only saying what generations of British working people knew in their bones.

Chapter Seven **The Welsh Miners' Libraries**

At a street corner in Tonypandy I heard two young miners discussing Einstein's Theory of Relativity. I know this was exceptional, but it is significant; and it is true.

—H.V. Morton, *In Search of Wales* (1932)

The miners' institutes of South Wales were one of the greatest networks of cultural institutions created by working people anywhere in the world. One would have to look to the Social Democratic libraries of Wilhelmine Germany or the Jewish workers' libraries of interwar Poland to find anything comparable.[1] Many of the Welsh miners' libraries began in the nineteenth century as mechanics' institutes, temperance halls, or literary societies, at first under middle-class patronage. Victorian colliers commonly authorized deductions from their wages to pay for their children's education, but when school fees were abolished in 1891, this flow of money (usually 1d. or 2d. per pound) was redirected toward the miners' institutes. They also received contributions from coal companies and other benefactors, but as the miners themselves usually covered the ongoing expenses, they controlled acquisitions. In 1920 Parliament set up the Miners' Welfare Fund, which taxed coal production and royalties and directed the revenue to fund pit baths, welfare halls, scholarships, and libraries. By 1934 there were more than a hundred miners' libraries in the Welsh coalfields, with an average stock of about three thousand volumes. In smaller villages the collection might consist of only a few hundred books, and the librarian was usually a miner who volunteered to mind the shop one evening a week.[2] The larger institutes were well-equipped cultural centers offering evening classes, lecture series, gymnasia, wireless rooms and photography labs for amateurs, and theaters as well as libraries.[3] They hosted concerts, amateur drama, traveling theatrical troupes, opera, dances, trade union and political meetings, choirs, debating societies, and eisteddfodau (Welsh cultural festivals), and about thirty of the Welsh workmen's halls were equipped with cinemas.[4] The pride of the movement was the Tredegar Workmen's Institute: by the Second World War its library was circulating 100,000 volumes a year. It boasted an 800-seat cinema, a film society, and a popular series of celebrity concerts, where the highest-priced tickets went for 3s.[5]

An Underground University

There were similar institutions in all the coal regions, many of them established by mine owners with the frank intention of making their workers sober, pious, and productive. Around 1850, nineteen out of fifty-four collieries in Northumberland and Durham had some kind of library or reading room.[6] Yet there was a special ferment in the South Wales coalfields, rooted in the peculiar cultural environment of the region. Wales had a tradition of weaver-poets, artisan balladeers, and auto-didact shepherds going back to the seventeenth century.[7] Welsh Nonconformity, Sunday schools, choral societies, temperance movements, and eisteddfodau all championed education and especially self-education. Penny readings had been especially popular in Wales, sponsored by chapels of all denominations, with a high level of participation by working-class members.[8] In 1907, thirteen out of fifty-three residential students at Ruskin College were South Wales miners.[9] Wales could also boast high concentrations of WEA students in 1938–39: 2.90 per 1,000 population in South Wales, and 6.25 (highest in the nation) in North Wales.[10] But in 1914 public libraries served only 46 percent of the Welsh population (compared with 62 percent in England), and most of the neglected areas were small towns and rural regions.[11] According to a 1918 parliamentary enquiry, "not a single municipally maintained public library is to be found in the central Glamorgan block of the coalfield."[12] Miners' libraries filled that vacuum: they were rarely established where public libraries already existed.[13]

Though affluent intellectuals denigrated the "Little Bethels" of the mining regions, collier-intellectuals recognized that they provided an enormous stimulus for debate and literary analysis, not unlike the yeshivas of Eastern Europe. Durham miner Jack Lawson conceded that "there were tendencies to narrowness and hypocrisy" in the chapels, but

> if Britain holds a comparatively advanced position in her social movements to-day [1932] it is largely because the eighteenth-century Methodist Revival saturated the industrial masses with a passion for a better life, personal, moral, mental, and social. … The chapel gave them their first music, their first literature and philosophy to meet the harsh life and cruel impact of the crude materialistic age. Here men first found the language and art to express their antagonism to grim conditions and injustice. Their hymns and sermons may have been of another world, but the first fighters and speakers for unions, Co-op. Societies, political freedom, and improved conditions, were Methodist preachers.

It was at a Methodist society that Lawson first found working people who shared his intellectual passions. One had been well into his thirties before his wife taught him to read: in his old age he was successfully tackling the New Testament in Greek and Nietzsche. Others ultimately became teachers, ministers, musicians, social workers, and even professors. Their houses were open to each other and they visited on impulse:

> We talked pit-work, ideals, the Bible, literature, or union business. The piano rattled, the choir was in action, and we sang with more abandon than any gang who has just learned to murder the latest film song. ... I was encouraged to express myself; to preach and to speak. I was given their warm, helpful friendship, and the hospitality of their homes. No longer was I "queer" or "alone." My thoughts and dreams were given direction. Even when they did not understand or agree they encouraged, and ignorant and intelligent alike combined to set my feet firmly on the road I had haphazardly been looking for.[14]

The parents of D. R. Davies (b. 1889) had no formal education and could not read English until fairly late in life, but his father (a collier) composed Welsh poetry and hymns, as well as a cantata performed by the chapel choir. Their home was often filled with neighbors discussing religion:

> Conversation was invariably about things that mattered, and ideas were the staple of intercourse. Without knowing it, I breathed a strong, stimulating intellectual atmosphere. In later years I realized what a great advantage I had enjoyed. It has been my lot to know at different times wealthy, polished and educated families amongst whom argument about great ideas was bad form. An entirely different and better start was mine. In my homelife, it was ideas that mattered. By their intellectual intensity my parents created in me a zest for ideas which gave direction to my life. ... My home did for me as a boy what the University is supposed to do, according to Newman, for youth—it awoke and encouraged a love of ideas for their own sake. And that advantage outweighed most of the handicaps under which I lived, handicaps neither few nor light.

All the children had music lessons and were singers, one with the Moody Manners Opera Company. "I was constantly listening to Bach, Handel, Mozart, Mendelssohn and Schubert—oratorios, cantatas and masses," Davies recalled. There was one schoolteacher who, in a class of sixty, "create[d] in his pupils an independent passion for knowledge," and inspired Davies to read Macaulay's *History of England* before his twelfth birthday. Because it was leavened with that spacious enthusiasm for music, literature, history, and theological debate,

> the Welsh Nonconformity in which I was reared did not make for narrowness and fanaticism of mind as so many of the frustrated, embittered critics of my generation have maintained. Today [mid-1950s] we are living upon the capital of those same "tin Bethels", and when that gives out (as it is now doing) the futility and leanness of our contemporary life will become more obvious and disastrous. It is true that our fathers, in Wales, taught us a religion of cast-iron

dogma, which, according to all the theories, should have made us obscurantists, inhabiting a very small world. But it did not. In some mysterious way we became freemen of a spacious world. Along beside the narrow dogma went a broad culture. What happened to me demonstrates that fact clearly. Can anything promote a wider interest than history? And history led to politics, which, in turn, opened the door on many intellectual horizons. And music. It fed the spirit as an instrument of perception, as an organ of knowledge. It made for inner refinement. We had few of the graces and polish of manners, characteristic of an affluent society, but music gave us something better. It created in us a fastidiousness of moral as well as literary taste. It gave us a sense of the necessary relation between content and form. I very much doubt whether, fundamentally, Eton or Harrow would have given me a better start, educationally, than the "tin Bethel", the elementary council school, and my home.

Even the perpetual Bible reading, in English and Welsh, stimulated an appetite for secular literature. "I defy any child of ordinary intelligence to read the Bible constantly (in the Authorized Version) without acquiring a genuine literary taste, a sense of style, and at least a feeling for the beauty of words. Before I was twelve I had developed an appreciation of good prose, and the Bible created in me a zest for literature," propelling him directly to Lamb, Hazlitt's essays, and Ruskin's *The Crown of Wild Olives*. Later, after a day of exhausting mine work, he would attend union meetings, chapel meetings, literary and debating societies, lectures, and eisteddfodau, and then do some fairly heavy reading. He joined the library committee of the Miners' Institute in Maesteg, made friends with the librarian, and advised him on acquisitions. Thus he could read all the books he wanted: Marx, Smith, Ricardo, Mill, Marshall, economic and trade union history, *Fabian Essays*, Thomas Hardy, Meredith, Kipling, and Dickens.[15]

If it still seems amazing that such a vital cultural life could flourish in the coalfields—that the Ton-yr-efail Workmen's Institute could spend £45 for the *Oxford English Dictionary*—one miner offered a fairly mundane explanation. As he saw it, all British workingmen were legendary hobbyists. Some gardened, played football, or bred dogs; others pursued literature, philosophy, or classical music with the same intensity.

Every miner has a hobby. Some are useful; some are not. Some miners take up hobbies as amateurs; some study to escape from the pit. I did .... Why do we do so many things? It's difficult to say. It may be a reaction from physical strain. The miner works in a dark, strange world. He comes up into light. It is a new world. It is stimulating. He wants to do something. It may be, in good times, pigeon racing, fretwork, whippet racing, carpentry, music, choral singing or reading. Think what reading means to an active mind that is locked away in the dark for hours every day! Why, in mid-Rhondda there are 40,000 books a month in circulation from four libraries ....[16]

Stephen Walsh (b. 1859), the Lancashire collier and Labour MP, offered another explanation:

> There is no place like a mine for promoting discussion. There is something in the never-absent danger, in being shut away underground, that draws men to each other, that makes them anxious to break the darkness and sense of loneliness by talk on subjects many and various.
>
> And so, in our discussions, I found that my book-learning, my ability to introduce fresh topics, gave me a status far beyond my years, and no doubt I caught something of the art of public speaking in delivering little expositions or lectures to my mates on things I had read about.[17]

Joseph Keating (b. 1871) read little but boys' magazines and 3d. thrillers until he stumbled across Greek philosophy. He was particularly struck by the Greek precept "Know thyself," and pursued that goal by reading until 3 a.m. As a collier he was performing one of the toughest and worst-paid jobs in the mine—shovelling out tons of refuse for a half-crown a day—when he heard a coworker sigh, "Heaven from all creatures hides the book of fate." Keating was stunned: "You are quoting Pope." "Ayh," replied his companion, "me and Pope do agree very well." Keating had himself been reading Pope, Fielding, Smollett, Goldsmith, and Richardson in poorly printed paperbacks. Later, he was reassigned to a less demanding job at a riverside colliery pumping station, which allowed him time to tackle Swift, Sheridan, Byron, Keats, Shelley, and Thackeray. Having acquired a violin, case, and bow from a housemaid for 18s., he took lessons and formed a chamber music quartet, playing Mozart, Corelli, Beethoven, and Schubert. Ultimately he became a journalist and novelist, yet he never forgot the almost sexual excitement that came from pursuing books and music in the coalfields:

> Reading of all sorts—philosophy, history, politics, poetry, and novels—was mixed up with my music and other amusements. I was tremendously alive at this period. Everything interested me. Every hour, every minute was crammed with my activities in one direction or another. New, mysterious emotions and passions seemed to be breaking out like little flames from all parts of my body. As soon as the morning sunlight touched my bedroom window, I woke. I did not rise. I leaped up. I flung the bedclothes away from me. They seemed to be burning my flesh. A glorious feeling within me, as I got out of bed, made me sing. My singing was never in tune, but my impulse of joy had to express itself.[18]

Welsh miners did not have to consult Matthew Arnold to recognize the liberating power of culture. They experienced it first-hand and saw it in their workmates. In the village of Penrhiwceiber the intellectual lights were Ted, a collier who read thirty books a year, and Jeff, an engine driver who played "The

Rustle of Spring" on the piano and invited his friends over to enjoy his impressive library of classical recordings:

> At such times we did not feel we were colliers doing menial and dangerous jobs in the bowels of the earth, but privileged human beings exposed to something extraordinary. Most of us were badly or barely educated, but such young men as Ted and Jeff who, alone and without help and encouragement, educated themselves, and having drunk the wine of knowledge they seemed to glow with pride. The work they were engaged in, lowly as it was, never depressed them. They neither grumbled about the work they did, nor did they envy others in better positions on the surface of the pit. These characteristics I noticed about men such as Ted and Jeff, and from the examples of such men I was able to develop my own pride, my own search for knowledge which eventually enabled me to leave such a dangerous and difficult occupation. ... These two characters, their attitudes, their personalities, their cheerfulness, their honesty and their kindness, I am sure made the rest of us feel that culture had done much to make them better men. They were never crude, never resorted to bouts of bad language and temper, or said mean things about others, although they took a "lot of stick" from many pit workers for being different.[19]

Nottinghamshire collier G. A. W. Tomlinson (b. 1906?) volunteered for repair shifts on weekends, when he could earn time-and-a-half and read on the job. On Sundays "I sat there on my tool-box, half a mile from the surface, one mile from the nearest church and seemingly hundreds of miles from God, reading the *Canterbury Tales*, Lamb's *Essays*, Darwin's *Origin of Species*, Wilde's *Ballad of Reading Gaol*, or anything that I could manage to get hold of." That could be hazardous: once, when he should have been minding a set of rail switches, he was so absorbed in Goldsmith's *The Deserted Village* that he allowed tubs full of coal to crash into empties. The pit corporal clouted him and snatched the volume away. He returned it at the end of the shift and offered a few poetry books of his own— "BUT IF THA BRINGS 'EM DARN T'PIT I'LL KNOCK THI BLOCK OFF." Tomlinson tried to write his own verses and concealed them from his workmates, until one of them picked up a page he had dropped and read it: "No good, lad. Tha wants ter read Shelley's stuff. That's *poetry!*" When, during the 1926 miners' strike, Tomlinson read "The Charge of the Light Brigade," an obvious political message

> crashed into my mind, mixing together the soldiers of the poem and the men of the pits, I was terribly excited. Why hadn't all the clever people found this out? Wasn't it plain enough for everybody to see? The very quality which was praised in the men at Balaclava was being decried in the men of the pits. Foolishness! they called it when speaking of the miners. Loyalty! they called it when speaking of the soldiers. As usual I invented a word for it. Britishness I called it.[20]

Wil John Edwards (b. 1888) recalled one miner who had practically memorized Shakespeare's works ("in a sense they had been grafted into his mind"), and another who dismissed Shaw as rehashed Ibsen ("Good ideas come to him and he chases them at speed, but his foot lands on the idea's train; there is a rending squeak as a bit comes away"). Edwards himself pursued Gibbon, Hardy, Swinburne, and Meredith. His reading was suggested by the literary pages of the *Clarion*, the librarian at the Miners' Institute (who directed him to *Don Quixote*), and a still more influential literary salon:

> Guidance in the choice of good books came to me deep down in the pit, in the darkness and dark dust of a narrow tunnel more than a thousand feet below the earth's surface. And it must not be thought that this guidance came through a grim atmosphere of serious, intellectual discussion. It was subject to inconsequential digressions; it was often interrupted by jokes that brought rough laughter and it was coloured, or stained, by what the rules call bad language, which, nevertheless, can flow naturally through the lips of good men. ... And what an inheritance was mine! This clean, glowing gift offered to me, and accepted by me, in the dimly relieved darkness is often taken for granted, if it is taken, by boys in more fortunate circumstances than mine were but, and here you have a paradox, when offered to me it had increased a thousand-fold in value perhaps because its light shone in the darkness though black coal-dust. ... Perhaps the sense of being forced to live in an invading darkness together with work, not always dull and mechanical, which demanded alertness to danger and resource, forced them to consider essentials without trimmings ....

It was in the pit that Edwards first heard the names of Spencer, Darwin, and Marx, as well as some fairly eloquent literary criticism: "Meredith is a poet who sings with a harp. Kipling is a nobody who sings what he can sing with a mouth-organ although he does talk of tambourines." That evening he tried to borrow Meredith's *Love in a Valley* from the Miners' Library, only to find twelve names on the waiting list for a single copy.[21]

"Apart from religion," recalled a Durham colliery blacksmith (b. 1895), "perhaps the most important influence at work in the village was the colliery institute. It provided some sort of alternative to the chapels, and churches, in that there was a Library."[22] Percy Wall (b. 1893) described his institute as a "blatantly utilitarian" building with a "square, cemented front" and a "drab and poorly lit" reading room, but it offered a wonderful escape from a dull Welsh village:

> I could view the future through the words of H. G. Wells, participate in the elucidation of mysteries with Sherlock Holmes, ... or penetrate darkest Africa with Rider Haggard as my guide. I could laugh at the comic frustrations of coaster seaman or bargee at the call of W. W. Jacobs. What a gloriously rich age it was for the story teller! ... When the stories palled there was always the

illustrated weeklies with their pictures of people and conditions remote from my personal experience but opening vistas of a large expanding world of architecture, art, travel and home life in foreign lands I could never expect to visit. I could laugh with *Punch* or *Truth*, although some of the humour was much too subtle for my limited education. Above all I could study the *Review of Reviews* and learn therein the complexities of foreign affairs.[23]

All that was fascinating if only because there were few other distractions in most Welsh mining towns. One housewife depended on Women's Co-operative Guild lectures to keep up her morale in a village where the only other recreations were a cinema, a British Legion hall, and some unfinished athletic fields.[24] Besides the institutes, the chapels, and the pits, there might be one other center of discussion in a mining town:

> As the Workmen's Institutes were considered the miners' Universities the shoemaker's sheds were considered their Common Room, and therein the young "listened to the wisdom of the ancients." … These village cobbler's shops, in fact, were often cells of flourishing cultural activity, the boot repairers themselves often being thoughtful and wellread men who played active parts in the cultural, social and religious life of the village, keen Eisteddfodwyr, nonconformists to the core, politically minded, displaying at all times an interest in current affairs generally and the world around them.[25]

Marx, Jane Eyre, Tarzan

Except for the occasional schoolteacher, shopkeeper, or clergyman, the miners' libraries served a working-class clientele; and miners determined acquisitions. The book selection committee at Tredegar was headed by that stalwart of the Labour Party's left wing, Aneurin Bevan. The borrowing records of these libraries—unlike those of public libraries—can therefore offer a profile of working-class reading preferences uncontaminated by middle-class cultural hegemony. Only three usable registers out of the hundred-odd South Wales miners' libraries have survived, but they are the best source we have to address the question that every study of reader response must begin with: Who read what?

Historians of the Welsh coalfields have offered three possible answers: *Das Kapital, Jane Eyre,* or *Tarzan of the Apes.* South Wales was a hotbed of labor militancy where, according to historians of the left, many workers were well-versed in the Marxist classics. Then there is *The Corn is Green* school of novels and memoirs, which describe a thriving autodidact culture in the coalfields, where colliers fervently studied the classics in adult education classes. The third answer was proposed in 1932 by Q. D. Leavis in *Fiction and the Reading Public.* Mrs. Leavis was nostalgic for a prelapsarian Elizabethan age, when the masses enjoyed

Shakespeare and Marlowe. In the Victorian period, however, the reading public began to divide between high and low literature, and after the First World War the two audiences were irreconcilably divorced. The masses now consumed rubbishy crime fiction and romances, while the great modernists—Lawrence, Joyce, Woolf, Eliot—were read only by small educated coteries.

Frankly, Mrs. Leavis's methods of literary sociology were crude. She dismissed out of hand the notion that you might ask people what they were reading and why they were reading it. Instead, she stationed herself in Boot's Circulating Libraries with a notebook: since Boot's specialized in light best-sellers, she got the results she was looking for. She also seized on the statistic that three out of every four books borrowed from public libraries were fiction, which she took as prima facie evidence of low literary tastes. (It proves more conclusively that Mrs. Leavis retained the Victorian literary prejudice against fiction.)[26]

We can test all these theories against three miners' libraries, beginning with the Tylorstown Workmen's Institute. We have the complete borrowing record for the year 1941, when there was a total of 7,783 loans.[27] Most of them fit Mrs. Leavis's definition of trash literature—books with titles such as *Corpses Never Argue* (13 loans), *Lumberjack Jill* (19), *A Murder of Some Importance* (24), *The Mysterious Chinaman* (18), *Anything But Love* (31), *The Flying Cowboys* (31), and P. G. Wodehouse's deathless *Right-Ho Jeeves* (17). The standard adventure novels also had their fair share of readers—Jack London's *White Fang* (17), Conan Doyle's *His Last Bow* (6) and *The Lost World* (15), Victor Hugo's *The Hunchback of Notre Dame* (12), Alexandre Dumas's *The Man in the Iron Mask* (4) and *The Three Musketeers* (11), John Buchan's *The Thirty-Nine Steps* (5), James Fenimore Cooper's *The Last of the Mohicans* (2), *Robinson Crusoe* (1), and *The Swiss Family Robinson* (5). There was considerable demand for such children's classics as *Little Women* (20), *The Prince and the Pauper* (8), and a remarkable Victorian survival, Hesba Stretton's *Jessica's First Prayer* (13).

On the whole, the greats and near-greats among the Victorians and Edwardians did not fare well. John Galsworthy's *A Modern Comedy* (4) and *The Forsyte Saga* (1), H. G. Wells's *Kipps* (1) and *The Island of Dr. Moreau* (3), Arnold Bennett's *Hilda Lessways* (2) and *Anna of the Five Towns* (2), Charles Reade's *Peg Woffington* (2) and *The Cloister and the Hearth* (1), Wilkie Collins's *The Woman in White* (5), Elizabeth Gaskell's *North and South* (1) and *Mary Barton* (2), and Rudyard Kipling's *Plain Tales from the Hills* (2) were all outpaced by A. J. Cronin's *The Citadel* (6) and Stella Gibbons's spoof *Cold Comfort Farm* (16). Bernard Shaw had a large number of readers, but they were spread thinly across his various works: *Man and Superman* (2), *Heartbreak House* (3), *Misalliance* (1), *Back to Methuselah* (1), *The Doctor's Dilemma* (4), *Androcles and the Lion* (2), *Pygmalion* (1), *John Bull's Other Island* (2), *Major Barbara* (1), *Plays for Puritans* (2), *Plays Pleasant* (4), *Plays Unpleasant* (1), and his novel *Cashel Byron's Profession* (1). Only one classic could compete with the best-sellers: *Pride and Prejudice* was loaned no less than 25 times, but that was in the wake of the 1940 film version starring Greer

Garson and Laurence Olivier, and Austen's popularity did not carry over to *Mansfield Park* (2). The only Dickens novel much in demand was *A Tale of Two Cities* (7), followed by *David Copperfield* (3), *Barnaby Rudge* (1), and *Oliver Twist* (1). Shakespeare's plays and a volume on Shakespeare's characters were borrowed a total of six times, *Gulliver's Travels* seven, *Anna Karenina* only three, Bacon's essays once, Longfellow's poems once. It may seem remarkable that Willa Cather's *Death Comes for the Archbishop* was checked out eight times, but a 1930 poll of readers of the *Sunday Dispatch* placed it among the postwar novels most likely to be read a generation hence.[28]

Mrs. Leavis bemoaned the indifference of the reading public to modernist literature, and Tylorstown confirms her pessimism. *A Passage to India* was borrowed once, Eugene O'Neill's *Strange Interlude* once, Robert Graves's *Goodbye to All That* twice. It seems extraordinary that all of five readers took out Virginia Woolf's *The Years*; but even including those, the fact remains that literary modernism accounted for barely one in a thousand loans.

Though Tylorstown was in what was supposed to be Britain's Red Belt, there was scarcely more interest in politics. The collection included biographies of Labour Party leaders George Lansbury (2 loans), Keir Hardie (1), and James Maxton (2). There were a few readers of foreign affairs, as represented by John Gunther's *Inside Europe* (5) and Michael Oakeshott's *Social and Political Doctrines of Contemporary Europe* (2). Beyond Reuben Osborn's *Freud and Marx* (2), there was hardly any demand for either these thinkers. Books by or about Lenin were taken out by six readers, Hewlett Johnson's *The Socialist Sixth of the World* by five, but the invasion of Russia on 22 June did not increase interest in the Soviet Union. Politics were more palatable if cast in the form of a dystopian thriller: there were eleven borrowers of Jack London's *The Iron Heel*, a prophesy of fascism that inspired Orwell's *Nineteen Eighty-Four*.

Closer to home, there were only two borrowers each for Walter Hannington's *The Problem of the Distressed Areas*, E. Wight Bakke's *The Unemployed Man*, and H. A. Marquand's *South Wales Needs a Plan*; and just one for Orwell's *The Road to Wigan Pier*. Miners were not much interested in reading about miners: only one of them checked out Richard Llewellyn's *How Green Was My Valley*, and two read *These Poor Hands*, a memoir by Welsh collier Bert Coombes. In contrast, there were ten borrowers for a more romantic kind of proletarian literature, W. H. Davies's *The Autobiography of a Supertramp*. The difference was that Davies took his readers away from the coalfields, recounting his wanderings through England, Canada, and America. "Yer writing about the pits?" a workmate asked J. G. Glenwright, a Durham mineworker with aspirations to authorship. "Nothing much to write about, is there? Just the muck and the dirt and that. An' perhaps a nasty accident, now and then."[29] The daughter (b. 1924) of an unemployed Rainton miner borrowed novels of social realism from the Carnegie Library, but her mother objected: "There's enough misery in the world without dwelling on it. Next time fetch a nice historical novel back."[30] As a WEA lecturer in the early 1930s, Roger Dataller found that emigrés from Staffordshire preferred that he did not discuss *The Old Wives' Tale*: "Having left the Five Towns they did not in the least wish to be reminded of the district again." *Sons and Lovers* provoked a more positive reponse among miners: one recalled vividly that he too, as a child, had listened cowering in his bedroom while his parents quarrelled.[31]

Fortunately, the catalogue to the Tylorstown library has survived, so we can compile a list of books the miners did not borrow but probably could have.[32] In 1941 they checked out nothing by Walter Scott, John Ruskin, or Thomas Hardy. They had no interest in the poetry of Keats, Shelley, or Siegfried Sassoon. They ignored *Women in Love*, *Testament of Youth*, and *A Portrait of the Artist as a Young Man*. The political writings of G. D. H. Cole, John Strachey, Bertrand Russell, and Ness Edwards's *History of the South Wales Miners* were left undisturbed on the shelves. And no one touched *Das Kapital*, Marx's *Critique of the Gotha Program*, or Engels's *Origin of the Family*.

Of course, there is a bias involved in any short-term study of library records. It can exaggerate the impact of a best-seller, which may enjoy a brief supernova of popularity and then, a year or two later, be forgotten. If a classic is borrowed at a slow but steady rate over the decades, it may eventually surpass the readership of the most popular light fiction. We can test that hypothesis against the Cynon and Duffryn Welfare Hall Library register, which records reading habits over a generation, from 1927 to the early 1950s. These records confirm the popularity of the authors Q. D. Leavis loved to hate: Edgar Rice Burroughs, Warwick Deeping, Jeffery Farnol, E. Phillips Oppenheim, Gene Stratton Porter, Edgar Wallace. But there was also some interest in the standard English classics. Demand for *Pride and Prejudice* (9 loans), *Wuthering Heights* (16), *Robinson Crusoe* (9), *Oliver Twist* (7), *Westward Ho!* (7), and *Vanity Fair* (10) was modest but sustained over many years. Even *Culture and Anarchy* had four borrowers, and there was a striking and continuing demand for some Victorian sensation novels and best-sellers—Grant Allen's *Dumaresq's Daughter* (18), R. D. Blackmore's *Lorna Doone* (13), Bulwer-Lytton's *The Disowned* (11), Florence Marryat's *Facing the Footlights* (20), and Mrs. Henry Wood's *East Lynne* (16). The last had nearly a million copies in print by 1909. In Welsh miners' libraries, Mrs. Wood was the fourth most frequently stocked novelist, behind only Dickens, Scott, and H. Rider Haggard.[33] She was also the most popular author among working people in Middlesbrough, as Florence Bell discovered in 1901.[34] In the Cornish working-class town of Megavissey in the early 1920s, *East Lynne* and *The Channings* "occupied half the population all the time," wrote a fisherman's daughter.[35]

There was not a trace of interest in modernist fiction at the Cynon and Duffryn Library. For these readers, the art of the novel culminated with Bennett, Galsworthy, and Wells. As for books on politics and social issues, only five can be located in the entire collection. Understandably, no one read what Lloyd George had to say about *The People's Will* in 1910, or a clergyman's report on *Ten Years in a London Slum*. What is more remarkable is that these miners, like those at

Tylorstown, cared little for books about themselves: only five borrowed James Hanley's *Grey Children*, a report on unemployed Welsh colliers. Wales was a pacifist stronghold, and the only political tracts that really engaged this community dealt with the horrors of war: H. L. Gates's *The Auction of Souls* (13 loans), an account of the Armenian massacres, and *Disarm! Disarm!* (15), a novel by pacifist Bertha von Suttner. Following that pattern, perhaps the most popular political book in Tylorstown was *The Bloody Traffic*, Fenner Brockway's 1933 exposé of the munitions industry. It had eight borrowers in 1941, when Britain's survival depended on her arms factories.

This neglect of politics was entirely typical. A survey of nineteen miners' libraries catalogues between 1903 and 1931 found that all the social sciences accounted for only 5.3 percent of book stock; at only one library did the proportion rise above 10 percent. There was nothing by Marx on the shelves at Treharris in 1925, Tredegar in 1917, or the Cwmaman Institute in 1911; and only 1.6 percent of stock at Cwmaman was in the "Politics, Economics and Socialism" section. Granted, many libraries built up their socialist collections over time, especially during the "Red Thirties," but though Tredegar eventually acquired the complete works of Lenin, he remained unread. At Cwmaman, as at other miners' libraries, readers mainly demanded fiction, which rose from 52.6 percent of loans in 1918 to 81.7 percent in 1939: politics never accounted for more than 0.5 percent. At the Senghenydd Institute library in 1925, on the eve of the General Strike, the proportions were 93.4 percent fiction, 0.4 percent economics.[36] Any historian of working-class culture in early twentieth-century Britain must deal with this inescapable fact: the readers of Marx and Lenin were infinitesimal compared with the fans of Mrs. Henry Wood.

Very revealing, in this context, is a 1937 survey of 484 unemployed men aged eighteen to twenty-five in Cardiff, Newport, and Pontypridd. Only 3 percent were involved in any kind of political organization, compared with 16 percent in religious groups, 11 percent in sports clubs, and 6 percent in adult education classes. One might expect these young men to be the shock troops of discontent, but none of them completely rejected Christianity. Though only 8 percent were active church members, 35 percent attended church or chapel at least once a month. Only seven of these men were politically active—either Labour, Communist, or Conservative. Fifty-seven percent identified reading as a major leisure activity, but it was usually the daily paper (if their family took in one), mainly for sports, news headlines, and the horoscope. They read books for escape (Westerns, aviation, crime and detective stories), purchasing cheap paperbacks, then exchanging them among friends, family, and comrades in the Employment Exchange queue. Hardly anyone was aware that such books were available at the public library—only 20 percent ever visited the libraries, and just 6 percent were regular borrowers. Another escape was the cinema: nearly everyone went at least once a month, 22 percent at least twice a week. Only 8 percent listened to anything on the radio but dance bands and variety: everything else was dismissed as "highbrow."[37]

Where, then, were the Marxist miners of South Wales? The most plausible answer is that the literary and political interests of Welsh working people could vary enormously from town to town. As an adult education bulletin noted in 1929, the Welsh valleys were remarkable for their isolation:

The miner or his wife may pay a visit to Cardiff once or twice a year, or spend Bank Holiday on Barry Island, but it is quite likely that he has never been into the next valley, while the one beyond that may be entirely *terra incognita* to him. Communications are bad, and the geographical isolation has led to a corresponding mental isolation. This is aggravated by the fact that the whole population of the valley is dependent on the coal industry. There is no variety in industrial life, and there is almost no differentiation into social grades such as may be found in any ordinary town. This makes for an extraordinarily friendly spirit; there is little shyness and much hospitality. But it has tended to make also for a narrowness of outlook. The miner may never have met an agriculturalist, a factory worker, or a docker, nor mixed with any society but that found in his own immediate surroundings. He never sees either the inside or the outside of a really fine building, be it church or office, public building or home. His horizon is formed by the tops of the bare hills which for so long have shut him away from the rest of the world. His middle distance is furnished with the seemingly endless rows of slate-roofed cottages, each as cramped and ugly as the one which he and his family occupy, and his foreground is the tiny kitchen, the untidy street, or the narrow seam of coal at which he expects to spend 47 hours every week between the ages of 14 and 70. Death is an ever-present possibility down the pit; life seems anyhow precarious when the chance of employment is, at the best, dependent on unknown forces and incomprehensible world movements, or, at the worst, dependent on the word of an unpopular manager, himself the tool of some remoter authority distrusted and disliked.

This cultural environment was hospitable to sectarian dogmas of various kinds: Welsh Nonconformity, miners' syndicalism, and the Marxism preached by the National Council of Labour Colleges (itself subsidized by the South Wales Miners' Federation). Steeped in the Welsh tradition of theological debate, miners plunged quite readily into adult classes in philosophy and history, though instructors often found them wedded to a simplistic economic determinism: "Any superstructure of Church or State, institutions or art, was disregarded as being irrelevant." A class that included some non-miners was likely to be receptive to a more complex view of historical causation.[38] The village of Mardy was a "little Moscow," where in 1933 ninety colliers were studying the proletarian philosopher Joseph Dietzgen at the Miners' Institute,[39] but reading tastes were very different in Tylorstown, just a few miles down the valley. Miners in the anthracite region to the west, around Llanelly, Swansea, and Port Talbot, were not so Marxist as those farther east;[40] and Aneurin Bevan's Tredegar was a moderate Labour town with hardly any Communists.[41] The intellectual climate could vary dramatically from mineshaft to mineshaft: as one collier explained, "The conveyor face down the Number 2 Pit was a university," where Darwin, Marx, Paine, and modernist theology were debated, while "the surface of Number 1 Pit a den of grossness."[42]

These extreme cultural variations can also be attributed partly to the fact that literary activities in a given community usually depended on the initiative of a few energetic individuals. Whatever their class, whether they patronized miners' institutes or Boot's Circulating Libraries, readers relied heavily on the advice of librarians in choosing books. A miner with a passion for the English classics was a likely candidate for institute librarian: in that capacity he could acquire the books he wanted to read himself and recommend them to his neighbors. In Penrhiwceiber the collier who supervised the Miners' Library three evenings a week steered a fellow pit worker toward Jack London, Gorky, A. E. Coppard, Chekhov, Maupassant, and Flaubert's *Madame Bovary* and *A Simple Heart*.[43] If Marxists were in charge of acquisitions (and they often were) they could do the same for leftist literature.[44] And if no one in town provided intellectual guidance, there was always *Tarzan of the Apes*.

Library acquisitions policies could shape reading habits, especially in isolated villages where there were few other sources of books. This pattern becomes apparent in the borrowing ledger of our third miners' library, maintained by the Markham Welfare Association. Here at last we find a coal town with classic literary tastes. In the first period covered by the ledger (September 1923 to December 1925), Jane Austen, the Brontës, Dickens, and George Eliot are the most popular authors. In Markham as in Cynon and Duffryn, no one borrowed Marx, but there was a continuing demand for Mrs. Henry Wood. Even in the depressed interwar years, there were still a few readers of Victorian self-help tracts: Samuel Smiles, James Hogg's *Men Who Have Risen*, and W. M. Thayer's *From Log Cabin to White House*.

Then there is a gap in the ledger. In September 1928 a new Markham Village Institute was opened, paid for mainly by the Miners' Welfare Fund.[45] The record resumes in March 1932, revealing that reading habits had hardly changed at all over nearly a decade. Indeed, judging from the borrowings, it appears that the Markham Library acquired very few if any new volumes. The probable cause was the prolonged and deep depression that crippled the coal industry from the early 1920s. After the boom years of the First World War and the immediate postwar period, demand for coal collapsed. French and German mines resumed full production, more efficient American mines captured markets, oil was becoming an increasingly important energy source. Daily wages, which averaged as much as 21s. 6¾d. in February 1921, were down to 9s. 5½d. by October 1922. Between 1920 and 1937, 241 pits closed in South Wales, the employed workforce shrank from 271,161 to 126,233, and total annual wages plummeted from £65 million to £14 million.[46] The Welsh unemployment rate was 13.4 percent in December

1925, 27.2 percent in July 1930, and in the Merthyr area as high as 47.5 percent by June 1935.[47]

The miners' institutes had been funded by deductions from miners' wages, the Miners' Welfare Fund, and by local governments. Now all these sources dried up. Between 1920 and 1928 the Cwmaman Workmen's Institute and Library saw its income cut from more than £2,500 to just over £450. At the same time, circulation more than doubled, from 14,966 to 31,054. That was a common pattern throughout South Wales, where armies of unemployed miners had plenty of time on their hands and few other distractions. If their libraries did not close down completely, librarians' wages were slashed, central heating was done without, and acquisitions of new books came to a dead stop. (Even in good times the Miners' Welfare Fund rarely subsidized the purchase of books.) The book budget for the Ferndale Workmen's Institute went from more than £315 in 1920 to zero in 1929. Under those conditions, the old stock would be borrowed over and over again until it was reduced to waste paper. By 1929, investigators for the Carnegie Foundation were reporting that, in the typical miners' library, 50 to 100 percent of the collection was unfit for circulation. By 1937, many libraries had bought no new books in the past decade.

A few miners of this era remembered reading every book in their library. Though the borrowing ledgers show that some volumes were never touched, these claims may not be much exaggerated. One library in Ynyshir was patronized by 300 out-of-work miners who borrowed a total of 500 books a week, an average of eighty-six books per miner per year.[48] Enduring prolonged structural unemployment, any one of them could have exhausted a collection of several hundred volumes. Out-of-work men commonly and quite plausibly claimed to read three or four books a week.[49] In a collective memoir of twenty-five unemployed people, eleven testified that the Great Depression gave them more time for reading (including a London fitter who went through a novel a day), four took up adult classes, and a colliery banksman used the opportunity to write a novel.[50] "It brought a bubbling sense of freedom at first," wrote dole-queue veteran Walter Greenwood, "a secret elation in being at liberty to indulge in a feast of uninterrupted reading at home, the public library or in those Manchester bookshops where, by tacit consent, the kindly proprietors permitted young men and students to browse among the new books."[51] "Thousands used the Public Library for the first time," recalled itinerant laborer John Brown, who read Shaw, Marx, Engels, and classic literature until he exhausted his South Shields library. "It was nothing uncommon to come across men in very shabby clothes kneeling in front of the philosophy or economics shelves."[52] If the library stocked Jane Austen (or Mrs. Henry Wood, for that matter) she would have been read, simply because she was on the shelves. "I just went through the catalogue," recalled Jack Lawson, and without any more guidance than that he was introduced to Dickens, Scott, Charles Reade, George Eliot, the Brontës, Hardy, Hugo, Dumas, Shakespeare, and Milton.[53]

The lack of new books only encouraged literary conservatism among the miners, who continued to read Victorian best-sellers into the 1930s. Even in prosperous times their libraries had relied partly on purchases and donations of used books, and they always tended to preserve their old stock. Of 1,433 volumes in the Treharris Institute library catalog in 1894, about 900 were still there 31 years later; and all but thirty of the 953 volumes in the 1896 Cymmer Institute catalog were in the 1913 catalog as well.[54]

Availability, according to Q. D. Leavis, explains why the masses attended Shakespeare in 1600: "Happily they had no choice." Except for bearbaiting and a few chapbooks, what else competed for their attention?[55] In the twentieth century, she argued, capitalism produced an ever-increasing flood of trash novels—and by virtue of their sheer volume, these diverted readers from the great books. In an isolated mining village, where there was nothing much to read but some tattered copies of Victorian classics, the corruption of reading tastes might be delayed, but inevitably *The Bowery Murder* and *The Slave Junk* would penetrate the remotest Welsh valleys. As if to confirm Mrs. Leavis, the Markham library acquired, by March 1935, a new batch of books by lowbrow authors: Warwick Deeping, Jeffery Farnol, E. Phillips Oppenheim, Edgar Wallace. The borrowing record up to October 1936 does indeed manifest a literary Gresham's Law, with bad books forcing out the good. In the rush to read *Anna the Adventuress*, *Captain Crash*, *The Sloane Square Mystery*, and *Pretty Sinister*, borrowings of the English classics drop precipitously.

The next phase in the ledger, from April 1937 to March 1940, reveals an even more striking shift in quite another direction, produced by a world in crisis. Ethiopia had been conquered, the Japanese had invaded China, a civil war was raging in Spain, a European war was on the horizon. In Markham, the escapist fiction that was so popular a few years before had dramatically given way to the literature of political commitment: Zola's *Germinal* (18 loans), Henri Barbusse's antiwar novel *Under Fire* (7), Walter Brierley's *Means Test Man* (11), Upton Sinclair's *Oil!* (22), Ralph Bates's *Lean Men* (on the Spanish Revolution of 1931, 13 loans), Mulk-Raj Anand's *The Coolie* (9), and Robert Tressell's bitter proletarian novel *The Ragged Trousered Philanthropists* (20). Markham miners read *Quiet Flows the Don* (10) and the socialist realism of Feodor Gladkov's *Cement* (22). *Salka Valka*, a portrait of Icelandic fishermen by Halldór Laxness, won a large following (18 loans) with its Christian communist message. The same readers still found Marx hard to tackle, but ten of them borrowed Engels's *The Origin of the Family*. Proletarian intellectuals like T. A. Jackson, Bert Coombes, W. H. Davies, Willie Gallacher, and Joseph Dietzgen had a few borrowers each. But even in this politically conscious phase, readers in all three communities were more interested in conflicts abroad than in issues closer to home. Ellen Wilkinson's polemic on unemployment in Jarrow, *The Town That Was Murdered*, had only one borrower. There was more interest in Agnes Smedley's *China Fights Back* (7), John Langdon-Davies's *Behind the Spanish Barricades* (3), and *Mein*

Kampf (6). Hywel Francis may have exaggerated the proletarian internationalism of the Welsh coalfields, but it certainly existed here, where the banner of the Markham Miners' Lodge proclaimed "The World is Our Country: Mankind are Our Brethren."[56]

The final section of the register covers July to December 1940—the Battle of Britain—and once again there is a marked change in borrowing habits. Now politics gives way to *Outlaws of Badger Hollow*, *Murder Must Advertise*, Sherlock Holmes, Edgar Wallace, and Marie Corelli. Perhaps the Nazi–Soviet Pact had dampened interest in Russia. The war had created new jobs, but not necessarily in the mines: many former colliers now made long and tiring commutes to munitions factories.[57] That might explain why the people of Markham now sought relief in easy reading. Only two of them borrowed anything as challenging as *Point Counter Point*—the only appearance of modernist literature in the entire ledger.

Decline and Fall

There were, then, intellectuals and Marxists among the Welsh colliers, but they were minorities concentrated in certain places and certain intervals in time. As the prime movers behind the miners' libraries, they represented the last efflorescence of the Victorian ethos of mutual improvement. When they died or moved away (between 1921 and 1931 more than a third of the population aged fifteen to twenty-nine left the Rhonnda valleys) there were no successors to carry on the institutes. By 1934 the signs of decline were obvious:

> To-day a number of the Institutes are dormant; housed in dull buildings, painted in sombre browns and deadly terra cotta; cinema and billiards going strong and education going weak; a complete neglect of the needs of women and girls, and more often than not of the younger generation of boys; no co-operation with other Institutes; a very small annual addition of new books; little or nothing being done to help the leisure problem of the unemployed.[58]

In 1937 the Blaina Institute had 300 to 400 members (down from 1,000) paying 3d. weekly. (The population of the district had fallen by more than a quarter since 1923.) Books could still be borrowed from the institute library for 1d. each, and nearly 400 individuals did so, but of those only thirty went in for any kind of serious or leftist literature: the rest only read escapist fiction. Lectures at the Blaina Institute still had a following, but adult education was much less popular and far less available than it had been before the war.[59]

Maes yr haf Educational Settlement, established in 1927, found a ready audience among unemployed miners for its courses in philosophy and history, and it succeeded in overcoming the isolation of the mining villages, where even diligent autodidacts knew little of towns in the next valley. Among its students, as one observer noted, it managed "to create a sense of confidence in the outside world, and so to help break through the reluctance and doubt of men trained from childhood with little or no idea of other places or other work beyond that of mining." In so doing, however, *Maes yr haf* encouraged the best minds to leave the coalfields. As early as 1929, it was apparent that

> The keenest people—those who are attracted by the prospect of further education—are also those who have, or who gain, the enterprise to embark on new ventures and a new life far removed from the old. Incidentally, this creates a real difficulty in the maintenance of attendance and standards of work in the classes .... *Maes yr haf* is continually losing some among its most promising students; it would be failing in duty if it did not encourage and help men to leave the stricken locality. It is only by working out to its own destruction continually in this sense, that the Settlement can make its fullest contribution to South Wales.[60]

Walter Haydn Davies, a colliery worker turned adult education teacher, recalled that most members of his miners' institute debating society aimed to acquire the intellectual skills necessary for upward mobility. "By the time the late Twenties came most of us had obtained positions in such institutions as the church, in teaching, the police force, the automobile industry, in electricity and chemicals, and in the distributive trades." There was also a singer, a labor relations officer with the National Coal Board, a miners' agent, some colliery officials, and a bookie.[61] In 1939 an investigator reported a general awareness among miners that the decline of coal was irreversible. Of fifty colliers' sons in an elementary school, he found only six who wanted to go into the mines, of whom four aspired to be foremen. All the students at a Junior Technical School were aiming at other lines of work, usually clerical, teaching, or skilled mechanical.[62]

"There are marvellous opportunities for educational and cultural development, of which we were deprived in our days," said an old miner-intellectual after the Second World War, "but they are not used." Only the least educated and ambitious remained in the pits, and their reading tastes ran to romances and crime stories.[63] Welfare institutes closed their libraries as the expansion of public library services made them superfluous. One Yorkshire coal town had no public library until 1925, and no full-time librarian until 1942. By 1953 the public library was issuing more than 5,000 books a month in a community of 14,000, and had effectively replaced the reading room at the imposing Miners' Welfare Institute, which was no longer used for that purpose.[64] In Bargoed the miners' institute only issued 2,661 books in 1961, down from 33,021 in 1931. The typical institute had become, said one ex-collier, a "stark waste of froth and strip-tease, surrounded by the slick decor of vinyl-covered easy chairs and formica-covered tables and glistening counters that click to the sound of glass."[65] The Tredegar Institute, which spent more than £1,000 a year on books in the late 1940s, was broken up in 1964. Nearly all of its magnificent collection is lost.[66] The last Rhonnda colliery (Mardy) closed in 1990. Only two Welsh miners' libraries (at the Cwmaman Institute and Trecynon Hall) survived to the end of the century.[67]

For comparison, one could look to the vast network of libraries maintained by the German Social Democratic Party and trade union movement. The trade unions alone supported at least 547 libraries in 1911. By then they were already reporting patterns of borrowing that would later show up in the Welsh miners' libraries. The Central Workers' Library in Gotha was typical: in 1909 light literature accounted for 1,818 loans, more than two-thirds of the total. There was limited demand for the classics (150 loans), science (162), history (239), and social science (66), and scarcely any interest in party literature (13) or trade unionism (6). A Mittweida library reported that in 1909 its 404 volumes of literature had been checked out 6,288 times, more than fifteen loans per volume, whereas 552 volumes on politics and economics were borrowed 1,076 times, just under two loans per volume. There is evidence, moreover, to support Mrs. Leavis's theory that increasing availability of light reading crowded out serious books. Between 1891 and 1911, loans of fiction from the Berlin Woodworkers' Library increased from 14.6 to 70.4 percent of the total; at the same time, natural science fell from 13.5 to 3.4 percent, social science from 22.7 to 2.2 percent, poetry from 12.6 to 4.3 percent. German workers did read novels with a social conscience, such as *Germinal* and Disraeli's *Sybil,* and they were interested in utopian literature, particularly August Bebel's *Woman Under Socialism* and Edward Bellamy's *Looking Backward.* But like their counterparts in South Wales, they found Marx difficult to digest. Friedrich Stampfer borrowed Karl Kautsky's popularization of *Das Kapital* and found only the first twenty pages heavily thumbed: the rest was "virgin purity."[68]

By and large, then, Mrs. Leavis was right, but with some qualifications. Though Welsh miners certainly had an enormous appetite for thrillers, Westerns, and tepid sex, they did not entirely ignore Charlotte Brontë. They did ignore the moderns, but in the late 1930s more than a few of them wanted to know more about Germany, Spain, the Soviet Union, and even Iceland. The "mass reading public" was not an undifferentiated mass: even within the circumscribed area of the Welsh coalfields, reading tastes could vary considerably over time and between communities. And after all, these conclusions are based largely on a sample of only three towns: they may well be upset when someone finds a fourth library ledger. Perhaps, across the valley, they were reading *Mrs. Dalloway.*

Chapter Eight The Whole Contention Concerning the Workers' Educational Association

The history of education, like literary history, has been written mainly from the perspective of the suppliers rather than the consumers. The scholarly spotlight has focused on teachers and administrators, bureaucrats and theorists, academic institutions and curricular policy. We have seen that a dramatically different history of primary education emerges when we shift our attention to the students; this perspective can also produce a new history of adult education. The Workers' Educational Association and Ruskin College were the most influential continuing education movements in twentieth-century Britain, and their institutional histories have been thoroughly chronicled. But here we pose different questions. Who were the students? Why did they enroll? What were their intellectual goals? What cultural equipment did they bring to their classes? What went on inside the classroom? Most importantly, how, if at all, did the WEA and Ruskin College change the lives and minds of its students?

All these issues are relevant to a controversy that erupted early in the twentieth century and continues today, a question that can only be resolved by studying WEA and Ruskin College students at close range. According to Marxist critics, these institutions played an important role in steering the British working class away from Marxism. Roger Fieldhouse has argued that the WEA's emphasis on objective scholarship and open-mindedness "could have the effect of neutralising some students' commitments or beliefs and integrating them into the hegemonic national culture."[1] As he sees it, "For all its occasional lapses, the adult education movement was welcomed by the establishment as a bulwark against revolutionism, a moderating influence and a form of social control. ... It attracted potential working class activists and leaders by its radical image, but diverted them from the communist or revolutionary politics to which they might otherwise have been drawn."[2] Stuart Macintyre makes much the same point, with more subtlety:

> Adult education is not an ideological neutral activity whose political character simply reflects the dispositions of teacher and student. Rather, the development of adult education in the inter-war years was an integral aspect of official social policy. ... The 1917 Commissions into Industrial Unrest ...

urged the provision of civic education in order to rectify the effects of Marxist classes. The WEA was the chief instrument of this state policy of adult education. In making this assertion, I do not mean to impugn the honesty of [A. D.] Lindsay, [R. H.] Tawney and others sympathetic to the labour movement who laboured in this field. It is their educational objective that lends itself to this characterisation. In essence the mission of the WEA was to break down the isolation of working-class students and integrate them in a national culture; in political terms the proletarian intellectual was encouraged to widen his narrow class horizons for a broader progressive polity; in cultural terms the old, dogmatic, autodidact knowledge was discredited in light of university studies.[3]

The weakness in this argument is a weakness common in theories of social control: it focuses on the controllers rather than the people who are supposed to be controlled. Fieldhouse in particular concentrates on discerning the intentions of educational officials and WEA tutors: his research is thorough but ultimately misdirected. Although Board of Education inspectors and Tory-dominated councils did occasionally accuse the WEA of teaching leftist propaganda, the latter generally stood up to that kind of pressure.[4] In the end, Fieldhouse has to concede that "there was little evidence of heavy censorship or control." He does produce what seems to be a smoking gun in the form of a 1925 memorandum by Lord Eustace Percy, president of the Board of Education:

In adult education there is a continual struggle between the Universities and those bodies, like the Workers' Educational Association, who work with the Universities, on the one hand, and the Communist or semi-Communist Labour Colleges on the other. Hitherto the Workers' Educational Association and the University Extension people have been able to make headway against these undesirable propagandists because, largely owing to Government assistance, they can offer better facilities. On the whole, too, I think the education that they do offer is extraordinarily useful. ... If we force the WEA and the Universities to cut down their work we shall not choke off the demand for local classes which is extraordinarily strong in all parts of the country, but we shall open a wide door to the Labour Colleges, and I believe that the result will be deplorable. In fact my own view is that £100,000 spent annually on this kind of work, properly controlled, would be about the best police expenditure we could indulge in .... [5]

But when we ask what the students were writing and thinking, it becomes apparent that Lord Percy is irrelevant to this discussion. He could not regulate them or their teachers. If he did fund the WEA as agent for social control, he was wasting the taxpayers' money.

The Ruskin Rebellion

Ruskin Hall was founded in 1899 by three Americans: Walter and Anne Vrooman, a philanthropic couple, and Charles Beard, who would later make a brilliant career as an iconoclastic historian. The principal was Dennis Hird, a former Anglican minister, temperance advocate, and socialist activist. Besides the Vroomans, Ruskin Hall garnered financial support from other well-to-do supporters and from trade unions. Based in Oxford, it offered correspondence courses, which in their first two years enrolled 1,800 students. But it was primarily a residential college: tuition and board were only £31 a year, though students had to do all the housecleaning and cooking. It affiliated with the WEA, and both dedicated themselves to offering a nonideological liberal education to working-class students in cooperation with the universities. Oxford academics lectured at Ruskin and served on its governing council, though it remained independent of the university.

By 1907, after it had been rechristened Ruskin College, political fissures were beginning to appear. The student body was becoming increasingly Marxist, and they could get large helpings of Marxism in Hird's classes in sociology. But H. B. Lees Smith, lecturer in economics, was an orthodox apostle of the free market. He dismissed Marx's labor theory of value, arguing that the wages offered in the marketplace (even in sweatshops) represented the true and fair value of the worker's labor, and could not be raised by unions or legislation without creating unemployment. Worse, he proposed to put some backbone into Ruskin's unstructured curriculum, introducing examinations, assigning more essays, and discontinuing Hird's sociology lectures. Nearly unanimous student protests preserved Hird's course, and most of the students refused to take the first exams.

Meanwhile, an Oxford-WEA joint committee was exploring proposals to allow Ruskin students to take Oxford diplomas in applied economics and politics. From the perspective of university representatives, this was a well-intentioned offer to open up Oxford to workingmen. The militant students, however, were suspicious: they perceived a plot by a bourgeois university to absorb a potentially troublesome working-class college and indoctrinate its students in capitalist ideology. In October 1908 the student rebels and their supporters organized themselves into the Plebs League, with a magazine to be edited by Hird. A struggle for control of the college ended with Hird's forced retirement, whereupon the majority of students voted to boycott classes: they demanded Hird's reinstatement and the dismissal of two anti-Marxist lecturers. The governors responded by shutting down Ruskin for two weeks, then readmitting only those students who signed a pledge to obey college regulations.

Some students, disgusted with the militants' disruptive tactics, remained with Ruskin College. Others seceded in August 1909, when the Plebs League founded the Central Labour College (CLC) in Oxford, with Hird as its warden. The CLC proclaimed that what distinguished it from Ruskin College and the WEA was

"Independence in Working-Class Education"—it would have no truck with universities that served the capitalists, and it frankly repudiated "impartial" liberal education for Marxist indoctrination. Relocated to London, the CLC enjoyed financial support from some unions which had backed Ruskin College, particularly the railwaymen's union and the South Wales Miners' Federation. To bring Marxist education to the rest of the country, the National Council of Labour Colleges (NCLC) was set up in 1921. The CLC and NCLC were therefore competing for the same students and the same trade union subsidies that went to Ruskin College and the WEA, with the result that the ideological differences between the two camps were magnified (as they always are in academia) by battles over enrollment and resources.

Ruskin College quickly recovered from its crisis and successfully prepared many of its students for the university diploma in economics and political science. Its governing council was reconstituted to include only representatives of working-class organizations: trade unions, Co-operative societies, and the Working Men's Club and Institute Union.[6] The college continued to attract militant (though not humorless) students, who sang to the tune of "Keep the Home Fires Burning":

Put the thing through quickly,
Wage the class war slickly,
Hang the rich to lampposts high—but don't hang me.
Stick to Marx, my hearties,
Damn the Labour Party,
Keep the hell fires burning bright for the bourgeoisie![7]

In the late 1930s Henry Smith, a resident tutor in economics, still had to deal with confrontational Communist students, though he had some sympathy with their politics. Their object was (still) "to discredit the teaching of anything but Marxism and to win converts," he recalled. "During the war I met a Cambridge don, a Communist Party member, who told me that he had written the admission essay for one of the cell, with mistakes carefully inserted."[8] As that last incident suggests, the question of whether there was enough Marx in the Ruskin curriculum was by then moot: students could now learn Marxism from the Oxford faculty. The same workingmen who, in 1920, regarded universities as ruling-class institutions, were often astonished by the hard leftism of the Oxbridge graduates they met in adult classes in 1946.[9] By then, of thirty-one adult education tutors based at Oxford University, at least ten (according to Roger Fieldhouse) and perhaps as many as fifteen were Communist Party members or fellow travelers. Now it was the students' turn to complain of Marxist indoctrination.[10] It was a neat reversal of the 1908 crisis, as well as a measure of changing intellectual trends.

One might see here enacted on a miniature stage the political struggles that would rock universities throughout the Western world sixty years later. Neither was purely a product of ideology. One Ruskin graduate complained that nothing was more grueling than "attempting to wade through a chapter of Marx. ... For some students the ordeal would be too much and copies of Marx would be thrown across bedrooms." The Ruskin protest may have been more a rebellion against the study load, the housekeeping chores, and the frictions that naturally arose when poor workingmen were cast among the gilded youth of Oxford, at a time when only one percent of undergraduates came from the working class.[11] Moreover, Ruskin students were grown men and trade union activists, who would not tolerate the disciplinary rules applied to adolescent undergraduates. (Women were not admitted until 1919.)

In fact the college could offer a sophisticated political education for Marxists like barber John Paton (b. 1886). He testified that a Ruskin correspondence course trained him in constructing a more organized frame of mind without dampening his political passions. (He went on to found the Glasgow Anarchist Group and became general secretary of the Independent Labour Party.)

> Many of the books I'd already read but I was coming to them now under guidance, and seeing them from new and unsuspected angles. ... I was acquiring knowledge now under discipline, and finding, while doing it, that the masses of undigested, unselected facts, with which my retentive memory teemed, were falling into form and place and becoming altogether more formidable weapons in my armoury. The fear so often expressed that the "tendentious teaching" of Ruskin College destroyed a revolutionary and created instead a spineless politician, was obviously groundless in my case. I ended more revolutionary than I began.[12]

Engineer George Hodgkinson (b. 1893), a militant shop steward who read Marcus Aurelius during a sit-down strike, likewise saw no conflict between liberal education and radical politics. For him a lecture on Dante "was a philosophical breeding ground in which grew up a spirit of revolt against capitalist competitive society which pitted man against man and put him at no higher level than the beasts of the field." He passed up a partnership in a new industrial company to enter Ruskin College. Though he adored the spires of Oxford, they only made capitalism seem worse by comparison, and highlighted the class barriers to education: "For me, Oxford had clearly defined what Disraeli called the 'two nations,' that the best education was a near monopoly and unless socialists could capture the Town and County Halls, the chances to open up the highway from the elementary schools to the Universities would be minimal."[13]

Many Ruskin students, like Welsh miner Jack Lawson, jumped at the chance to attend Oxford lectures. "We were never allowed to forget that we lived in a hostile centre," he admitted, but they did not withdraw into an embittered ghetto. They socialized with undergraduates who were friends of the working class, and cheerfully stepped into the ring with those who were not:

We were not cast down, but rather enjoyed the situation. In fact, we prided ourselves that we were not as other men, and sought means of showing it. We did not wear cap and gown, but rather delighted in emphasising the difference by deliberately wearing the dingiest clothes. We fixed up Socialist meetings at the Martyr's Memorial, well knowing that it would precipitate a conflict with masses of undergraduates, who would certainly regard the meeting as a challenge and joyously accept it. We used the most lurid language about the capitalist class, and pointedly included Oxford University, its Fellows, proctors, and undergraduates, in that class. I remember how one of our men, who spoke with a Cockney accent, at one meeting, with a sweep of the arms, included the assembled undergrads as the bourgeoisie. But he called it Bow-jer-wow-sie. Every time he said "Bow-jer-wow-sie" there was a bow-wow-wow like the bark of a dog from the men in cap and gown. The end of it was a free fight, flying Ruskin men, and the windows of the College smashed with bricks. That recurred fairly often.

Lawson's academic background, which consisted of reading his way through a miners' library, was sufficient to make him feel at home at Oxford:

Did we not stand on ground made sacred by Sir Walter Scott and see on the hill the trees associated with Arnold's "Scholar Gipsy"? Could we not wander in "the Broad" and imagine where Jude the Obscure had died reciting his Litany of Pessimism from Job, "Let the day be blotted out when it was said a man child is born"? Lincoln College spoke to us of Wesley; University of Shelley; and we walked with Addison in Magdalen .... If we trod this ground in shabby clothes, it was worth it, for the things and people we had read about as in a far-off time and distant land had become real and living to us. There was no hardship, for we companied in spirit with the great of the earth, and many of them had been poorer than we.[14]

Jack Ashley (b. 1922) found that liberal studies at Ruskin College were directly relevant to his work as a trade unionist and ILP activist: "Although I was impatient to study current controversies, rather than the ancient ones of Plato, Aristotle and Socrates, I appreciated that these gave philosophical depth and understanding to fundamental political problems of all times." He despised Communist dogmatism as much as he enjoyed teachers who used shock treatment to provoke debate. ("The Peterloo Massacre? But only a few old men and a dog were killed that day, so I don't know why they call it a massacre.") Ashley was less prepared for Ruskin than most of the students, having read only two books since leaving school: Jack London's *The Iron Heel* and the regulations of the Widnes Town Council. But principal Lionel Elvin "appreciated the profound difficulties facing working-class students":

When I stumbled through the intricacies of the political theories of Marx, Hobbes, Rousseau, Locke and T. H. Green, he marked my work frankly yet gave encouragement …. He was an excellent teacher, genuinely interested in discussing ideas and persuading students to express their own. It was rather like boxing with a far superior opponent who wants to encourage you and will not take advantage of his greater skill. Yet he never patronised or pretended ignorance; he treated students as his equals in intelligence, if not in knowledge.[15]

James Sexton, the dockworkers' MP, served on the Management Committee of Ruskin College, "whose products—let it be frankly admitted—varied a good deal when put to the test in the world." Some, like Jack Lawson, served the cause of labor admirably. Some were lockstep Marxists, and to others "Oxford imparted what would to-day be called a 'superiority complex' that simply made them unmitigated snobs, with a strong dislike for the work to which they had to go to when they left the University."[16] The only generalization one can make about Ruskin graduates is that they were not politically emasculated.

The Ruskin rebels as well defy easy categorization. They included men like Frank Hodges (b. 1887), future general secretary of the Miners' Federation, who by no means repudiated liberal education or Oxford University. Down in the pits, he had read the complete works of Shakespeare by an old safety lamp until the print was smudged beyond legibility: "The plays stirred my imagination, while the sonnets enlivened my emotions in an indescribable manner." At Oxford he noted well the hostility of undergraduates toward Ruskin men, but he applauded the Oxford Union for its tradition of fair play, and he thoroughly enjoyed the university, "which for the rest of my life I shall remember with generous affection." Even while studying at the breakaway Central Labour College, he was happy to accept invitations to tea from curious Oxford society ladies: "Whilst proceeding to discuss in our delightfully dogmatic fashion the right of the State to confiscate the capitalist system, we never allowed the discussion to prevent us from confiscating all the glorious eatables that were laid before us."[17]

Another of the Ruskin rebels, Wil John Edwards, offered a remarkable insight into their mentality, which could be more ambivalent than their professed Marxism might suggest. He came from a Welsh valley where miners combined a profound hostility to capitalists with a love of books, yet did not subject literature to political tests. A militant collier might "quote poetry to suit his politics; indeed, he often did so underground where he might be four hundred yards below criticism; but … when I heard him years later talking to an audience in the Workmen's Hall, this bias carried no weight. … He appreciated the true value of verse he quoted with no reference whatever to politics." On Saturdays Edwards browsed the Rationalist Press Association bookstall, but not only for its secularist propaganda: there he bought penny paperbacks of *Julius Caesar*, *Hamlet*, *The Merchant of Venice*, and Fitzgerald's *Rubiyat of Omar Khayyam*. He spent Sundays reading through the Miners' Library, though his sister thought it a sinful distraction from chapel.

It was in the pits—"the centre of culture amongst the miners"—that Edwards was introduced to Karl Marx. None of the miners could really understand him or satisfactorily explain the labor theory of value, but that did not limit their enthusiasm: "Marx was a prophet of the revolution; what he said went, and it could hardly matter where." Following closely on the heels of the 1904 Welsh evangelical revival, Edwards's Marxism became

> a crusade demanding all the devotion of a religion. It was less a political philosophy than a deeply spiritual cult …. I am bound to admit that in those days I was swayed more by emotion than understanding …. I was a socialist, but if anyone had asked me why I was a socialist, I could not have given a clear explanation. I was looking for a precisely drawn creed, perhaps for a gospel, something I could grip mentally.

At first, a liberal education appeared to be an essential part of the revolutionary struggle. "The opposing side could afford to buy the use of clever minds": obviously the workers had to educate themselves so that, "when the time came, the blind would not be led by the blind." Besides, his grievance against capitalism was that it condemned miners to intellectual as well as economic poverty, a life "without culture and without beauty." When he won a scholarship to Ruskin College, he leapt at the chance. Some of the women in his family, fearing that he would cease to support them, tried to prevent his going by kidnapping his desk, his bicycle, and his only two suits.

The moment he arrived at Oxford (with two new suits bought on credit) he was wrenched both ways. "What attracted me so much was the promised peace which would, I was certain, enfold my days—days of quiet reading and study, days of placid companionship with others who loved books as I loved books," he remembered. "There would be no disputes, no fierce arguments and clashing of temperaments, no strikes nor threats of strikes: the days of quiet study would be joined by nights of restful peace in the shadow of the spires of Oxford; and there would be delightful walks in the quadrangles." But how could that be reconciled with the solemn pledge that he and other Ruskin students had made: that their education "was never meant to be a relish or even a privilege; it was part of a grim plan whose object was the uplift of the workers of our country"? Moreover, his first experience of the university was precisely what John Ruskin had condemned as a monstrosity of industrial capitalism: the railway station. "Ugly exploitation which had so cruelly scarred the face of my lovely valley had placed a dirty hand on Oxford too," he mourned. "I did not expect that grinding of brakes, hissing of steam and all the noise which every other station can offer." The result was not a rejection of the university, but inner conflict and guilt:

I think we all secretly found Oxford a dream which had come true, even if we might talk contemptuously of Oxford as a nursery of privilege. We were on the threshold of a new world, a strange new world to us and a delightful one: Candide in his Eldorado was not more enchanted even if our Eldorado offered a less placid existence than his. ... The spires and quadrangles of my dreams were there ..., and as satisfying in their warm loveliness as I had known they would be. To me they told a love story, the story of a craftsman's devotion to his work: and I felt I could picture the faces of those early craftsmen when, at last, the great tapering spires they had built with their small hands might be left alone to point upwards for ever. All this was so different from the drab and uniform structure of our industrial villages; so different, indeed, that, in my mind, Oxford has never lost a quality of unreality.

At Ruskin he enjoyed complete freedom to read and study, but in college lectures "the first thing that struck me was the feeling that we were being treated as if we were children back again in an elementary school which needed only a cane to complete the picture." His economics instructor was biased against socialism: one of Edwards's papers was returned with the written comment "A jolly good essay spoilt by discussing the Marxian theory of Value." When he asked to be excused from the instructor's lectures, principal Dennis Hird told him that thirty-seven other students had applied for excuses already. In what was supposed to be a workingmen's college, Welsh colliers did not care to be told that mineowners' profits represented "the reward of ability." One student, Noah Ablett, offered his own informal lectures on Marxist economics, over the objections of the college authorities.

In retrospect, Edwards conceded that Ruskin students,

very naturally, had been so concerned with the class struggle that it had become a part of us and a big enough part to crowd out any suspicion that any of our opponents might have a point of view. And how could we, with our background in those days, possibly see any other point of view than our own, that we as a class were being exploited, kept deep in the earth as the foundation of privilege?

Consequently, when Oxford officials made a sincere overture to Ruskin College—offering financial aid and opportunities to matriculate at the university proper—the students rejected it as a sellout. Edwards remembered well his Sunday school lessons, which taught him how the Emperor Constantine had coopted and corrupted Christianity. When he returned home, he removed the family Bible and *Pilgrim's Progress* from the front room table and replaced them with *The Communist Manifesto*, *The Origin of Species*, and *Das Kapital*. A Plebs League activist, he taught a class in Marxian economics that attracted a dedicated cadre of students through the 1920s.

The difficulty, as Edwards admitted, was that his economic studies began to take on "the quality of mysticism in religions: invaluable to the elect and sometimes dangerous to the crowd." Typical of the Ruskin rebels, he developed "a picture of myself as an emancipated human being standing proudly as such on the top of a hill, a wonderful production developed by biological promotion, one who could look down on the lesser animals as poor and rather endearing relations." Occasionally that arrogance provoked a reaction. One Ruskin student, a fellow Welshman whose father had been killed in the mines, exploded when Edwards talked glibly of the inevitability of revolution: "Are you as Marx-mad as the rest of them in this confounded place? ... *Das Kapital* is your Bible and Marx your Jehovah .... All the Marxians in the world cannot tell you what is going to happen in the valleys tomorrow, or next year."

Edwards retained enough Christianity to be offended by Ruskin students who organized a mock revival meeting. When one of them prayed loudly for rain, he dumped a bucket of water on his head from a first-floor window. The weak point of all surrogate religions is that they can run up against their own crises of belief, and send their followers recoiling to the faiths they once abandoned. The failure of the 1921 coal strike and the 1926 General Strike, the emptiness of "mechanical materialism," and the disillusioning realities of Soviet Communism all ultimately convinced Edwards "that there are factors in Marxism that can produce more suffering to innocent human beings than has ever been inflicted by the most savage dictators."[18]

The Difficulty about That

Meanwhile, the Workers' Educational Association had become embroiled in similar ideological battles. The successor to the mechanics' institutes, the Working Men's College, and the University Extension movement, the WEA was more successful than any of them in bringing higher education to working people. Founded by Albert Mansbridge in 1903, it enrolled 111,351 students by 1948–49. A self-governing, democratic, decentralized organization, it was supported by trade unions, co-operatives, political groups (mostly Labour, some Liberal), churches, and chapels. It sponsored university summer schools, rural rambles, art exhibitions, training courses for Sunday school teachers, and lectures on topics ranging from Shakespeare and Ruskin to first aid and child care.

The centerpiece of the WEA was the University Tutorial Class. Under that scheme, university-trained lecturers came to working-class communities to teach three-year courses, ostensibly at the university level. With a maximum of thirty-two students, each class met for twenty-four two-hour sessions each year. One hour of lecturing was followed by an hour of discussion, with fortnightly essays assigned. These courses were funded mainly by the universities, the Board of Education, and local educational authorities.

There is no question that the WEA aimed to meliorate class conflict. R. H. Tawney, president of the organization from 1928 to 1944, strove to educate

British workers toward an Arnoldian ideal of a "common culture." The WEA disavowed propaganda in favor of "impartial" and "nonpartisan" education, but it enthusiastically affirmed that the simple act of bringing university teachers and working people together in the same classroom had a political objective. Like Toynbee Hall and other settlement houses, WEA classes were designed to open up communications across class lines, to allay working-class distrust of universities, to educate the "educated classes" in the realities of proletarian life, and to train workers to exercise power in a democracy.

That policy soon drew fire from the far left. When Tawney launched the first tutorial class at Longton in 1908, his students included several members of the Marxist Social Democratic Federation, who argued that his ideal of objective scholarship was designed to distract the workers from class warfare. In fact Tawney did what any conscientious teacher tries to do with dogmatic pupils: he suggested alternative points of view and defused confrontations. As one student remembered, "A pertinacious Marxian, arguing with the tutor, challenges point after point of his exposition, until at length baffled, but not defeated, the student retires from the tussle, saying to the tutor: 'It's no use; when I point my gun at you, you hop from twig to twig like a little bird'—and laughter comes to ease the strain." After class there was tea and good fellowship, with teacher and students discussing philosophy and reciting Whitman and Matthew Arnold.[19] In 1922 Board of Education inspectors confirmed that Tutorial Classes were indeed rubbing the rough edges off the most strident militants:

> Whilst it is impossible to conceive anything more crude, more violent or more absurd, than some of the opinions expressed in the essays of a small proportion of students, the gradual effect of the combined influence of the lectures, the discussions, the reading, the discipline of writing down their thoughts and the criticisms of the tutors, comes out in the essays as the session proceeds. Expression becomes more chastened, judgments become more moderate, a sense of the complexity of the facts shows itself. ... It is almost universally true that the effect upon students who remain in the classes is to make them reconsider their original crude generalisations, to make them aware of the complexity of the social and economic system in which they live, to make them more sceptical of ready-made nostrums, to introduce an element of cautiousness into their statesmanship.[20]

That was precisely what militant socialists dreaded. Rowland Kenney, the ILP journalist, accused Mansbridge of seducing workers into "the development of the Servile State":

> He refuses to see that the draining off of what brainy men the labour movement possesses, and the turning of these into university slimed prigs, is one of the most terrible wrongs a man can inflict upon the working classes. And so he

innocently pursues his evil course. He nets in hundreds of striving workers, and inoculates them with the virus of university "culture," and preaches a non-party, unsectarian doctrine which makes a fool of him every time he is lumped up against one of the brutal facts of our modern social system.[21]

(Apropos, a few years later Kenney would find himself working for the Ministry of Information and then for the Political Intelligence Department of the Foreign Office.) Ethel Carnie, the proletarian novelist, warned that the WEA would "chloroform" the workingman:

> After having had the best of his strength and brain power sapped during the day in the interest of the capitalist, in his limited time and valuable leisure, he is taken to look at his being exploited FROM EVERY POINT OF VIEW!... Why should I look on the fact that I am robbed, from "every point of view"? If a robber stole something valuable from me, I should not fall into a philosophical survey of the situation, but rush upon him, provided I was armed. ... What brain power we have left after being exploited we had better spend in concentration on the narrow, rigid, and distinctly not impartial facts deduced from the experience of our own exploited class. Any other form of "looking around" will be similar in effect to riding in a razzle-dazzle at a fair.

WEA students found these assaults enormously condescending, and their responses should make anyone think twice before using the word "hegemony." "Will Miss Carnie be good enough to show where the chloroforming process comes in?" shot back Lavena Saltonstall, a garment worker. "Greek art will never keep the workers from claiming their world; in fact, it will help them to realise what a stunted life they have hitherto led. Nothing that is beautiful will harm the workers." Moreover:

> The members of the tutorial classes are quite as able as herself to hear a lecture on industrial history, or economics, or Robert Browning, and remain quite sane. As a Socialist, as a trade unionist, as a suffragist—or a suffragette, if you like—I resent Miss Carnie's suggestion that the WEA educational policy can ever make me forget the painful history of Labour, or chloroform my senses to the miseries I see around me. ... I say that if Miss Carnie, and those from whom she has imbibed her views concerning the WEA, insist that a working man or woman is liable to be side-tracked or made neutral or impartial because they look at all sides of a question in order to understand it fully, then they are libelling the intelligence of the working classes.

"I am sufficiently class-conscious not to stoop to flatter my own class," sniffed Miss Carnie.[22] But letter-writers to the *Daily Herald* found something profoundly insulting in the assumption that the workers wanted nothing but propaganda:

Has not the student's individuality any claim to defence? Must he be put through an educational mould, and be expected to reappear as per pattern? Is the student a failure who reappears with his individuality strengthened?... The Socialist movement suffers from the extremists who recognise no teaching as being education which is not designed especially to confirm their views. ... The whole controversy has been marked by an arrogance scarcely surpassed by anything history can yield. One side has held up the principles of democracy in democratic education, whilst the other, holding up its two gods, Lester Ward and Karl Marx, has demanded, "Thou shalt have no other gods but these."

[The CLC has] a lamentably narrow conception of the value of education, for it is now generally admitted by progressive educationists that the main object should not be the cramming of predigested text-book information, but the development and culture of character and mental capacity. There is no class antagonism apparent in this. The working class in its struggle for emancipation will require self-reliant sagacious men with constructive and administrative ability; which policy is most likely to achieve satisfactory results in this direction—a course of study catholic in its scope, affording the student opportunities to develop his own mental powers (not his tutor's) or a course lopsided, narrow and doctrinaire, tending to produce a type of man utterly incapable of giving a considered judgement upon any matter outside his little sphere of knowledge.

The assumption of the CLC is that working-men cannot think for themselves, but will drink in, as truth, all that is told them. For the Socialist with no mental stamina the CLC is an ideal institution.[23]

The WEA succeeded famously in overcoming working-class distrust of the ancient universities. As the faculty of its 1911 Oxford summer school reported:

The general atmosphere was one of cheery good-fellowship; a certain breezy outspokenness not unwelcome. The public opinion of the meeting was very manifestly against class prejudice and intolerance, and against any approach to giving offence to others. It is true that the students often came up with the most erroneous ideas about the attitude of Oxford to the working classes, about the available resources of the University and colleges, and about the problems of facilitating the admission of poor men to a University course. But it is extraordinary how open their minds are to facts on those subjects. In the same way they are, like some other people, often the victims of formulas, captivated by half-truths, apt to repeat shibboleths, fond of crude generalisations; but it is astonishing how readily they accept criticism in these respects, and what a rapid improvement often begins at once.[24]

The students were virtually unanimous in applauding the program:

The tutors were very patient, with no "side," and more concerned to elicit my point of view than to impose their own.

Those who have only known Oxford at a distance, fear class and caste distinctions; as a matter of fact, it simply does not exist.

The idea (so common) that Oxford is out to "nobble" the workers, and to side-track their demands, is soon dispelled. Oxford, as I saw it, is honestly seeking to *learn* of the workers, and to guide any misdirected zeal of theirs along lines that will not lessen the zeal, but will make it effective, because of the knowledge gained.[25]

[I appreciated] the gentle and tactful way in which one was brought to see the narrow view that we workmen take of life and the broader and to me, more beautiful view, that our tutor put before us. ... It is not often that people can go gather and be free from political and spiritual bonds and differences. Here in the free and unfettered exchange of one's own thoughts with those of our fellow-workmen from other parts and very often with some of the finest scholars of our time, a lot of the rough corners are removed and one's ideas on many things are knocked into a reasonable shape.[26]

That sort of praise made Pleb Leaguers howl in vindication. They had fairly warned that once the workingman set foot in Oxford, he would be enthralled by the dreamy spires and gracious dons, and his soul would be lost forever. Their premise was correct, but their conclusion was a non sequitur. Even if summer school students fervently embraced the university, they did not change their minds about capitalism. One tutor drew that distinction clearly: his students showed "an actual increase in the power of impartial analysis, and ... less desire to make points or to get support for partizan views," but that did not mean that "any given creed is less keenly felt: far from it."[27] Though many students fell in love with the university, that epiphany only left them, as one of them wrote, with "a feeling of greater rebellion against our present cruel system, and with strength and courage to alter the lot of our co-workers, that they might also know and enjoy at some period of their existence the beauties of such places as Cambridge, instead of becoming mere human profit-making machines."[28] "I feel more keenly than ever the lack of opportunities of the workers for real education, and wonder how different the position of our class might have been had it been otherwise," concluded another student:

Perhaps at times the tutors may have thought us impatient and extreme, and the discussions somewhat crude, and perhaps rather cold and brutal, yet with it all there was a generous spirit and perfect freedom to express what one really felt. By such free discussions these men will know more of the real life of the worker, … the putrid atmosphere of the workshop and factory, and the deadening effect of much of the present-day labour, combined with the insecurity of livelihood. By these means I think they will better understand and appreciate our position, and wonder why we are not more extreme.[29]

The same undeferential determination to educate their tutors was displayed by the students in A. D. Lindsay's class on Plato's *Republic*: "We often attacked him as though he had written it himself," recalled Lavena Saltonstall. A don lecturing on conservatism came in for even rougher treatment: "We turned up in full force and endeavoured to crush him but he seemed no worse for his adventure, and no doubt enjoyed himself as much as we did."[30]

The atmosphere of those early summer schools appears to have been a mixture of confrontation and good humor, sharp dissent and mutual respect. Albert Mansbridge might describe it in treacly language ("the peer's son rejoices in the fellowship of the miner's son, and the casual labourer in the friendship of the don")[31] but it happened to be the truth: Lavena Saltonstall's favorite tutor was Gerald Collier, the son of Lord Monkhouse ("I never thought a lord's son could be so sensible or charming"). The essential point is that, in the same breath, Miss Saltonstall denounced the housing conditions of the servants and laborers who maintained Oxford ("one is reminded very forcibly of the pictures one sees in Dickens' books").[32] Much as she revered the old universities, they did not blunt her militancy. Briefly stranded by the 1911 railway strike, she remembered well that "All is not so serene as this old-world garden of Trinity would suggest. Outside … man has been fighting man with batons and bars and cudgels, and the end of the struggle is not yet in sight even if the strike is settled."[33]

"We do feel that we belong to the University," testified Oxford summer school student Sophie Green. "We have been really attached to some of the historic personages we have learned about and have walked with reverent steps over the ground they must have traversed years before in Oxford." Her class sponsored an entertainment that raised £23 for the Lady Margaret Hall Fellowship Fund: "We did it partly as a compliment to our tutor who was at Oxford University & partly to show we belonged." Yet that identification with Oxford went hand in hand with a surge of labor activism: she was elected to the Board of Guardians, while a classmate became a garment workers' union official. "After a visit to the summer school a group of our girls practically organised the Trade Union in our factory," Sophie Green boasted. The foremen were at once unsettled and impressed by the new intellectual climate at the works. "I admit this set of girls cultivate the social side of life a bit too much for my peace sometimes," said one, "but I don't like to be too severe as they talk sense, and you never see them bringing rubbishy literature into the place." One girl won two guineas for an essay submitted to the *Nation*, and two or three others published prize articles in a Co-operative magazine. Sophie

Green organized two village classes in Victorian literature, while her classmates pushed back the frontiers of knowledge in the domestic sphere: "They help small brothers and sisters, nephews & nieces who are still at school. It may sound like a small thing, but it isn't really when a boy at the secondary school, struggling with home work on social & historical subjects, says, 'Do you know, Dad, well I'll ask Aunt Nelly, I bet she will.' These are the sort of things I love to hear."[34]

Summer schools, however, only lasted a week or two. Could prolonged exposure to WEA instruction produce the kind of political neutralization that Fieldhouse warns against? Tutorial classes spent three years inculcating detachment and objectivity as academic virtues: did that, in the long run, pull students away from the militant left? Some tutors, like Raymond Williams, felt that the WEA carried open-mindedness to the point where it effectively discouraged any kind of political activism. Barbara Wootton complained that "The response to every positive suggestion put forward from any part of the room begins with the words 'Yes, but ....' And as often as not the next phrase will run '... the difficulty about that is that ....'"[35] A 1936 survey found a few students who agreed:

> In the discussions, the tutors never had any definite point of view, and seemed to restrain those who wanted to go to the left or the right. The student rapidly gained the idea that no problem was capable of solution, that there was so much to be said on all sides of a problem that one should take no action at all. It was only fools who gave adherence to a party, or had plans of action for changing the status quo.[36]

Fieldhouse's own evidence, however, points to a different conclusion: if the WEA had any influence at all, it encouraged political activity and drew some students farther to the left. Fieldhouse interviewed seventy-one persons who took WEA courses before 1951: one in four felt that their tutors influenced their politics, usually in the direction of Labour Party socialism, occasionally towards Marxism, never towards the political right or center. Only one student actually underwent a political conversion, from Liberalism to Labour; for the rest, the tutor only reinforced existing political convictions or spurred the student to greater activism. Eleven percent of the sample joined the Labour Party or became more active in it as a result of taking WEA classes, and 7 percent became Labour councillors.[37] Much the same conclusion is suggested by my own survey of twenty-eight autobiographies written by WEA students. Not one of them became politically quiescent, moderate, or conservative as a result of what they had learned in WEA classes, but seven became more militant.

Of course, many students were apolitical before and after taking adult classes. R. W. Morris (b. 1895), a Durham colliery worker, gave a very common reason for organizing a WEA class in economics: "None of us had any educational ambitions other than the pleasure of meeting together once a week in an atmosphere conducive to gaining some slight acquaintance with what made the world about us 'tick.'" He later won a scholarship to Ruskin College, but "as for politics," he admitted, "I am still rather vague about that even now."[38] The WEA opened up the world of literature to farm laborer Fred Kitchen without disturbing his political indifference.[39] His fellow students tried to interest him in an economics class, fruitlessly:

> Didn't he think it was important to study the way in which the wealth of the world was distributed, why he, a producer of essential food, should have to live on thirty-two and six a week? He did not. Thirty-two and sixpence was enough for any man to live on. He could get everything he needed for thirty-two and six a week. Why worry any more?[40]

At the same time, the WEA did nothing to cool the political passions of militant students like Harry Dorrell (a contributor to the *Daily Worker*) and Ronald Goldman.[41] The NCLC might accuse the WEA of nobbling the workers, but that argument is undermined by the fact that their student bodies overlapped considerably.[42] Seven autobiographers took courses with both organizations and, revealingly, they give no hint of any ideological differences between the two.[43] Aneurin Bevan denounced the WEA when he was an NCLC organizer: later he was happy to speak from WEA platforms, and his close friend Archie Lush taught for both groups.[44] At socialist hotbeds like the Manchester Clarion Club, where most of the members had attended WEA and/or Plebs League classes, there were strident debates over their different approaches to education, but that was hardly a typical case.[45] "The average worker-student does not care twopence about the WEA and NCLC squabble," observed one such student in 1925. "With most workers it is a matter of chance in which movement they eventually find themselves. They join a class in the first place because the time, place, or subject, is convenient to them, or because a fellow worker has persuaded them to join that particular class, the principles on which the class is organised are very seldom considered."[46] Scanning the first quarter-century of Oxford Tutorial Class reports, one is hard put to find much trouble created by Marxists. Here a modern history course is deadlocked between Labourites and Marxists, with each group of students talking past the other.[47] There a Communist leaves a politics class, accusing the tutor of "anti-Soviet bias"; no other students follow him.[48]

In Yorkshire in the early 1930s, WEA instructor Roger Dataller was sometimes accused of serving a "boss-class" organization and urged to "smash capitalism." He responded by pointing out "that the problems of society are not only economic and political, but biological and psychological, and that to interpret civilization in terms of one aspect alone is to interpret nothing. What of sex? What of religion? What of hero-worship? The cold body of Lenin on perpetual view in Moscow springs to my mind. ... But I feel I am getting nowhere." Among Marxist students, "Any suggestion of failure in the Five-Year Plan was laid to the malign intention of the lecturer." In a literature class one of them exploded:

"I am a wage-slave, and I am out for the class war. That's everything to me—the class war! *Antony and Cleopatra*? What do I want with *An-to-nee and Clee-o-patra*?... What does it mean to me?"

"Nothing," I said.

Overall, though, such clashes seem to have been a minor and occasional nuisance for the WEA. As a fellow collier and WEA activist told Dataller, the Communists were much less of an obstacle than some trade union officials: they feared that the WEA would train a new generation of labor leaders who could compete for their jobs.[49]

In any case, political militancy was as much at home in the WEA as in the NCLC. Bessie Braddock (b. 1899) credited both organizations with teaching her "the political and economic history I had been denied at elementary school. I began to find out how society evolved, and how trade unions grew up ... how the capitalists controlled money, business, and the land; and how they hung on to them."[50] Maurice Ridley, a blacklisted Durham miner, began a long series of WEA courses in 1929: he was not thereby diverted from studying with the NCLC and joining the ILP Guild of Youth, the Communist Party, and the Left Book Club Theatre Group.[51] Bill Horrocks (b. c. 1900), a Bolton millworker, insisted that his WEA and NCLC classes were both essential to the intellectual enfranchisement of working people:

It was common to hear working chaps say, "Oh aye, they've geet brains," when referring to men in authority. This implied that they themselves hadn't been endowed with nature's supreme gift. This was easy to understand when any one expressing any form of initiative was said by such beings to be "too damned forrod". I once heard a man say to his foreman, "Ah think ah've a better way ter do that" and the foreman replied, "Ah'm paid ter do t' thinkin' 'ere." That was an example of the old closed-shop philosophy .... With the advent of adult education there was a development towards self-expression by those who had become more enlightened.

Where suffragettes had once been heckled, townsfolk were now more receptive to public dissent:

The Bolton Town Hall steps became a public forum where two or three individuals expressed their opinions on subjects ranging from politics to religion. On summer evenings folk preferred to listen to these orators rather than cram themselves into a cinema .... I had my baptism of public speaking on those steps .... I gave the history of the circumstances which led to the first world war and how it led to the mass unemployment of the day. One could disagree with what I said, but if it wasn't for adult education I wouldn't have been capable of uttering a word on any subject. This form of education brought to light the subject of the Industrial Revolution; before then, all history taught in the schools was full-blooded patriotism, based upon wars and the lives of royalty. (That is why, when the first world war started, everyone thought we'd have Germany begging for mercy within six months.)[52]

In some cases the WEA moved students to the left, or at least did not discourage them from moving to the left. After taking classes in international relations, T. Dan Smith became a founding member of the Peace Pledge Union in 1936. He joined the ILP and, briefly, the Trotskyites before settling down as a mainstream Labour politician in the 1950s.[53] It was WEA classes—as well as hearing Major C. R. Attlee, MP speak from a coal cart—that spurred Marjory Todd to join the ILP in the early 1920s.[54] Attending Oxford on a Cassel Scholarship, John Allaway (b. 1902) found that his WEA training, far from fitting him into a university mold, enabled him to criticize the conventional curriculum. Assigned the orthodox economics texts of Alfred Marshall, he read them "with deep suspicion" and made a point of going beyond the set books to study J. A. Hobson, Henry George, Hugh Dalton, and John Maynard Keynes.[55]

There were some on the far left who argued that the WEA diluted working-class radicalism by diverting students away from economics to literature and the arts. "In the more extreme schools of WEA opinion," wrote one educationalist in 1938, "literature has become stigmatized as a 'right wing' or 'bourgeois' subject, and a good many undeviating 'proletarians,' continuing to work themselves into frenzies about Nazis and Communists, about distribution and exchange, profits of capital and business power, etc., despise those of their fellows who 'waste their time reading poetry.'"[56]

It is true that the proportion of WEA classes studying economics and economic history declined steadily, from 52 percent in 1913 to 32 percent a decade later. Between 1913 and 1933 literature rose from 11.7 to 21.4 percent, the arts from zero to 7.9 percent, natural science from 1.9 to 9.5 percent.[57] In part, this reflected a simple broadening of interests on the part of the students. They would commonly begin by organizing a course on economics, and then at the end of three years the class might stay together and tackle another subject. Between 1912 and 1934, for example, one Tunstall class started with industrial history and then took up in succession social and constitutional history, economics, political science, political theory, philosophy, psychology, intellectual history, and the history of science.[58] It is ironic that students of the 1930s considered economics a left-wing subject and English literature conservative, when today the two disciplines have reversed positions. But even back then, the study of literature could have revolutionary consequences, as it did for Nancy Dobrin (b. 1914).

Her father was an unemployed shipyard worker who loved to hear Ellen Wilkinson lash out at the Tories, and then voted Conservative. Many autodidacts grew up in homes where learning was valued, but not Nancy: "There was no such thing as discussion in our house, it was either a row or an order." She read avidly at the public library; but later, as a munitions worker, she managed to get through the Second World War without reading the newspapers or listening to the wireless.[59] (This was not unusual: in 1943, 19 percent of working women never read the morning newspapers, and only two out of three read them regularly.)[60] After the war, in London and unmarried, she joined the WEA out of sheer loneliness. "I hadn't a clue what the WEA was, but it was somewhere to go. Maybe there would be eligible males going too. I was thirty-seven, the years were clocking up on me." She enrolled in a literature class, which tackled *War and Peace*, James Joyce, and D. H. Lawrence's *The White Peacock*:

> Before the [first] session had finished I was hooked. To hell with fellows, this was interesting …. From then on I was reading and learning, I read with new eyes …. It was fascinating—everyone in the class seemed to be so well informed, to my astonishment I knew nothing. There was no stopping me, I was empty and needed filling …. [I] slowly realised what an ignoramus I had been and bigotted into the bargain.

That last sentence needs explaining: when she worked for a German Jew during the war, she demanded to know "What is he doing here when we are at war with them?" She had no idea what was happening to the Jews at the time. In another class she actually did met her future husband, a Viennese Jewish refugee who called himself a Christian Communist.[61] Without a WEA education, it is difficult to imagine her finding any rapport with such a man. Even if the WEA had no clear influence on her politics (narrowly defined), it emancipated Nancy Dobrin in the same way that it liberated Edith Hall, an overworked housemaid. Mrs. Hall recalled that she discovered Thomas Hardy in a WEA class in the 1920s, when

> *Punch* and other publications of that kind showed cartoons depicting the servant class as stupid and "thick" and therefore fit subjects for their jokes. The skivvy particularly was revealed as a brainless menial. Many of the working-class were considered thus and Thomas Hardy wrote in *Tess of the d'Urbervilles* that "Labouring farm folk were personified in the newspaper-press by the pitiable dummy known as Hodge …" and it was in this book that Hardy told the story of Tess, a poor working girl with an interesting character, thoughts and personality. This was the first serious novel I had read up to this time in which the heroine had not been of "gentle birth" and the labouring classes as brainless automatons. This book made me feel human and even when my employers talked at me as though I wasn't there, I felt that I could take it; I knew that I could be a person in my own right.[62]

Only a few students found WEA tutors patronizing.[63] Far more typical was George Gregory, a Somerset mine worker: the WEA helped him break the habit of mind that tends "to conform to an order, indulge in repetition, and find satisfaction as routine is successful," and it enabled him to work out his own criticism of capitalism. "Words fail to explain what that meant to me, and how I was assisted intellectually on the threshold of adult life."[64]

Albert Mansbridge was no shallow paternalist. He realized that the mechanics' institutes had failed because they "were largely the result of philanthropic effort, set on foot by some local magnate, ... rather than upon the initiative of the mechanics themselves."[65] As an activist in the Co-operative movement, Mansbridge designed the WEA to give working people a dominant share of control. Tutorial Class students chose the topics they would study, and they exercised a veto (rarely used) over the selection of tutors. No diplomas or certificates were granted: the idea was to eliminate competition and vocationalism from the classroom, as well as to ensure that the tutor could not intimidate his students. The Tutorial Class closely followed the mutual improvement model, but on a more advanced academic plane. "Its essential characteristic is freedom," Mansbridge argued. "Each student is a teacher, each teacher is a student."[66] The students, by all reports, felt few compunctions about challenging their teachers. In 1914 they badgered the Historical Association to write more about the everyday lives of working people.[67] The influence of the WEA on British historiography is another topic, but worth exploring: Tawney insisted that his classic *The Agrarian Problem in the Sixteenth Century* owed much to his Tutorial Class students.[68] Another instructor acquired from his Tunstall students a wealth of data for his research into the mining and pottery industries. As one alumnus remembered, the WEA became "a co-operative search for knowledge in which tutor learns as much as student."[69]

The best students often became teachers themselves. Some early Tutorial Class pupils in North Staffordshire developed their own local education program: by 1916 they were teaching thirty courses with a total of 650 students.[70] In 1927-28, thirty out of 103 instructors teaching shorter courses for the Yorkshire WEA branch were manual workers, most of them Tutorial Class alumni, compared with only eight university-trained lecturers.[71]

At the grass-roots level, the WEA created an articulate and obstreperous working-class intelligentsia. In their 1936 survey of 410 WEA students and 128 from Ruskin College, W. E. Williams and A. E. Heath found "hundreds" who had published articles in local papers, undertaking

> to provide antidotes to the sophistries of the local squire-archies, or to counter-act the log-rolling of the *condottieri* who misgovern the local Council. ... The adult student ... tackles the town Library Committee for banning Shaw's *Black Girl*, challenges the local clergy to show more social zeal; tells the mill-owners what is wrong with their policy; ventilates the local lack of facilities for cultural education; indicts the municipal fathers for their failure to provide a park or an adequate tram-service.

At least six students, and in some cases "scores," had written for each of the following: the *Manchester Guardian, Daily Herald, Daily Express, News Chronicle, Yorkshire Post, Sheffield Independent,* the *Nation, Westminster Gazette,* the *Listener, Economic Journal, Adelphi,* and *Contemporary Review.*[72]

Many students felt that the most valuable lesson they had learned in the WEA was to "see it whole."[73] That Arnoldian ideal addressed one of the most basic intellectual hungers of the working-class student: the need to understand how his individual life fitted into the larger society. "Instead of seeing my job in isolation as an individual postal worker, and from that angle only, it began to take shape as a planned industry with a complex structure; one of many in the social structure of the country I live in," explained George W. Norris, a student who rose to the executive council of the Union of Post Office Workers. "I could now spread my wings and begin to think intelligently about wage claims, hours of work, and conditions in industry, and to compare my industry with other industries." When he heard his first WEA lectures around 1909, "I discovered that my thinking was mostly propaganda and not thinking at all." That "propaganda" was not Marx, who was only a name to Norris before he joined the WEA. Rather he meant a general habit of resorting to formulas and slogans, which he found crippling when he became a trade union branch secretary: "It was easy work making propaganda speeches and giving stock answers to stock questions, but I soon found myself stumped for replies when questioned by trained thinkers." He could scarcely express himself on paper or in debate, until he learned that "to acquire knowledge in the university tradition meant a knowledge of how to use books as tools, and the necessity for bringing some order into my studies."

In that sense Stuart Macintyre is entirely right to conclude that "the mission of the WEA was to break down the isolation of working-class students and integrate them in a national culture." He is wrong, however, when he devalues that achievement and suggests that it clipped the political wings of the working-class autodidact. George Norris's WEA studies in industrial psychology enabled him to argue down postal supervisors who were eager to experiment with time-and-motion studies. After twenty-two years of WEA courses at a total cost of £10, he testified that

> I can now hold my own with the finest products of Eton, Harrow, Oxford and Cambridge whether it be in understanding problems of trade and commerce or in the realms of literature, art or music. ... I've learned how to analyse Government blue books and white papers, and to digest statistics; workshop practice, managerial problems, wage rates, currency problems, social planning, local and national government developments have all become understandable as a result of my studies. ... Training in the art of thinking has equipped me to see through the shams and humbug that lurk behind the sensational headlines of the modern newspapers, the oratorical outpourings of insincere party politicians and dictators, and the doctrinaire ideologies that stalk the world sowing hatred.[74]

In criticizing the WEA for assimilating independent autodidacts, Macintyre overlooks the loneliness of the self-educated worker. While the Williams–Heath survey found that many adult students enjoyed support and encouragement from their family and friends, there were just as many who encountered only suspicion, hostility, and contempt. Much like their bourgeois counterparts, they felt alienated from their class and pressured to conform to philistine values. For them, the WEA provided a haven—the proletarian equivalent of an artistic cafe, literary magazine, or university common room.[75] It offered Lavena Saltonstall a welcome escape from a suffocating hegemonic working-class culture:

> I am supposed to make myself generally *useless* by ignoring things that matter— literature, music, art, history, economics, the lives of the people round me and the evils of my day. … There are miles and miles of little-frequented paths on life's highway and faintly-marked pathways always attracted me more than the beaten road …. The world is suffering to-day because men and women merge their individuality into one orthodox mass. In my native place, the women, as a general rule, wash every Monday, iron on Tuesday, court on Wednesdays, bake on Thursdays, clean on Fridays, go to market or go courting again on Saturdays, and to church on Sundays …. The exceptions are considered unwomanly and eccentric people …. Should any girl show a tendency to politics, or to ideas of her own, she is looked upon by the majority of women as a person who neglects doorsteps and home matters, and is therefore not fit to associate with their respectable daughters and sisters. If girls develop any craving for a different life or wider ideas, their mothers fear that they are going to become Socialists or Suffragettes—a Socialist being a person with lax views about other people's watches and purses, and other people's husbands and wives, and a Suffragette a person whose house is always untidy. If their daughters show any signs of a craving for higher things than cleaning brass fenders or bath taps, they put a stop to what they call "high notions."[76]

One can always argue that the WEA should have devoted more attention to Marx. Fieldhouse's analysis of syllabi for Oxford and Cambridge extramural classes between 1925 and 1939 reveals a general slant toward the non-Marxist left. Most tutors seem to have been critical of Marxism, though the Marxist point of view was often discussed in class. Of the seventy-two WEA alumni interviewed by Fieldhouse, half described their teachers as Labour Party supporters; few tutors were characterized as Marxist, Liberal, or Conservative. But does it follow that Marx was treated unfairly in WEA classes? Most of the students Fieldhouse questioned felt that the politics of their lecturers had little or no influence on the way their courses were taught. More than a third of these students could not even guess the political stance of their tutors.

Like all questions of canonization, this one is endlessly debatable. How much Marx is enough? Why should there have been more Marxism in the curriculum?

After the implosion of world Communism and the 1997 "New Labour" landslide, the WEA emphasis on non-Marxian socialism seems admirably far-sighted. Besides, *Das Kapital* was frequently read in economic history classes, and Maurice Dobb's Marxist treatises sometimes appeared on WEA reading lists.[77] Among the leaders of the WEA, A. D. Lindsay, G. D. H. Cole, Harold Laski, and J. M. Mactavish (General Secretary from 1916 to 1927) were all non-Marxists who wrote with some sympathy about Marxism.[78] In the early 1920s the *Highway*, the WEA journal, made an effort to review books on Marx and encouraged students to read his works.[79] Though most WEA tutors were not Marxists, their treatment of capitalism could be quite congenial to Marxist students. In 1922 Board of Education inspectors protested that economics instructors often presented socialist doctrines as "scientific generalizations" rather than as one theory among many:

> Two ideas—the progress towards social democracy and the growth of trade unionism—tend to monopolise attention to the neglect of equally important aspects. ... The Industrial Revolution is frequently treated as a rapid trans-formation of society into two classes of capitalists and proletariat. The process is pictured as a process of the economic and social degradation of the people, relieved only in the latter stages by the rise of socialism and the promise of social democracy. Economic development is thus viewed very largely as a progress towards the socialist state.[80]

The WEA could hardly have steered many workers away from Marxism, if only because so few of its recruits were Marxists. A 1909 survey of thirty-four prospective students for a Tutorial Class found that nine of them had read Robert Blatchford's *Merrie England*, seven Henry George's *Progress and Poverty*, six Toynbee on the Industrial Revolution, five each Kropotkin's *Fields, Factories, and Workers* and at least parts of *The Wealth of Nations*; only one had even attempted Marx.[81] The batches of student papers saved from early WEA economics classes are equally free of Marxist influence.[82] A 1936 survey of London Tutorial Class students suggests their political distribution: nearly 45 percent read the *Daily Herald*, 26 percent the *News Chronicle*, 20 percent the *Daily Telegraph*, 7.5 percent *The Times*, and only about 5 percent the *Daily Worker*.[83]

In any case, the NCLC exaggerated its ideological differences with the WEA, which were steadily narrowing through the 1920s and 1930s. Its attacks on the WEA were largely motivated by competition for resources and students. The NCLC hoped to become the educational arm of moderate trade unions and the Labour Party. By 1925 it had twenty-five affiliated unions: it also received grants from the Labour Party, the Co-operative Union, and the Trades Union Congress. Consequently, it gradually played down the class struggle, shifting to practical training for trade unionists. It also had to fight off assaults on its left flank from the Communist Party. Ultimately, in 1964, the NCLC would be completely absorbed by the Trades Union Congress education department. Tellingly, it was the NCLC, not the WEA, which toned down its radicalism to please its financial patrons, until it offered little more than vocational training for labor functionaries in a welfare capitalist system.[84]

Nor should one assume that the WEA commitment to nonideological instruction was directed solely against Marxists. Before the Second World War, dissenting religion was still a more potent opponent of liberal education, and tutors had to take care to avoid theological controversies.[85] Given that most doctrinaire working-class Marxists began as doctrinaire Nonconformists, the parallels are unsurprising. In 1913–14 one tutor complained that many of the students in his industrial history class at Heywood were

> excessively engaged in religious work of a type that militates against good intellectual work. No man can study economic subjects who feels it is immoral to divorce, even for ease and insight, ethical from commercial and industrial questions, and in spite of more than one evening devoted to pointing out the subdivision and "abstraction" of the human sciences, I could not get ahead with the theory. Even apart from this, pious meetings evening after evening interfere with reading and essays.[86]

In 1924–25 T. W. Harries reported that, in his Tunstall philosophy class, "There is a genuine interest in philosophic thought, for which the strong Nonconformist tradition of the class is responsible. The same tradition is no doubt responsible for the unoriginality and unsensitiveness of the thought. Standard authors are too highly regarded, or rather regarded in the wrong way, being taken as substitutes for thought. Behind a claim of independence by certain members is concealed a lack of it."[87] In 1916, when a WEA organizer requested classroom space from the Clay Cross Education Committee, one member, a preacher and credit draper, objected that "surely coal miners had no reason to study Economics, Philosophy, or European History," or indeed anything other than "how to dig more coal, and get ready for the next world."[88] Here was the mirror image of the NCLC, which argued that miners should only study how to wage more class warfare, and get ready for the Brave New World. Construction worker Stan Dickens, who described his parents as "bigoted nonconformists," took WEA courses to get beyond the dogmas of the Plymouth Brethren, which he found "increasingly irksome and unsatisfying. I had tasted the fruit of the Tree of Knowledge and for good or ill wanted to eat more of it."[89] And just as the WEA mediated class and political conflict, so it could bridge religious differences. "Well, this is the first time Church and Chapel people in this village have ever met together for a common end," remarked a student in a rural history class. "And here we are, quite a happy family!"[90]

In his study of Antonio Gramsci, Harold Entwistle explained why a traditional liberal education can nurture radical thought more effectively than any program of indoctrination. Gramsci's educational program could have been taken out of any WEA pamphlet: "To the proletariat is necessary a disinterested school, a humanistic school, in short, as was intended by the ancients and more recently by the men of the Renaissance." One might call this quintessentially Arnoldian— except that similar definitions of culture were offered by Lenin ("the knowledge of all the wealth created by mankind") and Trotsky ("Culture is the sum total of … the whole knowledge and skill accumulated by mankind in its whole preceding history"). Lenin—the Lenin who regretted that young Bolsheviks were rejecting Pushkin for the futurist poet Mayakovsky—was convinced that proletarian culture had to be grounded in cultures inherited from the past, "the natural development of the stores of knowledge which mankind has accumulated under the yoke of capitalist society, landlord society and bureaucratic society."

Entwistle was criticizing—from the left—the "new sociology of education" that emerged in Britain in the 1970s, a doctrine echoed today by critics of the "cultural literacy" movement. It held that the content of education is problematic and socially constructed, that the learner is competent to define that content, that all subcultures are equally valuable, that academic knowledge is not superior to other kinds of knowledge. Rather than offering all classes the kind of education traditionally enjoyed by the elite, schools should value and preserve folk cultures. The difficulty is that all this closely resembles the theories of Giovanni Gentile, Mussolini's first minister of public instruction. His educational reforms of 1923 encouraged spontaneity and disdained intellectualism, emphasizing ideas and beliefs over facts, figures, names, and dates. "Teaching is formative, not informative," proclaimed one of Gentile's supporters. "The Italian school of today does not limit itself to the imparting of mere information and to the furnishing of cultural instruments. Its aim is to mould and fashion souls." It sounds deceptively progressive, but as Gramsci realized, it only made indoctrination easier. Without a knowledge of the past, students had no standards for judging the present. Without a fund of basic information, they could not intelligently form their own opinions or criticize what they were taught. And preserving traditional cultures meant, in effect, preserving the status quo. To say that classical education represents an imposition of middle-class culture on the masses overlooks an insistent working-class demand for that kind of culture. Gramsci noted that his proletarian colleagues experienced "a new feeling of dignity and freedom when they read poetry or heard references to artists and philosophers, and they asked, regretfully, 'Why didn't the schools teach these things to us as well?'"[91] "You can say what you like about the advantages or disadvantages of various forms of education," said one WEA student, a colliery blacksmith and published author, "but I think the point about public school and university education is that at their best they teach you to think."[92] As the next chapter will explain, Marxism failed to find a large working-class following in Britain for many reasons. The WEA was not one of them.

What Did the Students Want?

Why did students enroll in the WEA and Ruskin College? The 1936 Williams –Heath survey found that some pursued continuing education purely for individual cultural enrichment, and some were solely motivated by political concerns: equality, peace, social justice. The clear majority, however, mentioned both of these goals, convinced that one could not be attained without the other:

> To provide for the fullest expression of the faculties of the individual, and to direct energy towards the realisation of individual happiness through those faculties; and in addition to provide for the maximum co-operation of the individual towards the happiness of the group of which he is a part.

> Individually, to develop the student's personality and latent abilities so that he may be more effective in his spheres of work and influence. Socially, to encourage a critical but constructive attitude of mind towards social problems, etc. The quest for "pure knowledge" is futile unless others besides the student are influenced.

> First, to equip the student with adequate knowledge in order that he or she may make a more adequate and effective response to his or her social obligations. Secondly, to enable one to appreciate and cultivate a desire for the best in art, literature, music, etc., to more readily understand the significance of science, and generally to raise the level of intelligence in order that the student may enjoy a fuller and more harmonious existence, freer from the trammels of prejudice, superstition and dogmatism.[93]

Few believed that adult education should aim exclusively at building socialism. Even some of the most militant Marxists argued that only a broad liberal education could prepare the workers for political struggle:

> When education is purposely made available to fit the student, say for the class war, the result is mostly undigested dogma, consequently the class war suffers. Were Engels, Marx, Hyndman, Trotsky, Lenin, educated solely for the class war? Consider also the usefulness of Francis Place to the working-classes, and J. S. Mill, etc.[94]

Except for the occasional partisan of class warfare, students generally appreciated the impartiality of their teachers:

> He was always suggesting some other point of view which must be recognised. This has also struck me about other tutors: their desire that knowledge should be as wide as possible, and their ability to state, whenever opportunity offered, the opposite argument.

My tutor … did me most good because I disagreed with him. It led me into having to explain myself and to avoid too much speaking without thinking.

His habit of pointing out the ambiguous nature of one's contribution has taught me to consider well before committing myself.[95]

Intellectual independence was frequently cited as a prime educational goal:

The development of the whole man or woman, mental, spiritual, physical, particularly the remedial work necessary where deficiency in previous training is very marked. The stimulation of thought on all subjects … so that life may be lived according to one's own findings, making no ignominious compromise with the findings of other people whom one never knew.

To enable a man to stand on his own feet. To equip him to be able to endure his own company on occasions, communing with the inner world of his thoughts, instead of rushing out to mix with the crowd.

To teach people to think for themselves, to allow for the other person's point of view. To show how a great deal of pleasure and content can be obtained from the things inside us, and also to teach people a quiet enjoyment of the beautiful things of life which will provide a contrast and refuge from the everyday drabness.[96]

Alongside self-realization, the social motive was also a compelling reason for joining WEA classes:

It was something to do and I liked the friend who was already in the class.

I felt the need for social contact with men and women of similar tastes and ideas, and an association with them.

One good reason. To try to keep from too frequently visiting the village pub.[97]

One of the most commonly cited motives for pursuing adult education was very Arnoldian: "Disinterestedness." This involved not only the effort to overcome bias, though it certainly included that. It meant as well that education should be pursued with no thought of competitiveness or economic gain, that knowledge must be acquired for its own sake in an environment where students helped each other. Of course, WEA classes afforded excellent training for careers in the trade unions and the Labour Party, and WEA students often took vocational courses with other educational institutions. But the competitive pressures they faced in the workplace made them all the more insistent that the WEA should be completely noncompetitive and nonvocational:

It is the only movement available, for many, that considers non-material values. Religious bodies fulfil the function for some, but adult education should do it for many more.

The giving of prominence to things of the mind and spirit and the encouraging of an attitude of mind which places man first and his economic function second; freedom from commercialism; disinterestedness. All of which, I believe, go to stimulate the student to social service.

As helping to make it *disinterested*, it emphasises the group factor (the co-operative effort in search for truth) rather than a narrow personal outlook; it brings together workers from many trades and with varying experience, not from one limited circle.

I prefer it to be distinctly separated from the working-day affairs of students, because that leads to a disinterested attitude of enquiry, avoids the association of one's own selfish interest with matter that is being studied, and widens the outlook and corrects the perspective of the student.[98]

Many joined the WEA in search of an escape from the industrial machine:

With nothing but hard work and less than the real necessities of life, I felt there was something wrong with a system that condemned honest people to such a life. I had no personal or selfish ambitions, but I wanted to learn the "why and wherefore" of this system of society.

I was beginning to feel life a drudgery, a repetition of going to work and finding nothing to while away the time after it was over. On the other hand there was much I was wanting to know about life. Books written around so-called Socialist Problems, e.g. Shaw's *Man and Superman,* had come to me and after first shocking me (I had such child-like faith in the Bible then that I had never even thought of the problems it contained) had urged me to seek the truth of all things. ... By then I had realised that some people fully appreciated and enjoyed life, because, I thought, they had solved life's problems for themselves, and the rest of the world were mere drudges, slaves, and drunkards, and I did not wish to be classified with this latter class.

I thought (largely due to my intimate conversation with my WEA miner friend) that I could be developed into a more understanding and therefore intelligently useful human. I used often to listen to the idealism of this miner friend who had his eye in the heavens and his feet in the muck. As I look back upon our returning from the pit, in the early dawn of summer mornings, talking our way to a finer and higher economic and industrial and social world,

I experience certain feelings which almost cause me to say that there is an advantage in having plodded one's own way in the world from a school-leaving age of 13 years.[99]

Although the WEA always attracted more skilled than unskilled workers, it was the latter who insisted more vehemently on the value of a purely liberal education. Those with more interesting jobs—clerks, carpenters, metalworkers— often suggested that the WEA might relax its ban on vocational training: but there was "a chorus of 'Noes' from the machine-minders, from the coal-miners, from the hammer-and-file brigade of the engineering industry, from the telephonists, the postmen":

I would not. Knowledge for its own sake is a better principle. The working life of students is becoming more and more mechanical, and sectionalised, and technical education already looks well after that side. Adult education is often a way of escape from the tedious monotony of working life. Give as wide a range of subjects as possible and let the student follow his bent.

The actual working life of most manual workers is in the main semi-slavery, with the fear ever before them that even that will be taken away. My opinion is that adult education should be as far removed from the actual working life as possible. To simply use up all one's time and thoughts for the purpose of obtaining the necessaries of life is a very low standard of life for a human being.

No. Rightly or wrongly (it is possibly a defect of the present industrial system) many of us are disgruntled with our working life. We want freedom of mind, power and expression, and for that reason wish to dissociate work and study.[100]

One critic has argued that the WEA promoted a liberal education "hardly distinguishable from the conservatism of Newman."[101] But by Newman's definition, liberal education would prepare the student not for a particular vocation, but for any profession he chose to pursue. If he elected to become a labor activist, then the Arnoldian ideal of "seeing it whole" could have radical implications. One collier, having studied science and history via H. G. Wells (among others), found that he was

able to take a more intelligent view of the works where I earn my living. I never used to trouble about profits, machinery, etc. I was satisfied with my wages, never troubled how or where they came from. ... But when I had learned a little I wanted to know how profits were made, and why workers did not have a more reasonable share of them. So I think, on the whole, that education gives a desire for one to take an interest both technically and otherwise in the occupation they are engaged in.[102]

Residential institutions like Ruskin College had one drawback: full-time students could find themselves cut off from their old working-class milieu. Many of them were aiming for a white-collar job, even if it was usually as a trade union officer or adult education teacher.[103] As one woman conceded, her studies at Ruskin College had created

> a certain gulf due to lack of understanding on the one side and impatience or lack of understanding, on my part. These differences have grown less of recent years. At home they were always vexed that my promotion to my present post should have been so much delayed on account of my year in Oxford—particularly that I missed a good opportunity of promotion which fell vacant at the time I went to Oxford. Owing to the very intensive training at Ruskin College, I finished with (as I thought) a completely new outlook on life and was anxious that every one else should arrive at the same conclusion! I am afraid that I did not give sufficient thought to the fact that they had not had my opportunities of living at Oxford for a year and expected them to accept all I told them! As I was very enthusiastic I wanted to implant new ideas in every one with whom I came in contact. I imagine this made me somewhat of a nuisance at times, but after reflection and further reading, I settled down into wiser paths![104]

WEA students, who continued to work in their old jobs and remained in their communities, were less likely to feel that alienation. Nevertheless, a WEA course could have a very mixed impact on home life. The family that took classes together might grow closer. Sometimes a man would bring his wife into the WEA and make her, as one put it, "an intellectual pal." But women rarely persuaded their husbands to join. When one spouse enrolled in the WEA and the other did not, tensions were likely to develop as the educational gaps grew:

> My wife says I'm all blasted Economics and British working class. I have refused offers of better-paid jobs which would have made WEA work impossible. My wife does not think it is a good paying proposition and would prefer the flesh-pots to a place in heaven.

Having attended Ruskin College, a newsagent found himself drifting apart from his wife: he became a philosophic materialist while she took up spiritualism. "In later years of our married life we always seemed to see the opposite sides of almost every question that cropped up," he recalled, until she went to visit her sister in New Zealand and never came back. A laborer's wife with no formal schooling, after the birth of her tenth child, signed up for courses in Esperanto, psychology, economics, music, and geography, despite relentless ridicule and opposition from her husband. She stuck with it for at least ten years, though she had to smuggle public library books into her home. These were extreme cases, but many other students had to cope with lesser rifts:

We lost touch with each other with the result she ceased to be interested in my work as it advanced. She followed, but a long way behind. She found her interests in other ways and we settled the changed relation to accommodate each other: but much is lost in sympathy .... Our intellectual lives are separate and apart from each other and there is now little or nothing in common. This is a real loss to us both and I think the loss is mine mostly, since my wife has filled her life with her own domestic affairs and her own limited reading and conversation. I may share hers, but she never shares mine. She can't.

As a power-loom overlooker noted, a wife might not voice any objection when her husband went out to attend a mixed-sex class,

but behind the wifely mind there is—I won't call it a suspicion, or even a distrust, but it is there. It is an activity of which she either cannot or will not partake, it keeps her husband from home, and he is obviously enjoying himself. Thus there are two different streams of interest—the home, and immediate affairs in the case of the wife, the new field of knowledge in the case of the husband. And as time goes on they become more and more distinct; the husband becomes engrossed in something the wife cannot understand. ... I have raised this topic with several students of fairly long experience and they have all (and some painfully) been aware of the experience. ... The difference ... between acquiring knowledge almost surreptitiously—a sort of an interest which is alien from the family life—and paddling the cultural canoe together with the wife is tremendous.

The strains were not limited to married couples. One railway clerk (single) reported that his brother, a married commercial traveler, was concerned solely with supporting his family and therefore

finds my interest in education for its own sake rather puzzling. ... Art, literature, social conditions of the masses, politics, economics, even sport mean little or nothing to him. Hence there has been an ever-increasing divergence of opinion between us. His attitude towards my outlook is one of veiled hostility, and an unshakeable belief that I am none the better for the years I have spent with WEA classes. Once we were inseparable. Now we have practically nothing in common, though of course remain quite friendly.

Likewise, a young millworker protested that the WEA

has completely alienated my sister. She is the only one now who has not had educational training. I have tried in vain to get her to study, especially the 2½ years she was at home, unemployed. No use. She will not. Naturally she feels jealous to think we were both weavers and now I have a better position. She is making my life so intolerable with suspicion and jealousy that with my mother's consent I am seriously considering getting work away from home again. I am changed myself, that is why I cannot blame my sister. We have nothing whatever in common. She hates the WEA and all it stands for.

Male and female students alike often encountered a solid wall of family hostility:

My family think me an idiot, say I am wasting my time, call me funny names, and want to know where I am hoping to get to.

Doing something different from the rest of the family has made them regard my actions somewhat suspiciously.

They look on me as the prize rabbit.

They think you are a snob, and you have the conflict between intellectual isolation or running away from your family and friends.

That last respondent touched upon a common source of tension: adult students were often viewed as people who were getting above themselves, presuming to "improve" their kinfolk, disturbing the equilibrium of family life and the class hierarchy. "My early association with the WEA brought me into touch with people who were known to, but regarded by, my people as 'superior' folks," wrote one Ruskin student, "and their visits to my home were looked upon as, more or less, a move to 'uplift' the family and, as such were not encouraged." A typist complained that her insistence on gaining further education "led to many phrases of bitterness. I was accused of 'getting too big for my shoes,' learning to look down on my family, and filling my head with dangerous ideas, and certainly with ideas about things which were no concern of mine and ought to be left to my 'betters'." She was picking up notions about politics and religion quite unlike anything her parents had taught her. These new attitudes in turn "brought about desires for changes in my way of life, and most of these were resented—and often resisted." In a large family with children at several different educational levels (elementary school, secondary school, working) the tensions were compounded, with everyone accusing the one adult student of "showing off" and being "too bookish."

These frictions could be reduced by making adult education a family project. "My brother and I might not have been such good friends if we had not belonged to the same educational society," wrote one housewife. But in these cases another kind of tension might appear: instead of one student asserting her independence, there were several. Even if they were on a common intellectual plane, their differences had to be negotiated. One miner who had attended Ruskin College discovered that when he brought other family members into the WEA. "On the whole things go very smoothly at home, but I am constantly reminded that since my coming home from Ruskin College, our house is more like a debating shop than a dwelling-house," he wrote. His brothers were more ready to speak up at trade union meetings and where they had once turned their wages over to their mother, they now insisted on paying their board and handling their own personal budgets ("Those who control finance control policy").[105]

For growing numbers of women, the WEA provided the social and intellectual outlet that the mutual improvement society had provided for workingmen:

> I thought it would break the monotony of village life in winter for a mother of a family like me. It would keep my mind more active and prevent my feeling that I was getting into a rut. It would help me to understand more fully modern problems, and I have hopes that it will keep me advanced and thoughtful enough for me to be a help "intellectually" to my son as he grows older. I did not expect it to fulfil any social purpose, but I have found other people in the WEA who are glad to visit married stay-at-homes, and who are happy to arrange events, outings, and little social affairs and visits to suit the needs of married people with children or those handicapped by household ties.[106]

Another housewife "noticed that many marriages failed after several years, especially after children had grown up." The problem was that "too many women had not any interests outside the home, that they did no reading of any moment and that their conversation consisted of prices of food-stuffs and house-cleaning." Though she and another woman had young children, their husbands were agreeable to minding the kids while they attended classes.[107]

Female students had often been reluctant to speak up in early Tutorial Classes, especially where they were greatly outnumbered. A woman might find it difficult to disagree openly with a male student who was also a neighbor. Unlike the men, most women were not used to voicing their opinions on the shop floor, in offices, at trade union and Labour Party meetings. The WEA addressed this issue by setting up a Women's Advisory Committee in 1909, dedicating a full-time organizer to women in 1910, and sponsoring (as a temporary transition) some all-female classes.[108] Those policies, combined with liberal trends in society at large, brought more women into the WEA. By 1922 educational inspectors noted "that the extension of the franchise is producing a profound change in the attitude of women towards education and towards each other."[109] Women made up about 5 percent of CLC students[110] and, in 1935, only 4 percent of enrollment in NCLC correspondence courses,[111] but the proportion in WEA Tutorial Classes rose from 13.6 percent in 1911–12 to 44.2 percent in 1937–38.[112] This was partly the result of offering more courses in literature, always a favorite subject among women, but the percentage of female students was increasing in every discipline (Table 8.1, p. 290).

A 1936 survey of Tutorial Class students in the London area found that the women enjoyed cultural lives that were by any measure as rich and varied as the men's. The 200 men in the survey (mostly clerks, salesmen, and manual workers)

Table 8.1: Percentage of Female to Male WEA Students, 1913–28[113]

	Total	Economics	Politics	History	Science	Philosophy	Literature
1913–14	30.1	20.4	28.7	35.7	33.3	59.6	87.9
1927–28	65.0	27.2	33.0	54.8	62.9	89.3	145.5

worked an average of 43.3 hours per week, compared with 39.3 hours for the 236 women (mostly clerks and homemakers). Though 34.1 percent of the men and only 7.5 percent of the women worked more than 44 hours, the men generally devoted more hours to reading each week than women:

Table 8.2: Hours Per Week Devoted to Reading, London WEA Students, 1936

	Men	Women	Male Clerks	Female Clerks	Manual Workers	Housewives
Non-fiction	24.1	16.4	26.4	16.0	25.5	15.6
Newspapers	6.4	4.1	6.4	4.2	7.2	4.5
Fiction	12.1	17.5	13.0	17.4	12.4	13.3
Periodicals	3.2	2.4	2.5	2.1	3.9	2.4
Total	45.8	40.4	48.3	39.7	49.0	35.8

The results are equally unexpected on other counts. Male manual workers devoted as much time to reading as male clerks. (A century earlier Hugh Miller found that he accomplished less reading as a bank clerk than he had as a stonemason. The exhaustion that came from hours of adding up figures left little mental energy for study.)[114] It has been argued that the constant interruptions of housework left women less able to pursue serious study than men, who could at least count on large blocks of free time outside work hours. But women actually read more quickly—an average of 7.1 hours per non-fiction book compared with 10.0 hours for men—with the result that both sexes managed to read the same number of volumes (2.3 per month). Not many young mothers had the time for demanding courses: only 39.0 percent of all women students and 11.2 percent of women students under thirty were married, compared with 48.5 percent of all men. On the other hand, older women with grown children might find themselves with more leisure to devote to adult education. Under age twenty-five, men were more likely than women to enroll in the WEA, but the reverse was true after age forty-four, and such diversions as theatergoing and art galleries were most popular among women forty-five and over. It was men, not women, whose leisure activities tended to become narrower and more domestic with age. Overall, women were more likely than men to attend the theater (56.4 to 38.0 percent), lectures other than the WEA (51.3 to 38.0 percent), art galleries (31.8 to 19.5 percent), concerts (33.1 to 20.0 percent), and museums (28.8 to 24.5 percent). While fewer women than men devoted time to politics (16.5 to 28.0 percent) and trade union business (8.1 to 21.0 percent), women were more likely to indulge in singing (21.2 to 14.0 percent), photography (16.1 to 11.5 percent), and amateur theatricals (18.6 to 11.0 percent). They were far more likely to play a musical instrument (24.6 to 4.5 percent), just as likely to dabble in painting (about 5.0 percent each), and not much less fond of debating (20.3 to 27.0 percent).[115] Granted, a similar survey in the provinces might have yielded different results, but women throughout the country described Tutorial Classes as a liberating experience:

> I very often get chaffed since joining the WEA about what a lot I have to say and how prepared I am to argue. My husband and brothers obviously notice that I am much more ready to join in conversations on world outlook—economic problems and even political ones, which previously I dismissed as "men's subjects", but the WEA has taught me otherwise.
>
> Particularly with my husband, I fill a much more important place in the home and in his mind. He asks my opinion and likes to discuss vital things with me, which was entirely absent before I took WEA classes.
>
> It has not only given me more confidence in myself, but I *am* myself—I have an individuality of my own. It has made me understand my husband better: there is more comradeship in our lives, more give and take, more freedom for both of us.[116]

The most revealing question asked in the Williams-Heath survey was this: "Do you consider, on reflection, that your adult educational activity has made you less, or more, happy?" The replies were almost 95 percent positive, but what is most significant is that they often began by thinking about the meaning of happiness. Many, like John Stuart Mill, distinguished between higher and lower forms of happiness: adult education imparted depth along with pleasure. Far from doping the workers by imposing middle-class cultural hegemony, Ruskin College and the WEA did precisely the opposite: they made their students happier but less content.

> The more I know, the more I realise the mistakes one makes. ... When I look back I realise that, without my acquired adult knowledge, my life would have been blind, unconscious and animal-like. I now have a purpose in life. ... I did not know the joy of living until I was enabled to understand the problems of life. ... It has extended my range of thought and feeling. ... Even if it had made economic conditions more difficult for me, I think I would not regret the time given it. It has made life so much more interesting. ... As I grow older, and as I learn, I become more tolerant. This is happiness.
>
> Life came to mean something. It no longer consisted of going to work, bed or the pictures. ... When important things were reported in the newspaper, one

could have a shot at explaining them, and in doing so felt much happier than in merely resignedly saying "Such things are for other folk". ... I feel my work is a real contribution to progress. ... Since my life has led me into social and political and industrial movements I am glad that I discovered adult education in my early twenties. For it has added to the interest-content of my contacts, and has revealed subtle facts of knowledge and shades of understanding which could hardly have come to me otherwise. I am not necessarily happier, but my life is fuller.

I have found that education tends to make one more sensitive and to feel things more keenly. In a world where there is so much that hurts and leads to despair, as well as so much that delights and heartens, a sensitive nature touches deeper notes of unhappiness as well as higher ones of great happiness.

I have lost many illusions but I do not regret them, for education has taught me that it is better to see things as they are. I really cannot say that I am more or less happy; what I can say is that *the happiness is of a different kind.*

Adult education is its own reward—and its own revenge.[117]

The Reward

The WEA clearly succeeded in training an effective corps of working-class leaders. Of 303 students attending Oxford University Tutorial Classes in 1917–18, 195 were engaged in some kind of public work, including fifty-three trade union officials, twenty-six members of trades and labor councils, twenty-five Co-operative society officers, eleven members of local government bodies, thirty-eight involved in the Adult School movement, and twenty-six engaged in volunteer teaching.[118] By the 1930s the WEA was educating about 60,000 students, of whom one in five was enrolled in University Tutorial Classes. (In contrast, the NCLC peaked in the mid-1920s at 30,000 students, and was down to about 13,000 by 1937–38.)[119] An incomplete 1938 survey of England and Wales found more than 2,300 WEA students and alumni currently holding public office, including fifteen MPs.[120] The Labour victory of 1945 moved A. E. Zimmern to proclaim, "It is an England largely moulded by the WEA that has been swept into power."[121] The new prime minister, the chancellor of the exchequer, and twelve other members of the government had been WEA tutors or executives. A total of fifty-six WEA supporters, teachers, and students were sitting in the House of Commons.[122] John Langley, a railway coach builder elected a Brighton councillor in that *annus mirabilis*, credited his political consciousness to WEA lectures:

The subjects that we discussed were terrific. I got really fascinated by them, and the speakers were so good that I never missed a week. I went as regular as clockwork. I could read a newspaper much better after going to these classes. I could see behind what they were trying to pump into me. ... The working class has become educated. They can read the financial news in the newspaper, if they want to, and understand it. They wouldn't be able to get involved in it, but they could see which way the wind's blowing. They should know whether they're being done or not. ... We're more aware of the craftiness of things today [1976] than we were before. They could pull the wool over our eyes before, but they can't now.[123]

Building on a long autodidact tradition, the WEA had produced an army of postwar Labour politicians passionately committed to education, and thus contributed an all-party consensus for government aid to the arts. T. Dan Smith's father, a frequently unemployed miner, introduced him to opera, Chaliapin, Plato's *Republic*, Marx, and Bernard Shaw. His mother held down two cleaning jobs to buy a new piano for her children. Smith entered Newcastle politics on a personal mission to promote arts and culture in the north. He fought relentlessly to channel government money into libraries, public sculpture, and the Northern Sinfonia Orchestra. He took pride in building a university complex in the city center, though he admitted "we were uprooting a whole neighborhood." He provocatively installed abstract art in the Civic Centre Rates Hall, so that property owners could see where their taxes were going as they wrote out their checks. "How necessary for ballet dancers to communicate with footballers," he once wrote: it might have been his campaign slogan.[124]

Having accounted the real achievements of the WEA, it remains to acknowledge its limitations. Though Tutorial Classes accomplished much good work, the goal of educating students up to a university honors standard was, as even sympathizers conceded, "a polite fiction." Board of Education inspectors tried to be charitable, but in 1922 they were compelled to admit that the quality of written work in Tutorial Classes

varies so enormously as to make it impossible to generalise about it. ... Some essays are fully up to the standard of the best Honours work by University Students; and these are not always the work of men of previous good education. Some essays by mere beginners display remarkable power of clear and forcible expression. The essays of nearly the whole of one class of working women seen two years ago reached a remarkable standard both in expression and in the rarer academic quality of detachment. On the other hand another batch of essays from a small group of artisans were deficient in every good quality, and breathed only sound and fury. ...

On the whole, the essays show that at least half the students are profiting very much by the courses. As to the rest it is doubtful whether Tutorial class work—except for its political value—is the most appropriate means by which they can receive education. The treatment of the subjects is beyond them: they cannot read the best books with understanding, and they fail to make adequate progress.[125]

It could hardly have been otherwise. A Cambridge undergraduate reading for the English Literature Tripos might in three years attend 216 lectures and enjoy seventy-two hours of personal direction by his tutor. A WEA student, with far less leisure time at his disposal, had seventy-two hours each of lectures and of class discussion.[126] The first Tutorial Class, a 1908 seminar on economic history taught by R. H. Tawney, based in the Potteries town of Longton, became a legend in the WEA for the zeal of its students, but it was a struggle for many of them. Remedial classes in English industrial history and essay writing had to be organized for students unprepared for university-level work. Boom times in the Potteries meant more overtime, which depressed attendance. Recessions could be equally disruptive, as students became demoralized or left town in search of work. One pottery engineer recorded that, over a 26-week period, he worked an average of 74.5 hours a week and then wrote fourteen essays for the Tutorial Class, read another ten papers to the remedial class, and delivered a total of fifteen lectures to other workers' classes and a literary society.[127]

As the hard sciences were even more demanding, the WEA never developed a broad range of course offerings in that field. In 1938–39 all the natural sciences accounted for only 7.0 percent of WEA classes, compared with 58.4 percent for the social sciences (mainly politics, economics, history, and psychology) and 24.3 percent for literature and the arts.[128] (The sciences attracted a still smaller proportion of students in the less challenging adult courses offered by Local Education Authorities: only 1.8 percent of enrollment in 1927–28.)[129] Astronomy, physics, and chemistry were rarely offered by the WEA, because they required expensive equipment and sophisticated mathematical skills. Biology, botany, zoology, and geology were more feasible, since classes could resort to museums, zoos, botanical gardens, and country rambles. They could also draw on what remained of the dying tradition of working-class naturalists, who were meeting in pubs as late as the 1920s.[130] By then an instructor might still work with an occasional student "who has spent his Sunday mornings for twelve years collecting fossils from colliery tip-heaps with excellent results,"[131] or who had built his own microscope and chemical apparatus, but such versatility was increasingly rare.[132] As for the WEA policy of educating students up to an honors standard, "I must confess that I never took it seriously," wrote one biology tutor from Leeds University.

It could never have been intended to refer to Science Courses. How could a class meeting for two hours a week in town which provided, let us say, only one microscope and no other equipment whatever, be expected to reach Honours Standard ... in a Biology course? Science must be experienced and not read.

Midnight oil is of no avail. ... To merely lecture the students that offer themselves, or to get them to read books is to produce nothing but inflation and arrogance. An individual so trained would have a bad influence—I have seen it at work—and contact with him would be sufficient to make anyone hate science.

His university students in biology had to study botany, zoology, human physiology and histology, and pathology and bacteriology, each course consuming at least twelve hours a week (in practice much more) for three years. A Tutorial Class student would take seventy-two years to cover the same ground, not counting the introductory training university students received in chemistry and physics. At most a WEA tutor could offer a basic introduction to science. In place of real lab work he might bring specimens to class, share his research with the students, set up vivaria and aquariums, hold a class in his own laboratory, or conduct museum visits and nature walks.[133]

For some students, adult education produced more stress than gratification. When postal worker Paddy Molloy took his first class (in European history) in 1932–33, "An entire new field of learning was opened up for me, although I must confess that I understood very little of what was being taught." A few years later he attended Ruskin College, where he studied history and psychology, was introduced to classical music, and was immensely impressed by the objectivity and rigor of his tutor. But when he returned to his post office and trade union work,

Many of my colleagues did not know quite what to make of me. Coming from Ruskin I was not comfortable with them, nor they with me. It is difficult to portray the peculiar situation I found myself in. The WEA and Ruskin experience had, to put the matter bluntly, lifted me out of the relatively uneducated working class rut. They only knew I had been to college. It seemed odd that I should only be a postman. I felt often compelled to argue against, as I saw it, their unsubstantiated prejudices.

He defended Gandhi against a former sergeant major, who lashed back fiercely: "Don't argue with me you bloody educated nincompoop." "For some months after I left Ruskin I did not want to do any serious reading, or study at all," Molloy recalled. He recovered and became WEA organizer for Hertfordshire, only to face attack on another flank. One of his faculty was a German academic refugee, whose nerves had been shattered by Nazi persecution, but his classes were harassed by Communists who wanted him dismissed as an ideological traitor, and Molloy had to travel and argue past midnight to defend him.

By the end of the war Molloy was disillusioned with the WEA. He saw it becoming more and more a middle-class organization, steeped "in the high flown jargon of the University lecture, or Common Room."[134] The proportion of worker-students in the WEA had fallen from nearly half (48.2 percent) in 1937/38 to just under a third in 1949/50, and would decline further to 28.0 percent by 1958/59.[135] Autodidacts, the traditional constituency of the WEA, were becoming an endangered species, thanks to the (limited) opening up of secondary and higher education. In 1927 Board of Education inspectors in Yorkshire found that only in the smaller and more isolated towns was it "still possible to meet the old miner who knows his Butler's *Analogy*, the labourer who can recite most of Blake's poems, and who can enforce his points with apt quotations from the Bible."[136] By 1952 children at the same IQ level, regardless of their class background, had an equal chance of entering grammar school, though of course children from affluent families were likely to score higher on intelligence tests.[137]

Sidney Weighell (b. 1922), general secretary of the National Union of Railwaymen, enormously appreciated the educational routes that opened up after the Second World War. Where he had to rely on NCLC correspondence courses and study "after work literally by the guttering candle," his son acquired a doctorate, and his two nephews became, respectively, a metallurgist and an aeronautical engineer. But as he admitted, "With this sort of change, the traditional pool of working-class brains and talent has been siphoned off," and the intellectual level of NUR leaders had unmistakably declined.[138] Pearl Jephcott's 1945–46 survey of 103 teenage girls was hard put to find a working-class intellectual among that generation. There was the daughter of Methodist trade unionists, a Sunday school teacher who managed the library at her Girls' Life Brigade Company, who knew *Madame Butterfly* and the *Messiah*, who read everything from *Wuthering Heights* and *The Water Babies* to Walter de la Mare and Adolf Hitler. But she was literally one in a hundred: the other girls in the survey were devoted to the cinema, indifferent to current events, and positively hostile to "big books."[139]

Adult Education: Why This Apathy? was the telling title of a 1953 report by WEA official Ernest Green. By then it was clear that the wartime enthusiasm for culture had worn off. Green discovered that, in a typical town in 1949–50, only one adult in forty-six was taking an evening institute course, and only one in 265 was taking a class in the liberal arts. Each year since 1948 the National Coal Board had offered a hundred university scholarships to miners to train as mining engineers: it never found more than fifty-five takers. A newspaper explained that one could hardly expect young men to give up £12 in wages for an £11 university stipend. "Shades of Jack Lawson, who sold up his home to go to Ruskin College!" snorted a disgusted Green.[140]

A 1962 Gallup Poll in North Staffordshire found that 83 percent of working-class respondents had never heard of the WEA, and 91 percent did not know what it was. When asked where they would go for information about adult education, nearly half did not know: none mentioned the WEA or a university.[141] A 1965–66 survey in Chester and Eccles found that only 5 percent of persons aged fifteen or over, and only 1 percent of semi-skilled and unskilled workers, had ever taken a WEA or university extramural course. Though only 25 percent of all adults were professionals or managers, they accounted for 65 percent of all WEA and extramural students. Put another way, 23 percent of all university and college of education graduates had attended WEA or extra-mural courses, compared with 8 percent of grammar school graduates and only 3 percent of those who had attended secondary modern schools, though secondary modern students accounted for 35 percent of all WEA/extra-mural students.

One encouraging sign was the fact that educational broadcasts on radio and television regularly reached 24 percent of skilled workers, 30 percent of the semi-skilled, and 18 percent of the unskilled.[142] That pointed the way toward the Open University, launched in 1969, and reaching more than 200,000 students by the 1990s. Though most of them were not working-class, in the 1970s, 52 percent of the fathers of Open University students were manual workers, and another 28 percent were lower-rung white-collar employees.[143] Even in the Thatcher decade, observed Richard Hoggart, adult students were still seeking the best that is known and thought in the world:

They express that need in lovely old-fashioned ways. They speak of wanting to be better educated so as to live a fuller life, so as to be more whole, so as to be able to understand their experience better, and the way their society is going. They want to understand and to criticise, but from a larger and less febrile perspective than they are generally offered; they are Arnoldians before they are anything else. Jude and his sister are not dead nor necessarily at university; they probably have Filofaxes; but they are still looking for larger meanings.[144]

Chapter Nine Alienation from Marxism

"Why was there no Marxism in Great Britain?" Historian Ross McKibbin has posed the question, and he suggests a number of inhibiting influences: smaller factories where owners knew employees, layer upon layer of caste and craft subdivisions within the working class, a persistent attachment to church and chapel, loyalty to a depoliticized monarchy, the legitimacy of Parliament as a reformed institution based on a broad suffrage, opportunities for social mobility up to the House of Lords, education in democratic procedure via model parliaments and trade unions, faith in the rule of law, and a government that had withdrawn from industrial relations to permit unfettered collective bargaining. McKibbin particularly focuses on another necessary "condition for the emergence of a Marxist party ... an active 'socialist' leadership whose own values and way of life are largely outside and hostile to the ruling values of civil society." That was certainly not to be found among the first Labour MPs: all had been born into the working class, nearly all had been industrial workers, none had a university education. "The sort of men who were so prominent in European socialist parties —marginal bourgeois, journalists, 'theoreticians', professional orators—were comparatively rare in Britain." The British working class had forged its own organizations and its own leaders, who did not care to accept middle-class patronage, even under the name of socialism.[1]

Everything McKibbin says is true, but he and other historians have missed other factors which may be at least as important, and which only become visible when working people themselves explain why they were not (or had ceased to be) Marxists. They rarely mention such global issues as the purge trials, the Nazi-Soviet Pact, the invasion of Hungary, or Khrushchev's "secret speech" of 1956. Instead, they emphasize philosophical, ethical, and literary problems. Put bluntly, the trouble with Marx was Marxists, whom British workers generally found to be dogmatic, selfish, and antiliterary. These complaints cannot be dismissed as the sour edge of post-Hungary disillusionment—though the disillusioned deserve to be heard here. The memoirs of those who were never disenchanted and of those who were never Marxists, as well as a revealing sociological study, point to the same conclusion, though most of them were written before 1956. British working people judged Marxism by the Marxists they knew, and concluded, with good reason, that such people were not going to make a better world.

The Labour Party rather than the Communist Party would attract mass support, for reasons that can be traced back to their religious and literary roots. In the first half of the twentieth century "Practical Christianity"—a vague but sincere belief in charity, equality, and doing good—was the consensus theology of British working people, whether or not they attended church.[2] It was a doctrine entirely at home in the Labour Party, but difficult to reconcile with orthodox Marxism. Stuart Macintyre has highlighted the contrast: where Labour socialism was ethical, idealist, and undogmatic, early British Marxism embraced a more "scientific," materialist, and rigid world view. If a more humane and flexible Marxism failed to take root, that was largely a result of the availability of Marxist literature in English. By 1933 much of the later Engels had been published, but little of the early Marx; plenty of Lenin, Trotsky, and Stalin, but no Lukács or Gramsci. Hence, early British Marxists dismissed as "bourgeois" the same canon of English classics that inspired generations of autodidacts, thus alienating the very proletarian intellectuals who might have been the driving force behind a more creative Marxism. Where Marxists defined exploitation in purely economic terms, Labour socialists, brandishing their Everyman's Library volumes, promised beauty in life, joy in work, a moral vision in politics. Following a long line of radicals and mutual improvers, they proclaimed that knowledge (rather than ownership of the means of production) is power.

"Thus," Macintyre concludes, "the Labour leaders preached and practised on the basis that there was no other impediment to socialism than the backward mentality of the masses—no Foreign Office officials with a penchant for circulating documents of doubtful provenance; no newspaper proprietors ready to publish them; no bankers with ultimatums concerning government spending."[3] That last remark is not fair to the WEA, which certainly did teach working people to read critically the pronouncements of diplomats, press magnates, and financiers. Yet the respective ideologies taken up by the Labour and Communist parties did create a self-sorting mechanism, with idealists and self-improvers attracted to the former, cynics and authoritarians to the latter. This, it should be emphasized, is only a rough generalization with plenty of exceptions: no single cause can entirely explain the membership of any political movement. The Labour Party certainly had its share of careerists, and the early Communists in particular included many genuine crusaders, such as Helen Crawfurd. But even she once confided to a comrade, "Mary, Communism is all right, though there are scoundrels in the Communist Party!"[4] My point is that there was something inherent in Communism that put the scoundrels in control. The ideology attracted them to the point where they came to dominate the Party, and most of the idealists either left in disgust or were pushed out.

Evangelical Materialism

The establishment of a Marxist stronghold in the South Wales coalfields can be traced to the great Welsh Evangelical Revival of 1904. Many miners who were swept up in that enthusiasm soon found a more worldly outlet for their spiritual passions in Keir Hardie's socialism, while others turned to Marxism.[5] South Wales Nonconformity could be as dogmatic as it was literate, grounded in close readings of an authoritative text. That mentality was readily transferable to Marxism or, for that matter, any number of other surrogate religions. Collier D. R. Davies briefly embraced the 1904 revival and then, in rapid succession, turned to fund-amentalist Unitarianism, orthodox atheism, and evangelical Marxism. For a time, he recalled, the Independent Labour Party "satisfied my religious yearnings, for socialism became a religion in which I developed an unquestioned, dogmatic faith. Its future triumph I never doubted. It would solve all problems and put everything right." When it didn't, he resorted to psychoanalysis, which, "it seemed, had achieved a comprehensive formula, according to which men could be made automatically good." When they weren't, he returned to Marxism, fought in the Spanish Civil War, and finally came full circle, taking orders in the Church of England.[6]

The dogmatic tendencies of working-class Marxists were reinforced by two authors they often studied side by side with Marx. One might assume that Adam Smith and Charles Darwin gave aid and comfort to unbridled capitalism, but they were also read enthusiastically (and very differently) by the partisans of the Plebs League and the NCLC. Smith, Darwin, and Marx all offered materialist theories of evolution based on struggle and exploitation. They all suggested that the existing social order was not divinely ordained, but had progressed according to certain scientific laws. Once those laws were understood, society could be reconstructed along different lines. For Dunfermline housepainter James Clunie (b. 1889), *Das Kapital* and *The Wealth of Nations* both demonstrated that industrialism inevitably increased economic inequality, the exploitation of labor, and class conflict. To this *The Descent of Man* added "the great idea of human freedom. ... It brought out the idea that whether our children were with or without shoes was due to poverty arising from the administration of society."[7]

The difficulty was that this combination of theological absolutism and scientific certainty could produce a pharisaical type of Marxist who alienated his potential followers. Frank Goss described his own father, an SDF activist, in those terms:

My father's socialism might be considered in somewhat the same plane as being a Plymouth Brother or a Seventh Day Adventist, except that it was by a more scientific and materialistic approach that the millennium was to be achieved on earth rather than the hope of achieving a heaven after death.

A mixture of Marx and the Sermon on the Mount with a greater or less degree of each in the mixture, made up the outlook of most of the socialists of those days. They looked forward to a new world in which all people of the earth would be equal, brothers who would use the earth and its products for the benefit of all, each contributing in effort according to his ability and receiving according to his needs. A good socialist was one who acted in his everyday life in his relations to others in the sense of this hope in the brotherhood of man. To them, the sanity of their proposition was so obvious that it only needed explaining sufficiently for all people to adopt it. Each socialist would become the nucleus of a snowball of revelation which, gathering momentum, would soon embrace all the world.

The immediate set-back to this theory was that ... there were large numbers of people on whom the blinding light of socialist sanity had been projected who did not seem capable of absorbing it. From this it was simple reasoning for socialists to classify themselves as the enlightened and all others, for whom the light had not proved to be of any lasting value, were lumped together as "the unenlightened". Socialists became the chosen people all over again.[8]

Even true believers were compelled to admit that this was a problem. Glasgow foundryman Thomas Bell (b. 1882) discovered as much agitating for the Socialist Labour Party, a precursor of the Communist Party. "With cold, hard scientific logic and quotations from Marx and Engels, we usually reduced all opposition to silence," he assured his readers, "but we never made members." He suspected "our sectarianism had something to do with it." Apparently the workers "thought we were terribly intellectual, and that they had to have a knowledge of Karl Marx and science before they could join the Party."[9] Walter Citrine (b. 1887), who passed through an early Marxist phase, noted that a workmate on a Liverpool construction site, an SDF man, was "cordially hated by most of the other workmen because of his sarcastic manner, and perhaps because he always defeated them in argument."[10]

Not many working people were prepared to accept dictates from such men, especially when Communist discipline went beyond matters of ideology. As Hymie Fagan (b. 1903) recalled, the Party closely policed the daily lives of its members, dictating their dress and even instructing them to pay their bills: "We did not want our members to appear queer, in the original sense of the term, in the eyes of the working class." As manager of the Party bookstore in King Street, he once committed the astonishing indiscretion of putting Trotsky's autobiography in the shop window. He fought back when Party boss Harry Pollitt accused him of deviationism: "Bugger you mate, I'm not going to invent a confession." After that experience, he was duly skeptical of Stalin's show trials.[11] One particularly rigid Sheffield Stalinist devoted his memoirs (titled "We Tread But One Path") to proclaiming his invariable rightness on all issues, though he did confess to one terrible disappointment: for reasons he could not comprehend, his son had become a political cynic and emigrated to the land of apartheid.[12] As one woman told J. T. Murphy, "Before I joined the party all the comrades used to come to me and say what a good worker I was and tell me that I ought to join; that I was the type which they wanted in the ranks of the party. But after I joined, although I do more work than before, they never cease to tell me what a fool I am." On that point, Murphy ruefully quoted T. A. Jackson: "The party line is always moving in a circle." Murphy himself quit the Party in 1932 over an obscure doctrinal dispute. That ended his career as a journalist for the Soviet and domestic Communist press, forcing his wife to go back to work. "And, strange as it may seem, we were happier," he concluded.

> It was as if we had been released from a condition of continuous tension, common to the life of Communists, wherein all one's thoughts are concentrated on the party and its work, its associations, its people, its doctrine, to the exclusion of the larger world around us. The more I have thought about the way in which we lived previously the less surprised I am that the Communist Party made so little headway.[13]

The primary motive of autodidacts had always been intellectual freedom. Few of them would sacrifice it to a Marxism that submerged individuals in the massing of masses and clashing of classes. James Griffiths (b. 1890), the Welsh collier and MP, attended the Central Labour College, but steeped as he was in the "religious idealism" of the ILP, "I could not bring myself to accept the materialist concept of history: my Welsh temperament recoiled against such an arid doctrine. At the end of each lecture on the M.C.H. I would join a fellow student, who shared my revulsion, in singing: 'I am the master of my fate, I am the captain of my soul.'"[14] Taxi driver Herbert Hodge (b. 1901) was at first impressed with the intellectuals he met in the Soho branch of the Communist Party, but soon realized that they treated workers as unthinking objects. One recent university graduate blandly repeated the Leninist notion "that the less the unemployed got to eat, the quicker they'd revolt. I suggested he should try a few months of semi-starvation himself, and see how revolutionary it made him feel. But he only smiled the university-graduate's superior smile which makes the non-university man feel such a fool." From his own work with the unemployed, Hodge knew that years on the dole only produced apathy, and that out-of-work men wanted practical help in dealing with the Board of Guardians far more than ideology. That experience, plus his eclectic reading (Bergson, Nietzsche, William McDougall, Bertrand Russell, the New Testament, and Herbert Spencer as well as Marx) led him out of the Party towards a socialism that would be brought about by individual volition, not "human masses, social systems, and economic forces. We've become so used to thinking in these terms that we've forgotten the root of them all is the human individual."[15]

More idiosyncratic still was R. M. Fox (b. c. 1894), a factory laborer who was published by the Hogarth Press and lectured for the WEA. He found both Marxists and the Labour Party too confining, casting his lot instead with Irish nationalists, militant suffragettes, conscientious objectors, and the Industrial

Workers of the World. He frequented Charlie Lahr's anarchist secondhand bookshop in Holborn, a mecca for down-and-out Nietzscheans and scruffy poets, where he could freely indulge his "crush on philosophic Germans, gloomy Scandinavians, sour Swedes and analytical Russians." Fox always insisted that economic deprivation made intellectual liberty all the more valuable to the poor. He hailed Maxim Gorky for realizing that "men who have felt the burden on their backs ... appreciate freedom"; only bourgeois socialists like Sidney Webb wanted more state control.[16] Any political system that denied working people "beauty, colour, and adventure from life" was treating them like machines. Therefore Fox rejected the crude "pamphleteering" of *The Ragged Trousered Philanthropists*, much as he admired its brutal truthfulness:

> Some who speak of working-class literature mean only churned-up political rhodomontade. But while working-class literature is in the political manifesto stage it is not literature and it is not working class. The literature of wage-earners only reaches maturity when it ceases to be pitched in a wholly aggressive key and expresses the life of the workers as something of intrinsic worth and interest apart from polemical purpose. ... Such a literature cannot be confined to the workshop for it is not only or chiefly with the worker as a worker, but with the worker as a man or woman that we are beginning to be pre-occupied.[17]

Communism, of course, was not the sum total of Marxism, and at this point one might ask about the possibilities for developing a humane proletarian Marxism outside the Communist Party. The answer is that the logical sites for building an alternative Marxism were the Central Labour College and the National Council of Labour Colleges, but they clung to an ideology that was, in its own way, as ossified as Communism. Many CLC students, among them Aneurin Bevan, came to feel that its simon-pure Marxism was too dogmatic and not entirely relevant to the twentieth century.[18] Even a sympathetic historian concedes that its lecturers simply and tediously "reproduced the work of leading marxists, very often with little or no commentary" beyond the repeated mantra that it was all "scientific." Marxism was thus treated as "a compendium of answers to set questions, without enough emphasis being placed upon its ability to identify new questions and problems."[19] By 1923 CLC students were protesting the neglect of *non*-Marxist economics.[20] Later, Communist students would attack the school from the left for not submitting to Party control, and moderate trade unionists concluded that the college was turning out irresponsible agitators. A succession of financial scandals and internal battles over educational resources finally led to the CLC's closure in 1929.[21]

Harold Heslop, the Durham miner-novelist, attended the CLC in 1925–26 and found the curriculum dismally propagandistic. "They insisted that there was no viable reasoning on economics before Marx, and none whatever since," so the students learned nothing of Adam Smith, David Ricardo, or John Stuart Mill.

Instead, they were plunged cold into the bewildering mental theories of proletarian philosopher Joseph Dietzgen without any preparatory work in philosophy. "For us, Aristotle was some ancient Greek who had written a book about babies ..., but never were we offered even a potted biography of Kant, Locke, Butler, Hume, Hegel and all the tribe of German philosophers. All we were instructed to do was to locate them and reject them on the grounds that they were not relevant to the needs of the working class." Heslop was in search of a working faith, "obsessed by a deeper hunger than I had hitherto known for salvation," and he was profoundly affected by Marx's outrage, his pity, the "crashing force in the simplest of his observations." But that side of Marx was lost in CLC lectures.[22]

Likewise, many students found NCLC lecturers intellectually contemptible. According to Jack Hilton (b. 1900), a militant agitator for the unemployed who had been imprisoned for rioting,

> They are hatless and suffer from cerebral fever; they look high-brow and sordidly live on economic rigidity. Marx, Dietzgen and Engels are their food and they eat it up like gluttons. ... They're overripe single-trackers, they lack human nature. They are merely book socialists, their ferocity is confined to the iron rigidity of terminology. Really they are as useful ... as a group of feminine sissies when playing cave man stuff. ... Their lectures are parrot-like and have mathematical precision. To them Bill Shakespeare would be taboo. ... History is just to emphasise the obvious fact that the "haves" some time ago diddled the "have nots," and its purpose is in the last analysis proved conclusively and indubitably to be "That the only remaining class to rise, will rise," and so become dominant in the we-are-the-boss stakes.

For all their talk of "international solidarity ... whenever one or two dogs of party fractionalism meet for common action, they nearly always snarl and chew one another up."[23] Even T. A. Jackson, the most brilliant NCLC lecturer, eventually admitted that their ideological track had been far too narrow: "'What do they know of England, that only England know?' And for 'England' read 'Marxism' and you have a truth of ten times the dimensions."[24]

Harry McShane, a Glasgow engineering worker, was an early recruit to the Communist Party but left it before the great disillusionment of 1956. The more he read of the young philosophical Marx, the more impatient he became with the Party's "mechanical materialist view" that "history makes men." Lenin and Bukharin, he noted, thought otherwise: "Action is changed by ideas," and the workers are "not just an economic force," but thinking individuals "who hold and discuss ideas." Socialism is not simply the outcome of inexorable historical development, but "the creative act of the working class to solve the economic crisis of capitalism. Because it is creative, it isn't inevitable; the capitalist system can end up in fascism, as in the thirties in Germany, rather than socialism." And because socialism is creative, "it isn't about state planning …; it is about the working class owning the means of production and planning their lives for themselves." The key to building socialism, then, was creating an intellectually sophisticated working class, though that seemed a remote prospect by the 1970s. "The intellectuals are writing for one another instead of for working-class people," McShane complained, "they seem to think that workers can't read!"[25]

Have You Read Marx?

In fact, most workers did have great difficulty reading Marx and Marxists. Unlike John Ruskin, William Morris, and Robert Blatchford, the Marxists generally and glaringly failed to produce literature accessible to the working classes. If Ross McKibbin is right—that there was no British Marxism because Britain lacked an alienated intelligentsia, but developed a working-class party and trade union movement independent of the middle classes—that amounts to saying that Marxism is inherently a movement of the educated classes rather than the laboring classes. The latter were effectively and, one could argue, deliberately excluded by the difficulty of Marxist language. Any number of autodidacts registered that complaint.[26] As Harry McShane asked, how can human beings be emancipated by a doctrine they cannot understand and have no role in creating? McShane began his education in Marxism by reading *Justice* and the *Socialist*, the respective organs of the Social Democratic Federation and the Socialist Labour Party. But the former, he found, preached "a narrow stupid Marxism," while the latter printed page after grey page on the materialist conception of history. Even with A. P. Hazell's penny pamphlet, *A Summary of Marx's "Capital"*, it took him a full week to master the labor theory of value. Like most working-class readers, he much preferred Blatchford's *Clarion*, where an unideological socialism was leavened with breezy articles on literature, freethought, and science.[27]

Of the Labour MPs surveyed by the *Review of Reviews* in 1906, only two mentioned Marx as a formative author. Walter Hampson (b. 1866), the wandering socialist fiddler, complained that whenever he lent out his *Das Kapital*, it came back with the latter pages uncut.[28] In fact it is difficult to locate anyone who even claimed to have read all three volumes. T. A. Jackson doubted that fifty people in all of Britain had persevered to the end,[29] and according to J. T. Murphy few Communist Party members "had more than a nodding acquaintance with the writings of Marx."[30] Robert Roberts (b. 1905) remembered

> a course which opened with fanfare and fifty-four students in a room over the bar at the local trades club, to study (under a man with a large red beard) the "first nine chapters of *Das Kapital*." After a month only three of us remained, and one was a girl whose father (standing guard in the bar below) insisted on

her attendance. This class was the prototype of innumerable similar fiascos which occurred right through the '20s. Of Marxism the proletariat wanted not even the "first nine chapters."[31]

Even the Ruskin College Marxists, A. E. Coppard recalled, were living "the sweetest Surreyside melodrama": all earnestly preparing for the Revolution, "and there was not enough hot blood in the lot of them to fill a flea." They answered every criticism with the same conversation-stopper: "Have you read Karl Marx?" Coppard finally learned how to trump that card: "Have you?"

> Then inevitably came the lame admission, "Some of it, all that's really necessary, the first five chapters of *Das Kapital*, they contain the essence, all you want." Yet to them the Revolution was truly a mystic ideal; as vague as heaven it was, and in that identical vagueness lay its kindred power to sway them.[32]

Few common readers could penetrate the smokescreen of jargon. Glasgow MP George Barnes (b. 1859) had unpleasant memories of the language used at an SDF meeting. "I was so belaboured with words about exploitation, proletariat, bourgeois and others of learned length and thundering sound just then imported from Germany that I believe I retired sore all over and determined to go no more to Social Democratic Federation branches. And I never have."[33] Others persevered with Marx, whose very difficulty might suggest a kabbalistic power to transform a desperate economic situation. Ewan MacColl recalled a fellow Communist in Depression-era Manchester, a seaman who sold the *Daily Worker* until he was found in the local party headquarters, literally starved to death. Confronted with that, MacColl could only talk about one thing: "Politics—there seemed to be nothing else in life, nothing else that was worth a damn. All the time I was living on a thread of anger which was eating me away." The girls he tried to date were not charmed by his conversation, "and who could blame them. You were talking such fucking jargon! But the jargon meant something to you—it was a code that you'd cracked."[34] It also cut off Marxists from the class they were supposed to be mobilizing. Communist Party of Great Britain (CPGB) founder J. R. Campbell organized Marxist study circles for Glasgow slumdwellers who, as his stepson remembered, "had not the faintest idea what he was talking about. ... I watched the knitted brows and perplexed looks in the eyes of his students and wondered if they had the slightest inkling of Karl Marx's message." In a very general way they sympathized with Campbell, but they could not even master the catechism: when asked "What is a capitalist?" one ship-welder answered, "A capitalist is a bastard of the first water!"[35]

Margaret McCarthy was at first dazzled by young Communists who reeled off words like "dialectical," "empiric," "formalistic," and "materialist conception." Only later did it become apparent that "the intensive application of confusing hieroglyphic verbal terms and high-sounding political phraseology" was an encryption device to exclude newcomers like herself from Party discussions. "I have since, of course, realised that most human institutions, and particularly political bodies, do tend to freeze out the new recruit, despite the professed desire to attract the masses," she explained, "but the Communist Party members had a particularly suspicious attitude, due partly to jealousy for place and power which the newcomer, especially one with any gift of eloquence, might eventually challenge, and partly to vague motives of security."[36]

The fact that working-class readers did respond to Marx's rare concessions to wit suggests a missed opportunity. In 1925 Ifan Edwards was driven by unemployment to read *Das Kapital* in the public library. "It took him about four hundred pages of close print to come to the crux of his argument in the classic illustration of the labourer looking for a job in a factory, and, as he said, 'expecting nothing but a hiding,'" Edwards remembered. "This little aside appealed to me very much, as I had had one or two hidings myself."[37]

Unethical Socialism

If an ideology offers a rationalization for a type of unacceptable behavior, it will often (though not invariably) attract followers with that kind of moral weakness. Such formulas as "Self-interest is the greatest virtue" or "Your anger is not a personal failing, but a healthy response to social injustice" or "All human relations are power relations" will exert a gravitational pull on selfish, hostile, or dictatorial personalities. Early British working-class Marxism was all too often a vulgar Marxism that glibly dismissed morality in capitalist society as bourgeois morality, or resorted to the easy excuse "capitalism has made us what we are." In contrast the Labour Party preached a kind of twentieth-century Wesleyanism. Socialism would be brought about by an ethical revolution based on broadly Christian principles, just as nineteenth-century evangelicalism had transformed a brawling, hard-drinking proletariat into respectable chapelgoing Victorians. Working people rooted in this tradition were repeatedly appalled by the behavior of individual Communists, most of whom seemed to lack the moral commitment that had built the Methodist Church, the trade union movement, and the Labour Party.

After the failure of the General Strike, cotton-weaver William Holt (b. 1897) "dipped into *Das Kapital*" and joined the Communists—though a veteran radical, with the works of Marx and Lenin lining his homemade bookshelves, warned "that I should not find them quite as heroic and admirable as I believed." Holt organized a Todmorden chapter of the National Unemployed Workers' Movement, but it fell victim to internal bickering and a general unwillingness to volunteer for organizational work. Tellingly, Communist activity in the town came to a halt while Holt was in jail for leading a demonstration against the Means Test. "One of the local men who called himself a Communist complained that the reason why nothing had been done in Todmorden while I was in gaol was because I had not trained cadres of leaders. As a matter of fact, I had spent hours trying to teach this very man, but he was a born grouser and incorrigible," explained an exasperated Holt. "Why don't you do something yourself?" he shot back, "I'm not Atlas." In fact his Communist cell attracted "a few ragged, well-known loafers" who "began to use me as a tool for furthering their own ends." He hated the "conspiratorial" climate of Party meetings where, "in an atmosphere of strange antipathy, one speaker after another ... gave humourless speeches criticizing their own actions and passionately admitting their mistakes."[38]

Such complaints are registered fairly consistently in workers' memoirs. A. T. Collinson (b. 1893), a founding member of the Communist Party in Middlesex, left it partly because too many had joined up "to gain personal advantage, and when successful in this respect they fade out."[39] Frank Chapple became a member in 1939, but as a ship-repair electrician he noticed that Communist organizers "didn't appear like true Communists to me. ... Why should leading Communists always get the good numbers to work at, corner weekend work at overtime rates, have something more important to do when it was time to get out and sell the *Daily Worker?*"[40] Lathe-turner Les Moss (b. 1901) admitted that he spent a lot of company time discussing Marxism ("it's true we hardly did any work sometimes") and he left the Party in 1947 because, he felt, it was run by intellectuals who kept power in their own hands but would not back workers in their confrontations with bosses.[41] ILP activist Jack Ashley found Communists not only dogmatic, patronizing, and addicted to jargon, but plain dishonest as well. When a Communist friend argued that the exploitive practices of capitalist publishers justified his stealing books from an Oxford bookshop, Ashley saw it as "a rationalisation of a selfish action."[42] Though John Brown was a student of Marx and an NCLC official, he saw "that the type of man who was joining the Communists was very obviously not the self-sacrificing martyr type so largely responsible for the creation of the Labour Party." As a Ruskin College student (1932–34) he was no more impressed with Oxford undergraduates

who had swallowed chunks of Marx and Lenin whole, and repeated their undigested paragraphs *ad nauseum* whenever politics was discussed. They looked upon Cole as a hopeless reactionary, and spoke continually of "mass action" by the workers. What form this "mass action" was to take was never clearly defined, and I noticed that when it came to doing any propaganda or canvassing work for the local movements, those who had been shouting the hardest were not to be found.[43]

Margaret McCarthy noted a marked change in the calibre of Accrington Communists between 1926, when she joined the Party, and 1932, when she returned from a sojourn in Russia. At first it attracted real idealists:

… active people from the trade unions, students from the National Council of Labour Colleges, ILPers who had been driven leftward by the General Strike, and such types as generally form the active core, the local intelligentsia of the Labour movement. But these people had drifted away from the Party and a new class of individuals had entered, who rather frightened me. They were not only unemployed, which was not surprising in our depressed district, but often distinctly unemployable people, with a turn for violent language and a yearning for violent action. On one occasion I found a heavy wooden truncheon in the Party rooms and at once demanded a meeting of the local members, where I lectured them on the stupidity of Communists carrying weapons and had the thing thrown out. There was a protest to the District Headquarters of the Party against my speech at that meeting and I found myself again in trouble for inferring nasty things against Party members. Some time later, three-quarters of these self-same members in Accrington went over *en bloc* to the local branch of the Fascists which was opened by Mosley himself, and I knew that my estimation of their characters and intentions had been correct. But in the meantime it was they who had the ear of the Party.

"I wanted to clean the Party of such types," she wrote, but "in due course I was to learn that the Party and they were one; that it was such characters as my own which were alien and astray in the Communist Party." When idealists attempted to reform Party bureaucracy and corruption, "they usually found this a sure and quick way right out of the Party." Assigned to the Party's Scottish office in 1930, she was appalled to find the kind of tyranny and gross mismanagement one associates with a Five-Year Plan. "It soon became clear to me that such Party organisation as functioned was maintained by one factor only: namely the untiring, loyal, self-sacrificing devotion of the members who worked at innumerable unpleasant, exhausting and time-devouring jobs." They had to endure

the petty bullying and domination of the Party bosses, whose inefficiency and muddling they resented but concealed, maintaining the leadership through a real, if grumbling, sense of duty to the Party. … The District Secretary was a typical example, being physically large, loud, rude and brutal in his manner, jealous of his power, notoriously mean and ungenerous, and cringing before the national leadership in London. In him I saw typified the new individuals rising to power in the Party, the species of new "Party boss".

This is what ultimately drove her out of the Party. It was not so much the suffocating repression in Stalin's Russia, nor her realization that the Leninists had distorted Marx's original vision, nor even "the obvious fact that the average unemployed worker in Britain, existing as miserably as he did on the dole, still enjoyed an infinitely higher standard of life than the average Russian worker in

Moscow working full-time." What finally made her snap was the spectacle of loyal Party workers railroaded by their superiors for some minor error or ideological deviation. Even before Stalin's terror moved into high gear in 1934, she had seen a miniature show trial in a Party chapter in Glasgow:

> I sat in that small meeting, in that filthy room, looking at the squalid people as they disparaged and abused our comrade, not in the Party's interests but from some obscure motive of power, relishing the opportunity to badger and humiliate, to rend and vilify. I sat among them, sensitive to the atmosphere of the meeting, furtive, shifty, thick with moronic bigotry, and it seemed to me that I could not breathe, that I was choked and blinded by the fug of imbecile, foul and unnecessary conspiracy, the conspiracy of comrade against comrade. Then suddenly all became cold and clear to me. THIS was the Party! This cluttered room, these mean, perverse people, the silent, shamed victim of their mindless, pointless venom. This was the Party. This room full of filth and ignorance was the cell of the Party, the Party in essence. The Party was just this, multiplied a thousandfold, a millionfold. And it was because the Party had become like this that it had withered, the workers wanting none of us .... [44]

ILP agitator Jennie Lee favored a Popular Front alliance with the Communists, and was even inclined to view the great Soviet famine of the early 1930s in a favorable light, but it was a personal incident of gross callousness that left her unforgettably bitter toward the Party. Her grandfather had been a dedicated trade union organizer and socialist who suffered victimization. Even in retirement he daily visited the Fife Miners' Union headquarters in Dunfermline. One day he ran into a young Communist delegate arriving for a miners' meeting who sneered: "What are *you* doing here? I thought we had got rid of all you old buggers!"

> He might just as well have lifted his fist and struck the old man physically. He could not have hurt more. My grandfather did not go again to the office. His union, his life, all the pride and the labour and hopes he had put into it! Then to end up sitting looking into the fire, sad, perplexed, afraid to go near his old workplace lest he should be spat on. I walked down Rose Street, Dunfermline, the evening I heard of that encounter, with murder in my heart. I think if I had met a known communist I would have been gaoled for manslaughter. That sort of incident told in bald outline may sound silly and trivial. Multiplied a thousand times and repeated all over Great Britain in a thousand different variations, it goes far to explain the dislike and distrust of the Communist Party that balks all their efforts to achieve friendly relations with the rest of the working-class movement. [45]

Around 1939 Mary Craddock succumbed to an adolescent passion for Communism. "I loved the slogans, the little pills of wisdom that went down my gullet painlessly—'The best for the most'—'From each according to his ability, to each according to his need.'" But any mention of Communists made her father spit: "Riff-raff, that's what they are. Corner enders. Them as wouldn't work if they could. On the look-out for something for nowt. Them's communists." A Durham miner crippled by rheumatism, on the dole since age fifty, a founding member of the Labour Party, he had precious little stake in capitalism. What sharply distinguished his Labour doctrine from Communism was, first, a belief in individual freedom and a hatred of bureaucracy. He distrusted even the local all-Labour urban council, which he regarded as a swamp of inefficiency and patronage. More than that, he retained the old Labour Party's Victorian faith in personal moral responsibility. His daughter discovered that side of him when she pointed out a particularly filthy slum:

> "Look at it," I said. "That's what capitalism did for you."
> Father and I surveyed in silence the grim ugly street that had been put up to house the pitmen. It was incredibly ugly, drab with gaping windows and rotting doorways propping up slatterns in sack aprons and curling-pins. Inside one could glimpse disorder born of despair. I saw it as a failure of the System. Father had a different view. He was looking at the slatterns and their filthy little kids.
> "Aye," he agreed. "It's a very bad area this. It's a terrible thing to see the way people let themselves go when they've lost their self-respect."[46]

Several factors alienated George Scott from Communism—Harry Pollitt's rabble-rousing, the Soviet invasion of Finland, not to mention his own upward mobility as a young reporter in Yorkshire—but the moral issue was preeminent. He was disgusted by the "immature but clever cynicism" practiced by Stan, a fellow journalist. Stan sneered equally at the "opiate of the masses" and at men who put themselves in harm's way in wartime ("I shall join Intelligence and get a nice, comfortable, safe chair in an underground cellar in Whitehall"). He had read *Das Kapital* (or parts of it) and could talk slickly about dialectical materialism. His own dialectic was derived from *Straight and Crooked Thinking*, a guide to identifying faulty logic, but he "enjoyed it because it taught him how to twist truth to his own ends. He put what he learned into practice and his methods of debate were skilful, muscular, witty and deliberately crooked. … He had a cold, well reasoned appreciation of the blessings of benevolent despotism as a form of government. Naturally he saw himself as the despot."[47]

Though he passed through a "near-extreme left" phase as a telegraph messenger boy, R. L. Wild (b. 1912) was not impressed by the local Party man in Winchester. He was one of those "small men with big ideas," who worshipped Stalin and read little beyond Marxist dogma, but what decisively condemned him in Wild's eyes was the fact that he lived comfortably by sponging off his family. "Were his dreams of power, of some sort of niche in an English Kremlin, or a commissarship in

Hampshire?" Wild wondered. "How much of all this was for an ideal, a cause? How much was through greed and laziness and conceit?"[48]

Sociologist G. H. Armbruster investigated that question in a Welsh mining town in 1939. It is significant that the locals were acutely suspicious of Armbruster, variously denouncing him as a Tory, a German spy, a social worker, or a Communist—all of which they regarded with equal hostility. He found that in spite of prolonged unemployment and the circulation of Marxist literature, colliers still manifested "a strongly individualistic bias" and a desire "to be recognized as just a bit better than their neighbors." Though the out-of-work miner could offer "a ready explanation for his misfortune in terms of the evils of capitalism and the necessity for economic transformation," on another level he still viewed unemployment as a personal failing, in a culture where "respectability" meant having a job. Armbruster concluded that the "spontaneous collectivism" of the Welsh miners was a myth: they were generally skeptical of proposals to nationalize the mines or place them under workers' control. Most miners professed a kind of socialism, but it scarcely resembled any socialist theory developed by intellectuals. It was in fact welfare capitalism based on inherited moral principles of "practical Christianity":

> For the majority of workmen who call themselves socialists, aside from the strong religious note of "brotherhood," socialism partakes of the character and aspirations of the existing order. Their ideal is really more closely akin to the program of the Liberal Party than that of a clear cut socialism as we understand it; the security of their jobs, adequate wages, the improvement of housing conditions, increased pensions, social insurances, etc. are the tangible contents of these aspirations. The question of common ownership of production is even looked upon with a healthy skepticism. ... There are those who speak of socialism almost purely in religious terms who may even vote Conservative, and regard it as a sort of benevolent exchange of brotherhood, of charitable giving, for whom it means a universal association in spirit of kindliness, and with the realization of which all problems will end.

The chapels had always reinforced this doctrine of Christian benevolence and individual responsibility. But as a schoolmaster involved in charity distribution noted, these values were now increasingly confined to the older generation: "This new one that's being raised on [handouts] and has never worked, never will. They won't do a thing for themselves but grab any charity that's given to them. They spend the rest of the time quarrelling among themselves over who got more than they deserved." For some of those who had lost the old ethic of sturdy independence, Communism offered a refuge and a rationalization, though as Armbruster noted, they were strikingly incapable of real selflessness:

> Their communism is clearly one of psychological necessity, of some integrating faith in utter contradiction to their former outlook and behavior. They have

transferred self condemnation to the convenient condemnation of "the capitalist system which makes us as we are". ... For those ... who are versed in the verbiage of socialist and communist doctrines, there is a surprisingly clear recognition that a gap exists between their principles and their ability to live them. I have a good number of statements to the effect, spontaneously rendered by such men. They understand that their habits have been conditioned by living in an entirely different society. "Aye, it will come [socialism], but not in our time; we'd all be too much capitalists; we are too selfish." Another: "It won't be with us, we'd just come to believe in it, we can't change our ways, we must come to it gradually," and another, "we have progress, evolution as Darwin says; you or I won't see socialism, we aren't socialists at heart, but our children will know it because they will really be socialists."

Employed colliers belonged to a community that provided a living frame. Their workmates, chapels, and trade unions interpreted events in the larger world and offered a clear set of moral and political principles to live by. Plunged into the mass unemployment and political turmoil of the 1930s, these miners lost that frame and were profoundly disoriented:

The unemployed man slowly loses his anchorage in institutions such as trade unions which provide attitudes and some understanding of his relation to wider economic and social forces. The trade unionist can at least measure his reactions toward events as they affect his primary aspirations. The workless lack concrete organizations of their needs and are without the hard practical guidance of daily labour and the vigilant struggle to ensure the conditions of their jobs.

Cut adrift, the unemployed increasingly resorted to "systems" for winning football pools, millenarian Christianity, millenarian Communism, and (among women especially) astrology. All these panaceas offered short-cuts to salvation involving no real individual effort: as Armbruster noted, the unemployed conspicuously "lack the capacity to act upon any of their convictions." Even when they denounced capitalism or condemned the moderation of the trade unions and the Labour Party, this was "a rationalization for inaction. Many is the man I found vociferous in his denunciation of 'the system' and the conduct of his own organizations who when the time came for demonstrations, hunger marches, etc. was not present." Of the 3,000 voters in this district, the Communist Party could claim only thirty-five members, all unemployed. Armbruster got to know eight of them well:

They were known by their fellows as bad trade unionists, and as workmen concerned only with the promotion of their own interests. They possessed little of the fellowship which they now profess, and even at present I have seen these men conducting themselves in a fashion which was in direct contradiction to their avowed belief in brotherhood and equality. I am certainly not extending this as a generalization for all communists among the miners. I knew several members sincere in every respect, but I think it is evident that as an all-embracing philosophy, particularly in the naive fashion in which it is interpreted here, it fulfils a definite psychological function for many among the unemployed who deeply require a precisely formulated attack on the "system" to externalize their personal guilt feelings. ... There was, I found, a great deal of truth in the popular observation that the communists were poor workers and trade unionists. I knew two leaders of the party, each of whom was discontent with work in the mines and found in communism a justification for their attitude and often callous indifference for the safety and welfare of their butties in the colliery.

There was, for example, a former preacher, traumatized by ten years of unemployment, who now proclaimed that "Marx has replaced God" and regularly read the *Daily Worker*: "While in the mine he was not regarded as a faithful trade unionist and was a 'company man' insofar as he would pass remarks to officials about so and so's conduct, in return for favours." His brother was transformed from an apolitical chapelgoer to a Communist by six years of unemployment: "Was not liked when working, looked after his own interests to the detriment of others. ... Spends his time trying to get as much charity as he can from the social services, much to the dislike of many of his fellows. Recognizes that his conduct has not corresponded to his beliefs and rationalises it ... by reference to the 'conditions that make us as we are,' and the hope that 'evolution' will remake man."[49]

The criticisms offered by Armbruster, William Holt, and Margaret McCarthy are largely corroborated by Andrew Thorpe's research in recently opened CPGB archives. Except for a blip following the 1926 General Strike, the Party had fewer than 10,000 members before 1936. Membership then surged to unprecedented levels during the worst phase of Stalin's terror, and rose again in the months following the Nazi-Soviet Pact. General disillusionment among Party members was produced not by events in Moscow, but by failings much closer to home. Internal CPGB documents frankly admit that grass-roots organization was "so rotten" that it alienated potential recruits. New members were likely to find that local chapters were run by incompetent hacks, or dominated by cliques that froze them out. Others were driven away by ideological sectarianism, or by the endless labors (meetings, trade union agitation, activity in front organizations, selling the *Daily Worker*) demanded of party members. As a result the CPGB, like the Communist parties of the United States and Weimar Germany, had an enormous and rapid membership turnover.[50] No doubt victimization was a contributing factor, but the early organizers of the Methodist Church, the trade union movement, and the Labour Party had suffered similar bouts of persecution. They each nevertheless succeeded in building a movement with a mass working-class base, in large part because of their moral appeal. Lacking that attraction, the CPGB was never more than a marginal political force.

If the failure of British Communism was a moral failure, the exception that proves that rule was Rhondda East. Here, as Chris Williams has shown, a series of scandals left the local Labour Party vulnerable to charges of corruption and nepotism. Communist councillors and activists were able to seize the moral high ground by attending to the everyday concerns of their constituents, including medical clinics, free milk, and child welfare. As a result, the Communists came close to capturing this parliamentary seat, polling 31.9 percent of the vote in 1931, 38.2 percent in 1935, and 45.5 percent in 1945. But most of these votes represented a protest against Labour malfeasance, not an endorsement of Marxist ideology, which (as the borrowing patterns in miners' libraries suggest) was largely ignored outside of a few "little Moscows."[51]

More typically the Party emphasized doctrine and slogans rather than practical assistance in dealing with the problems of poverty. When Communists attempted to recruit tramps by taking over the National League for the Abolition of Vagrancy, they did not address such mundane issues as improving shelter conditions. "One talked of the theory of Dialectical Materialism, and another appealed to us to take our hands off the Chinese," recalled a baffled hobo. "Exactly what they thought they were getting at has puzzled me ever since."[52]

Stalin Reads Thackeray

"It is an extraordinary thing to see an out-of-work man arguing his head off about the fate of a Trotsky, in the midst of sheer misery and poverty," James Hanley reported from South Wales in 1937. "The ordinary voice has given way to the loud Quack, the most skull-splitting theories upon Politics, Art, Literature, Painting and the rest are trumpeted into the ear, all things are ordained with the assurance of a Caesar." Here the Communist attitude to literature could be particularly blinkered. "'Unless your writing has in it the Marxian viewpoint it is valueless,' etc. etc., and they quoted Marx and Balzac by the yard, though I'm sure the latter's droll stories would have shocked them considerably," Hanley protested. "Many of these people hold that all literature that has ever been written is valueless."[53] Given that most autodidacts were devoted to the literary canon, nothing could have done more to drive them away from Marxism.

In 1938 an adult educator suggested that most Marxist literary critics could learn a great deal from reading Marx, who did not rule out the role of individual genius in authorship, who denied that literature could be reduced to a by-product of economic conditions, who disliked socialist propaganda novels, who admired a whole range of classic authors (Homer, Aeschylus, Dante, Shakespeare, Goethe, Scott, Thackeray, Charlotte Brontë, Dickens) regardless of their politics.[54] But doctrinaire British Marxists of the 1920s and 1930s generally refused to see any value in art apart from propaganda. The National Council of Labour Colleges sponsored agitprop theater groups, and from that platform Ness Edwards denounced Shakespeare and nearly all other important playwrights as reactionaries: only Shaw and Ibsen won his guarded approval. There was also a Workers' Theatre Movement, affiliated with the Communist Party, whose aims were laid out in a 1930 manifesto: "It rejects decisively the role of raising the cultural levels of the workers through contact with great dramatic art which is the aim of the dramatic organizations of the Labour Party and the ILP. ... The task of the WTM is the conduct of mass working-class propaganda and agitation through the particular method of dramatic representation."

As Raphael Samuel pointed out, that dogma effectively cut off these movements from everything vital in drama. Sean O'Casey would have been the ideal playwright for a proletarian theater, but he was never performed by any WTM troupe: T. A. Jackson disapproved of his "pessimism." While the ILP and Co-operative societies sponsored dozens of thriving theatrical groups, the WTM failed to find much of a following in the working class.[55] WTM propaganda even repelled some of its own performers, who could not forever suppress their unpolitical love of literature. Ewan MacColl remembered his father, a Communist ironfounder, as someone who was always giving him secondhand books. He "belonged to the generation who believed that books were tools that could open a lock which would free people. He really did believe that." At age eight MacColl received the works of Darwin. By fifteen he had read Gogol, Dostoevsky, and the entire *Human Comedy*:

> They were a refuge from the horrors of the life around us. ... Unemployment in the 1930s was unbelievable, you really felt you'd never escape. ... So books for me were a kind of fantasy life. Books, however abstruse their theories were, were an escape. For me to go at the age of fourteen, to drop into the library and discover a book like Kant's *Critique of Pure Reason* or *The Mistaken Subtlety of the Four-Sided Figure* ... the titles alone produced a kind of happiness in me.
>
> I fell in love with books. When I discovered Gogol in that abominable translation of Constance Garnett with those light-blue bindings (I can remember them to this day), I can remember the marvellous sensation of sitting in the library and opening the volume, and going into that world of Akaky Akakievich Bashmachkin in *The Overcoat* or in *The Nose*, or *The Madman's Diary*. I thought I'd never read anything so marvellous, and through books I was living in many worlds simultaneously. I was living in St. Petersburg, and Paris with Balzac, I really was. And I knew all the characters, Lucien de Rubempré and Rastignac as though they were my own friends.

By then MacColl had also read Engels's *The Peasant War in Germany* and *The Origins of the Family*. He joined the Young Communist League and the Workers' Theatre Movement, organizing a troupe of his own called the Red Megaphones.

But the tension between art and sectarianism was never resolved. For the Red Megaphones, and particularly for someone as well read as MacColl, WTM scripts were an insult:

> We had a strong feeling that we were being written down to. ... We were beginning to doubt the efficacy of the endless sloganizing. I've noticed frequently among middle-class party people that I've worked with, over the years, that there's an idea that workers will accept anything, providing the message is OK. The quality doesn't matter, the form doesn't matter. All that matters is that we agree on the correct slogans.

The group performed satiric songs and sketches, "but we always felt uncomfortable because they seemed to be written from the outside. Saying things like 'the workers', but we *were* the workers. It seemed false for us to be standing there singing 'the workers'. Christ! We couldn't have been more the workers!" MacColl firmly believed in class solidarity, but he saw that identity politics erased identity, submerging him in "the masses":

> From the time I began to think—about the age of twelve or thirteen—I resented people who talked about us as "you people", or "you workers". I felt reduced, as if my identity was being taken away. "You people", you great enormous mass of nobodies who produce all the riches of the earth, you people, my people, me![56]

T. A. Jackson spent a lifetime struggling with that conflict. He wrote his autobiography to prove "that a man can be a Communist and still remain *human*"—implying that it was not easy to reconcile the two.[57] Though it was issued by Lawrence and Wishart (the Party's publishing arm) in the depths of the Stalinist chill, the title, *Solo Trumpet*, was shamelessly individualistic. Jackson's habit of running afoul of Party discipline (he was removed from the Central Committee in 1929) was not unconnected with his hopeless love of the English classics, which he had mastered thoroughly by age fourteen. At that point in life, as a reading-boy in a London printing works, socialism made no impression on him, largely because he was exploring the metropolis through the frame of secondhand classics:

> It was truly a wonder-world, for I was seeing it not merely with eyes of flesh but with the eyes of heightened imagination;—seeing it not only through spectacles manufactured by an optician, but through glasses supplied by magicians named Charles Dickens, Walter Scott, William Makepeace Thackeray, Joseph Addison, Daniel Defoe, Harry Fielding, Toby Smollett, Sam Johnson and Will Shakespeare himself ... —and that was the trouble. I was book-hungry and I found a land where books were accessible in a quantity

and variety sufficient to satisfy even my uncontrolled voracity. How could anyone expect *me* to even begin to contemplate the complete overturn of a world as wonderful as this?[58]

Was an education in the classics really a vaccination against Marxism? That certainly was not the case with Marx—or Tommy Jackson, for that matter. Yet it is telling that Jackson's unpublished memoirs devote much more attention to his literary pursuits than the version published by Lawrence and Wishart. His comrade Helen Crawfurd, in her own unpublished manuscript, likewise had far more to say about literature than the usual authorized Party autobiography. She derived lessons in socialism and feminism from Carlyle, Shaw, Wells, Galsworthy, Arnold Bennett, Ibsen's *Ghosts* and *A Doll's House*, Dickens, Disraeli's *Sybil*, *Mary Barton*, *Jude the Obscure*, *Tess of the d'Urbervilles*, *Under the Greenwood Tree*, Tennyson's *The Princess*, Longfellow, Whitman, Burns, Elizabeth Barrett Browning, George Eliot, George Sand, the Brontës, *Les Misérables*, and *The Hunchback of Notre Dame*.[59]

As a published proletarian author, William Holt did not appreciate party hacks telling him that "There can be no proletarian art until after the revolution." On a tour of the USSR he found much to admire in Soviet industrial and social organization, but Russian agitprop films struck him as devoid of creativity or individuality. Conversation among Communists was "dreary—obsessed as we were by politics—humourless and barren. ... The tension of party life was unnatural, and a growing suspicion began to haunt me that Bolshevism was a horrible disease." He described it as an antiliterary psychosis, occasionally relieved when his comrades "unconsciously revealed to me the repressed, more human side of their nature," as when Page Arnot introduced him to Stendhal. Holt was ultimately expelled from the Party for writing articles that "described mill-girls laughing and talking of what they were going to wear at Blackpool."[60]

Jack Jones (b. 1884) became aware of the conflict between ideology and literature as a boy miner in Merthyr Tydfil, when he earned a few extra shillings selling sweets in the theater. There he saw the opera and whole history of English drama, from Shakespeare to Oscar Wilde. All of it was eroding the puritanical culture of Nonconformity, "making inroads on the narrowness of the outlook of different sections of the town's growing population." After the First World War he became an early Communist Party member, as well as a South Wales Miners' Federation official in the godforsaken town of Blaengarw, but the two roles inevitably clashed: he resented the endless stream of Party dictates and, when he failed to carry them out, the constant attacks by local Communists. Then in 1923, in his capacity as bookbuyer for the Blaengarw Miners' Institute Library, he discovered the great peace of the Cardiff Central Library. "I'd like to do a year's reading in the quiet of this room," he told a librarian.

I left school the day before my twelfth birthday to go and work underground with my dad. For a dozen years after I started work I don't think I read one good book. I remembered bits of Bible-stories which I had been told in Sunday School—but those somehow got mixed up in my mind with Sexton Blake and Jack, Sam and Pete. Not until I married did I do any real reading—bought a number of volumes of Everyman's Library, which were all sold to a second-hand bookseller during the hard times which came after the lock-out of the miners the year before last. Since then it's mostly Marxist books I've been reading. But as a miners' leader I must stock my mind with more than what Marx and Engels and those of their school have written.

Once a month, when his duties took him to Cardiff, he would exchange twelve to twenty books and take them home in an old suitcase. He read Tolstoy and Gorky, and raced through most of Dostoevsky in a month. He was guided by a librarian who, like a university tutor, demanded an intelligent critique of everything he read. Disdaining "books of the month" and "best-sellers", Jones was anxious to distill "the quintessence of the great minds of all time, the imperishable intellectual substance of the ages." Back at the Blaengarw Workmen's Hall, he brought in a stock company to present a one-week Shakespeare festival, followed by stripped-down opera and even a Shaw repertory. They all attracted large crowds, but local Communists attacked him for neglecting his duties to "mess about with bloody actors." In 1928 he quit his post as miners' representative and moved closer to the library that had been "my university." He finally left the Communists for the Liberal Party and became a successful novelist, beginning with *Rhondda Roundabout* in 1934.[61]

Jones was reacting against the attitude typified by Communist Willie Gallacher, who began his first volume of autobiography (1936) by stating outright that he would not discuss anything that did not have "a definite bearing upon my becoming a working-class agitator."[62] Starting in the Popular Front years, that hostility to literature abated. Gallacher loosened up in later installments of his memoirs (1951, 1966), where he confessed a liking for Burns, Scott, the Brontës, Mrs. Gaskell, children's comics, and Olivier's film of *Hamlet* (he once played Second Gravedigger for an amateur society). Of course he admired Dickens, and not only the obvious *Oliver Twist*: the Communist MP was prepared to admit that he appreciated the satire of the Circumlocution Office in *Little Dorrit*.[63]

Especially during the wartime alliance with the Soviet Union, Communists became more anxious to embrace the British literary heritage. They noted that Marx had admired *Tom Jones* and Robert Burns; that Engels had learned much about English social conditions from Carlyle's essays, Disraeli's novels, and the poetry of Elizabeth Browning; that Stalin, in his youth, read Shakespeare, *Vanity Fair*, and *The Origin of Species*. They cited exhaustive production figures for English classics published in the USSR, where "There is no Board of Censors nor any official censorship." There was even a glowing report of a Moscow Art Theatre dramatization of *The Pickwick Papers*. True, the audience was not quite sure how to respond to its quintessentially bourgeois hero.[64] But if Stalin was a devotee of Thackeray, surely it was safe to applaud.

Chapter Ten **The World Unvisited**

What we now call "cultural studies" can be traced back to George Orwell's classic essay "Boys' Weeklies" (1939). Orwell was one of the first intellectuals to subject popular culture—in this case the *Gem*, the *Magnet*, and other story papers for boys—to serious critical analysis, focusing on their political implications. These magazines, read largely by working-class children, specialized in public school stories suffused with a frolicsome Toryism, and otherwise oblivious to the political storms of the past twenty-five years. Orwell concluded that the *Gem* and *Magnet* had successfully indoctrinated their readers in the ideology

> of a rather exceptionally stupid member of the Navy League in the year 1910.
> … Here is the stuff that is read somewhere between the ages of twelve and eighteen by a very large proportion, perhaps an actual majority, of English boys, including many who will never read anything else except newspapers; and along with it they are absorbing a set of beliefs which would be regarded as hopelessly out of date in the Central Office of the Conservative Party. All the better because it is done indirectly, there is being pumped into them the conviction that the major problems of our time do not exist, that there is nothing wrong with *laissez-faire* capitalism, that foreigners are unimportant comics and that the British Empire is a sort of charity-concern which will last for ever.[1]

Since then, historians and literary scholars have become increasingly obsessed with the ideologies of race, class, empire, and gender embedded in all kinds of texts, canonical literature as well as popular magazines. According to this new conventional wisdom, a whole generation was converted to imperialism by the novels of G. A. Henty, children's magazines, and classroom propaganda. "At school, in church groups, in recreational associations—at almost every turn boys were exposed to the imperial idea," observes Patrick Dunae. "In the late nineteenth and early twentieth century most British youths were acutely aware of their imperial heritage. They could scarcely have been otherwise."[2]

In reality, they often were otherwise. The majority of those youths were working-class, and they seem to have been strikingly unaware of their empire. There is no denying that textbooks, popular literature, and later the cinema were supersaturated with imperialist propaganda.[3] But did these messages get through to their intended audience? Too often, those who examine literature for evidence of imperialism, racism, or male supremacy assume that these values were unproblematically transmitted to its readers, as if literature were a kind of political drug, with predictable and consistent effects. In fact, the ideological impact of popular literature is far more complicated and often fairly surprising.

An illustration of that point is offered by Guy Aldred (b. 1886), a socialist anarchist who devoted his political life to denouncing other socialists and anarchists as sellouts. William Morris, Bernard Shaw, the SDF, the ILP, the Soviets—all had betrayed the true Marxist faith. So had Marx, for that matter. ("In practice he deviated badly very often. I would not consider him a sound revolutionist.")[4] Remarkably, one of the very few unblemished heroes in Aldred's pantheon was Nick Carter, an American dime novel detective who tracked down criminals in a thousand stories published between 1886 and 1990.[5] "My interest in the exploits of Nick Carter was intense and so thoroughly had I studied him that I could have written his biography," he asserted. "*Nick Carter* kept me sane and certainly did me no harm. It did not make me believe in prison or crime …. I merely saw in Nick Carter a champion of Right. I idealised the tales and adventures. I am quite sure that this reading made nothing but a good impression on me …. It was good fun, kept my mind healthy and clear and saved me from much hypocrisy."

How could one worship such a pillar of law and order and remain an incorruptible radical? Aldred had no difficulty explaining it: "We often get out of our reading what we put into it."[6] The same uncertainty principle was at work in that vast genre of pulp fiction that glorified the English public school and the British Empire. To a remarkable extent, these stories did transmit a public school ethos to Board school children, but they generally failed to make them imperialists. Even after a half-century of unrelenting indoctrination, most working people knew little of the Empire and cared less. This case study illustrates, once again, that reader response depends entirely on the frame of the audience, which in turn depends on their education and their other reading experiences.

Greyfriars' Children

Public school stories were a staple of children's papers, and they had an enormous readership. *Boys of England,* founded in 1866, within a few years had an estimated circulation of 250,000, and gave rise to a number of imitations, all of which reworked the themes and values of *Tom Brown's School Days.*[7] In 1879 the *Boy's Own Paper* had a print run of 200,000 and an audience that cut across class lines. Correspondents reported that it was read by students at Wellington College, half the pupils at a Birmingham grammar school, and sixty-eight out of eighty-four boys working at a Scottish branch of the Technical Department of the Post Office.[8] By 1940, one of every eight books read by boys whose education was due to terminate at age fourteen was a school story. Among girls, the proportion was one in four—well ahead of love stories, which accounted for less than 10 percent.[9]

Beginning in 1907, the celebrated Frank Richards stories in the *Gem* and *Magnet* were tremendously popular. But how successful were they in communicating conservative values down the social scale? That question can only be answered by consulting the memoirs of Richards's fans. It may be objected that none of them would say outright "These stories indoctrinated me in bourgeois cultural hegemony, and I'm a better man for it"—but that, in effect, is what some of them did say. London hatter Frederick Willis asserted that they taught him to be "very loyal" to the headmaster and teachers at his old Board school:

> We were great readers of school stories, from which we learnt that boys of the higher class boarding schools were courageous, honourable, and chivalrous, and steeped in the traditions of the school and loyalty to the country. We tried to mould our lives according to this formula. Needless to say, we fell very short of this desirable end, and I attributed our failure to the fact that we were only board school boys and could never hope to emulate those of finer clay. Nevertheless, the constant effort did us a lot of good. We thought British people were the salt of the earth. ... The object of our education was to train us to become honest, God-fearing, useful workmen, and I have no complaints against this very sensible arrangement.[10]

Edward Ezard (b. c. 1900) admitted that he and his friends read the *Gem* and *Magnet* for "the public school glamour." They thoroughly absorbed all the stock phrases and attitudes associated with Greyfriars, Frank Richards's mythical school, conducting playground fights strictly according to Marquess of Queensberry rules. The headmaster was "firm but just and he had our wholesome respect." One teacher "gave we lads from that poorish neighbourhood a pride in themselves, so that we carried ourselves well anywhere and wouldn't for all the world let him or the school down." If they did, then "caning round the school" was clearly "a salutary experience."[11] (Of course boys' papers also authorized high jinks, within limits: Richard Hoggart claimed they inspired him to throw a stink-bomb in grammar school.)[12] For Paul Fletcher (b. 1912), a colliery winder's son in a Lancashire mining town, the *Magnet*'s appeal lay precisely in that "code of schoolboy honour." "Although I never realised it at the time, it proved to influence me more about right and wrong than any other book," he recalled. "And that includes The Bible." After all, the Greyfriars code "was as well defined as the scriptures [were] nebulous." Writing in 1972, Fletcher conceded that some,

> rejoicing under the name of intellectuals, would find it difficult to stifle their mirth at yarns which had a beginning and an end, and were completely free of drugs, dolls, crude Americanisms, and lavatory wall adjectives. But they don't matter. Harry Wharton and the Famous Five set an example of how to "play

the game" (and here there will be a slight pause for merriment by some soccer players and their followers), and their code of honour, effete as it may seem now, was something which society as a whole could now do with.[13]

Where no other code existed, Frank Richards supplied one. A. J. Mills, a charlady's son, recalled that his teachers made a pathetic attempt to teach an honor system, but "the nearest any of us got to knowing about the honor system was to read the *Magnet* to find out how the other half lived."[14] Robert Roberts described this phenomenon in wonderful detail:

The standards of conduct observed by Harry Wharton and his friends at Greyfriars set social norms to which schoolboys and some young teenagers strove spasmodically to conform. Fights—ideally, at least—took place according to Greyfriars rules: no striking an opponent when he was down, no kicking, in fact no weapon but the manly fist. Through the Old School we learned to admire guts, integrity, tradition; we derided the glutton, the American and the French. We looked with contempt upon the sneak and the thief. Greyfriars gave us one moral code, life another, and a fine muddle we made of it all. I knew boys so avid for current numbers of the *Magnet* and *Gem* that they would trek on a weekday to the city railway station to catch the bulk arrival from London and buy first copies from the bookstall. One lad among us adopted a permanent jerky gait, this in his attempt to imitate Bob Cherry's "springy, athletic stride." Self-consciously we incorporated weird slang into our own oath-sprinkled banter—"Yarooh!" "My sainted aunt!" "Leggo!" and a dozen others. The Famous Five stood for us as young knights, *sans peur et sans reproche.* Any idea that Harry Wharton could possibly have been guilty of "certain practices" would have filled us with shame. He, like the rest, remained completely asexual, unsullied by those earthy cares of adolescence that troubled us. And that was how we wanted it.

With nothing in our own school that called for love or allegiance, Greyfriars became for some of us our true Alma Mater, to whom we felt bound by a dreamlike loyalty. The "mouldering pile," one came to believe, had real existence: of that boys assured one another. We placed it vaguely in the southern counties—somewhere between Winchester and Harrow. It came as a curious shock to one who revered the Old School when it dawned upon him that he himself was a typical sample of the "low cads" so despised by all at Greyfriars. Class consciousness had broken through at last. Over the years these simple tales conditioned the thought of a whole generation of boys. The public school ethos, distorted into myth and sold among us weekly in penny numbers, for good or ill, set ideals and standards. This our own tutors, religious and secular, had signally failed to do. In the final estimate it may well be found that Frank Richards during the first quarter of the twentieth century had more influence on the mind and outlook of young working-class England than any other single person, not excluding Baden-Powell.[15]

Much as the actual public schools created a common culture for affluent children, public school stories created a common frame of morality, ritual, and literary references that enabled working-class children to socialize with one another. "We knew the same families in a way," as one Glasgow boy put it.[16] "How my eight year old mind boggled at the heroic antics of Harry Wharton and Tom Merry," recalled the son of a Camberwell builder's laborer, "and how determined I was to emulate their true blue behaviour by my conduct in the more prosaic atmosphere of St. George's [Church School], even if I sometimes wore no shoes and the arse was out of my trousers."[17] These readers were entirely aware that they could never hope to enter the world of Greyfriars School, as the son of a Walworth telephone linesman noted:

They were the sons of rich fee-paying parents; many of our parents were on the dole! They had a splendid sports ground with a "Pav"—we managed with an asphalt-covered yard and an open shed. They did prep and attended lectures in exotic things like French, biology and maths. We had lessons in "the three Rs" and a few other things and were sometimes given homework. In case of misdemeanour, they were given "lines", "six of the best" in the Master's study or, in extreme cases, expelled. We didn't have the luxury of expulsion: there might have been a queue for it. … Our homework competed for a place on the kitchen table; they had "studies." What was a "study"? This was an idea so foreign to us that we didn't know how to pronounce the word.

And yet, he added, "There was no envy on our part." Quite the contrary, "to paraphrase the Indian pal of Harry Wharton and Bob Cherry, the interestfulness was terrific!"[18] And where class resentment did exist, the stories could act as a salve. Joseph Stamper, a Lancashire ironmoulder's son, might publicly ridicule private school boys as "Jane-Anns." But privately, in what he called an act of "frustration-compensatory-escapism," he projected himself into the Fifth Form at Greyfriars.[19] Bermondsey boys saw no inconsistency in taunting actual Eton and Harrow students they occasionally encountered in the street ("Does yer muv'ver know yer out?" "Where did yer git that 'at?") while devouring the antics of Billy Bunter in the *Magnet.*[20] Lionel Fraser (b. 1895), the son of domestic servants, dreamt of Oxbridge but had to settle for a commercial course at Pitman's School. He certainly got on, rising into the higher altitudes of merchant banking, but he always regretted the lack of university education. Whatever resentment he may have felt was mollified by the *Gem* and *Magnet,* which "brought brightness into my rather humdrum existence giving me an insight into the hitherto unknown life of upper-class children." Making sense of the school slang and rituals was not easy, but Tom Merry and Harry Wharton "became my idols and I longed to be like them. They behaved themselves so admirably, they were so clean-limbed, they set a high tone, yet were strong and brave, never bumptious or priggish, and they commanded my respect and admiration." They also produced a contented boy who loved the Boy Scouts and unquestioningly accepted the Church of England.[21]

Charwoman's son Bryan Forbes "devoured every word, believed every word" of the *Magnet* and *Gem*, "surrendering to a world I never expected to join." As an adult he appreciated that they rehashed the same plot week after week, all to buttress "our indestructible class system." Nevertheless, he reviled Orwell's "politically slanted hatchet job." It was Richards who "won the contest hands down," Richards who "was the first author to cement my love of the printed word." As far as Forbes was concerned, Orwell's essay was only the first in a long series of "literary papal bulls," usually

> issued by some self-appointed arbitress, signposting crimes that were never intended and which young readers would never suspect of their own accord. Every so often these crabbed (and I suspect childless) pundits fire a salvo in the direction of Enid Blyton; dark Freudian and racist undertones are unearthed for the unwary. The shot scatters, peppering the likes of A. A. Milne and Kenneth Grahame—the young, we are told, will be in danger of having their values corrupted for life by indiscriminate exposure to such works. All balls, of course.

That arbitress might have replied that Frank Richards had done his job more thoroughly than even Orwell imagined: as a television director, Forbes worked for the Conservative Party to refurbish the public images of Edward Heath and Margaret Thatcher. Forbes also endorsed corporal punishment: if he was caned at school, it must have been for a good reason. "My own nefarious exploits included tumbling through the skylight of the girls' changing room and riding an upright piano down an incline until it crashed straight through the door of the headmaster's study, there to disintegrate."[22]

Those incidents sound suspiciously like episodes in a Frank Richards story. If Forbes was consciously or unconsciously fictionalizing here, that shows how far Richards influenced his readers and moulded their treatment of reality. On the other hand, if he really did toboggan on a piano and so forth, that might help to explain Richards's popularity: in certain important ways, his stories captured the essence of school life (pranks and all) even as it was experienced by working-class boys. Certainly those boys were able to project themselves into the world of Greyfriars. As one of them wrote, "the exploits of Tom Merry and Harry Wharton were better than the 'comics' of today [1979], in that we could at least imagine ourselves as the heroes in the stories."[23] It was much easier to identify with Billy Bunter than the Incredible Hulk, if only because the fans of the former probably attended schools that had much in common with Greyfriars. Edward Balne's school memoirs are filled with rosy recollections of "spacious playing fields, country lanes, extensive farm lands, which included a wide variety of fruit trees, a well-kept cricket ground and a football pitch; the School Band practice room ..., a spacious swimming bath, ... the school church—a surprisingly fine building," as well as a dedicated headmaster who offered the brightest boys special tutelage in his office. Reading this, one has to remind oneself that Balne, an orphan who never knew any of his relatives, is describing a London Poor Law school at the turn of the century. He knew well that the poor "were at a great disadvantage from an educational point of view," and he did not deny that school discipline was strict even by the standards of the day. But he thoroughly absorbed the conservatism that the school inculcated, and came to harbor unlimited contempt for the progressive education of the 1970s.[24]

When Thomas Burke was sent to a West Country orphanage, he anticipated a school like those in the boys' papers, and he was not disappointed:

> In retrospect I see it as others see Winchester or Rugby or Westminster, and can never pass a certain station beyond the Gloucester boundary without a gush of sentiment. Except for its uniform and its drills, there was little to distinguish it from the public school. It had its own tone and tradition, and its own slang, and it had much to give that was good. ... For four years it fed me and clothed me and trained me, and while the discipline was a constant fret, I recognise that they had a mixed crowd to deal with, and that it was necessary. ... They had called it a happy family, and it was. ... They gave me a school to look back upon with affection, a contact with tradition: old walls and lighted windows that enclose the faint perfume of our mornings. Their buildings are something more than buildings; their masters something more than men with degrees; and if their system hurt me in places, it armoured me in others, and set me on the right way. For me it was at first hard, but it helped by hardening me. It taught me to cultivate a hide and preserve my soul intact from the crowd. In short, they built me; and in going back to the old school—a sentimental indulgence which every man grants himself once—I went back to distant spires and antique towers, and wondered how I could ever have been unhappy there.[25]

When he entered the House of Lords, veteran miner and Board school graduate Bernard Taylor (b. 1895) could join his colleagues in the same kind of nostalgia, recalling with pride the inspiring headmaster, the lifetime friendships among the old boys, the "strong school patriotism," the football and cricket rivalries—everything, in fact, except the green playing fields, which in Taylor's case were asphalt.[26] "Who doesn't remember the absorbing tales from Greyfriars School," a railwayman's son (b. 1907) reminisced. "These boys went on for years, and never went past the Remove, and never grew up, for which we were truly grateful." That message was daily reinforced by the headmaster of his Walthamstow school, whose motto was "Play up, play up, and play the game."[27] A council school in the slums of Sheffield taught the same maxim: "Even today," one alumnus recalled in 1979, "it still holds a proud place for me."[28] One grimy Salford school sat next to a railway siding, and the pupils were constantly distracted by shunting trains and flurries of coal dust; but even there boys were required to wear Eton collars, and the respected headmaster ("a good sort, but very strict") would give one to anyone who could not afford it.[29] According to Yorkshire journalist George Scott, a young fan of the *Gem* and *Magnet*, "that self-esteem which is supposedly acquired on the playing fields of Eton" could just as easily take root in "the back alleys and the stony recreation grounds, the gravel football pitches and our own peculiar and exclusive wall games played against the sides of houses with wickets or goals marked out in chalk." Rugby men might pity him for his gritty childhood—or envy his early immersion in what they chose to call "real life"—but

> when I recall the absorption of self into the games I played and even into the stories in those boys' comics I cannot believe that my imagination was stunted in its growth. ... Every child has in common the construction of a private world of fantasy, compounded of a variety of extravagant wishes which he can fulfil in his games. What we loosely call reality—meaning the bread and butter facts of life which are the burden and responsibility of parents—impinge upon a child's life only lightly except in the most grievous circumstances. Unless poverty bears down so hardly upon a family that the child is forced to give up his dream-life for the *real* life of the pit or the factory, as in the early days of the industrial revolution, then there is little enough difference between the life of the prep.-school boy and the elementary school child.[30]

Even a delinquent (b. 1910) happily recalled that "My favourite reading was of middle-class boys who attended ancient academies, threw Liddell and Scott's lexicons at each other, and carried the public-school spirit into the most fantastic situations." So when he was sent to an industrial school, he found it astonishingly familiar:

> A two-storied red building, gabled and tiled, stood in a billow of green foliage, restful as a grazing cow. About it stretched an extensive demense of orchards, farm-land, chicken-runs and meadows. In a large playing field some boys were kicking about a football, and as the train passed another group came into view who were practising the jump across a sunken stream. In this brief glimpse there was nothing to suggest the grim and repressive institution I had feared; it was obviously a school, but a school, it seemed, of the idyllic sort one had read about in boys' papers.

Later, at a Borstal, he got on famously because he was so clearly a Greyfriars type: "A spirited fellow, not too amenable to discipline, good in sports, ruthless in fights, hard-working and sociable. It will be seen that this tallies pretty well with the 'Public School' *persona*; and ... this is what the Borstal authorities set out to impose."[31]

One has to conclude that, in early twentieth-century Britain, there was a common schoolboy culture that largely (though of course not entirely) transcended

---

class. The secret of Frank Richards's success was that he uncannily understood that culture and was able to guide his readers through it. Louis Battye (b. 1923), the spastic child of former millworkers, was at first utterly bewildered by the *Gem* and *Magnet*, because he was being educated at home and had no school experience of any kind. The boys of Greyfriars and St. Jim's

> wore long trousers like men and most peculiar collars and jackets. The teachers, too, seemed very odd: they were all men and wore square hats and long black cloaks. And what strange things went on there! What queer lessons were taught! What on earth was Latin, for instance? And the customs, the caning and flogging and fighting, the inexplicable moral taboos (why was it bad to smoke and drink and play cards?—quite nice people came to the pub every day to do all three)! No wonder I was baffled.
>
> But I persevered and eventually familiarised myself with the conventions of the form. I accepted Harry Wharton, Tom Merry and the other "decent chaps" as heroes, I learned to accept their standards as my own even when I couldn't see the reason for them, I learned to hate the "cads" and "rotters" and laugh at Billy Bunter and Arthur Augustus D'Arcy, to fear Mr. Quelch and respect Dr. Holmes. I even began to wonder if the stories were actually true, and if they were I rather wished I could go to one or other of these schools, in spite of the thrashings, kickings and other personal violences I would have to suffer if I did. …
>
> I have dwelt at some length on this peculiar mythology because it really did have a profound effect on my mental development. I continued to read the *Gem* and *Magnet* religiously until I was fourteen or fifteen, and from them I received what might be called the Schoolboy's Code.

That code was, contrary to what one might expect, immensely useful to a poor and severely disabled child. It enabled him to get along with other children when he was sent to Heswall Hospital: "I had absorbed a certain amount of theoretical know-how on the business of living with boys from my Greyfriars and St. Jim's training which helped me to avoid major gaffes, although on the surface the Boys' Surgical Ward at Heswall hadn't a great deal in common with those mythical academies." Later, at the school for the handicapped at Chailey, this same code

> was of great value in enabling me to settle down in what would otherwise have been a completely strange and bewildering society. True, Chailey was far from being Greyfriars, but at certain points there was sufficient resemblance for what I had learned of public school life to apply. To a certain degree I knew what to expect and what was expected of me. And what would otherwise have been a terrifying ordeal was made quite bearable.[32]

Well before the Teddy Boys, school stories created a youth culture powerful enough to challenge parental authority. Though uniforms were not compulsory at her Exmouth council school, Patricia Beer wore hers with pride and immersed herself in girls' school stories, particularly *Ursula's Last Term*. "It was an addiction," she confessed, and even temporary deprivation brought on "what must have been withdrawal symptoms." Her mother dismissed them with the ultimate expression of parental contempt: "I could write that kind of thing myself." They were both stunned when Patricia shot back, "Then why don't you?" It was appallingly defiant behavior for a young girl in the 1930s, but "it never once occurred to me that my mother's point of view about *Ursula* could embody any integrity or taste." These stories, which strike us today as laughably wholesome, may have threatened working-class parents "because all the girls in them went away to boarding schools and were out of their mothers' clutches. Certainly, I fervently wanted to go to boarding school myself and might well, after a period of conditioning to middle-class ways and speech, have been very happy there. Perhaps Mother sensed this wish and disposition."[33] Angela Brazil inspired Kathleen Betterton (whose father operated a lift in the London Underground) to ascend the scholarship ladder to Christ's Hospital in Hertford and thence to Oxford University. The Brazil stories, she wrote,

> conjured up muddled visions of midnight picnics, sweet girl prefects, hockey, house-matches, and exploits that saved the honour of the school. It never occurred to me that Mother and Father might be hurt by my anxiety to leave home, or feel that in letting me go they were losing a part of me. With the heartless self-absorption of childhood I was longing for a different world, less circumscribed than the one I knew.[34]

The fact that many parents banned such stories only enhanced their appeal for children. John Macadam (b. 1903) had to read them in secret and, forty years later, could still quote freely from them.[35] V. S. Pritchett furtively devoured the *Gem* and *Magnet* with a compositor's son: both adopted Greyfriars nicknames and slang. Pritchett's father eventually discovered them, burnt them in the fireplace, and ordered the boy to read Ruskin, though there was no Ruskin in the house. As far as the father was concerned, boys' weeklies were pornography—and Pritchett later realized he was entirely right:

> The crude illustrations, the dirty condition of the papers, indicated that they were pulp and sin. One page and I was entranced. I gobbled these stories as if I were eating pie or stuffing. To hell with poor self-pitying fellows like Oliver Twist; here were the cheerful rich. I craved for Greyfriars, that absurd Public School, as I craved for pudding. There the boys wore top-hats and tail-coats—Arthur Augustus D'Arcy, the toff, wore a monocle—they had feasts in their "studies"; they sent a pie containing a boot to the bounder of the Remove; they rioted; they never did a stroke of work. They "strolled" round "the Quad" and rich uncles tipped them a "fivah" which they spent on more food.[36]

Though Orwell faulted Frank Richards for banishing sex from his stories, perhaps they were capable of a more suggestive reading. Amy Gomm, an electrician's daughter, discovered the erotics of the text in some old *Gems* and *Magnets* she found in a cupboard. "What a joy to share my bed with Tom Merry and his chums, and that other band of derring-doers, Harry Wharton & Co. My excitement knew no bounds. My indiscretion was equally boundless." When she told her parents about the papers, they naturally burned them.[37]

Yet fathers often read comics with their children and absorbed the Greyfriars mythology.[38] After Dennis Marsden won an exhibition to St. Catherine's College Cambridge his parents, solid Labour supporters,

found supreme happiness sitting on the Backs looking over the river and towards King's College. For my father, Lord Mauleverer (of Billy Bunter and the *Magnet*) might have walked that lawn; Tom Brown must have been there, and the Fifth Form from St. Dominic's. He had read *The Adventures of Mr. Verdant Green at Oxford*, and saw that I had a "gyp" (as Verdant Green had a "scout"). He imagined how my gyp would shake his head and say (as Verdant Green's scout *always* said), "College gents will do anything." All I could say— and I said many bitter things—couldn't convince my parents that that powerful Cambridge image of my father's schoolboy reading wasn't *my* Cambridge. "We'll have to start learning to talk proper now," my father would quip, not wholly joking. How I writhed when he asked me, not completely facetiously, how soon Lord Mauleverer was coming home with me! How I ranted when my parents and family listened to Union debates on the wireless, watched "our boat" in the Boat Race, or waited eagerly for "our team" to score in the Varsity Match! To no effect. Actually, the only Public-School friends of mine they met seemed to them comically distasteful. But they never lost their dream. I came slowly to accept that when I questioned it, just as when I expressed my doubts about a scientific future, they became frightened, hurt or puzzled, and said that I had a funny attitude to things.[39]

Adolescent Propaganda

Though school stories appeared to be blatantly conservative, they were not always an effective vaccination against leftist politics. One could enjoy Frank Richards and still become a socialist or even a Communist. Walter Citrine won, as a Sunday school prize, a volume of school stories from the *Captain*, including one by P. G. Wodehouse. "The lady who gave this prize awakened in me a thirst for good literature," eventually leading to the works of Karl Marx and his followers.[40] George Scott left school and the boys' weeklies behind at fifteen: in barely a year he had absorbed enough Shaw, Wells, Dos Passos, John Steinbeck, and (second-hand) Marx to lecture his parents on the evils of capitalism and to flirt with the

Communist Party.[41] C. H. Rolph, a member of the Left Book Club and later director of the *New Statesman*, felt Orwell had been terribly unfair: "I do not believe that any writer has ever given me greater pleasure than this incredibly many-sided man Frank Richards."[42] One of the Famous Five's greatest fans, Harry Young (b. 1901), would become a leading organizer of the Communist Party. Their appeal, he concluded, was a matter of

> sheer gut affluence and opulence. Christmas at Greyfriars; all those Puddings and Pies. Toast in front of the blazing fire in "their own study" where incidentally they never studied anything! The "fivers" from "Pater"!! All the games, fights and japes. But above all !NO WORK! which we all had to do. ... None of the Greyfriars boys ... were ever going to be anything, or do anything. There was never the slightest suggestion that they MIGHT work at something. They were fifteen but the thought of a career or profession just didn't occur. They were true parasites—non workers.[43]

Even Hymie Fagan, an East End Jewish Communist, picked up public school ethics from the *Gem*, the *Magnet*, and the stories of Talbot Baines Reed. He once declined to run in an athletic event because "It seemed to me, under the influence of the boys' books I had read, that it was dishonourable to run for money."[44]

There are no real paradoxes here. These responses simply demonstrate that whether a text is "conservative" or "subversive" depends on the context in which it is read and the larger literary diet of the reader. The same reader can enjoy Karl Marx and Frank Richards in separate compartments, bringing a different frame to each. As a boy Percy Wall (b. 1893) adored the *Magnet*, the *Boy's Own Paper*, and G. A. Henty novels; he collected cigarette cards of Baden-Powell, Kitchener, and Redvers Buller; and, in a South Wales miners' library, he loved to "penetrate darkest Africa with Rider Haggard as my guide." Nevertheless, he regarded Cleopatra's Needle as a "symbol of Britain's predatory attitude to the African continent" and later spent thirty months in prison as a conscientious objector. While he read Henty for enjoyment, he studied the *Clarion*, the *Freethinker*, *The Struggle of the Bulgarians for Independence*, and *The Philippine Martyrs* for their politics, and did not allow one body of literature to affect the other.[45]

It is equally possible for the same reader to adopt different frames for the same story, relishing it on one level while seeing through the claptrap on another. In his youth Aneurin Bevan enjoyed the *Magnet* and *Gem* surreptitiously (his father forbade them) and devoured H. Rider Haggard at the Tredegar Workmen's Institute Library. But during the "Phoney War" he blasted the government's stupidly optimistic predictions in precisely the same terms: "Immediately on the outbreak of war, England was given over to the mental level of the *Boys' Own Paper* and the *Magnet*. ... If one can speak of a general mind in Britain at all just now, it is sodden and limp with the ceaseless drip of adolescent propaganda." In 1944 Bevan freely admitted that "William Le Queux, John Buchan and Phillips Oppenheim have always been favourite authors of ours in our off-moments. Part of their charm lies in their juvenile attitude." But in his public speeches Winston Churchill seemed incapable of switching off this boys' paper frame: "It is this refusal to grow up which is part of the Prime Minister's attraction for the general public."[46]

As human beings are flooded with far more empirical data than they can possibly process, they must invent strategies for *preprocessing*, admitting some kinds of information while screening out others. This is one of the functions of the frame: like an intelligence analyst, it must first sift "signals" from a much larger body of irrelevant "noise" before it can interpret the former. As one London East Ender explained in 1911, he developed an internal censor to edit "the flood of goody-goody literature which was poured in upon us. Kindly institutions sought to lead us into the right path by giving us endless tracts, or books in which the comparative pill of religious teaching was clumsily coated by a mild story. It was necessary in self-defense to pick out the interesting parts, which to me at the time were certainly not those that led to the hero's conversion, or the heroine's first prayer."[47]

Marx encountered that filtering mechanism at work in Greek dramas. They condoned slavery, and in that sense were political; yet modern audiences could still be riveted by these plays, without in any way diminishing their horror of slavery as an institution. "There is then a problem when we discover that work pronounced ideologically incorrect or unsound is found to be enjoyable, technically excellent, or in some other way 'aesthetically' good," Janet Wolff writes. She is disturbed by her own enjoyment of, "first, the classical ballet, many of whose works of repertory are based on reactionary and sexist (not to say silly) stories, and secondly, the paintings of Emil Nolde, a German expressionist painter who was a Nazi sympathiser." If she appreciates these works in spite of their politics, "what is it that I am appreciating?"[48] The answer is that all audiences at all times employ frames that focus selectively on some types of data while de-emphasizing or disregarding others. A cultural critic may choose to address the ideology of the dance, but a balletomane would probably lay down an opposite set of interpretive rules: ignore the story, and concentrate on the beauty of the body in motion. In that case, it hardly matters whether *Swan Lake* or the *Magnet* is broadcasting reactionary propaganda, because the audience has tuned out that message.[49]

Harry Wharton and Bob Cherry could inspire passionate loyalty in the Jewish East End, where some immigrants' sons wore Eton caps.[50] Even in the roughest streets of that district there was a steady market for back issues of the *Magnet*, which could be a spur to literary creativity: Willy Goldman (b. c. 1911) recalled that the cheap weeklies inspired his circle of young toughs to create their own handwritten magazine.[51] With Orwell's essay in mind, Chaim Bermant (b. 1929) described the enormous acculturating power of children's magazines. His father was an ordained rabbi, but when he emigrated to Glasgow he had to work as a poor *schochet* (slaughterer). "Provincial Jewish life in the 1930s was still in the hands of immigrants who, if only to establish their own bona fides as Englishmen, demanded one quality above all others from their Rabbis, that they speak 'mit a gutten Englis', which was the one quality father lacked." It was a skill that the next generation would acquire rapidly. The Bermant family arrived in Scotland when Chaim was eight: before his ninth birthday he had mastered enough English to read Beatrix Potter in the Mitchell Library. Her stories were not so alien to him as one might imagine: somehow the animal characters reminded him of the Latvian village from which he had come.

Chaim soon became a fan of the *Beano*'s Lord Snooty, an aristocrat who inexplicably consorted with a gang of working-class kids: "The strip fulfilled every schoolboy's fantasy of finding himself among wealthy people in a noble setting." Thanks to school stories, his everyday conversation was filled with student slang he barely understood— "prep", "fag", "prefect", "close", "quad", "remove", "poor show", "well-played". So far he was no different from his gentile schoolmates, but for Chaim there was a special added appeal: "The comics as a whole provided my sole entry into the non-Jewish universe." Even a working-class comic hero like Deed a Day Danny was a cultural model to emulate, for he always "came home at the end of the day to an orderly house with a set tea, whereas with the exception of the Sabbath and festivals, we rarely sat down at a table together as a family."

Later in life, Bermant wondered why the public schools enthralled him. "Was it that I was so embarrassed by our domestic circumstances that I wanted to leave home? Or was it, perhaps, that I was already finding the closeness and intensity of Jewish life overpowering, that I longed to be away from parental eyes and parental concern?" If we ask whether he realized that these schools did not take immigrant boys, the answer is that, just three years after his family stepped off the boat onto Scottish soil, "I found myself in a public school of sorts." It was a Jewish school near Castle Douglas in Dumfriesshire, another of those institutions that acquired enough public-school trappings to reinforce the messages sent by the *Magnet* and *Gem*.

> The building itself helped, for although it could not have been more than fifty years old, it had battlements and turrets and dark cellars which were out of bounds to the boys, which, given the schoolboy's imagination, could easily have functioned as dungeons. There were also extensive grounds, including a good cricket pitch, and a couple of water-towers mocked up to look like ancient keeps. We had pillow fights with adjoining dorms, cricket matches with a number of third-rate boarding schools in the vicinity, and I imbibed something of the public school ethos.

Like most Glasgow Jews, Bermant assimilated to England, not Scotland. Children's magazines were nearly all Anglocentric, even when they were published in Scotland, and BBC announcers spoke south-of-the-Severn English. Later he had some passing sympathy for the Scottish National Party, but what was the point of leaving one's own ghetto for someone else's? His father owned no books other than religious texts, he never read a novel or saw a play, and his only exposure to classical music was an accidental encounter with Beethoven's Egmont Overture on the radio.

For his son, the BBC and school stories offered an escape from a suffocatingly narrow culture. And there would be no turning back: though Bermant later emigrated to Israel, he soon returned home, incapable of living without tea shops, gothic churches, hedgerows, Bishop's Stortford, and 'soft mellowness on summer afternoons.'"

Bermant once told the joke of the Jewish immigrant who yearns to become a British subject, and finally applies for naturalization, only to return home shattered and in tears. His wife assumes that his application has been turned down, but no: her distraught husband has just learned that "They've given India away." All that was deadly serious to young Bermant as he followed the progress of the Second World War in the *Glasgow Herald* and *Manchester Guardian*. The war, the school, the boys' weeklies were all "building up new obsessions to replace the old and drawing reassurance and pride from the Empire." He dreamt of a postwar world where that Empire would be mightier still, until "gradually the whole of Africa glowed pink before my eyes." No wonder he loved singing "There'll Always be an England" and "Rule, Britannia": he sensed that his own survival depended on the survival of the British Empire.[52]

Marlborough and All That

That attitude was common among assimilating Jews, but not typical of British working people in general. Few of them were imperialists; many of them were only vaguely aware that the Empire existed; most of them would have been hard put to name a couple of British colonies. Once again reader response was highly selective: the public school stories, which were so successful in converting slum children to Rugbeian values, dramatically failed to make them love the Empire, even when reinforced by relentless imperialist evangelizing in the schools.

Grass-roots working-class activists in the Liberal, Labour, and Communist parties were almost uniformly anti-imperialist, while those who were less interested in politics generally brought a healthy apathy to imperial issues. It is revealing that most plebeian memoirs do not mention the Empire, and those that do usually view it through a skeptical frame. A Lancashire silk millworker who took up the study of Roman history in the 1840s noted that Caractacus, "when taken a prisoner to Rome, could only ask in astonishment why his captors living in palaces should envy him a hut in Britain: and we wondered how many Asiatic, African, and other chieftains had asked the same question, as they, and all belonging to them, successively fell into the hands of their English captors."[53] Working in a Leeds boot and shoe factory, George Ratcliffe (b. 1863) studied the courses of great empires (Babylonia, Persia, Carthage, Rome) and concluded that of all these, "the action of British Government regarding America [in 1776] was the most foolish I had ever read of."[54]

Some time ago Richard Price scotched the myth of working-class support for the Boer War. Only a handful of trades councils and workingmen's clubs expressed any opinion at all on the conflict, and those that did often formed branches of the National Democratic League, an anti-imperialist pressure group within the Liberal Party. The clubs tolerantly heard both prowar and antiwar lecturers, but the war was widely regarded as a distraction from social reform and a violation of national self-determination, fomented by a conspiracy of South African capitalists. Jingoist celebrations like Mafeking Night were carried on by middle-class clerks, apolitical young men out for a lark, and some workingmen expressing both their patriotism and genuine relief for the safety of British boys.

As a general rule, the attitudes of working people toward the Boer War were shaped by a profound instinct of loyalty—not to the Empire, but to their families and neighbors. Workingmen's clubs naturally felt a community obligation to local men who had gone off to fight in South Africa, and often raised money to support their families. For the same reason, resolutions denouncing British atrocities were often opposed by antiwar workers, since they implied a slur on their friends and sons. There would of course be boisterous celebrations when the troops came home, but these reflected a familial concern for the safe return of their boys rather than military triumphalism.[55] David Livingstone, who once worked in a Lanarkshire cotton mill, had inspired the same fraternal sentiment. He enjoyed "universal popularity among the masses," a Glasgow power-loom tenter recalled. "When he was lost in Africa and H. M. Stanley went out in search of him, our first question every morning was: 'Any news of Dr. Livingstone?' When at last we heard he had been found there was a day of rejoicing like a coronation."[56]

Workers' memoirs sometimes discuss family members who fought in South Africa, but with no apparent awareness of what they were fighting for.[57] "It was so far away it didn't seem real somehow," remembered one charwoman. "It was a story-book sort of war: George and the Dragon stuff. We heard bits about individual bravery, but we really had no idea why it was being fought and we thought the Boers were a lot of stupid savages not wanting to be in the Empire."[58] "But for George Brown," recalled a resident of the Lincolnshire hamlet of Digby, "the Boer War might have passed unnoticed in the village." Brown was a local laborer and ne'er-do-well, but his enlistment "had the effect of transforming him overnight from a black sheep into a village hero," Digby's only soldier at the front.

> We on our part were very conscious of the honour and responsibility which had been thrust upon us. We were now personally represented, and it became Digby's war.
>
> I remember the change taking place. From the moment of George Brown's arrival in South Africa everybody took a lively interest in the fighting. … Everything in the village was now on a war footing. The women had sewing meetings to make Army comforts. The children learned patriotic songs. … Children were christened with the names of war heroes. … We followed with keen interest the news of the famous sieges, and when word came through that Mafeking had been relieved there was great excitement.[59]

A Birmingham glass-blower's son described the return of a local veteran—and the anticlimax that followed:

> The whole street prepared to give him the welcome befitting to a public hero. Flags and streamers linked up every window, and excitement ran high when the news flashed round that the hero had arrived. Presently he came like the Sultan of Turkey, mounted on a chair, with the South African sun beaming from under a broad-brimmed hat and crowds of people jostling and joking and cheering him along in a mad frenzy of delight. I was among the drummer-boys who tapped tin-cans and marched to patriotic singing but was finally put to bed in tears because I could not join further in the festivities. Soon after the celebrations the hero became an ordinary man again who received only ordinary notice from the people who had cheered him, which made me wonder whether he was a hero at all.[60]

War fervor did produce a swing to the Unionists among the lower working class in the election of 1900, but that support quickly evaporated, and skilled workers remained solidly Liberal or Labour. After the military victories of mid-1900, working-class jingoism and army enlistments faded away.[61] Tom Tremewan was eleven when the conflict broke out, working on his grandfather's farm in Cornwall. He was boyishly patriotic, until one of their horses was killed in combat: "I have hated war ever since."[62] Initially London hatter Frederick Willis supported the war: "As a citizen of the great British Empire, earning six shillings a week, I felt I could never face the world's scorn if we ceased to exist as a first-class power." The hysteria of Mafeking Night, however, later gave way to "admiration for the rebels who refused to surrender."[63] Young Manny Shinwell was one of the few men in his Glasgow neighborhood who backed the war, and even he had no awareness of the Empire. He felt properly patriotic "when I saw men marching to the docks on their way to South Africa, though I could hardly be expected to understand the reason for their departure." In that he was entirely typical: "My patriotism was of the subconscious variety—I just believed Britain was the best country."[64]

When Welsh miner Jack Jones enlisted, his father was disgusted: "Boy, you ought to be ashamed of yourself. Only them that runs from the p'lice, an' them that are too lazy to work, goes to the army." Shortly after arriving in South Africa, he deserted.[65] One Manchester slum boy remembered that soldiers in those days were objects of contempt: his aunt would never have gone out with one.[66] Robert Roberts noted that jingoistic ditties, though hugely popular, did not

> alter the common soldier's social status one iota. With us, as with the rest of the working class, "regulars", ex-regulars and their families stayed unquestionably "low". One eldest son, I remember, who after a row at home walked out and joined the Fusiliers was considered by his father (a joiner) to have "brought shame and disgrace on all the family." Yet the same parent, solid Conservative

like the ex-soldiers he despised, drank himself into insensibility to celebrate the accession of George V.

"Except in periods of national crisis or celebration," Roberts explains, "industrial labourers, though Tory, royalist and patriotic, remained uninterested in any event beyond the local, horse racing excepted." This is a critically important distinction which is often blurred or overlooked. The same workers who cheered when the king visited Bolton were indifferent when he visited Delhi. Any direct threat to their homeland, as during the two world wars, would arouse in them a fervent, visceral patriotism, but their love of England stopped at Dover, and did not imply any special affection for Somaliland. In that respect, G. K. Chesterton had a better sense of the popular pulse than Rudyard Kipling. Coronations were celebrated as national, not imperial, holidays: "One felt the coming together of a whole country for a day of contentment and freedom," Roberts recalls. For most children, Empire Day meant nothing more than a recitation of "a lot of inconsequential facts on India [and] parts of Africa, ... all ruled over by Edward the Peace-maker (pacemaker, my father called him)."[67]

Empire Day was, in fact, instituted to combat that kind of apathy among Board school pupils. First officially observed on 24 May 1904, the holiday was still going strong into the 1950s, and then quickly disappeared with decolonization. Though working-class memoirs frequently mention Empire Day, they also reveal that these celebrations did little to enhance awareness of the colonies. Only occasionally did the propaganda work as it was supposed to, as in the case of the son of a Bristol engineer:

> They used to encourage us to be proud of the flag, salute the flag when we was at school. Yes, I was proud of being British. We was always taught to be proud of the Queen and King. We was the people of the world, wasn't us? ... I knew we 'ad to have somebody in charge, I knew, same as having a teacher or headmaster in charge of the school. You 'ad to have somebody up there, didn't you? I was proud of the school, I used to play football for the school. ... "St. Silas for honour, for loyalty, for courage, for courtesy. Play up, play fair, play the game."

More typical was a Fulham baker's daughter, who remembered Empire Day mainly as a school sporting event: "We had to have small Union Jacks, and the address before the sports started was very patriotic, but it was completely lost on us, all we wanted was to get on with the excitement of winning for our colour."[68] "I regret to say that the glories passed over our collective heads," Hymie Fagan recalled. "What we celebrated on Empire Day was that we had a half-day's holiday."[69] Stephen Humphries concluded, from oral interviews, that the strongest memories were of "the chocolate buns and mugs that were distributed freely on such occasions."

Some children came away with more subversive thoughts, like the laborer's daughter who had to recite a poem about the great merchant ships bringing England her bread and butter. "And somehow or other it stirred a bit of rebellion in me. I thought, where's my bread, where's my butter? And I think it sowed the first seeds of socialism in me, it really did." When the standard imperialist history was taught, recalled engineer's son Jim Flowers (b. 1905), "It was all dates and names and battles, the Spanish Armada, Nelson, Marlborough and all that. ... It didn't make much impression on me though. It went into my brain and I stored the facts because you had to, but patriotism never struck me as being very clever." His trade unionist father had given him Tom Paine to read, so he took an internationalist republican view of history. During the First World War, when the headmaster read aloud rosy dispatches from the *Daily Chronicle*, "It struck me that if ever the British had to go backwards they wouldn't say it was a retreat, it was a strategic withdrawal so that they could swallow up the enemy later on."[70] Grace Foakes (b. 1901), daughter of an East London dockworker, could not remember exactly how many children her mother had (probably fourteen) but was certain that only five survived infancy. On Empire Day "We sang of our lands and possessions overseas. We sang of 'Deeds of Glory.' We sang, and believed we were the mightiest nation on earth. But ... I sang with my mouth only, not from the heart. For I saw only those same high walls and thought to myself, 'We sing of our possessions, while not one of us here owns as much as a flowerpotful of earth.'"[71] A. J. Mills, son of a disabled First World War veteran and a charlady, was frankly contemptuous of school lessons in military glory and hated reciting "The Charge of the Light Brigade." On Empire Day "The Mayor always seemed to tell us how fortunate we were to be born British, or words to that effect. It must have taken a bit of doing on his part considering how many of us nippers had fathers who were unemployed. Anyhow, as it was followed by a halfday's holiday for us kids, it must have been a good country to live in."[72]

Most memoirs of Empire Day do not mention specific colonies, and those that do often seriously confuse them. A Cornish farmworker's daughter (b. late 1920s) remembered a classroom map with the British Empire in pink, but she could never tell the East from the West Indies.[73] Alfred S. Hall (b. 1910), son of a Camberwell bus conductor, was enlisted in a school pageant where the children were draped in the flags of the various colonies. "I was representing Montenegro," he wrote, "not only did I not know who or where they were, I couldn't even say the word." (Nor did he remember it correctly: Montenegro was never a part of the British Empire.) One teacher completely baffled the pupils when she spoke about the Far East: "Most of us didn't even know which way was East, those that were Scouts of course did, there were few of those, couldn't afford the uniform. The Far East to our mob was Whitechapel, East of London, many had never even been there."[74]

For some, Empire Day meant only the embarrassment of impersonating a Jamaican banana in the school pageant.[75] Fairly representative was Dorothy Burnham (b. 1915), whose father was an irregularly employed French polisher. In geography classes she picked up very quickly that Britain imported butter from New Zealand and pineapples from Australia: "the subject of food was of the greatest possible interest to me," given that she had to go home to "two slices of bread and marge and a handleless cup of weak tea. ... It really didn't seem much of a meal for a proud citizen of the most Important Capital of the Greatest Country of the Mightiest Empire in the Whole World!" While her catechized classmates would all shout in unison that London was the world's greatest city, few hands went up when they were asked to explain why, though they all lived there. They were keenly patriotic, but

> Patriotism in those days was an ideal of love and service to one's country. It did not conjure up pictures of an intolerably supercilious British raj arrogantly wielding the big whip on cowering, depressed natives. Rather, it inspired courage, promoted unselfishness and a concern for others which overrode purely private considerations. For my father army drill was not a chore to be endured; it was an article of faith to be constantly renewed by devoted practice. ... Not till the grey decades of the 'thirties did patriotism become identified with an aggressive nationalism, when the emergent dictators stripped the word of its idealism and flung it in the dirt to be trampled by succeeding post-war generations.[76]

What Dorothy Burnham and her classmates embraced was a specifically English patriotism, not an attachment to impossibly remote colonies. One seaman's daughter went home for her half-holiday "with no understanding of anything we had done, but aware that we were exceptional because we were English."[77] Granted, even if this English exceptionalism did not make slum children imperialists *per se*, it could sometimes endow them with an imperial sense of assurance. Empire Day conveyed to Louis Heren (b. 1919), a poor boy in Shadwell, "that London was the seat of the Empire and beyond question the greatest city in the world. We took a vicarious pride in goings-on such as the Opening of Parliament, royal garden parties, Henley and Wimbledon." Since he scarcely knew where Henley and Wimbledon were, he was not likely to absorb much from geography lessons about the North-West Frontier and the Federated Malay States.

> It made no lasting impression on me except—and this is a very large qualification—to establish that I was a freeborn Englishman and the world was my oyster. I developed an expansive and proprietory view of the world which has never quite left me. I am certain that it helps to explain why years afterwards I could fly into India, Palestine, Korea, Singapore, Indo-China and many other exotic and occasionally dangerous places and feel equipped to report and comment on the goings on of the natives.

As a correspondent for *The Times*, he could coolly cross from Jordan to Israel via the Mandelbaum Gate in 1948, when most Israelis were still hostile to the British.

One Israeli "said how he admired the confidence of the British public school man ... I did not tell him that my confidence, or whatever it was, was nurtured in a slum school."[78]

What those schools failed to create was any real feeling of imperial comradeship toward Canadians, Australians, New Zealanders, and South Africans. A young attendant in a Liverpool military hospital during the First World War recalled endless slanging matches and punch-ups between English and Commonwealth soldiers, even among the wounded, mainly because the colonials were much better paid and competing for local girls:

> They taught us at school about the unity and solidarity of the far-flung British Empire; but when I was a kid I never saw any evidences of it in the conduct and talk of these men. ... Although I don't think it will be found in any official version of the Great War as fought at home, I know from actual experience that much real trouble occurred between the wounded of the Colonies and the Homeland. ... We looked upon the British Empire Unity as a myth: we could do no other. Teachers might rave and yammer of "brothers" from beyond the seas standing shoulder to shoulder with the brothers from the Homeland. We knew such was not the case. Instead of shoulder to shoulder, it was hand to throat and feet to belly, and kick him when he's down.[79]

A Map of the World

Why, then, did the working classes care so much for Greyfriars, and so little for the Empire? Two memoirs in particular suggest an answer. In one, Walter Southgate set down his recollections of Mafeking Night in the East End. His father, a quill-pen maker, treated the celebrations with unbridled contempt ("How much of the Empire do these cockneys think they own I should like to know?"). The children enjoyed it purely for the fireworks and bonfires. They played "English versus Boers" and wore celluloid buttons of Baden Powell and Lord Roberts, but "Mafeking for all I and other children knew might have been in Timbuctoo." The world beyond their local streets was unknown: Southgate never saw the English countryside until age nine. That is why working-class memoirists were able to reconstruct their communities in such amazing detail: they dealt every day with the same circle of neighbors, friends, and shopkeepers until the memories became indelible. As Southgate wrote, "So self-contained was that North Street community (and this applied to other East End streets too) that even after 60 years, I was able to recall most of the names of the neighbours and the men's occupations," a total of fifty-three individuals.[80] This intense localism also explains why another East Ender, Phyllis Willmott (b. 1922), could scarcely grasp the concept of a British Empire:

Firmly bounded as it was by the geography of the locality, and underpinned by the local sub-culture based on the rules and unquestioned authority of the adult world, this was my complete and self-contained universe. At school, of course, we learnt about the far-flung countries of the British Empire, and at Sunday school about the missionaries who "saved" savages in "darkest Africa" and other frighteningly strange places. But in contrast to the solid reality of our own circumscribed world these were to me as awesome and unreal as a story from *Grimm's Fairy Tales.*

Far less of a mental leap was involved in winning a scholarship to a Greenwich grammar school: a more affluent world than the one she lived in, but otherwise not much different. After she graduated and found work with the Times Book Club, she discovered the West End. It was a thrill to visit the galleries and theaters, but she felt as disoriented as a tourist in a foreign capital. She never thought to buy a street map: she had no idea that such things existed, and in any case would have considered it "an unacceptable extravagance."[81]

The frame of the reader includes a mental map of the world, and a story that cannot find a place on that map will be difficult to grasp. With remarkable consistency, British working people described their mental maps in terms that call to mind a Saul Steinberg cartoon. The center ground was dominated by the streets where they grew up, drawn to enormous scale and etched in fine detail. Nearby towns hovered vaguely in the middle distance. Foreign countries, if they existed at all, were smudges on the horizon. When Alison Uttley's Peak District Board school tried to instill pride in the four nations of the Kingdom by singing "Men of Harlech," "Blue Bells of Scotland," "The Minstrel Boy," and "Rule Britannia," the children all dutifully applauded, but "nobody knew anything of those far regions Scotland, Ireland, and Wales, except the Scottish head gardener."[82] British working-class memoirs are predominantly works of local history, announcing their parochial focus in their titles: *A Sheffield Childhood; Newlyn Boyhood; Memories of Old Poplar; Salford Boy; Ancoats Lad; A Love for Bermondsey and Its People; Jipping Street; 36 Stewart Street, Bolton; Lark Rise.*

Any excursion beyond those boundaries could be bewildering. In search of work, John Clare once walked just twenty-one miles to Grantham, "and I thought to be sure I was out of the world." Proceeding to Newark-on-Trent "I felt quite lost .... I had never been from home before scarcely farther than out of sight of the steeple I became so ignorant in this far land that I could not tell what quarter the wind blew from and I was even foolish enough to think the sun's course was altered and that it rose in the west and set in the east."[83] A century later remarkably little had changed, even in cosmopolitan cities. Harry Watkin (b. 1909) was one of those memoirists who could recollect the names of all his schoolmates, but he also related a more painful memory: when a painting he had done in art class was accepted for a student exhibition at the Manchester Art Gallery, he never told his parents. Though it was only a tramride away "it seemed a preposterous idea.

Mother had never been to town in my lifetime. Would she have gone on the tram? She couldn't walk there and I couldn't imagine her trying to get on a tram. Could she have found her way there? And wearing what? A shawl? And Dad. A ridiculous thought .... So they never knew about their son's work being shown in the Art Gallery."[84] Until the Maharajah of Jeypore visited London in 1902, Guy Aldred, a Clerkenwell office boy, never fully appreciated that some human beings were not Londoners:

> The world to me was London; and, as I realised to my surprise, not all London. The other countries of the world did not exist for me. The dominions of the British Empire meant nothing to me. Scotland was a kind of no-man's land, a hidden and impossible Tibet beyond some mighty wall, leagues upon leagues distant from the place in which I lived. I realised that there was a country called England because I lived in the chief city of that country. I knew, of course, that there were other cities in England. I knew their names but they were not nearly so important as the names of the shops in the small part of London in which I had been born and reared. England was but a suburb of London just as London itself was but a suburb of Clerkenwell. ... I did pay a faint tribute to the reality of Highgate but as a place I sometimes visited on a horse tram. This seemed the back of beyond to me and merely gave character and reality to the part of the city in which I lived. I was thoroughly ignorant and rejoiced in my ignorance. I was indeed the perfect London villager .... I accepted that there must be a world peopled even as Clerkenwell was peopled. It was all gloriously vague. History, geography, everything beyond the immediate locality of my experience was an indefinable alienism. My mind refused to form any impression of a true wide-view of the past, just as it declined to form any impression of the distant in point of space. For all practical purposes, the world outwith London and the world before now was a ghost-land. I understood that there was a world that was not Christian. But it was not the world in which I lived. It was not the world of my experience. I could not conceive of it having any connection, any practical transport association with that real world of my understanding, the world called Christian. It was a wonderful world of magic and myth; and it seemed to me that in order to enter into relations with it, I would have to possess Aladdin's lamp.[85]

In 1934 more than 95 percent of London East End residents had been born there or in neighboring boroughs.[86] A labor exchange clerk found it pointless to inquire if an applicant would emigrate overseas: "'Overseas? Where's that?' would ask the girl who had never been further than the London Hospital."[87] This was the audience for Empire Day and Rudyard Kipling.

Through the nineteenth century and well into the twentieth, little news from the outside world penetrated working-class communities. In 1863 few popular newspapers or cheap books circulated in Oldham, where there were only six postal deliveries per capita per year: one of the lowest rates in England, but fairly typical of northern manufacturing towns.[88] Consequently, recalled J. R. Clynes,

> Millions of men and women died in their towns and villages without ever having travelled five miles from the spot where they were born. To them the rest of the world was a shadowy place merging into the boundaries of unreality. … Old cotton-spinners in Oldham, when I was a lad, used to debate with immense gravity on the destination of the tons of cotton the mills turned out, and lived in permanent fear lest the world should be overloaded with cotton goods and all the mills suddenly have to close down.[89]

The isolation was worse in rural areas, where the Marian martyrs might seem more newsworthy and immediate than Khartoum. In the 1880s, according to Richard Pyke, farm workers of Devonshire had access to few books or periodicals, beyond a weekly paper that was handed from house to house and read aloud by one of the educated children: "Rumours might reach us of a war with the Zulus, or the tragedy of General Gordon: but it was all too distant to disturb our sleep, or excite our fear."[90]

By the turn of the century urban workers were reading evening, Sunday, and sporting papers as well as local weeklies, but these usually did not carry much national or world news. Even when they did report global events, recalled a Lancashire textile worker's son, "these were remote from our little sphere, and only affected us like stories in books; they were not in our daily lives."[91] As a result, notes Robert Roberts, "A national morning newspaper had little appeal. Some workers hardly ever went into their own city, and London was a place where royalty lived, that and little more. Having no official connection with national government beyond an occasional election, they did not feel the State as a reality at all."[92] No national commentator sympathized with working-class culture so well as Wilfred Pickles, BBC newsreader and stonemason's son. But even he admitted that the hours he spent in the public library, reading Shelley, Keats, Shaw, and Galsworthy, represented a desperate breakout from the stultifying provincialism of his native Halifax:

> I found a depressing narrowness of outlook and resented my family's unquestioning judgment that everything they did was right and anything to the contrary was to be condemned. People who had coffee for breakfast were peculiar and not to be trusted, while folk living on the other side of North Bridge had none of our earthy qualities, it was believed. Bradford, eight miles away, was another world which could not be a nice place …. I was grappling with my first big personal problem—how to escape from this world of mean streets.[93]

Before the advent of bus travel in the 1930s, Northumberland mining communities were so isolated that each one developed a distinctive accent. That self-containment, one local boy recalled, left "miners vulnerable to a belief that those who lived in the wider world beyond their circumscribed own were in contempt of them."[94] Though Welsh colliers maintained miners' libraries and impressive personal collections of books, "the lack of public transport ... meant that one's world often consisted of a library of one's own," in the words of one ex-coalworker.[95]

Even communities with a lively literary and musical culture could be suffocatingly insular. The father of Labour politician T. Dan Smith, a Wallsend miner, was fascinated by travel books, Twain's *Innocents Abroad*, Chaliapin, Caruso, and European affairs. But hardly anyone in their neighborhood ever ventured outside it. "A hundred yards for shopping, a couple of hundred yards to the church, made up much of my world," wrote the younger Smith, who, like his father, was a fervent anti-imperialist.[96] John Macadam, the son of a Greenock lathe operator, recalled that his relatives and neighbors regularly came over to discuss everything under the sun. "Such talk there was! The wild generalizations we would make! The tremendous arguments there would be as to whether Burns was a greater poet than Shakespeare, or Scott the master of Dickens, or John Kerr of Greenock Glenpark a greater bat than Hobbs. There was a lot of pawky wit in it and a lot of laughter and, thinking back on it now, a surprising range of subjects." Yet this intellectual depth did not translate into geographical breadth. Macadam was an apprentice shipyard plater, and never

did it ever occur to me in those days [c. 1920] that there was much prospect of any other life for me than the one I was leading. Thirty-odd years ago life was much more localized than it is now. We were much more inclined to stay put. Until I was sixteen a day out in Glasgow, twenty-six miles away, was a great annual event. London was a mirage and beyond London a vast void that one filled at will with imaginings spiced by reading. Mr. Cook was as unreal—or, maybe as real—as Captain Marryat or Fenimore Cooper. Years later, when I got into newspaper work, I met a considerable character called William Power who wrote a book titled *The World Unvisited*, a very fascinating survey of the world from his own fireside. It was only when I read Power that I realized that this is what I had been doing subconsciously all my short life.[97]

The same intellectual vitality could be found in the Jewish East End of the 1930s, a short ride on the Underground from central London. But it was still, as Bernard Kops described it, "a self-imposed ghetto. ... It was my world, and Aldgate East was the outside frontier of that world, a world that consisted mainly of Jewish people. I had no chip on my shoulder about being Jewish, because I knew of nothing else that existed."[98]

Even the most ambitious autodidacts rarely ventured far beyond the bounds of English and American literature. With the exception of Hugo and Dumas, and sometimes Cervantes, Balzac, and Tolstoy, there was little interest in continental authors. James Hanley's workmates laughed when he taught himself French by reading the *Mercure de France*. When he lectured to an audience of railwaymen on realism in modern French literature, the response was still more discouraging. Working the night shift at a railway station, Hanley withdrew into the work of Molière, Hauptmann, Calderon, Sudermann, Ibsen, Lie, and Strindberg, until he grew quite cozy in his literary shell. His parents were appalled that he had no friends. "But I've hundreds of friends," he protested. "Bazarov and Rudin and Liza and Sancho Panza and Eugènie Grandet." His father countered with Squeers, Nickleby, Snodgrass, and Little Nell: "And they're a healthy lot I might say, whereas all your friends have either got consumption or are always in the dumps."[99]

That isolation could produce enormous contrasts in culture between neighboring working-class communities. As far back as the Regency, a strolling actor noted the phenomenon as his company moved from town to town:

> Nothing is more surprising than the difference of taste and of manners in the inhabitants of adjoining villages. Sometimes I have observed this marked difference in the short space of two miles; and without any outward thing whereby to indicate the cause, you might find the people at one place seeking their pleasure in the ale-house, and making bets upon the next prize-fight, ... playing at cards for a quart, ... earnestly debating the age and qualities of a bull-dog, or quarrelling over the bets upon a cock-fight. ... In such places the inhabitants generally show an utter contempt for everything associated with literature: they can find amusement in coarse oaths, in insulting and harassing, by every means in their power, anybody who professes to love literary refinement or science. In a neighbouring village, or hamlet, on the other hand, you may find the bulk of the inhabitants fond of reading, and conversant with the poets,—panting to gain a better acquaintance with our Shakespeare, and quoting his writings,—singing out the songs of the Ploughman Bard, "A man's a man for a' that," having their occasional music-meetings, and taking pleasure in the theatre, because they can appreciate the author's work, and can find religion beaming in the soulfulness of his expressions.[100]

Geography was always a conspicuously weak subject in English popular schooling. James Bonwick (b. 1817), a carpenter's son, received what was, by contemporary standards, a fine education at the Borough Road School in Southwark, but it did not go far beyond the King James Bible. Biblical history and geography were taught thoroughly: Lord Brougham, inspecting the school, was impressed by a boy who sketched from memory a detailed map of ancient Palestine. "We learned what happened to a small and but partially civilized nation two to three thousand years ago," wrote Bonwick, but "of Egypt, Assyria, India, Greece, Rome, or even England, we knew nothing. Of the war with France we retained the memory of three events,—the battles of the Nile, Trafalgar, and

Waterloo." This was hardly the education of an imperialist: "We were genuine *Little-Englanders.*" Bonwick later became an amateur Egyptologist, fond of pointing out "how much our Western Civilization is indebted to Orientals"; and a pioneer anthropologist who condemned the destruction of the Tasmanians by "the Christian civilized Whitefellow!"[101] Scottish primary education had its strengths, but one shepherd's son (b. 1825) from North Esk wrote that geography was "unheard of in our school. ... I well remember my idea was, that our little glen constituted the whole universe,—that the tops of the hills which surrounded it were the ends of the earth,—and that the opening between them which allows the river to escape to the sea, was nothing else than the road out of the world away into the unknown."[102]

Even as the government began to invest more in education, the quality of instruction in geography did not improve dramatically. Between 1856 and 1859, roughly 3,800 state-aided primary schools ordered 902,926 reading lesson books and 163,512 arithmetic and math texts. In contrast, they bought only 82,836 geography texts, plus 14,814 school atlases and 14,369 wall maps. Only 67,272 history texts were ordered, and they would not convey much sense of the larger world, since nearly all of them focused on Britain. What was worse, recently published geography texts contained maps that were up to fifty years out of date. Population figures were hopelessly obsolete, the United States did not extend west of the Rockies, the European settlement of New Zealand was just beginning, many other new colonies were omitted altogether, railways were a new invention, and mail coaches were still described as the main means of transport. All that, it should be underscored, could be found in newly printed texts, quite apart from the thousands of older geography books still in use.[103]

Even in the 1880s, Flora Thompson's village school had no geography books and no formal instruction in geography or history, other than readers offering stock tales about King Alfred and the cakes and King Canute ordering the tide to retreat. There were good maps on the walls, and her *Royal Reader* offered thrilling depictions of the Himalayas, the Andes, Greenland, the Amazon, Hudson's Bay, and the South Pacific, as well as scenes from Washington Irving and James Fenimore Cooper. She also remembered borrowing a decrepit copy of Belzoni's *Travels* and enjoying intensely the excursion through Egyptian archaeology. But she was an unusually self-motivated reader: her less-educated neighbors were only hazily aware of the existence of Oxford, just nineteen miles away.[104]

Alfred Williams (b. 1877), the Swindon railway worker and poet, recalled that shortly after he left school, a chargeman offered him and five friends pennies for answering simple geographical questions. "During these tests the chargeman was astonished to learn that Salisbury is a county, Ceylon is the capital of China, and that Paris stands on the banks of the river Liffey. ... Only one out of six could give the names of ... six [English] counties. ... Not one of the half-dozen, though all were born in the town, could give the name of a single Wiltshire river."[105] In the early twentieth century Cornish schools tried to instill some sense of the county's

Celtic heritage, but according to one Newlyn boy, "For most of us who rarely travelled further than St. Ives or Hayle the names of places on the map of Cornwall were, to all intents and purposes, as remote-sounding as Babylon or Vladivostok."[106] Boys' weeklies were the powerful agents of acculturation for R. L. Lee (b. 1921), an impoverished half-Chinese boy in Merthyr Tydfil. He once caught a five-inch trout and tried to cook it on a spit, "like they did in the Canadian Rockies—and as I'd read about in the *Wizard*." In contrast, his school geography lessons left no imprint. "Who cared where France was? We'd never be going there anyway—the furthest we were ever likely to go would be to Barry; didn't really know where that was, but the bus driver did. And what about Sir Walter Scott going to all that trouble to find the South Pole, when it wasn't even lost in the first place."[107]

So housepainter's son Harry Burton might sing patriotic songs on Empire Days, "but it did us no harm because it never went very far," and no one knew where the Empire was. His headmaster "once came into a geography lesson and explained how the Pyrenees got their name; it is almost the only fact that I still retain from that or any other geography lesson in that school. ... On the other hand we wallowed in *Eric* and *St. Winifred's* and other school stories, especially Talbot Baines Reed's." They described a world very like his own, except that Reed's boys had more money. Burton's London Board school promoted the same games ethic and *esprit de corps*, and by age eleven he had written his own school story. He, like other working-class children, preferred Frank Richards to Empire Day simply because the former was a more reliable guide to the reality he knew. When Burton won a secondary school scholarship, he inevitably found himself facing, on his very first day, a "tall hatchet-faced master" exactly like the one in the *Magnet*.[108]

The geographic and historical literacy that the schools did not provide could be acquired from the staggeringly popular stories of G. A. Henty. In the slums, Edwardian boys' club libraries reported that Henty was among the most frequently borrowed authors.[109] He may have sold as many as a quarter million books a year in the 1890s; his publishers estimated that they had disposed of a total of 25 million copies by the 1950s.[110] Today, Henty's works appear to be bumptious imperialist tracts, but a century ago they were often read quite differently: for readers with educational deficits, they supplied a clear introduction to the grammar of history and geopolitics. For that reason, Henty was widely admired among men of the left—in the Labour Party, the ILP, even the Communist Party.[111] As Roger Dataller explained, while Board school history lessons were largely lists of dates, Henty provided

for youthful readers the only historical information they were ever likely to encounter. Through Henty, I discovered for the first time that there was a Frederick the Great, a Gustavus Adolphus, and a William the Silent; that nations did not live in a vacuum, but were tied up—often very closely—one with another; that statesmen and diplomatists were important in the background; and that the seeds of one conflict often developed into the fruit of a second. I sensed pervasively his lack of characterization; but stereotyped as his situations and language was ("With a shout they ran forward," "He fell with a sharp cry," "Young sir, you have saved your country"), Henty did for me what my teachers had been unable to do. He made me ask for more.[112]

Since they filled those gaps, classic travel books could produce the same kind of epiphanies as other classic literature. Anson's *A Voyage Round the World* performed that magic for Alexander Somerville (b. 1811) and for the Scottish turnip-hoers he read it to.[113] A Scottish flax-dresser (b. 1803) gained his "first or incipient idea of localities and distances" when he was assigned to read aloud at work from Anson, Cook, Bruce, and Mungo Park: "I am not aware of having at any time since, enjoyed a similar treat with higher zest." These authors sparked an intellectual awakening that ranged far beyond geography. He was inspired to read widely in fiction, drama, poetry, and history. He joined a mutual improvement society and a choral club, attended scientific lectures, spoke at public meetings, agitated for parliamentary reform and temperance.[114] A 1946 survey of Tottenham residents, 95 percent of them working-class, found that their favorite category of nonfiction reading was travel and adventure. "Maybe that's because I've never been outside England but I would like to go to some of them countries you read about," explained one manual worker with an elementary education.[115]

If working people knew little of the world beyond their local communities, perhaps the only effective means of promoting the Empire was to bring bits of it home. The 1924 British Empire Exhibition at Wembley attracted more than 27 million visitors, equivalent to 60 percent of the population of the United Kingdom, and it was only one of several such imperial festivals.[116] Reading the memoirs of those who attended, one cannot help but conclude that these were by far the most persuasive vehicles of imperialist propaganda. School lessons only instilled the haziest consciousness of colonialism, but once the discussion turns to Wembley, it jumps into sharp and memorable focus.[117] The physical reality of those exhibition pavilions hit home as no literature could. "Until this visit, apart from those annual school parades, my only other knowledge of the Empire was what I had seen on maps of the world showing all those pink portions," wrote Moorside plate-moulder Fred Scholes, but this "one-in-a-lifetime" day left indelible impressions of a Maori village, South African ostriches, Burmese carvings, Maltese lace, a Hong Kong restaurant, models of the Taj Mahal and the residence of the Rajah of Sarawak. "Never before, or since, has there been an exhibition to come up to the British Empire Exhibition of 1924. Alas, there will never be another."[118] "Sheep shearing in the Australian pavilion, the Canada Pacific railways, miniature rolling stock, the very tall African Nationals, people up to eight feet tall, and little Africans as well," exclaimed the son of an Oxfordshire farm laborer. "I am doubtful as to whether there has ever before or since been such a marvellous show."[119] The daughter of a Herefordshire gardener could not forget "The beautiful antique temples of India, the cleverly architectured buildings of Burma, the elaborate buildings of Ceylon, the primitive buildings of the Gold Coast, ... the wonderfully realistic Canadian Pacific Railway, running amidst wild, rugged mountains, and the fertile prairie lands, and orchard lands, all looked very lifelike. ... We felt, I remember, very proud to belong to the Mother Country."[120] The African village at the 1929 North East Coast Exhibition in Newcastle could infect even miners' daughters with a touch of imperial condescension:

> The authenticity of this section was never questioned, and we were convinced that a whole village of Africans had been moved lock stock, and barrel to the town moor. Despite all the poverty around us, perhaps this was our first injection of a superiority complex. With furniture in our homes and desks in our classroom, surely we were very fortunate! Home cooking did not vary very much, but leek puddings and tettie hash were certainly more appetising than anything the Africans were eating.[121]

Building Jerusalem

The geography of one country, at least, was taught well and thoroughly to Victorian schoolchildren. Though it was not yet a British colony, these lessons would have consequences for future imperial policy. Disraeli's *Tancred* and George Eliot's *Daniel Deronda*, which both envisioned a Jewish return to Palestine, prepared elite opinion for the Balfour Declaration. Among the masses, the same role was performed by the Sunday schools and church-related day schools, which, while they neglected modern geography, meticulously taught the landscape of the Holy Land. That biblical education could produce a kind of Anglo-Zionism, where children conflated contemporary England and ancient Israel to the point where they merged into a common homeland. One anonymous schoolboy of the early nineteenth century described the tremendous impact of those lessons:

> The wish to travel became painfully strong; and the impossibility of gratifying that wish only added fuel to the spark which had been kindled. The East, the famous, celebrated, mysterious East, especially claimed my thoughts. To see Palestine, Bethlehem, Nazareth, Jerusalem, was my daily wish. To describe the absorbing interest with which I regarded the City of David at that time is literally impossible. ...
>   ... Men cannot forget the East. The lapse of ages, the rise and fall of dynasties, and the birth, growth, and decay of mighty empires are unable to erase from the *memory*—shall I call it?—of humanity that the *East* is its native place. ... It is not the Jew only, but also the Gentile, who experiences this strong feeling. Undoubtedly, the Bible has much to do with this clustering of the affections around the scenes of sacred story ...; but sometimes, in our wild day-dreams, we imagine that our acquaintance with Biblical geography and story is *but the renewal* of knowledge which has accidentally slipped from memory.

The fact that Scripture provided the foundation of English literature and the modern English language perpetually reinforced the idea that Palestine was the promised land of the English people. That sentiment extended down to the bottom of the social pyramid. One day, returning from school, this same schoolboy heard an elderly beggar woman singing:

> O, mother dear, Jerusalem!
>   When shall I come to thee?
> When shall my sorrows have an end?
>   Thy joys when shall I see?

He found her living in "poverty in its absolute sense"—a hovel with no furnishings but some straw and a ragged blanket, nothing to eat but a few potatoes. "And yet this old woman was happy. What made her so? What was the secret of her contentment? The song I had heard on the moor suggested the secret, and it was confirmed by her own aged lips" when she asked him to read from her New Testament.[122]

In a Norfolk rural school at the end of the nineteenth century, geography was still a matter of memorizing the cities, mountains, and rivers of Europe. "As far as our knowledge of its various inhabitants was concerned—their occupations and even their appearance—they might never have existed," wrote a farmer's son. But the Bible was taught so thoroughly at Sunday school that, "Though I was wholly unaware of it, the language of the Authorized Version became somehow a part of me. What I read was never unnatural," and for that reason, he accepted Bible tales without question. "To me these stories were as real as if I had been a participant. Saul and the witch of Endor: David and Jonathan and the tragedy of Gilboa: Elijah and Elisha and Naboth's vineyard and Mount Carmel were more real to me than the history stories in our *Readers* at school."[123] In the warm community of his Cumberland Methodist chapel, tailor's son Norman Nicholson enjoyed the same comforting sense that

we all belonged to the same country. And that country was the Holy Land. The landscape of the Bible was far more familiar to us than the geography of England. We had news of it twice every service in the lessons; the preachers preached about it; the hymns depicted and extolled it. Jerusalem, Jericho, Bethlehem, Canaan, the Sea of Galilee, Mount Carmel, Mount Ararat, Gilead, Moab, the Brook Cherith and cool Siloam's shady rill—all these seemed no further away from home than, say, the Duddon Valley. They were like a private estate to which all chapel people had a key, a secret but accessible region, where they could call in and visit and rest for a while at any time of the day. It was not only that the Bible lands seemed near to home: in some ways they *were* home. And they looked like home. To me the shepherds keeping watch over their flocks were men like the Watsons of Millom Farm, or the Tysons of

Beck Farm, or the Falconers of Water Blean. … And once, I remember, a Sunday School teacher gave us a lesson on the Good Samaritan. … "Now there was a man," he said, "sent out on a walk from Jerusalem to Jericho, just as he might have been going from Foxfield to Broughton"—mentioning two villages eight or nine miles from Millom, just over the Lancashire side of the old County boundary. And even today, I cannot walk or drive along those two miles of highway, without seeing the man left half-dead, lying in the dyke bottom at the roadside.[124]

As M. K. Ashby noted, late Victorian farm laborers projected themselves into Scripture, where they found not imperialism, but a radical liberalism:

They were on the side of the Prophets, rather than of the Kings, the institutions. The grounds of self-respect their fathers had lost in England they found afresh in Palestine. There were no two nations of the ancient Jews and there should be no great cleavage among Englishmen. They had read the injunction to the King of the Jews that "his heart be not lifted up above his brethren". The great men of Israel were but farmers like their own cousins and ancestors. David had been a shepherd, Amos a herdsman, Christ himself a carpenter. For the more imaginative, the gorse bushes on Old Lodge could be on fire with the flames that do not consume. They could imagine the Saviour walking on the blue brick causeway the Feoffees were laying along the street, and were certain that saintly followers of his had walked and would yet walk the Tysoe lanes.[125]

Michael Gareth Llewelyn remembered his mother, a £60-a-year schoolmistress in South Wales, teaching Bible tales with such a literary flair that

All these scriptural personages and scenes … were identified in my mind with people and places I knew. The widow whose cruse became inexaustible was old Marged Emmwnt, who lived in a small cottage near the brook "Kedron" in the wooded valley below the village. The walls of Jericho were the high walls around the churchyard. David, the Shepherd King, was my cousin, a young sheep farmer of Cilymynydd. Moses was one of the bearded deacons who came to the Lebanon Chapel, where the Calvinistic Methodists gathered to worship.[126]

One Catholic millworker from Bolton remembered a brother who served in Palestine with General Allenby: "Exploring the Holy Places of history wholly absorbed and enthralled him, and eventually turned his spirit back to his childhood faith."[127] As late as the 1920s, according to one chauffeur's daughter, the schools ensured that "the map of the Holy Land … became almost as familiar to us as the map of England."[128]

To the West

British working people were equally enthralled by the geography, literature, and culture of another promised land. One of the sharpest ideological divisions between the classes involved their attitudes towards America. That country has always fascinated the proletariat as much as it has repelled the European educated classes, because it promised the former a measure of freedom and affluence that the latter was not prepared to grant. In the 1790s, London Corresponding Society radicals, inspired by Paine's *Rights of Man*, idealized the young republic as a pastoral paradise without kings, lords, or bishops, where all enjoyed economic independence and none was too wealthy.[129] Meanwhile, an Aberdeenshire clergyman warned that young emigrants were writing effective and dangerous propaganda for the new nation:

> By comparing (in their letters) their present with their former condition in this country, they have done much to excite others to follow their example. Such examples, and some late publications, may do much hurt, unless seasonably prevented. America is represented to be a wholesome and pleasant country, where the people, enjoying the rights of freemen, have a vote in the election of their legislators, pastors, and magistrates: a country provided by divine providence, to afford a comfortable habitation to those who are ill used at home; where the land is good in its quality, cheap, and gratuitously bestowed; and the passage to it unexpensive, and made in a few weeks. As migration is begun in this lowland country, something should be done to put a stop to its progress.[130]

The 1830s, hard times in England, were the Age of Jackson across the Atlantic, making emigration all the more attractive. As a Slapton carpenter recalled:

> One of the farmers who had emigrated some years ago to America wrote a glowing account of the country and its prospects, urging all who could to come over to Iowa. The letter was read in almost every cottage. It was read at the village inn and at the Methodist chapel every Sunday until it was nearly worn out. The Lord had now opened a door of escape. Special prayer-meetings were held to know the Lord's will, which was that they should go. For several weeks nothing was thought about or talked about but going to America. The whole village was at work in packing and mending clothes. A farewell service was held in the Methodist chapel, which was crowded, and the services lasted through night until daybreak. The following evening, in the glorious springtime of May, some thirty-three men, women, and children knelt down in the street, and, after a short prayer-meeting, marched through the village singing hymns. The whole village turned out, and many accompanied them for miles. "Good-bye; God bless you!" rang from every cottage door. Every eye was wet. Mr. Tapper leaned over the Rectory gate and was visibly affected with this

melancholy procession of his best parishioners. Prayers in the Methodist chapel were regularly offered up for the exiles until news came of their safe arrival and settlement. This induced others, in batches of threes and fours, to follow for several years.[131]

By mid-century, one of the most popular songs among British workingmen, including the father of Andrew Carnegie, was

To the West! to the West! to the land of the free,
Where the mighty Missouri rolls down to the sea;
Where a man is a man if he's willing to toil,
And the humblest may gather the fruits of the soil.[132]

Those who remained behind could immerse themselves in American literature. The United States failed to sign an international copyright agreement until 1891, leaving Charles Dickens and Thomas Hardy defenseless against piracy, but British publishers were equally free to steal the works of American authors and sell them at rock-bottom prices. *Chambers's Edinburgh Journal* frequently published American stories, partly because they were accessible to readers and partly because they cost nothing in royalties.[133] Within two weeks in October 1852, at least ten English editions of *Uncle Tom's Cabin* appeared: it has been estimated that, in one year, a total of 1.5 million copies were sold throughout the Empire.[134] By the 1860s Routledge was selling *Uncle Tom* and *The Last of the Mohicans* for 6d.[135] Thanks to this availability, the literary conservatism so common among the working classes was reversed in the case of American authors, who were enjoyed by common readers long before they acquired respectability in critical circles. Washington Irving was published in English school anthologies as early as the 1820s, Longfellow and William Cullen Bryant in 1833, Poe in 1836, Whittier in 1851.[136]

All varieties of British radicals—abolitionists, humanitarians, temperance reformers, peace agitators, feminists, champions of public and adult education—drew inspiration and support from their American counterparts.[137] Chartist newspapers aggressively hailed the United States as a model of the blessings of democracy, a free press, cheap government, and separation of church and state, though they did not overlook the evils of slavery. When Chartists applied political tests to literature, they generally passed American poets with high marks for their democratic values. W. J. Linton was an early promoter of Longfellow in England, and the *People's Paper* published fiction by Poe, Hawthorne, and Harriet Beecher Stowe.[138] As American authors seemed to address themselves to a plebeian audience, they were often hailed as brother workers, even when their credentials were questionable. Sid Chaplin, a Durham blacksmith, was inspired to write poetry by "Walt Whitman, who was *my* poet. I recognized a person like myself in Walt Whitman, a kindred spirit. He was a working man. I knew that from the start, it came out of everything in his poetry. A working man with a great feeling for his fellow working men, and fellow citizens as well when it came to the Civil War."[139]

As the tramp-poet W. H. Davies wrote, America was a wonderful territory for beggars.[140] The celebrated singer Sir Harry Lauder, when he was still a mineworker, acquired a fair knowledge of American history: "George Washington and Abraham Lincoln ranked second only in my estimation to Robert Burns and Walter Scott." One of his (and Keir Hardie's) favorite books was a popular biography of James Garfield, *From Log Cabin to White House* (1881).[141] By 1893 it had gone through forty British editions, and it was quite capable of inspiring a Cornish tin miner to emigrate.[142] Coming of age in Shadwell, Louis Heren intently followed news of the New Deal on the radio—liberal journalist Raymond Gram Swing reporting from Washington, Alistair Cooke broadcasting folk songs recorded by the Works Projects Administration (WPA), the labor struggles of Walter Reuther and John L. Lewis—and ever since he "felt at home in the United States."[143] Mary Lakeman, a Cornish fisherman's daughter, confirmed what George Orwell had written in "Riding Down from Bangor": *Little Women, Good Wives, What Katy Did, Avonlea, Tom Sawyer, Huckleberry Finn*, and *The Last of the Mohicans* all created a romantic childhood vision of unlimited freedom and open space. "For me Jo, Beth and Laurie are right at the heart of a permanent unalterable American scene," she wrote, "and I can turn on Louisa M. Alcott and others so powerfully that Nixon and Watergate are completely blacked out."[144]

In a country where few were educated intensively, the American alternative of broadly educating the many appealed to autodidacts. V. S. Pritchett's "popular educator" was the literary section of the *Christian Science Monitor*.

> It was imbued with that unembarrassed seriousness about learning things which gives American life its tedium but also a moral charm. In Europe the standards have been high for the few, the path of education has been made severe. If we learn, if we express ourselves in the arts, we are expected to be trained by obstruction and to emerge on our own and to be as exclusive, in our turn, as our mentors; willingness and general goodwill are—or have been until very lately—despised.[145]

Though Pritchett did not attend a university until he was fifty, he was permitted to teach at Princeton, Berkeley, Smith, Vanderbilt, Brandeis, and Columbia. "From my earliest days I have liked the natural readiness and openness of the American temperament and I had been brought up in childhood a good deal on the classic American writers and their direct response to the world they lived in," he recalled. "Good luck to escape, by going abroad, the perpetual British 'no' to the new boy; good luck to meet the American 'yes' to my first bits of writing."[146]

On a 1910 tour, trade unionist Margaret Bondfield was deeply impressed by students who cheerfully worked their way through the University of Wisconsin as waiters: "I wondered what sort of attitude one would find for a similar case, say in

Eton or Harrow." There was much in the United States that repelled her: yellow journalism, labor violence, the unbridled constitutional right to bear arms. But American literature had always been a beacon to British labor: back home, while organizing shop assistants, she kept up her courage by reciting Whitman, and in New England she visited the homes of Emerson, Thoreau, Hawthorne, and Louisa May Alcott. Speaking from a lorry in the Massachusetts mill town of Lawrence, she was surprised to discover that half her audience was from Yorkshire or Lancashire. When she asked one woman why she remained in America, "with a very dramatic gesture she swept the horizon with her arm and said, 'Just look at this, and then think of that hell upon earth, Bradford.'" Miss Bondfield had to admit that "The Lawrence Mill was as clean as when it was first built. The windows were clean. The mill was surrounded with grass verges, and here and there tree-lined streets. The girls wore clean overalls, tidy feet and shoes, with their hair beautifully clean and nicely dressed. A mill crowd in Lawrence certainly would compare most favorably with Bradford."[147]

The memoirs of Margaret McCarthy convey the magic of New England for a Lancashire millgirl. When her family relocated from Oswaldtwistle to New Bedford for two years in the 1920s, "our whole existence, our way of life and thought, our outlook and ambitions were irrevocably revolutionised." Though the mill where she worked was a non-union shop, the employees enjoyed something approaching affluence:

> We noticed the smart, expensive-looking clothing, the careless, unconcerned spending of money, the easy hire-purchase way of the workers' lives, with surprise. Inside the factories, too, the workers' existence seemed transformed. The broken stone floors of Lancashire, steeped in water and oil, were replaced by smooth hardwood; automatic appliances relieved the weaver of so much labour that one worker could operate up to thirty looms, as against the four which was normal per weaver in Lancashire; technical appliances reduced breakages of the threads, but when such troubles occurred help was available to repair the damage. The unhealthy Lancashire habit of "kissing the shuttle" had been abolished, and in the factory were supplies of purified water, even iced water in summer, on tap in the weaving-sheds, for the workers' convenience. Other facilities astonished us, as, for example, the music and dancing provided in the warehouses during the luncheon breaks.

As a girl she had identified closely with Tom Sawyer, and New Bedford, an old whaling town, conjured up Herman Melville. She took art classes which allowed far more scope for creativity than such courses at home, and she enjoyed friends of a variety of ethnic groups. Forced to return to Oswaldtwistle—"a grey trap, a straggling, gloomy, lifeless, forgotten place, which continued to exist from the dead past to the present by some oversight of Nature"—she was so embittered that she became a passionate Communist. She spent several hard years studying and working in the Soviet Union, enduring the privations and the repression, but in one respect she was always a deviationist: she insisted that she would return to America given the opportunity, even if the Party forbade her. There, to the West, was the Workers' State.[148]

According to Robert Roberts, the Russian Revolution went almost unnoticed in Salford, except among socialists and a butcher's wife who named two pups Lenin and Trotsky. In contrast, the arrival of American troops was electrifying:

> One sunny evening, to our wild astonishment, the cattle sidings were suddenly alive with soldiers, thousands of tall, clean, upstanding men—from the "Middle West," they said—in boy scout hats and spick and span uniforms—all dumped in the heart of a northern English slum. They marched with a band, friendly and smiling, along our main way—and sang, too: "Over there, over there. We won't get back till it's over over there!" Everyone who could move poured from the slits of streets on to the high road to see them pass, screaming with joy: for so long now we had had so little to cheer. … We followed them far into the dusk until they turned into one of those great barracks built a hundred years before to intimidate the half-starved workers of the North. In the shop for days after people repeated the same things—"Did you see them? Wonderful fellers! They'll show the Germans! It won't be long now."[149]

A Liverpool dockworker's son, who lost a brother and two uncles in the war, warmly remembered the arrival of American troops: "To the working class kids they were great guys, they would throw coins to us from their open trucks as they went by."[150] According to a London tobacco worker's son, whose brother died in the conflict, "Those were the days when people within our social class were looking to the new world of the American continent for relief from their existing poverty. A new world of prosperity and promise to which many emigrated."[151] For proletarian novelist Jack Common, that world was an alluring melange of Thoreau's philosophy, Jack London's socialism, and Bernarr MacFadden's bodybuilding. He found the most authentic expression of British working-class culture in the Hollywood movie:

> The popular imagination was now emigrant to America and the moving-picture was its Mayflower. A feat of modern technology had revived the ancient Gothic fascination of the cave with the lit drama at its end. This new thing that incorporated some very old things put a glow into many lives especially in need of such a mind-charmer at that distressed time.

> The picture they looked at night after night was often American. So much the better, perhaps, for America was then a bright land, far, far away, the Golden West, the reborn Atlantis. *There* was the larger, truer, simpler democracy that England for all its revolutions and natural insurgence had never quite managed to make. America had fun, we all believed. Even its rich men were happy and

unafraid; its poor could strike it lucky or be sure of an handout. A good rough working-class kind of world run openly to a gambler's set of rules and tempered by a domestic morality of late-Victorian sweetness—that was our America of the dark final winter in World War One.[152]

That combination of domesticity and limitless opportunity fascinated boys like R. L. Wild, an illegitimate child, whose family served doughboys in a small Eastleigh cafe: "Americans, to me, *had* something. They were different; more masculine, more romantic, all at the same time. I know now what they had, what they have to-day. A great deal more money than our own boys, no doubt. But this they also had—a sincere appreciation of the four walls of a home. ... For years I was convinced that only the Americans could put a lighted match into their mouths, close the lips and bring the thing out, still flaming. Wonderful."[153]

Aldous Huxley in *Brave New World* and George Orwell in *Coming Up for Air* typified the horror felt by middle-class intellectuals when they confronted the prospect of flashy, chrome-plated, materialistic "Americanization."[154] But denunciations of "Fordification" were not likely to resonate with workers like Margaret McCarthy: what most impressed her in New Bedford was the parking lot by the mill, where she discovered that the weavers and spinners owned cars. Thomas Burke, a poor boy from Poplar, was convinced that old England needed more rampant American consumerism. Movie palaces, snack bars, chain stores, and the resulting mixing of social classes had "done so much good that we now regard the zest and pungency of London life, which the States gave us, as our own growth."[155] The informal, enthusiastic doughboys who arrived during the Great War had been a shot of adrenaline.[156] They could also send over more American girls, who, far from the stereotype of the hard-boiled businesswoman, were wittier than the English and more chic than the French.[157]

American films had captured almost 60 percent of the British market by 1914, rising to 85 to 90 percent after the war, much to the distress of elitist critics.[158] The invasion, of course, was spearheaded by a son of England's proletariat: Charlie Chaplin once told Thomas Burke that the British class system would never have allowed him to do what he had done in California.[159] An Irish laborer's son in Clapton explained the enormous impact of Hollywood:

After *The Big House*, I ran straight home and informed my surprised and amused mother that I wanted to join the convicts when I grew up. To me they seemed to live a better life in their Big House than the heroes who joined the army or the Flying Corps. In the army you stood a good chance of ending up as a pair of bloody hands clinging to a barbed wire fence, while every single person in the Flying Corps crashed in flames. That was a fact—we saw it in the film, so I would be a convict or nothing, until I saw *The Vagabond King*. I spent days after that in despair, convinced that I had been born in the wrong century.[160]

Of course it was escapist fantasy: but when your parents and teachers indoctrinated you in a class fatalism, squelching any hope that you might have some direction over your own life, Hollywood conveyed an intoxicating sense of possibility. Wally Horwood grew up in Walworth between the wars, the son of a barely literate telephone lineman and a mother who never neglected to remind him that

> The world was ruled by a mysterious THEY whose sole purpose was to prevent ignorant people like US from making any headway in life. From boyhood onwards, any original endeavour that I might tentatively consider would be met with, "THEY won't like it!" or "THEY won't let you do that!" or a completely deflationary "THEY won't take no notice of YOU!" Making every allowance for the double negative it will be seen that she was in no way a soul of encouragement.

The movies brought home an entirely different message. Horwood was particularly struck by one film about "some kind of American Officer Training Corps and the humiliations of a boy from a poor home attempting to become a member. Eventually, he triumphed, became the chief cadet, or whatever, and, in a magnificent uniform led the passing-out parade on horseback. I used to daydream myself as being in that position." Horwood fully recognized that Hollywood was mass-producing "the opium of the people," an endless output of "fantasy and unreality. In days when many lived almost on the bread-line, we saw people living in the most opulent affluence. Yet I personally felt no resentment; neither did I ever hear of anyone that did." The reason, clearly, was the relentless optimism of the New Deal cinema. *It Happened One Night, The Thin Man, Easy Living,* and *The Philadelphia Story* portrayed a society where class barriers existed but could be hurdled by anyone with determination.[161] Some movies conveyed a more radical message. Jim Wolveridge, a costermonger's son from Stepney, and formerly a guest of the Brentwood Workhouse, was electrified by *Wild Boys of the Road.*

> It was set in the American depression, and was about groups of American boys riding the rails and going from town to town in search of work, and it showed the kids' struggles with strong arm railway guards and officials who tried to keep them off the trains and away from the towns which might have to support them temporarily. It also showed the kids fighting back. Our crowd were too young to be marxists or bolshies, but knew enough about the struggles of the unemployed, and to see the kids hitting back at the law got our noisy support.

Fury, The Black Legion, Dead End Kids, I am a Fugitive from a Chain Gang, All Quiet on the Western Front—"There were quite a few American films of the time dealing with social problems," Wolveridge recalled, "but damn few English ones." In British movies "poverty and unemployment didn't exist and they gave the impression that we all spoke with posh Oxford accents, wore nothing but evening dress and spent all our time dining at the Savoy. If the working class were shown at all they were depicted as dimwitted clowns who spoke with a phoney accent that was even worse than the real thing." Wolveridge was so offended by the ersatz cockneys of *Bank Holiday* that he walked out in the middle of the film. So predictable was this treatment that when he saw the English thriller *They Drive by Night*, he was stunned by the rare authenticity of the East End dialogue: "Blimey somebody's been doing his homework."[162]

One could swallow Hollywood myths whole without blunting one's political radicalism, perhaps because both were based on similar kinds of adolescent idealism. Ted Willis was swept away by Tom Mix and Pearl White:

The simple morality of those silent Westerns and other dramas made a deep impression on me. As I left the cinema I would resolve to make myself as bold and selfless as the stars I had seen, to protect the weak and defend the innocent at no matter what cost in personal sacrifice, and to emphasize my resolution I even tried to imitate the distinctive walk and mannerisms of the hero.

He brought the same righteous melodrama to socialist politics, lecturing his scandalized father "that I would rather that my three sisters become prostitutes than that they should be exploited as wage-slaves in a sweatshop for twelve or fourteen hours a day." (Ted was also a great fan of *Mrs. Warren's Profession*.) He identified completely with a film about a young surgeon who falls in love with a crippled girl and performs a dangerous operation to help her walk again: "For a long time after this I dreamed of finding a crippled girl of my own, to whom I could devote my life." He did not plan to become a doctor—hardly a realistic ambition for the son of a London Transport worker and a washerwoman. "No, I simply wanted to sacrifice myself, to love and protect and serve someone weaker than myself, to perform an act of utter and complete unselfishness." He found that vocation as a full-time organizer for the Labour Party League of Youth. "We'll abolish poverty and misery and ignorance. And war, we'll abolish war," he assured his mother, in words that might have been composed by a Los Angeles screenwriter of the 1930s. "We'll build beautiful new cities, and people will be happy, and there'll be singing in the streets, and the children will grow up with a real chance." ("That's nice," she replied.)[163]

Sociological surveys of film audiences carried out around 1945 illustrated in detail the impact of American movies. One Swinton girl wished she were old enough to date Americans, and not only because GIs gave her sweets and tinned fruits: "Anyone from America, in my books, must be glamorous because all the film stars were, and I judged all Americans by them."[164] Mass Observation found that 64 percent had a positive opinion of American films (including 26 percent who rated them "better than ours"), compared with only 20 percent negative. Though most filmgoers realized that Hollywood presented an unrealistic portrait of America, they also broadly perceived the United States as more democratic than Britain.[165] What the working classes found alluring in these movies was a society where, it seemed, everyone could be bourgeois, where middle-class affluence and values were apparently the norm. Hollywood taught an unemployed Irish shop assistant to adopt American table manners.[166] An engineer and an army postal worker wanted to model their own families after the Andy Hardy movies,[167] which left a sixteen-year-old clerk profoundly discontented: she wanted to hang out in corner drug stores like an American college girl, and she wished that English boys would treat her with the gallantry of Mickey Rooney.[168] A butcher's son longed to become a band singer in America, "which in my opinion is the greatest place on the map of the world. Where everybody is classed as one, which (if you don't mind my saying so), is not a policy generally carried out by all of the English people at the present day."[169] A nineteen-year-old munitions worker, who had kept a record of every film she had seen since age four (a total of 1,350), was entranced by portrayals of affluent American homes with their labor-saving devices.[170] Respondents of both sexes confirmed that Hollywood glamor left them dissatisfied and somewhat envious of the American way of life, even if they realized that the tinsel was fake. "I know that all the stories are not true, and the characters merely exist on celluloid—I have told myself that hundreds of times," said a miner's daughter, "but somehow my brain refuses to accept it and I am more dissatisfied than ever. Films are like a drug—the more one has the more one wants, and yet, after seeing a film there is no satisfaction. Everything seems flat and dull when the last scene flickers out, and knowing that—I still go."[171]

The complexities of the working-class perspective on America were most perceptively untangled by Herbert Hodge, author and taxi-driver. During the Second World War he had the rare privilege of a speaking tour across the United States, and he could see that it was not a model of egalitarianism. University of Wisconsin students asked him about the British class system, but seemed oblivious to gross economic inequality at home. Labor–management hostility in Detroit was worse than anything he had seen in Britain. He was outraged when the Chicago police ransacked the home of an elderly black lady, disgusted by the American "dollar complex" and success-at-any-cost ethic. Yet, he concluded, in one important sense this was a genuinely classless society. American business executives eagerly asked him for advice on public speaking, something their English counterparts would have been embarrassed to do. In Britain

You will find earnest ex-public school boy members of even the Communist Party writing little tracts for each other on how to get on with the "workers"—as if the "workers" were a different biological species.

In the States there is no such caste division. The American boy grows up in a community "dedicated to the proposition that all men are born free and equal." In cold fact they may be no more free and equal in the U.S. than we are in Britain. But because they are all of them dedicated to the proposition they do tend to behave in their social intercourse as if it were so. And that is at least the beginning of true democracy. We'll never get as near as that to democracy in Britain until we've abolished our caste system of education.

Hodge recalled *The Autobiography of a Super-Tramp*, where W. H. Davies "presented himself as a confident, tough guy when a hobo in the States, and as a timid, diffident chap in England." He found exactly the same transformation in himself. The public school boy might be repelled by American "vulgarity," but

The council school boy ... will warm and glow in this new social atmosphere. He will feel himself blossoming like a plant brought out of the cellar into the sunshine. For the first time in his life, he will feel free to chuck out his chest to its fullest capacity. ... He will simply notice that he feels a lot better than he ever did at home, both mentally and physically, and that he has suddenly acquired an enormous confidence in himself.

It is only when he comes back to England and goes through the old, old process of being quietly snubbed and put in his place that he realizes that the difference between the vital, ebullient self he knew in America and the soggy self he knows in England is due almost entirely to this difference in social atmospheres.[172]

Recessional

Perhaps the most damning conclusion one can reach about British imperial propaganda is that it utterly failed to alert the working classes to the greatest threat the Empire would ever face. As Orwell noted in 1939, the boys' weeklies were stuck in 1910, scarcely conscious of the rise of the European dictators and the approach of war.[173] "Nazi Germany and the war in Abyssinia as seen in jerky clips on British Movietone News had little or no meaning for us," recalled one fan of the *Magnet* and Sexton Blake. "The Spanish Civil War and the tribal warriors of Ethiopia aiming spears at the Italian Air Force seemed like an episode from *Sanders of the River*. People didn't really die on films, they only fell down. Chamberlain dressed and looked like any of the other comics, and the goose step was better than Charlie Chaplin."[174]

For all our complaints about the superficiality of the Television Generation and the Internet Generation, the Movie Generation was far less aware of current events. They could scarcely have been otherwise, given that the typical newsreel consisted of five one-minute stories. Growing up in a family that read newspapers only for sport and scandal, Vernon Scannell knew all the great prize fighters by age thirteen, "but I could not have named the Prime Minister of the day or his political party. When, in 1935 I saw at the cinema newsreels showing the destruction of the Abyssinian warriors by the tanks and dive-bombers of

Mussolini it was with little interest and less comprehension, and a few months later when Hitler's troops invaded the Rhineland no minatory sound of war drums reached my ears." The history and geography he was taught at school were never related to contemporary events. Remarkably, Scannell had read widely about the last war: the poetry of Siegfried Sassoon and Wilfred Owen, Edmund Blunden's *Undertones of War* and Robert Graves's *Goodbye to All That*. The Penguin edition of *A Farewell to Arms* so overwhelmed him that he tried to write his own Great War novel in a Hemingway style. But none of this translated into any awareness that another war might be on the way. He could not have found the Sudetenland on a map.[175] That part of the world was never discussed on Empire Day. "Instead of teaching us about how one-fifth of the world was red and British, we should have been taught something about Hitler, Mussolini and their kind," complained the daughter of a Southampton longshoreman.[176]

The only history Alf Strange learned at school consisted of "vague kings and dates": he much preferred helping his father (a Shropshire village blacksmith) at the forge. Consequently, "Hitler and Europe and Chamberlain and the whole threat of war seemed another world away. We were all terribly ignorant of the storm that was building up across the horizon."[177] For seventeen-year-old Margaret Perry, a Nottingham store clerk, the declaration of war meant only "the prospect of beautiful young men in uniform."

I didn't read newspapers in those days, had no idea what had been happening across the channel during the last six years. Germany was far, far away and Poland even further. Where was Poland anyway? I knew Austria was next to Germany and Czechoslovakia around there somewhere but our lessons in Geography at school hadn't included a map of Europe. The British Empire, yes, I remember that. Tea came from India and Africa was full of little black pygmies, but Europe, that was full of foreigners who couldn't speak English. Another world of which I was completely ignorant.[178]

Two polls conducted in 1948 provide hard statistical evidence of that ignorance. A government survey found that only 33 percent of those earning £4 a week or less could correctly name a single colony, though another 36 percent mentioned a dominion. After forty years of Empire Day propaganda, 63 percent of all respondents could not think of a single raw material imported from the colonies. Among unskilled workers, 59 percent had little or no interest in colonial matters and only 15 percent a high level of interest, compared with 54 percent of the middle classes.[179] When Mass Observation asked 2,078 people which countries belonged to the Empire, 17 percent could not name any. The dominions scored reasonably well: Australia was mentioned by 78 percent, Canada 67 percent, New Zealand 52 percent, South Africa 40 percent. But India and Pakistan together were named by only 18 percent, Malaya 9 percent, and the rest of Africa combined by only 9 percent. A mere 8 percent cited any of the strategic Mediterranean bases of

Malta, Gibraltar, and Cyprus, so critical during the Second World War. No other colony was mentioned by more than 1 percent. Fully 65 percent could not name any recent event in any part of the Empire: 20 percent mentioned India and Pakistan (which had just become independent amidst terrible turmoil) and 15 percent cited South Africa. Imperial literacy was lower still among the working class. Those with higher education could name on average 4.25 countries in the Empire, compared with only 2.75 for those with an elementary education. More strikingly, 71 percent of those with higher education, but only 24 percent of those with an elementary education, could explain the difference between a dominion and a colony.[180]

This is not to say that Empire Day, Frank Richards, and *Sanders of the River* were complete failures as propaganda. They undoubtedly found a receptive audience among middle-class schoolboys, who could realistically look forward to a career commanding Africans or Indians. But they simply did not have the same relevance for working-class children, who rarely ventured far from home. After all, how much of the Empire did they own?

Chapter Eleven **A Mongrel Library**

The academic pioneer of popular culture studies was raised by a widow on public assistance. Richard Hoggart (b. 1918) granted that his mother "was certainly not an intellectual," but he was exposed to the autodidact tradition through his grandmother, who made sure he did his homework and claimed that they were related to "poet Longfellow" and "painter Hogarth." He profited little from his Hunslet elementary school, where a bully attacked him for being a Jew (he wasn't) and "talking posh" (he hardly did). Though he failed the scholarship examination, he was admitted to a "brick cube" grammar school. There the teachers were more inspiring, but Hoggart never ventured beyond the assigned work until the day the headmaster confronted him outside his study. He had read one of Hoggart's essays, which began with the sentence "Thomas Hardy was a truly cultured man," and he asked—in a conspicuously southern and middle-class accent—"What is 'a truly cultured man,' Hoggart?"

> I was baffled. I thought he was playing me up, because if our headmaster didn't know what a truly cultured man was, if the phrase wasn't absolutely cast-iron, where were we? And he said, "Am I one? I don't think so. I don't feel myself 'truly cultured.'" This was my first sight of a mind speculating, of thought as something disinterested and free-playing, with yourself outside it. I usually thought of a master as somebody who said, "This is what such-and-such a verb is, or this is what happened in 1762, and you have to learn it". ... One of the things ... my headmaster ... did for me, and perhaps this is where my interest in cultural change starts, was to give me a feeling for cultural comparisons, between the cultures of the North and South in England, and between different social classes.[1]

Once he had broken free of the idea that culture was something set in stone, Hoggart began to think seriously about the relative worth of various levels of culture. While he admired *Fiction and the Reading Public*, he felt that Mrs. Leavis had too easily dismissed popular literature:

> Helped by Orwell and C. S. Lewis, I became more and more drawn to the question of what people might make of that material, by the thought that

obviously poor writing might appeal to good instincts, that the mind of the reader is not a *tabula rasa* but has been nurtured within a social setting that provides its own forms and filters and judgements and resistances, that one had to know very much more about how people used much of the stuff which to us might seem merely dismissable trash, before one could speak confidently about the effects it might have.

In 1964, with money from Allen Lane of Penguin Books, he set up the Centre for Contemporary Cultural Studies at the University of Birmingham. At the time he was impatient with professors devoted to the standard canon, "as though that was not itself a cultural construct but a prescription from heaven." Within a few years, however, he began to wonder what he had created. There was the doctoral student who denounced Hoggart's Arnoldian humanism and demanded that the Centre only admit students from the hard left. There was the spreading plague of jargon and abstractions used as "props or crutches, substitutes for thought, ways of showing others and assuring themselves that they belong to an inner group." And then there was the monster that he himself had inadvertently midwived: "'The Beatles are in their own way as good as Beethoven' nonsense." Hoggart unfortunately lived long enough to hear an Oxbridge academic proclaim that "Lavatorial graffiti are not to be distinguished in any qualitative way from the drawings of Rembrandt," and a BBC executive declare "There is no longer art. There is only culture—of all kinds."

"Here the far Left meets the slick entrepreneurs," Hoggart sighed. "Some of our arguments come back to haunt us." In fact Hoggart had never been an uncritical populist: he originally intended to title his most famous book *The Abuses of Literacy*.[2] His definition of culture combined a reverence for great books, a lesser but real admiration for not-so-great books, and a sociological interest in the uses of all levels of literature. It avoided the sharp dichotomies drawn by the Romantics, Victorians, and Modernists, who tended to make a fetish of the highest art and dismiss everything else as pernicious rubbish. It equally rejected the postmodernist notion that "the comic strip cannot be treated as *qualitatively* inferior to a Shakespeare play or any other classic text."[3]

This Third Way was a distinctively working-class approach to literature, what could be called critical populism. Autodidacts certainly worshipped the classics, but they could also be charitable toward the lesser ranks of literature. While they generally had a conservative sense of literary hierarchies, they tended to grade books on a sliding scale rather than pass-fail. Once the old Evangelical hostility to secular literature had been overcome, even serious autodidacts could treat fairly rubbishy books with remarkable tolerance, and they were not distressed by the jumbling together of high and low culture. As proletarian author Thomas Burke put it, the ideal reader was one who could enjoy Virginia Woolf and Somerset Maugham and sportswriters.[4] Though a Primitive Methodist lay preacher, miners' MP John Johnson (b. 1850) insisted he was never an "objectionable young prig, scorning anything in the shape of light literature. … On the contrary, I eagerly devoured the best novelists and poets, and am strongly of opinion [sic] that if a man does not judiciously vary his reading he is likely to suffer from literary indigestion, whilst if I took a serious view of life and its duties I hope that did not preclude me from much innocent enjoyment."[5] These readers tended to approach any literary work on its own terms, from *Julius Caesar* to advertising bills, and take from it whatever they found valuable. After all, as one workhouse veteran noted, there was more mental stimulus in a boys' weekly than in the typical Victorian schoolbook.[6]

From the nineteenth century up to the present day, popular culture has been blamed for promoting a variety of social evils: juvenile crime, racism, violence, male supremacy, consumer capitalism, not to mention bad taste. None of these accusations is completely groundless, far from it, but the actual uses of literacy may be much more complicated and ambiguous than most students of cultural studies imagine. They typically approach popular culture by selecting a work or genre (say, boys' weeklies or romance novels), assuming these texts are read by a defined audience (in these cases, boys or women), and then trying to discern the attitudes of the presumed audience by studying the texts they are supposed to have read. But can we so neatly match up text and audience? Boys' weeklies were also read by girls. Many women never read romances, and most women read much else besides. Children often read books far above their presumed level of comprehension. Moreover, can we understand the impact of a particular work or genre in isolation, without considering all the other intertextual influences at play? If not, then we must make some attempt to reconstruct the entire literary diet of the audience. If we do that for the British working classes in the nineteenth and twentieth centuries, we find that no two individual reading histories were alike. Each one was a unique jumble of ephemera, junk, and often some classics. And if every one of the newspaper articles, sermons, penny novelettes, advertisements, movies, and Everyman's Library volumes was open to individual interpretation by everyone in an audience of millions, how can we possibly arrive at any reliable generalizations about popular culture? The only workable method is to consult the readers themselves, and let them explain how they made sense of it all.

The Function of Penny Dreadfuls

In the late nineteenth and early twentieth centuries, the penny dreadful (cheap crime and horror literature for boys) created something approaching panic among middle-class observers, who were certain that it encouraged juvenile delinquency.[7] Working-class critics, however, were inclined to be much more easygoing. "Demoralizing literature? Well, none of us in after life adopted highway robbery as a profession," noted Thomas Okey (b. 1852), "although each desired to possess a Black Bess and to effect exciting escapes from pursuing Bow Street Runners by 'rides to York.'" As a basketweaver who became professor of Italian at Cambridge

University, Okey recognized that much of the clamor over penny dreadfuls grew out of a longstanding prejudice against teaching the poor to read. To those who protested that the Board schools were producing semi-literates, Okey countered that they were probably as well-read as the Cambridge undergraduate he found absorbed in the "Pink 'Un" (the *Sporting Times*).[8] A South Wales miner (b. 1875?), raised in an orphanage, acknowledged that "Robin Hood was our patron saint, or ideal. We sincerely believed in robbing the rich to help the poor." (Actually he stole from a old widow's tuck shop.) "Our real heroes were robbers like Jack Sheppard, Dick Turpin, and Charles Peace, whose '*penny-dreadful*' biographies we knew by heart." Yet in later life, even as a Calvinistic Methodist minister, he did not condemn that genre:

> It introduced me to a romantic world when pennies were scarce, and libraries seemed far beyond my reach. We read the badly printed booklets in all sorts of places, even in church; they gave us glimpses of freedom, abandon, and romance, heroism and defiance of fate, whilst we chafed at restrictions and shut doors. True, our heroes ... were outlaws. But what boy is not a bandit, a rebel, a pirate at heart! As a corrective to natural law-breaking propensities, the '*penny-dreadful*' always ended with the punishment of crime.[9]

Others argued that even junk literature stimulated the reading habit.[10] An ironworker's son (b. 1866) who rose to the upper ranks of the British Medical Association attributed his "budding love of literature ... to an enthusiastic reading of Penny Dreadfuls which, so far from leading me into a life of crime, made me look for something better."[11] Though miners' MP Robert Smillie (b. 1857) surreptitiously gorged on *Dick Turpin* and *Three-Fingered Jack* as a boy, they too "led to better things": by fourteen he had seen *Richard III*, read some of the Sonnets, discovered Burns, Scott, and Dickens.[12] "They were thrilling, absolutely without sex interest, and of a high moral standard," explained London hatmaker Frederick Willis. "No boy would be any the worse for reading them and in many cases they encouraged and developed a love of reading that led him onwards and upwards on the fascinating path of literature. It was the beloved 'bloods' that first stimulated my love of reading, and from them I set out on the road to Shaw and Wells, Thackeray and Dickens, Fielding, Shakespeare and Chaucer."

Children's papers could lead readers to great literature in more direct ways. As Willis noted, *Union Jack* serialized abridgements of Walter Scott novels, with more sensational titles, and the *Chatterbox Christmas Annual* for 1890 introduced him to Dr. Johnson.[13] Barber John Paton (b. 1886) remembered that the *Boys' Friend* "ran a serial which was an enormously exciting tale of Alba's oppression of the Netherlands, and gave as its source, Motley's *Rise of the Dutch Republic*." He borrowed it from the public library and, with guidance from a helpful adult, also read J. R. Green, Macaulay, Prescott, Grote, and even Mommsen's multivolume *History of Rome* by age fourteen. "There must have been, of course, enormous gaps in my understanding of what I poured into the rag-bag that was my mind, particularly from the bigger works," he conceded, "but at least I sensed the important thing, the immense sweep and variety and the continuity of the historical process."[14]

Thomas Frost (b. c. 1821), who wrote several penny dreadfuls, argued that they were the direct descendants of those charming chapbooks that had entranced earlier generations of common readers. While they could be "very trashy," as a genre they were no more horrifying than some of Shakespeare's plays and less immoral than many of the sensation novels available at Mudie's Select Circulating Library. One could, he noted, find similar kinds of sensationalism in Ann Radcliffe, Smollett's *Count Fathom*, Harrison Ainsworth's *Rookwood*, Bulwer Lytton's *The Last Days of Pompeii*, and Charles Dickens. Frost did not gloss over the qualitative differences here. He saw that Dickens and Bulwer Lytton represented a great improvement in popular taste over *Dick Turpin* and, following Wilkie Collins, he was certain that the mass reading public would eventually learn "the difference between a good book and a bad."[15] All the same, he recognized that even classics could appropriate themes and devices from trash literature. If that seems a remarkably modern critical insight for the 1880s, it was shared by a number of working-class readers. East End socialist Walter Southgate (b. 1890) remembered that Dick Turpin and Buffalo Bill stories "were condemned by our teachers (all from middle-class backgrounds) who would confiscate them," but he appreciated their generic similarities to *Robinson Crusoe*, the Waverley novels, and *The Last of the Mohicans*.[16] As a boy George Acorn, a fellow East Londoner, read "all sorts and conditions of books, from 'Penny Bloods' to George Eliot" with "some appreciation of style," enough to recognize the affinities of high and low literature. Thus he discerningly characterized *Treasure Island* as "the usual penny blood sort of story, with the halo of greatness about it."[17]

"I do not see why the poor old public should be flouted for preferring *The Prisoner of Zenda* to *Hedda Gabler*," protested Robert Blatchford in 1903. He confessed to a boyish weakness for pirate stories and adventure tales. Had not Defoe, Scott, and Dumas worked in essentially the same genre? Literary men have always bewailed the deterioration of literary taste, but Blatchford's reply to them would probably hold true for any generation: yes, the presses are churning out more rubbish nowadays, but also more good literature. "What about Dent's Temple Shakespeare, what about the innumerable new editions of English and foreign classics now appearing? Frankly, I do not believe there were ever so many lovers of real literature, in this country at any rate, as there have been within the last ten years."[18]

Neither Blatchford nor any other working-class memoirist seriously questioned traditional literary hierarchies. Their tolerant affection for low literature coexisted with a conviction that the great writers were objectively great. Following Matthew Arnold, Blatchford affirmed that only the "abnormally dull" could prefer poetaster Martin Tupper to Milton. For anyone with an innate sense of discrimination, "it is well-nigh impossible ... ever to mistake a bad book for a good one."[19] Most books had some value, but they could be definitively ranked on a scale. In the following paragraph by gardener's son Howard Spring (b. 1889) one can discern five distinct strata of literary taste:

> From the *Magnet* it is no great step to G. A. Henty, and from that hearty friend of so much British youth, from Henty, I say, and from Ballantyne, Kingston and the rest, the passage to *Treasure Island* and *Robinson Crusoe* is not difficult. I know. The boy who has read *Treasure Island* and has been tempted thereby to sample *Kidnapped* and *Catriona* is ripe for Scott and Dumas, and thence there is nothing less than the infinite to step into.[20]

Spring knew exactly what belonged in that highest category. When he won a University College Cardiff prize worth £3 in books, he lugged home sixty Everyman's Library volumes, to cheers and laughter from the audience.[21] Weaver-novelist William Holt extolled the standard greats ("Noble Carlyle; virtuous Tolstoi; wise Bacon; jolly Rabelais; towering Plato...") and, having taught himself German, memorized Schiller while working at the looms. But he did not limit himself to classics: "I read omnivorously, greedily, promiscuously," from dime novels and G. A. Henty to Hardy and Conrad. Holt disparaged popular authors such as Ethel M. Dell and Elinor Glyn for "peddling vulgar narcotics," yet he was closely attuned to the mass reading public. His own autobiography sold a quarter of a million copies, and he once owned a fleet of bookmobiles. He reconciled taste with populism through this logic: though most readers consume a certain amount of junk, it does them no harm because they recognize it as junk. He recalled the protest of an old age pensioner in clogs, when a bookmobile offered him Edgar Wallace: "Dammit! Ah've seen me, when Ah've bin readin' Edgar Wallace, sit up till three o'clock in t' mornin'. Ah'd finish it, and then wuzz it across th' house. *Gor*-yonnit! Ah doan't know what Ah want readin' sich rubbish for! But 'e could tell a good tale, could Edgar."

In the 1940s Mass Observation surveys confirmed that fans of cheap thrillers commonly acknowledged they were facile and not to be compared with classics.[22] William Holt appreciated what many scholars of popular culture today have yet to recognize: that the impact of literature cannot be measured by sales figures alone. Some books are chewing gum, consumed in mass quantities but leaving no taste behind; others transform the lives of the readers. That observation lay behind his own definition of a great book:

> I believe that the humble person is the touchstone by which the true classic can be told. Surely a book cannot be truly great if it makes no impression at all on the mind of a humble man or woman? Great books evoke response in circles high and low, readers responding in their own way according to their own lights and in due proportion to the measure of their spirit and what they are able to bring to the book themselves, both innate and acquired.[23]

Autodidacts widely recognized that essential difference. Only canonical literature could produce epiphanies in common readers, and specifically, only great books could inspire them to write. Lancashire millworker Ben Brierley (b. 1825) read penny fairy tales and horror stories as a boy, but they did not contribute to his work as a dialect poet: "I must confess that my soul did not feel much lifted by the only class of reading then within my reach. It was not until I joined the companionship of Burns and Byron that I felt the 'god within me.'"[24] When young, ironmoulder-novelist Joseph Stamper devoured penny dreadfuls as well as Stead's Penny Poets, and in an economy of scarcity he sometimes had to "ponder whether to buy Thomas à Kempis or *Deadwood Dick*." Still, in one vitally important sense the cowboy hero could not be equated with cheap editions of Homer, Keats, Tennyson, *Hiawatha*, and *Evangeline*, for only the latter impelled him to write his own poetry, something that was not encouraged at school.[25]

Poverty and Indiscrimination

We must therefore break the habit of treating high culture and popular culture as two distinct categories with mutually exclusive audiences. In fact, a promiscuous mix of high and low was a common pattern among working-class readers of all regions, generations, and economic strata. Their approach to literature was a random walk. As Pierre Bourdieu notes, autodidact culture is commonly ridiculed for its unsystematic organization and acquisition.[26] Even a sympathetic observer like Arnold Freeman, of the Sheffield Educational Settlement, was "astonished" by "the indiscriminate character of the reading even of the best of the workers," who appeared "to read almost anything that is put into their hands."[27] If that seems to be middle-class condescension, it was consistently confirmed by working-class readers:

… when I think of books and myself I seem to have played the butterfly rather than the bee …. [Warehouseman, b. 1861][28]

It began, as all writers' lives begin, by copious, catholic, and indiscriminate reading. From the age of eight or nine I was allowed to read anything I wanted to, although I remember my father's taking away from me *Peregrine Pickle*, saying I could read it when I was older. I got hold of it again within a week and read it clandestinely and avidly …. [Shipbuilder's son turned professional author, b. 1887][29]

I read voraciously, without direction, desultorily, in a panic of fear I would never have time to read all that I wanted to read; I picked up books and cast them away unread if they did not immediately appeal to me. And slowly out of this welter of reading I began to discover the few books which I could go on reading and re-reading. [Barrow steelworker, b. 1914][30]

Most working people in the eighteenth and nineteenth centuries, and even some in the twentieth, faced an absolute poverty of reading matter. That is, the literature available to them could not fill up their leisure time, even if they read it all. There was no room for selectivity. As Cornish carpenter George Smith (b. 1800) had little access to libraries, he "read every sort of book that came in my way"—novels, history, biblical criticism. He particularly liked mathematics because it was slow reading: "A treatise on algebra or geometry, which cost but a very few shillings, afforded me matter for close study for a year."[31] Methodist millworker Thomas Wood (b. 1822) attended a school where there was only one book, the Bible, which was never read beyond the first chapter of St. John. Therefore he later "read everything I could lay my hands on," which was precious little. At this time "A cottage library in a fairly well-to-do family would seldom exceed half-a-dozen volumes, and consisted of such books as Doddridge's *Use and Progress of Religion in the Souls* [sic], Bunyan's *Works*, particularly the *Pilgrim's Progress*, Cook's *Voyages*, *News from the Invisible World*, etc., and a volume, or perhaps two, of magazines." He worked his way through most of the library at an independent Sunday school, and joined a mechanics' institute for 1½d. a week. His reading, though "very heterogeneous" and undirected, could be quite intensive, as when he devoted almost a year to the six volumes of Rollin's *Ancient History*. That "left an impression on my mind which 40 years of wear and tear has not effaced."[32]

A half century later Edwin Whitlock (b. 1874) faced much the same shortages. A farmer on Salisbury Downs, he had plenty of time to read while shepherding: "The difficulty was to get hold of books. The only ones in our house were the Bible, a few thin Sunday School prizes, which were mostly very pious publications, one or two more advanced theological works, and a Post Office Directory for 1867, which volume I read from cover to cover." Whitlock also borrowed books from a schoolmaster and from neighbors:

> Most of them would now be considered very heavy literature for a boy of fourteen or fifteen, but I didn't know that, for I had no light literature for comparison. I read most of the novels of Dickens, Scott, Lytton and Mrs. Henry Wood, *The Pilgrim's Progress* and *The Holy War*—an illustrated guide to Biblical Palestine, *Uncle Tom's Cabin*, several bound volumes of religious magazines, *The Adventures of a Penny*, and sundry similar classics.

With few books competing for his attention, he could freely concentrate on his favorite reading, "a set of twelve thick volumes of Cassell's *History of England*."[35] For Durham colliery worker Sid Chaplin, the bitterest memory of poverty— worse even than the miners' strike of 1926—was "a perpetual starvation of books. ... You went with half a crown in your pocket and scoured the town like a lean book-hungry bloodhound, ... fit to bay in the covered market because the book was sixpence more than you possessed. ... I remember sneering at passing

[Newcastle University] students because they had everything, which is to say all the books they desired, and I had nothing."[34]

Readers who read whatever came to hand would unavoidably stumble across a certain percentage of classics amidst the rubbish. Growing up in Clapton during the Depression, Michael Stapleton needed a signature from his father (an Irish navvy) for a public library card,

> but I asked him on the wrong evening and he merely shouted at me. ... So I ... started examining every book in the house, ransacking forgotten cupboards and the hole under the stairs. I read everything I could understand, and begged twopenny bloods quite shamelessly from the boys at school who were fortunate to enjoy such things. I absorbed an immense amount of useless information, but occasionally a treasure came my way and I would strain my eyes under the twenty-watt bulb which lighted our kitchen. A month-old copy of the *Wizard* would be succeeded by a handbook for vegetarians, and this in turn would be followed by *Jane Eyre. Tarzan and the Jewels of Ophir* was no sooner finished than I was deep in volumes three and four of a history of *The Conquest of Peru* (the rest of the set was missing). I would go from that to *Rip Van Winkle* and straight on to a tattered copy of the *Hotspur*.[35]

Under those conditions, one inevitably read much that was not age-appropriate, far above or below one's comprehension level. James Williams (b. c. 1900) admitted that, growing up in rural Wales, "I'd read anything rather than not read at all. I read a great deal of rubbish, and books that were too 'old', or too 'young' for me." He consumed the *Gem, Magnet*, and Sexton Blake as well as the standard boys' authors (Henty, Ballantyne, Marryat, Fenimore Cooper, Twain) but also Dickens, Scott, Trollope, the Brontës, George Eliot, even Prescott's *The Conquest of Peru* and *The Conquest of Mexico*. He picked *The Canterbury Tales* out of a odd pile of used books for sale, gradually puzzled out the Middle English, and eventually adopted Chaucer as his favorite poet. The *Royal Readers* school anthologies published by the firm of Nelson in fact "made only slight concessions to youth" in their verse selections. Though we regard W. H. G. Kingston as a children's writer, his lavish use of nautical jargon was a challenge to the young reader: "In common with other Victorian authors, he made no concession by way of a simplified vocabulary for children. The age of 'pappy' children's books had not yet come. If I had time I'd look up hard words in a dictionary, but more often than not I guessed their meaning from the context." In 1971 Williams argued that such a sturdy literary diet stretched the minds of Edwardian schoolchildren. He denounced "a deplorable tendency in the last 30 years to keep the child away from difficulties. Too many failed teachers have become inspectors with power to institute easy reading and working in all subjects. Every child is a shorn lamb, for whom all winds have to be tempered. It is the failures who get the V.I.P. treatment. In my day we took the hard stuff neat."[36]

In fact younger plebeian readers often tackled difficult books, even if they read them through an unsophisticated frame. W. E. Adams enjoyed *Pilgrim's Progress*, *Gulliver's Travels*, and the *Arabian Nights* at quite a young age, though "the religious meaning of the first, the satirical meaning of the second, and the doubtful meaning of the third were, of course, not understood. The story was the thing—the trials of Christian, the troubles of Gulliver, the adventures of Aladdin."[37] George Acorn read George Eliot at age nine, but "solely for the story. I used to skip the parts that moralized, or painted verbal scenery, a practice at which I became very dextrous."[38] Bookbinder Frederick Rogers read *Faust* "through from beginning to end, not because I was able at sixteen to appreciate Goethe, but because I was interested in the Devil." Moving on to *Don Quixote*, "I did not realize its greatness till long after; but its stories of adventure and its romance and humour appealed to me strongly enough."[39] Stella Davies's father would read to his children from the Bible, *Pilgrim's Progress*, Walter Scott, Longfellow, Tennyson, Dickens, *The Cloister and the Hearth*, and Pope's translation of the *Iliad*, though not in their entirety: "Extracts suitable to our ages were read and explained and, when we younger ones had been packed off to bed, more serious and inclusive reading would begin. ... We younger ones often dipped into books far beyond our understanding. It did us no harm, I believe, for we skipped a lot and took what we could from the rest."[40]

Harry Burton (b. late 1890s), a housepainter's son who became a Cambridge don, affirmed that "a child can never be too young for almost any work of genius—provided it *is* a work of genius. ... *Hamlet*, for example, undoubtedly touches on problems with which little boys or girls cannot, or certainly should not, be familiar by experience," but educators had to take account of "the incredible elasticity of the child's understanding, which at one moment will fail to grasp some of the simplest conceptions and at the next seems to encompass the profoundest mysteries." There were few books at home when he was a boy, but one of them was *Don Juan*. He read it before he was eleven—through a prepubescent frame, of course.

> I saw nothing in it but comic adventures, sunny shores, storms, Arabian Nights interiors, and words, words, words. Many of the words I did not understand, but I did not therefore jump to the conclusion that they were indecent! All of them—or nearly all—jogged happily through my unreceptive brain leaving vaguely pleasing sensations in their wake. ... Genius speaks to all hearts and to all ages; the very greatest work in any medium brings its own credentials and is its own interpreter, and even if it says something different to every single worshipper, what it says is always valid and always true.[41]

In fact some uneducated readers had an uncanny knack for recognizing greatness in literature. Growing up in Lyndhurst after the First World War, R. L. Wild regularly read aloud to his marginally literate grandmother and his completely illiterate grandfather—and it was his grandparents who selected the books. Wild's mother, who "never read a book in her life," would also periodically bring home a 6d. volume from Woolworth's.

> I shall never understand how this choice was made. Until I started reading to them they had no more knowledge of English literature than a Malay aborigine. … I suppose it was their very lack of knowledge that made the choice, from *Quo Vadis* at eight, Rider Haggard's *She* at nine. By the time I was twelve they had come to know, intimately, a list of authors ranging from Shakespeare to D. H. Lawrence. All was grist to the mill (including Elinor Glyn). The classics, poetry, essays, *belles lettres*. We took them all in *my* stride. At times we stumbled on gems that guided us to further riches. I well remember the Saturday night they brought home *The Essays of Elia*. For months afterwards we used it as our road map.
>
> "Now, this 'ere Southey bloke," [Grandad] would say, after an evening with Lamb. "We ain't 'ad 'e, 'ave us? This 'ere Mr. Lamb, 'e seems to go for 'n, don't 'e?"
>
> Perhaps that's how we got round to poetry. I don't know how often they would want to listen, again and again, to Lawrence on Poverty.

> The only people I ever heard talk about my Lady Poverty
> Were rich people, or people who imagined themselves rich.
> Saint Francis himself was a rich and spoiled young man.
> Being born among the working people
> I know that poverty is a hard old hag,
> And a monster, when you're pinched for actual necessities.
> And whoever says she isn't, is a liar.

> The family silently took that in, until Grandad spoke: "God, 'e must 'ave known what it was like, eh, Matey?"[42]

Thus it was possible for a naive reader, flying blind, to home in on the classics. George Howell, bricklayer and trade unionist, explained how: "I read promiscuously. How could it be otherwise? I had no real guide, was obliged to feel my way into light. Yet perhaps there was a guidance, although indefinite and without distinctive aim." Howell groped his way through literature "on the principle that one poet's works suggested another, or the criticisms on one led to comparisons with another. Thus: Milton—Shakespeare; Pope—Dryden; Byron —Shelley; Burns—Scott; Coleridge—Wordsworth and Southey, and later on Spenser—Chaucer, Bryant—Longfellow, and so on."[43] By following these intertextual links, autodidacts could reconstruct the literary canon on their own.

Certainly, some readers selected authors simply because they had picked up their names from critics and schoolteachers. Edwin Muir (b. 1887), an Orkney crofter's child, admitted he "followed up with a sort of devotion every reference I found in my school-books or in the weekly paper to great writers. I worshipped their names before I knew anything of their work. Spenser, Shakespeare, Milton, Dryden, Swift, Goldsmith, Wordsworth, Coleridge, Tennyson, Swinburne, Macaulay, Carlyle, Ruskin—these names thrilled me." But this canon was hardly a hegemony imposed on Muir. On the contrary, everything in his cultural milieu conspired against the pursuit of literature. Books were still expensive: a coveted biography of Carlyle was on sale in Kirkwall for 1s. 3d., which was 3d. more than he had. There was a lending library in town, but with no education or guidance in English literature he wasted valuable reading time. Then there was opposition from his father, who made him return a study of "the Atheist" David Hume. And when his brother gave him 3d. to spend, he was almost insulted to learn that the money had gone to purchase Penny Poets editions of *As You Like It*, *The Earthly Paradise*, and Matthew Arnold. At home there was nothing to read except the Bible, *Pilgrim's Progress*, *Gulliver's Travels*, an R. M. Ballantyne tale about Hudson's Bay, back numbers of the *Christian World* ("They contained nothing but accounts of meetings and conferences, announcements of appointments to ministries, and obituary notices; yet I read them from beginning to end"), a large volume documenting a theological dispute between a Protestant clergyman and a Catholic priest, a novel that was probably *Sense and Sensibility* ("I could make nothing of it, but this did not keep me from reading it"), *The Scots Worthies* in monthly parts (a thousand pages in all), the *People's Journal* and other cheap magazines. "I read a complete series of sentimental love tales very popular at the time, called *Sunday Stories*," as well as a raft of temperance novels. Consequently, when he stumbled across Christopher Marlowe or George Crabbe in that literary junkyard, "it was like an addition to a secret treasure; for no one knew of my passion, and there was none to whom I could speak of it."[44]

The most heroic chapter of this history recounts the struggle of ordinary readers, in the face of tremendous obstacles, with no meaningful help or preparation, to discover literary greatness on their own. The education Neville Cardus received at his Manchester Board school was worthless. His parents (who worked in a home laundry) owned no books other than *East Lynne*, the Bible, "somebody's Dream Book," a Marion Crawford novel, and an odd volume of Coleridge poems. Cardus read only boys' papers until quite suddenly, in adolescence, he dove into Dickens and Mark Twain. "Then, without scarcely a bridge-passage, I was deep in the authors who to this day I regard the best discovered in a lifetime"—Fielding, Browning, Hardy, Tolstoy, even Henry James. He found them all before he was twenty, with critical guidance from no one: "We must make our own soundings and chartings in the arts ... so that we may all one day climb to our own peak, silent in Darien."[45]

"Reading for me then was haphazard, unguided, practically uncritical," recalled boilermaker's daughter Marjory Todd. "I slipped all too easily into those traps for the half-baked—books *about* books, the old *John o' London's Weekly*, chit-chat of one kind or another." Yet in a few years she had advanced to *Moby Dick*, *Lord Jim*, *Crime and Punishment*, and *Wuthering Heights*.

Whether I knew it or not, curiosity was being sharpened, knowledge absorbed, mental frontiers pushed back. Sitting alone on a seat on the Common one Sunday afternoon, putting off the time when I must go home and get the tea, I remember I experienced that sudden awareness of identity and purpose which I suppose comes to most adolescents. Perhaps to some it comes only gradually. For me the moment was caught and held on that Sunday afternoon, so that now [1960], nearly forty years later, I can remember exactly the angle of the slanting sun, a clump of pine trees, the rough worn grass and a few small pine cones at my feet.

The revelation was almost negative—or rather, it showed me that what I had been up to that moment I would never be again. Colours would be bolder, outlines more sharply defined; the new energy which was tingling through me would demand new outlets, the nature of which I could not yet guess. I did not want to go home immediately to the bustle of getting tea; I wanted to be alone. Something was going to happen; I did not yet know what. I would, I suppose, have been ripe for revivalism, for conversion, had any proselytising force been at hand, but it was not. I might even, I dare say, have fallen in love.[46]

Derek Davies (b. 1923) could not recall that his mother had ever read a book. His father, a die-caster in an automobile factory, read only local and sports papers and two novels a week—a Western or a detective thriller.

Yet quite unintentionally he gave me ... a love of reading. ... He never seemed to vary the diet, he never discussed either the books he read or newspaper items, and he never urged me to read for myself. Often my mother would accuse him of being "dead to the world with your nose stuck in a book," yet behind her chiding lay a note of admiration for an achievement which for her was incomprehensible. I rapidly assumed that reading was manly, cheerfully risked the same forgiving rebuke, and was soon reading everything he read. By the age of eleven or twelve I must have read a couple of hundred of his novels. ... Obviously nobody moulded my reading habits. I never had stories read to me at bedtime, and the children's classics remained for me to discover when my own children came along. In one unplanned leap I plunged into reading and found myself simultaneously reading voraciously on several widely differing levels.

In addition to the newspapers and his father's novels, he consumed books for younger children and travel books for adults ("Tibet, I remember, was one passionate preoccupation"). He jumped from the *Wizard* and *Hotspur*, which his parents considered "trash," to their twenty-two bound volumes of *The Illustrated News History of the 1914–18 War*.

Undeterred by the fact that I had neither the space nor the money to embark on even the most modest layout, I consumed book after book on the building of model railways. Gradually, as I found out how to use the School Library and the Public Library, some degree of selection took place, but as nobody at school before the Sixth Form advised me what to read the selection remained distinctly erratic. I remained ignorant of whole areas of likely books, and I constantly read books far ahead of my understanding. At about fourteen, for example, I read every word of T. E. Lawrence's *Seven Pillars of Wisdom*, although I had only the faintest glimmering of its real significance.

All this wildly random reading had concrete value for Davies. Even his father's rubbishy novels "provided me with a reading fluency and a vocabulary which gave me a flying start in the Grammar School." For his first public speaking engagement, before his chapel mutual improvement society, he offered to lecture on T. E. Lawrence. "I can still remember the polite disapproval of the elderly Secretary …, for in my youthful audacity I started the talk like a sensational newspaper with the moment of Lawrence's dramatic death on the speeding motorcycle." But perhaps his dad's newspapers had taught him a cinematic sensibility: years later he was astonished to find the same opening in David Lean's film.[47]

Any consideration of twentieth-century mass culture must take into account the most popular proletarian author of all time. Charlie Chaplin was a classic autodidact, always struggling to make up for a dismally inadequate education, groping haphazardly for what he called "intellectual manna." Once, in New York, he suggested that someone ought to compile a new kind of dictionary that would specify the precise word for every idea, whereupon a black truck driver directed him to Roget's Thesaurus. Then there was the waiter at the Alexandria Hotel who quoted William Blake and Karl Marx as he delivered courses to Chaplin's table; and the acrobatic comedian who advised him to read *The Anatomy of Melancholy*, explaining (in a Brooklyn accent) Burton's influence on Shakespeare and Dr. Johnson. Chaplin could be found in his dressing room studying a Latin-English dictionary, Robert Ingersoll's secularist propaganda, Emerson's "Self-Reliance" ("I felt I had been handed a golden birthright"), Irving, Hawthorne, Poe, Whitman, Twain, Hazlitt, all five volumes of Plutarch's *Lives*, Plato, Locke, Kant, Freud's *Psychoneurosis*, Lafcadio Hearn's *Life and Literature*, and Henri Bergson—his essay on laughter, of course. Bergson had argued that the essence of comedy is the mechanization of human behavior: it is not difficult to see this theory dramatized in *Modern Times*. Chaplin also spent forty years reading (if not finishing) the three volumes of *The World as Will and Idea* by Schopenhauer, whose musings on suicide are echoed in *Monsieur Verdoux*. In fact Chaplin translated to the screen the same mongrelization of philosophy and melodrama, high culture and low comedy that characterized the typical literary diet of autodidacts. Thus he successfully appealed to mass audiences as well as sophisticated critics.[48]

True, the large majority of working-class readers were less motivated than Chaplin, and for them it was even more necessary to dilute serious books with large helpings of subliterature. Managing a comprehensive school library in the

1950s, Edward Blishen appreciated that slum residents were "profoundly suspicious of books." If they happened to acquire one (usually "as a second-class Christmas present") they commonly donated it to the school:

> And I was glad to accept books of this kind. Cheap annuals, poorly written children's novels—I needed to have such things on the shelves. Oh, those school libraries that contained nothing but the best, or the very good! Could one expect boys like mine to reach out at once, in all their inexperience, for books so sophisticated and demanding? The presence of familiar bad books made them feel at home in the library ...; and the more familiar, informal, boy-managed it seemed to be, the more likely they were to use it.

> If I wanted them to become real readers, I argued, then I must ask myself what made anyone whatever a real reader. And surely part of the process was the discovery, for yourself, of bad, better, best. Literature, like life, was a mongrel business. That was the delight of it. So I must have a mongrel library.[49]

Boys' Stories for Girls

Female reading was no less mongrelized. Alongside the *Gem* and *Magnet*, girls had their own parallel universe of school stories, where a miner's daughter could imagine herself "the Heroine of St. Catherine's, and even the Richest Girl in the School."[50] But as Orwell correctly guessed, many girls chose to read boys' weeklies. Some of them passionately identified with the young gentlemen of Greyfriars,[51] even to the point of mimicking their manners and catchphrases.[52]

Like more canonical male authors, Frank Richards and other boys' writers could have a liberating influence on their girl readers. As a railway clerk's daughter, Muriel Box (b. 1905) enjoyed borrowing her brother's *Magnet*, *Gem*, and *Boy's Own Paper*: she later became a leading feminist activist and a pioneer woman film director.[53] That hunger for adventure, according to M. K. Ashby, may explain why girls as well as boys fought over the *Boy's Own Paper*: "Perhaps the long voyages of the boys in the stories, over mountains or in sailing boats, and the wonderful expeditions to collect tropical birds and plants compensated the children for their continually interrupted adventures and the severe usefulness of their errands."[54] Domestic servant Dorothy Burnham (b. 1915) never read girls' stories ("I found them insipid and meaningless") but she and her older sister were fixated on the *Magnet*, to the point of mimicking the school uniform (blazer, straw hat, shirt and tie). This partly reflected their new found interest in the opposite sex. Dorothy identified particularly with that subversive fellow the Bounder, who smoked, gambled, and even "split an infinitive or two."[55]

Just as their foremothers had been inspired by Pope, Carlyle, and Lord Chesterfield, these girls suffered no psychological damage when they assumed the male perspective. At a time when literature offered few truly emancipated heroines, girls could leap out of constricting female roles by identifying with adventurous male characters. As a child Pat Phoenix found escape in Arthurian legends, assuming the role of Arthur rather than Guinevere.[56] One chauffeur's daughter alternated effortlessly between heroes and heroines: "I have plotted against pirates along with Jim Hawkins and I have trembled with Jane Eyre as the first Mrs. Rochester rent her bridal veil in maddened jealousy. I have been shipwrecked with Masterman Ready and on Pitcairn Island with Fletcher Christian. I have been a medieval page in Sir Nigel and Lorna Doone madly in love with 'girt Jan Ridd.'"[57] Jennie Lee likewise worked through her family bookcase, and "Before I quite realized what was happening I was the Count of Monte Cristo tapping away desperately in an effort to establish communication with the prisoner in the next cell. Or I was Liza fleeing from slavery across the broken ice and carrying a child in my arms. Or Burning Daylight swaggering into town, the toughest and whitest man in all the North."[58] None of that prevented her from becoming an admirer of Mary Wollstonecraft, Olive Schreiner, and George Sand, as well as a Labour MP.[59]

Schoolgirl crushes on romantic poets were not unusual, but Angela Rodaway (b. 1918), whose father worked in a garage and a soap factory, fully assumed their personae: "I 'lost' my tie so that the collar of my school blouse gaped Byronically. I was determined to die by the time I was thirty [like Shelley] and to look pale and ethereal for most of the years preceding this. I learnt that Byron had fed himself on rice and vinegar in order to achieve such an effect and I tried to do the same." Her adolescent appetite soon got the better of her and, having read Boswell on Johnson, she decided to emulate instead the great doctor's diet and personal hygiene. Yet between meals, she was capable of assuming a feminist spirituality, writing poems to an "unknown, unnamed goddess, a mysterious and omnipotent 'she.'"[60] Even Annie Kenney, the most militant of the working-class suffragettes, began her autobiography by quoting "A man is not all included between his hat and his boots" (Whitman) and "Man, know thyself."[61] The fixation on ungendered language was a late twentieth-century fetish: an earlier and sturdier generation of feminists concentrated their energies on more meaningful issues.

Nor were these exceptional cases. A 1940 survey of working-class girls aged thirteen and fourteen found that about a quarter of the adolescent magazines they read were, in fact, written for boys. Adventure stories accounted for 54 percent of books read by working-class boys aged twelve and thirteen, but also 21 percent of books read by girls, compared with less than 7 percent for love stories.[62] In an 1888 survey of mainly middle-class adolescents, the favorite book among girls turned out to be Charles Kingsley's preposterous *Westward Ho!* Jules Verne, W. H. G. Kingston, and Whyte Melville, who are generally typed as adventure writers for boys, were actually more popular with girls than Louisa May Alcott, Harriet Beecher Stowe, Mrs. Gaskell, Lewis Carroll, Jane Austen, and all the Brontës. The girls rated *The Girl's Own Paper* their favorite magazine, but *The Boy's Own Paper* took second place. As one young woman remarked,

A great many girls never read so-called "girls' books" at all; they prefer those presumably written for boys. Girls as a rule don't care for Sunday-school twaddle; they like a good stirring story, with a plot and some incident and adventures—not a collection of texts and sermons and hymns strung together, with a little "Child's Guide to Knowledge" sort of conversation. ... People try to make boys' books as exciting and amusing as possible, while we girls, who are much quicker and more imaginative, are very often supposed to read milk-and-watery sorts of stories that we could generally write better ourselves. ... When I was younger I always preferred Jules Verne and Ballantyne and *Little Women* and *Good Wives* to any other books, except those of Charles Lever.[63]

Marjory Todd was initially put off by the title of *Little Women* ("it sounded like just another goody-goody book such as those ... which were all our Sunday School could provide") but discovered a new and exciting world in Marryat's *Poor Jack*.[64] The 1888 survey concluded that many girls' books sold well only because they were given as presents by adults: "If girls were to select their own books ... they would make a choice very different from that which their elders make for them." Sure enough, when London elementary schoolchildren of both sexes selected prize books in 1910, the only "girls' book" high on the list was *Little Women* (1,625 choices), along with *Robinson Crusoe* (2,283), *David Copperfield* (1,114), *Ivanhoe* (1,096), and *Westward Ho!* (1,136).[65] All this parallels what Barbara Sicherman found among female readers in late Victorian America: they were equally fond of "boys' books" which, far from indoctrinating them in any male ideology, reinforced their independence.[66]

The Dog That Was Down

Popular literature and movies have also been indicted for communicating racist attitudes to their audiences. Boys' papers in particular stand condemned for routinely depicting the Chinese as villainous and blacks as comical or vicious.[67] George Orwell cataloged the predictable stereotypes:

FRENCHMAN: Excitable. Wears beard, gesticulates wildly.
SPANIARD, MEXICAN etc: Sinister, treacherous.
ARAB, AFGHAN etc: Sinister, treacherous.
CHINESE: Sinister, treacherous. Wears pigtail.
ITALIAN: Excitable. Grinds barrel-organ or carries stiletto.
SWEDE, DANE etc: Kind hearted, stupid.
NEGRO: Comic, very faithful.[68]

Yet that list, on the face of it, is unfair to Frank Richards. Though his stories were densely populated with ethnic cartoons, the least attractive were arrogant white

Americans. Richards forthrightly condemned Jim Crow laws in the United States and public-school anti-Semitism in Britain, and he introduced an Indian school-chum to make a statement against racism:

> The dark eyes of Hurree Jamset Ram Singh had a flash in them now. "Did you call me a nigger," he asked quietly. … "I have a great respect for negroes, as much esteemfulness as I have for other persons. … But if the intention is to insult—"[69]

Even artifacts of British popular culture that seem obviously racist may, on closer examination, appear more ambiguous, especially when we consider the response of the audience. In nineteenth-century Sunday school literature one can certainly find contemptuous treatments of Eastern religions and horror stories about the Sepoy Mutiny, but also denunciations of racial bigotry.[70] "Nigger" minstrel shows were enormously popular in the Victorian period, but how were they read by working-class spectators? As Michael Pickering suggests, the answer is not as clear as it might seem today. A tradition of blackface performers can be traced back to the court of Richard II, not to mention *Othello*, and they often affirmed universal or antislavery themes.[71] When a minstrel pranced about the stage wearing the costume of an aristocratic dandy, whose pretensions were being mocked: the "nigger's" or the gentleman's? Unlike his white American counterpart, the British workingman was not yet competing with a large black labor force, and consequently did not need to proclaim his racial superiority. On the contrary, Chartist agitators and trade unionists frequently compared the condition of free English workers with that of American slaves. Joseph Arch, organizer of the Agricultural Labourers' Union and staunch anti-imperialist, protested that "the life of poor little Hodge was not a whit better than that of a plantation nigger boy."[72] Given that most minstrel singers were whites in blackface (Henry Mayhew found that only one of fifty "Negro Serenaders" in the streets of London was actually black),[73] it is not improbable that working-class audiences identified with "Jim Crow." In Victorian Britain, blackface minstrelsy may have represented a poor white homage to and appropriation of black American music—not so very different from what Elvis Presley did a century later. In that spirit, the millworker-poet Joseph Burgess adopted a minstrel song as his personal anthem:

> I will live as long as I can, ha! ha!
>   Or I'll know de reason why,
> For as long as dere's breff in pore old Jeff,
>   Dis nigger will never say die, ha! ha![74]

Though the labor press (e.g., *Reynolds's Newspaper*, the *Bee-Hive*, the *Working Man*) supported the Confederacy in the American Civil War, their readers tended to side with the North.[75] One ex-weaver from Stockport enlisted in the Grand

Army of the Republic, partly because he was unemployed, but also because "I detested slavery of every kind whether among the white factory operatives at home or among the negroes of America. I always went with the dog that was down."[76]

Those sentiments were fired by the spectacular popularity of *Uncle Tom's Cabin*. It captivated working-class audiences like no other literary work of the nineteenth century, and it continued to rouse them well into the twentieth. It appears in the catalogs of ten out of twenty South Wales miners' libraries, not counting the translation *Caban F'ewyth Twm*.[77] As late as 1940, it was one of the most widely read books among working-class schoolgirls. When they recalled the dark ages of child labor, workingmen often framed their protests in those terms: they had been treated as brutally as Uncle Tom.[78] The book inspired radicals like Samuel Fielden, an emigrant from Lancashire, executed in connection with Chicago's Haymarket riot of 1886,[79] as well as Communists Willie Gallacher and Helen Crawfurd.[80]

In the memories of ordinary readers, *Uncle Tom's Cabin* stands out as a devastating experience. It was practically the only literary work that moved a Forest of Dean colliery storekeeper to comment in his diary: "Was struck most impressively with some of its beautiful contrasts and the extensive range of mind of the author."[81] A warehouse clerk kept it open under his desk lid, "snatching a few pages in the intervals of working a numbering machine. Many a salt tear fell into the desk, or was with difficulty concealed when duty called."[82] "Oh, the reality of the escape over the crackling ice, and of black Topsy who wasn't born but 'just growed'—never, never to be forgotten!" recalled a Dundee bookkeeper's daughter. "And the sense of sin—never to be quite expiated."[83] "Reality" may not be the word that *Uncle Tom's Cabin* brings to mind today, yet audiences before the First World War found in it a heart-stopping realism. In stage versions it could effectively abolish the proscenium, erasing the boundaries between drama and life, actors and spectators. In one North Wales mining village, audience identification with black slaves was complete and thoroughly harrowing:

> *Uncle Tom's Cabin* played absolute hell with our emotions. We felt every stroke of the lash of the whip. It cut us to the quick, heart and soul. In the audience some people wept unashamedly like the Greeks of old who considered it manly to give vent to their feelings when moved. Others with obvious effort restrained themselves by the exercise of great control from rushing on the stage, taking the whip out of the hand of the cruel task master and giving him a taste of his own medicine. One or two were only repressed with the reminder that it was on the stage—and not in real life. Not so Mrs. Whalley. In the middle of the sixpennies ... she was loudly sobbing, looking up and calling out, "Oh, oh" as each lash discordantly cut the air and Tom's poor body. At one juncture her grief was awful to behold and as she was sympathetically escorted out to the back ... she was still sobbing and crying and would not be comforted. As if motivated all the more by the compassion of the audience, the cruelty on the

stage was intensified and the accompanying words were savagely added on as salt to the wounds. There was not a dry eye in the Pavilion that night. ... [Afterwards] the people moved out into what was to them the *unreality* of the world outside, to such a degree had the events of the past two hours taken hold of them. Outside Mrs. Whalley was still giving vent to her feelings as the crowd gathered round, some people had come running from near the Miners' Institute over a hundred yards away. Again sympathizers were trying to tell her that it was only a play, on the stage. "It wasn't for real," they pleaded. And then she moved off into the night homewards, still crying and moaning.[84]

C. H. Rolph recalled that his father "had a romantic admiration for the Zulus, even though they killed his father (a private in the South Wales Borderers) at the Battle of Isandhlwana." There may well have been a touch of class resentment behind that sentiment: "My father used to say that ... Isandhlwana and its 900 British dead showed 'the blacks' that spears and courage could win against rifles, and that well-trained *impis* could outwit upper-class English duffers like Lord Chelmsford." Rolph himself picked up a similar message from S. Clarke Hook's stories of Jack, Sam, and Pete in the *Boys' Friend Threepenny Library*. Jack and Sam were white boys, and their friend Pete was a black superhero, "who was not only stronger than Samson but richer than Croesus. Pete picked up objectionable characters with one hand and dropped them into ponds, and if a railway company refused to put on a special train for him he bought the railway and ran it himself."[85]

There is some evidence that British working people were able to identify with other colored races as well. The American Indian in particular offered a romantic escape from dreary industrial civilization. James Fenimore Cooper and (after 1907) the Boy Scout movement both had armies of working-class followers, and both idealized American Indian culture.[86] For a boy in a Lancashire mining village around 1880, where there were few books to read (other than twenty volumes of Methodist Conference minutes), W. H. G. Kingston's *Dick Onslow among the Red Indians* could be hypnotic: "I was entranced. I no longer lived in Hindley. In imagination I turned native and lived among red men and hunters, tomahawks and scalps."[87] Ramsay MacDonald was one of a number of poor boys who, when playing Cowboys and Indians, chose to be the latter.[88] Once the Hollywood Western reached British screens, attitudes began to change. "We cheered the cowboys like mad and hissed and booed the Indians, for they were always the baddies" is a typical comment.[89] One Bermondsey boy could not bring himself to shake hands with an actual Indian, having seen too many scalpings at the flicks: "It was difficult for us to understand that the pictures we saw at the movies were all make-believe."[90] "Them be devils, them be," exclaimed a woman at a South Wales cinema, "but don't you worry, boy *bach*; ours will be here in a minute." ("Ours were the cowboys," a miner explained helpfully.)[91]

My point, then, is not to exonerate any social class of racism. The complicated reality is that prejudice against and identification with nonwhite people could coexist in working-class culture, often in the same individuals. Patrick McLoughlin, growing up in Depression-era Sunderland, had a friend, Ernie, who fancied himself a kind of White Oriental. "Ernie avidly read any story that had to do with the Chinese." Though he picked up the worst pulp-fiction bigotries ("he always wanted to see a Chinese woman stripped ... to see if it was true what they said") at the same time

> He liked the inscrutable Orientals. I'm sure he would have wished he was Chinese, or maybe Red Indian. The only real Chinese we knew were a family who kept a laundry about a mile from [our] street and any time we were passing we'd spend a full half hour with our noses pressed up against the window, watching the expressionless faces as they plied their smoothing irons to shirts and underclothes, wondering what was going on in their Oriental minds. There was something about them that fitted in with Ernie's own outlook on life. We went to see all the Fu Manchu films they ever made and read all the Sax Rohmer novels. Ernie even started to pull at his right ear lobe with his fingers, the same as Nayland Smith did in the Fu Manchu stories.[92]

The conventional working-class idea of Africa at the time was equally cartoonish: a remote place "where the people were black and lived in the jungle. It was very hot there, and these people, who were called niggers, didn't wear clothes. Some of them were savage and carried spears, and some would even eat you if they caught you. Also living in the jungle were wild animals like lions and tigers and elephants which would also eat you if they got the chance .... "[93] Yet however demeaning these attitudes were, they were not imperialistic: no one who thought Africa was like that would want to spend his life policing the continent. And while East-of-Suez movies were loaded with stereotypes, working people could view them skeptically. "Such films as *Rainbow Island*, *Sudan*, *Kismet*, *Cobra Woman* and *The Thief of Bagdad* are to me just ridiculous, and an insult to our intelligence," complained a young female textile worker.[94] One eighteen-year-old girl was "revolted" by *White Cargo*: "Not the immorality of Tondalayo who can hardly be blamed for it. But the contemptuous way men seem to seduce and undermine coloured girls in a way that they wouldn't have the courage to try on European girls, and yet they are as much entitled to respect as we." She offered a perceptive reading of a scene in *Son of Fury*, where Ben (Tyrone Power) "is teaching one of the island girls how to eat with a knife and fork; she drops the food and exclaims I am stupid, Ben reflected and said he was the stupid one for trying to alter their way of life. With all that they lack in culture, this film brought home to me, that the uneducated people are the happiest, provided their associates are equally ignorant."[95]

Before the First World War, the working classes in Britain were considerably less racist than the governing classes. They rarely engaged in racial violence, and they had not absorbed the scientific racism fashionable among the university-educated.

Black American abolitionist speakers and Africans who visited England in the mid-nineteenth century generally reported a high level of racial tolerance. After 1918, as racism became less acceptable among educated people, it became more common among British workers, as they increasingly competed with immigrants for jobs.[96]

Uses and Gratifications

If the classics were an unambiguously emancipating force for working-class readers, it is far more difficult to generalize about the political effects of the much vaster body of literature that was less than classic. Throughout most of the twentieth century, leftist intellectuals regarded "mass culture" with suspicion. The Frankfurt School and the postwar American critics of consumer culture had their precursors among the pre-1914 generation of British socialists, who warned that music halls, the cinema, professional sports, and the popular press were narcotizing the proletariat.[97] Politically motivated workers like Bert Coombes were careful to explain to their brother miners "the difference between a serious novel and one of the 'hug me, sugar' romances." (The former category might include Zola's *Germinal* or Jack London.)[98] A more benign view of mass culture is offered by the "Uses and Gratifications" school of sociologists. Through audience interviews, they have shown that viewers of (for example) soap operas are neither passive nor brainwashed, but actively engaged in what they are watching. Entertainment that seems empty to academics may be stimulating, socializing, and educational for a less sophisticated audience.

This study clearly has a much closer affinity with the "Uses and Gratifications" approach, which has rescued us from the habit of treating mass audiences as herds of pathetic sheep. All the same, its limitations must be acknowledged.[99] If you ask viewers what they gain from soap operas, they will naturally emphasize the positive: they are not likely to mention (or even be aware of) subtle forms of indoctrination. Though most working-class memoirists defended low literature as harmless and enjoyable, they were probably more discerning than the average reader, who may well have been more passive and credulous. And while the autobiographers are generously forthcoming about responses to some forms of popular literature (such as school stories) they tell us almost nothing about others (notably women's magazines). In any case, the realm of "mass culture" is so vast and various that even an army of sociologists could not reliably generalize about its political effects. The most we can do is focus selectively on a few literary or nonliterary works, and even then we may find their political influence was mixed.

It is reasonably safe to say that certain kinds of popular literature communicated profoundly conservative values to working-class readers. Especially effective were the pious works of Hesba Stretton, Mrs. O. F. Walton, and Amy Le Feuvre, stories with titles like *Little Meg's Children, Jessica's First Prayer, Christie's Old Organ,* and *Froggy's Little Brother.* In an Oxfordshire village of the 1880s, Flora Thompson recalled that children and mothers alike borrowed them from the Sunday School library and cried over them. Though these sentimental tales dealt with slum life, they served "not so much to arouse indignation at the terrible conditions as to provide a striking background for some ministering lady or child." The dual message was, first, that benevolent ladies and clergymen were doing their best for depraved and almost subhuman slumdwellers. And second, "Saddening as it was to read about the poor things, it was also enjoyable, for it gave one a cheering sense of superiority. Thank God, the reader had a whole house to herself with an upstairs and downstairs and did not have to 'pig it' in one room; and real beds, and clean ones, not bundles of rags in corners, to sleep on." It all reinforced the sense, so common among the "respectable" working class and even Thompson's impoverished rural laborers, that they were "typical," at the midpoint of the economic pyramid rather than at the bottom. "On one side of that norm were the real poor, living in slums, and, on the other, 'the gentry'. They recognized no other division of classes."[100]

Growing up among the Plymouth Brethren in the late 1920s, Patricia Beer drew the same conclusion from the same books: the working classes were incapable of moral improvement, intellectual culture, or spiritual salvation without the intervention of the altruistic upper classes. In poor families, fathers left their children "in unsavoury lodgings to starve, while mothers were produced only that they might immediately die or go off on a permanent spree, abandoning their children to destitution." Their slum neighbors

were always a "bad crew" who drank, brawled and cursed. They neglected the sick of their community, leaving them to die with no food, no covering and no light, and if any inmate's children appeared decently dressed they would be stripped before they reached the shelter of the larger streets so that their clothes might be pawned for gin. The women ill-treated and over-worked any child who might be running errands or drudging for them.

The rich, in dramatic contrast, were self-evidently

superior beings, marked out by their manners and their attitude to life, particularly their attitude to the poor. They had been brought up on the motto, "Remember the poor," and the good rich did remember them, systematically, though they found it difficult to remember their names: even Miss Mabel, when she knew Christie quite well, tended to address him as "organ-boy," while Miss Winnie and Miss Jane always called Jessica "little girl". ... It never once occurred to them, as it never occurred to me, or to my parents, or to Hesba Stretton, Mrs. O. F. Walton and Amy Le Feuvre, that anything could or should be done beyond tears and the hand-out and the prayer in the wretched attic. Into neither the world of books nor the real world in which I lived did ideas of socialism and social reform ever enter. The authors of the books not only believed, as did the Brethren, that being washed in the blood of the Lamb was the only thing that mattered but also that God Himself had ordained who should be rich and who should be poor, so that to tamper with the existing social order would have been both a frivolous sideline and a grave sin.

Those lessons were reinforced by the counter-revolutionary ideology of *The Scarlet Pimpernel*, which Patricia's family swallowed whole. "For one thing it was by a Baroness, and so both begetter and begotten were of noble blood. We all identified absolutely with the persecuted aristocrats of the story. It seemed not to occur to one of us that had we lived then we should by reason of our social status have been *sans-culottes* dancing round the guillotine, rather than *vicomtes* escaping in carts." Patricia's father, a stationmaster for the Southern Railway, belonged to the thoroughly respectable upper-working class. What he imbibed from Baroness Orczy and the Plymouth Brethren was reinforced by the *Daily Mail*: he "not only recited its news and views without the slightest attempt at personal judgement or interpretation, but also blindly accepted its pronouncements on matters that he could have checked from his own observation." His company rail pass made possible occasional family excursions to London, but everything they had read left them terrified of the world beyond the West End:

> It was surprisingly easy to fit in the picture of London which these books gave with the London I really knew. ... A mile to the east of St. Paul's Cathedral ... were the dark gullies, the labyrinthine alleys and courts, where Jessica and Christie lived. ... The buildings reeked with fumes of gin and tobacco and rang with the sounds of groans, curses and sobs. ... We would mix with the fashionable people in and out of the well-appointed shops and then, when we got to a suitable place, stand fearfully at the street corners beyond which the slums were supposed to lie, peering into the dark world of Meg, Jessica and Christie, at much the same spot where they had peered out into our lighter realm and with equal panic. What went on in these poor districts was thought to be unspeakably evil and menacing, and was therefore, by definition, unstated, but the mere impression was enough to keep us safely out of its clutches. ... Here again the books both shaped and bore out our forebodings.[101]

Yet Marjory Todd read the same literature, with very different results. "I would not now willingly expose a child of mine to the morbid resignation of any of these books," she wrote in her mature years, "yet I think that children, when their home life is secure and happy, can take a lot of that debilitating sentiment—the implication that life is tragic here below, but a better time awaits above; even those dreadful deathbed scenes—without a lot of harm. We sharpened our teeth on this stuff and then went on to greater satisfaction elsewhere," including *Pride and Prejudice, Jane Eyre, Alice in Wonderland*, Captain Marryat, Kenneth Grahame, and E. Nesbit.[102] While Patricia Beer was relishing Hesba Stretton and Baroness

Orczy, she was also absorbing an opposing viewpoint from the Canadian stories of L. M. Montgomery. Her heroines Anne and Emily were writers, models of female emancipation, and Prince Edward Island was a classless society where everyone had chores to do.

And if some authors were doing their best to prop up the class system, they were surely undermined by Victorian melodrama, which was overpopulated with nefarious aristocrats and virtuous factory lasses.[103] Even the cheapest sentimental fiction could inspire murderous class resentment. Leslie Halward (b. c. 1904), a Birmingham toolmaker, remembered how his Aunt Clara would become engrossed in the tales of the *Home Companion* weekly:

> One evening I was present when she was reading a chapter and she came to the bit where the young son of hard-working parents, having risen in the world, one day when walking out with a fine lady passed his old mother without any sign of recognition. At this point Aunt Clara paused, glared at me over the top of her spectacles, and said slowly and awfully: "If ever you grow to be ashamed of your mother I'll—*kill* you." I assured her that she had no cause to worry, and she went on reading.[104]

As for the influence of the cinema, here again the evidence is mixed. Marxists and near-Marxists of the 1930s characterized Hollywood movies as capitalist dope, and surveys around 1945 suggest that audiences may in fact have absorbed attitudes congenial to the Conservative Party. Films inculcated deferential habits in employees, such as the shop girl who wanted a marriage like Mrs. Miniver's ("Often I've longed to tell customers off but thought 'the girl in the film didn't get nasty she remained polite'") and the messenger boy who saw *An American Romance* ("I suddenly decided to be good natured and hard working"). As a shorthand typist explained, "*The First of the Few* made me resolve to be more efficient at my work and to study more, whereas after seeing *Pride and Prejudice* I tried to be more sociable and pleasant with people."[105] A factory girl carefully copied the smart manners and dress of screen actresses ("I think this is useful especially if one is apt to have an inferiority complex")[106] and a fifteen-year-old welder's son affirmed that

> In films I have imitated lots of things in my manner. For instance since I have been going to the pictures I always touch my hat when I meet anybody. I always greet everybody with a smile. When I bump into anybody I always say I am sorry. If I pass in front of anybody I always say excuse-me. I have also learned to become better mannered at the dinner table. In dress I always have a crease in my trousers. I always put grease on my hair and have a parting in it. I always keep my clothes clean and I do not have any pins in them. I always strip to the waist when I wash. I clean my teeth every morning. ... Films have [also] given me knowledge and a lot more ideas in lovemaking.[107]

On the other hand, as we have seen, working-class audiences were equally impressed by Hollywood "message" films. For many young women during the Second World War, the cinema was liberating. They resolved to become an aviatrix after seeing a movie biography of Amy Johnson, or Irene Dunn as a ferry pilot in *A Guy Named Joe*.[108] Women-in-uniform films made one sixteen-year-old shop assistant want to join the auxiliary services, though she did not swallow musicals in which "the girl has both career and her man when in fiction it works out but not in life usually."[109]

Most of the role models were male, of course, but that presented no difficulty to female moviegoers, who could identify with ruggedly masculine characters. The same girls who crossed over to boys' weeklies quite effortlessly imagined themselves as Ray Milland in *Ministry of Fear*, Joseph Cotten in *Journey into Fear*, Frederick March battling gladiators in *The Last Days of Pompeii*, even American marines in *Bataan* and *Guadalcanal Diary* ("I came out of the cinema exhausted because I had been fighting their battle for them" reported a breathless typist).[110] A munitions worker testified that *The Adventures of Mark Twain* reinforced her desire to become a writer.[111] *Trader Horn* "awakened a yearning for travel" in a railwayman's daughter—one of several women who said that the movie made them want to explore the world.[112] A number of working women identified strongly with the Gauguin figure in *The Moon and Sixpence*, played by George Sanders: they too were struggling to escape boring jobs and humdrum homes. "His ambition, determination to get what he wanted and his very unsettled ways impressed me very much, insomuch that I determined to achieve my ambition and become an artist also," explained an ex-nurse. "Not to be the same as him, an artist, but something more, for the love of art itself and for the joy one can gain by expressing one's feelings in paint."[113] One passionate fan of the film was an eighteen-year-old girl stuck at home with well-meaning but suffocating parents, who did not let her use the scholarships she won. Now studying English and elocution, with hopes of becoming an author, she felt that George Sanders

> seemed to me to be in my position. Tied to a home, that was not a home to him, and to a wife who didn't love him for what he was but for what she wanted him to be. He had the courage (I seem to lack it) to cast aside convention and pursue his course whatever the cost to himself or others. The cost was not great, the love he had for his last wife and the joy he got from his achievements made his tragic death seem worth while. This film made me realise more than ever, never to ignore inspiration, whether or not I receive acclaim.[114]

Of all popular media, advertising acquired the most poisonous reputation among the British intelligentsia.[115] H. G. Wells's *Tono-Bungay* (1909) and George Orwell's *Keep the Aspidistra Flying* (1936) portrayed the industry as an insidious and well-financed machine for mass manipulation. But here again an unconscious class bias may have been at work. Since advertising tells the educated classes nothing that they do not already know, and competes for the attention of popular audiences, they inevitably find it banal and mind-numbingly repetitive, an endless blare that drowns out the true and the beautiful. To the uneducated classes, however, it may offer much that is genuinely new and informative. An educated person can reproduce this effect by turning off the television and studying advertisements from an unfamiliar culture or historical period, which can be fascinating to sociologists and inspirational to graphic artists. The evidence here is sketchy and inconclusive, for only a few plebeian memoirists discuss the subject, but they do suggest that advertising could supply Victorian workers with much of the useful knowledge that their betters took for granted, including basic literacy. The tailor-poet Jacob Holkinson (b. 1822), with only three weeks of formal schooling, taught himself to read by studying signboards, handbills, and booksellers' windows.[116] Printer Charles Manby Smith (b. 1804) recognized that cities enjoyed higher literacy not because they necessarily offered better schools than rural areas, but because reading skills were taught and constantly reinforced by the billsticker:

> His handiwork stares the public in the face; and it is a sheer impossibility for a lad who has once learned the art of reading, to lose it in London, unless he be both wilfully blind and destitute of human curiosity. To thousands and tens of thousands, the placarded walls and hoardings of the city are the only school of instruction open to them, whence they obtain all the knowledge they possess of that section of the world and society which does not lie patent to their personal observation. It is thence they derive their estimate of the different celebrities—in commerce, in literature, and in art, of the time in which they live, and are enabled to become in some measure acquainted with the progress of the age. Perhaps few men, even among the best educated, could be found who would willingly let drop the knowledge they have gained, although without intending it, from this gratuitous source.[117]

Even for the destitute, the shopwindows of mid-Victorian London offered a

veritable Great Exhibition, which is perpetually open to all comers, and of which nobody ever tires. It is an awful blunder to suppose that those only profit by the display in shop-windows who are in a position to purchase. Every shop-front is an open volume, which even he that runs may read, while he that stands still may study it, and gather wisdom at the cheapest source, which may be useful for a whole life. To the moneyless million, the shops of London are what the university is to the collegian: they teach them all knowledge; they are history, geography, astronomy, chemistry, photography, numismatics, dynamics, mechanics—in a word, they are science in all its practical developments—and, glorious addition, they are art in all its latest and noblest achievements. While to one class of observers they are a source of inexhaustible amusement, to another they are a source equally inexhaustible of instruction. Therefore it is that the mechanic and artisan, out of work and out of money, wanders along the interminable miles of shop-fronts, peering here, puzzling there, guessing in this place, solving in that, some one or other of the mechanical problems presented to his view. A common thing with men and lads thus circumstanced, is to sally forth in groups, to dissipate the weary hours of enforced idleness by gazing in at the shop-windows, and speculating upon this or that unknown material or contrivance; and guessing or, if practicable, inquiring into the circumstances of its produce or construction.[118]

Thomas Carter was one of the most priggish proletarian evangelists of "useful knowledge:" he extolled Addison and Steele as literary models while denouncing fairy tales as "fabulous and foolish." But in relaxed moments he admitted that he owed his love of reading largely to chapbooks, and he seriously argued that newspaper advertisements were more informative—and not quite as misleading—as the editorial columns. Since they forthrightly trumpeted a bill of goods and made no pretense of objectivity, he could

learn more of human nature and of the tangled web of affairs from these sources than I am able to learn from the most laboured statements of either editors or paid correspondents. While these, in order to bring grist to their mill, are forced to comply with party views and to suppress their own; or are induced to mystify plain questions, so that they may seem to be profoundly learned in political knowledge; the advertising parties write for themselves—throw aside the veil of mystery—ask in good plain English for the reader's cash, and generally give a fair view of what is going on in the regions of their inner man.

Of course advertisers sometimes resorted to "cabalistic phrases" and misleading language, but the ordinary reader could learn to decode these and, in so doing, develop his defenses against all kinds of propaganda.[119] These few examples hardly settle the question, but they do suggest that historians should study audience response directly before they leap to conclusions about the "ideological work" of advertising or any other medium. This chapter has deliberately put forward more questions than answers, more cautions than definitive statements. But at least one clear conclusion does emerge from the available evidence: from *Chambers's Journal* to *The Moon and Sixpence*, British common readers were remarkably adept at appropriating enlightenment and (mostly) harmless entertainment from popular culture.

Chapter Twelve What Was Leonard Bast Really Like?

All the centuries-old tensions between the educated classes and the self-educated classes seem to point toward the conclusion that John Carey reaches in *The Intellectuals and the Masses* (1992). A blunt populist, Carey argues that the fundamental motive behind the modernist movement was a corrosive hostility toward the common reader. Nietzsche, Ortega y Gasset, George Gissing, H. G. Wells, Bernard Shaw, T. S. Eliot, Virginia Woolf, Sigmund Freud, Aldous Huxley, Wyndham Lewis, D. H. Lawrence, Ezra Pound, and Graham Greene all strove to preserve a sense of class superiority by reviling the mean suburban man. They convinced themselves that the typical clerk was subhuman, machinelike, dead inside, a consumer of rubbishy newspapers and canned food.

The intellectuals, Carey argues, had to create this caricature to maintain social distinctions in an increasingly democratic and educated society. By the early twentieth century the Board schools had introduced great literature to the masses, who were buying the shilling classics of Everyman's Library by the million. Workers and clerks had by no means caught up with the educated classes, but some of them were coming uncomfortably close. Many intellectuals felt threatened by the prospect of a more equal distribution of culture: it is telling that the epithet they loved to spit at the masses was not "uneducated," but "half-educated." One could feel a patronizing fondness for the unlettered peasant, but in a society where every man supplies his own philosophy, the philosopher becomes redundant. In 1883 *Punch* published a stunningly frank expression of these anxieties in the form of a cartoon, "Education's Frankenstein—A Dream of the Future." While Board school kids read Ruskin, spout Shakespeare, and sing Wagner, middle-class authors, critics, artists, and lawyers are rendered unemployable and banished to the workhouse. No irony was intended here: the fear was that the 1870 Education Act would succeed in creating an enlightened proletariat.[1] The friction between Hannah More and Ann Yearsley was being repeated on a mass scale.

Some modern writers dispensed with the masses through fantasies of wholesale extermination, often rationalized on eugenic grounds. A more practical means of restoring their elite status was the creation of modernism, a body of literature and art deliberately made too difficult for a general audience. The old autodidacts had built on a foundation of English classics partly because they were so accessible. Robert Collyer grew up in a blacksmith's home with only a few books—*Pilgrim's Progress, Robinson Crusoe*, Goldsmith's histories of England and Rome—but their basic language made them easy to absorb and excellent training for a future clergyman. "I think it was then I must have found the germ ... of my lifelong instinct for the use of simple Saxon words and sentences which has been of some worth to me in the work I was finally called to do."[2] That kind of self-education was possible in the nineteenth century; but in the twentieth, autodidacts discovered that the cultural goalposts had been moved, that a new canon of deliberately difficult literature had been called into existence. The inaccessibility of modernism in effect rendered the common reader illiterate once again, and preserved a body of culture as the exclusive property of a coterie.[3]

Restricting Literacy

Carey is addressing, then, a question of intellectual property. Who should control access to culture and participate in its creation? If knowledge is power, then power, wealth, and prestige depend on preserving inequalities of knowledge. Anthropologist Mary Douglas notes that the drive to maintain differentials of information is present in all societies: "Ethnography suggests that, left to themselves, regardless of how evenly access to the physical means of production may be distributed, and regardless of free educational opportunities, consumers will tend to create exclusive inner circles controlling access to a certain kind of information."[4] Charles Knight missed the mark when he wrote that "knowledge is the common property of the human family—the only property that can be equally divided without injury to the general stock."[5] Like all other goods, the market value of knowledge increases with scarcity. We pay investment analysts, art critics, and clairvoyants for unique insights, not to tell us what everyone already knows. This is not to say that universally distributed knowledge is necessarily valueless. If we were all thoroughly trained in French literature or automotive repair, that knowledge would still have use value to us as individuals; but it would have no exchange value in the marketplace, and professors of French and car mechanics would have to enter job retraining programs. Conversely, the exchange value of knowledge can be enhanced by creating artificial scarcities, monopolies, or oligopolies, through such devices as copyright, encryption, and professional accreditation. As Douglas concludes, the rational economic strategy of the information class is "to erect barriers against entry, to consolidate control of opportunities, and to use techniques of exclusion." Each member of that class must strive to control the discourse, whether it concerns biblical interpretation or women's fashions or literary theory: "Otherwise, his project to make sense of the universe is jeopardized when rival interpretations gain more currency than his own, and the cues that he uses become useless because others have elaborated a different set and put it into circulation."[6]

Jack Goody has shown how "restricted literacy" was used to corner the information market in pre-print societies. The limited circulation of the Koran in West Africa, the magic treatises of medieval Europe, the mysterious religious books of ancient Egypt and Mesopotamia, obscure Pythagorean tracts, Indian gurus claiming special access to spiritual truth, the repudiation of written texts in favor of oral instruction—all are attempts to maintain control over the transmission of knowledge and protect intellectual property.[7] In societies that have not yet invented copyright or the footnote, to publish is to perish: unless the dissemination of literature is restricted, anyone can steal it without paying a user's fee. When India's Mithila College possessed the only manuscript of Gangesa's great work of logic, the *Chintamani*, students were prohibited from copying it— until one of them memorized it and used that knowledge to start a school that effectively competed with Mithila.[8]

In modern societies academics do not hesitate to publish their work, because copyright and rules of citation ensure that they will receive their due professional rewards. But certain kinds of intellectual property are still vulnerable to appropriation. One can copyright literary works but not literary genres: though *The Waste Land, Howl,* and *Of Grammatology* are all protected, anyone is free to enter the business of producing *vers libre*, beat poetry, or deconstructive criticism. Such literature can be protected from imitators, popularizers, critics, and rival schools only through various forms of encryption, such as Latin bibles, Marxist jargon, modernist obscurantism, or postmodernist opacity.

Consumers, however, take a different view of the information marketplace. They prefer to maximize choice and availability, and they will regard claims to special knowledge as an unfair monopolistic practice. The theory of information advanced by Goody and Douglas was in fact laid out much earlier in another anthropological treatise, which was widely read among the British working classes. When Robinson Crusoe learns that Friday worships Benamuckee, a deity who lives in the mountains,

> I ask'd him if he ever went thither, to speak to him; he said no, they never went that were young Men; none went thither but the old Men, who he call'd their *Oowocakee*, that is, as I made him explain it to me, their Religious, or Clergy, and that they went to say *O*, (so he called saying Prayers) and then came back, and told them what *Benamuckee* said: By this I observ'd, That there is *Priestcraft*, even amongst the most blinded ignorant Pagans in the World; and the Policy of making a secret Religion, in order to preserve the Veneration of the People to the Clergy, is not only to be found in the *Roman*, but perhaps among all Religions in the World, even among the most brutish and barbarous Savages.
>
> I endeavour'd to clear up this Fraud, to my Man *Friday*, and told him, that the Pretence of their old Men going up the Mountains, to say *O* to their God *Benamuckee*, was a Cheat, and their bringing Word from thence what he said, was much more so.[9]

Throughout the history of education, Lawrence Stone found the same strategy of intellectual exclusion at work:

> It is precisely because education is so powerful a force in preserving existing social distinctions, that change is always a highly explosive political issue, and is always so bitterly resisted and resented. Thus an upper-class of gentry and successful businessmen securely entrenched in classics-based private schools and universities, and consequently enjoying a monopoly of all the key positions in the society (as in England) is unlikely to welcome the extension and improvement of grammar school facilities for the middle class. Similarly, an urban middle class which monopolizes an extensive classics-based lycée system (as in nineteenth-century France) may well not look favourably on an extension of elementary education, and will certainly oppose any integration of that system into its own. Again, a lower middle class of farmers and shopkeepers enjoying the privilege of education in writing and account-keeping (as in eighteenth-century England) is likely to obstruct any improvement in elementary education which would make the poor their equals and competitors.[10]

One can see that macrohistorical process at work on a microhistorical level in the career of William Gifford (b. 1756). He was apprenticed to a Presbyterian shoemaker who read nothing but religious tracts, all preaching the same dogma, which he used to crushing effect in theological discussions. Armed with Fenning's dictionary, he knew how to encode information in jargon: "His custom was to fix on any word in common use, and then to get by heart the synonym, or periphrasis by which it was explained in the book; this he constantly substituted for the simple term, and as his opponents were commonly ignorant of his meaning, his victory was complete." If the shoemaker's hoard of knowledge capital was meagre, his apprentice had next to none. At this point Gifford had read only some ballads, the black-letter romance *Parismus and Parismenus*, some odd loose magazines of his mother's, the Bible (which he studied with his grandmother), and *The Imitation of Christ* (read to his mother on her deathbed). He then learned algebra by surreptitiously reading Fenning's textbook: his master's son owned the book and had deliberately hidden it from him. Gifford still could not afford pen or paper, so he scratched out algebraic problems on odd bits of leather with a blunted awl.

Even at this abysmal level of poverty, Gifford was able to set up as a small-scale intellectual entrepreneur. He began composing occasional verses—to celebrate the painting of an alehouse signboard, for example. His workmates invited him to recite his poems, and sometimes took up collections that earned him as much as 6d. an evening. "To one who had lived so long in the absolute want of money, such a resource seemed a Peruvian mine," Gifford recalled. His objective in writing poetry was neither truth nor beauty: it was cash, or more precisely, intellectual capital. Everything he earned he reinvested in paper and mathematical texts: "Poetry, even at this time, was no amusement of mine: it was subservient to other purposes; and I only had recourse to it when I wanted money for my mathematical pursuits."

His master could not have been more antagonized if Gifford had set up a rival shop across the street. The apprentice's growing intellectual powers presented a real economic threat: the shoemaker once exploded at Gifford "for inadvertently hitching the name of one of his customers into a rhyme." Gifford tried to conceal his work, without success. The master finally demanded that he surrender his papers, searched his garret, confiscated his books, and warned that any more poetry would bring fearsome consequences. Gifford's literary career would have been strangled at birth, except for an extraordinary change in his fortunes. A local surgeon recognized his talent and organized a subscription to buy him out of his apprenticeship. He attended Exeter College Oxford and went on to translate Juvenal under the patronage of Earl Grosvenor (pension £400 a year). He became editor of the *Anti-Jacobin* and first editor of the *Quarterly Review* (annual salary £1,500, plus two government sinecures worth another £900). As a richly endowed intellectual, he became the most bigoted of Tory critics, notorious for damning any authors who happened to have the wrong politics.[11]

As Francis Place had learned, it was not prudent for a workingman to know more than his employer. George Smith had mastered algebra and geometry at a Lancastrian model school around 1810: he later worked for a Quaker tanner who was stumped by Euclid and asked him to explain it all. Smith agreed, though he was a bit put out that his employer expected free lessons on his employee's time. The tanner immediately ran aground on the first proposition of the first book. "I had strange forebodings of our fate with the second proposition," Smith remembered,

so on the next day I disposed of my dinner as quickly as possible and went to my pupil. As I approached the front of the house I saw him looking out for me with his face pressed against the glass of the window, and before I reached the parlour door I heard him lock it. I turned the knob, but it was fast. I knocked, but got no answer. Euclid, geometry and I were locked out together, and I heard no more from him on the subject.[12]

Until the early nineteenth century, literacy alone had been enough to confer some intellectual distinction. The subsequent expansion of literacy was regarded with apprehension by the educated classes, because it diminished their caste status: a pattern discerned by Alan Richardson among the Romantics[13] and Patrick Brantlinger among the Victorians.[14] By 1830 G. L. Craik noted that,

Among the highest orders of society, the very cheapness of literary pleasures has probably had the effect of making them to be less in fashion than others of which wealth can command a more exclusive enjoyment. Even such distinction as eminence in intellectual pursuits can confer must be shared with many of obscure birth and low station; and on that account alone has doubtless seemed often the less worthy of ambition to those who were already raised above the crowd by accidents of fortune.[15]

Another response to the growing numbers of self-educated workers was to ignore their existence. No such characters appear in any English novel before 1880, except Felix Holt and Alton Locke, who are presented as highly exceptional minds among a generally debased proletariat. Workers might be depicted as respectable, impoverished, depraved, eccentric, pitiable, or criminal—but not thoughtful.[16] The stonemason-poet Hugh Miller noted this blind spot as early as 1849. The lower classes, who once entered literature only as buffoons or pastorals, were now indeed playing a wider range of roles:

The reading public are invited to sympathize in the sorrows and trials of aged labourers of an independent spirit, settling down, not without many an unavailing struggle, into dreaded pauperism; overwrought artizans avenging their sufferings upon their wealthy masters; and poor friendless needle-women bearing up long against the evils of incessant toil and extreme privation, but at length sinking into degradation or the grave. We are made acquainted in tales and novels with the machinery and principles of strike-associations and trades' unions; and introduced to the fire-sides of carriers, publicans, and porters. ... There is no lack of a hearty sympathy on the part of the writers with the feelings of our humbler people; but we are sensible of a feebleness of conception when they profess to grapple with their intellect.

The works of Robert Burns and the autobiography of Benjamin Franklin had portrayed working people with brains, sketching them

in terms very different from what the modern novelist or tale-writer would employ. ... Were a modern tale-writer to describe a poor weaver, forced by lack of employment to quit his comfortless home, and cast himself with his wife and children upon the cold charity of the world, he might bestow upon him keen sensibilities, a depressing sense of degradation, and a feeling of shame; but his thoughts on the occasion would scarce fail to partake of the poverty of his circumstances. When, however, the weaver Tom tells exactly such a story of himself, not as a piece of fiction, but as a sad truth burnt into his memory, we find the keen sensibility and the sense of shame united to thinking of great power, heightened in effect by no stinted measure of the poetic faculty. Now, from our knowledge of such cases, and from a felt want, in our modern fictitious narratives, of what we shall term the inner life of the working-classes, what we would fain recommend is, that the working-classes should themselves tell their own stories.[17]

At the same time and for the same reason, shoemaker-poet John Younger felt compelled to explain in print "how we really subsist, think, feel, and act, in our most circumscribed circumstances, in comparison with the way we have so often been represented in the novels of late years." He had

> to account for, or to make excuse for, one in my circumstances having attempted to write at all, that taste, agreeably to the opinion of many, lying out of the line of a working man's occupation. Indeed, I have often been censured for it by neighbours, even by some professing themselves scholars, as if I were taking undue indulgence from the bondage of circumstances, or intruding as a poacher upon the manor of their appropriation.[18]

Thomas Hardy hardly offered more sympathy to Jude Fawley. His efforts to gain admission to Christminster are depicted as an exercise in futility, motivated partly by selfish social ambition, partly by "the modern vice of unrest." Clearly, he should give up his quest for "special information" and be content with "ordinary knowledge."[19] A novel with that outlook was bound to be less than inspirational to poor scholars. One Coventry millworker and WEA student claimed that he pushed his son to educate himself for a better life, until one morning the boy was found dead in his room, with a phial of poison beside him and *Jude the Obscure* under his pillow. He feared he would fail his examinations, and the story apparently deepened his depression.[20] Another Cornishman, A. L. Rowse, found that the novel only "increased my growing exasperation with the circumstances of my home-life and with the difficulties, indeed the improbability, of my getting to Oxford"—though he did eventually get there.[21]

While the pursuit of literature was emancipating for autodidacts, they did occasionally notice that they were ignored or reviled by some of their favorite authors. V. S. Pritchett ran up against that in a collection of articles by Marie Corelli:

> I read and then stopped in anger. Marie Corelli had insulted me. She was against popular education, against schools, against Public Libraries and said that common people like us made the books dirty because we never washed, and that we infected them with disease. I had never been inside a Public Library but now I decided to go to one. ... I got out [my notebook] and I wrote my first lines of English prose: hard thoughts about Marie Corelli.[22]

Coachman's daughter Anne Tibble was enraged by *The Waste Land*, which she read as a scholarship student at a redbrick university:

> Eliot's neurosis of disillusion was horrifying ... almost utterly invalid. I could even call it evil. ... I didn't care whether *The Waste Land* was an oriental,

unsentimental poem taking hope as psycho-neurosis. I only knew that it was almost utterly without feeling for others, therefore invalid. Eliot showed people as ugly, stupid, shabby, vulgarian, squalid, somehow indecent. But people such as some of those in *The Waste Land* I had been looking at all my life: the "broken fingernails of dirty hands" was meant to repel, to startle readers into seeing working people as rats—slimy, mean, ugly. ... Weren't these my father's and my mother's hands? Hands therefore of so many like them. *The Waste Land* marked the beginning of an era of cynicism and disillusion under which we still labour.

The experience of reading it plunged her into depression, but in the late 1920s it was difficult to express her real feelings about one of the greatest living poets. "I was too much a coward and a cretin to say that in my essay," she later confessed. Instead, she channelled her scholarly energies toward the poetry of John Clare, whose work affirmed the literacy of working people.[23]

This condescension was not always immediately obvious to autodidacts. They considered themselves respectable and intelligent, so when they came across allusions to the uneducated masses, they might assume that the author had others in mind. Joseph Stamper grew up in a rich Lancashire proletarian culture, where workers organized debating clubs and literary societies in pubs, contributing 2d. or 3d. a week toward the bulk purchase of books. His parents patronized the public library, and his mother made him a lifelong opera fan when she took him to Gounod's *Faust*. Young Stamper enjoyed public readings of Dickens, Thackeray, and Scott; and (alongside the *Police News* and *Deadwood Dick*) he consumed W. T. Stead's penny editions of Homer, Pliny, Keats, Longfellow, and Tennyson. Yet in the course of his wide-ranging reading

> I came across phrases that puzzled me, such as "sans-culotte", "shiftless rabble", "dregs of humanity", "ignorant masses". I wondered where all these worthless people lived. I could only think it must be in London or some such place outside my ken. Then one day it dawned on me, these scornful and superior writers were writing about me, and the people who lived in our street. It knocked me sideways for a little time ....

Later, while working at a steel foundry, he went to the public library to ask permission to borrow, for study purposes, three nonfiction books at a time (the usual limit was one). The Chief Librarian was skeptical: "Where *is* the need for study ... in a steel foundry?" "Thinking to sway him to granting the privilege, I told him I'd had two books published," Stamper recalled. "It was a false step, I saw his manner harden, accusation swam into his severe eyes. I was an offender against the unwritten law, I had no right to have books published, I was not a member of the book-writing class. He closed the interview ...."[24]

"Nothing angers me more than to hear some critics dismiss millions of people as the great unthinking 'Admass', or refer to them with contemptuous arrogance as though they had no more sense or sensitivity than a school of mackerel," protested Ted Willis (b. 1918), Bakelite moulder and novelist. "Behind the condescension is the presumption that the critic's own tastes, standards, and way of life are so much more rewarding, so much more elevated and worth while, than those of the man in the street. I must confess that I have not always found this to be so." As a newsboy he had worked for a newsagent who liked to discuss the *Meditations* of Marcus Aurelius and the *Moral Discourses* of Epictetus. With the Labour Party League of Youth he had seen John Gielgud in *Julius Caesar* at the Old Vic, in the 9d. seats.[25]

The Insubordination of the Clerks

For a prime example of the attitude that exasperated Ted Willis, one can turn to Virginia Woolf. Introducing a volume of autobiographical essays by members of the Women's Co-operative Guild, she duly praised their passion for self-education. But she was a touch condescending about their literary talents ("This book is not a book") as well as their undisciplined tastes in reading: "They read Dickens and Scott and Henry George and Bulwer Lytton and Ella Wheeler Wilcox and Alice Meynell and would like 'to get hold of any good history of the French Revolution, not Carlyle's, please,' and B. Russell on China, and William Morris and Shelley and Florence Barclay and Samuel Butler's Note Books—they read with the indiscriminate greed of a hungry appetite, that crams itself with toffee and beef and tarts and vinegar and champagne all in one gulp."[26] One Guildwoman highlighted the cultural chasm separating her from Mrs. Woolf when she described her own bookshelves, crammed with all the standard Victorians: "Nothing modern you see," she conceded. She had read some contemporary novelists, venturing as far as Conrad and Wells, but "in many cases the characters do not 'stay with' me." Her son made the mistake of presenting her with Michael Arlen's *The Green Hat*, and compounded it by asking her opinion, "which he got very forcibly."[27] And when Mrs. Woolf later argued (in *Three Guineas*) that women should refuse to work in munitions factories, Mary Agnes Smith, a weaver who had taken courses with the WEA and Hillcroft College, reminded her that that was not an option for someone on the dole.[28]

　　Leonard Woolf shared his wife's snobberies. He had lived for a time in Ceylon with a magistrate named Dutton, who was reviled by some of the resident Englishmen as "A bloody unwashed Board School bugger, who doesn't know one end of a woman from the other." Though a socialist, Woolf cheerfully agreed that "there was some truth in the portrait." Bad enough that they were professional colleagues, but Dutton had the presumption to write dreadful poetry, play Mozart and musical comedy on the same piano, and read Home University Library books. Of course, Woolf assures us, there is no comparing his own Cambridge education with Dutton's self-education: "Literature, art, poetry, music, history, mathematics, science were pitchforked into his mind in chaotic incomprehensibility. When later on in Ceylon I became an extremely incompetent shooter of big game and, in cutting up the animals killed by me, saw the disgusting, semi-digested contents of their upper intestines, I was always reminded of the contents of Dutton's mind."

Dutton also reminded Woolf of Leonard Bast, the clerk of E. M. Forster's *Howards End*.[29] For all his gentle liberalism, Forster embraced the class prejudices of modernist intellectuals. Bast is anxious and envious among the rentier intelligentsia, and his attempts to acquire culture are hopeless. Forster frankly stamps him "inferior to most rich people." He is "not as courteous as the average rich man, nor as intelligent, nor as healthy, nor as lovable." He plays the piano "badly and vulgarly," and what is worse, he plays Grieg.[30] In literary conversations he is only capable of repeating cant phrases and dropping names. The problem, says Margaret Schlegel, is that "His brain is filled with the husks of books, culture—horrible; we want him to wash out his brain."[31] (Note that the term "brainwashing" did not originate in the Korean War.)

Bast is literally crushed and killed by books. He really should have been a mindless shepherd or ploughman like his grandfather. Unfortunately, sighs Forster, rural laborers today are typically "half clodhopper, half board-school prig," but get rid of that education and "they can still throw back to a nobler stock, and breed yeomen."[32] Of course, they would be mowing hay for Squire Forster, who thinks there is much to be said for "the feudal ownership of land."[33] Though it is usually read as a critique of the class system, *Howards End* is fragrant with nostalgia for a rigid social hierarchy. "It is part of the battle against sameness," Margaret assures us. "Differences—eternal differences, planted by God in a single family, so that there may always be colour; sorrow perhaps, but colour in the daily grey." And what advice does she offer Helen about Leonard, the murdered father of her child?

"Forget him."
"Yes, yes," says Helen, "but what has Leonard got out of life?"
"Perhaps an adventure," shrugs Margaret.
"Is that enough?"
"Not for us. But for him."[34]

What more does the man want? And that is the last we hear of Leonard Bast.

Forster succumbed to cultural despair after the First World War, which raised both wages and income taxes. "The class to which ... I belong is sliding into the abyss," he protested, rather prematurely, in 1919.

A certain amount of precious stuff, a certain tradition of behaviour and culture will perish. ... At Cambridge scarcely any one takes Classics—it's all Science. Salaries of Professors and Readers remain stationary while those of boiler-makers, plate rollers go up, are reaching them, passing them. There's nothing to be done—and as a matter of fact I do record my unenthusiastic vote for Labour, because, for the wrong reasons, it wants some of the right things, and having attained the right things, it may possibly adopt the right reasons. But it's so puzzling and queer to feel that one's the last little flower of a vanishing civilisation, so exasperating to know that one doesn't understand what is happening, so chilling to realise that in the future people probably won't mind whether they understand or not, and that this attempt to apprehend the universe through the senses and the mind is a luxury the next generation won't be able to afford.[35]

He remained convinced that boiler-makers could not use their senses and minds properly, even when his own senses told him otherwise. A year later he spent a weekend in Ramsgate with one of his lovers, a miner named Frank Vicary:

We sat about in shirt sleeves and loafed at street corners talking to other miners, also went to a party where the host (a miner) played Scriabine, Grieg, &tc—with no great charm, but with thunderous execution. I liked the miners personally, but could not see that they were after anything but money of which (if you compare them with the other manual labourers and even make allowance for the special discomfort and risk) they have already their fair share, I think. Sentimentally I am on their side, but my intellect argues that clerks, university teachers &tc, are really the oppressed class today.[36]

Forster evidently forgot what he had written in the first sentence while he was writing the second. Obviously, the miners *were* after something other than money—modern music, for example. Though Forster had a number of working-class lovers, he consistently chose men who were his intellectual inferiors, and then sneered at their insensitivity: "Imaginative passion, love, doesn't exist in the lower classes."[37] He could only deal comfortably with them on a feudal basis, as peasants to be patronized. In that spirit he set up Frank Vicary as a Gloucestershire farmer. After the venture failed Forster admitted that it was a self-serving fantasy: he imagined himself "toddling there in old age, looked after by the robust and grateful lower classes."[38] Yet he was horrified by a very successful effort to send millions of city workers back to the land—as dreadful suburbanites rather than picturesque yeomen. In a 1946 broadcast talk he complained that an unspoilt area around Stevenage was to be the site of a satellite town: "Meteorite town would be a better name. It has fallen out of a blue sky." He knew this was Leonard Bast's chance to escape his slum flat, assuming he had not been rendered homeless by the Luftwaffe. "I think of working-class friends in north London who have to bring up four children in two rooms, and many are even worse off than that. But I cannot equate the problem."[39] (Perhaps he was going to say "I cannot connect.")

But was Leonard Bast so culturally impoverished? Was the character Forster created an authentic representation of that vast and growing army of Edwardian clerks? For an answer, we can look to the memoirs left by young men who were born into the working classes around 1890, attended Board schools, read cheap editions of the classics, enjoyed 2s. concerts, and took one step up the social ladder into the lower reaches of the middle class. The contrast is astonishing. Those of us who only know Leonard Bast from *Howards End* would scarcely recognize the man in his self-portrait.

Forster could not believe that a clerk might be genuinely thrilled by literature. (That prejudice is not dead among academics even today.) Aping his betters, Bast pathetically grinds away at his Ruskin and puts in time at concerts. They mean nothing to him, yet he is always hoping for a "sudden conversion, a belief ... which is particularly attractive to a half-baked mind. ... Of a heritage that may expand gradually he had no conception: he hoped to come to Culture suddenly, much as the Revivalist hopes to come to Jesus."[40] Yet that is precisely how Culture came to autodidacts: their memoirs commonly climax with The Book That Made All The Difference. For the leisured classes, a gradually expanding intellect is certainly a preferable approach to learning, but the self-educated have only limited time to make up enormous gaps. They must move more quickly, they have hungrier minds, and they will passionately embrace any book that opens up a new intellectual landscape. For W. J. Brown (b. 1894), a plumber's son, the epiphany happened around age ten, when an elderly sea captain at Margate allowed him to use his personal library. "It wasn't an incident," Brown explained

It was, in an almost religious sense, an "experience". ... Consciousness does not expand slowly and regularly, but, as it seems to me, in great leaps. The mind forms a certain conception of the world it lives in. ... Then one comes across a fresh writer—ancient or modern—or a new acquaintance—and suddenly there is a vast expansion of consciousness, a lifting of the mind to a new level, ... a thrill beyond description, ... a moment of triumphant ecstasy. So with my admission into the world of books.[41]

The author most likely to produce that kind of inspiration was, sure enough, John Ruskin. Forster considered him hopelessly irrelevant to Bast's mean little life, but if the clerk had been allowed to speak for himself, he might have been surprisingly eloquent:

... here was another valiant, another innovator, another pioneer, staking out new claims for individual identity. The fact of Ruskin's gallant and successful defence of Turner the great landscape painter, and his still more valiant stand against the orthodox economists, cast a spell over me which was irresistible. ... To read *Modern Painters, The Seven Lamps of Architecture, The Stones of Venice, The Crown of Wild Olives,* was a kind of aesthetic intoxication. It was an experience in which the glamour of his rich literary style held sway over the critical sense. He says things with a beauty that enamours the mind of the idea that they must be true. No one—it appeared to me—ever laid out the long passages of prose with a nearer approach to those subtle delicacies of structure, the balancings and castings forward and glancings back by which musicians take and keep the ear. He had that singular gift of writing audibly. As one reads some of his sentences, the lips moved to frame the words they seemed to set to sound. Some of those sentences have a sheer sensuous loveliness that almost silences the mind's demand for intellectual significance; like that most beautiful passage written late in life and beginning: "morning breaks, as I write, over these Coniston hills", which in its pensive and mournful lustre is as glorious as a great painting or a great song. ... He takes us out on a day's journey from the dusty towns, and shows our affinity with the flowing stream, and excites our soul to commune with the rustling leaves. ... Ruskin strenuously combated the tendency to confine art to within its own domain. This art prophet looked at art as a philosopher, not merely as an art critic. He saw how art is inextricably bound up with all phases of human life. ... The longer he lived the farther he was carried away from the conception of art as a something to be confined within stereotyped borders; to be nurtured to appeal to certain specified tastes. ... Art must justify itself by human service. ... We are left to choose as to whether art is to be confined to the whim and caprice of the connoisseur; to while away the time of the merely indolent; to serve the purpose of a merely aesthetic taste; or whether it shall be used as a vehicle for the purpose of educating, elevating, and ennobling human character.[42]

The actual author was Chester Armstrong (b. 1868), a checkweighman in a Northumberland mining village. The lesson he derived from Ruskin strikingly resembles the message of *Howards End*: a rejection of the rentier aestheticism of the Schlegel sisters for an art that is connected with philosophy, connected with social service, connected with men and women of all classes, connected with life itself. Perhaps Forster's real anxiety was that Bast would find nothing new in *Howards End*—that clerks could discover on their own much the same truths in the Everyman *Unto This Last*.

In 1906 the first Labour MPs cited Ruskin, more often than anyone else, as the author who had moulded their minds. Will Crooks quoted him in support of old age pensions,[43] while *Unto This Last* inspired F. W. Jowett to agitate for improved primary education.[44] Oldham millworker J. R. Clynes, the future lord privy seal, spent 1s. he could ill afford for a secondhand copy of *The Seven Lamps of Architecture*:

How that book enthralled me with the great beauty of its style! For even then, when I was not yet eighteen years of age, the suggestiveness of sound, the grace and nobility of phrase with which these authors clothed their thoughts, impressed me far more deeply than did the thoughts themselves. ... For many weeks I read and re-read this one book, and so illumining was the love I held for it that, before I had perused it the third time, its every subtlety of meaning was as much my own intimate possession as a young lover's memory of his virgin kiss is his. ... To this day that one volume of Ruskin's is the dearest book in all English literature to me![45]

The intellectual awakening of one Beeston engineer (b. 1893) took place when his father-in-law, a trade unionist, presented him with *Unto This Last* and *The Seven Lamps of Architecture*. Up until this moment his reading had been limited to penny dreadfuls, his father's newspaper, and a Sunday school prize biography of Abraham Lincoln, but now

> Ruskin began to implant in my mind a positive philosophy, the virtue of work, the need for a new standard of values, that man is a creative being, hammered in subsequently by the thoughts of Benedetto Croce, digested at Ruskin College. I became an honest seeker after truth rather than a rebel with a chip on his shoulder, and one with a growing appetite for reading and for study opportunities.[46]

A lab assistant (b. c. 1872) could not afford *Unto This Last*, but found it such "a revelation" that he copied it out and bound it by hand.[47] As late as 1950, Roger Dataller overheard two steelworkers discussing Ruskin on a South Yorkshire bus.[48] One silk millworker quoted Ruskin's preface to *The Story of Ida* to legitimize the whole project of working-class autobiography: "The lives we need to have written for us are of the people whom the world has not thought of, far less heard of, who are yet doing most of its work, and of whom we can best learn how it can best be done."[49]

For autodidacts, almost any one of the English classics could produce that kind of epiphany—but not usually anything modernist. W. J. Brown was introduced to literature by *Robinson Crusoe, She, The Last of the Mohicans*, and *Around the World in Eighty Days*, and he never moved far beyond that level. He tried *The Idiot* and *The Brothers Karamazov*, but found them too depressing, perhaps because his life was anything but Dostoevskian.[50]

Brown worked as a boy clerk in the Post Office Savings Bank at West Kensington for something under 15s. a week. Modernist texts, from *Howards End* to Bernard Shaw's *Misalliance*, have consistently depicted the clerk as a prisoner, trapped in a suffocating office and a mind-killing job. The clerks themselves, however, offer a radically different portrayal of Edwardian office life. A surprising number of them found their careers intellectually stimulating. Granted, we are relying here on autobiographical evidence, which may be untypical. No doubt there were thousands of clerks whose brains were numbed by years of desk work, and therefore lacked the energy for memoir-writing or any other creative activity.

Those clerks who did leave behind literary works probably also had the drive and imagination to rise above the kind of office routine that would have anaesthetized others. One correspondent to *T. P.'s Weekly*, a penny literary review for self-improvers, inspected several branches of his bank and reported that "practically every bank clerk" read the paper; while another letter to the editor complained that many of his fellow bank clerks were interested in nothing but sports, crime news, and perhaps a popular novel.[51] We can conclude that many Edwardian clerks were intellectuals: their memoirs are simply too numerous and too enthusiastic to dismiss entirely. The authors were not isolated or alienated: they depict themselves as part of a large and lively community of philosopher-accountants. Along with schoolteaching and journalism, clerical work attracted the brightest Board school graduates, if only because no better careers were yet open to them. Already, the best minds were being skimmed off the working classes and concentrated in offices, where they often achieved a critical intellectual mass.

W. J. Brown, for example, would arise early each morning, study for an hour, row a bit on the lake in Battersea Park, breakfast at 8:00 a.m., take a brisk forty-minute walk to work, and do his routine but painless job from 9:00 a.m. to 4:00 p.m. Then, after tea, he would enjoy "five glorious hours of freedom" reading Darwin, Huxley, and Tennyson's *In Memoriam* at the Battersea Public Library: "I had then, I think, the happiest days of my life." Brown worked in a huge room with 200 other boy clerks. That recalls the opening scene of Billy Wilder's film *The Apartment*, which conjures up the darkest nightmare of the twentieth-century intellectual: the fear of submergence in a mass of unthinking humanity. But working-class writers usually felt quite at home in that situation. As Brown put it,

> I had the elementary schoolboy's love of crowds, the slum kid's love of the prolific life of the mass. And here I was back in the mass .... There was no rule against talking, and as, after a while, the work itself could be done mechanically, without engaging more than a fraction of one's conscious mind, conversation went on all the day long. Two hundred boys, coming from many different parts of the country, freely intermingling, exchanging experiences and ideas with each other, can act as a tremendous educational force one upon the other. We discussed, argued, and disputed interminably; approving, questioning and debating every proposition under the sun, and in the process adding enormously to our stock of ideas and knowledge.[52]

The West Kensington Post Office Savings Bank was Brown's university, and his Oxford Union as well, for his debating skills won him recognition among his fellow boy clerks. He organized 3,000 of them into a union, persuaded a Royal Commission to redress some of their grievances, and went on to become an important trade unionist and Labour MP.[53] No wonder Brown failed to appreciate Dostoevsky. He much preferred the autobiography of Benjamin Franklin.

Another boy clerk at the Post Office Savings Bank confirmed that it was not difficult to "do more than an hour's work in an hour, and then surreptitiously read a study book or a novel. Kindly bosses generally winked at this proceeding." In a few years he had worked through all of Carlyle ("even his indigestible *Frederick the Great*, and that twice") and advanced to the Second Division of the Civil Service, which,

> in unexpected ways, … led to a fuller life. No one who has not lived the life of a young man in a big office can realize how intensely the life can be led. True, there are hours of dull work, though even that can be mitigated by devising rapid methods of doing it. But there is the association of a number of young and eager minds, all reaching out in different directions, a number of characters in the shaping, all experimenting.

A coworker was familiar with the art galleries of Europe, as well as French and Italian literature:

> It was a pleasure to listen to his talk and I am sure I sucked in more knowledge than any professor at a university could have imparted. No doubt it was less perfectly digested, but it was his, acquired by himself and poured out like a fresh and untroubled spring.
> There were many readers amongst us. We philosophised, we talked history and politics and literature and were altogether gloriously uplifted.

There was a certain quota of mindless routine,

> but most of us had two halves to our brains. One went on rapidly calculating, or directing the hand in its writing, while the other launched out on the splendid adventures of the mind. I myself could cast up long columns of figures, or rather cast them down, which is a quicker method, with perfect accuracy, and talk incessantly with my neighbour about Oliver Cromwell or Mahomet. Most of us had this capacity in greater or less degree, and the quicker workers often lent a hand to the slower. It was a good life, though exasperating at times.[54]

V. S. Pritchett found the same adventure of the mind as an office boy for a leather factory. He relished the disinterested intellectual pleasure of learning the business, much as Defoe had in *The Complete English Tradesman*. And far from stifling his dreams of becoming a writer, his work brought him into contact with customers and workers who had serious literary interests:

> There was the tycoon with his Flaubert—whom I did not read for years—there was Beale, the leather dresser, who recited Shakespeare at length, as we went

through the skivers on the top floor; there was Egan, our foreman, ... who, in between calling orders to the men and going over his weighing slips, would chat to me about Dickens and Thackeray. ... There was a leather belting manufacturer who introduced me to literary criticism.[55]

One of the most successful of the intellectual clerks was Joseph Toole (b. 1887), the son of a Salford tramworker, who became a Labour MP and Lord Mayor of Manchester. After a miserable Catholic school education ("merely instruction classes with a view to one's later removal to a factory or any blind-alley job") periodic unemployment allowed him to study in the Manchester Reference Library. There he discovered Adam Smith, Ricardo, Herbert Spencer, Huxley, Mill, Emerson, Dickens, Morris, Blatchford, Shaw, Wells, and of course John Ruskin, without suffering any of Leonard Bast's literary indigestion. Quite the opposite: "Study always left me with a deep feeling that there was so much amiss with the world. It seemed that it had been started at the wrong end, and that it was everybody's business to put the matter right." His mates, who saw no value in the great books, accepted the status quo "as God-given and never to be altered. Fatalism run riot."

Toole found liberation in the insurance business. "This was the period when the fortunes of most of the large insurance companies were laid," he later recalled, "and the offices were keen to find any man who could use a pen, tell a plausible story, look presentable, work well, and was all the better if he had the confidence of his neighbours." Moreover, "No job a man can undertake will give him the same insight into the everyday life of the common people as does the insurance business," which offered an unequaled education in economics and sociology. Toole hated squeezing premiums out of poor clients, hated the constant pressure to round up new customers, but otherwise "I had a good time in the insurance world. In no time promotion came my way, but the great feature about the work was that you were not tied to a clock or the buzzer of the workshop. The liberty it gave one presented wonderful chances to study, either by delving into books or attending at the theatre and improving one's mind." Toole enjoyed productions of Sudermann, Galsworthy, Shaw, Stanley Houghton, and Harold Brighouse at Miss Horniman's Repertory Company. He even saw private subscription performances of Ibsen plays that had been banned by the Lord Chamberlain. Though doing well in the insurance business, he was not uncritical of capitalism: for a time he read Marx and joined the Social Democratic Federation.[56]

In the same city, Neville Cardus was equally enjoying his work as a junior clerk for a marine insurance agent. He scented nautical romance in the phrase he copied out in every policy: " ... of the seas, storms, floods, pirates, jettison, letters of marque." Nominally the office hours were 9:30 a.m. to 5:00 p.m., but often there was not much work, so he read at his desk or escaped to the Manchester Reference Library. For Cardus, whose clerk's salary never rose above £1 a week, Manchester was a city of inexhaustible cultural riches. One could attend a new Galsworthy play on Monday, a Brodsky Quartet concert on Tuesday, see the French actress Réjane at a Wednesday matinée, the Hallé Orchestra on Thursday, and on Friday Ibsen's *Ghosts*.[57] He met with friends at a Lyons café for poached eggs on toast and tea (6d.) and argued passionately over

> Elgar, Shaw, Wells, Ibsen, Nietzsche, Strauss, Debussy, the French Impressionists; our first tastes of Stendahl, the de Goncourts, J-K Huysmans—these last were rather late reaching England, or at any rate, Manchester; then, before our sight had become accustomed to the fresh vista, the Russians swept down on us—Dostoevsky, Turgenev, Tchekov, Moussorgsky, Rimsky-Korsakov, and the ballet. It was a renaissance; the twentieth century opened on a full and flowing sea; thus we emerged from the Victorian Age.
>
> There were not enough hours to the day for a young man. We never went straight home after a new play by Shaw, after *Gerontius*, after the A flat symphony, after Kreisler had played the Elgar violin concerto for the first time, after *Tristan*, after Strauss's *Salome* with Aino Akté in it. We walked the city streets; we talked and talked …, not to air our economic grievances, not to "spout" politics and discontent, but to relieve the ferment of our minds or emotions after the impact of *Man and Superman*, *Elektra*, *Riders to the Sea*, *Pélleas and Mélisande*, *Scheherazade*, *Prince Igor*.[58]

Why isn't there a scene like that in *Howards End*? Thomas Burke, who grew up in poverty in Poplar, hated the condescension of "sleekly prosperous West End novelists" toward East Enders. As he wrote in 1932, "One of our 'intellectual' novelists recorded recently, with a note of wonder, that on his visiting a Whitechapel home the daughters of the house were reading Marcel Proust and a volume of Tchekov's comedies. Why the wonder?" Burke pointed to the Bethnal Green and Whitechapel Art Galleries, the well-used public libraries, the proliferating literary circles, and the popular concerts at the People's Palace.[59]

Forster's novel stands in a long tradition of anti-urbanism in English literature, traced by Raymond Williams in *The Country and the City*. In Q. D. Leavis one sees the same nostalgia for the rural dialects recorded by Hardy and George Bourne, coupled with denunciations of "the suburban idiom spoken around us and used by journalists."[60] But it was not a tradition that extended to the working-class intelligentsia. Eager for self-education, they embraced the brilliance of metropolitan life. Where a middle-class intellectual might feel engulfed and oppressed by the urban masses, the same crowds could be endlessly stimulating to proletarian writers, many of whom were refugees from the provinces. "Wonderful London! What a school for learning! What a field for training! What a sphere for service!" sang printer William Lax (b. 1868), brought up in a small Lancashire mining village.[61] Why, asked Thomas Burke, had no English composer attempted to capture the spirit of a city crowd, as Massenet did in "Southern Town"? "I do not want the flowery mead or the tree-covered lane or the insect-ridden glade—

at least, not for long," he protested, "and I hate that dreadful hollow behind the little wood. Give me six o'clock in the evening and a walk from the City to Oxford Circus, through the soft Spring or the darkling Autumn, with festive feet whispering all around you, and your heart filled with that grey-green romance which is London."[62]

V. S. Pritchett enjoyed nothing more than errands to exotic Bermondsey:

I had a special pleasure in the rank places like those tunnels and vaults under the railway: the smells above all made me feel importantly a part of this working London. Names like Wilde's Rents, Cherry Garden Street, Jamaica Road, Dockhead and Pickle Herring Street excited and my journeys were not simply street journeys to me: they were like crossing the desert, finding the source of the Niger. London was not a city; it was a foreign country as strange as India.[63]

Chaim Lewis found that his small Jewish neighborhood in Soho "seemed to grow up with me and keep pace with my own expanding interests. It was as though my awakening senses had set the sleeping neighbourhood throbbing by its ears. It rose to greet and nourish each new interest," as when he discovered the bookshops of Charing Cross Road. Forster was certain that Leonard Bast would be better off as a peasant, but Lewis knew that "Only the multilateral life of a city's centre can rise to the occasion of an adolescence."[64] V. W. Garratt, who migrated to London from Birmingham after the First World War, immersed himself in the "brotherhood of books" at the British Museum. Far from T. S. Eliot's city of faceless masses, London offered ordinary people unequaled scope for identity and liberty:

From the moment I entered it it became my spiritual home. The splendid paradox of sharing its surging life and law and order, with a fuller sense of one's individuality and freedom than is to be gained in the smallest village, gives it an atmosphere from which no provincial visitor can ever escape. Enter London with a friendly heart and the way is open for it to be friendly to you. No other city shows such good manners, and whether you want to draw on the knowledge of a bus conductor or on the patience and goodwill of the multifarious drivers on the road, you will get what you want without fuss or excitement. And where else can you find such large-hearted tolerance of freaks and foibles that help to make up its cosmopolitan life? Individuality can spread its plumage without public restraint and you can as well stand on your head in the Strand as use it to express an opinion without the danger of having it knocked off. Wherever I live I shall be a naturalized Londoner to the end of my days.[65]

Frederick Rogers (b. 1846), the East End bookbinder, felt as keenly as Jude Fawley the sense of being a "trespasser" in Oxford. But he was not envious, because "London and its opportunities were educating me as universities do other men." It too had dreamy spires: as a sandwich-boy he had found shelter in historic churches, which "became centres of historical knowledge to me as I grew older." Later, he made good use of the Guildhall Library and the University Extension movement, studying history, English literature, and enough physiology to publish an article in a medical journal. At Toynbee Hall he joined a Shakespeare class and organized an Elizabethan Society.[66] "In modern London a navvy's lot is not so much worse than a millionaire's," observed William Margrie (b. 1877), a Camberwell paperhanger. "The navvy can feast his eyes on the world's masterpieces at the National Gallery, Hampton Court, Tate Gallery, and Dulwich. He can obtain Shakespeare, Dante, Shelley, Milton, Dickens, Scott for a few shillings, or read them in the public library for nothing. He can enjoy grand opera and Shakespeare at the Old Vic for sixpence. London is a perpetual feast of architecture, and that costs nothing at all."[67] Printer's apprentice T. A. Jackson found the cityscape saturated with literary allusions:

> To walk Fleet Street and to explore the Temple was to live again in the *Fortunes of Nigel*—was not I, too, a London apprentice as was jolly Jan Vin?—or in *Pendennis*, or more sombrely, in *Bleak House*. The street and alleyway names took on the life of the novels and the novels took on the life and movement of the streets. And the river beyond, with ships visible from Blackfriars and beyond the Southwark and London Bridge ... was near enough to the veritable ocean to add its confirmation to Marryat, Smollett, and Defoe. There were still coffee-houses, so-called, sufficiently like those of the *Spectator* to bring its pages back to life, and to receive from those pages their benediction of grace.[68]

There were female Basts as well, though opportunities for young women only really opened up during the manpower shortages of the First World War. On 18s. a week Stella Davies paid 12s. for room and board in the southern suburbs of Manchester, 3d. for her National Insurance premium, "and managed to have a very good time indeed with the remaining five and ninepence." She attended free organ recitals at the Town Hall and concerts at the University Settlement in Ancoats. For 6d. she could get standing room at the Hallé Orchestra or gallery seats at Miss Horniman's Gaiety Theatre.[69] Baker's daughter Edna Bold (b. 1904) found Manchester's "Lowryesque townscape" more stultifying, but she attended a vast range of cultural events: midday concerts at Houldsworth Hall and opera conducted by Sir Thomas Beecham, as well as public lectures on lexicography, More's *Utopia*, educational reform, "Russia before the Revolution," art appreciation, and "Modern Woman."[70] Raised by a Lancashire farm worker, Margaret Penn (b. 1896) was thrilled to emigrate to Edwardian London and work in a grim bookstore accounting office. The pay was miserable, but she enjoyed the attention of the otherwise all-male staff, attended meetings of the Fabian Society and the Women's Social and Political Union, was invited to bohemian parties and the Cafe Royal, even modeled for artist Nina Hamnett.[71]

"I'm so fed up with reading and hearing about the doleful thirties," Elizabeth Ring protested in 1975. "Looking back on that time, ... I am reaffirmed in my belief that every poor person should live in London. ... We had the cultural world on our doorstep." Starting at age eight, she attended free concerts at Northampton Institute, Grotrian Hall, and Wigmore Hall. From its 1931 opening she saw opera and ballet three times a week at Sadler's Wells, in the wildly appreciative 6d. gallery. "We had no technical knowledge, no discrimination, nothing by which to judge these young dancers," she admitted, "but we felt that something wonderful had happened in Islington, and we were prepared to become hysterical in support of it. The Sadler's Wells wasn't just a theatre to my generation, it was more a way of life." There was also outdoor Shakespeare and ballet in Regent's Park, Prom Concerts at Queen's Hall, and Gielgud's *Hamlet* on twofers. Her father, an unskilled laborer, periodically disappeared on sexual escapades, but between times he took her to see *The Beggar's Opera* and introduced her to the work of Bernard Shaw. She summed it up by quoting the philosopher-longshoreman Eric Hoffer: "It is in the city that man became human. In the crowded, stinking little streets. No noble conception, no great idea, was conceived outside a city."[72]

The Bridge

Modernists were not always insensitive to the wonders of mass urban life (one thinks of *Mrs. Dalloway*) but they rarely had anything positive to say about the suburbs. John Carey has analyzed that phobia in some depth.[73] While millions, in Britain and the United States, voted with their mortgages for suburban villas, the university-educated intelligentsia looked on in horror. Matthew Arnold set the tone with his classic dismissal of commuters shuttling endlessly "from an illiberal, dismal life at Islington to an illiberal, dismal life at Camberwell."[74] In *The Waste Land*, the army of clerks trudging toward London Bridge Station are the living dead:

A crowd flowed over London Bridge, so many,
I had not thought death had undone so many.

What is remarkable is how many plebeian writers seized on that passage and insisted that Eliot had it all wrong. As an office boy V. S. Pritchett went home each night from that station, and found truth and beauty in the porters' announcements:

To myself, at that age, all places I did not know, seemed romantic and the lists of names were, if not Miltonic, at any rate as evocative as those names with which the Georgian poets filled up their lines. I would stare admiringly, even enviously, at the porter who would have to chant the long line to Bexley Heath;

or the man who, beginning with the blunt and challenging football names of Charlton and Woolwich would go on to comic Plumstead and then flow forward over his long list till his voice fell to the finality of Greenhythe, Northfleet and Gravesend; or the softer tones of St. Johns, Lewisham, and Blackheath. And to stir us up were the powerful trains—travelling to distances that seemed as remote as Istanbul to me—expresses that went to Margate, Herne Bay, Rochester and Chatham. I saw nothing dingy in this. The pleasure of my life as an office boy lay in being one of the London crowd and I actually enjoyed standing in a compartment packed with fifteen people on my way to Bromley North.[75]

Thomas Burke went so far as to write a travelog of the London suburbs, places

that every good Londoner, and every student of the human heart, should visit. You go and stare at some crumbling pile made by some predatory prelate some five hundred years ago, and from your rubber-necking you offer yourself some manufactured thrill. It's all wrong. The true thrill should come when you look at the new suburb and its half-built roads and houses, and remember that Mr. Wilkinson has taken that little house which still wants windows and is not yet connected to the main drainage, and is waiting to take his bride into it; that there they will begin their married life, and there will the young Wilkinsons be born. ... To ignore such places as these is to mark yourself Philistine.[76]

In what was supposed to be a cultural wasteland, Burke found an array of literary societies attended by clerks, shop assistants, and workers. True, like Leonard Bast, these people often resorted to "the worn platitudes upon the worn novelists and essayists, the cobbled summaries of the messages of the philosophers, the solemn introductions to the beauties of established poets. But to the pupils and teachers alike," Burke reminds us, "these things are shockingly new."[77]

Over the Bridge, the title of Richard Church's autobiography, not only alludes to Eliot: it reminds us to consider which end of the bridge we are entering. For a metropolitan intellectual, it may be the portal of a suburban Hades. For Church (b. 1893), educated and raised in south London (as for Alfred Kazin, born on the wrong side of the Brooklyn Bridge), it was the high road to literary success. Here was a Leonard Bast who bought Ruskin's *Lectures on Architecture and Painting* when it was first published in Everyman's Library (1907) and, contra Forster, found it an "explosive" revelation. His parents never purchased a book, but a few years later, with his first wage packet of 15s., he bought Palgrave's *Golden Treasury* in the World's Classics edition. A postman's son, Church remembered his inner-suburban world as warm and secure, "a pocket of civilisation utterly quiet and self-sufficient."[78] He once entertained adolescent dreams of becoming a "mephisthophelean" artist, "ready to claim a larger authority over my fellow-creatures, over circumstances kind or averse, over the very laws of right and wrong," but that was not to be. Though he won a scholarship to Camberwell Art School, his father pressured him to give it up and sit for the Civil Service exam. Church dreaded the day he had to report for work at the Land Registry, which he imagined to be something out of *Bleak House*.

He was gratefully surprised to discover that the living death of clerkdom was more a literary cliché than a reality: "The multitudes of cultured men whom I met in the Civil Service, friends, advisers, monitors, served me in those first years in lieu of a university, helping me to educate myself, to enlarge my range of mind and experience, and finally supporting me in the heady and dangerous adventure of commencing author." Church rose every morning at 5 a.m., read until 7 a.m., clocked in at the office from 9 a.m. to 4 p.m., did a bit more reading on His Majesty's time, was home again by 5 p.m., and continued to read until midnight. He attended lunch-hour organ recitals at St. Clement Dane's on The Strand. He could stand and read in bookshops as long as he occasionally bought a shilling classic. He transferred to the Custom House in Billingsgate Market, where his colleagues up to the rank of director supported his work in poetry. One officer subsidized his first book of verse; another gave him Marlowe's plays for his twenty-first birthday. The offices were just below Eliot's London Bridge. Far from being a wasteland, they provided Church with the raw material for his first novel, *The Porch* (1937), which won the Femina Vie Heureuse Prize.[79] He had no reason to envy Oxbridge, because the Civil Service offered a livelier literary milieu:

> The ghosts of Charles Lamb, Thomas Love Peacock, Anthony Trollope, and Austin Dobson still haunted its corridors. A living novelist lurked in its inner shrine, the Treasury, and a young poet in the Board of Trade, both of them later to rise to eminence in the hierarchy of the administration. Dramatic critics, black-and-white artists, longshore writers, roosted in the Government departments, pretending to ignore the larger reputations which they were making in the outside world. Indeed the Civil Sevice was recognised as a shelter for younger sons, cranks, eccentrics, misfits, and persons with a vocation; members incapable of holding their own, and unwilling to compete, in an increasingly commercial and industrial world. ... Painters, musicians, fellow-poets, revealed themselves [in the Custom House canteen], and I had to exert myself to debate with them to justify my curiously isolated manias, to display and protect my juvenile verse-making. These contests and encouragement heaped fuel on my inward fire.

Returning late from these lunchtime symposia, he would be reprimanded by the Deputy Chief Analyst, only to discover that the supervisor was solidly grounded in rationalist philosophy and eighteenth-century French and English literature. Like Trollope, Church found that compiling bureaucratic reports "was good technical training for a young writer. It taught me verbal concision and precision, a fundamental virtue in a poet. The necessary impersonality and objective accuracy were health-giving antidotes to the flamboyance and self-concern with which most young poets set off on the career which in the long run must consume them." In his extramural lectures on literature, Israel Gollancz once challenged his students to compose a sonnet in the style of Milton: he awarded the prize to Richard Church.

There lay the strength and the weakness in his poetry: it read too much like Milton. Following Lessing's *Laokoon* and Schopenhauer's *The Art of Literature*, Church had firmly conservative views "about the relationship between the arts and where the frontiers between them should stand. As I consider what has happened in music, painting, sculpture, and letters since Mallarmé and his followers broke down those fences, I think it may be fortunate that I fixed my prejudices, as a practitioner, thus early in life, upon the resolution never to force words to forsake meaning, in the effort to imitate the possibilities of music or paint." Modernists had made poetry "an esoteric game with verbal symbols," when its real mission should be "the improvement of human society." Modernist pessimism was being forged in 1917, the darkest phase of the war, but at the time, Church remembered, "I was especially active and burning with hope." In that year he published his first volume of verse which, thanks to the wartime poetry boom, sold out. He conducted his own experiments in *vers libre* which T. S. Eliot published at Faber and Faber, yet Church always found Eliot's poems "too dialectical and loaded with learning. The fact that I have said so, in the press, from time to time over the past thirty-five years, has done me no good amongst the fashionable younger critics." Though he liked Eliot as a friend,

> I have distrusted the Montparnasse influence in his verse and doctrine, his sponsoring, even out of loyalty, of the writings of Ezra Pound. The dreadful self-consciousness of so many *déraciné* Americans, aping the hyper-civilized European decadents, has always given me the sensation of being in the presence of death, of flowers withered because the plant has been torn from its taproot in a native soil. Even the novels of Henry James have for me this dessicated atrophy, unsimple and pretentious.

Church was a populist who aimed to broadcast culture as widely as possible. He hailed the radio for whetting the public appetite for museums, books, and classical records: "The awakening has been a powerful renaissance, as effective as that which followed the dispersal of the libraries of Constantinople in the middle of the fifteenth century." His literary tastes were, in a word, proletarian, derived largely from the old *Clarion*, which published his first verses. "I saw art as I saw religion, from a non-conformist point of view," he explained. "Both these vast fields of consciousness were, for me, prospects of worship, of adoration, before the living manifest of Nature, and of the Christ who first touched my eyes when I was a child of ten years." For him, as for Leonard Bast, literature was a matter of "revelation," an intensely personal response not subject to "the claims and disciplines of authority, especially academic authority."

Belletrist Augustine Birrell taught him that a truly literate person must have a library of at least 2,000 volumes, and "that a part of literary education was to sit surrounded by one's books, absorbing them through one's skin, as sun-starved aspirants to health absorb ultra-violet rays from a lamp." Of course, the 2,000 volumes had to be classics. Church was taken aback when someone asked if he read contemporary authors. ("That was a novel idea. I felt that it was a step downwards.") His was an Everyman's Library definition of literature. Twenty of his own books would be published by the Dent firm, which later employed him as poetry editor. One of his discoveries was Dylan Thomas, who privately libeled Church as "a cliché-riddled humbug and pie-fingering hack." The realization that Leonard Bast had become an important literary gatekeeper may have been too much for Thomas to bear.[80]

By Office Boys for Office Boys

Richard Church and Neville Cardus were among the many clerical and distributive workers who frankly confessed to improving their minds during office hours. As a £1-a-week warehouse clerk in the early 1920s, H. E. Bates spent most of the workday with Conrad, Hardy, Wells, Bennett, Galsworthy, Edith Wharton, and Willa Cather.[81] Shop boys who worked for newsagents or lending libraries enjoyed tremendous opportunities for self-education.[82] As a 10s.-a-week office boy in a Clydeside shipyard, John Macadam (b. 1903) felt "vastly overpaid" and profoundly bored, but on errands he could escape to the public library to read travels and biographies. Later, as an apprentice plater, he would sometimes "slip into a quiet corner of a hold somewhere and scribble away in grubby little notebooks." He even tried to write an industrial novel, inspired by Maxim Gorky. He was thrilled when the *Greenock Telegraph* published a sketch he had written about a tinkers' encampment, which proved to be his entrée into journalism. Macadam lived near Colin Milne, literary editor of the *Glasgow Evening Citizen*, and regarded him with the same awe that Leonard Bast felt for the Schlegels: "Somehow he seemed a daily visitor from a world I vaguely felt to be delectable but closed to me." In fact the class barrier, though quite real, was permeable at that point: on Milne's recommendation the *Citizen* hired Macadam as a telephone boy. "What a jolly, exciting world I found myself in, a strange free world full of bawling, Rabelaisian men who smoked long pipes and laughed a lot and cursed us with tremendous oaths when we were slow or slipshod." From there Macadam was propelled into a thrilling journalistic career: reviewing Anna Pavlova, writing up Jacob Epstein, discussing pugilism with Bernard Shaw.[83]

Forster hardly knew or cared for that world of telegrams and laughter. He depicts Bast as a man hopelessly trapped in his cubicle, capable of doing only one specialized kind of insurance work. When he loses that job, he inevitably and helplessly plummets into destitution. But why not try his hand as a writer?

Margaret Schlegel does detect something of the poet in him, but she is certain that if he put his thoughts on paper—if he ever presumed to compete with E. M. Forster—"it would be loathesome stuff."[84]

Even if it were, it probably could have found a publisher. Opportunities for freelance writers were growing explosively. The Newspaper Press Directory listed 2,531 magazines published in 1903, four times as many as in 1875.[85] The census recorded 687 authors, editors, and journalists in 1861, leaping to 3,434 in 1881 and 13,786 by 1911.[86] The "New Journalism", the cheap papers that proliferated from the 1880s onwards, was dismissed by Forster and other intellectuals as the "gutter press".[87] Lord Salisbury's oft-quoted sneer—"Written by office boys for office boys"—accurately summed up a revolutionary social fact: journalism had opened an escape hatch for Board school graduates with a literary flair. With no special training, Neville Cardus could become music critic for the *Manchester Guardian*. Tramp seaman J. E. Patterson explained how he made an easy transition to "literary tramp," contributing to about fifty periodicals and newspapers, "from half-crown reviews to half-penny 'dailies' and boys' papers." During an earlier stint as an underworked law clerk he mastered Greek, Celtic, and German literature in translation at the Cardiff Public Library. With those slender credentials he became "a critic of drama, edited an illustrated journal, and reviewed general literature for three of the principal ones of those days."[88]

Thomas Burke paid for Queen's Hall concerts by writing for *Ally Sloper's Half-Holiday*, a deliciously vulgar comic paper. Professional authors warned that he could never succeed as a writer without connections, and referred him to Gissing's *New Grub Street*. But Burke found that, with no connections at all, he could easily pick up an odd guinea placing a sketch or a short story. Gissing's complaints about literary hackwork utterly baffled Burke, who found scribbling in a garret a wonderful liberation from the thrall of clerkdom.

Burke conceded that most popular periodicals had low literary standards, but that allowed anyone with a limited education to take up journalism.[89] One example was Patrick MacGill (b. 1890), son of an illiterate Donegal peasant. After leaving school at age ten, he picked potatoes and worked as a navvy. He read virtually nothing, not even the daily papers until, working on the rail line, he happened to pick up some poetry written on a page from an exercise book. Somehow it spoke to him, and he began to read "ravenously." He brought *Sartor Resartus, Sesame and Lilies*, and Montaigne's essays to work. *Les Misérables* reduced him to tears, though he found *Das Kapital* less affecting. Each payday he set aside a few shillings to buy secondhand books, which after a month's use were almost illegible with rust, grease, and dirt. He fervently embraced the great books as his own:

> For me has Homer sung of wars,
>   Aeschylus wrote and Plato thought
>   Has Dante loved and Darwin wrought,
> And Galileo watched the stars.

His reading inspired him to write poetry, solely for the enjoyment of his workmates. When a fellow navvy was killed in a work accident, MacGill scribbled an account on a bit of tea-paper, with no thought of publishing it. He was about to toss it away when he noticed a page of the *Dawn*, a ½d. London newspaper, which had been used to wrap beef. Though he had never heard of the paper, he scrounged up a filthy envelope and sent off his story. The editor printed it and offered two guineas for his next article. His workmates were astonished, impressed, and amused to learn that one could earn so much simply by writing. MacGill soon had a regular job with the *Dawn* at £2 a week, and went on to become a popular novelist.[90]

Thomas Thompson (b. 1880) managed to write his way out of the mills of Lancashire, starting with gossipy paragraphs for local newspapers at a half-crown apiece. He discovered "easy money" when the *Cotton Factory Times* paid him 7s. 6d. for a column, and was thrilled to get 26s. from the *Sunday Chronicle* for a humorous story. "Provided one has talent there is an expanding market," he affirmed in 1940. "For the writer new avenues open out. He may write short stories and articles, novels or other books; he may, if he is commercially minded, write advertisements, and if he is versatile he may find more than just adventure in the theatre, in writing for radio, and in writing for the films."[91] At age thirteen Robert Clough (b. c. 1910) found work with the *North Mail* measuring the length of local news items, to ensure that the stringers (some of them Durham colliers) were paid their 1d. a line. He was soon reporting on his own village to several local papers, earning more than the 5s. a week he was paid at his day job. From there he ascended to the pinnacle of Newcastle journalism. In retrospect, Clough did not regret missing his chance for a grammar school scholarship.

> Extended years at school may have qualified me for no more than an uncongenial job at some clerk's desk, thus denying me fifty engrossing years in newspapers. ...
> It was once no novelty for the office boy to be seated in due course at the boardroom table. Now [1970s] it is unlikely that a boy who has known only the village school, and consequently is unable to parade academic honours, will easily gatecrash the certificated queue at the personnel officer's door.[92]

In this context, it is tremendously significant that so many late Victorian popular papers sponsored essay contests. For slum children with some writing talent, these offered the essential first rung up the ladder of literary success. Lancashire journalist Allen Clarke (b. 1863), the son of a Bolton textile worker, avidly read his father's paperback editions of Shakespeare and ploughed through the literature section (Chaucer, Marlowe, Jonson, Beaumont and Fletcher, Milton, Pope, Chatterton, Goldsmith, Byron, Shelley, Burns, Wordsworth, Leigh Hunt) of the public library. With that preparation, he was winning prizes for poems in London papers by age thirteen. In 1881 he bought the first issue of *Tit-Bits*, where he began publishing verses and humorous sketches, and then went on to found and edit several Lancashire journals.[93] The first literary prizes won by Neil Bell (b. 1887), a Southwold boatbuilder's son, included a fountain pen, a bronze medallion, a multibladed knife, and a parrot. (Within a week this parrot had ceased to be, but Bell sold the cage for 5s.) When *Yes and No* offered a prize for a true travel story, he fabricated (and partly plagiarized) something about an escapade in southern Italy and won half a guinea. He sent children's verses to *Chatterbox* for 7s. 6d., published light verse in *London Opinion* for a half-guinea, and was ecstatic when he broke into the highbrow *English Review* with a fake-Shakespearean sonnet. In 1912 he was earning almost £5 a week from writing and schoolteaching. By 1955 he had published about eighty books, mostly novels and children's stories, and was earning nearly £2,000 a year from writing alone.[94]

The growth of popular journalism, public libraries, and Board schools in the late nineteenth century all conspired to create an office-boy intelligentsia paralleling—and often opposing—the modernist intelligentsia. A representative figure of the former was A. E. Coppard (b. 1878), a laundrywoman's son who grew up in dire poverty, left school at nine, ascended the ranks of clerkdom, and became (at age forty) a professional author. At fourteen he was still enjoying *Deadeye Dick*, by twenty he was reading Henry James and had submitted a poem to the *Yellow Book*. He secured a literary education at the Brighton Public Library, and as a professional runner he used prize money to buy Hardy's poems, Shakespeare, Mackail's translation of *The Odyssey*, and William Morris's *The Earthly Paradise*. In an undemanding job (at 12s. a week) he read on company time, though there was a row when his supervisor found *Jude the Obscure* on his desk. Not until he was thirty, and moved to Oxford, did he know anyone except his wife with whom he could intelligently discuss literature. Yet he never felt the lack, because his outsider position offered him complete intellectual freedom:

> In the pursuit of culture and understanding of literature I had no tutor or mentor or fellow-seeker after such righteousness. I had continued to follow my instinct. What else could I have done? There were no night schools or evening classes for my purpose, I had to find my own way and my instinct seldom misled me. Certainly I was never bored, I have never in my life experienced that so common malaise. Nobody could order me to study some book because it was renowned or esteemed: I was not set to prepare any papers for scholarly or examination reasons on subjects that were of no interest to me; I obeyed no alien direction, my own was good enough always. Assiduously I kept to my instinctive channel and was never conscious of a lack of benevolent guidance. I felt no want of assistance or instruction from anybody and always wanted to be alone in this. I was not thwarted by our family poverty, poverty was the environment I had been born into and I had an admirable adaptability .... Such preparation of course left me undisciplined, self-willed, opinionated, and intolerant, but I suppose it nourished whatever spark of original talent I had.

His instincts directed him to the standard poets, but not modern verse which depended on "the omission of the capital letters from the beginnings of each line and of poetry from whatever remained." His artistic tastes stopped at the borders of Bloomsbury. He felt an aversion toward Cézanne, "contempt" for Van Gogh, and "comfortably allergic ... to the art in general that has proliferated by a sort of artificial insemination since the First World War." Duncan Grant was "no good," nor did he care for the criticism of Roger Fry and Clive Bell. For a time he was a neighbor of Lady Ottoline Morrell: "Most of her followers scared me as a bunch of Bloomsbury assumers. By assumers I mean a ceaseless chatterer who takes it for granted that you understand what he is talking about." Living near Oxford, he retraced the steps of Jude Fawley. It was not that he felt inferior among the undergraduates, several of whom (Aldous Huxley, Harold Laski, L. P. Hartley, J. B. S. Haldane) he counted as acquaintances. But his literary ambitions were driven by "a deepening feeling of friendly rivalry with them." Coppard was a populist who enjoyed producing a works magazine because "it deepened my awareness of many mundane matters. Most of the men were friends with me, I played football in their team, went to their annual beanfeasts—roast goose and barrels of ale at some far-off country inn—I knew a good deal of their domestic affairs." Though he published a couple of poems in Eliot's *Egoist*, he put in a

> plea against authority and expertise for the good average man who feels a response to art or any other forms of *Kultur*, but having no time to spare for study and instruction is content with what he likes and rejoices when he finds it for himself. The artist, the poet, the musician, are creating precisely for him and not to please other artists, poets, and musicians; nor do they ever labour to satisfy, as is often urged, simply the souls of their artistic selves. ... As a "young man mad about poetry" I did not feel at all out of place in a commercial office chiefly concerned, as mine was, with iron-founding and the casting of street lampposts for the City of Wolverhampton. Nor did I experience—perhaps I ought to have done—any of the "square peg in a round hole phases" supposed to be inevitable in such cases. I liked the hole! I fitted it well and enjoyed office work.[95]

The Better Hole

Not only was Leonard Bast becoming an author: he was outselling E. M. Forster. Howard Spring's *My Son, My Son!* (1938) sold 750,000 copies and was translated into several languages. His *Fame Is the Spur* (1940), a fictional treatment of the temptation and damnation of Ramsay MacDonald, was made into a major motion picture. Spring was the son of a Cardiff gardener who bought his children secondhand copies of *Tom Jones* and *Swiss Family Robinson*, and read aloud from *Pilgrim's Progress, Robinson Crusoe,* and Charles Dickens. ("My father abhorred rubbish.") Spring failed his scholarship examination and left school at twelve,[96] but he had a second chance at a literary career as a newspaper office boy. His job was to cull racing tips from the major London and provincial papers for reprinting in the *South Wales Echo*, after which he was free to peruse their literary pages:

> I read them all, and, almost from infancy, was steeped to the eyebrows in information about books. Nothing that was to do with books seemed to me in those days to be unimportant. That the *Cardiff Times* was publishing as a serial story Mr. Max Pemberton's *Beatrice of Venice* presented itself as an event of importance; and I could have enumerated then, though my mind has since happily unburdened itself, the titles of works by such improbable authors as David Christie Murray, Mrs. Caffyn, and Maclaren Cobban. From these groundlings to the stars: Wells and Bennett, Henry James, Conrad and Hardy, scarcely a novel was published that I did not know from its reviews, scarcely a review was written that I did not cut out and file.[97]

He launched himself as a writer when he produced a school story (borrowing freely from Talbot Baines Reed) and placed it with a new boys' weekly. To his amazement, he received £1 12s. 6d. for two evenings of easy work.[98] Spring would become an arbiter of middlebrow taste, succeeding Arnold Bennett and J. B. Priestley as book reviewer for the *Evening Standard*. His model was Bennett, "a man who got on with writing his books instead of bothering his friends with long explanations about why he was not at the moment getting on with the writing of the books which he was going to get on with." As a popular author, Spring resented the modernist assumption that literary quality necessarily had an inverse relationship to sales: "For myself, I think that in the immortality stakes *Ulysses* hasn't a dog's chance with *Kipps*, or *Orlando* with *The Old Wives' Tale*." And who, he asked in 1941, was "to blame for the inertia, the sloth and the blindness that made contemptible the decades between the wars," when aesthetes couldn't be bothered with the problem of mass unemployment? The guilty man was Lytton Strachey:

> Look at the celebrated portrait of him by Henry Lamb: the dry, dessicated, juiceless, cynical man whose very contact is enough to freeze all generous emotion and immobilise all noble endeavour. And we took him to our hearts! He bowled over our idols, and we applauded him. He jeered at nobility, pretending it was humbug, and we said: "Yes, of course it is humbug." Florence Nightingale, Arnold of Rugby, anyone who had opposed endeavour to sluggishness, faith to despair, was an appropriate butt of his harsh, despairing and faithless creed. He raised the banner of negation, and we were all ready to enlist beneath it. A war had been won, or so we thought, and peace was here; and what was a man to do with peace save enjoy the plenty that proverbially accompanies it? ... The Rhondda was a long way to the west and Jarrow a long way to the north. They need not disturb us. The great thing was that here, at

last, was Peace, and this time we were going to keep it. Therefore, away with all talk of endeavour, ardour, endurance; away with eminent Victorian virtues.[99]

These cultural tensions are symmetrically illustrated in the careers of two coalfield intellectuals, South Wales politician Aneurin Bevan and South Yorkshire novelist Roger Dataller. They began at opposite poles on the populist–elitist spectrum, then immersed themselves in (respectively) haute bohemian and autodidact milieux, until they eventually reversed their starting positions.

It is not difficult to understand Bevan's voracious hunger for books. His father was a quintessential miner-autodidact. Though his mother learned to read and write in school, she had ten children and became illiterate ("As the children came there was far too much to do. ... I lost the knack"). Their son consequently burrowed through the Tredegar Workmen's Institute Library, and acquired his characteristically grandiose vocabulary through close study of Roget's Thesaurus. "The relevance of what we were reading to our own industrial and political experience had all the impact of a divine revelation," he proclaimed, though his tastes inclined toward abstract philosophy. When he chaired the Tredegar Library Committee, £60 of its £300 acquisitions budget was delegated to a colliery repairman to buy philosophy books. Bevan could quote Nietzsche, discuss F. H. Bradley's *Appearance and Reality*, and deeply impress an Oxford tutor with his critique of Kant's Categorical Imperative. He became the most confrontational figure in the Labour Party leadership, particularly on the cultural front, where he liked to challenge professors and intellectuals on their own turf. "The people are excluded from forming judgement on various matters of public interest on the ground that expert knowledge is required, and that of course the people cannot possess," he protested in 1938. "The debunking of the expert is an important stage in the history of democratic communities because democracy involves the assertion of the common against the special interest. ... The first weapon in the worker's armoury must be a strongly developed bump of irreverence. He must insist on the secular nature of all knowledge."

The elite classes, then, maintained their prestige through the conspicuous display of intellectual wealth as well as material goods. If that sounds Veblenesque, Bevan was in fact deeply influenced by *The Theory of the Leisure Class*.[100] Yet as his political career progressed, he developed a taste for another kind of conspicuous consumption. He loved hobnobbing at the Cafe Royal with bohemian artists like Jacob Epstein, Matthew Smith, and Michael Ayrton. He increasingly saw himself as a natural aristocrat, inspired by the Uruguayan philosopher José Enrique Rodó, who combined economic egalitarianism with intellectual elitism. Rodó warned that mass education in the United States had produced "a sort of universal semi-culture and a profound indifference to the higher. ... The levelling by the middle classes tends ... to plane down what little remains of *intelligentsia*: the flowers are mown by the machine when the weeds remain." He feared "that abominable brutality of the majority which despises the greater moral benefits of liberty and annuls in public opinion all respect for the dignity of the individual." Given his thumpingly proclaimed faith in the wisdom of the common man, it seems odd that Bevan would enjoy quoting Rodó to his dinner guests: the Rodó who feared that democracy would abolish the "legitimate superiorities" of Carlylean heroism. "All in civilisation that is more than material excellence, economic prosperity," wrote Rodó, "is a height that will be levelled when moral authority is given to the average mind."[101]

This fear of "middlebrow" culture has been endemic in the modern intellectual left, which has generally despised the cultural classlessness of the United States. Bevan lived comfortably with the contradiction, just as he had no difficulty dining at the Cafe Royal and drinking Lord Beaverbrook's champagne while he vilified capitalists. It drove Brendan Bracken beyond all endurance: "You Bollinger Bolshevik, you ritzy Robespierre, you lounge-lizard Lenin!" he exploded. Bevan coolly explained that he was simply engaging Tories on their own ground, but less educated members of his own party felt (with some justification) that he was talking down to them with all those words culled from the thesaurus. Another drawback, as one biographer notes, is that after a flaming youth of intense self-education, Bevan appears to have ceased reading books and fallen back on quoting Rodó, until by the 1950s his socialist thinking had become ossified and sterile.[102]

While Bevan was moving up and out of autodidact culture, Roger Dataller passed him in the opposite direction. In the early 1920s Dataller was reading Osbert Sitwell in the pits and, with the encouragement and advice of John Middleton Murry, complaining that his mates were wretched philistines. None of them, apparently, had heard of Debussy, Picasso, Chaliapin, or J. M. Synge. Stuck in the "sepulchral hole" of a mining town, he compared himself to Oscar Wilde in Reading Gaol. "All my life I have been bound within the turgid flow of mediocrity," he sighed. "What a twist of fate it is to find yourself a time-keeper, when you want to be an artist with a flowing tie, a broad-brimmed sombrero, and a villa in Capri." Dataller wrote off his neighbors as reminiscent of Gogol's *Dead Souls*—though he admitted that "we haven't gone even half-way to meet the people of our acquaintance."[103]

When he did meet them, as a WEA instructor, he was stunned by their energy for learning. The students, "including a mother with her baby, are intellectually eager to sit upon hard benches for three hours of torrid sunshine, in order that they may listen to a lecture on 'Modern Tendencies in Industry.'" Granted, one could not assume any knowledge on their part: "It is not unusual to meet a collier very fierce for learning, but whose study has been gravely warped by lack of direction. Single-track education, if you like—sometimes a passionate knowledge of Carlyle, or Ruskin, or Burns, or Milton, and little else." But there was no denying the passion. After class, one student would follow Dataller on a four-mile bus ride all the way to the railway station, just to continue the discussion.[104] As Dataller became more thoroughly integrated into this community of students, he found it ever harder to maintain the pose of an alienated intellectual. By 1932 the typical working-class couple seemed much more likeable, even if they were indifferent to the WEA:

> Spruce and tidy—he with clean pocket handkerchief, she with her shopping basket and air of modest efficiency—they take their seats in the bus for the weekly jaunt into town. There is something so inoffensive and fundamentally decent about them. And a vast indignation arises against the legion of scamps and curs that would endeavour to trade upon that decency. ... And yet, in another mood and moment, as one remembers their indifference to great issues, their mental lethargy, their unabashed credulity, one finds oneself in an attitude of unutterable disgust. We bring the whole heritage of culture, in fee for the asking, and lay it at their feet. They are not interested. We introduce those figures who alone make human history of real significance, and without a "by your leave" they stream away for intimate communion with Jean Harlow or with Wallace Beery. ... "The people, sir? The people is a great beast!" ... Please hand me my Carlyle.[105]

Dataller taught "modern fiction"—which, in WEA classes, meant Galsworthy, Bennett, Wells, and Conrad. He also tried out Woolf, Joyce, and Hemingway with his students, but they preferred Dickens and Trollope for their ability to tell a straightforward story. When introduced to Auden and Eliot, "their attitude was that if a poet took little trouble to make himself understood, he must not complain of comparative neglect. They felt there was an obligation in the artist as well as in the reader." By 1934 Dataller was growing tired of seeing the label "very good but very difficult" inevitably attached to modernist literature: it was like "saying of some kind of food that it is very good but that most people cannot eat it." Tolstoy had proclaimed that true art must produce unity of feeling among an audience, and in Dataller's classroom only a few literary episodes (none of them modernist) passed that test: Sophia pulling Mr. Povey's tooth in *The Old Wives' Tale*, the meeting of Ishmael and Queequeg in *Moby Dick*, Huck and Jim floating down the Mississippi, the fight and wedding scenes in *The History of Mr. Polly*, Artemus Ward's *The Shakers* and *Prince of Wales*, *A Christmas Carol*, the storm in *David Copperfield*, the trial in *The Pickwick Papers*, J. B. Priestley's *The Good Companions*, and Shakespearean tragedy. He was ever more infuriated by Mrs. Woolf's serene confidence that literary genius could not arise from the working classes. What about Burns and Sean O'Casey? Among his students Dataller saw plenty of potential talent, most of it stifled for lack of an outlet.[106]

He also noticed a refreshing lack of deference. Much as the workingman valued education, he was not afraid to deflate academics. "Like Mark Twain, he will poke an irreverent finger at the antics of philosophers and scholars no less than at those of Kings and Emperors ... and he holds tightly to his bosom that precious thing of which he will not allow the sophists to cheat him, the validity of his own experience." Supported by this earthy self-confidence, students disregarded jargon that would either exclude them from the discussion or force them to engage the issue only on the instructor's terms. In their essays, they aimed at

> the elimination as far as possible of aesthetic terms, or definitions which in the opinion of the essayist (being a man of action first and of thought afterwards!) tend to obscure the issue upon which he is writing. "Classical" and "Romantic" movements may be fully outlined within the syllabus; but once a deferential gesture has been made to the tutor's requirements, let us get down (it would seem) to the pertinent business of the evening! What *kind of a man* was Wordsworth, and what impelled him to turn from Revolution to Reaction? What *kind of a man* was Byron? Did he become a rebel because he comprehended injustice, or merely because poor, he became neglected, and lame, the object of female commiseration? Was Shelley *really* a revolutionary? And if so, why did he elect to live in Italy instead of with the liberty lads of England? The same shrewd, commonsensical sort of question, not labels and classification (necessary for working purposes though these may be), but an ardent student inquiry, pouring into, and bursting through, the flimsily constructed framework.
>
> In a word, the student with a point of view![107]

By 1940 Dataller had completed the transition to populism, repudiating the modernists he had taught and admired only a few years before. Now he clearly sided with Mr. Bennett against Mrs. Woolf. Now he blamed "clique and coterie" for boosting the "sterile obscurantism" of James Joyce. Now he was ready to argue that Charles Dickens, though out of fashion among modernist critics, in fact passed the only true test of literary greatness—borrowings from the public library.[108]

What if the modernists had shared Dataller's willingness to meet his audience halfway? In *Who Paid for Modernism?*, Joyce Wexler recently argued that, contrary to "the myth of the suffering artist," there was a substantial potential audience for the work of Joyce and Lawrence. In their later careers, however, they wrote increasingly obscure books for private publishers and a coterie readership. Had they heeded the advice of their editors and submitted to the disciplines of the literary marketplace, they might have produced more structured and accessible work: another *Sons and Lovers* rather than *The Plumed Serpent*, another *Portrait of the Artist as a Young Man* instead of *Finnegans Wake*. Thus Wexler answers her own question: "Authors paid for modernism by giving up the wide audience their ambition desired and their talent deserved."[109] The success of Arnold Bennett in explaining highbrow literature to general readers suggests that she may have a point. Even a remote Cumberland village in the 1920s was not impervious to modernism. When Edward Short was growing up in Warcop, one of the local residents was artist Donald Wood, who actually deigned to explain contemporary art to country folk.

Whenever he was spotted a crowd of children and old men assembled behind him and watched every stroke, commenting among themselves, often in a highly critical way and in loud whispers. But we soon discovered that neither our presence nor our comments worried him in the slightest or made him self-conscious, indeed he seemed to enjoy having an audience for he was a young man of great good humour, enthusiasm and modesty. Neither criticism nor acclaim put him off. He would chat with us as he painted and ask our views on his work. ... Looking back, I do believe he taught us to see the village with different eyes, to see forms and colours that, before his coming, we had never noticed. To us trees had always been green, sheep white and water blue. In our paintings at school, where quite progressive, indeed almost avant-garde methods, were used in teaching art, strange new colours, purple trees, green sheep, orange water began to appear. Donald ... was transforming our powers of observation and our ability to record what we saw, and—more important— what we felt about what we saw.[110]

The plebeian intellectual was likely to remain a populist as long as he belonged to a circle of other plebeian intellectuals. The mutual improvement societies, the WEA, or even a gang of like-minded clerks could offer such a congenial cultural home. Those who failed to find such a home—or who chose to avoid it—were liable to gravitate toward the more exclusive orbit of modernism. Leicester bottlewasher Tom Barclay was just such a marginal figure, forever scolding the proletariat for preferring Ethel M. Dell and *Tarzan of the Apes* to Eugene O'Neill and *A Portrait of the Artist as a Young Man*. He felt more rapport with the middle-class Fabian socialists, and like them he dismissed the working classes as beer-sodden and petit bourgeois. He liked to quote Bernard Shaw to the effect that "if it were not for the working man we would have had Socialism established long ago."[111]

An important base for the populist intelligentsia was Robert Blatchford's *Clarion* and the affiliated Clarion Scouts, which offered a refuge for Edwin Muir (b. 1887) when he held down a depressing job as a Glasgow clerk at 16s. a week. Blatchford's hearty socialism allowed Muir to idealize the uncouth workers at his beer-bottling plant: "I no longer saw them as they were, but as they would be when the society of which I dreamed was realized. ... For the first time in my life I began to like ordinary vulgar people, because in my eyes they were no longer ordinary or vulgar, since I saw in them shoots of the glory they would possess when all men and women were free and equal." Those charitable impulses, however, gave way to sour irony when he turned to the Nietzschean elitism of the *New Age*, A. R. Orage's high bohemian weekly:

Reading it gave me a feeling of superiority which was certainly not good for me; I can still remember with some embarrassment a phrase of the editor to the effect that the paper was "written by gentlemen for gentlemen." But it stimulated my mind. It also sharpened my contempt for sentimentality, since, except for Orage's own political and literary notes, the tone of the paper was crushingly superior and exclusive, and some of the contemporary writers for whom I was in danger of contracting an admiration were treated there with surprising rudeness. On the strength of this I acquired a taste for condemnation to which I had no right, and when any of my friends came to see me, filled with enthusiasm for some new book, I could crush him with a few words, though his enthusiasm was genuine and my condemnation borrowed.

Muir still belonged to the Clarion Scouts, but now he gravitated to a clique within that organization known as "the intellectuals." Its members were drawn mostly from the no-man's-land between the working and lower-middle classes: teachers, clerks, salespeople, government employees, engineers. They disdained "the superstitions of the mob":

> We followed the literary and intellectual development of the time, discovering such writers as Bergson, Sorel, Havelock Ellis, Galsworthy, Conrad, E. M. Forster, Joyce and Lawrence, the last two being contributed by me, for I had seen them mentioned in the *New Age* by Ezra Pound. ...
>
> It was the first time I had listened to or taken part in intelligent conversation. Up to now my mental life had been quite solitary, and though I was always reading and discovering new books to read, there was no one to whom I could talk of them. I lived two lives, a quite private life of intellectual discovery, and another in which the name of a book never escaped my lips and I was careful to behave like everybody else. Now that I could speak and listen freely I was filled with a deep sense of relief and gratitude.

But he was also succumbing to intellectual arrogance, fed by an intense study of Nietzsche:

> The idea of a transvaluation of all values intoxicated me with a feeling of false power. I, a poor clerk in a beer-bottling factory, adopted the creed of aristocracy, and, happy until now to be an Orkney man somewhat lost in Glasgow, I began to regard myself, somewhat tentatively, as a "good European." I was repelled by many things that I read, such as the counsel to give "the bungled and botched" a push if I found them going downhill, instead of trying to help them. My Socialism and my Nietzscheanism were quite incompatible, but I refused to recognize it. I did not reflect that if Christianity was a "slave morality" I was one of the slaves who benefited by it, and that I could make no pretension to belong to the "master class." But I had no ability and no wish to criticize Nietzsche's ideas, since they gave me exactly what I wanted: a last desperate foothold on my dying dream of the future. My heart swelled when I read, "Become what thou art," and "Man is something that must be surpassed," and "What does not kill

me strengthens me." Yet it swelled coldly; my brain was on fire, but my natural happiness was slipping away from me. ... I tried, when I came to Nietzsche's last works, *The Twilight of the Idols* and *Ecce Homo*, to ignore the fact that they were tinged with madness. ... I adopted the watchword of "intellectual honesty," and in its name committed every conceivable sin against honesty of feeling and honesty in the mere perception of the world with which I daily came into contact. Actually, although I did not know it, my Nietzscheanism was what psychologists call a "compensation." I could not face my life as it was, and so I took refuge in the fantasy of the Superman. Already I was beginning to see that my job was at the mercy of any chance; yet I could look forward only to the life of a clerk; and when I thought that I might grow middle-aged and round-backed and grey at that work I was overcome with dejection.

In fact, a wave of dismissals at his company impelled him to find another clerical job in a bone factory, which cloaked the town with the stench of rotting flesh. There his only intellectual companion was a fellow clerk and *New Age* reader, who professed to be a friend of the workers but "never referred to them except in abusive terms, and pounced on sentimentality as if it were a deadlier enemy than Capitalism itself." In that waste land, Muir began writing "lonely, ironic, slightly corpse-like poems."[112] The *New Age* printed them, along with some aphorisms he later published in book form as *We Moderns*:

Art is at the present day far too easy of comprehension, far too obvious. Our immediate task should be to make it *difficult*, the concern of a dedicated few. Thus only shall we win back reverence for it .... A democratic familiarity with it—such as exists among the middle classes, *not* among the working classes, in whom reverence is not yet dead—is an abomination. ...

The cult of the average man ... is nothing but the exaltation of men at the expense of Man. In due time all ideals perish, only an aspiration towards averageness remains, and equality is everywhere enthroned. ... Well, we must weigh men again; we must deny equality; we must affirm aristocracy. ...

How unhappy must all those poor mortals be who are not poets! ... Cloddish and fragmentary, they are scarcely human, these poor mortals.

All this came from a crofter's son, who was not above taunting proletarian writer Patrick MacGill:

Sure, Patrick, ne'er were style and matter knit
More trim than yours: here is the proof of it.
Your theme's a navvy posing in a hovel,
And 'tis quite clear you scribble with a shovel.

His greatest contempt was reserved for Arnold Bennett, for finding the stuff of literature in the Potteries:

Why, pray, so garrulous of wood and leather,
Eating, the clock, the bathroom, and the weather?
Why on *existence* do you always dwell?
Is it because you've naught of *Life* to tell?[113]

If that seems to be a four-line summary of "Mr. Bennett and Mrs. Brown," which was published some years later, perhaps Mrs. Woolf was elaborating what had already become commonplace among the modernist intelligentsia. (As a poet, Muir would be discovered by the Woolfs and published by their Hogarth Press.)[114]

Those pretensions could indeed offer compensation for isolated and marginal plebeian intellectuals: for example, a Nietzschean milkman in Glasgow, who lived in a filthy room with hordes of books and worked for an unsanitary milk company. "He was in no movement and had a supreme distaste for all," recalled a coworker. "He was completely contemptuous of the masses, to whom he used to refer in the sneering phrase of the Master as 'the dear people.'"[115] Inspired by *New Age* Nietzscheanism Hugh MacDiarmid, a poet hovering precariously between the educated classes and the destitute classes, became a self-described "intellectual snob of the worst description." He applauded the 1911 anti-Jewish riots in South Wales, denounced Robert Burns for preaching democracy and brotherhood, called for "a Scottish Fascism," and complimented the Soviet secret police ("What maitters 't wha we kill ...?"). The Scotland he grew up in still had a strong autodidact tradition, which MacDiarmid preferred to ignore. He despised the Shetland Islanders, among whom he lived for a time, and yearned to get back to "civilized people" in Edinburgh or Glasgow—though at times he denied that there were civilized people in Glasgow. He professed to enjoy "the company of quite illiterate people" as well as the creators of "difficult high-brow literature" like T. S. Eliot and Ezra Pound, "but never half-educated mediocrities!" As John Carey might have predicted, his bitterest fulminations were reserved for those who took popular courses in English literature: "third-hand and fourth-hand generalities ... a stock of details swept up by the industrious housemaids of literature." In the course of an erratic literary career, he reassured himself by quoting Pound ("A nation which does not feed its best writers is a mere barbarian dung heap") and Kierkegaard ("The literary and social and political situation requires an exceptional individual—the question is whether there is anyone in this realm who is fitted for this task except me"). A founder of the Scottish National Party, he was the kind of ultranationalist who denounces nearly all of his countrymen as sellouts: "I am speaking for Scotland in a way which few men, if any, have ever been qualified to speak." Later, he found in the Communist Party the same assurance that he belonged to a vanguard elite: "Here lies your secret, O Lenin—No' in the majority will that accepts the result ...."

MacDiarmid conceded that it was not easy to "reconcile my use of a linguistic medium utterly unintelligible to 'the mob', and my highbrowism generally, with my Communism—the extremes of High Tory and Communist meeting." It was in fact a kind of shabby intellectual gentility, desperately striving to distinguish itself from the masses. This insecure elitism may explain why he could quote, in almost the same breath, Lenin on the true Marxist intellect and Clive Bell on the awfulness of best-sellers; why he supported the Soviet invasion of Hungary in 1956; why he recognized a kindred spirit in Malcolm X, and teamed up with him in a televised Oxford Union debate; why neither his Scottish separatism nor his Communism made him averse to accepting a Civil List Pension from the king. His memoirs were mostly given over to name-dropping, quoting favorable reviews, and explaining his own failures as a refusal to run with the herd. When the masses occasionally came into his line of vision, he either extolled them in the abstract or vilified them in reality. The son of a 37s.-a-week postman, he cultivated "*eutrephelia*, well-bred arrogance—the over-weening blue eye arched in the bony face. ... That is how I reconcile my highbrowism and my Communism."[116]

Cultural Triage

In the first half of the twentieth century, then, two rival intelligentsias squared off against each other, competing for audiences and prestige. One was middle-class, university-educated and modernist, supported largely by patronage and private incomes; the other was based in the working and clerking classes, mainly Board school graduates and the self-educated, more classical in their tastes, but fearlessly engaged in popular journalism and the literary marketplace. One appealed to an elite audience; the other wrote best-sellers and feature films. One was inspired by Marx, Nietzsche, and Freud, the other Carlyle, Dickens, and Ruskin. One read and wrote for the *New Age* and *New Statesman*, the other *T. P.'s Weekly* and *John o' London's*. The labels that they adopted (or were forced upon them) were "highbrow" and "middlebrow." Until about 1950 the highbrows could reasonably claim to be beleaguered and misunderstood in a culture dominated by middlebrows. But thereafter government patronage, the BBC, and the expansion of higher education gradually created a mass audience for Forster, Eliot, Woolf, Pound, Joyce, and the entire Bloomsbury group. They were canonized in the university curriculum, while the counterintelligentsia of Arnold Bennett, Neville Cardus, Ethel Mannin, Richard Church, A. E. Coppard, V. S. Pritchett, Thomas Burke, and Howard Spring is mostly ignored even by academic specialists. If they treat middlebrow culture at all, they usually dismiss it as superficial and middle-class,[117] and to a considerable extent it was. But it was also the direct descendant of Victorian self-improvement, produced for and by thinking people with working-class roots. In the second half of the century, with the decay of the autodidact tradition, the decline of the industrial working class, and the opposition of an increasingly popular and confident modernist culture, middlebrow culture would lose its audience and disappear.

In her essay "Middlebrow" Virginia Woolf formulated a general theory of cultural stratification that concisely explains the tensions generated by the rise of

Leonard Bast.[118] For the past two centuries, intellectuals in the West have generally sorted culture into three bins,[119] and Mrs. Woolf followed this pattern. At the top, naturally, is the "highbrow," defined simply as a member of the thinking classes: "He is the man or woman of thoroughbred intelligence who rides his mind at a gallop across country in pursuit of an idea." Conversely, the "lowbrow is ... of course a man or woman of thoroughbred vitality who rides his body in pursuit of a living at a gallop across life." In other words, he belongs to the nonthinking classes, though in fairness Mrs. Woolf includes in this category admirals and duchesses as well as miners, cooks, and clerks. Lowbrow culture is now usually called, less pejoratively, "popular culture" or "folk culture." Far from disparaging it, intellectuals have usually admired popular culture as earthy, authentic, indigenous, unselfconscious, vital, traditional, natural, free of the taint of commercialism, a source of inspiration for high art. Why, protested Mrs. Woolf, does the press perpetuate the myth that highbrows disdain lowbrows, "when highbrows need lowbrows, when lowbrows need highbrows, when they cannot exist apart, when one is the complement and the other side of the other!" Lowbrows provide the two essentials every highbrow needs: subject matter and an audience.

> You have only to stroll along The Strand on a wet winter's night and watch the crowds lining up to get into the movies. These lowbrows are waiting, after the day's work, in the rain, sometimes for hours, to get into the cheap seats and sit in hot theatres in order to see what their lives look like. Since they are lowbrows, engaged magnificently and adventurously in riding full tilt from one end of life to the other in pursuit of a living, they cannot see themselves doing it. Yet nothing interests them more. Nothing matters to them more. It is one of the prime necessities of life to them—to be shown what life looks like. And the highbrows, of course, are the only people who can show them. Since they are the only people who do not do things, they are the only people who can see things being done.

As long as these two castes remain in their proper stations, where one produces culture while the other consumes it, there is a happy equilibrium. T. S. Eliot had no objection to proletarian culture within a strict social hierarchy: he was genuinely fond of the lowbrow antics of Groucho Marx and music hall star Marie Lloyd. Trouble arises only with the intrusion of a third cultural stratum, which has been called by various names, all of them derogatory: "bourgeois," "petit bourgeois," "mass culture," "midcult," "admass," "suburban," "middle-class," "middlebrow."[120] From Ortega, Pound, and Eliot on the political right to Adorno, Marcuse, the Leavises, and Dwight MacDonald on the left, modernist intellectuals shared an obsessive loathing of middlebrows. Mrs. Woolf defines them as lowbrows who invade the territory of highbrows, practicing authorship without a license. They occupy a dubious place in the class system, "betwixt and between," confusing neat intellectual hierarchies. They are promiscuously democratic, associating on equal terms with both lowbrows and highbrows. They pursue, "rather nastily, ... money, fame, power, or prestige"—unlike highbrows. Where highbrows embrace the avant-garde ("to buy living art requires living taste"), middlebrows prefer "bound volumes of the classics behind plate glass," a clear dig at Everyman's Library and at the parlors of the self-improving working classes. But middlebrows are a menace primarily because they poach on the reading audiences that highbrows once considered their own:

> I often ask my friends the lowbrows, over our muffins and honey, why it is that while we, the highbrows, never buy a middlebrow book, or go to a middlebrow lecture, or read, unless we are paid for doing so, a middlebrow review, they, on the contrary, take these middlebrow activities so seriously? ...
>
> To all this the lowbrows reply—but I cannot imitate their style of talking—that they consider themselves to be common people without education. It is very kind of the middlebrows to try to teach them culture. And after all, the lowbrows continue, middlebrows, like other people, have to make money. There must be money in teaching and in writing books about Shakespeare. We all have to earn our livings nowadays, my friends the lowbrows tell me.

Mrs. Woolf did not dispute that. "Even those of us whose Aunts came a cropper riding in India and left them an income of four hundred and fifty pounds, now reduced, thanks to the war and other luxuries, to little more than two hundred odd, even we have to do that." Rentier modernists were no longer completely insulated from the literary marketplace, where they had to compete with more popular authors. Modernists could carve out a market niche among sophisticated readers and earn a modestly good living writing for them. But among the larger public of common readers, they could not compete with populist authors, nor could they come close to the stupendous royalties of an Arnold Bennett. Mrs. Woolf worried that prosperous middlebrows might move into Bloomsbury, drive up the rents, and force her out—an anxiety that afflicts every artist living in a bohemian quarter.

Journalists who wrote low literature were less of a problem for highbrows, since they offered no direct competition for readers. But middlebrow authors like Bennett had an appalling habit of writing clear across the intellectual spectrum. V. W. Garratt, a former factory worker, pursued what he called a "Jekyll and Hyde" literary career, producing articles for the sophisticated *English Review* and the downmarket *John Bull*, on topics ranging from Mayan sculpture to association football. A poet himself, he enjoyed hearing Ezra Pound and Harold Munro read their work at the Poetry Bookshop, but he was also a freelance journalist, always looking to spin the raw stuff of human interest into saleable copy. As Garratt explained it, "Fleet Street has always had a soft heart for the 'gate-crasher' who has something to offer,"[121] but cultural gatekeepers were scandalized. Q. D. Leavis looked back to a golden Elizabethan age when "the masses were receiving their amusement from above (instead of being specially catered for by journalists, film-directors, and popular novelists, as they are now)."[122]

One cannot help but think that the impoverishment and death of Leonard Bast represent wish fulfillment on the author's part, disposing of yet another aspiring middlebrow. The unpleasant reality was that clerks belonged to a rising and increasingly articulate class. Of course they were vulnerable to economic downturns, when some clerks were, like Bast, precipitated into poverty. The autobiographies discussed here are admittedly Dick Whittington stories, written by the exceptionally successful. Still, clerkdom was a growth industry that offered social mobility, expanding job opportunities, and rising salaries. Of 388 clerks marrying in inner London parishes between 1898 and 1903, 42.8 percent had working-class fathers. Commercial, bank, and insurance clerks accounted for 3.8 percent of male workers over age fifteen by 1911, up from 0.7 percent in 1851. Insurance clerks in particular tended to enjoy good pay, relatively high prestige, and an open path for promotion to managerial positions.[123] Someone like Bast, at the beginning of his career, would have a meagre wage; but unlike the Schlegel sisters, he could look forward to a sharply rising earnings curve. One sample of ten insurance clerks, earning an average of £121 a year in 1890, were making £423 by 1914—enough to afford a comfortable suburban home, a couple of full-time servants, and private schools for their children.[124] Compare that with Virginia Woolf's private income of under £400;[125] Forster's inheritance of £8,000 probably earned even less. And Everyman's Library was promising those clerks a complete literary education for £50. Economically as well as culturally, the clerks were breathing down the necks of the rentier intellectuals. The latter could only preserve their cultural prestige by creating a new literature inaccessible to Board school graduates.

Meanwhile, a similar transition was under way in the United States. Once middlebrow culture began to flourish, modernism was created to distance intellectuals from the increasingly educated public. Among professors of American literature, the old popular canon of Longfellow, Whittier, Lowell, and Holmes was superseded by Thoreau, Whitman, Dickinson, Melville, and Poe. The former had been taught by an older generation of generalists, the latter were promoted by younger academics who had received more specialized training as Americanists. Their modern canon, as Richard Brodhead observes, served "to underwrite their own new cultural authority. If there is anything the second or modern American canon is that the first or genteel canon was not, it is difficult. (The substitution of Dickinson for Longfellow is symptomatic.) *This* version of our literature requires the aid of expert assistance to bring it home to the common mind—and so helps support the value of expertise more generally."[126]

In Britain, T. S. Eliot drew that line when he taught extension courses in English and French literature during the First World War. The students were interested though passive, and Eliot acknowledged that they were doing their best, given the difficulty of the syllabus and wartime conditions. Privately, he wrote that

"These people are the most hopeful sign in England, to me." But when he publicly addressed a modernist audience, he assumed more snobbish airs. In the April 1918 *Egoist* he wrote off Alice Meynell's middlebrow *Hearts of Controversy* as "what a University Extension audience would like; but it is not criticism." In "The Function of Criticism" he would be even more arrogant: "I have had some experience of Extension lecturing, and I have found only two ways of leading any pupils to like anything with the right liking: to present them with a selection of the simpler kind of facts about a work—its conditions, its settings, its genesis— or else to spring the work on them in such a way that they were not prepared to be prejudiced against it."[127]

The office-boy intelligentsia could not flourish in that climate. Neville Cardus had little in common with the next generation of anxiously modern critics: "The mandarins, as though to assure us or themselves that they were not things of the past, frisked about with the very latest in verse, prose, atonalism and surrealism, like so many old bucks ogling desperately the contemporary scene."[128] For his own cohort, criticism was a matter of describing one's own electric (if naive) response to the arts, without fretting too much about "bourgeois escapism." But once university men entered journalism, he felt elbowed out by a "fashionable Bloomsbury-Chelsea highbrowism which does not understand that genius is a miracle to be revered whether in fashion or not."[129] Richard Church had always been committed "to accuracy, to a reverence for tradition and an avoidance of eccentricity. ... Poetry, and indeed all art, should in its first purpose be a communication, as direct and simple as possible." This straightforwardness "made my work uninteresting to experimentalists, and those critics who have fostered the fashion for puerilism and obscurity in the arts and literature during the second quarter of the twentieth century." The problem with accessibility is that there is no profit in it for the intelligentsia: "It ... leaves the critics nothing to say."[130]

The modernists used difficulty to fence off and protect literary property. In 1914 Ezra Pound proclaimed that the old aristocracies of blood and business were about to be supplanted by "the aristocracy of the arts." This new elite, he argued with breathtaking frankness, should be no less cynical in gulling the ignorant masses: "Modern civilisation has bred a race with brains like those of rabbits and we who are the heirs of the witch-doctor and the voodoo, we artists who have been so long the despised are about to take over control. ... And the public will do well to resent these 'new' kinds of art."[131] Pound coined the term "Imagist" as a kind of brand name for modern poetry,[132] but he soon saw a problem in his marketing strategy: if the point of Imagist poetry was to overawe the masses, what was to prevent them from learning the trick of it and producing their own? Amy Lowell considered copyrighting the name "Imagist" to keep out inferior imitators, but intellectual property law has never permitted a poet to register his movement as a trademark. Sure enough, by 1917 Eliot was complaining that "now it is possible to print free verse (second, third, or tenth-rate) in almost any American magazine."[133]

The irony is that this hostility to the masses was a response to an increasingly sophisticated audience. If most American magazines were printing free verse, America could hardly have been the philistine wasteland portrayed by Sinclair Lewis and H. L. Mencken. In fact the reading public on both sides of the Atlantic was becoming more affluent and more educated. That growing audience could support an ever-expanding corps of writers, artists, critics, and academics. That growing body of intellectuals could, in turn, become more specialized: they could earn a living by rejecting the mass audience and writing for coteries of sophisticated readers. The modernists were among the first authors to carve out that market niche, and to secure it they had to become ever more innovative, complex, and difficult—partly to frustrate imitators, partly to appeal to the exclusivity of their readers. That is why mass education, even mass higher education, never produces a "common culture," however noble that dream may be. Whenever the masses are educated up to a given level of culture, elite audiences and intellectuals will have already pressed on to the next and more challenging level.

The BBC's Third Programme, founded in 1946, illustrates that process. The company had successfully offered the general public classical music and quality newscasts, along with lighter programing, but Virginia Woolf disdained this mix as the quintessence of middlebrow. The BBC, she snorted, really stood for "the Betwixt and Between Company."[134] The Third Programme was created as a closed shop for intellectuals, which would deliberately exclude the self-educated. The company's Director-General William Haley, backed by BBC governors Harold Nicholson and Lady Violet Bonham-Carter, was determined not to compromise with public taste as, he believed, his predecessors had. He publicly identified his target as "the alert and receptive listener, the listener who is willing first of all to make an effort in selection and then to meet the performer half-way by giving his whole attention to what is being broadcast." An internal memo, however, defined the audience more selectively: it was "already aware of artistic experience and will include persons of taste and intelligence, and of education. ... The programme need not cultivate any other audience, and material that is unlikely to interest such listeners should be excluded." In 1949 Harman Grisewood, second controller of the Third Programme, was still more elitist: his aim was not to bring culture to the masses (the objective of Matthew Arnold and John Reith) but to exclude them, to appeal to the already educated while making no concessions to "aspirants." George Barnes and John Morris, the first and third controllers, had both been educated at Bloomsbury's nursery, King's College Cambridge; Barnes was a friend of Forster and a disciple of Keynes.

In its first week, the Third Programme made clear that there would be no concessions. It broadcast complete productions of Shaw's *Man and Superman*, Milton's *Comus*, and Sartre's *Huis Clos*. Interludes between programs were filled with readings from Henry James selected by Desmond MacCarthy. What is amazing is that the channel managed to attract as many as 7 percent of evening listeners, a third of them working-class. During those first weeks, 19 percent of working-class listeners found the Third Programme "very attractive" or "moderately attractive," compared with 55 percent of the lower-middle class and 70 percent of the upper-middle class.[135] By 1949, 21 percent of the working class at least sometimes listened in, compared with 63 percent of middle-class and artisan households.[136]

Radio Times published letters from its proletarian fans. "Many of my work-mates who have never seen the inside of a university common room were introduced to the higher aspects of literature, music and philosophy," wrote a Glasgow ironmoulder. BBC producers knew that there was a still larger potential audience of "aspirants" who would "prefer the Third Programme to be a little more on familiar ground. After all, we are not all University Students," explained one unemployed miner. The self-educated pleaded for study guides and background information that might help them digest a heavy diet of high culture, but the BBC sternly rejected "dilution," "hearing aids," or (Haley's word) "crutches."[137]

Notwithstanding Mrs. Woolf, the great virtue of betwixt and between programming was that it inevitably exposed all listeners to a certain amount of high culture. Chaim Bermant recalled that "in the days before good music was segregated from bad"—before the Third Programme—he could turn on the radio in search of a dance band and stumble across a symphony orchestra. His father's only encounter with classical music happened when, "switching on too early for the news, he heard a snatch of Beethoven's Egmont Overture and remarked: *Dos is doch fun himmel*—but this is from heaven!"[138]

That opportunity was lost with the increasing specialization of cultural life, which appears to be a pervasive secular trend in modern societies. Something similar happened to the theater around 1900, when the common Victorian audience for Shakespeare divided between sophisticated drama and the movies. By the late 1950s art critic Harold Rosenberg recognized that this process of cultural segregation was unstoppable. Mass education had produced the "inexorable liquidation of the proletariat into the intellectual caste." As this educated class grew, it inevitably subdivided into increasingly specialized professions, artistic movements, schools of psychology, theories of literary criticism. In order to be taken seriously, each of these subgroups developed a distinctive jargon: "The more incomprehensible this lingo is to outsiders, the more thoroughly it identifies the profession as such and elevates it out of the reach of mere amateurs and craftsmen. The continued use of Latin by the medical profession appears as simple-minded compared to what newer professions have been able to accomplish in 'English'." Rosenberg saw that "The segregation of occupations within the mazes of their technical systems increasingly demolishes the old mental cohesions of class." That, he argued, is why Leninism had failed to take root in the most economically developed societies. (It might also help to explain why Leninism crumbled when professional specialization developed in Communist societies.) Each profession— whether Freudian, Beat, feminist, or deconstructionist—claims to have an ideology that explains the human condition. Each proclaims itself a "vanguard" ("a word that turns up everywhere," Rosenberg noted, though today "cutting-edge" is preferred). And each profession uses its private language and theories to criticize other professions, in an endless competition for prestige and economic rewards.

Always working against this "Balkanization" are the popularizers, the cultural "middlemen" who explain the professions to the general public. Because they cut through jargon, popularizers tend to deglamorize intellectual "vanguards" and effectively steal their intellectual property: why should a mass audience struggle with highbrow culture when middlebrow commentaries are more readable? Rosenberg recognized that the "alienation of the artist," academics' contempt for colleagues who write for "the general reader," the loathing of couturiers for retailers who copy and mass-market their designs, are all of a piece. For them, popularization is theft, "a work totally taken away from its creator and totally falsified."[139]

The problem is still more acute at the start of the twenty-first century, when laborers in the avant-garde must continually accelerate cultural innovation to keep up with demand. The rentier intelligentsia is gone, but its functions have been taken over by tenured professors. Their incomes are equally secure, but they earn less than Leonard Bast, who has become a middle-management insurance executive. Worse, he is now thoroughly familiar with modernism. He was assigned *A Portrait of the Artist as a Young Man* in college, he works in a Corbusier-style office building, he assumes that a modern painting ought to look like a Jackson Pollock. He may well know E. M. Forster, whose audience has grown exponentially with each generation. *Howards End* sold just under 10,000 copies in its first three years, *A Passage to India* only 23,000 in twelve years; but sales of the first Penguin editions were 250,000 and 300,000 respectively,[140] and the film versions were seen by millions.

When modernism became mass culture, the avant-garde had to move on to something more modern still—postmodernism, which strove to recapture the opacity and difficulty that once cloaked modernism. Postmodernists reproduced Mrs. Woolf's cultural triage, with some necessary updating. In their hierarchy, the highbrows were postmodernists themselves. (Of course they avoided the term "highbrow," preferring to speak of "high theory"). Like earlier generations of highbrows, they admired and patronized "popular culture," though now they meant television, rock, and hip-hop rather than peasant verse or folk music. The canon of literary classics—now including the modernist classics—in turn became middlebrow culture. In the age of Penguin Books and mass higher education, Shakespeare, Melville, and Lawrence were devalued by overproduction: too many people had read them and too many academics had written about them. Therefore the advanced intelligentsia had to relocate once again, like a genteel household that moves to ever more remote suburbs, to escape the crowds of the encroaching inner city.

Chapter Thirteen **Down and Out in Bloomsbury**

"Il faut tant d'argent pour être bohême aujourd'hui" (It takes so much money to be bohemian today), sighed Maurice Barrès in 1888.[1] More than a century later, residents of even the grottier reaches of Camden Town or the East Village would ruefully agree that not everyone has the capital to set up shop in Bohemia. It is more than a matter of rent: one has to invest heavily in education, social connections and, above all, location. Bohemian Paris, writes Jerrold Seigel, fancied itself the adversary of bourgeois France, and yet, "Like positive and negative poles, Bohemian and bourgeois were—and are—parts of a single field: they imply, require, and attract each other." Bohemians were recruited from the bourgeoisie, patronized by the bourgeoisie, and (when successful) absorbed back into the bourgeoisie. Bohemia (to offer a working definition) has always served the bourgeoisie as a laboratory for cultural research and development, experimenting with new sensibilities in literature, art, music, couture, cuisine, design, erotics, and narcotics.

In that sense, Bohemians are as essential to a dynamic capitalist economy as research scientists, with some important differences. Because Bohemia produces new culture rather than new technologies, it must be adversarial: if bohemian aesthetics and moralities were not transgressive, they would be part of the larger culture, and we do not pay inventors to invent what we already have. Therefore the Bohemian must exploit the liberal freedoms of bourgeois society somewhat farther than the respectable bourgeois is prepared to go—at first. But the ultimate goal of the Bohemian is to get past that initial shock, to change bourgeois tastes and thus create a larger market for his avant-garde art.[2]

On the Fringe

While shocking and selling to the bourgeoisie, Bohemia also had to deal with the working classes: as neighbors, as mistresses, as literary subjects. Here were people who seemed to offer an earthier sensibility, a more honest morality, a fascinating potential for violence and revolution—or at least, that much could be projected on them. From Henri Murger to Jean-Paul Sartre, Bohemians have written with authority about the workers. But what did the workers have to say about the Bohemians? Though admission to the avant-garde usually required an elite education and some family money, a few proletarians managed to find a precarious foothold in London's Bohemia. The poet Clare Cameron, born (1896) Winifred Wells to a London blacksmith, was a 15s.-a-week clerk given to artistic ecstasies that Leonard Bast was never permitted to experience. *L'Après-midi d'un faune* at a Queen's Hall concert moved her to rhapsody: "What strange tale of the hot earth and sky was running under the faint midsummer noon?" She ate cheap lunches at Lyons to save money for volumes of Tennyson, Shelley, and Ruskin. She found the "kindling glow" of words and ideas in Tolstoy, Shaw, Ibsen, Nietzsche, and Marx. She churned out poetry that no one would publish, "verses about trees, the moon, the sea, the rain, the wind; of that ever-present need to open a gate within that would never yield more than an inch to let my emotions escape in song." She found beauty in country walks but also in "the tall chimneys of West Ham, slim and graceful and smoky against the rosy sunset sky, suggesting Whistler, Turner, Pennell." At the end of the day, she had to go home to a Nonconformist mother who admonished her that she could not afford such artistic tastes. But once she read Murger's novel and saw Puccini's opera, she could not turn back:

Ah, *there* was the life we craved! There was expression of and answer to all our fumbling desires and half-formed dreams. Our rebellious hearts beat high. Life could be so easy like that; so flowerlike and fragrant; so light and laughing and care-free; a song, a dance, a caper, instead of the dull jog-trot we were used to; passionate, high-hearted, expressive, free; and brave and content when the petals fell and the song ended and the tired feet could dance no more. People lived like that in Chelsea; *that* was life, not the grey and prosy existence we knew.

At her first Bohemian party (it was actually in St. John's Wood) she was dazzled and intimidated by the easy conversation, the poise, the confidence, the wit. And she was not unaware that it might all be a matter of class:

How did one attain to that long-desired level? Must one be born with it or for ever go unsupported; was it the result of achievement, or thought, or education, or self-discipline, or—or—accident? ... I took rapid survey of the prints and water-colours and plaques on the buff walls, of the tapestries and pottery and the gentle air of comfort which soothed and satisfied the spirit. A harbour from the world—soft lights, soft sounds, soft colours, with an occasional bright splash of scarlet orange or green in cushion or jar to stimulate and enchant. ... A truly harmonious home.

It was painful to compare her own dismally "respectable" East End home, with its inevitable aspidistra and kippers, pink-rose wallpapers and antimacassars, where they read Mrs. Henry Wood and *News of the World*. Nothing was so pathetically bourgeois as working-class domesticity. Yet she could not feel at ease in Bohemia either. Clothes were an obvious problem: something "shabbily picturesque" would have passed for artistic, but hers were shabbily proletarian, which was quite another matter. Nor was it easy to discuss Italy, France, Brussels, or the Ballet Russe with an artist in a Soho restaurant: "I had never known anyone who had been farther than Eastbourne or Yarmouth." The class system did not stop at the boundaries of the artistic quarter. "We could not belong," Clare recognized, "but we would go to the studios if we were invited, and live on the fringe."

That marginal position allowed her to study Bohemians from an ideal vantage point. Like the Irish writer in London or the Jewish writer in America, the proletarian writer in Bohemia was at once an insider who knew the culture and an outsider who could criticize it. Once dazzled by artistic types, Clare eventually saw they were "conventional rebels, poseurs, hangers-on, freaks, slavish followers of fashion wherever fashion led."[3] This pattern would repeat itself again and again. From their precarious economic perch, working-class writers were able to produce a remarkably perceptive—and disillusioning—sociology of Bohemia.

In the 1920s, London's Bohemia offered plenty of inexpensive diversions for the working girl. Marjory Todd, a labor exchange clerk, attended chamber music (4d.) at the People's Palace in Mile End Road, the St. Matthew Passion at St. Clement Danes Church, lectures by Julian Huxley and Prof. Soddy, Fabian Society meetings, a tutorial class in political theory taught by C. E. M. Joad at Toynbee Hall. She could afford to attend the theater twice a month, indulge in a spaghetti and minestrone dinner in Charlotte Street for 1s., talk for hours at the Cafe Royal while she nursed a tall glass of coffee (9d.). At a WEA Summer School where G. D. H. and Margaret Cole taught, she could briefly enjoy something resembling university life: "All of us students, miners, clerks or mill-workers … felt it was a holiday to be able to work in seminars in the morning and spend the rest of the day in the country, walking, swimming, playing cricket or just loafing in the grounds of Easton Lodge—taking out a pile of books, and then not reading them but lying in the sunshine and talking or just simply idling as undergraduates do."

But even here, she repeatedly bumped up against class obstacles. For the Fabians she knew, the slums provided sociological specimens to be examined or perhaps, more deliciously, a vacation from bourgeois mores. Their ears pricked up when she mentioned she lived in Limehouse: "They had heard about sinister Chinese and opium dens. When I told them that I only saw the Chinese—the most law-abiding people—changing their books at the Public Library and that I often walked home all the way from Westminster to Limehouse late at night but unmolested, they looked politely skeptical." Only when she inherited £70 from her grandmother could she afford to move from Limehouse to an unfurnished room in Fitzroy Square. Once there, the social stratifications became all the more glaring. She joined the 1917 Club, a haunt of the Woolfs and the Stracheys and their followers, and was shocked to find, at what was supposed to be a gathering place for socialist intellectuals, an aristocratic high table reserved for the elect. Once she saw some friends off for a Paris holiday, and on impulse they urged her to come along. "It tore me in half. I had my passport ready and I could have gone with them. … But I knew then that I would come back to find my livelihood lost through an act of folly. And in those days I could not take such a risk." It was a lark to mingle with painters (some of whom actually produced pictures) and several authors of "Bloomsbury novels," but they clearly did not have to report to work on Monday:

> The Slade girls wore long picture-dresses after the fashion set by Dorelia John—with high fitted bodices, long full skirts, strings and strings of amber beads and Victorian jewelry bought in the Caledonian Market or at Cameo Corner. … Many of them looked lovely in them, especially at a time when fashion was so graceless. But it was a caste distinction all the same. They had to have an allowance of some sort from somewhere. No one who had to work could have dressed as they did. I could not have done so in my working hours at Tottenham.
>
> There was also, as always, an outer fringe of alcoholics, drug addicts, remittance men, women who lived on alimony, "artists' models," students who had given up working and were merely hanging round until their allowances were cut off. … Most of the young men I knew were the products of public schools and universities, in academic jobs, or beginning a career at the Bar, or living on an allowance from their parents while they found out if in fact they could become artists or writers, sowing oats as wild as they dared until supplies were cut off and they had to leave the group. … I can think of several knights, one Chairman of Quarter Sessions, one Recorder, several professors, one or two Members of Parliament whom I first knew over a half pint of bitter in those days.

She was also befriended by the linguist C. K. Ogden, who had developed a plan to reduce the English vocabulary to 850 words and wanted her to become the "original Basic English girl." It all came to an end when the Civil Service transferred her to Rawtenstall. Though she hated to leave Soho and the man she loved, hard economics left her no choice. Ogden offered her a job in one of his Cambridge bookshops, "but he wouldn't pay me enough to live on. … Dons' daughters who needed only pin money could work for less than I." "*Why* must you go?" asked her boyfriend. "Why must you always be so working-class? You should say 'I *can't* starve.' You should be able to take a risk." The "upper-class arrogance" of it all infuriated her: "It's because I *am* working-class that I know I *can* starve and I *won't*. Because I haven't got a rectory behind me if I come a cropper as you would have, and I am *always* going to pay my rent."[4]

That cultural conservatism was an insuperable barrier separating the working classes from the professional avant-garde. Working people could not afford permissiveness; for Bohemians it was and is a professional necessity. "The artist must experience everything" because he can put that experience into his art and sell it. All that is part of the cost of doing business in new sensibilities, especially erotic sensibilities. Angela Rodaway, daughter of a garage and soap factory worker, saw that immediately in a fascinating student teacher who introduced her to the Bohemia of the 1930s:

> She wore sandals, full skirts and bright shirt blouses, buttoned very low. Out of doors she wore a voluminous black cloak. Her hair was cut in the style of a boy of the sixteenth century and was the colour of birch leaves in autumn. She looked like a birch tree, slim and beautifully shaped with fine wrists and ankles and her clothes seemed somehow to cling to her, so that one saw her naked.

It was a lark when she took Angela to vegetarian restaurants and discussed psychology, but a visit to a Bohemian cottage in Norfolk came as a nasty shock. The floors could hardly be seen beneath the compost of books, scattered papers, old loaves of bread, dust, cobwebs, and soot: "It all looked like the archives section of a government department through which a tornado had passed and had long been stilled." One must understand that generations of British working women had waged a relentless class struggle against dirt. A coal-fired economy produced a perpetual drizzle of soot, which would overwhelm any home without constant scrubbing and cleaning. Bohemian children might rebel against bourgeois parents by effecting a studied slovenliness, especially when they found themselves living without servants, but for those who spent a lifetime doing dirty work, cleanliness was a radical affirmation of self-respect. Thomas Carter remembered that his mother "carried her dislike of dirtiness so far as to request every person coming into her house to be careful not to soil, or otherwise put out of order, the well scrubbed and 'neatly sanded floor'."[5] "Until that year," Angela Rodaway commented, "I had found that intellectual and aesthetic interests were always the concomitant of some degree of social graciousness. The two things had seemed to me inseparable." But in these "aggressive, left-wing political intellectuals, some of whom slept on the floor and ate vegetarian meals off orange-boxes ... I saw the total rejection of at least half of all I had hoped to aspire to."[6]

For a time Angela joined the young Bohemian crowd at the Cafe Royal. She ploughed through Freud and Jung, saw *The Cabinet of Dr. Caligari* ("it seemed merely grotesque"), and decorated her Battersea room with portraits of Bernard Shaw, Aldous and Julian Huxley, Marx, Walter de la Mare, and James Joyce. But she never fitted in with this herd of nonconformists. Bohemians are professional dissenters, defining themselves in opposition to the bourgeoisie, or at least their own cartoon of the bourgeoisie. Consequently, they often back themselves into an alternative conformity, becoming slaves to counterfashions. Everyone in her crowd, Angela noted, somehow had the idea that it was bourgeois to smoke but not drink, so they drank but did not smoke. "The talk was all of capitalism (with the stress on the second syllable and the glottal stop following), vegetarianism (boiled corn and lumps of cheese), sex and prenatal influences (though none of them liked children), and free love, no one apparently having heard the axiom that the great lover never really loves at all. It seemed to me that they missed the one great emotional experience." Though they put on airs of poverty, many of them had considerable financial reserves. What was even more appalling:

> Some deliberately went on the dole for half the year while they followed vocations as writers, painters, composers, or while they were studying for external degrees. I found this shocking. I lived in much the same way, going in and out of jobs, which I despised, and writing during the "rest" periods but I would not go on the dole. I had lived on it for too long in my childhood and I could not dissociate it from the means test.

Only after she fainted from hunger on an Underground platform did a leftist magazine editor persuade her to go on public assistance.[7] That persistence of Victorian respectability may explain why the British working classes never produced an outlaw intellectual like Jean Genet. A possible candidate might have been Mark Benney (b. 1910), a literary burglar. Bohemia, he found, would accept anything—"Whatever one did, Freud would excuse, and Bloomsbury would approve"—except yesterday's fashions, and there he disqualified himself. His tastes in art (and thievery) ran more to Louis XIV. He admired *The Decline and Fall of the Roman Empire* and *The Idylls of the King*, and scrounged Hampstead bookshops for secondhand Brownings and Rossettis. In prison he toyed with becoming a professional critic, but on his release he attended the opening night of O'Neill's *Strange Interlude*, and found it harder to bear than semi-solitary confinement. "The truth was, I had conceived culture as meaning an intimate knowledge of Greek literature, familiarity with the works of Leonardo, the ability to appreciate Beethoven," he conceded. For him, Shaw, Wells, Butler, Wilde, Kipling, and Masefield were still thrillingly new. He knew little of Freud except that everyone seemed to be talking about him at Soho's Cafe Vert, where artists and writers

> spent eloquent hours arguing about Proust, Pirandello and paederasty. All my preconceived notions were upset, all I had honoured became irrelevant, all my laboriously acquired knowledge was out of date. Joyce, Eliot, Rilke, Mann; Picasso, Gaudier, Wyndham Lewis; Keyserling, Spengler, Jung, Croce; Stravinsky, Bloch, Sibelius, Schönberg. These were the lords of the new culture; these had outshone the older artists, writers, thinkers, musicians till their work was reduced to the status of a clumsy child's ineptitudes. And not one of this hierarchy was I acquainted with.[8]

Charlie Lahr, a German anarchist who ran a scruffy Hammersmith bookshop, rejected all popular writers as inherently bourgeois. "Any writer earlier than

D. H. Lawrence, who had just come into prominence with *Sons and Lovers*, was out of date," recalled Bonar Thompson, who had left his job as a railway worker to become an itinerant orator. Lahr lent Thompson André Gide and *A Portrait of the Artist as a Young Man.* "It was wonderful for me to feel that I belonged to the elect who had read these giants of the future," wrote Thompson, who credited Lahr with introducing him to "writers of whom I should not otherwise have heard until years later." The difficulty was that "As soon as authors did become well known, Charlie had done with them. He felt, I suppose, that they had been bought over, or had taken to writing for the mob, else why were they popular with the wrong kind of readers?"[9]

That attitude infuriated Ethel Mannin, one of the most industrious authors of the century, who produced upwards of one hundred books over a lifetime. She broke into Bohemia only after serving an apprenticeship with the archenemy: the advertising industry. That was not an uncommon career path in modern literature (take for example Sherwood Anderson, F. Scott Fitzgerald, Hart Crane, Allen Tate, Allen Ginsberg)[10] but Mannin never apologized for her years on the job. She became a kind of anti-Woolf, sweating a living by her pen. She ground out romantic novels at a guinea per 1,000 words, and picked up another £20 a month writing for the women's pages of London and provincial newspapers.[11]

Her formula was to write frankly for readers who were "Philistines, and proud of it." Her definition of the term, however, did not include anyone who disparaged great literature and art, for Mannin was firmly rooted in the autodidact tradition. In her father's library she enjoyed Gissing and Wells, *Adam Bede* and *The Cloister and the Hearth.* A Clapham letter-sorter, he collected Nelson's Sevenpenny Classics, which she applauded as "a great boon to poor people." (In the 1930s she would advise Allen Lane on the Penguin Books project.)[12] By age fifteen she was quoting Wilde, Dr. Johnson, Francis Bacon, Shakespeare, Milton, Elizabeth Browning, Omar Khayyam, Anatole France, Emily Brontë, Shaw, Hazlitt, Stevenson, Scott, W. E. Henley, and Schopenhauer in her commonplace book. Yet Mannin was also stubbornly committed to "recognizing neither class nor intellectual distinctions," which she regarded as two related and equally arrogant forms of elitism. She repudiated the highbrow as well as the lowbrow: the latter was "merely a Highbrow gone wrong and become an intellectual pervert," who fetishized junk culture as the highbrow fetishized high culture. No, the saving remnant was neither highbrow nor lowbrow:

> They do not clutter up their lives with a lot of ideas about themselves; they do not wallow in a muck of idealism; they do not spell art with a capital A or beauty with a capital B. ... They do not measure success in terms of money, breeding in terms of blood, or culture in terms of learning. ... They are not literary; they strike no mental attitudes. They do not say, "This is good; this is bad; this is right; this is wrong; this is beautiful; this is ugly." They say, "If you like that sort of thing, that's the sort of thing you like," and "that's all right

for you; this is all right for me." They do not attempt to establish criteria; they are not concerned with accepted standards. They are Philistines, and do not care ....[13]

It was that cultural catholicism which Mannin so much admired in Arnold Bennett: "He is interested in literally everything—shops, football matches, seaside piers, music, literature, ill-health, dramatic critics, Greek plays—why not limericks?"[14] Except *Orlando*, she read nothing of Virginia Woolf, whom she found "too intellectual, too subtle and complicated and remote from reality."[15] In the 1930s she became a temporary admirer of the Soviet Union and turned to producing novels of social significance, but she still wrote in the same populist style, using her old reliable romantic devices to sell socialism.[16]

Mannin also reported on Bohemian doings for the popular papers. Billed as "a modern George Sand," she assumed some of the essential trappings of the avant-garde. She advocated trial marriages and got drunk in Greenwich Village. Her daughter began sex education at age three and was packed off to Summerhill, A. S. Neill's progressive school. Mannin made sure to read *Ulysses* (or at least the final chapter)[17] and she admired Gertrude Stein. But in the end she lost all patience with modernist obscurity:

Me, I did not and do not want a language that burns black the tongue of one who speaks it and scars the one who listens: I wanted—and want—a language that will make meaning clear, that will speak with the tongues of men and of angels, language that does not merely photograph actuality but interprets it. ... But there, apparently, it all was; there seemed to be some virtue in obscurity; obscurity of style and in you yourself being obscure, religiously avoiding the vulgarity of success, or even of recognition outside of the immediate circle, the sacred inner circle of the coterie; your work, it seemed, must be esoteric or you were in the outer darkness of a shoddy fame.

Mannin completely rejected the Bohemian portrait of the artist as "a creature apart." She embraced instead the popular craftsmanship championed by William Morris, her father's hero:

As much creative impulse may go into the making of a chair as the writing of a book. ... It is the mediocre people who are most insistent on spelling art with a capital A. They talk about "my work," and with every piddling little production imagine themselves one degree more removed from the common run of humanity. ...

There are poets who have never written a line of poetry; artists who are completely unaware that they have ever in their lives fulfilled more than the daily round, the common task, illuminated by enjoyment of such simple things as days of sun, pints of beer, and being in love. They have put beautiful craftsmanship into the making of a gate, thatching a roof, mending a pair of boots; poured out a wealth of creative love in the making of a garden. ... Many a writer of books and painter of pictures is less of an artist than many such simple inarticulate people in whose veins, unknown to them, flows the poetry of the earth, the rhythm of life itself.[18]

Where Is Bohemia?

But if all good workmanship is art, and if creative people are everywhere, we must inevitably confront a disorienting question: "Where is Bohemia?" It was asked and perceptively answered by hatter Frederick Willis:

Writers and artists of a certain type are under the impression that it exists in Chelsea, Bloomsbury, and St. John's Wood; young journalists think it is to be found in the Savage Club and the Cafe Royal, and respectable people from the suburbs used to pin their faith to the Bullfrog Club, the Gargoyle Club, the Poets' Club, and similar places. The fashion for spending dreary evenings in crazy apartments situated in West End mews flourished between the wars, and may continue for all I know, but this is only a counterfeit Bohemia.[19]

Willis personally preferred the proletarian Bohemia of railway station coffee-stalls and Islington carnivals. But this much is agreed on: Bohemia is always in a great metropolitan center, on the *rive gauche*, in Greenwich Village, along the Bloomsbury–Chelsea axis. A suburban Bohemia seems a contradiction in terms, even an obscenity. Bohemia defines itself as an anti-suburbia. But, Willis suggested, is suburban philistinism not a self-serving myth created by Bohemians?

Suburbia, the butt of most self-styled intellectual writers; dull suburbia, soulless suburbia, snobbish suburbia. But I can testify, being a suburbanite myself, there was happiness, contentment, and morality in Victorian and Edwardian suburbia that it would be hard to find in equal proportion anywhere else. ... When I was young there was hardly any masterpiece of literature written in English that was not available in a sixpenny or shilling edition. The very fact that we had no radio or television made us tremendous readers and talkers. Publishers turned out these books in millions and we paid our money and took our choice. There were no book societies to make a choice for us. ... I have spent many pleasant hours discussing these books with my friends with the same enthusiasm that modern youth discusses the merits of football teams or film stars.[20]

As other plebeian writers testified, there was plenty of culture in suburbia. The difficulty was that it was a classic Everyman's Library culture, which has no economic value for professionals in the business of producing new culture. They cannot do their job unless they have news about galleries, artists, theatrical directors, designers, undiscovered authors—and they must have it sooner than anyone else. There are four industries that must cluster in metropolitan centers fairly close to each other: the arts, finance, the national media, and the garment trade. Bloomsbury, the City, Fleet Street, and Whitechapel (or Greenwich Village, Wall Street, Sixth Avenue, and Seventh Avenue) are located where they are because they are all extremely sensitive to fashion, continually retooling to exploit the latest trends. Entrepreneurs in all these businesses therefore must have absolutely up-to-the-minute information, which can only be picked up "on the street." If they remain in the suburbs and wait until the press reports on a new artistic movement or oil strike or style in evening wear, that news will be stale and worthless. Putting it in anthropological terms, Mary Douglas explains that the Bohemian, like anyone else, has "to get the best information that is available, and to get near its sources so as to have it reliably and quickly." If he is physically remote from "information about the changing cultural scene ... other people can tamper with the switchboard, he will miss his cues, and meaning will be swamped by noise"—that is, Bohemia will move on to a new trend that he cannot comprehend. "So his objective as a rational consumer also involves an effort to be near the center of transmission and an effort to seal off the boundaries of the system."[21] The elite Bohemians of the Bloomsbury Group and the Fabian Society were perfectly positioned to achieve both objectives.

In theory, one might create the same critical mass in the suburbs by building a planned community for artistic people. Bedford Park was a late Victorian experiment in that direction; a garden suburb for academics, artists, theater people, and authors, among them W. B. Yeats. Another resident, G. K. Chesterton, recalled

When by the windows (often bow)
Or on the stairways (seldom strong)
Summoned (perhaps) by copper gong
Fixed up by Craftsmen pure and stark,
We met in that amazing throng,
People we met in Bedford Park.[22]

But as Frederick Willis recognized, Bedford Park Bohemians could not escape a fundamental contradiction by moving out of the city. Though they disdained traditional suburbs, they were producing cultural goods and services ultimately destined for suburban consumption. "Paradoxically," Willis noted in 1960, "Bedford Park merely became the pattern for conventional suburbia. The craze for oak beams and artificial quaintness spread from Bedford Park to all the new suburbs as rapidly as does the Colorado beetle," to the point where the community lost all its distinctiveness.[23]

The cultural contradictions of Bohemia were most penetratingly analyzed by East End novelist Thomas Burke, a former hotel boot-cleaner. He was fascinated by the artistic community when he discovered it before the First World War, and repeatedly returned to the subject throughout his literary career. As early as 1915, however, he saw that it was becoming a theme park. Soho snookered young Fabians and secretaries with overpriced restaurants, serving indifferent food and not much Parisian gaiety. The high-rent Bohemia of Chelsea was all "painfully manufactured."[24] Poseurs were still dressing up like the characters in Murger's novel and Puccini's opera. Even Augustus John "looks and dresses like a comic-paper Bohemian." Bohemia, he concluded, could not deliver the creative freedom it promised because it was essentially a business, a factory for manufacturing aesthetics. Like any other business it had its own work rules, dress codes, product lines, marketing strategies, professional jargon, and corporate culture. "In all my experience," Burke protested, "I have met few real poets, artists, or musicians who are bohemians. I have usually found them to be as precise and formal as lawyers are supposed to be." That is why those who escape to Bohemia in search of self-realization are usually disappointed. Bohemia organizes nonconformity, standardizes eccentricity, plans spontaneity, lays down rules for creativity, industrializes artistic innovation, markets a repudiation of consumer capitalism. A true Bohemianism, as Burke argued, would be

> simply the habit of being oneself at all times and occasions. ... [But] in the
> professional Bohemia individuality has little play. At Art balls and revels ...
> everybody is alike, all must conform to the prevailing mood and taste, and be
> gay or eccentric according to the occasion. ... All is considered and deliberate;
> a spectacle of solemn young people trying to be "different," wearing the absurd
> trappings of Murger's country, which existed only at the point of his pen, and
> trying to invoke the Russian oversoul with thin drinks; young men with pink
> socks and pink voices fumbling with the arts, and trying to forget that they
> came from Liverpool.

Only the homosexuals saved it from hopeless dullness, and even they were no longer fulfilling their quota of outrageousness. The irony was that all that Bohemia promised—freedom, creativity, novelty, diversity, color—could be found in every part of the metropolis *outside* the artistic quarter:

> Bohemia lies everywhere about you, except in studios, for these are serious
> workshops; you are as likely to find it there as behind the grille of the Bank of
> England. But you will find it in the East India Dock Road, among the marine
> students; in Smithfield and Bermondsey, among the mad medicals; in South
> Kensington, among the science men. ... The four-ale bar is Bohemia. The
> suburban monkey's parade is Bohemia. Hampstead Heath at night is Bohemia.
> ... In every corner of the great bazaar of London the ardent shopper of

humanity will find the stalls loaded with bunches of Bohemian bananas, not to be bought or bargained for, but to be had for the taking.

Any New Yorker today would be struck by the force of that: a random walk through the city offers sensations far more various and fascinating than anything one can find in Soho. For Burke, the only true Bohemians were the workers, because they could pursue art and literature without concern for sales or image. For an authentic Bohemian restaurant, Burke recommended the Newspaper Workers' Club off St. Bride Street, with a bar open till 4 a.m., great meals for 1s., wonderfully coarse printers and writers, and billiards and darts. There was also a workingmen's cafe near Great Queen Street, the haunt of unsuccessful men of letters from nearby council flats, whose scruffiness was a function of poverty rather than a fashion statement. There you could find the kind of carefree individuality that only failure can preserve.[25] Where is Bohemia? In Stepney, where every Russian immigrant family seemed to have a piano, and factory girls played Sibelius.[26] "It proves what the artists have not yet learnt," Burke proclaimed, "that one can lead the Bohemian life, if one wishes to, in strict decency, and that muddle and drunkenness are no necessary part of it."[27]

Burke wrote his own guide to Bloomsbury, which scarcely mentioned the Group. Without naming Lytton Strachey, he debunked "the fables started by various commentators on the Victorian age," in particular the notion that "the Victorians were stifled by repressive fetishes and sat tamely in captivity, and that we of this generation demolished those fetishes and marched into sunlight and freedom." This, he argued, was one of Bohemia's class-bound illusions. The anti-Victorians only knew Victorians in their own social stratum, assuming "that all the life of the middle nineteenth century could be represented by Cabinet Ministers' wives in dolman and chignon." But Burke, who made a hobby of collecting low nineteenth-century literature, knew that the Victorian underworld had been more coarse than anything contemporary Bohemia had to offer. Penny dreadfuls, music hall songs, scandal sheets, the earthier competitors of *Punch*, the works of G. W. M. Reynolds "would be regarded as Terribly Bad Taste," if not suppressed outright, in the twentieth century. Today academics would find this a very postmodern treatment of the Victorians, but Burke was doing it in 1939.[28]

All the same, the working-class Bohemian might feel as alien in his own community as in Bloomsbury. Willy Goldman's 1940 memoir *East End My Cradle* is a necessary corrective to romantic treatments of Jewish Whitechapel, where, as in other working-class communities, there were rough as well as respectable elements. The widow's sons who prepared for scholarship examinations in the public library coexisted with street gangs, wife-beaters, tawdry sex, and, in some quarters, a suspicious contempt for education. The East End did occasionally give rise to unmistakably Bohemian eccentrics, but their neighbors tended to label them "queer." "They may read books surreptitiously, or adopt some other 'intellectual' pursuit," Goldman explained. "Sometimes they are thwarted artists.

... People point them out in the street: 'See that long-haired fellow?' They tap their foreheads significantly. 'Some say he's supposed to be clever.' This last is added from a sense of fairness rather than conviction." Goldman knew one of these characters, Ephraim Wise, who appeared to be a half-wit and down-and-outer until he revealed himself to be a talented artist. Some autodidacts were loyally supported by their families, but the reaction of Wise's relatives was equally common:

> To his people he was a "problem"—but not a psychological one. He was merely the ordinary problem of the "no-good." That was their explanation of his artistic ambitions. He was "too big for his boots." They felt he had no right to be "different." People with warped lives will forgive you anything but being different from themselves. They will deny it as long as they can: label you "no-good," "snob," "stuck-up," and all the rest of it—until you prove your difference. Then they will hate you with a mean, murderous hate. That is the greatest honour they can do you. It is the reward of the artist who rises from adversity.

But Wise could never rise very far. After two years as a garment worker he resolved, at any cost, to attend an art school, where he seemed to be the only student without a car. His family opposed and ridiculed him at every turn, always needling him about the "sacrifices" they were making. He had saved enough for the first term's tuition, but when he came up £3 short for the second term's, neither his relatives nor the school would make up the difference. His back to the wall, Wise became a gatecrasher. He had always been the type who was regularly evicted from public libraries: now he continued to attend art school until the porter threw him out. He then invited himself to stay with a friend in Stepney Green. He tried breaking and entering to cadge commissions: Bernard Shaw allowed him ten minutes of sketching, and he once successfully infiltrated the office of an art journal editor. Occasionally West Enders were amused by this reverse slumming and engaged him for a portrait, until he ended up dead from delirium and exhaustion in Colney Hatch Asylum. Totally indifferent to basic material concerns, he stands as a reminder that some artists really are willing to starve for their work.

He also demonstrates that modernist fears of the mob—the people who censored Lawrence, Joyce, Radclyffe Hall, and Henry Miller—were not absolutely groundless. The fate of Ephraim Wise left Willy Goldman deeply alienated from his working-class community, and parts of his memoir were published in the journals of high Bohemia—Osbert Sitwell's *Life and Letters* and John Lehmann's *New Writing*. But he was no more at ease in Bloomsbury. With wholly sardonic intent, he titled one chapter of his memoirs "A Room of One's Own." For authors who had to work in cramped tenements, Mrs. Woolf's essay was a sour middle-class joke.[29] Working-class aspirants to Bohemia faced an even greater barrier: without leisure time, a university education, or social contacts among the avant-garde, it was almost impossible to master the modernist canon. Though Goldman joined the public library, he could not bring himself "to ask for a 'serious' or 'intelligent' book, for it sounded snobbish and highbrow." What he wanted, really, was "to read what great minds think of our crazy world," and that he could only find in the older classics. While engaged in writing he "had a sudden reversion from the moderns to the Masters, finding more in every way of what I wanted in Dostoievsky and Balzac than in any except the most outstanding contemporaries. I have always since favoured rather those writers who get into a passion about life than those who lay it bare before you like a dissected corpse." His taste in English novelists started with Defoe and ended, abruptly, with Wells.[30]

The early career of V. S. Pritchett shows that a Council school boy could not easily acquire the credentials for admission to Bohemia, and was likely to find himself stranded betwixt and between. His grandfather had been a classic Victorian autodidact, steeled by Carlyle and Ruskin. Pritchett himself was really a cut above the working classes (his father was a Micawberish businessman) and at Rosendale Road School near Herne Hill he received a remarkably progressive education from an unusually innovative teacher, W. W. Bartlett. "Mr. Bartlett's methods were spacious," Pritchett recalled. "A history lesson might go on for days; if it was about early Britain and old downland encampments he would bring us wild flowers from the Wiltshire tumuli." He illustrated lessons with his own paintings and sketches, and then set the pupils to make their own. But the real "revelation" came in his English classes, where Bartlett took the revolutionary step of introducing his students to the latest in contemporary literature. Dispensing with textbooks, he handed out Ford Madox Ford's *English Review* and discussed Bridges, Masefield, and John Davidson. "For myself," Pritchett wrote,

the sugar-bag blue cover of the *English Review* was decisive. One had thought literature was in books written by dead people who had been oppressively over-educated. Here was writing by people who were alive and probably writing at this moment. They were as alive as Barlow Woods. The author was not remote; he was almost with us. He lived as we did; he was often poor …. The art of writing became a manual craft as attractive—to a boy—as the making of elderberry pipes or carpentering. My imagination woke up. I now saw my grandfather's talk of Great Men in a new light. They were not a lot of dead Jehovahs far away; they were not even "Great"; they were men.

Soon Pritchett was reading Penny Poets editions of *Paradise Regained*, Wordsworth's *Prelude*, Cowper, and Coleridge. He formulated plans to become Poet Laureate by age twenty-one, until he realized that his education had not prepared him to become a poet of any kind, official or Bohemian. On the one hand, he failed his grammar school scholarship examination: Bartlett's creative curriculum had neglected basic grammar and spelling. He was equally unprepared for the intimidating greatness of Ruskin's *Modern Painters* and the Dulwich

Gallery: "It was the old story …. There was too much to know. I discovered that Ruskin was not so very many years older than I was when he wrote that book." Later, as an office boy, Pritchett tried to read widely and dreamt of an escape to Bohemia. But his knowledge of the Latin Quarter was gleaned not from Flaubert, only from third-raters like George du Maurier, W. J. Locke, and Hilaire Belloc. He could not escape the sense that "all my tastes were conventionally Victorian. … I seemed irredeemably backward and lower class and the cry of the autodidact and snob broke out in me in agony 'Shall I never catch up?'"[31]

Before the Youth Culture

"It is one thing to be 'socially mobile,'" observed Leslie Paul (b. 1905), whose father was rising out of the working classes into the lower depths of the advertising profession, "but it is another thing to catch up culturally. That takes longer," especially in a home environment where "there was not much talk of writers beyond Dickens and Scott and the lady who wrote *The Lamplighter*, and nothing at all about music and poetry or the arts." Paul made an embarrassing debut in Bohemia, wearing yesterday's fashions. Having developed an adolescent passion for the nature writer Richard Jefferies, he edited a hiking monthly, acquired a Harris tweed suit and hat, and even "prospected a bungalow at Caterham, preparing to become a poet-editor-country gentleman in the already defunct Georgian style."[32] Jefferies had enjoyed a prewar following of nature-lovers, but by 1923 he had passed into his "rubbish" phase, and Georgian pastoral had been abandoned for the bleak modernism of Eliot.[33]

Nevertheless, Paul persevered. With autodidact diligence, he closed in on the avant-garde. He read "Prufrock" and *The Waste Land*, though not until the 1930s. He smuggled *Ulysses* and *Lady Chatterley's Lover* past customs. In *John o' London's* and the *Nation*, in William MacDougall's Home University Library volume on *Psychology* and F. A. Servanté's *Psychology of the Boy*, he read up on Freud. In a few years he knew enough to ghost-write BBC lectures on modern psychology. By age sixteen he already knew "the terrible sentence passed upon my world by those Freudian words of judgement: censor, repression, Oedipus complex, compensation, sublimation, neurosis; which rendered every emotion suspect and convicted almost every life of being lived in bad faith."[34]

Out of those Oedipal influences, Paul would create the Woodcraft Folk, a working-class youth movement that nearly caught up with Bohemia. Though never large, it was a fascinating anticipation of the youth culture that would germinate in the 1950s and blossom in the 1960s. It may seem paradoxical that the roots of the Woodcraft Folk lay in the Boy Scout movement, which taught loyalty to king, country, and employers. But as Paul recognized, scouting inadvertently sparked a grass-roots generational rebellion that would have shocked Sir Robert Baden-Powell, had he been aware of what slum boys were thinking. Many of them read his *Scouting for Boys* (1907) through their own subversive frame:

> British youth by the thousands were electrified. With an astonishing perception they leapt at Scouting as at something for which they had long been waiting, divining that this was a movement which took the side of the natural, inquisitive, adventuring boy against the repressive schoolmaster, the moralizing parson and the coddling parent. Before the leaders knew what was happening groups were springing up spontaneously and everywhere bands of boys, with bare knees, and armed with broomsticks, began foraging through the countryside. But for the generalship of which Baden-Powell was a master, the Boy Scout movement might have led to the defiant experiments characteristic of German youth; as it was, under his leadership it became orderly, constitutional and imperialist. ... In the decade from 1908 to 1918 no other influence upon British boyhood came anywhere near it. In this decade I grew up, with the Scout movement as my real spiritual home, learning to despise the work of classrooms in favour of the open air pursuits the Scout movement glorified, and hopeful that I might build my whole life upon them.[35]

Playing Trotsky to Baden-Powell's Stalin was John Hargrave, a charismatic veteran of Gallipoli who called himself "White Fox" and preached an ideology of "Red Indianism." His book *The Great War Brings It Home* (1919) called on the coming generation to make a revolutionary break with European civilization and embrace the cultures of indigenous peoples. He rose to the upper ranks of the Boy Scouts, but when he called for less militarism and more democracy in the movement, he was purged. In 1920 he organized his own band of youth, the Kibbo Kift Kindred, which was supposed to mean "Proof of Great Strength." The Kibbo Kift made a cult of the new, though the doctrines they promoted were the shopworn enthusiasms of the prewar avant-garde. Following Edward Carpenter, they viewed Western civilization as a disease and the simple life as its cure. Like H. G. Wells, they advocated a world government led by an enlightened and selfless elite, i.e., themselves. Inspired by William Morris, they encouraged handicrafts and looked forward to a postindustrial green utopia.[36] Paul, who edited a Kibbo Kift paper, found it all intoxicating: "We were the elect. In my small lodge we were absorbed with the sense of being chosen. We were going to change the world. ... We talked of the Silent Places, and scorned the common herd living in the Big Smoke."[37]

Hargrave proved no less autocratic than Baden-Powell, and in 1925 Paul broke away to organize the Woodcraft Folk, a splinter of a splinter based on the educational theories of Rousseau's *Emile*. Paul's manifesto *The Child and the Race* (1926) proclaimed the younger generation as the true revolutionary class. His group sang ersatz folk songs and rejected book learning for the immediate experience of adolescence. They adopted American Indian names, though the

Indians had never done them any harm. They repudiated traditional Christianity for a vague but fervent pantheism that would today find a home in the more mystical corners of the environmental movement. They were passionate pacifists who admired the Russian Revolution, and never saw the contradiction. And just as the Beatniks defined themselves in opposition to Madison Avenue, Paul "loathed" his father for pursuing the "degrading occupation" of advertising salesman.[38]

In short, the Woodcraft Folk had all the ingredients that made up the youth culture of the 1960s, except sex, drugs, rock-and-roll, and (let us not forget the Fourth Horseman) designer clothes. Contraception, narcotics, Carnaby Street, and the endless consumption of perishable pop records required a level of affluence that would only be attained a generation later. Much as the new French bourgeoisie of the 1830s gave rise to the *rive gauche* Bohemia, the great postwar expansion of the middle class throughout the Western world produced a mass-market Bohemia, making available to millions of teenagers the moral freedoms and experimental lifestyles that had once been confined to a few elite intellectuals. In the Great Depression, the Woodcraft Folk could not have imagined any of this. They belonged to a strong tradition of working-class puritanism which, after the Second World War, was doomed by rising incomes and modern permissiveness. In 1938 they had a total membership, including adults, of 4,521 (compared with 438,713 for the Boy Scouts) and they declined steadily from there.[39] It was profoundly disillusioning to see their German counterpart, the Wandervögel, submerge themselves in the Hitler Youth; and Stalin's purges ended their infatuation with the Soviets. Their woolly Edwardian bohemianism seemed, in the Second World War, worse than irrelevant. The traditional civilization Leslie Paul had denounced—with its "values of truth, justice, mercy, creativity"—was now fighting for survival against two fascist leaders of mass youth movements. In his memoirs, Paul wrote off the Woodcraft Folk as an embarrassing episode, a childhood disease.[40]

What Went Wrong?

The title of Paul's autobiography, by the way, was *Angry Young Man*. It was published in 1951—a lean year for Bohemia, with Britain still in the grip of economic austerity and cultural conservatism. Yet it is a curious phenomenon: whenever an idea has been finally and thoroughly discredited, then the moment has come for its revival. Five years later Paul's label was stuck on a new generation of writers, starting with John Osborne, Kingsley Amis, and John Wain. The Angry Young Men had almost nothing (certainly not anger) in common except that their careers were swept along by a new and much more powerful wave of youth rebellion propelled, in part, by the diffusion of modernism. If indeed working-class culture consistently lags a generation behind avant-garde culture, then the Teddy Boys were due to discover *The Waste Land* around 1952. They would not read the original, of course. Rather, the modernist mood of disillusionment, disaffection, dissent, and dissonance would gradually permeate popular culture and eventually trickle down the social scale. Originating in Bohemia, it would be picked up by academics and highbrow periodicals, and then (after a decent interval) relayed to the masses by middlebrow journalists, screenwriters, and novelists. When that sensibility, once confined to Bloomsbury, reached the secondary modern schools, it would inspire what we now call "the youth culture," which we have come to accept as the inevitable price of adolescence. In 1952 an adult educator explained that

> the peculiar autumnal feeling of disintegration felt by intellectuals in the late 20's and 30's and expressed in *The Waste Land* ... would seem utterly strange—outlandish is still the best word—to an average working-class audience. For to them the middle 30's were a time of hope and excitement—growing signs of the Welfare State, emancipation of women, international idealism, hopes of a Labour Government with real power—they were the February days before the spring. Auden and the Red poets were as far off the mark as Eliot and despair.

That Victorian earnestness, which sustained the WEA and autodidact culture as a whole, survived largely intact up until 1945. Only the next generation, too young to remember the idealistic Thirties, would catch up with modernist pessimism:

> The ideas of intellectuals do in fact seep down through society, in over-simplified and distorted forms, but with a curious rough and ready veracity. The cynicism and debunking of Aldous Huxley in the 20's, even the far-off influences of Darwin and Freud, eventually reach the young shop assistant or the lorry driver and they are thrown back in the face of the intellectuals in the kind of cynicism revealed by Lavers and Rowntree or Professor Zweig. Press, radio, popular novels, films on schizophrenia, finally even the "penny dreadfuls" pass along psychology, popular science, criticisms of religion, electronic brains and mechanical tortoises, whether the educationists like it or not.[41]

Jim Turnbull loathed it. A blacksmith, the child of drunks, almost totally deprived of formal education, he became a teetotaler, a socialist, and an insatiable self-improver in Jarrow, where two-thirds of the work force were on the dole in 1934. His library included Chesterton, Belloc, Bradlaugh, Darwin, and *The Pickwick Papers*, as well as a collection of classical records. He debated Aquinas and Hume with a Dominican stump-speaker. He bought his nephew Bacon's essays at a 3d. bookstall, took him to his first opera (*La Bohème*), and (though an atheist) taught him to appreciate the architecture of St. Nicholas's Cathedral. He believed absolutely in the essential goodness of working people and their capacity for enjoying great literature and music. Presented with contrary evidence, he invariably asserted that a more equitable society would fix all that. And he had a specific blueprint for the socialist utopia: it was going to be a permanent free symphony concert. "You'll see the time, son, when the symphonies of Beethoven and the operas of Mozart will be played in public halls everywhere"—this in a town where hardly any classical music was ever heard. "The bits of bairns'll be whistling Schubert and Chopin, and Handel'll be a household word. ... One day, son, one day, we'll all take in great music like a bairn takes in its mother's milk." Jim Turnbull's tragedy, his nephew wrote, was that he lived to see the 1960s:

He looked up from a famous review, pushing back a pair of steel-rimmed spectacles, and delivered a sharp tirade against scientific humanism and angry young novelists. We looked out of the window at the street. Forty years hadn't made all that difference to the houses. There were a few fancy front doors with glass panels and chromium knockers, a forest of television aerials and a car of sorts at every other house. Uncle Jim sighed. He looked like a defeated general. He turned sadly back to his pile of penny poets and his 1920 *Clarions*, an old fighter whose victory had turned sour, a rebel without a cause.
"What went wrong, hinney?" he asked.[42]

"I knew how my grandfather's, even my father's, generation felt about education," wrote Jennie Lee.

They were very romantic about it. They thought of it as a kind of lamp to light the feet of their children, so that we need not stumble and hurt ourselves as they had done, or as armour buckled around us so that we could meet in fair fight all who stood in our way. ... That fight was all part of the struggle to build a self-confident working-class. Jude the Obscure, fearful of his own limitations and impressed by the training of his superiors, vowed that his children should be numbered among the Initiated. ... It is very hard on the old idealistic socialist when he sees graduates from the working-class homes turn into small-town snobs. He had counted on them to be his invaluable allies. He cannot understand what has gone wrong.[43]

H. E. Bates, who bitterly remembered living on the dole when the streets were full of jobless disabled veterans, considered John Osborne a pampered kid who did not know the meaning of the word "angry." "Look Back in Self-Pity" was more like it.[44] Ethel Mannin walked out after the first act of *Look Back in Anger* which she had seen somewhere before: "The sort of half-baked stuff about Life, Society, the Social System, Love, Sex, fashionable with the progressive-minded young *circa* 1915."[45] Herbert Morrison belonged to a generation of Labour politicians who loved their old Board schools for teaching strict discipline and great literature, who denounced the abolition of school prizes as the "silliest and meanest" of the Depression-era spending cuts. "Fortunately for us this desire to create a better world and to get rid of the bad old one did not exhibit itself in some anti-social activities which so aggravate the situation today," he scolded the younger generation in 1960. "Thanks to the flood of books and pamphlets by wise and far-seeing writers"—Morrison was a great fan of Nelson's Classics and Stead's Penny Poets—"we had our thoughts harnessed to purposeful and feasible ambitions."[46]

The Sixties were equally hard on Communist Jack Dash, who always had a limitless faith in the intellectual capacity of the proletariat. Before the premiere of *Look Back in Anger*, a half-dozen other longshoremen and he had formed "a sort of industrial Socrates discussion forum." They would report themselves available for work and, if there was none, retreat to a park or coffee shop. "Heated discussions would then take place on subjects such as political economy, dialectical materialism, what was meant by qualitative change and quantitative change and in what order they appeared in the class struggles of a capitalist society." One docker had a superb knowledge of English literature and could discuss Hobbes, Locke, and Nietzsche. A second would plunge into Bishop Berkeley and the purpose of art under capitalism, and there was a former professional wrestler who was an expert in biology and photography. Dash himself was an amateur artist, who staunchly believed "that all art began with an altruistic purpose." On that count, the age of Warhol was deeply disillusioning. Dash could admire collier's son Henry Moore, but the fact that the Greater London Council had paid £7,000 for a sculpture of a woman with a head looking in three directions only convinced him that modern artists had been corrupted by commodification, enslaved to "gimmickry and fad." His tastes still ran to art with a moral, like Rodin's *The Burghers of Calais*—a "symbol that there are humans who do not live for themselves alone." He could take pride in visiting the Royal Festival Hall, "conscious that this beautiful hall was built by my class," but he had to admit that "the percentage of wage-workers attending to enjoy the concerts is like a spit in the Thames."[47]

Bernard Kops (b. 1926), the son of an immigrant leather worker, had a special understanding of the transition from autodidact culture to old Bohemia to youth culture, because he experienced all three. He grew up in the ferment of the Jewish East End, attended *Faust* at Sadler's Wells, read *The Tempest* at school, and cried over "The Forsaken Merman." At fifteen he became a cook at a hotel, where the staff gave him Karl Marx, Henry Miller, and *Ten Days That Shook the World*. A neighbor presented him with the poems of Rupert Brooke, and "Grantchester" so resonated with the Jewish slum boy that he went to the library to find another volume from the same publisher, Faber and Faber. Thus he stumbled upon T. S. Eliot. "This book changed my life," he remembered. "It struck me straight in the eyes like a bolt of lightning." Most working-class readers found it more difficult to leap into modernism, but because Kops had not yet become accustomed to more traditional poetry, he was not locked into an old frame: "I had no preconceived ideas about poetry and read 'The Wasteland' and 'Prufrock' as if they were the most acceptable and common forms in existence. The poems spoke to me directly, for they were bound up with the wasteland of the East End, and the desolation and loneliness of people and landscape. Accidentally I had entered the mainstream of literature."

Having entered it, he plunged ahead at full throttle. After Stalingrad, he immersed himself in Russian literature. A GI dating his sister introduced him to Walt Whitman and Emily Dickinson. At Speakers' Corner he recited *The Ballad of Reading Gaol*. But he was not encouraged by his family: "My father told me that books would get me nowhere fast." He was right, as Kops later admitted: "Books took me away from the family as I sat amongst them. Farther and farther away." Now he regarded them all through an Eliotic frame: "I would sit on the settee as they played cards and I'd look up and see them, wonder where I fitted in. I had fantasies."

When rows broke out in his overcrowded slum apartment, Kops took refuge in the Whitechapel Public Library, reading Garcia Lorca, Sean O'Casey, and Shakespeare. Eventually he escaped to Soho, but he could not entirely fit in there either.[48] Up to a point Bohemia was "a place where I could be myself," but it was also a "largely terrifying and sordid" world inhabited by "tearaways, layabouts, lesbians, queers, mysteries, and hangers-on … the would-be poets, the sad girls from Scotland, the artists without studio or canvas. The kinky men searching for kinky love." There were four Trotskyites who perpetually quarreled until they formed two antagonistic parties. Beatniks appeared in Soho in 1950, and then "Bohemia became depressing. … Soho suicides were merely people who couldn't face up to mediocrity." (Remember that the Beat Generation was first called that because they seemed beaten down.) Kops knew "many humanitarians who beat their wives, or socialists who are fascists to their children. It's so easy to hide behind a banner. Maybe they need to love the masses because they can't love people." At one orgy a girl methodically worked her way through every man in the room and then, at 4 a.m., broke down in tears and told him that her Jewish mother lived just up the road by Stepney Green Station ("Do you think I should go and see her?").

Kops frequently went home for a hot meal. He came to feel that the East End, for all its limitations, was "a happy world. And there was a spirit of community as in a village. People were involved in each other's lives, and not for the wrong reasons. Now [1963], looking back, I see it was a desperate time—but then it meant security and happiness." There was poverty but no competitive materialism, a world where Woody Allen would have been incomprehensible: "I cannot remember the excitable neurosis that pervades bourgeois Jewish communities today."[49] Perhaps Kops was unduly nostalgic for laboring-class domesticity and too hard on creative-class artiness, but those themes had by then become a tradition in proletarian literature. A circle of working-class poets would carry that tradition forward into the 1960s, celebrating the suburban respectability of "Penny Lane," while uneasy amidst the brittle promiscuity and Scandivanian decor of Swinging London:

I once had a girl
or I should say

she once had me.
She showed me her room,
isn't it good?
Norwegian wood.[50]

Ultimately Kops gave up the grottiness of Soho for marriage and fatherhood, very like Gordon Comstock in *Keep the Aspidistra Flying*, but with one important difference. In 1936 Orwell's half-hero had no choice but to turn bourgeois and take a job in advertising. Two decades later Kops could carry on as a state-subsidized Bohemian with a £500 Arts Council grant.[51] He saw that affluence was transforming Bohemia, and not for the better:

> The American civilization had caught up with us. Everything was speeded up and slicked up, and there was a great deal of violence in the streets. A wave of bitterness and cynicism broke out. The whole surface seemed to be cracking. Prostitutes were thronging the pavements of Old Compton Street and policemen were walking around with hands open behind their backs for their dropsy and the Pornbrokers were raking it in. Cafés that we knew started closing, the leisurely ones where artists and anarchists argued all day. Coffee bars were opening in their place. The object was to get you in, make you feel uncomfortable under the harsh lighting, and then get you out as quickly as possible.

Soho was overrun by kids with guitars, and already the buzz on the street was that

> the great revolution of youth would break out at any moment. ... And we, the old crop of the gone poets, sauntered the West End streets still thinking we would set the place alight and march on the citadels of the philistines. ...
> The age of the week-end Bohemian had arrived! ...
> For the old-timers of Soho things got desperate. Some tried to fit into the new coffee-bar society, became characters, dispensing old anti-social tales to the newly lost. They held court, were lionized but remained pathetic. Most of them died alone somewhere, at night in a lousy room, and they were forgotten within days. ... Soon I started recalling the old blissful really gone bohemian days. I was already part of that past and still hadn't begun.

We are all weekend Bohemians now, patronizing the "creative industries" that occupy much of London and the better part of lower Manhattan. Kops saw Bohemia mutate into a form that is recognizable today, right down to the artists in search of a marketable gimmick ("I must find next year's trend now") and the coffee bars with "bad paintings on the wall and good girls trying to look bad around the walls."[52] Through the 1940s, all forms of consumption had been strictly limited by wartime rationing and postwar austerity, as well as an asceticism rooted in the Nonconformist churches and still potent within the Labour Party. Only in the early 1950s could housewives at last burn their ration books. The green light had been given not only to washing machines, automobiles, and television sets, but also to fashion designers, interior decorators, artists, boutiques, rock entrepreneurs, experimental playwrights, and trendy restaurants. One has to be on guard against a false nostalgia here: superannuated Beatniks do tend to go on about the good old days, and the old Bohemia certainly had its share of phonies, as Kops knew well. What had changed was the fact of more disposable income, which called into existence the Bohemian shopping malls one now finds in London's Camden Town or New York's Soho. As early as 1931, Aldous Huxley discerned the "modernity-snobbery" now so glaring in metropolitan boutiques, where the bourgeoisie could purchase the trappings of Bohemia.[53] This pursuit has become an increasingly expensive competition for status involving rapid obsolescence, as cultural styles supersede one another with dizzying speed. As Pierre Bourdieu explains it, "The old-style autodidact was fundamentally defined by a reverence for culture which was induced by abrupt and early exclusion." The next generation of leftist academics and cultural entrepreneurs was not excluded from higher education, and therefore "acquired a relation to legitimate culture that is at once 'liberated' and disabused, familiar and disenchanted." They avoided traditional academic fields, for the very rational economic reason that these disciplines were already controlled by older scholars. Rather than attempt to break into a market dominated by established firms, a shrewder business strategy is to develop new products—in this case, by producing monographs on comic books, jazz, environmentalism, or parapsychology.[54] In this dynamic economy the autodidact is left hopelessly behind, like a traditional craftsman made redundant by new technology. His Everyman's Library will be rendered obsolete by critics who insist that everyone must buy this year's model of the literary canon, or else subject the old canon to increasingly opaque methods of reinterpretation. How can he possibly catch up, when even well-educated cultural professionals are hard pressed to keep pace with the constant acceleration of fashion? "When there is a very competitive market for the marking services they provide," observes Mary Douglas,

> there will be a premium on originality and artistic creativity. Any newcomer who wants to break through into big earnings, say as a playwright, ballet dancer, or writer, will have to challenge the supremacy of the established set of names in his field and replace it with a newly fashionable set. There will be constantly renewed reflection upon society and the human lot, again disturbing the value of the total stock of information that any one person can hold or survey. Most art critics are sensitive to these switches of judgment .... In these circumstances the problem of controlling or disseminating information is made more difficult by continual change in the stock of information itself. When the whole

environment is one in which inventiveness is being encouraged and paid for, there will be a great sense of shortage of time.

Arts trends may have as brief a shelf life as stock exchange trends, and they depreciate rapidly if one fails to catch the latest wave in architecture or literary theory. The names that Bohemia adopted for itself—*avant-garde*, *advanced*, *progressive*, *le dernier cri*, *new wave*, *cutting edge*, *modernist*, *postmodernist*—all reflect the Anxiety of Cool, the relentless struggle to get out in front and control the production of new cultural information. Bohemia is "subversive" only in that it seeks to wean consumers away from older cultural products in order to sell them new ones. In that sense it exemplifies "creative destruction," the rapid innovation and obsolescence that Joseph Schumpeter identified as the essence of mature capitalism. Everywhere and always, concludes Mary Douglas, "in the top consumption class the attempts of some to control the information scene are being foiled by others who stand to gain by changing it. But since this is the class that both uses and fabricates the information, naturally they cannot help but outbid each other and speed up the game, turning the society into a more and more individualistic and competitive scene ... which increases the differences between their class and those at the bottom." Far from undermining capitalism, Bohemians are selling ever newer and more expensive cultural products as status markers, thus "extending the distance between poor and rich. They are shortening everyone's time perspective for the sake of their own competitive anxiety, generating waste while at the same time deploring it."[55]

By the 1960s, this process produced middle-class youths who so thoroughly embraced Bohemian values that they grew frankly contemptuous of a culturally conservative working class. Though they styled themselves members of the radical left, they could be outrageously arrogant toward the people who had to clean up after them. The senior porter at the University of East Anglia, who had won a grammar school scholarship but had to pass it up, was disgusted by the student culture of drugs, drunkenness, vandalism, promiscuous sex, and general laziness. Most offensive of all, for all their professions of "ideological socialism," was their exploitation of working people:

> Porters, cleaning ladies and the kitchen staff, who all worked for the benefit and comfort of students, were quite often treated shamefully and with derision. ... These young students are the victims of false indoctrination in our State schools where they have been taught that all that matters is their personal expectations and rights. ... I found that many students, just because they had obtained a place in a university, used it as a kind of backcloth for acting out their personalities.

Working people had long observed that kind of behavior in exclusive Bohemian circles: now Bohemianism was permeating the larger culture. These students, the porter noted, were looking forward to successful careers in the new-sensibility industry. They "spent many hours convincing themselves that they had occupied advanced posts in all kinds of positions, politics, photography, the arts, business executives, financial wizards, etc. ... Listening to them at times was like being in a mental hospital where everyone was pretending to be someone else."[56]

In fairness to the students, they correctly anticipated Britain's shift to a postindustrial economy, where there would be plenty of new jobs in the creative professions. Today, as the prime minister likes to remind us, pop music employs many times more people than coal and steel. The "creative industries" (publishing, media, visual and performing arts, design, music, software) generate more than one million jobs, £50 billion in goods and services, and a vigorous export sector, eclipsing the declining heavy industries.[57] In Cool Britannia, it makes good political sense for the Labour Party to find a new base here. The old classics-oriented autodidacts have disappeared with the factories that employed them.

Glyn Hughes—whose father, a bus conductor, read Shaw, Wells, and Bertrand Russell late into the night—mourned the change in the early 1970s. He spoke with one of the last survivors of the self-education tradition, an old spinner in the Pudsey mills, working at machines that were about to be junked. She despised television, and had just donated her personal library of 4,000 books to a hospital: "My walls are very damp so I had them all in polythene bags behind a curtain in the bedroom. There's not much point in that, is there?"

Saddleworth, a Yorkshire woollens mill town, had by then been gentrified by professional newcomers who brought their weekend Bohemianism with them: *Vogue* and the *Sunday Times*, art festivals and galleries, boutiques and restaurants, saunas and Spanish classes for tourists. Once Saddleworth had produced working-class militants like suffragette Annie Kenney, dialect poets like John o' Grinflint and Ammon Wrigley. But Hughes realized that for those who still worked in the factories, the new culture was utterly foreign:

Inarticulate; educated to fear such places as doctors' surgeries, headmasters' waiting rooms, lawyers' offices, and to cover that fear with bravado; not knowing what "environment" and "comprehensive education" and "élitism" were; not learning the modern techniques of "protest" from the newspapers that *they* read; not having learnt to form groups the modern way, through coffee mornings, women's lib., Tupper-ware parties, and meetings after the keep-fit class, they were largely unable to affect public decisions. ...

To remember a tradition is not enough. Now, if these people were to survive, they had to enter another culture.

And they couldn't do it. They wouldn't do it. That new culture was about them, but they couldn't get into it; it mocked them, with its glitter.[58]

And they were bypassed by Britain's state-supported Bohemia. In the early 1980s the Greater London Council directed more subsidies to community arts groups, but less than 1 percent of them operated in working-class housing estates. Though these groups were more leftist and experimental than the Royal Opera House or the London Festival Ballet, their audience was equally bourgeois and university-educated. A 1981 report found that 63 percent of Arts Council grants for writers went to applicants who had attended Oxford or Cambridge. Arts institutions marketed themselves exclusively to the professional and artistic classes, with nearly total success. In the 1980s only 3 percent of attendees at the Institute for Contemporary Arts were blue-collar workers, while manual and clerical workers together accounted for only 8 percent of members of the National Film Theatre. Working-class youths knew that such sites were off-limits. "They'd tell me where to get off … I've been told to fuck off, I've had things thrown at me," one of them told an investigator. "Theatre goers? Someone well-off," concluded another. "Not just your ordinary worker … it's a class thing."[59]

However often today's literary scholars repeat the mantra of race, class, and gender, they clearly have a problem with class. A search by subject of the on-line *MLA International Bibliography* for 1991–2000 produces 13,820 hits for "women," 4,539 for "gender," 1,826 for "race," 710 for "postcolonial," and only 136 for "working class." The *MLA Directory of Periodicals* lists no academic or critical journals anywhere in the world devoted to proletarian literature, and the subject is very rarely taught in universities. In Tony Blair's Britain as in many other Western nations, professionals in the creative industries have success-fully reconciled bourgeois and Bohemian values. Affluent and ambitious, profit-motivated and style-conscious, they are sincerely committed to women's equality and genuinely interested in the literature, music, art, and cuisines of non-Western peoples. But the boutique economy they have constructed involves a process of class formation, where the accoutrements of the avant-garde are used to distance and distinguish cultural workers from more traditional manual workers.[60]

For both these classes, the withering away of the autodidact tradition has been a great loss. We forfeited some important knowledge about ourselves when we shut out or forgot the working-class observers of Bohemia. Even if they never caught up, they saw, more clearly than any of us, where our culture was moving.

Notes

Abbreviations

The following abbreviations are used in the endnotes throughout:
AM   Albert Mansbridge Papers, British Library
BBC British Broadcasting Corporation Written Archives Centre
BUL Brunel University Library
IWM Imperial War Museum
JMD J. M. Dent Records, Wilson Library, University of North Carolina at Chapel Hill
MO   Mass Observation Archive
OUA Oxford University Archives, Bodleian Library
RCL Rotherham Central Library
SLSL Southwark Local Studies Library

A Preface to a History of Audiences

1. David Perkins, *Is Literary History Possible?* (Baltimore: Johns Hopkins University Press, 1992), 25–27.
2. Jeffrey Richards, *Happiest Days: The Public Schools in English Fiction* (Manchester: Manchester University Press, 1988), 2.
3. Robert Darnton, *The Kiss of Lamourette* (New York: Norton, 1990), 212.
4. Ibid., 157.
5. For an anthology and bibliography of recent work in the field, see Guglielmo Cavallo and Roger Chartier, eds., *A History of Reading in the West* (Amherst: University of Massachusetts Press, 1999). The Supplemental Bibliography in Richard D. Altick, *The English Common Reader 1800–1900*, 2nd edn. (Columbus: Ohio State University Press, 1998) focuses specifically on Britain.
6. See, for example, Louise L. Stevenson, "Prescription and Reality: Reading Advisors and Reading Practice, 1860–1880," *Book Research Quarterly* 6 (1990–91): 43–61.
7. See, for example, David Vincent, *Literacy and Popular Culture: England 1750–1914* (Cambridge: Cambridge University Press, 1989), ch. 3.
8. See Joseph McAleer, *Popular Reading and Publishing in Britain 1914–1950* (Oxford: Clarendon Press, 1992), ch. 3.
9. Janice Radway is one of the few reader-response critics who has interviewed actual readers, in *Reading the Romance: Women, Patriarchy, and Popular Literature* (Chapel Hill: University of North Carolina Press, 1984). Where Radway's readers were contemporary,

Martyn Lyons and Lucy Taska showed that the same method could be used to explore recent history in *Australian Readers Remember: An Oral History of Reading 1890–1930* (Oxford: Oxford University Press, 1992).

10. Ronald J. Zboray, *A Fictive People: Antebellum Economic Development and the American Reading Public* (New York: Oxford University Press, 1993).

11. David Paul Nord, "Reading the Newspaper: Strategies and Politics of Reader Response, Chicago, 1912–1917," *Journal of Communication* 45 (Summer 1995): 66–93.

12. Clarence Carr, *Authors and Audiences: Popular Canadian Fiction in the Early Twentieth Century* (Montreal: McGill-Queens University Press, 2000).

13. In addition to Carlo Ginzburg's *The Cheese and the Worms: The Cosmos of a Sixteenth-Century Miller*, trans. John and Anne Tedeschi (Baltimore: Johns Hopkins University Press, 1980), see Sara T. Nalle, "Literacy and Culture in Early Modern Castile," *Past & Present* 125 (November 1989): 65–96.

14. Altick, *Common Reader*, 244.

15. David Vincent, *Bread, Knowledge and Freedom: A Study of Nineteenth-Century Working Class Autobiography* (London: Methuen, 1982), 109–95.

16. John Burnett, David Vincent, and David Mayall, eds., *The Autobiography of the Working Class: An Annotated, Critical Bibliography*, 3 vols. (New York: New York University Press, 1984–89). For scholars who want to investigate upper- and middle-class readers, the potential sample is even larger: more than 6,000 entries in William Matthews, comp., *British Autobiographies* (Hamden, CT: Archon, 1968).

17. A. E. Coppard, *It's Me, O Lord!* (London: Methuen, 1957), 9.

18. Joel Wiener, *William Lovett* (Manchester: Manchester University Press, 1989), 2. Barbara English, "Lark Rise and Juniper Hill: A Victorian Community in Literature and History," *Victorian Studies* 29 (1985): 7–35.

19. See also Chester Armstrong, *Pilgrimage from Nenthead* (London: Methuen, 1938).

20. Robert Collyer, *Some Memories* (Boston: American Unitarian Association, n.d.), 14–15, 23–24.

21. Literary theorists have speculated about hypothetical readers—Wolfgang Iser's "implied reader," Stanley Fish's "informed reader," Jonathan Culler's "qualified reader," Michael Riffaterre's "superreader"—but they are not relevant here.

22. Janice Radway, "The Book-of-the-Month Club and the General Reader: On the Uses of 'Serious' Fiction," *Critical Inquiry* 14 (Spring 1988): 518, 538.

23. Barbara Herrnstein Smith, *Contingencies of Value: Alternative Perspectives for Critical Theory* (Cambridge, MA: Harvard University Press, 1988), 52–53.

24. George Haw, *The Life Story of Will Crooks, MP* (London: Cassell, 1917), 22.

25. Smith, *Contingencies of Value*, 50–53.

26. Bryan Forbes, *A Divided Life* (London: Heinemann, 1992), 8.

27. Nancy Sharman, *Nothing to Steal: The Story of a Southampton Childhood* (London: Kaye & Ward, 1977), 137.

28. Margaret Perry, untitled TS (1975), BUL, p. 9.

29. T. J. Jackson Lears, "Making Fun of Popular Culture," *American Historical Review* 97 (December 1992): 1417–26. My criticisms of Lears, and my approach to the history of audiences, were anticipated by Lawrence W. Levine in "The Folklore of Industrial Society: Popular Culture and Its Audiences" and "Levine Responds," *American Historical Review* 97 (December 1992): 1369–99, 1427–30.

30. For example, in James Curran, Anthony Smith, and Pauline Wingate, eds., *Impacts and Influences: Essays on Media Power in the Twentieth Century* (London: Methuen, 1987), only Curran's essay, "The Boomerang Effect: The Press and the Battle for London 1981–6," gives us any real sense of audience response.

31. Roger Chartier, *The Cultural Uses of Print in Early Modern France*, trans. Lydia G. Cochrane (Princeton, NJ: Princeton University Press, 1987), 3–8.

32. Erving Goffman, *Frame Analysis: An Essay on the Organization of Experience* (Cambridge, MA: Harvard University Press, 1974), introduction.

33. Robert Darnton, *The Forbidden Best-Sellers of Pre-Revolutionary France* (New York: Norton, 1995), 186–87.

34. Thomas Hardy, *Jude the Obscure* (New York: New American Library, 1961), 121.

35. McAleer, *Popular Reading*, ch. 3.

36. Shils defined "ideology" as an intellectual system marked by a high degree of "(a) explicitness and authoritativeness of formulation, (b) internal systemic integration, (c) acknowledged affinity with other contemporaneous patterns, (d) closure, (e) imperativeness of manifestation in conduct, (f) accompanying affect, (g) consensus demanded of exponents, and (h) association with a corporate collective form deliberately intended to realize the pattern of beliefs." Edward Shils, "Ideology," in *The Intellectuals and the Powers and Other Essays* (Chicago: University of Chicago Press, 1972), 23.

37. Matthew Arnold, *Culture and Anarchy*, in *The Complete Prose Works of Matthew Arnold* (Ann Arbor: University of Michigan Press, 1965), 5:95–100, 109–12, 233–34.

38. M. K. Ashby, *Joseph Ashby of Tysoe: A Study of English Village Life* (Cambridge: Cambridge University Press, 1961), 5–7, 12–14, 21, 26–28, 30, 34, 57–58, 82, 93–95, 108–109, 115, 122, 243–44, 258.

Chapter One: **A Desire for Singularity**

1. Arnold, *Culture and Anarchy*, 112–13.

2. Margaret Aston, *Lollards and Reformers: Images and Literacy in Late Medieval Religion* (London: Hambledon, 1984), 193–217. Anne Hudson, *The Lollards and Their Books* (London: Hambledon, 1985), 141–63.

3. T. Wilson Hayes, "The Peaceful Apocalypse: Familism and Literacy in Sixteenth-Century England," *Sixteenth-Century Journal* 17 (Summer 1986): 131–33.

4. J. W. Martin, "Miles Hogarde: Artisan and Aspiring Author in Sixteenth-Century England," *Renaissance Quarterly* 34 (Autumn 1981): 379–81.

5. Hayes, "Peaceful Apocalypse," 133–43. J. W. Martin, "Christopher Vitel: An Elizabethan Mechanick Preacher," *Sixteenth Century Journal* 10 (Summer 1979): 17–18.

6. Margaret Spufford, *Small Books and Pleasant Histories: Popular Fiction and Its Readership in Seventeenth-Century England* (Athens: University of Georgia Press, 1981), xvii, 30–34.

7. Christopher Hill, *The English Bible and the Seventeenth-Century Revolution* (London: Allen Lane and The Penguin Press, 1993), 14–31, 188, 198–200, 246–47, 428, 432.

8. David Cressy, *Literacy and the Social Order: Reading and Writing in Tudor and Stuart England* (Cambridge: Cambridge University Press, 1980), 132–35.

9. Peter Laslett, "Scottish Weavers, Cobblers and Miners Who Bought Books in the 1750s," *Local Population Studies* 3 (Autumn 1969): 7–15.

10. Ned Landsman, "Evangelists and Their Hearers: Popular Interpretation of Revivalist Preaching in Eighteenth-Century Scotland," *Journal of British Studies* 28 (April 1989): 120–49.

11. David Kirkwood, *My Life of Revolt* (London: George G. Harrap & Co., 1935), 3–4.

12. Joseph Livesey, *Autobiography of Joseph Livesey* (London: National Temperance League, 1886), 4–7.

13. William Thom, *Rhymes and Recollections of a Hand-Loom Weaver*, 3rd edn. (London: Smith, Elder & Co., 1847), 13–15.

14. John Sinclair, *The Statistical Account of Scotland* (Edinburgh: William Creech, 1791–99), 1:456–57.
15. Ibid., 4:524.
16. Ibid., 14:483.
17. Ibid., 3:597–600.
18. Ibid., 7:59–60. See also *The New Statistical Account of Scotland* (Edinburgh and London: William Blackwood & Sons, 1845), 4:433.
19. Sinclair, *Statistical Account*, 15:171–72.
20. Henry Mayhew, *London Labour and the London Poor* (New York: Dover, 1968), 1:295.
21. Patrocinio P. Schweickart, "Reading Ourselves: Toward a Feminist Theory of Reading," in Elizabeth A. Flynn and Schweickart, eds., *Gender and Reading: Essays on Readers, Texts, and Contexts* (Baltimore: Johns Hopkins University Press, 1986), 41.
22. Joseph Wittreich, *Feminist Milton* (Ithaca, NY: Cornell University Press, 1987). Claudia N. Thomas, *Alexander Pope and His Eighteenth-Century Women Readers* (Carbondale: Southern Illinois University Press, 1994), 1–3, 10–13, 26, 45, 152–59, 188–93, 199–204, 240–45.
23. Donna Landry, *The Muses of Resistance: Labouring-Class Women's Poetry in Britain, 1739–1796* (Cambridge: Cambridge University Press, 1990), 12–22, 43–55, 123–30.
24. Ibid., 154–58.
25. Ann Yearsley, "To Those Who Accuse the Author of Ingratitude," in *Poems on Various Subjects* (Oxford and New York: Woodstock Books, 1994), 57–60.
26. Mary Waldron, *Lactilla, Milkwoman of Clifton: The Life and Writings of Ann Yearsley, 1753–1806* (Athens, GA and London: University of Georgia Press, 1996), 37–46.
27. Ann Yearsley, "Addressed to Ignorance, Occasioned by a Gentleman's desiring the Author never to assume a Knowledge of the Ancients," in *Poems*, 93–99.
28. G. L. Craik, *The Pursuit of Knowledge under Difficulties Illustrated by Female Examples* (London: C. Cox, 1847), 7–18.
29. Mary Ann Ashford, *Life of a Licensed Victualler's Daughter* (London: Saunders & Otley, 1844), iii–iv.
30. Janet Hamilton, *Poems, Essays, and Sketches* (Glasgow: James Maclehose, 1870), 265–66.
31. Ellen Johnston, *Autobiography, Poems and Songs* (Glasgow: William Love, 1867), 9.
32. *Quarterly Review* 35 (December 1826): 149.
33. Charles Campbell, *Memoirs of Charles Campbell* (Glasgow: James Duncan, 1828), 3–6, 19.
34. Hugh Miller, *My Schools and Schoolmasters*, 14th edn. (Edinburgh: William P. Nimmo, 1869), 416–20.
35. Francis Place, *The Autobiography of Francis Place (1771–1854)*, ed. Mary Thale (Cambridge: Cambridge University Press, 1972), 222–23, 275–76.
36. Christopher Thomson, *The Autobiography of an Artisan* (London: J. Chapman, 1847), 5–8, 19–24, 319, 335–42.
37. George Howell, draft autobiography (1898–1908), Bishopsgate Institute, volume C/a, p. 22.
38. Jean Rennie, *Every Other Sunday: The Autobiography of a Kitchenmaid* (London: Arthur Barker, 1955), 47–48, 88, 162, 181–82, 196–99.
39. Dorothy Burnham, *Through Dooms of Love* (London: Chatto & Windus, 1969), 174, 184–87, 192.
40. Ben Adhem [Allen Clarke], *Liverpool Evening Post* (30 November 1935): 2.
41. John MacDonald, *Travels* (London: Author, 1790), 100, 141–43. John Jones, *Attempts in Verse* (London: John Murray, 1831), 173, 176. William Lanceley, *From Hall-Boy to House-Steward* (London: Edward Arnold, 1925), 25, 161. Louise Jermy, *The Memories of*

a Working Woman (Norwich: Goose & Son, 1934), 84–86, 92–93, 144. Lavinia Swainbank, autobiographical extract in John Burnett, ed., *Useful Toil* (Harmondsworth: Penguin, 1984), 221–24.

42. Margaret Powell, *Below Stairs* (London: Peter Davies, 1968), 114, 128–29, 139–40.

43. Margaret Powell, *The Treasure Upstairs* (London: Peter Davies, 1970), 33–38, 134–36.

44. Marshall McLuhan, *Gutenberg Galaxy: The Making of Typographic Man* (Toronto: University of Toronto Press, 1962), 158.

45. Walter J. Ong, *The Presence of the Word* (New York: Simon & Schuster, 1970), 54.

46. Bernard Capp, *Astrology and the Popular Press: English Almanacs 1500–1800* (London: Faber and Faber, 1979), 215–16, 221–22.

47. Thomas Hardy, "Memoir of Thomas Hardy," in *Testaments of Radicalism: Memoirs of Working-Class Politicians 1790–1885*, ed. David Vincent (London: Europa, 1977), 101.

48. J. R. Clynes, *Memoirs: 1869–1924* (London: Hutchinson, 1937), 35, 45.

49. William Johnson, "How I Got On: Life Stories by the Labour MPs," *Pearson's Weekly* (1 March 1906): 613.

50. "The Labour Party and the Books That Helped to Make It," *Review of Reviews* 33 (1906): 573–74 (a survey of the reading tastes of early Labour MPs).

51. Robert Roberts, *The Classic Slum* (London: Penguin, 1990), 177–78, 228.

52. George Bourne, *Change in the Village* (New York: George H. Doran, 1912), 194, 244–59, 297–303.

53. Ann Kussmaul, ed., *The Autobiography of Joseph Mayett of Quainton (1783–1839)* (n.p.: Buckingham Record Society, 1986), 1–2, 40–42, 48, 52, 70–72, 75–77, 86, 96.

54. Uriah Plant, *An Account of the Principal Events in the Life of Uriah Plant* (London: Published for the author by Thomas Griffiths, 1829), xi–xii, 4–9, 27–28, 31–42, 56–58, 73, 99, 107, 282–83.

55. John Clare, *John Clare's Autobiographical Writings*, ed. Eric Robinson (Oxford: Oxford University Press, 1983), 9, 25–26.

56. John Clare, "Journal", in *The Prose of John Clare*, ed. J. W. and Anne Tibble (London: Routledge & Kegan Paul, 1951), 7 September 1824.

57. John Clare, "Self-Identity," in *The Prose of John Clare*, 239.

58. Altick, *Common Reader*, 35–37, 108–23. Valentine Cunningham, *Everywhere Spoken Against: Dissent in the Victorian Novel* (Oxford: Clarendon Press, 1975), 48–56.

59. Elizabeth Mary Wright, *The Life of Joseph Wright* (London: Oxford University Press, 1932), 20–21.

60. Thomson, *Autobiography of an Artisan*, 65–67.

61. Joseph Barker, *The History and Confessions of a Man* (Wortley: J. Barker, 1846), 140, 149–52, 186–87, 193–95, 209.

62. Elisabeth Jay, *The Religion of the Heart: Anglican Evangelicals and the Nineteenth-Century Novel* (Oxford: Clarendon Press, 1979), 192–95.

63. Samuel Westcott Tilke, *An Autobiographical Memoir* (London: Author, 1840), xiv–xvi.

64. J. Barlow Brooks, *Lancashire Bred* (Oxford: Author, 1950–51), 1:156.

65. Altick, *Common Reader*, 123–28, 160–61.

66. Thomas Jones, *Rhymney Memories* (Llandysul: Gwasg Gomer, 1970), 48, 77–81, 97, 116–17, 121–22, 147–50.

67. John Johnson, "How I Got On: Life Stories by the Labour MPs," *Pearson's Weekly* (10 May 1906): 787.

68. Cunningham, *Everywhere Spoken Against*, 56–62.

69. Edwin Muir, *The Story and the Fable* (London: George G. Harrap & Co., 1940), 113–14.

70. Richard Pyke, *Men and Memories* (London: Epworth, 1948), 18, 36–41, 47, 100.

71. Paul Thomas Murphy, *Towards a Working-Class Canon: Literary Criticism in British*

Working-Class Periodicals, 1816–1858 (Columbus: Ohio State University Press, 1994), 15–18, 36–40, 45, 49–53, 98–104.

72. Joel H. Wiener, *Radicalism and Freethought in Nineteenth-Century Britain: The Life of Richard Carlile* (Westport, CT: Greenwood, 1983), 8, 27–29, 65, 68–69, 111–12, 121, 208, 258–59.

73. Murphy, *Working-Class Canon*, 40–43.

74. "Preface," *Labourer* 1 (1847), quoted in H. Gustav Klaus, *The Literature of Labour: Two Hundred Years of Working-Class Writing* (Brighton: Harvester, 1985), 49.

75. Murphy, *Working-Class Canon*, 10.

76. Wiener, *Lovett*, 44–48, 82–86, 99–102, 120–25.

77. William Lovett, *The Life and Struggles of William Lovett* (New York: Knopf, 1920), 44–46.

78. Murphy, *Working-Class Canon*, 54–61, 125–47.

79. Thomas Frost, *Forty Years' Recollections: Literary and Political* (London: Sampson, Low, Marston, Searle, and Rivington, 1880), 14–15, 38–39.

80. Thomas Frost, *Reminiscences of a Country Journalist* (London: Ward & Downey, 1886), 225–26.

81. Robert Lowery, "Passages in the Life of a Temperance Lecturer," in Brian Harrison and Patricia Hollis, eds., *Robert Lowery: Radical and Chartist* (London: Europa, 1979), 54–60, 67–72, 82.

82. Thomas Cooper, *The Life of Thomas Cooper* (New York: Humanities Press, 1971), 37–39.

83. Thomas Cooper, "Moral and Political Lessons of *Gulliver's Travels*," *Cooper's Journal* (11 May 1850): 297–99.

84. Samuel Bamford, *Early Days* (London: Simpkin, Marshall & Co., 1849), 192–95, 209–10, 280–82.

85. The Independent Labour Party—which was, in effect, the left wing of the Labour Party until it broke away in 1932.

86. Edward Milne, *No Shining Armour* (London: John Calder, 1976), 13–14, 47.

87. Catherine Cookson, *Our Kate* (London: Macdonald, 1969), 158–60, 211. Obituary, *New York Times* (12 June 1998):A19.

88. Murphy, *Working-Class Canon*, 77–78.

89. "Labour Party and Books," 577.

90. John Birch Thomas, *Shop Boy* (London: Routledge & Kegan Paul, 1983), 58–59, 64.

91. Walter Hampson, "Reminiscences of 'Casey,'" *Glasgow Forward* (26 September 1931): 12.

92. T. A. Jackson, "Walter Scott—Who Made the Novel a Necessity," *Plebs* 26 (January 1934): 4–7.

93. Ernie Trory, *Mainly About Books* (Brighton: Crabtree, 1945), 18–19, 70–72.

94. T. A. Jackson, TS autobiography, Marx Memorial Library (London), pp. 68–69, 72–73.

95. "Labour Party and Books," 568–82.

96. Ben Batten, *Newlyn Boyhood* (Penzance: Author, n.d.), 54–56.

97. Jack Goring, untitled MS (1938), BUL, pp. 158–60.

98. Allen Clarke, "Should Young Courting Couples Go Holiday-Making Together," *Liverpool Weekly Post* (4 August 1934): 2.

99. Sir Henry Jones, *Old Memories* (London: Hodder & Stoughton, n.d.), 68, 95.

100. Fred Gresswell, *Bright Boots* (London: Robert Hale, 1956), 122–24.

101. Henry Edward Hawker, *Notes of My Life* (Stonehouse: Star Press, 1919), introduction.

102. George Acorn, *One of the Multitude* (London: William Heinemann, 1911), 193, 239–40.

103. V. W. Garratt, *A Man in the Street* (London: J. M. Dent & Sons, 1939), 80–81, 92–99, 161.

104. G. J. Wardle, "How I Got On: Life Stories by the Labour MPs," *Pearson's Weekly* (22 February 1906): 597.

105. Frederick Rogers, *The Seven Deadly Sins* (London: A. H. Bullen, 1907), 29.

106. Ben Tillett, *Memories and Reflections* (London: John Long, 1931), 77.

107. Edmund Stonelake, *The Autobiography of Edmund Stonelake*, ed. Anthony Mor-O'Brien (Bridgend: Mid Glamorgan County Council, 1981), 57–58.

108. "Labour Party and Books," 570–71. Caroline Benn, *Keir Hardie* (London: Hutchinson, 1992), 11–12.

109. C. A. Glyde, "Memories of an Agitator," *Yorkshire Factory Times* (22 February 1923): 2.

110. George Lansbury, *My Life* (London: Constable, 1928), 266–68.

111. Helen Crawfurd, TS autobiography, Marx Memorial Library (London), pp. 58–59, 129.

112. Mary Smith, *The Autobiography of Mary Smith, Schoolmistress and Nonconformist* (London: Bemrose & Sons, 1892), 16–18, 26–41, 94–95, 132–35, 145, 156, 161–65, 209, 242–47, 256–60.

113. Elizabeth Bryson, *Look Back in Wonder* (Dundee: David Winter & Son, 1966), 80–81, 124–25, 213–15.

114. Sam Shaw, *Guttersnipe* (London: Sampson, Low, Marston & Co., 1946), 120, 163–66.

115. W. J. Linton, *Threescore and Ten Years 1820 to 1890: Recollections* (New York: Charles Scribner's Sons, 1894), 114.

116. George Jacob Holyoake, *Sixty Years of an Agitator's Life* (London: T. Fisher Unwin, 1892), vol. 1, ch. 36.

117. Fenner Brockway, *Socialism over Sixty Years: The Life of Jowett of Bradford (1864–1944)* (London: George Allen & Unwin, 1946), 28.

118. Robert Blatchford, *My Eighty Years* (London: Cassell, 1931), 169–70.

119. Robert Blatchford, *The Nunquam Papers* (London: Clarion Newspaper Co., 1895), 15–19.

120. Richard Hillyer, *Country Boy* (London: Hodder & Stoughton, 1966), 135–37.

121. Blatchford, *Eighty Years*, xiii, 43–44, 139, 150, 196.

122. Annie Kenney, *Memories of a Militant* (London: Edward Arnold, 1924), 23–24.

123. J. Bruce Glasier, "How I Became a Socialist," *Labour Leader* (10 May 1912): 299.

124. Robert Blatchford, *My Favourite Books* (London: Clarion Press, [1911]), 223–32.

125. Kenneth O. Morgan, *Keir Hardie* (London: Weidenfeld & Nicolson, 1975), 7.

126. John Ward, "How I Got On: Life Stories by the Labour MPs," *Pearson's Weekly* (15 March 1906): 655.

127. Philip Inman, *No Going Back* (London: Williams & Norgate, 1952), 35–36, 45–47.

128. Frederick Rogers, *Labour, Life and Literature: Some Memories of Sixty Years* (London: Smith, Elder & Co., 1913), 137–39.

129. Robert Roberts, *The Classic Slum* (London: Penguin, 1990), 177–79.

130. James Murray, "To Pashendaele and Back" (c. 1976), IWM, p. 23. See also J. T. Murphy, *New Horizons* (London: John Lane The Bodley Head, 1942), 32; and Bill Naughton, *On the Pig's Back: An Autobiographical Excursion* (Oxford: Oxford University Press, 1987), 3.

131. J. R. Clynes, "The Use of Books to Working Men," *Everyman* 2 (18 April 1913): 5.

132. Raphael Samuel, *East End Underworld: Chapters in the Life of Arthur Harding* (London: Routledge & Kegan Paul, 1981), 274–75.

133. Haw, *Will Crooks*, 19–20. Tillett, *Memories*, 190. See also G. H. Roberts, "How I Got On: Life Stories by the Labour MPs," *Pearson's Weekly* (17 May 1906): 806; John Wilson, *Memories of a Labour Leader* (London: T. Fisher Unwin, 1910), 51; Lansbury, *My Life*, 129–30; Brooks, *Lancashire Bred*, 1:30; Arthur Fredrick Goffin, "A Grey Life" (1933), BUL, ch. 7.

134. "Labour Party and Books," 575.

135. James Clunie, *The Voice of Labour* (Dunfermline: A. Romanes & Son, 1958), 19–20, 33, 39, 42.
136. James Clunie, *Labour is My Faith: The Autobiography of a House Painter* (Dunfermline: A. Romanes & Son, 1954), 82.
137. Percy Wall, "Hour at Eve," BUL, chs. 1–2, 8, 17–18.
138. R. M. Fox, *Smoky Crusade* (London: Hogarth Press, 1937), 236, 239, 256–58.
139. Emrys Daniel Hughes, "Welsh Rebel," National Library of Scotland, pp. 113, 128–31, 140, 151–54, 178–80, 190.
140. Jack Lawson, *A Man's Life* (London: Hodder & Stoughton, 1932), 77–81, 102–4, 119–20, 129.
141. Alice Foley, *A Bolton Childhood* (Manchester: Manchester University Extra-Mural Department, 1973), 55, 59–61, 65–73, 91–92.
142. Rudolf Rocker, *The London Years* (London: Robert Anscome, 1956), 144–45, 160–61, 177–79. William J. Fishman, *East End Jewish Radicals 1875–1914* (London: Duckworth, 1975), 254–75.
143. Chaim Lewis, *A Soho Address* (London: Victor Gollancz, 1965), 18, 66–67, 93–99, 124.
144. Thomas Thompson, *Lancashire for Me* (London: George Allen & Unwin, 1940), 22–25.

Chapter Two: **Mutual Improvement**

1. Harold Begbie, *Living Water: Chapters from the Romance of the Poor Student* (London: Headley Bros., 1918), 114–18.
2. Altick, *Common Reader*, 205–206. E. P. Thompson, *The Making of the English Working Class* (New York: Vintage, 1963), 743–44.
3. *Fifty Years' History of the Gallatown Mutual Improvement Association (1863–1913)* (Kirkaldy: East End Printing Works, 1913), 117.
4. Eric Hopkins, *Working-Class Self-Help in Nineteenth-Century England* (London: UCL Press, 1995), 24, 51.
5. Vincent, *Bread, Knowledge and Freedom*, 30–31.
6. Jane Rendall, *The Origins of the Scottish Enlightenment, 1707–1776* (London: Macmillan, 1978), 62.
7. James Mackenzie, *Life of Michael Bruce* (London: J. M. Dent, 1905), 11–13.
8. John C. Crawford, "The Origins and Development of Societal Library Activity in Scotland" (MA thesis, University of Strathclyde, 1981), pp. 177–89, 210–14, 220–21.
9. R. A. Houston, *Scottish Literacy and the Scottish Identity: Illiteracy and Society in Scotland and Northern England 1600–1800* (Cambridge: Cambridge University Press, 1985), 38–40, 174–78. Paul Kaufman, "A Unique Record of a People's Reading," *Libri* 14 (1964): 227–42. *The Statistical Account of Scotland* (9:588–93) records twenty wrights as heads of households in 1792, but given the growth in Crieff's population and industry, there were probably only half as many at mid-century.
10. Crawford, "Societal Library Activity," pp. 28–31.
11. *Scots Chronicle* (25 October 1796): 3, (30 December 1796): 3, (20 January 1797): 3, (10 February 1797): 4, (19 May 1797): 4.
12. Samuel Brown, *Some Account of Itinerating Libraries and Their Founder* (Edinburgh: William Blackwood & Sons, 1856), 58–59, 63–64.
13. East Lothian Itinerating Libraries, Fourth Annual Report, 1824–25, p. 6.
14. Robert Skeen, *Autobiography of Mr. Robert Skeen, Printer* (London: Wyman & Sons, 1876), 5.
15. Alexander Bethune, *Memoirs of Alexander Bethune* (Aberdeen: George & Robert King, 1845), 231–32.

16. Alexander Bethune, "Sketch of the Life of John Bethune," in John Bethune, *Poems* (Edinburgh: Adam & Charles Black, 1840), 44–47.

17. Ian R. Carter, "The Mutual Improvement Movement in North-East Scotland in the Nineteenth Century," *Aberdeen University Review* 46 (Autumn 1976): 383–92.

18. William Donaldson, *Popular Literature in Victorian Scotland: Language, Fiction and the Press* (Aberdeen: Aberdeen University Press, 1986), 5, 11, 21–32, 102–106.

19. David Marquand, *Ramsay MacDonald* (London: Jonathan Cape, 1977), 30.

20. Jane Cox, ed., *A Singular Marriage: A Labour Love Story in Letters and Diaries: Ramsay and Margaret MacDonald* (London: Harrap, 1988), 10–11.

21. G. E. Elton, *The Life of James Ramsay MacDonald* (London: Collins, 1939), 24–28.

22. Samuel Bamford, *Passages in the Life of a Radical* (Oxford: Oxford University Press, 1984), 14.

23. Thomas Walter Laqueur, *Religion and Respectability: Sunday Schools and Working Class Culture 1780–1850* (New Haven, CT: Yale University Press, 1976), 88–89, 92–93, 96, 117–18, 154–58, 246. S. J. D. Green, "Religion and the Rise of the Common Man: Mutual Improvement Societies, Religious Associations and Popular Education in Three Industrial Towns in the West Riding of Yorkshire c. 1850–1900," in *Cities, Class and Communication: Essays in Honour of Asa Briggs*, ed. Derek Fraser (New York: Harvester Wheatsheaf, 1990), 29.

24. Place, *Autobiography*, 131, 175–76, 198–200.

25. John Buckley, *A Village Politician: The Life-Story of John Buckley*, ed. J. C. Buckmaster (London: T. Fisher Unwin, 1897), 98–99.

26. Joseph Constantine, *Fifty Years of the Water Cure* (Manchester and London: John Heywood, 1892), 5–9, 15.

27. Lovett, *Life and Struggles*, 21–22, 35–37, 58–59, 138–50.

28. Lowery, "Passages in the Life," 72–73.

29. John Bedford Leno, *The Aftermath: With Autobiography of the Author* (London: Reeves & Turner, 1892), 42, 49–50.

30. William Farish, *The Autobiography of William Farish* (privately printed, 1889), 11–12, 46–47, 59–60.

31. Frost, *Forty Years' Recollections*, 198–203.

32. T. B. Graham, *Nineteenth Century Self-Help in Education—Mutual Improvement Societies. Volume Two: Case Study: The Carlisle Working Men's Reading Rooms* (Nottingham: Department of Adult Education, University of Nottingham, 1983), 8–11. Robert Elliott, "On Working Men's Reading Rooms, as Established since 1848 in Carlisle," *Transactions of the National Association for the Promotion of Social Science* (1861): 676–79. Mary Brigg, ed., *The Journals of a Lancashire Weaver* (Liverpool: Record Society of Lancashire and Cheshire, 1982), viii–xi.

33. Joseph Greenwood, "Reminiscences of Sixty Years Ago," *Co-partnership* (December 1910): 182, (January 1911): 6, (February 1911): 22.

34. A Student of the Working Men's College, London, "How to Make Colleges," *Working Men's College Magazine* 2 (June 1860): 98–99.

35. Mabel Tylecote, *The Mechanics' Institutes of Lancashire and Yorkshire before 1851* (Manchester: Manchester University Press, 1957), 230–31, 241–46.

36. Frank Curzon, "Some Statistics of the Huddersfield Mechanics' Institution," *Transactions of the National Association for the Promotion of Social Science* (1859): 344–47.

37. Ben Brierley, *Home Memories* (Manchester: Abel Heywood, 1886), 35–36.

38. Charles Shaw, *When I Was a Child* (London: Methuen & Co., 1903), 221–23, 228.

39. Laqueur, *Religion and Respectability*, 193–94, 216–25.

40. J. F. C. Harrison, "The Victorian Gospel of Success," *Victorian Studies* 1 (December

1957): 155–64; Kenneth Fielden, "Samuel Smiles and Self-Help," *Victorian Studies* 12 (December 1968): 154–76.

41. Robert Blatchford, *A Book About Books* (London: Clarion Press, 1903), 233–54.

42. "Labour Party and Books," 576. Thomas Summerbell, "How I Got On: Life Stories by the Labour MPs," *Pearson's Weekly* (22 March 1906): 675.

43. Paul Davies, *A. J. Cook* (Manchester: Manchester University Press, 1987), 2.

44. Beckles Wilson, "Library London," in *Living London*, ed. George R. Sims (London: Cassell, 1902–1903), 3:97.

45. John Britton, *The Auto-Biography of John Britton F.S.A.* (London: Author, 1850), 1:2. Livesey, *Autobiography*, 81–82. William Marcroft, *The Marcroft Family* (London: John Heywood, 1886), 41–42. Thomas Burt, in "Labour Party and Books," 569. John B. Turnbull, *Reminiscences of a Stonemason* (London: John Murray, 1908), 65–69. Robert Watchorn, *The Autobiography of Robert Watchorn*, ed. Herbert Faulkner West (Oklahoma City: Robert Watchorn Charities, 1958), 2. George Rowles, "Chaps among the Caps" (1968), BUL, p. 21.

46. Henry Coward, *Reminiscences of Henry Coward* (London: J. Curwen & Sons, 1919), v–vii. Thomas Burke, *The Sun in Splendour* (New York: George H. Doran, 1926), 232. Lansbury, *My Life*, 99. Edgar Wallace, *Edgar Wallace: A Short Autobiography* (London: Hodder & Stoughton, 1930), 53. Frank Steel, *Ditcher's Row: A Tale of the Old Charity* (London: Sidgwick & Jackson, 1939), 60. J. G. Graves, *Some Memories* (Sheffield: Author, [1944]), 42–43.

47. George Gregory, untitled TS, BUL, pp. 2, 36–37, 60–65, 71–103, 111, 115–23, 126–27.

48. Samuel Smiles, *Life of a Scotch Naturalist: Thomas Edward*, new edn. (London: John Murray, 1882), v–vii, 78–80, 91, 253–54, 323.

49. Samuel Smiles, *Men of Invention and Industry* (New York: Harper & Brothers, 1885), 321–63.

50. Henry H. Cawthorne, "The Spitalfields Mathematical Society (1717–1845)," *Journal of Adult Education* 3 (April 1929): 155–166.

51. Timothy Claxton, *Memoir of a Mechanic* (Boston: George W. Light, 1839), 34–36.

52. Gwyn A. Williams, *Rowland Detrosier: A Working-Class Infidel 1800–34* (York: St. Anthony's, 1965), 3–4, 7–9, 15–16.

53. G. E. Maxim, "Libraries and Reading in the Context of the Economic, Political and Social Changes Taking Place in Manchester and the Neighbouring Mill Towns, 1750–1850" (MA thesis, Sheffield University, 1979), pp. 569–72.

54. Anne Secord, "Science in the Pub: Artisan Botanists in Early Nineteenth-Century Lancashire," *History of Science* 32 (1994): 269–315. Anne Secord, "Corresponding Interests: Artisans and Gentlemen in Nineteenth-Century Natural History," *British Journal of the History of Science* 27 (1994): 383–408.

55. Lowery, "Passages in the Life," 77–78, 114–15.

56. Allen Davenport, *The Life and Literary Pursuits of Allen Davenport* (Aldershot: Scolar, 1994), 26–28.

57. John A. Leatherland, *Essays and Poems* (London: W. Tweedie, 1862), 9–16.

58. Thompson, *Lancashire for Me*, 25.

59. *Gallatown Mutual Improvement*, 59–60, 63, 71–72, 76, 90–98, 103, 107–11, 120–27.

60. Green, "Religion and the Common Man," 36–37.

61. Armstrong, *Pilgrimage from Nenthead*, 17–18, 42–43, 57–60, 70–71, 82–84, 87–90, 93–95, 101–103, 109–10, 118–23, 127–28, 201–4, 258, 261–67.

62. David Willox, "Memories of Parkhead, Its People and Pastimes," Mitchell Library, pp. 100–102.

63. Inman, *No Going Back*, 44–45, 147.
64. F. H. Spencer, *An Inspector's Testament* (London: English Universities Press, 1938), 78, 83–85, 100, 108–14.
65. Crawford, "Societal Library Activity," 110, 238–40.
66. David Chadwick, "On Free Public Libraries and Museums," *Transactions of the National Association for the Promotion of Social Science* (1857): 575.
67. Elizabeth Rossiter, "A Student's Wife's Notion of College and Classes," *Working Men's College Magazine* 1 (October 1859): 153–54.
68. A Student's Wife, "Will College Night Classes Be of Any Use to Women?" *Working Men's College Magazine* 2 (January 1860): 2–4.
69. George Eliot, *Felix Holt the Radical* (Harmondsworth: Penguin, 1972), 212.
70. Graham, *Nineteenth Century Self-Help*, 23, 38–39.
71. Green, "Religion and the Common Man," 33.
72. "Metropolitan Associations," *Union Review* 1 (January 1882): 13.
73. Vincent, *Literacy and Popular Culture*, 24–26.
74. Barbara J. Blaszak, *The Matriarchs of England's Cooperative Movement: A Study in Gender Politics and Female Leadership, 1883–1921* (Westport, CT: Greenwood, 2000), 75–78.
75. Margaret Penn, *Manchester Fourteen Miles* (Cambridge: Cambridge University Press, 1947), 74–80. Stella Davies, *North Country Bred: A Working-Class Family Chronicle* (London: Routledge & Kegan Paul, 1963), 76.
76. Foley, *Bolton Childhood*, 44–46, 55–56.
77. Gillian Scott, *Feminism and the Politics of Working Women: The Women's Co-operative Guild, 1880s to the Second World War* (London: UCL Press, 1998), 68.
78. D. H. Lawrence, *Sons and Lovers* (Cambridge: Cambridge University Press, 1992), 69.
79. Deborah Smith, *My Revelation* (London: Houghton Publishing, 1933), 18, 48–62, 84–85, 92, 97.
80. Elizabeth Andrews, *A Woman's Work is Never Done* (Ystrad Rhondda: Cymric Democrat Publishing Society, n.d.), 6.
81. Ian Inkster, "Introduction: The Context of Steam Intellect in Britain (to 1851)," in *The Steam Intellect Societies—Essays on Culture, Education and Industry circa 1820–1914* (Nottingham: Department of Adult Education, University of Nottingham, 1985), 11–16.
82. Tylecote, *Mechanics' Institutes*, 67–68.
83. Green, "Religion and the Common Man," 29–33.
84. James Dellow, *Memoirs of an Old Stager* (Newcastle: Andrew Reid & Co., 1928), 38–39.
85. T. Lloyd Roberts, *Life Was Like That* (Bala: A. J. Chapple, n.d.), 11–13.
86. Working Men's Club and Institute Union, Annual Report, 1874–75, pp. 10–11, 20–21.
87. Richard Price, *An Imperial War and the British Working Class* (London: Routledge & Kegan Paul, 1972), 47, 61–62.
88. Jean Everitt, "Co-operative Society Libraries," *Library History* 15 (May 1999): 33–40.
89. John Attfield, *With Light of Knowledge: A Hundred Years of Education in the Royal Arsenal Co-operative Society, 1877–1977* (London: RASC/Journeyman Press, 1981), 6–9, 12, 40, 45–48.
90. Alexander Hartog, *Born to Sing* (London: Dennis Dobson, 1978), 44–45.
91. Adult Education Committee of the Board of Education, *The Drama in Adult Education* (London: HMSO, 1926), 75–103, 113–20, 152–54, 163–69. C. O. G. Douie, "The Drama in Prisons," *Journal of Adult Education* 1 (September 1926): 61–69. Beresford Ingram, "Education in Prisons," *Adult Education* 10 (September 1937): 37. Winifred Albaya, *Through the Green Door: An Account of the Sheffield Educational Settlement,*

Shipton Street: 1918–1955 (Sheffield: Sheffield District Education Committee, 1980), 169–72.

92. Arthur Gill, "I Remember! Reminiscences of a Cobbler's Son" (1969), BUL, pp. 2–3, 144–46.
93. C. H. Rolph, *Living Twice* (London: Victor Gollancz, 1974), 84–88.
94. Hymie Fagan, "An Autobiography," BUL, pp. 44–51.
95. Ralph L. Finn, *No Tears in Aldgate* (London: Robert Hale, 1963), 150–56.
96. Family Life and Work before 1918 Oral History Archive, Department of Sociology, University of Sussex.
97. Samuel Taylor, *Records of an Active Life* (London: Simpkin Marshall, 1886), 2–4, 9, 22–24.
98. Samuel Taylor, "Literary and Musical Entertainments for the People," *Transactions of the National Association for the Promotion of Social Science* (1858): 644–45.
99. Flora Thompson, *Lark Rise to Candleford* (Harmondsworth: Penguin, 1987), 43–44, 109–11, 192, 252–53, 331–32, 350–59, 413–16, 433–36.
100. Ruth Johnson, *Old Road: A Lancashire Childhood 1912–1926*, compiled and written by Alfred E. Body (Manchester: E. J. Morten, 1974), 112–13, 116–17.
101. J. G. Glenwright, *Bright Shines the Morning* (London: Martini, 1949), 138–40.
102. Henry Byett, "Richard Jefferies and Alfred Williams—A Comparison," AM.
103. Margaret Thomson Davis, *The Making of a Novelist* (London: Allison & Busby, 1982), 3–6.
104. Foley, *Bolton Childhood*, 11–12, 25.
105. H. M. Burton, *There Was a Young Man* (London: Geoffrey Bles, 1958), 35, 39–41, 47–49.
106. John Allaway, in Ronald Goldman, ed., *Breakthrough: Autobiographical Accounts of the Education of Some Socially Disadvantaged Children* (London: Routledge & Kegan Paul, 1968), 14–17.
107. Derek Davies, in Goldman, *Breakthrough*, 35–39.
108. Elizabeth Flint, *Hot Bread and Chips* (London: Museum Press, 1963), 108–109.
109. Jack Lawson, *Peter Lee* (London: Epworth, 1949), 211.
110. Dennis Marsden, in Goldman, *Breakthrough*, 107–17.
111. Brian Jackson and Dennis Marsden, *Education and the Working Class* (London: Routledge & Kegan Paul, 1962), 100–103.
112. Jeremy Seabrook, *Mother and Son* (London: Victor Gollancz, 1979), 39, 151–53, 165.

Chapter Three: **The Difference Between Fact and Fiction**

1. Chartier, *Cultural Uses of Print*, 335–36.
2. David D. Hall, "The World of Print and Collective Mentality in Seventeenth-Century New England," in *Cultures of Print: Essays in the History of the Book* (Amherst: University of Massachusetts Press, 1996), 87.
3. Spufford, *Small Books*, esp. ch. 9. The Harvard College Library has a collection of 2,800 chapbooks, mostly from the mid-eighteenth to the early nineteenth centuries, of which just over a third are romances, folk stories, and fairy tales, while 5 percent deal with the supernatural. The rest offer songs, humor, history, biography, travel, crime, or religion. See Susan Pedersen, "Hannah More Meets Simple Simon: Tracts, Chapbooks, and Popular Culture in Late Eighteenth-Century England," *Journal of British Studies* 25 (January 1986): 99–106.
4. Clare, *Autobiographical Writings*, 5.

5.   Ibid., 42.
6.   George Deacon, *John Clare and the Folk Tradition* (London: Sinclair Browne, 1983), 38.
7.   Thomas Burt, *Thomas Burt, MP, DCL, Pitman and Privy Councillor* (London: T. Fisher Unwin, 1924), 115. See also John Britton, *The Beauties of Wiltshire* (London: Author, 1825), 3:xvi–xvii; Robert Owen, *The Life of Robert Owen* (London: Frank Cass, 1967), 3–4; Anonymous, *Chapters in the Life of a Dundee Factory Boy* (Dundee: William Kidd, 1887), 44.
8.   Ashby, *Ashby of Tysoe*, 34.
9.   Albert Charles Adams, *The History of a Village Shopkeeper* (Edinburgh: John Menzies, 1876), 8–11.
10. Doreen M. Rosman, "'What Has Christ to Do with Apollo?': Evangelicalism and the Novel, 1800–1830," *Studies in Church History* 14 (1977): 301–11. Elisabeth Jay, *Religion of the Heart* 195–202.
11. Pat Rogers, "Classics and Chapbooks," in *Literature and Popular Culture in Eighteenth Century England* (Brighton: Harvester, 1985).
12. Miller, *Schools and Schoolmasters*, 28–30.
13. Bamford, *Early Days*, 40–41, 89–91.
14. Barker, *History and Confessions*, 116–18.
15. J. Campkin, *The Struggles of a Village Lad* (London: William Tweedie, 1859), 21–22.
16. James I. Hillocks, *Life Story: A Prize Autobiography* (London: William Tweedie, 1863), 30.
17. Leatherland, *Essays and Poems*, 4–5.
18. Thomas Carter, *Memoirs of a Working Man* (London: Charles Knight, 1845), 19–21, 24–31, 74–76.
19. Robert Roberts, *The Life and Opinions of Robert Roberts, a Wandering Scholar*, ed. J. H. Davies (Cardiff: William Lewis, 1923), 17–18, 46, 49, 105–106, 196.
20. Thompson, *Lark Rise*, 259–60.
21. V. S. Pritchett, *A Cab at the Door* (London: Chatto & Windus, 1968), 47–48.
22. Jones, *Rhymney Memories*, 42–43.
23. Fred Kitchen, *Nettleworth Parva* (London: J. M. Dent & Sons, 1968), 40.
24. Fred Kitchen, *Brother to the Ox* (London: J. M. Dent & Sons, 1942), 11, 13, 149–51, 199, 224.
25. Edward Storey, *A Right to Song: The Life of John Clare* (London: Methuen, 1983), 225.
26. William Miles, *An Autobiography: From Pit Bank to Balliol College* (London: Author, 1972), 18.
27. William Glynne-Jones, *The Childhood Land* (London: Batsford, 1960), 81–82.
28. Samuel, *East End Underworld*, 39–40.
29. Goffman, *Frame Analysis*, ch. 5.
30. Thomson, *Autobiography of an Artisan*, 94–101, 288–94.
31. Thomas Wright, *Some Habits and Customs of the Working Classes* (London: Tinsley Brothers, 1867), 165.
32. Philip Boswood Ballard, *Things I Cannot Forget* (London: University of London Press, 1937), 108–109.
33. Alfred Gilchrist, *Naethin' at A'* (Glasgow: Robert Gibson & Sons, n.d.), 50.
34. Acorn, *One of the Multitude*, 134.
35. Roberts, *Classic Slum*, 176.
36. Harry Blacker, *Just Like It Was: Memoirs of the Mittel East* (London: Vallentine, Mitchell, 1974), 28.
37. Ted Willis, *Whatever Happened to Tom Mix?* (London: Cassell, 1970), 47–50.
38. Jack Common, *Kiddar's Luck* (London: Turnstile, 1951), 64.

39. Emlyn Williams, *George: An Early Autobiography* (New York: Random House, 1961), 152–58.
40. William Stott, *Documentary Expression and Thirties America* (New York: Oxford University Press, 1973), ch. 5.
41. Thompson, *Lancashire for Me*, 15.
42. Garratt, *Man in the Street*, 114.
43. Hillyer, *Country Boy*, 31–32.
44. John Paton, *Proletarian Pilgrimage* (London: George Routledge & Sons, 1935), 41.
45. Thomas, *Shop Boy*, 139–40.
46. A Factory Girl, *The Unfortunate Genius* (London: Bookseller, 1852), 41. Cooper, *Life*, 8. Andrews, *Woman's Work*, 2.
47. James Edwin Saunders, *The Reflections and Rhymes of an Old Miller*, ed. W. Ridley Chesterton (London: Hodder & Stoughton, [1938]), 32–34.
48. Common, *Kiddar's Luck*, 60–61, 94–95.
49. T. A. Jackson, *Solo Trumpet* (London: Lawrence & Wishart, 1953), 14–15.
50. Leatherland, *Essays and Poems*, 5.
51. Robert Story, *Love and Literature* (London: Longman, Brown, Green & Longmans, 1842), 60–61.
52. Rogers, *Labour, Life and Literature*, 6, 15.
53. William Heaton, *The Old Soldier* (London: Simpkin, Marshall, 1857), xvi–xvii.
54. Herbert Hodge, *It's Draughty in Front* (London: Michael Joseph, 1936), 62.
55. Anonymous, *Struggles for Life* (London: W. & F. G. Cash, 1854), 40.
56. Elizabeth Rignall, "All So Long Ago" (1973), BUL, ch. 2. For a similar account, see Hughes, "Welsh Rebel," pp. 19–20.
57. Harry Alfred West, "The Autobiography of Harry Alfred West: Facts and Comment," BUL, pp. 11, 15, 44–45.
58. Janet Fyfe, *Books Behind Bars: The Role of Books, Reading, and Libraries in British Prison Reform, 1701–1911* (Westport, CT: Greenwood, 1992), 181, 195–96.
59. Bamford, *Passages*, 14, 363–64.
60. Klaus, *Literature of Labour*, 1985), 51–52.
61. John James Bezer, "The Autobiography of One of the Chartist Rebels of 1848," in David Vincent, ed., *Testaments of Radicalism: Memoirs of Working Class Politicians 1790–1885* (London: Europa, 1977), 167.
62. Hughes, "Welsh Rebel," pp. 19–20, 128–31, 140.
63. "Labour Party and Books," 573, 578.
64. Blatchford, *Favourite Books*, 191, 208.
65. Clunie, *Labour is My Faith*, 11–13.
66. Annie Kenney, *Memories of a Militant* (London: Edward Arnold, 1924), 106.
67. Rowland Kenney, *Westering* (London: J. M. Dent & Sons, 1939), 27–28.
68. Crawfurd, TS autobiography, pp. 49–53.
69. Edward Salmon, *Juvenile Literature as It Is* (London: Henry J. Drane, 1880), 15.
70. Robert W. Lovett, *Robinson Crusoe: A Bibliographical Checklist of English Language Editions (1719–1979)* (New York: Greenwood, 1991).
71. Kevin Carpenter, *Desert Isles & Pirate Islands: The Island Theme in Nineteenth-Century English Juvenile Fiction: A Survey and Bibliography* (Frankfurt: Peter Lang, 1984).
72. Martin Green, "The Robinson Crusoe Story," in *Imperialism and Juvenile Literature*, ed. Jeffrey Richards (Manchester: Manchester University Press, 1989), 35–37.
73. Daniel Defoe, *Robinson Crusoe* (Oxford: Oxford University Press, 1981), 171–73.
74. Ibid., 217–22.
75. Erhard Dahl, *Die Kürzungen des* Robinson Crusoe *in England zwischen 1719 und 1819*

vor dem Hintergrund des zeitgenössischen Druckgewerbes, Verlagswesens und Lesepublikums (Frankfurt: Peter Lang, 1977).

76. Rogers, "Classics and Chapbooks".

77. In H. T. Dickinson, ed., *The Political Works of Thomas Spence* (Newcastle: Avero, 1982), 5–15.

78. Clare, *Autobiographical Writings*, 13.

79. Ebenezer Elliott, "Autobiography," in John Watkins, ed., *Life, Poetry and Letters of Ebenezer Elliott* (London: John Mortimer, 1850), 12.

80. Greenwood, "Reminiscences of Sixty Years Ago," 51.

81. "Labour Party and Books," 571.

82. Campkin, *Village Lad*, 22. Allen Clarke, "Some Memories of Old-Time Excursions," *Liverpool Weekly Post* (5 May 1934): 2. Eric Horne, *What the Butler Winked At* (London: T. Werner Laurie, 1923), 47–48.

83. Hartley Kemball Cook, *In the Watch Below: The Books & Hobbies of Seamen* (London: J. M. Dent & Sons, 1937), 60–61.

84. Thomas Jordan, untitled MS (1976), BUL, pp. 2, 9.

85. Louis Battye, *I Had a Little Nut Tree* (London: Secker & Warburg, 1959), 95–96.

86. Murray, "To Pashendaele and Back," pp. 5, 15–16, 21.

87. Ian Watt, "Robinson Crusoe as Myth," *Essays in Criticism* 1 (April 1951): 101.

88. Michael Gareth Llewelyn, *Sand in the Glass* (London: John Murray, 1943), 13.

89. Spike Mays, *No More Soldiering for Me* (London: Eyre & Spottiswoode, 1971), 173–74.

90. Alison Uttley, *The Farm on the Hill* (London: Faber and Faber, 1941), ch. 3.

91. J. R. R. Adams, *The Printed Word and the Common Man: Popular Culture in Ulster 1700–1900* (Belfast: Institute of Irish Studies, Queen's University of Belfast, 1987), 168–69.

92. Helen Small, "A Pulse of 124: Charles Dickens and a Pathology of the Mid-Victorian Reading Public," in *The Practice and Representation of Reading in England*, ed. James Raven, Helen Small, and Naomi Tadmor (Cambridge: Cambridge University Press, 1996), 271–74, 280–81.

93. P. R. Catchside, "Loveclough Printworks Library," *Library History* 2 (Autumn 1970): 46–51.

94. Christopher M. Baggs, "The Miners' Libraries of South Wales from the 1860s to 1939" (PhD diss., University of Wales, Aberystwyth, 1995), 510–11.

95. Charles H. Welch, *An Autobiography* (Banstead: Berean Publishing Trust, 1960), 33.

96. Acorn, *One of the Multitude*, 28–35.

97. John Sykes, *Slawit in the 'Sixties* (Huddersfield and London: Schofield and Sims, n.d.), 23–29.

98. Gilchrist, *Naethin' at A'*, 14.

99. Wright, *Habits and Customs*, 166.

100. Allan Jobson, *The Creeping Hours of Time* (London: Robert Hale, 1977), 102.

101. G. A. W. Tomlinson, *Coal-Miner* (London: Hutchinson, 1937), 64.

102. Mrs. Preston, in *Life as We Have Known It*, ed. Margaret Llewelyn Davies (London: Hogarth Press, 1931), 119.

103. Eleanor Hutchinson, "The Bells of St. Mary's," BUL, ch. 3.

104. Grace Foakes, *My Part of the River* (London: Shepheard-Walwyn, 1974), 48.

105. Pritchett, *Cab at the Door*, 109.

106. Wall, "Hour at Eve," ch. 1.

107. Neville Cardus, *Second Innings* (London: Collins, 1950), 45–47.

108. Norman Nicholson, *Wednesday Early Closing* (London: Faber and Faber, 1975), 142–45.

109. Samuel, *East End Underworld*, 47, 74–75, 274. The same criticism is offered in the

anonymous "Autobiography of a Journeyman Shoemaker," *Saturday Evening Commonwealth* (22 November 1856), 3.

110. Frost, *Reminiscences of a Country Journalist*, 151–53.
111. Frank R. Argent, "No Medals for Frankie," SLSL, p. 22.
112. R. L. Lee, *The Town That Died* (London: Author, 1975), 88.
113. Ashby, *Ashby of Tysoe*, 94.
114. Donaldson, *Literature in Victorian Scotland*, 32.
115. Brierley, *Home Memories*, 21–22.
116. Nora Hampton, "Memories of Baptist End, Netherton, Dudley in the Period 1895–1919," BUL, p. 1. Walter Citrine, *Men and Work* (London: Hutchinson, 1964), 11. James Whittaker, *I, James Whittaker* (London: Rich & Cowan, 1934), 15. See also Edward Blishen, *This Right Soft Lot* (London: Thames & Hudson, 1969), 74.
117. Walter Haydn Davies, *The Right Place—The Right Time* (Llandybie: Llyfrau'r, 1972), 52.

Chapter Four: **A Conservative Canon**

1. Pierre Bourdieu, *Distinction: A Social Critique of the Judgement of Taste*, trans. Richard Nice (Cambridge, MA: Harvard University Press, 1984), 260–67.
2. Crawford, "Societal Library Activity," 36–40, 48–50, 85–88, 112–18, 232–33, 246–51.
3. Lord Cockburn, *Journal of Henry Cockburn* (Edinburgh: Edmonston & Douglas, 1874), 1:73–74.
4. Hamilton, *Poems, Essays, and Sketches*, vii–ix, 235–36, 244–46, 361–63, 371.
5. Alexander Somerville, *The Autobiography of a Working Man* (London: C. Gilpin, 1848), 93.
6. Carter, *Memoirs*, 40–42, 57–58, 79–82, 117–18.
7. Clare, *Autobiographical Writings*, 45–46.
8. Story, *Love and Literature*, 96, 127–33, 167–68.
9. Robert White, *Autobiographical Notes* (Newcastle-upon-Tyne: Eagle, 1966), 3–5, 21–22.
10. Harry Hanham and Michael Shortland, introduction to *Hugh Miller's Memoir: From Stonemason to Geologist*, ed. Shortland (Edinburgh: Edinburgh University Press, 1995), 3–4.
11. Miller to Miss Dunbar, 25 October 1834, quoted in ibid., 16.
12. Miller, *Schools and Schoolmasters*, 51–56.
13. Jim Bullock, *Them and Us* (London: Souvenir, 1972), 69.
14. Jackson, TS autobiography, p. 90.
15. Patrick J. Dollan, untitled TS, Mitchell Library, pp. 26, 169–70, 191–93, 197–99.
16. Cardus, *Second Innings*, 70–71.
17. Mayhew, *London Labour*, 1:293–96.
18. Michael Thompson, *Rubbish Theory: The Creation and Destruction of Value* (Oxford: Oxford University Press, 1979).
19. Charles Knight, *Passages of a Working Life* (London: Bradbury and Evans, 1864–65), 3:12.
20. Janet Hitchman, *The King of the Barbareens* (London: Putnam, 1960), 113–14.
21. MO file 47, pp. 22–23; file 48, pp. 26.
22. Emanuel Shinwell, *Conflict without Malice* (London: Odhams Press, 1955), 24–25.
23. Joseph Keating, *My Struggle for Life* (London: Simpkin, Marshall, Hamilton, Kent & Co., 1916), 65–66, 72–74, 99, 112–14.
24. Rogers, *Labour, Life and Literature*, 39–40, 43–45.
25. Charles Manby Smith, *Curiosities of London Life* (London: A. W. Bennett, [1853]), 102.
26. Russell Jackson, ed., *Victorian Theatre* (London: A. & C. Black, 1989), 45–50. Douglas A. Reid, "Popular Theatre in Victorian Birmingham," in David Bradby, Louis James, and

Bernard Sharratt, eds., *Performance and Politics in Popular Drama* (Cambridge: Cambridge University Press, 1980), 74–77, 82–85.

27. R. W. Morris, "Autobiography of R. W. Morris," BUL, p. 43.

28. F. W. Jowett, "Bradford Seventy Years Ago," in Brockway, *Socialism over Sixty Years*, 20.

29. Brooks, *Lancashire Bred*, 1:136–37.

30. Jeremy Crump, "The Popular Audience for Shakespeare in Nineteenth-Century Leicester," in Richard Foulkes, ed., *Shakespeare and the Victorian Stage* (Cambridge: Cambridge University Press, 1986), 271–82.

31. Samuel Westcott Tilke, *An Autobiographical Memoir* (London: Author, 1840), xv.

32. Thompson, *Working Class*, 736.

33. Joss Marsh, *Word Crimes: Blasphemy, Culture, and Literature in Nineteenth-Century England* (Chicago: University of Chicago Press, 1998), 111–12.

34. R. G. Kirby and A. E. Musson, *The Voice of the People: John Dougherty, 1798–1854: Trade Unionist, Radical and Factory Reformer* (Manchester: Manchester University Press, 1975), 175.

35. Shinwell, *Conflict without Malice*, 72–73.

36. Clynes, *Memoirs: 1869–1924*, 30–32, 49–50, 80–82. Edward George, *From Mill Boy to Minister: An Intimate Account of the Life of the Rt. Honourable J. R. Clynes, MP* (London: T. Fisher Unwin, [1918]), 41–42, 60–61.

37. Robert Smillie, *My Life for Labour* (London: Mills & Boon, 1924), 49–52.

38. Alice Foley, Interview 72, Family Life and Work before 1918 Archive, Department of Sociology, University of Sussex.

39. Crump, "Popular Audience for Shakespeare," 279–80.

40. Johnson, *Old Road*, 107–109.

41. Crump, "Popular Audience for Shakespeare," 278. Jackson, *Victorian Theatre*, 13.

42. Walter Freer, *My Life and Memories* (Glasgow: Civic Press, 1929), 132.

43. Rogers, *Labour, Life and Literature*, 128–33.

44. Blatchford, *Nunquam Papers*, 119–22.

45. W. E. Adams, *Memoirs of a Social Atom* (London: Hutchinson, 1903), 233–34, 378–81, ch. 57.

46. Steel, *Ditcher's Row*, 130–31, 238–39.

47. Nicholson, *Wednesday Early Closing*, 172–79.

48. Patricia Beer, *Mrs. Beer's House* (London: Macmillan, 1968), 177–85.

49. Hillyer, *Country Boy*, 29–30, 134–35.

50. Clare Cameron, *Rustle of Spring: Simple Annals of a London Girl* (New York: George H. Doran Co., 1927), 118. Garratt, *Man in the Street*, 174. Williams, *George*, 180. David Scott Blackhall, *This House Had Windows* (London: Max Parrish, 1961), 61–62. Dennis Marsden, in Goldman, *Breakthrough*, 109. Amy Langley, untitled TS, BUL, part 1. Harold Brown, *Most Splendid of Men: Life in a Mining Community 1917–25* (Poole: Blandford, 1981), 175. Vernon Scannell, *Drums of Morning: Growing up in the Thirties* (London: Robson, 1992), 188. Hampton, "Memories of Baptist End", pp. 43, 49.

51. Thomas Burke, *The Wind and the Rain* (London: Thornton Butterworth, 1924), 143–45.

52. Martha Salmon Vogeler, "The Victorians and the Hundred Best," *Texas Quarterly* (Spring 1968): 184–98.

53. C. H. Rolph, *London Particulars* (Oxford: Oxford University Press, 1980), 82–84, 95–96, 132.

54. N. N. Feltes, *Literary Capital and the Late Victorian Novel* (Madison: University of Wisconsin Press, 1993), 41–55.

55. Bonar Thompson, *Hyde Park Orator* (London: Jarrolds, 1934), 208–9.

56. Harold Heslop, "From Tyne to Tone: A Journey," BUL, pp. 167–68.

57. Jackson, TS autobiography, pp. 4–5, 25–26, 48–49, 125–27.

58. Jackson, *Solo Trumpet*, 18–19.

59. Murphy, *New Horizons*, 215–16.

60. Kathleen Woodward, *Jipping Street: Childhood in a London Slum* (New York: Harper & Brothers, 1928), 135–38.

61. Alan Gibson, *A Mingled Yarn* (London: Collins, 1976), 53.

62. J. W. and Anne Tibble, *John Clare: A Life*, rev. edn. (London: Michael Joseph, 1972), 164. Carter, *Memoirs*, 97.

63. Richard D. Altick, "From Aldine to Everyman: Cheap Reprint Series of the English Classics, 1830–1906," in Altick, ed., *Writers, Readers, and Occasions: Selected Essays on Victorian Literature and Life* (Columbus: Ohio State University Press, 1989).

64. Joseph O. Baylen, "Stead's Penny 'Masterpiece Library'," *Journal of Popular Culture* 9 (Winter 1975): 710–25.

65. John R. Turner, *The Walter Scott Publishing Company: A Bibliography* (Pittsburgh: University of Pittsburgh Press, 1997), ix–xvi.

66. J. M. Dent, *The House of Dent 1888–1938* (London: J. M. Dent & Sons, 1938), 4–6, 9–11, 22–23.

67. Frank Swinnerton, *Swinnerton: An Autobiography* (London: Hutchinson, 1937), 220.

68. Dent, *House of Dent*, 4–26.

69. Ibid., 61–64, 75–77.

70. Ibid., 123–26.

71. John R. Turner, "The Camelot Series, Everyman's Library, and Ernest Rhys," *Publishing History* 31 (1992): 27–46.

72. Hugh Kenner, *A Sinking Island: The Modern English Writers* (New York: Knopf, 1988), 29–35.

73. Donald Armstrong Ross, ed., *The Reader's Guide to Everyman's Library*, 4th edn. (London: J. M. Dent & Sons, 1976) is a complete bibliography of the series.

74. E. F. Bozman, *Everyman's Library 1906–1956* (London: J. M. Dent & Sons, 1956), 6.

75. J. M. Dent to A. Harvey-Smith (18 September 1909), Box 111, JMD. J. M. Dent to M. A. DeWolfe Howe (30 July 1920), Box 117, JMD.

76. C. J. Hogarth to J. M. Dent (5 November 1923) and J. M. Dent to C. J. Hogarth (8 November 1923), Box 129, JMD.

77. J. M. Dent to Miss H. Black (26 June 1919), Box 115, JMD. J. M. Dent to P. L. Elliott (25 October 1921), Box 123, JMD. J. M. Dent to J. M. Jones (19 December 1924), Box 133, JMD.

78. J. M. Dent to Eric S. Pinker (24 January, 26 February, 31 August, and 19 October 1923), Box 130, JMD.

79. J. H. Willis, Jr., *Leonard and Virginia Woolf as Publishers: The Hogarth Press 1917–41* (Charlottesville: University Press of Virginia, 1992), 314.

80. J. M. Dent to Anton Bertram (5 September 1921), Box 122, JMD.

81. It published *Their Eyes Were Watching God* (1938), *Voodoo Gods* (1939), and *The Man of the Mountain* (1941).

82. See a review of forty Everyman volumes in *Highway* 5 (October 1912): 17–18.

83. Author's interview with Frederick Padley, 24 August 1987.

84. For a more detailed discussion of this journal, see Jonathan Rose, "*Everyman*: An Experiment in Culture for the Masses," *Victorian Periodicals Review* 26 (Summer 1993): 79–87.

85. Charles Sarolea to G. Bell and Sons, (24 October 1913), file 2, Charles Sarolea Papers, Edinburgh University Library.

86. C. B. Purdom, memorandum to Hugh Dent (2 February 1932), pp. 5–7, Box 174, JMD.

87. Letters to the editor from A. J. Key (21 November 1912); F. W. Gray (23 March 1913); Robert Boswell (26 June 1913); Sidney B. Reed (17 November 1913); and Robert J. Phalp (3 March 1914), file 17, Charles Sarolea Papers, Edinburgh University Library.

88. Murray, "To Pashendaele and Back," pp. 27–31, 115–16.

89. Ernest Rhys, *Wales England Wed* (London: J. M. Dent & Sons, 1940), 273–74.

90. Ballard, *I Cannot Forget*, 26–28, 35–43, 94–97, 155–56.

91. D. R. Davies, *In Search of Myself* (London: Geoffrey Bles, 1961), 47–78.

92. Roger Dataller, *Oxford into Coalfield* (London: J. M. Dent & Sons, 1934), 103–104.

93. Roger Dataller, "A Yorkshire Lad," RCL, p. 133.

94. N. B. Dolan, letter to the editor, *Highway* (February 1934): 20.

95. Tomlinson, *Coal-Miner*, 69–71.

96. Fred Bason, *Fred Bason's Diary*, ed. Nicolas Bentley (London: Allen Wingate, 1950), 58–59, 144.

97. Q. D. Leavis, *Fiction and the Reading Public* (London: Chatto & Windus, 1932), 71.

98. Bristol Public Library, Annual Report, 1944–45, pp. 27–28.

99. "The Leisure of the Adult Student—A Sample Investigation in London," *Adult Education* 9 (March 1937): 203–16.

100. MO file 2018, p. 100.

101. Marion Springall, "An Approach to Adult Education in a Rural Area," *Adult Education* 17 (March 1945): 121.

102. Common, *Kiddar's Luck*, 90–91.

103. Agnes Cowper, *A Backward Glance at Merseyside*, 2nd edn. (Birkenhead: William Brothers, 1952), 96–97.

104. Brian Maidment, ed., *The Poorhouse Fugitives* (Manchester: Coronet, 1987), 13–14, 97–98.

105. Alexander Baron, autobiographical note in Stanley J. Kunitz, ed., *Twentieth Century Authors*, First Supplement (New York: H. W. Wilson, 1955), 49.

106. K. T. Wallas, review of Alfred Williams, *Songs of Wiltshire*, *Highway* 2 (December 1909): 36–37.

107. Leonard Clark, *Alfred Williams: His Life and Work* (Newton Abbot: David & Charles, 1969), 15–22, 28, 45.

108. W. H. Davies, *Later Days* (London: Jonathan Cape, 1925), 38–39.

109. Bernard Shaw, preface to W. H. Davies, *Autobiography of a Super-Tramp*, 2nd edn. (London: A. C. Fifield, 1908), ix.

110. Peter Donnelly, *The Yellow Rock* (London: Eyre & Spottiswoode, 1950), 213–14.

111. Kathleen Betterton, "White Pinnies, Black Aprons …," BUL, pp. 5, 33–35, 54–55, 117–18, 126–28, 148, 154–57, 167, 179–81, 186–87, 191–92, 205, 233.

112. Jane Mitchell, in Goldman, *Breakthrough*, 125–41.

113. Ronald Goldman, in Goldman, *Breakhrough*, 73–89.

Chapter Five: **Willingly to School**

1. G. A. N. Lowndes, *The Silent Social Revolution* (London: Oxford University Press, 1937), 13–20; Brian Simon, *Education and the Labour Movement, 1870–1920* (London: Lawrence & Wishart, 1965), 112–20.

2. Edmund Holmes, *In Quest of an Ideal: An Autobiography* (London: Richard Cobden-Sanderson, 1920), 63–64.

3. Phil Gardner, *The Lost Elementary Schools of Victorian England* (London: Croom Helm, 1984), 211.

4. Even "scientific" polling cannot entirely escape subjectivity. Not only are poll results open to interpretation: the interviewees must first interpret the questions put to them, usually without as much opportunity for probing, clarification, elaboration, and qualification as oral history affords. Poll interviewers, moreover, have been known to garble questions and (accidentally or deliberately) misrecord answers. See Paul Thompson, *The Voice of the Past*, 2nd ed. (Oxford: Oxford University Press, 1988), 122–23.

5. A glaring example is Stephen Humphries's *Hooligans or Rebels? An Oral History of Working-Class Childhood and Youth, 1889–1939* (Oxford: Basil Blackwell, 1981), which is also based on the Thompson–Vigne project as well as other oral history archives. Humphries has a right to focus on discontented youth, if discontent is his subject, but *Hooligans or Rebels?* obscures the fact that most working-class children were neither, and it gives the highly misleading impression that *none* of these children enjoyed school.

6. Alec Ellis, *Educating Our Masters: Influences on the Growth of Literacy in Victorian Working Class Children* (Aldershot: Gower, 1985), 97–98, 114, 151–56.

7. Simon, *Education*, 118–19.

8. H. C. Dent, *1870–1970: Century of Growth in English Education* (London: Longman, 1970), 18–19, 69–70. For a similar view, see Pamela Horn, *The Victorian and Edwardian Schoolchild* (Gloucester: Alan Sutton, 1989), 184–93.

9. George Orwell, "Such, Such Were the Joys," in *The Collected Essays, Journalism and Letters of George Orwell*, ed. Sonia Orwell and Ian Angus (New York: Harcourt, Brace and World, 1968), 3:330–69; Cyril Connolly, *Enemies of Promise* (London: George Routledge & Sons, 1938).

10. Gardner, *Lost Elementary Schools*. See also J. H. Higginson, "Dame Schools," *British Journal of Educational Studies* 22 (June 1974): 166–181; and D. P. Leinster-Mackay, "Dame Schools: A Need for Review," *British Journal of Educational Studies* 24 (February 1976): 33–48. Higginson and Leinster-Mackay based their positive assessments mainly on the testimony of middle-class sources, who in fact attended relatively superior private schools rather than true dame schools.

11. "Second Report of a Committee of the Statistical Society of London, appointed to enquire into the State of Education in Westminster," *Journal of the Statistical Society of London* 1 (August 1838): 194–96.

12. For a couple of exceptionally positive accounts, see Mary Weston, *The Story of Our Sunday Trip to Hastings* (London: S. W. Partridge, 1879), 8; and Israel Nichols, "Sixty Years in Suffolk: The Observations of an Ordinary Man," S Knodishall 9, Suffolk Record Office, Ipswich, pp. 2–3.

13. John Askham, *Sketches in Prose and Verse* (Northampton: S. S. Campion, 1893), x–xiii, 10–17.

14. Collyer, *Memories*, 12.

15. William Gifford, *Memoir of William Gifford* (London: Hunt & Clarke, 1827), 7. Place, *Autobiography*, 30.

16. W. J. Hocking, *Bench and Mitre: A Cornish Autobiography* (London: Wells Gardner, Darton & Co., 1903), 27–29.

17. W. J. Francis, *Reminiscences* (Southend-on-Sea: Francis & Sons, 1926), 9–10.

18. William Cameron, *Hawkie: The Autobiography of a Gangrel*, ed. John Strathesk (Glasgow: David Robertson, 1888), 11, 15.

19. Sykes, *Slawit in the 'Sixties*, 20–29.

20. Jobson, *Creeping Hours*, 93–94.

21. John Harris, *My Autobiography* (London: Hamilton, Adams & Co., 1882), 23–26.

22. Joseph Burgess, "Nineteenth Century Lancashire Textile Operatives' Tribulations, 1800–1895," National Museum of Labour History, p. 105.

23. George H. Barber, *From Workhouse to Lord Mayor* (Tunstall: Author, 1937), 3–4.

24. Thomson, *Autobiography of an Artisan*, 35–37.

25. Rogers, *Labour, Life and Literature*, 5, 50, 58–59.

26. Shaw, *When I Was a Child*, 1–6, 132. For workingmen who expressed similar sentiments, see also Joseph Gutteridge, *Lights and Shadows in the Life of an Artisan* (Coventry: Curtis & Beamish, 1893), 274; William J. Milne, *Reminiscences of an Old Boy* (Forfar: John MacDonald, 1901), 40; Ben Turner, *About Myself 1863–1930* (London: Cayme, 1930), 22–23; Blatchford, *Eighty Years*, 38–40; Henry Hughes, "Short Biography of Henry Hughes" (1896), trans. (1947) Albert B. Hughes, Newport Reference Library, p. 25; Joseph Arch, *The Autobiography of Joseph Arch* (London: MacGibbon & Kee, 1966), 27–29; Tom Mann, *Tom Mann's Memoirs* (London: McGibbon & Kee, 1967), 4.

27. Freer, *Life and Memories*, 128–29.

28. Lansbury, *My Life*, 20–21.

29. James Edwin Saunders, *The Reflections and Rhymes of an Old Miller*, ed. W. Ridley Chesterton (London: Hodder & Stoughton, [1938]), 24–27.

30. Flint, *Hot Bread and Chips*, 67–68.

31. "Autobiography of a Suffolk Farm Labourer," *Suffolk Times and Mercury* (18 January 1895): 6.

32. Frank Galton, "Autobiography," revised draft (1944), Coll Misc 315: Galton, British Library of Political and Economic Science, ch. 2. See also Burton, *There Was a Young Man*, 58.

33. John Eldred, *I Love the Brooks* (London: Skeffington, 1955), 47.

34. Lord Taylor of Mansfield, *Uphill All the Way: A Miner's Struggle* (London: Sidgwick & Jackson, 1972), 7.

35. E. Ellis, *As It Was and Twenty-One Today* (n.p.: Author, 1978), 6.

36. Winifred Albaya, *A Sheffield Childhood* (Sheffield: Sheffield Women's Printing Co-operative, [1984]), 2.

37. William J. Belcher, untitled MS (1936), BUL, p. 5.

38. Garratt, *Man in the Street*, 21–25.

39. John Edmonds, "The Lean Years" (1970), BUL, pp. 77–79.

40. Frank Goss, "My Boyhood at the Turn of the Century: An Autobiography," BUL, pp. 74–79.

41. For example, Robert E. Hayward, *Where the Ladbrook Flows: Memories of Village Boyhood in Gastard, Wiltshire* (Corsham: Chris J. Hall, 1983), 56.

42. Spike Mays, *Reuben's Corner* (London: Eyre Methuen, 1980), 64–66, 75–76.

43. Quoted in John Burnett, ed., *Destiny Obscure* (Harmondsworth: Penguin, 1984), 159.

44. H. M. Tomlinson, *A Mingled Yarn* (London: Gerald Duckworth, 1953), 11–13.

45. Wallace, *Wallace*, 16–18, 21–23.

46. John Allaway, in Goldman, *Breakthrough*, 7–9.

47. Mark Grossek, *First Movement* (London: Geoffrey Bles, 1937), 25–33.

48. George Hitchin, *Pit-Yacker* (London: Jonathan Cape, 1962), 51.

49. Alfred Green, *Growing Up in Attercliffe* (Sheffield: Urban Theology Unit, 1981), 36–37, 78–85.

50. Jackson, TS autobiography, pp. 13–14.

51. Gresswell, *Bright Boots*, 33–37, 66.

52. Joseph Stamper, *So Long Ago …* (London: Hutchinson, 1960), 191–92, 211–16.

53. Goffin, "Grey Life," ch. 5.

54. Argent, "No Medals for Frankie," pp. 39–46.

55. Elizabeth K. Blackburn, *In and Out the Windows* (Burnley: F. H. Brown, n.d.), 26–27, 48–50, 58.

56. Elizabeth K. Blackburn, *When I Was a Little Girl: A Bunch of Childhood Memories 1907–1916* (Burnley: F. H. Brown, n.d.), 64–65.

57. Elizabeth K. Blackburn, *When I Grew Up* (Accrington: Ward Knowles, n.d.), 12–14, 17–18, 21–24.

58. Richard Hoggart, *A Local Habitation* (London: Chatto & Windus, 1988), 196.

59. Amy Frances Gomm, "Water Under the Bridge," BUL, pp. 39–40.

60. Alfred S. Hall, "I Was a Camberwell Boy," SLSL, p. 15.

61. Rolph, *London Particulars*, 29. For similar complaints about the teaching of history and geography, see A. Gordon James, "A Soul Remembering," BUL, pp. 9–10; and Belding Colman, "Autobiography 1901–1951," RCL, pp. 19–20.

62. Common, *Kiddar's Luck*, 89–90.

63. For example, Brooks, *Lancashire Bred*, 1:53.

64. Edna Bold, "The Long and the Short of It: Being the Recollections and Reminiscences of Edna Bold" (1978), BUL, pp. 1, 14–15, 36.

65. Jack Lanigan, "Thy Kingdom *Did* Come," BUL, p. 6.

66. Joseph H. Armitage, "The Twenty-Three Years; or, the Late Way of Life—and of Living," BUL, pp. 29, 66.

67. Henry George Lock, "An Old Man Tries to Remember" (1956), BUL, pp. 1–2.

68. Catherine McLoughlin, untitled MS, BUL, p. 5.

69. Edward Balne, "Autobiography of an Ex-Workhouse and Poor Law Schoolboy" (1972), BUL, pp. 7–21.

70. Hilda Rose Fowler, "Look after the Little Ones" (1976), BUL, p. 11.

71. P. A. Heard, *An Octogenarian's Memoirs* (Ilfracombe: Arthur H. Stockwell, 1974), 39–40.

72. Ernest Ambrose, *Melford Memories: Recollections of 94 Years* (Lavenham: Long Melford Historical and Archaeological Society, 1972), 2.

73. Batten, *Newlyn Boyhood*, 16.

74. Derrick V. Rugg, *Across Cobble-Stones* (Padstow: Tabb House, 1983), 38.

75. In Goldman, *Breakthrough*, 132.

76. Beer, *Mrs. Beer's House*, 177.

77. Wally Horwood, "A Walworth Boy: Looking Back on Growing Up, 1922–1939," SLSL, p. 206.

78. Hayward, *Where the Ladbrook Flows*, 58–59, 63.

79. T. Dan Smith, *An Autobiography* (Newcastle-upon-Tyne: Oriel, 1970), 8.

80. Nancy Day, untitled MS, BUL, pp. 40–41.

81. Lottie Barker, "My Life as I Remember It, 1899–1920," BUL, pp. 24, 30.

82. Elsie Elizabeth Goodhead, *The West End Story* (Derby: Derbyshire Library Service, 1983), 32.

83. Lowndes, *Social Revolution*, 16–17, quoted in Simon, *Education*, 115.

84. Paul Thompson, *The Edwardians: The Remaking of British Society* (Chicago: Academy Chicago, 1985), 73.

85. Standish Meacham, *A Life Apart: The English Working Class, 1890–1914* (London: Thames & Hudson, 1977), 171.

86. For example, Douglas Jennings, "Solarium: The Diary of a Nobody" (1955), BUL, p. 349; and Stan Dickens, *Bending the Twig* (Ilfracombe: Arthur H. Stockwell, 1975), 19–20.

87. George H. Gallup, ed. The Gallup International Public Opinion Polls, Great Britain, 1937–1975 (New York: Random House, 1976), 192.

88. Taffy Lewis, *Any Road: Pictures of Small Heath, Sparkbrook and Further Afield 1902–39* (Birmingham: Trinity Arts, 1979), 10.

89. William Campbell, *Villi the Clown* (London: Faber and Faber, 1981), 17–18.

90. Edward Ezard, *Battersea Boy* (London: William Kimber, 1979), 103–104.

91. Thompson, *Lark Rise*, 182–86.

92. Edmonds, "Lean Years," pp. 70–71.

93. Rolph, *Living Twice*, 30–31.

94. Gladys Teal, *Grasp the Nettle* (Leeds: Arthur Wrigley & Sons, [1978]), 9.

95. Kenney, *Westering*, 12, 311–15.

96. Ernest James Bourne, "Some Reminiscences of My Boyhood 1905–14," Waltham Forest Local Studies Library, p. 19.

97. Aubrey S. Darby, *A View from the Alley* (Luton: Borough of Luton Museum and Art Gallery, 1974), 5, 9–10.

98. Thompson, *Edwardians*, 74.

99. Meacham, *Life Apart*, 174–75.

100. J. S. Hurt, *Elementary Schooling and the Working Classes 1860–1918* (London: Routledge & Kegan Paul, 1979), 212.

101. Flint, *Hot Bread and Chips*, 108–11, 140, 143.

102. Tom Tremewan, *Cornish Youth: Memories of a Perran Boy (1895–1910)* (Truro: Oscar Blackford, 1968), 22–23.

103. MO file 2047, pp. 2, 8, 14, 19.

104. Ernest Green, *Adult Education: Why This Apathy?* (London: G. Allen & Unwin, 1953), 28–34, 52–59.

105. John H. Goldthorpe et al., *The Affluent Worker in the Class Structure* (Cambridge: Cambridge University Press, 1971), 137–40.

106. Elizabeth Roberts, *A Woman's Place: An Oral History of Working-Class Women, 1890–1940* (Oxford: Basil Blackwell, 1984), 37.

107. W. Gareth Evans, *Education and Female Emancipation: The Welsh Experience, 1847–1914* (Cardiff: University of Wales Press, 1990), 166–68.

108. Jill Liddington and Jill Norris, *One Hand Tied Behind Us: The Rise of the Women's Suffrage Movement* (London: Virago, 1985), 35.

109. Ashby, *Ashby of Tysoe*, 246–47.

110. Elisabeth Dale, "School, Day and Sunday," BUL.

111. See, for example, Annmarie Turnbull, "Learning Her Womanly Work: The Elementary School Curriculum, 1870–1914," in *Lessons for Life: The Schooling of Girls and Women 1850–1950*, ed. Felicity Hunt (Oxford: Basil Blackwell, 1987).

112. Ellen Wilkinson, in *Myself When Young: By Famous Women of To-Day*, ed. Margot Oxford and Asquith (London: Frederick Muller, 1938), 403–404, 408–10.

113. Roberts, *Woman's Place*, 1–2, 30–34.

114. Gallup, *Polls*, 209, 223–24.

115. Joanna Bourke, *Working-Class Cultures in Britain 1890–1960: Gender, Class and Ethnicity* (London: Routledge, 1994), 62–71.

116. Andrews, *Woman's Work*, 11.

117. Kathleen Betterton, "White Pinnies, Black Aprons …," BUL, pp. 27, 117–18.

118. Adeline Hodges, "I Remember," BUL, p. 31. See also Hamilton, *Poems, Essays, and Sketches*, ix; and Hannah Mitchell, *The Hard Way Up*, ed. Geoffrey Mitchell (London: Faber and Faber, 1968), 52–54, 57.

119. Roberts, *Classic Slum*, 50–51, 55.

120. D. H. Lawrence, "Education of the People," in *Phoenix: The Posthumous Papers of D. H. Lawrence (1936)*, ed. Edward McDonald (New York: Viking, 1968), esp. 594–613.

121. Vernon Scannell, *The Tiger and the Rose* (London: Hamish Hamilton, 1971), 81–82. Scannell, *Drums of Morning*, 30.

122. Kenney, *Westering*, 76–79.

123. Michael Pickering and Kevin Robins, "The Making of a Working-Class Writer: An Interview with Sid Chaplin," in *The British Working-Class Novel in the Twentieth Century*, ed. Jeremy Hawthorn (London: Edward Arnold, 1984), 143.

124. Lennox Kerr, *The Eager Years* (London: Collins, 1940), 102, 108–109.

125. William Harry Sutton, untitled MS, BUL, pp. 6–7, 31.

126. John T. Macpherson, "How I Got On: Life Stories by the Labour MPs," *Pearson's Weekly* (1 March 1906): 613.

127. Martha Martin, "The Ups and Downs of Life," BUL, pp. 57–58.

128. Anita Elizabeth Hughes, "My Autobiography" (1977), BUL, pp. 4–5.

129. Shaw, *When I Was a Child*, 21.

130. Davies, *Right Place*, 90–91.

131. Wil John Edwards, *From the Valley I Came* (London: Angus & Robertson, 1956), 16.

132. Bernard Taylor, *Uphill All the Way* (London: Sidgwick & Jackson, 1972), 11.

133. J. E. Patterson, *My Vagabondage* (London: William Heinemann, 1911), 64.

134. Thompson, *Lancashire for Me*, 21–25.

135. Foley, *Bolton Childhood*, 33–34.

136. Anne Kynoch, *The King's Seat* (Letchworth: Wayfair, 1961), 12, 111–23.

137. Roberts, *Classic Slum*, 25.

138. Bernard Crick, *George Orwell* (Boston: Little, Brown, 1980), chs. 2–3. Jonathan Rose, "Eric Blair's School Days," in *The Revised Orwell*, ed. Rose (East Lansing: Michigan State University Press, 1992), 75–84.

139. Thompson, *Voice of the Past*, 112–13, 138–41.

Chapter Six: Cultural Literacy in the Classic Slum

1. Carl Philip Moritz, *Journeys of a German in England in 1782*, trans. and ed. Reginald Nettel (London: Jonathan Cape, 1965), 42–44, 59, 187.

2. William Chambers, *Memoir of William and Robert Chambers*, 9th edn. (Edinburgh: W. & R. Chambers, 1876), 228–34. Sondra Miley Cooney, "Publishers for the People: W. & R. Chambers—The Early Years, 1832–1850" (PhD diss., Ohio State University, 1970), 52–56, 97–98.

3. Cooney, "Publishers for the People," 107–10. Altick, *Common Reader*, 336–38.

4. Newcastle-upon-Tyne Working Men's Club Library Register 1871–74, Newcastle Central Library.

5. Sinclair, *New Statistical Account of Scotland*, 13:37, 52–53.

6. Cooper, *Life*, 252. Bethune, *Memoirs*, 37–39, 43–52. Adams, *Social Atom*, 100–101. Holyoake, *Agitator's Life*, 1:77. Richard Church, *Over the Bridge* (New York: E.P. Dutton, 1956), 130. Eldred, *I Love the Brooks*, 102.

7. Adrian Desmond, "Artisan Resistance and Evolution in Britain, 1819–1848," *Osiris* 3 (1987): 89.

8. Harry Watkin, *From Hulme All Blessings Flow: A Collection of Manchester Memories* (Manchester: Neil Richardson, 1975), 56.

9. Benn, *Keir Hardie*, 38.

10. Elton, *Ramsay MacDonald*, 27.

11. John Wilson, *Memories of a Labour Leader* (London: T. Fisher Unwin, 1910), 83.

12. Smillie, *Life for Labour*, 52–54.

13. Adams, *Social Atom*, 112–13. Jones, *Old Memories*, 69. Allen Clarke, "Adventuring in 'The Realms of Gold'," *Liverpool Weekly Post* (26 May 1934): 2. Alexander Falconer Murison, *Memoirs of 88 Years* (Aberdeen: Aberdeen University Press, 1935), 80. J. G.

Graves, *Some Memories* (Sheffield: Author, [1944]), 43–44. Willox, "Memories of Parkhead," pp. 102–103.

14. Wright, *Joseph Wright*, 38–41. K. M. Elisabeth Murray, *Caught in the Web of Words: James Murray and the Oxford English Dictionary* (New Haven and London: Yale University Press, 1995), 25.

15. Goss, "My Boyhood," pp. 9–10.

16. See, for example, C. W. Bowerman and Arthur Henderson, "How I Got On: Life Stories by the Labour MPs," *Pearson's Weekly* (8 February 1906): 563, (8 March 1906): 613.

17. Dennis Smith, *Conflict and Compromise: Class Formation in English Society 1830–1914* (London: Routledge & Kegan Paul, 1982), 138–41.

18. Thomson, *Autobiography of an Artisan*, 21.

19. [Arnold Freeman], *The Equipment of the Workers* (London: George Allen & Unwin, 1919), chs. 1–3.

20. Ibid., ch. 8.

21. Florence Bell, *At the Works* (London: Virago, 1985), 144–45.

22. Florence Bell, "What People Read," *Independent Review* 7 (1905): 426–40.

23. C. B. Hawkins, *Norwich: A Social Study* (London: Philip Lee Warner, 1910), 307.

24. [Freeman], *Equipment*, 235.

25. Thompson, *Lark Rise*, 198–99, 365, 415.

26. Wilfred Wellock, *Off the Beaten Track: Adventures in the Art of Living*, 2nd edn. (Rajghat: Sarva Seva Sangh Prakashan, 1963), 43, 195.

27. Stamper, *So Long Ago*, 185–86.

28. Chris Waters, *British Socialists and the Politics of Popular Culture, 1884–1914* (Manchester: Manchester University Press, 1990), 109–10.

29. Shinwell, *Conflict without Malice*, 44–46, 72–73.

30. Wilfred Pickles, *Sometime…Never* (London: Werner Laurie, 1951), 20, 27–28.

31. "The Public for Poetry Broadcasts," 27 October 1941, BBC R9/9/5/LR/392.

32. G. Launders, "Reminiscences: B.B.S.W. and Its Surroundings" (1936), Sheffield Local Studies Library, pp. 18–20.

33. Roger Elbourne, *Music and Tradition in Early Industrial Lancaster 1780–1840* (Totowa, NJ: Rowman & Littlefield, 1980), 27–30.

34. William Millington, *Sketches of Local Musicians and Musical Societies* (Pendlebury: Pendlebury Journal, 1884).

35. Laqueur, *Religion and Respectability*, 177.

36. John Shinn, "A Sketch of My Life and Times" (1923), BUL, pp. 17–23, 26, 28, 32–37, 41, 44.

37. Ambrose, *Melford Memories*, 12.

38. Francis Anthony, *A Man's a Man* (London: Duckworth, 1932), 63, 68–70.

39. Dave Russell, "'What's Wrong with Brass Bands?': Cultural Change and the Brass Band Movement, 1918–c. 1964," in Trevor Herbert, ed., *Bands: The Brass Band Movement in the 19th and 20th Centuries* (Milton Keynes: Open University Press, 1991), 58–60, 75.

40. Marjory Todd, *Snakes and Ladders* (London: Longmans, Green, 1960), 106–107.

41. E. D. Mackerness, *A Social History of English Music* (London: Routledge & Kegan Paul, 1964), 200–203.

42. Reginald Lennard, "Music in an Oxfordshire Village," *Highway* 1 (February 1909): 76–77.

43. Davies, *Right Place*, 65–66.

44. Peter Crossley-Holland, ed., *Music in Wales* (London: Hinrischen, 1948).

45. Jennie Lee, *My Life with Nye* (London: Jonathan Cape, 1980), 16, 22.

46. Brown, *Most Splendid of Men*, 85, 110, 139.

47. Whittaker, *I, James Whittaker*, 174–76.

48. Waters, *Socialists and Popular Culture*, ch. 4.

49. William Martin Haddow, *My Seventy Years* (Glasgow: Robert Gibson & Sons, 1943), 48–49, 145–46, 163–64.

50. Jeremy Seabrook, *What Went Wrong?: Working People and the Ideals of the Labour Movement* (London: Gollancz, 1978), 136–37.

51. Arthur Barton, *Two Lamps in Our Street* (London: New Authors Limited, 1967), ch. 6.

52. Walter Greenwood, *There Was a Time* (London: Jonathan Cape, 1967), 59–60, 124–26, 171–73, 243–44.

53. Cardus, *Second Innings*, 99–108, 127.

54. Neville Cardus, *Autobiography* (London: Collins, 1947), 16–17.

55. Coppard, *It's Me, O Lord!*, 91.

56. Blackburn, *In and Out*, 32.

57. Patrick McLoughlin, *The Johnson Street Bullies* (Bognor Regis: New Horizon, 1980), 256.

58. Elsie Gadsby, *Black Diamonds, Yellow Apples: A Working-Class Derbyshire Childhood between the Wars* (Ilkeston: Scollins & Titford, 1978), 1, 11.

59. Herbert Mannion, "I Was in a Gas Works," in *Seven Shifts*, ed. Jack Common (New York: E. P. Dutton, 1938), 168.

60. J. R. Clynes, *Memoirs: 1924–1937* (London: Hutchinson, 1937), 57.

61. Rolph, *London Particulars*, 112–13, 136–37, 162, 168.

62. Rolph, *Living Twice*, 39.

63. A. J. Mills, "Coward or Fool," IWM, p. 13.

64. J. Ronald Andrew, *The Wharncliffe Gardens Story* (Hastings: Author, 1981–83), 1: 187–88, 195.

65. Sid Chaplin, *A Tree with Rosy Apples* (Newcastle-upon-Tyne: Frank Graham, 1972), 155–57.

66. J. P. Mayer, *Sociology of Film* (London: Faber and Faber, 1946), 259. J. P. Mayer, *British Cinemas and Their Audiences: Sociological Studies* (London: Dennis Dobson, 1948), 106, 169, 175, 181, 183, 219.

67. Michael Stapleton, *The Threshold* (London: Hutchinson, 1958), 223–27.

68. Percy Edwards, *The Road I Travelled* (London: Arthur Barker, 1979), 22.

69. William Abington, "Thus It Was: Kimbolton in the Early 1900s," County Record Office Huntington, pp. 60–61.

70. Louis Heren, *Growing up Poor in London* (London: Hamish Hamilton, 1973), 42.

71. Georgie Wood, *I Had to Be "Wee"* (London: Huthinson, 1948), 58, 181–82.

72. "Listeners' Living Habits, Autumn 1939," 22 December 1939, BBC R9/9/3/LR/86.

73. "What Listeners Like," May 1939, Table 1, BBC R9/9/3/LR/71.

74. F. M. Leventhal, "'The Best for the Most': CEMA and State Sponsorship of the Arts in Wartime, 1939–1945," *Twentieth Century British History* 1 (1990): 299–301.

75. *The Fifth Year: The End of the Beginning: Report on the Work of C.E.M.A. for 1944* (London: CEMA, 1945), 7, 31.

76. Gallup, *Polls*, 142.

77. Frank Chapple, *Sparks Fly! A Trade Union Life* (London: Michael Joseph, 1984), 23–24, 37.

78. MO file 2427, pp. 1–10.

79. MO file 2576, pp. 1–4.

80. MO file 3005, pp. 24–25.

81. Stan Dickens, *Bending the Twig* (Ilfracombe, Devon: Arthur H. Stockwell, 1975), ch. 21.

82. Fred Blackburn, *George Tomlinson* (London: William Heinemann, 1954), 5, 30.

83. Leslie Paul, *Heron Lake: A Norfolk Year* (London: Batchworth, 1948), 83.

84. Sidney Harrison, *Teacher Never Told Me* (London: Elek, 1961), 119–24, 168–71.
85. Capp, *Astrology and the Popular Press*, 120–22.
86. Roy Porter and Lesley Hall, *The Facts of Life: The Creation of Sexual Knowledge in Britain, 1650–1950* (New Haven: Yale University Press, 1995), pp. 6–7, 103–105 and ch. 2.
87. James Lackington, *Memoirs*, 7th edn. (London: Author, 1794), 95.
88. Jones, *Rhymney Memories*, 63.
89. Pritchett, *Cab at the Door*, 129.
90. Common, *Kiddar's Luck*, 181.
91. John Paton, *Proletarian Pilgrimage* (London: George Routledge & Sons, 1935), 58–59.
92. Gibson Cowan, *Loud Report* (London: Michael Joseph, 1938), 63.
93. Dickens, *Bending the Twig*, ch. 16.
94. Edith Hinson, *Mary Ann's Girl: Memories of Newbridge Lane* (Stockport: Stockport Metropolitan Borough Recreation and Culture Division, 1984), 8.
95. Mary Bertenshaw, *Sunrise to Sunset* (Manchester: Pan Visuals, 1980), 99.
96. Porter and Hall, *Facts of Life*, esp. 8–9, 128–31.
97. Vincent, *Bread, Knowledge and Freedom*, 42–43.
98. David Vincent, introduction to J. D. Burn, *The Autobiography of a Beggar Boy* (London: Europa, 1978), 31.
99. John Strathesk, preface to Cameron, *Hawkie*, 6–7.
100. Michael Mason, *The Making of Victorian Sexual Attitudes* (Oxford: Oxford University Press, 1994), 117–78. See also Michael Mason, *The Making of Victorian Sexuality* (Oxford: Oxford University Press, 1994), 133–56.
101. Place, *Autobiography*, 45–47.
102. Barker, *History and Confessions*, 119–20.
103. James Bonwick, *An Octogenarian's Reminiscences* (London: James Nichols, 1902), 31.
104. Thomas Okey, *A Basketful of Memories* (London: J. M. Dent & Sons, 1930), 11–12.
105. Ruth B. Bottigheimer, *The Bible for Children: From the Age of Gutenberg to the Present* (New Haven and London: Yale University Press, 1996), ch. 8.
106. Bonwick, *Reminiscences*, 32.
107. Garratt, *Man in the Street*, 20.
108. Frank Richards, *Old Soldier Sahib* (n.p.: Harrison Smith & Robert Haas, 1936), 133–34.
109. Harry John Belsey, *Bromley Memories: A Working-Class Childhood 1917–1921* (Chislehurst: Author, 1977), 42.
110. Robert Roberts, *A Ragged Schooling* (Manchester: Manchester University Press, 1976), 197–98.
111. Tom Barclay, *Memoirs and Medleys: The Autobiography of a Bottle-Washer* (Leicester: Edgar Backus, 1934), 19–20, 32.
112. Penny Summerfield, "An Oral History of Schooling in Lancashire 1900–1950: Gender, Class and Education," *Oral History* 15 (Autumn 1987): 25–30.
113. Mrs. P. Marrin, untitled TS (1978), BUL, p. 1.
114. Woodward, *Jipping Street*, 93–96.
115. Jim Bullock, *Bowers Row: Recollections of a Mining Village* (Wakefield: EP Publishing, 1976), 100–101.
116. Hodge, *Draughty in Front*, 33–34.
117. Allen Clarke, "Adventuring in 'The Realms of Gold,'" *Liverpool Weekly Post* (26 May 1934): 2.
118. Harry Dorrell, "Falling Cadence: An Autobiography of Failure," BUL, p. 24.
119. Mary Bentley, *Born 1896: Childhood in Clayton and Working in Manchester and Cheshire* (Manchester: Neil Richardson, 1985), 32.

120. Margaret Wharton, *Recollections of a GI War Bride: A Wiltshire Childhood* (Gloucester: Alan Sutton, 1984), 132–33.

121. Nicholson, *Wednesday Early Closing*, 159–60, 168, 171.

122. Batten, *Newlyn Boyhood*, 24.

123. Forbes, *Divided Life*, 5–8.

124. Leslie Paul, *First Love* (London: SPCK, 1977), 19–20, 41.

125. Edna Bold, "The Long and the Short of It: Being the Recollections and Reminiscences of Edna Bold," in *Destiny Obscure*, ed. John Burnett (Harmondsworth: Penguin, 1984), 119–20.

126. Edith L. Evans, *Rough Diamonds* (Bognor Regis: New Horizon, 1982), 75–76.

127. Mays, *Reuben's Corner*, 66–67.

128. Thompson, *Lark Rise*, 46, 56.

129. Grossek, *First Movement*, 30, 135–39.

130. Thomas Bell, *Pioneering Days* (London: Lawrence & Wishart, 1941), 32–33.

131. Elsie Gadsby, *Black Diamonds, Yellow Apples: A Working-Class Derbyshire Childhood between the Wars* (Ilkeston: Scollins & Titford, 1978), 51.

132. Joseph Stamper, *Less Than the Dust: The Memoirs of a Tramp* (London: Hutchinson & Co., [1931]), 8–9.

133. Taylor, *Uphill All the Way*, 23–24. Williams, *George*, 186–87.

134. Garratt, *Man in the Street*, 107–108. Sir Ronald Gould, *Chalk Up the Memory* (Birmingham: George Philip Alexander, 1976), 20.

135. Foley, *Bolton Childhood*, 69.

136. F. Reid, "Socialist Sunday Schools in Britain, 1892–1939," *International Review of Social History* 11 (1966): 29–30.

137. Margaret Bondfield, *A Life's Work* (London: Hutchinson, 1948), 25–26, 127–28.

138. Ethel Mannin, *Confessions and Impressions* (London: Jarrolds, 1930), 39–41.

139. Harry McShane and Joan Smith, *Harry McShane: No Mean Fighter* (London: Pluto, 1978), 34–35.

140. Edmonds, "The Lean Years," pp. 83–84.

141. Jennie Lee, *The Great Journey* (London: Macgibbon & Kee, 1963), 57–58. Lee, *Life with Nye*, 49–50.

142. Todd, *Snakes and Ladders*, 119–20.

143. Tierl Thompson, *Dear Girl: The Diaries and Letters of Two Working Women 1897–1917* (London: Women's Press, 1987), 18–20, 39, 48, 50–52, 56, 60, 90.

144. Ibid., 57–58, 61–62, 95, 98.

145. Ibid., 74–75, 90, 95–98.

146. Ibid., 134–38, 160–64, 226.

147. Ibid., 133, 151–54, 168–69, 174–87, 211.

148. Ibid., 138.

149. Ibid., 174.

150. Ibid., 232.

151. Ibid., 95–96.

152. Ibid., 261–62.

153. Ibid., 203–205, 282–83.

154. Porter and Hall, *Facts of Life*, 208–209, 220.

155. Roberts, *Classic Slum*, 52, 231–32.

156. Teal, *Grasp the Nettle*, 14–15.

157. Margaret Powell, *Climbing the Stairs* (London: Peter Davies, 1969), 79. Margaret Powell, *Albert, My Consort* (London: Michael Joseph, 1975), 73.

158. Claire Davey, "Birth Control in Britain during the Interwar Years: Evidence from the

Stopes Correspondence," *Journal of Family History* 13 (1988): 329–45.

159. Marie Stopes, *Mother England* (London: John Bale, Sons & Danielsson, 1929), 99, 100, 115.

160. June Rose, *Marie Stopes and the Sexual Revolution* (London: Faber and Faber, 1992), 144–45, 156.

161. Hall, "Camberwell Boy," p. 30.

162. Alfred S. Hall, untitled TS, SLSL, p. 19.

163. Elizabeth Ring, *Up the Cockneys!* (London: Paul Elek,1975), 61–63, 88.

164. Eliot Slater and Moya Woodside, *Patterns of Marriage: A Study of Marriage Relationships in the Urban Working Classes* (London: Cassell, 1951), 165–76, 292.

165. Ibid., 194–213, 294.

166. MO file 3110B, p. 11.

167. MO file 3110, pp. 28–29, 31, 42, 45, 72, 76.

168. Rolph, *London Particulars*, 82–86, 120–27.

169. Hall, "Camberwell Boy," p. 17.

170. Aubrey Cyril Hicks, "Boyhood Memories 1902–1914" (1972–73), Buckinghamshire County Record Office, D/X 667, pp. 2, 125–27, 132, 152.

171. Henry Snell, *Men, Movements, and Myself* (London: J. M. Dent and Sons, 1936), 16.

172. George Bourne, *The Bettesworth Book* (London: Lamley, 1901), 276.

173. Bessie Harvey, "Youthful Memories of My Life in a Suffolk Village," ed. A. M. Hassall, *Suffolk Review* 2 (October 1963): 201.

174. James Stevens, *A Cornish Farmer's Diary*, ed. P. A. S. Pool (Penzance: Editor, 1977).

175. W. J. Paddock, *A Country Boy: A Celebration of Life* (Corsham: C. J. Hall, 1984), 8.

176. Roger Dataller, "Self-Expression in the Student," *Adult Education* 9 (June 1937): 253–54.

177. "Winter Listening Habits: A Report on the First Random Sample Scheme, January 1938," 1 September 1938, part 2, pp. 48–56, BBC R9/9/2/LR/67.

178. MO file 1209, pp. 1–7.

179. MO file 686, pp. 14–16; file 948, p. 9.

180. S. P. Mackenzie, *Politics and Military Morale: Current-Affairs and Citizenship Education in the British Army, 1914–1950* (Oxford: Clarendon Press, 1992), 87–88, 184–85.

181. MO file 305, pp. 1–2.

182. Alberto Manguel, *A History of Reading* (New York: Viking, 1996), 180–83.

183. Bernard Capp, *The World of John Taylor the Water-Poet* (Oxford: Clarendon Press, 1994), 49–54.

184. Mayhew, *London Labour*, 1:27–28.

185. Cooper, *Life*, 55–57.

186. Secord, "Science in the Pub," 286–88, 297–99.

187. Adult Education Committee, *Natural Science in Adult Education* (London: HMSO, 1927), 28–29, 47.

188. Abington, "Kimbolton in the Early 1900s," p. 51.

189. F. G. and D. Irene Thomas, "'Fresh Woods and Pastures New': Adult Education in Rural Devon: II," *Journal of Adult Education* 5 (October 1931): 261–63, 269–75.

190. Quoted in Murphy, *Working-Class Canon*, 36–39.

191. Storey, *Right to Song*, 223. Clynes, *Memoirs: 1869–1924*, 34. See also Kerr, *Eager Years*, 102, 135; and Pickering and Robins, "Interview with Sid Chaplin," 146.

192. Howard Spring, *Heaven Lies About Us* (London: Constable, 1939), 69–71.

193. Robert Blatchford, *English Prose and How to Write It* (London: Methuen, 1925), 2–4.

194. Jackson, TS autobiography, p. 182.

195. Emanuel Shinwell, *Lead with the Left: My First Ninety-Six Years* (London: Cassell, 1981),

25, 29, 32–35, 50–51, 71.

196. J. H. Thomas, *My Story* (London: Hutchinson, 1937), 30.

197. Haw, *Will Crooks*, 17.

198. Hillyer, *Country Boy*, 148–50, 176–77.

199. Todd, *Snakes and Ladders*, 61.

200. Okey, *Basketful of Memories*, 100–101.

201. Ronald L. Cohen, "The Influence of Jewish Radical Movements on Adult Education among Jewish Immigrants in the East End of London 1881–1914" (MEd thesis, Queen Mary College, 1977).

202. Blacker, *Just Like It Was*, 31–32, 54, 86–88, 97–99, 163–64, 173–74, 181–83.

203. Arnold Wesker, in Goldman, *Breakthrough*, 176–79.

204. Finn, *No Tears in Aldgate*, 157–61, 188. Ralph L. Finn, *Spring in Aldgate* (London: Robert Hale, 1968), 73–74, 85–87.

205. Bill Naughton, *A Roof Over Your Head* (London: Pilot, 1945), 8–9. Naughton, *On the Pig's Back*, 4–8, 19, 34–35.

206. Rose Gamble, *Chelsea Child* (London: British Broadcasting Corporation, 1979), 143.

207. D. Felicitas Corrigan, *George Thomas of Soho* (London: Secker & Warburg, 1970), 49.

208. J. H. Engledow and William C. Farr, *The Reading and Other Interests of School Children in St. Pancras* (London: Mary Ward Settlement, [1933]), 9.

209. Bowles Fripp, "Report of an Inquiry into the Condition of the Working Classes of the City of Bristol," *Journal of the Statistical Society of London* 2 (October 1839): 371.

210. MO file 2018, pp. 1–4, 16.

211. A. J. Jenkinson, *What Do Boys and Girls Read?* (London: Methuen, 1940), chs. 2, 16.

212. Ibid., 103–104, 244–45.

213. Ibid., 109–11, 251–52.

214. Ibid., 114, 255.

215. MO file 48, pp. 16–17, 26.

216. City and County of Bristol, Annual Report of the Public Libraries Committee, 1944–45, pp. 27–28.

217. MO file 2018, pp. 58, 69–71, 76, 79–82.

218. "Education in Industry," *Adult Education* 15 (June 1943): 198–200.

219. Mary Craddock, *Return to Rainton* (London: Hutchinson, 1963), 109.

220. P. C. Vigor, *Memories Are Made of This* (Luton: Borough of Luton Museum and Art Gallery, 1983), 133–37.

221. Ferdynand Zweig, *Labour, Life and Poverty* (London: Victor Gollancz, 1948), 52–58, 127–98. Ferdynand Zweig, *The British Worker* (Harmondsworth: Penguin, 1952), 217–18, 229–31.

222. Ferdynand Zweig, *The Worker in an Affluent Society* (New York: Free Press of Glencoe, 1961), ch. 16.

223. Gallup, *Polls*, 1457.

Chapter Seven: The Welsh Miners' Libraries

1. For an account of the latter, see David Shavit, *Hunger for the Printed Word: Books and Libraries in the Jewish Ghettos of Nazi-Occupied Europe* (Jefferson, NC: McFarland, 1997), ch. 1.

2. Baggs's "Miners' Libraries" is the definitive history of the movement. See particularly ch. 8 for the tricky calculations involved in estimating the number of libraries and the size of their collections. See also his "'Well Done, Cymmer Workmen!': The Cymmer Collieries Workmen's Library, 1893–1920," *Llafur* 5 (1990), no. 3: 20–27.

3. James Hanley, *Grey Children* (London: Methuen, 1937), 32–37.

4. Peter Stead, "Wales and Film," in *Wales Between the Wars*, ed. Trevor Herbert and Gareth Elwyn Jones (Cardiff: University of Wales Press, 1988), 166.

5. D. J. Davies, *The Tredegar Workmen's Hall 1861–1951* (n.p., 1952), 80–93.

6. John Benson, *British Coalminers in the Nineteenth Century* (London: Longman, 1989), 152–54. J. Ginswick, ed., *Labour and the Poor in England and Wales 1849–1851* (London: Frank Cass, 1983), 2:57–60.

7. Geraint H. Jenkins, *Literature, Religion and Society in Wales, 1660–1730* (Cardiff: University of Wales Press, 1978), 24, 129–30, 198–99, 209–10, 254, 288–90, 293–99, 303–304.

8. Davies, *Right Place*, 206–10.

9. Richard Lewis, *Leaders and Teachers: Adult Education and the Challenge of Labour in South Wales, 1906–1940* (Cardiff: University of Wales Press, 1993), 62.

10. Harold Marks, "Some WEA Statistics: How Efficient are the Districts?" *Highway* 32 (March 1940): 64.

11. Alec Ellis, "Rural Library Services in England and Wales before 1919," *Library History* 4 (Spring 1977): 69.

12. Commission of Enquiry into Industrial Unrest, No. 7 Division, *Report of the Commissioners for Wales, including Monmouthshire*, Parl. Sess. Papers, 1917–18, vol. XV, Cd. 8688, pp. 12, 19, 28, 30.

13. Baggs, "Miners' Libraries," pp. 141, 148–50.

14. Lawson, *Man's Life*, 109–15.

15. Davies, *In Search of Myself*, 18–19, 27–31, 36, 51–52.

16. H. V. Morton, *In Search of Wales* (London: Methuen, 1932), 247–49.

17. Stephen Walsh, "How I Got On: Life Stories by the Labour MPs," *Pearson's Weekly* (29 March 1906): 691.

18. Keating, *Struggle for Life*, 26–27, 55–56, 65–66, 72–74, 81–83, 99, 110–13.

19. Robert Morgan, *My Lamp Still Burns* (Llandysul: Gomer, 1981), 90–91.

20. Tomlinson, *Coal-Miner*, 74–77, 119–20, 123–25.

21. Edwards, *From the Valley I Came*, 44–48, 67, 96–97, 138–39.

22. Morris, "Autobiography", p. 8.

23. Wall, "Hour at Eve," ch. 15.

24. Mrs. F. H. Smith, in Davies, *Life as We Have Known It*, 71–72.

25. Davies, *Right Place*, 104–105.

26. Leavis, *Fiction and the Reading Public*, 4–7, 43.

27. The complete borrowing record for Tylorstown, the nearly complete record for the Markham Welfare Association Library, and a discussion of the methodological problems involved in using such documents, are in Jonathan Rose, "Marx, Jane Eyre, Tarzan: Miners' Libraries in South Wales, 1923–52," *Leipziger Jahrbuch zur Buchgeschichte* 4 (1994): 187–207. The borrowing records for all three miners' libraries are held by the library of the University of Wales, Swansea.

28. Leavis, *Fiction and the Reading Public*, 36.

29. Glenwright, *Bright Shines the Morning*, 82–83.

30. Mary Craddock, *A North Country Maid* (London: Hutchinson, 1960), 151.

31. Dataller, *Oxford into Coalfield*, 130, 180.

32. I write "probably" because not every book listed in a library catalog is actually on the shelves. Also, the catalog was apparently compiled in 1945, and some of these books might have been acquired in the interim.

33. Baggs, "Miners' Libraries," 510.

34. Bell, *At the Works*, 165–66.

35. Mary Lakeman, *Early Tide: A Megavissey Childhood* (London: William Kimber, 1978), 172.

36. Baggs, "Miners Libraries," 386–92, 403, 423–30.

37. A. J. Lush, *The Young Adult* (Cardiff: University of Wales Press Board, 1941), 47, 50, 72, 79–82.

38. "Adult Education in the Rhondda Valley," *Bulletin of the World Association for Adult Education* 40 (May 1929): 19–21.

39. Fagan, "An Autobiography," p. 93.

40. T. Brennan, E. W. Cooney, and H. Pollins, *Social Change in South-West Wales* (London: Watts, 1954), 69–70.

41. Dai Smith, *Aneurin Bevan and the World of South Wales* (Cardiff: University of Wales Press, 1993), 209.

42. Davies, *Right Place*, 102–104.

43. Morgan, *My Lamp Still Burns*, 116.

44. The activity of Marxists on miners' library committees is charted in Hywel Francis, "The Origins of the South Wales Miners' Library," *History Workshop* 2 (Autumn 1976): 183–205, esp. Appendix 6.

45. Miners' Welfare Fund, Annual Report, 1929, pp. 38–39.

46. Hywel Francis and David Smith, *The Fed: A History of the South Wales Miners in the Twentieth Century* (London: Lawrence & Wishart, 1980), 33, 48.

47. Kenneth O. Morgan, *Rebirth of a Nation: Wales 1880–1980* (New York: Oxford University Press, 1981), 211–12.

48. Baggs, "Miners' Libraries," 178. David E. Evans, "Report on the Condition of Libraries in the Aberdare Urban District Council, and County Borough of Merthyr Tydfil," 17 May 1929; and Brinley Thomas, "Report on the Condition of Workmen's Libraries in the Rhondda Urban District," in South Wales Miners' Library, Swansea.

49. B. L. Coombes, *These Poor Hands: The Autobiography of a Miner Working in South Wales* (London: Victor Gollancz, 1939), 221–22. Jimmy O'Connor, *Memories of a Market Trader* (Peterborough: Minimax, 1984), 20. Alexander Baron recalled a sergeant in a Wessex battalion who spent his unemployed years in the public library reading Dickens, Thackeray, and Jane Austen: "Four books a week was nothin' to me in those days." Alexander Baron, *From the City, From the Plough* (New York: Ives Washburn, 1949), 160–62.

50. H. L. Beales and R. S. Lambert, eds., *Memoirs of the Unemployed* (London: Victor Gollancz, 1934), 79, 95–96, 105, 119, 127–28, 133–34, 145–46, 154, 170, 176–77, 208–209, 234, 239–40, 262.

51. Greenwood, *There Was a Time*, 184–85.

52. John Brown, *I Was a Tramp* (London: Selwyn & Blount, 1934), 201, 208, 215.

53. Lawson, *Man's Life*, 77–80.

54. Baggs, "Miners' Libraries," 167–68, 268–71, 330.

55. Leavis, *Fiction and the Reading Public*, 83–85.

56. Hywel Francis, *Miners Against Fascism: Wales and the Spanish Civil War* (London: Lawrence & Wishart, 1984), 29–39.

57. E. D. Lewis, *The Rhondda Valleys* (London: Phoenix House, 1959), 260–61.

58. Thomas Jones, "Workmen's Libraries and Institutes," in *Leeks and Daffodils* (Newtown: Welsh Outlook, 1942), 137.

59. Philip Massey, "Portrait of a Mining Town," *Fact* 8 (1937): 10, 27, 50.

60. "Adult Education in the Rhondda Valley," 22, 27.

61. Davies, *Right Place*, 239.

62. G. H. Armbruster, "The Social Determination of Ideologies: Being a Study of a Welsh

Mining Community" (PhD diss. University of London, 1940), 154–57, 161.

63. Ferdynand Zweig, *Men in the Pits* (London: Victor Gollancz, 1949), 90–92, 108–109.

64. Norman Dennis, Fernando Henriques, and Clifford Slaughter, *Coal Is Our Life* (London: Eyre & Spottiswoode, 1956), 127, 167–68.

65. Davies, *Right Place*, 226–28. Zweig, *Men in the Pits*, 90–92, 108–109.

66. *South Wales Coalfield Project*, National Register of Archives, pp. 237–39.

67. They were nearly closed in 1998, and were saved only by a last-minute restoration of a subsidy from the Rhonnda Cynon Taff County Borough Council. Rob Thompson, "Village Libraries Win a Stay of Execution," *Western Mail* (4 March 1998).

68. Hans-Josef Steinberg, "Workers' Libraries in Germany before 1914," trans. Nicholas Jacobs, *History Workshop* 1 (Spring 1976): 166–80.

Chapter Eight: The Whole Contention Concerning the Workers' Educational Association

1. Roger Fieldhouse, "The Ideology of English Adult Education Teaching 1925–1950," *Studies in Adult Education* 15 (September 1983): 29–30.

2. Roger Fieldhouse, "Conformity and Contradiction in English Responsible Body Adult Education, 1925–1950," *Studies in the Education of Adults* 17 (October 1985): 123.

3. Stuart Macintyre, *A Proletarian Science: Marxism in Britain, 1917–1933* (London: Lawrence & Wishart, 1986), 89–90.

4. Geoff Brown, "Independence and Incorporation: The Labour College Movement and the Workers' Educational Association before the Second World War," in Jane L. Thompson, ed., *Adult Education for a Change* (London: Hutchinson, 1980), 113–15.

5. Public Record Office T. 161/186/S. 17166, Lord Eustace Percy to Walker Guiness, 7 October 1925, quoted in Fieldhouse, "Conformity and Contradiction," 123.

6. Bernard Jennings, "Revolting Students—The Ruskin College Dispute 1908–9," *Studies in Adult Education* 9 (April 1977): 1–16. Harold Pollins, *The History of Ruskin College* (Oxford: Ruskin College Library, 1984), 14–25, 42. Richard Lewis, "The South Wales Miners and the Ruskin College Strike of 1909," *Llafur* 2 (Spring 1976): 57–72. Lawrence Goldman, *Dons and Workers: Oxford and Adult Education Since 1850* (Oxford: Clarendon Press, 1995), ch. 5.

7. Roger Dataller, *A Pitman Looks at Oxford* (London: J. M. Dent & Sons, 1933), 135–36.

8. Henry Smith, *The Impersonal Autobiography of an Economist* (Exeter: Henrietta Quinnell, 1992), 100.

9. Harold M. Watkins, *Unusual Students* (Liverpool: Brython, 1947), 82.

10. Roger Fieldhouse, *Adult Education and the Cold War: Liberal Values under Siege 1946–51* (Leeds: Department of Adult and Continuing Education, University of Leeds, 1985), 33. Goldman, *Dons and Workers*, 266–86.

11. Harmut Kaelble, *Social Mobility in the Nineteenth and Twentieth Centuries: Europe and America in Comparative Perspective* (Leamington Spa: Berg, 1985), 52.

12. Paton, *Proletarian Pilgrimage*, 205–206.

13. George Hodgkinson, *Sent to Coventry* (London: Robert Maxwell, 1970), 41, 43, 54–66.

14. Lawson, *Man's Life*, 161–69.

15. Jack Ashley, *Journey into Silence* (London: Bodley Head, 1973), 68–73.

16. James Sexton, *Sir James Sexton, Agitator: The Life of the Dockers' M.P.* (London: Faber and Faber, 1936), 211.

17. Frank Hodges, *My Adventures as a Labour Leader* (London: George Newnes, 1925), 13–15, 25–38.

18. Edwards, *From the Valley I Came*, 48, 67, 79, 103–105, 123–25, 154–85, 227–30, 243–44, 258–61.

19. An Old Student, "Looking Backwards: A Tutorial Class Anniversary," *Rewley House Papers* (February 1929): 72–73.

20. J. Owen, J. Dover Wilson, and W. S. Dunn, *Report on University Tutorial Classes in England* (n.p.: Board of Education, 1922), 15–16, 18, 24.

21. Rowland Kenney, "Education for the Workers," *New Age* (26 March 1914): 652–53.

22. Ethel Carnie and Lavena Saltonstall, letters to the *Cotton Factory Times*, 20 March, and 3, 10, 17 April 1914.

23. F. Cox, R. C. Carton, and A. W. Humphrey, letters to the *Daily Herald*, 8 July 1912.

24. Oxford University Extension Delegacy Tutorial Classes Committee Report, 1912, pp. 11–12.

25. Ibid., pp. 15, 24–28, 59–60.

26. "The Invasion of a University," *Highway* 3 (September 1911): 187–88.

27. Oxford Tutorial Classes Report, 1912, p. 42.

28. "Summer Classes, 1912," *Highway* 5 (October 1912): 15–16.

29. "Invasion of a University," pp. 189–90.

30. Ibid., pp. 188–89.

31. Albert Mansbridge, *University Tutorial Classes* (London: Longman, Green, 1913), 13.

32. Lavena Saltonstall, letter to *Halifax Evening Courier*, 19 July 1910.

33. "Invasion of a University," p. 188.

34. Sophie Green to Albert Mansbridge, 28 August 1922, AM, Add. 65265.

35. Barbara Wootton, "A Plea for Constructive Teaching," *Adult Education* 10 (December 1937): 96–104.

36. W. E. Williams and A. E. Heath, *Learn and Live* (Boston: Marshall Jones, 1937), 206.

37. Fieldhouse, "Ideology of Adult Education," 29.

38. Morris, "Autobiography," part 2, pp. 120, 124.

39. Kitchen, *Brother to the Ox*, 244.

40. Marjorie Randle, "Brother to the Ox," *Highway* 32 (January 1940): 71.

41. Harry Dorrell, "Falling Cadence," pp. 152–55. Goldman, *Breakthrough*, 85–88.

42. Brown, "Independence and Incorporation," 117.

43. For instance, George Brown, *In My Way* (London: Gollancz, 1971), 27–29, leaves the reader with the extremely misleading impression that his summer course at Balliol was sponsored by the NCLC as well as the WEA. See also Jack Jones, *Union Man* (London: Collins, 1986), 35, 48–49.

44. Lewis, *Leaders and Teachers*, 184, 225.

45. Davies, *North Country Bred*, 193–95.

46. L. C. Stone, letter to the editor, *Highway* 18 (November 1925): 30. This point was confirmed by one of the earliest WEA recruits, Frederick Padley, in an interview with the author, 24 August 1987.

47. Oxford University Tutorial Classes Committee, Class Reports, OUA, DES/RP/2/2, 1924–25, p. 38.

48. Ibid., 1937–38, p. 78.

49. Dataller, *Oxford into Coalfield*, 25, 71–75, 99.

50. Jack and Bessie Braddock, *The Braddocks* (London: MacDonald, 1963), 10–11. See also Edward Cain, "Memories," BUL, p. 11; Davies, *Right Place*, 88, 97, 105–107; James Griffiths, *Pages from Memory* (London: J. M. Dent & Sons, 1969), 19, 24–25, 48; Harold Finch, *Memoirs of a Bedwellty MP* (Newport: Starling Press, 1972), 12–13, 37.

51. Durham Strong Words Collective, *But the World Goes on the Same: Changing Times in Durham Pit Villages* (Whiteley Bay: Strong Words, 1979), 62–65.

52. Bill Horrocks, *Reminiscences of Bolton* (Manchester: Neil Richardson, 1984), 27–32.

53. Smith, *Autobiography*, 16–20, 28–30.

54. Todd, *Snakes and Ladders*, 108–109. See also Whittaker, *I, James Whittaker*, 310–11.

55. John Allaway, in Goldman, *Breakthrough*, 17–20.

56. H. Edmund Poole, *The Teaching of Literature in the WEA* (London: Workers' Educational Association, 1938), 8.

57. D. B. Halpern, "The Balance of Subjects in WEA Classes, 1913–58," *Rewley House Papers* 3 (1959–60): 24–25.

58. "The History of the Tunstall II Tutorial Class: 1913–34," *Rewley House Papers* 8 (March 1935): 350–53.

59. Nancy Dobrin, *Happiness* (London: Regency, 1980), 13–14, 26–27, 31, 36, 50–51.

60. Louis Moss and Kathleen Box, *Newspapers: An Inquiry into Newspaper Reading Amongst the Civilian Population* (Wartime Social Survey, n.s. 37a, June–July 1943), 12.

61. Dobrin, *Happiness*, 59–60.

62. Edith Hall, *Canary Girls and Stockpots* (Luton: WEA Luton Branch, 1977), 39–40.

63. John Petty, *Five Fags a Day* (London: Secker & Warburg, 1956), 85–87; Harry Benjamin, *Adventure in Living: The Autobiography of a Myope* (London: Health for All Publishing, 1950), 39–45, 58–59; Williams and Heath, *Learn and Live*, 111–18.

64. Gregory, untitled TS, pp. 99–100.

65. Albert Mansbridge, *The Trodden Road* (London: J. M. Dent & Sons, 1940), 49–50.

66. Albert Mansbridge, "University Tutorial Classes," in *The Kingdom of the Mind: Essays and Addresses 1903–37* (London: J. M. Dent & Sons, 1944), 28.

67. "The Historical Association," *Western Daily Press*, 12 January 1914.

68. Ross Terrill, *R. H. Tawney and His Times* (Cambridge, MA: Harvard University Press, 1974), 39–40.

69. "Tunstall Tutorial Class," 352.

70. Old Student, "Looking Backwards," 70–71.

71. *Report on Adult Education in Yorkshire for the Period Ending on the 31st July, 1927* (London: HMSO, 1928), 41.

72. Williams and Heath, *Learn and Live*, 129–31.

73. Ibid., 49–52.

74. George W. Norris, "The Testament of a Trade Unionist," *Highway* 39 (May 1948): 158–59.

75. Williams and Heath, *Learn and Live*, ch. 5

76. Lavena Saltonstall, "The Letters of a Tailoress," *Highway* 3 (January–February 1911): 52, 77.

77. Fieldhouse, "Ideology of Adult Education," 14–19, 23–27.

78. For example, J. M. Mactavish, "Karl Marx and Modern Socialism," *Highway* 13 (June 1921): 149–51.

79. Anonymous review of M. Beer, *The Life and Teachings of Karl Marx*, *Highway* 14 (October 1921): 4.

80. Owen, Wilson, and Dunn, *University Tutorial Classes*, 17–18.

81. Henry Clay, "What Workpeople Read," *Highway* 1 (September 1909): 182–83.

82. Box labeled "Early Tutorial Classes," WEA Central Office Library, London.

83. "Leisure of Adult Student," 212.

84. J. Corfield, *Epoch in Workers' Education: A History of the Workers' Educational Trade Union Committee* (London: WEA, 1969), ch. 3. Brown, "Independence and Incorporation," 109–25. Chushichi Tsuzuki, "Anglo-Marxism and Working-Class Education," in *The Working Class in Modern British History*, ed. Jay Winter (Cambridge: Cambridge University Press, 1983).

85. Watkins, *Unusual Students*, 27–28.
86. Oxford University Tutorial Classes Committee, Class Reports, OUA, DES/RP/2/2, 1913–14, p. 34.
87. Ibid., 1924–25, pp. 55–56.
88. Miles, *From Pit Bank to Balliol College*, 48–50.
89. Dickens, *Bending the Twig*, 20, 160–61, 174.
90. "What the WEA Means to Its Members," AM.
91. Harold Entwistle, *Antonio Gramsci: Conservative Schooling for Radical Politics* (London: Routledge & Kegan Paul, 1979), 18–21, 43–44, 47–48, 78–86, 180–81.
92. Pickering and Robins, "Interview with Sid Chaplin," 144.
93. Williams and Heath, *Learn and Live*, 3–13.
94. Ibid., 17.
95. Ibid., 108–10.
96. Ibid., 3–6.
97. Ibid., 19–23.
98. Ibid., 16.
99. Ibid., 21–23.
100. Ibid., 24–25.
101. Ibid., 19–23.
102. Ibid., 40–42.
103. J. E. Thomas, *Radical Adult Education: Theory and Practice* (Nottingham: Department of Adult Education, University of Nottingham, 1982), 15–16, 60.
104. Williams and Heath, *Learn and Live*, 49–52.
105. Ibid., 13–16, 92.
106. Ibid., 159–60, 163–65.
107. Ibid., ch. 6.
108. Mary Stocks, *The Workers' Educational Association: The First Fifty Years* (London: George Allen & Unwin, 1953), 52–53.
109. Adult Education Committee, *The Development of Adult Education for Women* (London: HMSO, 1922), 3–7.
110. Roseanne Benn, "Women and Adult Education," in *A History of Modern British Adult Education*, ed. Roger Fieldhouse (Leicester: NIACE, 1996), 381.
111. *Plebs* 28 (March 1936): 68.
112. H. Edmund Poole, "English Literature as a Subject in WEA Classes," *Adult Education* 12 (June 1940): 170.
113. Joseph J. Senturia, "Sex and Subject Selection," *Journal of Adult Education* 4 (April 1930): 166–73.
114. Miller, *Schools and Schoolmasters*, 514–15.
115. "Leisure of the Adult Student," 203–16.
116. Williams and Heath, *Learn and Live*, 168–69.
117. Ibid., ch. 3.
118. Oxford University Tutorial Classes Committee, Class Reports, OUA, DES/RP/2/2, 1918–19, pp. 5–7.
119. Brown, "Independence and Incorporation," 109.
120. They are listed in the WEA annual report for 1938, pp. 110–60. G. F. Brown, "Working Class Adult Education," in A. H. Thornton and M. D. Stephens, eds., *The University and Its Region: The Extra-Mural Contribution* (Nottingham: Department of Adult Education, University of Nottingham, 1977), 54.
121. A. E. Zimmern to Albert Mansbridge, 29 July 1945, AM, Add. 65258, f. 106v.
122. Stocks, *Workers' Educational Association*, 143.

123. John Langley, *Always a Layman* (Brighton: QueenSpark, 1976), 31, 39–40.

124. Smith, *Autobiography*, 8–10, 16–20, 35, 40–41, 68–71, 74–76, 140–42.

125. Owen, Wilson, and Dunn, *University Tutorial Classes*, 15–16.

126. Poole, *Teaching of Literature*, 11. See also *Report on Adult Education in Yorkshire*, 26–29.

127. Linden R. West, "The Tawney Legend Re-examined," *Studies in Adult Education* 4 (October 1972): 105–19.

128. WEA Annual Report, 1939, p. 71.

129. Adult Education Committee, *The Scope and Practice of Adult Education* (London: HMSO, 1930), 77–79.

130. Secord, "Science in the Pub," 280.

131. Adult Education Committee, *Natural Science in Adult Education* (London: HMSO, 1927), 33–34.

132. Williams and Heath, *Learn and Live*, 139–40.

133. Association of Tutorial Class Tutors, "Report on the Teaching of Science in Tutorial Classes," memorandum to Central Joint Advisory Committee on Tutorial Classes, 18 July 1924, AM, Add. 65198, ff. 183–84.

134. Paddy Molloy, "The Ugly Duckling (that Never Became a Swan)," TS, Ruskin College Library, chs. 8–9.

135. E. W. F. Malone, "The WEA—A New Phase II," *Adult Education* 23 (September 1960): 117.

136. *Report on Adult Education in Yorkshire*, 25.

137. J. E. Floud, A. H. Halsey, and F. M. Martin, *Social Class and Educational Opportunity* (London: Heinemann, 1957), 44–61.

138. Sidney Weighell, *A Hundred Years of Railway Weighells* (London: Robson, 1984), 43, 87–88.

139. Pearl Jephcott, *Rising Twenty: Notes on Some Ordinary Girls* (London: Faber and Faber, 1948), 11–16, 62–63, 108–13.

140. Green, *Adult Education*, 28–34, 52–59.

141. Roy Shaw, "Adult Education and the Working Class," *Studies in Adult Education* 2 (1970): 3.

142. Bryan Luckham, "The Characteristics of Adult Education Students," *Studies in Adult Education* 3 (October 1971): 118–36. Bryan Luckham, "The Image of Adult Education," *Studies in Adult Education* 4 (April 1972): 2–5.

143. Naomi Sargant, "The Open University," in Fieldhouse, *British Adult Education*, 290–93.

144. Richard Hoggart, *A Sort of Clowning* (London: Chatto & Windus, 1990), 137.

Chapter Nine: **Alienation from Marxism**

1. Ross McKibbin, "Why Was There No Marxism in Great Britain?" in *The Ideologies of Class: Social Relations in Britain 1880–1950* (Oxford: Clarendon Press, 1990), 32–36.

2. Hugh McLeod, "New Perspectives on Victorian Class Religion: The Oral Evidence," *Oral History* 14 (Spring 1986): 35.

3. Macintyre, *Proletarian Science*, chs. 2–3.

4. Mary Brookshank, *No Sae Lang Syne: A Tale of This City* (Dundee: Dundee Printers, n.d.), 36.

5. Davies, *Right Place*, 88.

6. Davies, *In Search of Myself*, 38–44, 53, 139–40.

7. Clunie, *Labour is My Faith*, 30–31. Clunie, *Voice of Labour*, 30–31.

8. Goss, "My Boyhood," pp. 188–89.

9. Bell, *Pioneering Days*, 69.
10. Citrine, *Men and Work*, 30.
11. Fagan, "Autobiography," pp. 71, 74, 83–87.
12. T. H. James, "We Tread But One Path" (1966), RCL, p. 32.
13. Murphy, *New Horizons*, 61, 181–83, 307–308.
14. James Griffiths, *Pages from Memory* (London: J. M. Dent & Sons, 1969), 13–14, 197–98.
15. Hodge, *Draughty in Front*, 64–66, 76–77, 86–87, 258–60, 280–82.
16. Fox, *Smoky Crusade*, 136–37, 176–85, 353.
17. R. M. Fox, *The Triumphant Machine* (London: Hogarth Press, 1928), 2, 85–87.
18. Smith, *Bevan and South Wales*, 200–9.
19. John Atkins, *Neither Crumbs nor Condescension: The Central Labour College 1909–1915* (Aberdeen: Aberdeen People's Press and London: Workers' Educational Association, 1981), 13.
20. Macintyre, *Proletarian Science*, 151.
21. Lewis, *Leaders and Teachers*, 156–67.
22. Heslop, "From Tyne to Tone," pp. 118–19, 130–34, 138–39.
23. Jack Hilton, *Caliban Shrieks* (London: Cobden-Sanderson, 1935), 125–28.
24. Jackson, TS autobiography, pp. 125–27.
25. McShane and Smith, *Harry McShane*, 264–66.
26. For example, Shinwell, *Conflict Without Malice*, 27; George Hardy, *Those Stormy Years* (London: Lawrence & Wishart, 1956), 28; Dorrell, "Falling Cadence," pp. 50.
27. McShane and Smith, *Harry McShane*, 29–30, 36.
28. Hughes, "Welsh Rebel," p. 223.
29. Quoted in Davies, *In Search of Myself*, 153–54.
30. Murphy, *New Horizons*, 181.
31. Roberts, *Classic Slum*, 220.
32. Coppard, *It's Me, O Lord!*, 149–50.
33. George N. Barnes, *From Workshop to War Cabinet* (London: Herbert Jenkins, 1924), 42.
34. Ewan MacColl, "Theatre of Action, Manchester," in Raphael Samuel, Ewan MacColl, and Stuart Cosgrove, eds., *Theatres of the Left 1880–1935: Workers' Theatre Movements in Britain and America* (London: Routledge & Kegan Paul, 1985), 222.
35. Campbell, *Villi the Clown*, 16.
36. Margaret McCarthy, *Generation in Revolt* (London: William Heinemann, 1953), 78–79, 96.
37. Ifan Edwards, *No Gold on My Shovel* (London: Porcupine Press, 1947), 173–78.
38. William Holt, *I Haven't Unpacked* (London: George G. Harrap, 1939), 194–252.
39. A. T. Collinson, "One Way Only: An Autobiography of an Old-Time Trade Unionist" (1966), BUL, pp. 158–59, 173–74.
40. Chapple, *Sparks Fly!*, 34–35.
41. Les Moss, *Live and Learn: A Life and Struggle for Progress* (Brighton: QueenSpark, 1979), 20–23, 74–81.
42. Ashley, *Journey into Silence*, 73.
43. Brown, *I Was a Tramp*, 225–26, 249.
44. McCarthy, *Generation in Revolt*, 148–49, 159–61, 192, 238–41, 244, 252–53.
45. Jennie Lee, *This Great Journey* (New York: Farrar & Reinhart, 1942), 154–56, 177–78.
46. Craddock, *North Country Maid*, 46–48, 132–33.
47. George Scott, *Time and Place* (London: Staples, 1956), 86–89, 93–97, 102.
48. R. L.Wild, *Wild Oats* (Edinburgh and London: William Blackwood & Sons, 1959), 31, 141–44.
49. Armbruster, "Social Determination", 63–73, 85–92, 96–110, 120–23, 173–75, 187–90,

198, 215–17, 224–26, 250–51.

50. Andrew Thorpe, "The Membership of the Communist Party of Great Britain, 1920–1945," *Historical Journal* 43 (September 2000): 777–800, esp. 781, 795–99.

51. Chris Williams, *Democratic Rhondda: Politics and Society, 1885–1951* (Cardiff: University of Wales Press, 1966), 168–204.

52. W. A. Gape, *Half a Million Tramps* (London: George Routledge & Sons, 1936), 325–26.

53. Hanley, *Grey Children*, 168, 211–12.

54. H. L. Elvin, "Marx and the Marxists as Literary Critics," *Adult Education* 10 (June 1938): 266–73.

55. Raphael Samuel, "Workers' Theatre 1926–36," in Bradby, James, and Sharratt, eds., *Performance and Politics*, 216–28; Raphael Samuel, "Theatre and Socialism in Britain (1880–1935)," in Samuel, MacColl, and Cosgrove, *Theatres of the Left*, 21, 27–34, 50–54, 58.

56. Ewan MacColl, "Theatre of Action," 208–10, 231, 240, 254.

57. Jackson, *Solo Trumpet*, vii.

58. Ibid., 11–12.

59. Crawfurd, TS autobiography, pp. 58–63, 71–73, 174, 203.

60. Holt, *I Haven't Unpacked*, 194–252.

61. Jack Jones, *Unfinished Journey* (London: Hamish Hamilton, 1937), 61, 192–97, 207, 215–17; and *Give Me Back My Heart* (London: Hamish Hamilton, 1950), 173–77.

62. William Gallacher, *Revolt on the Clyde* (London: Lawrence & Wishart, 1936), 1.

63. William Gallacher, *Rise Like Lions* (London: Lawrence & Wishart, 1951), 129–30, 181. William Gallacher, *The Last Memoirs of William Gallacher* (London: Lawrence & Wishart, 1966), 25, 35.

64. Trory, *Mainly About Books*, 18–19, 25, 54–55, 66–68, 98–99.

Chapter Ten: **The World Unvisited**

1. George Orwell, "Boys' Weeklies," in *Collected Essays*, 1:481–82.

2. Patrick A. Dunae, "Boys' Literature and the Idea of Empire, 1870–1914," *Victorian Studies* 24 (1980): 105–21.

3. John M. MacKenzie, ed., *Propaganda and Empire: The Manipulation of British Public Opinion, 1880–1960* (Manchester: Manchester University Press, 1984).

4. Guy A. Aldred, *No Traitor's Gait!* (Glasgow: Strickland, 1955), 111–14, 145–47, 269, 274–81.

5. J. Randolph Cox, "Paperback Detective: The Evolution of the Nick Carter Series from Dime Novel to Paperback, 1886–1990," in *Pioneers, Passionate Ladies, and Private Eyes: Dime Novels, Series Books, and Paperbacks*, ed. Larry E. Sullivan and Lydia Cushman Schurman (Binghamton, NY: Haworth, 1996), 119–32.

6. Aldred, *Traitor's Gait!*, 39–40.

7. Louis James, "Tom Brown's Imperialist Sons," *Victorian Studies* 17 (September 1973): 90–93.

8. P. W. Musgrave, *From Brown to Bunter: The Life and Death of the School Story* (London: Routledge & Kegan Paul, 1985), 142–43.

9. Jenkinson, *What Do Boys and Girls Read?*, 16, 174.

10. Frederick Willis, *Peace and Dripping Toast* (London: Phoenix House, 1950), 56–57.

11. Ezard, *Battersea Boy*, 98–102.

12. Hoggart, *Local Habitation*, 166.

13. Paul Fletcher, *The Clatter of Clogs: Life in Lancashire during the Twenties as Seen through*

the Eyes of a Boy (Bolton: Clog-Lamp Press, 1972), 102–4.

14. Mills, "Coward or Fool," p. 19.
15. Roberts, *Classic Slum*, 160–61.
16. Clifford Hanley, *Dancing in the Streets* (London: Hutchinson, 1958), 64–65.
17. Argent, "No Medals for Frankie," p. 5a.
18. Horwood, "Walworth Boy," p. 100.
19. Stamper, *So Long Ago*, 178–79, 182.
20. Percy S. Bustin, "My Two Square Miles of London: Reminiscences of a Bermondsey Boy" (1970–74), SLSL, pp. 29–30, 47–48.
21. W. Lionel Fraser, *All to the Good* (London: Heinemann, 1963), 19, 24–25.
22. Forbes, *Divided Life*, 6–8, 114–24.
23. John Harrison, *My Village: Sheriff Hill, County Durham* (Gateshead: Author, 1979), 17.
24. Balne, "Poor Law Schoolboy," pp. 6–8, 11–15, 18–21, 35.
25. Burke, *Wind and the Rain*, ch. 3.
26. Taylor, *Uphill All the Way*, 8–9.
27. W. F. Turner, "The Pleasures of the Young in the Early Twenties," Waltham Forest Museum Local Studies Library, pp. 3, 9.
28. Ted Furniss, *The Walls of Jericho* (Sheffield: Rebel Press, 1979), 3.
29. Richard Heaton, *Salford: My Home Town* (Manchester: Neil Richardson, 1982), 1.
30. Scott, *Time and Place*, 25–28.
31. Mark Benney, *Low Company: Describing the Evolution of a Burglar* (London: Peter Davies, 1936), 88, 134–35, 218–19.
32. Battye, *Little Nut Tree*, 97–98, 136.
33. Beer, *Mrs. Beer's House*, 97–98.
34. Betterton, "White Pinnies, Black Aprons ...," p. 65c.
35. John Macadam, *The Macadam Road* (London: Jarrolds, 1955), 18.
36. Pritchett, *Cab at the Door*, 109–10, 113–14.
37. Gomm, "Water under the Bridge," p. 127.
38. Common, *Kiddar's Luck*, 35–36. Scannell, *Tiger and the Rose*, 74. Jackson and Marsden, *Education and the Working Class*, 92.
39. Dennis Marsden, in Goldman, *Breakthrough*, 118–19.
40. Citrine, *Men and Work*, 24–25, 33, 37, 46.
41. Scott, *Time and Place*, 27–28, 99–101.
42. Rolph, *London Particulars*, 59–61.
43. Harry Young, "Harry's Biography," BUL, chapter titled "Boys' Magazines, Boys' Weeklies," p. 2.
44. Fagan, "Autobiography," pp. 16–17, 37–38, 54–55.
45. Wall, "Hour at Eve," chs. 1, 7–8, 15, 17.
46. Michael Foot, *Aneurin Bevan* (London: McGibbon & Kee, 1962), 1:22, 307, 395, 448.
47. Acorn, *One of the Multitude*, 50.
48. Janet Wolff, *Aesthetics and the Sociology of Art*, 2nd edn. (Ann Arbor: University of Michigan Press, 1993), 23–24.
49. The field of mass media studies has grappled with the same problems of audience reception. See John Eldridge, Jenny Kitzinger, and Kevin Williams, *The Mass Media and Power in Modern Britain* (Oxford: Oxford University Press, 1997), part 3.
50. Blacker, *Just Like It Was*, 66.
51. Willy Goldman, *East End My Cradle* (London: Faber and Faber, 1940), 43, 66–69.
52. Chaim Bermant, *Coming Home* (London: George Allen & Unwin, 1976), 39–40, 54, 79–89, 116–17, 124, 134–35.
53. Adam Rushton, *My Life* (Manchester: S. Clarke, 1909), 107.

54. George Ratcliffe, *Sixty Years of It* (London: A. Brown & Sons, n.d.), 79.

55. Price, *Imperial War*, 14, 67, 75–95, 145–47, 172–73.

56. Freer, *Life and Memories*, 131–32.

57. Rose Gibbs, *In Service: Rose Gibbs Remembers* (Orwell: Ellison's Editions, 1981), 1–2.

58. Margaret Powell, *My Mother and I* (London: Michael Joseph, 1972), 50.

59. Gresswell, *Bright Boots*, 81–84.

60. Garratt, *Man in the Street*, 63–64.

61. M. D. Blanch, "British Society and the War," in *The South African War: The Anglo-Boer War 1899–1902*, ed. Peter Warwick (London: Longman, 1980), 210–38.

62. Tremewan, *Cornish Youth*, 12, 17.

63. Willis, *Peace and Dripping Toast*, 132–35.

64. Shinwell, *Lead with the Left*, 23, 32.

65. Jones, *Unfinished Journey*, 97–101.

66. Cardus, *Autobiography*, 21.

67. Roberts, *Classic Slum*, 140–44, 162–63, 179–82.

68. May A. M. Rainer, "Emma's Daughter" (1977), BUL, p. 31.

69. Hymie Fagan, in Margaret Cohen and Hymie Fagan, eds., *Childhood Memories*, Ruskin College Library, p. 36.

70. Humphries, *Hooligans or Rebels?*, 41–44.

71. Grace Foakes, *Between High Walls: A London Childhood* (London: Shepheard-Walwyn, 1972), 18–19.

72. Mills, "Coward or Fool," pp. 17–18.

73. Ethelwyn Watts, *How Long is Forever: Memories of a Cornish Maid* (Redruth: Dyllansow Truran—Cornish Publications, [1982]), 21.

74. Hall, "Camberwell Boy," pp. 13, 15. Hall, untitled TS, p. 20.

75. Angela Hewins, *Mary, After the Queen: Memories of a Working Girl* (Oxford: Oxford University Press, 1985), 12–13.

76. Burnham, *Dooms of Love*, 33–34, 37–38, 208–9.

77. Gamble, *Chelsea Child*, 60–61.

78. Heren, *Growing Up Poor*, 18–20, 57–59.

79. Whittaker, *I, James Whittaker*, 121–25.

80. Walter Southgate, *That's the Way It Was: A Working Class Autobiography 1890–1950* (Oxted: New Clarion, 1982), 32–34, 45.

81. Phyllis Willmott, *A Green Girl* (London: Peter Owen, 1983), 10–11, 121–22.

82. Uttley, *Farm*, 148–49.

83. Clare, *Autobiographical Writings*, 63.

84. Watkin, *From Hulme*, 51, 70, 74–75.

85. Aldred, *Traitor's Gait!*, 41.

86. Bourke, *Working-Class Cultures*, 139.

87. Todd, *Snakes and Ladders*, 132.

88. Vincent, *Literacy and Popular Culture*, 39–42.

89. Clynes, *Memoirs: 1869–1924*, 33.

90. Pyke, *Men and Memories*, 17–18.

91. Allen Clarke, "A Romance That Staggered the Nation," *Liverpool Weekly Post* (27 October 1934): 2.

92. Roberts, *Classic Slum*, 162–63.

93. Wilfred Pickles, *Between You and Me* (London: Werner Laurie, 1949), 29–30.

94. Robert Clough, *A Public Eye* (London: Hamish Hamilton, 1981), 17.

95. Davies, *Right Place*, 236–38.

96. Smith, *Autobiography*, 1–3, 9–10.

97. Macadam, *Macadam Road*, 21–22.
98. Bernard Kops, *The World is a Wedding* (New York: Coward-McCann, 1963), 15.
99. James Hanley, *Broken Water* (London: Chatto & Windus, 1937), 253–61.
100. Thomson, *Autobiography of an Artisan*, 226–28.
101. Bonwick, *Reminiscences*, 6–7, 12–13, 16–19, 51–52, 55–57, 112–13, 178–79.
102. Anon., "Life of a Blacksmith," *Saturday Evening Commonwealth* (Glasgow), (17 January 1857): 3.
103. James Tilleard, "On Elementary School Books," *Transactions of the National Association for the Promotion of Social Science* (1859): 388–89, 393–96.
104. Thompson, *Lark Rise*, 33–34, 110, 180–81.
105. Alfred Williams, *Life in a Railway Factory* (London: Duckworth, 1915), 157–58.
106. Batten, *Newlyn Boyhood*, 18.
107. Lee, *Town That Died*, 29–30, 41.
108. Burton, *There Was a Young Man*, 40–41, 63–64, 73, 99.
109. Charles E. B. Russell and Lilian M. Rigby, *Working Lads' Clubs* (London: Macmillan, 1908), 187–91.
110. MacKenzie, *Propaganda and Empire*, 220.
111. Herbert Morrison, *Herbert Morrison: An Autobiography* (London: Odhams, 1960), 19–20. Fagan, "Autobiography," p. 41. Sam Smith, "Bosley Cloud: A North Country Childhood," BUL, p. 33. H. J. Bennett, *I Was a Walworth Boy* (London: Peckham Publishing Project, 1980), 30–31. William Holt, *Under a Japanese Parasol* (Halifax: F. King and Sons, 1933), 111–12. Lanigan, "Thy Kingdom *Did* Come," pp. 22, 63. John Allaway, in Goldman, *Breakthrough*, 9. John Edwin, *I'm Going—What Then?* (Bognor Regis: New Horizon, 1978), 8–9.
112. Dataller, "Yorkshire Lad," pp. 11–13.
113. Somerville, *Autobiography*, 89–92.
114. "Jacques," "Glimpses of a Checquered Life," *Saturday Evening Commonwealth* (Glasgow), (1 November 1856): 3, (15 November 1856): 3.
115. *Reading in Tottenham* (Tottenham: Borough of Tottenham Libraries and Museum Department, 1952), 22–24.
116. MacKenzie, *Propaganda and Empire*, 101.
117. For example, Daisy England, *Daisy England* (London: Regency, 1981), 102; Maggie Newberry, *Reminiscences of a Bradford Mill Girl* (Bradford: City of Bradford Metropolitan Council, Libraries Division, 1980), 82; Blackburn, *When I Grew Up*, 16.
118. Fred Scholes, in *Oldham Chronicle* (1 November 1975): 21.
119. Denis A. Gibson, "The Struggle for Existence," Ruskin College Library, p. 32.
120. Edna Matthews, "Looking Back: Village Life in the Early 20's," BUL, pp. 8–10.
121. Mary Wade, *To the Miner Born* (Stocksfield: Oriel, 1984), 57–59.
122. ˉAnonymous, *Struggles for Life*, 72–81, 256–57.
123. Michael Home, *Winter Harvest: A Norfolk Boyhood* (London: Macdonald, 1967), 73, 78–79.
124. Nicholson, *Wednesday Early Closing*, 94–95.
125. Ashby, *Ashby of Tysoe*, 114.
126. Michael Gareth Llewelyn, *Sand in the Glass* (London: John Murray, 1943), 5.
127. Foley, *Bolton Childhood*, 78.
128. Wharton, *GI War Bride*, 77.
129. Colin Bonwick, *English Radicals and the American Revolution* (Chapel Hill: University of North Carolina Press, 1977).
130. Quoted in Sinclair, *Statistical Account*, 6:145–46.
131. Buckley, *Village Politician*, 47–49.

132. Samuel Gompers, *Seventy Years of Life and Labour* (New York: E. P. Dutton, 1925), 1:18–21.

133. Cooney, "Publishers for the People," 81.

134. Altick, *Common Reader*, 300–301.

135. Ellis, *Educating Our Masters*, 131.

136. Ian Michael, *The Teaching of English: From the Sixteenth Century to 1870* (Cambridge: Cambridge University Press, 1987), 220–38.

137. G. D. Lillibridge, *Beacon of Freedom: The Impact of American Democracy upon Great Britain 1830–1870* (Philadelphia: University of Pennsylvania Press, 1955). Frank Thistlewaite, *The Anglo-American Connection in the Early Nineteenth Century* (Philadelphia: University of Pennsylvania Press, 1959).

138. Murphy, *Working-Class Canon*, 91, 125–26.

139. Pickering and Robins, "Interview with Sid Chaplin," 142.

140. W. H. Davies, *Beggars* (London: Duckworth, 1909), 90–91.

141. Harry Lauder, *Roamin' in the Gloamin'* (London: Hutchinson, 1928), 133. Morgan, *Keir Hardie*, 7.

142. George Cocking, *From the Mines to the Pulpit* (Cincinnati: Author, 1901), 64–66. See also Penn, *Manchester Fourteen Miles*, 55.

143. Heren, *Growing Up Poor*, 13–14, 203.

144. Lakeman, *Early Tide*, 170–71.

145. Pritchett, *Cab at the Door*, 161–62.

146. V. S. Pritchett, *As Old as the Century* (New York: Random House, 1982), 38, 42–43.

147. Bondfield, *Life's Work*, 37, 93, 96, 111–14.

148. McCarthy, *Generation in Revolt*, 49–64, 95.

149. Roberts, *Classic Slum*, 213–14.

150. Joe Ayre, "The Socialist," BUL, p. 11.

151. Dorrell, "Falling Cadence," p. 5.

152. Jack Common, *The Ampersand* (London: Turnstile Press, 1954), 61–62.

153. Wild, *Wild Oats*, 4–5.

154. This fear was pervasive among the interwar intelligentsia. See D. L. LeMahieu, *A Culture for Democracy: Mass Communication and the Cultivated Mind in Britain between the Wars* (Oxford: Clarendon Press, 1988), ch. 3.

155. Thomas Burke, *London in My Time* (London: Rich and Cowan, 1934), 35–36.

156. Thomas Burke, *Out and About London* (New York: Henry Holt, 1919), 176–90.

157. Thomas Burke, *Living in Bloomsbury* (London: George Allen & Unwin, 1939), 29.

158. Kevin Williams, *Get Me a Murder a Day!: A History of Mass Communication in Britain* (London: Arnold, 1998), 78–79.

159. Kenneth S. Lynn, *Charlie Chaplin and His Times* (New York: Simon & Schuster, 1997), 96.

160. Stapleton, *Threshold*, 113–14.

161. Horwood, "Walworth Boy," pp. 26, 91–92, 97.

162. Jim Wolveridge, *"Ain't It Grand" or "This Was Stepney"* (London and West Nyack: Journeyman, 1981), 20, 41–42, 65–66.

163. Willis, *Tom Mix*, 3, 47–49, 144.

164. Dorothy Tildsley, *Remembrance: Recollections of a Wartime Childhood in Swinton* (Manchester: Neil Richardson, 1985), 21–22.

165. MO file 1095, pp. 14–17; file 1569, p. 30.

166. Mayer, *Sociology of Film*, 182–83.

167. Ibid., 197–98. Mayer, *British Cinemas*, 140–41.

168. Mayer, *Sociology of Film*, 183.

169. Mayer, *British Cinemas*, 118–19.
170. Mayer, *Sociology of Film*, 258.
171. Mayer, *British Cinemas*, 33, 38, 57, 66–70, 74, 122.
172. Herbert Hodge, *A Cockney on Main Street* (London: Michael Joseph, 1945), 33–34, 59–61, 65–66, 70, 78–87, 117.
173. Orwell, "Boys' Weeklies," 478–79.
174. Bryan Forbes, *Notes for a Life* (London: Collins, 1974), 28–29, 37–38.
175. Scannell, *Drums of Morning*, 36–37, 73–74, 77–78.
176. Sharman, *Nothing to Steal*, 85.
177. Alf Strange, *Me Dad's the Village Blacksmith* (Denbigh: Gee & Son, 1983), 18, 155.
178. Perry, untitled TS, p. 27.
179. G. K. Evans, *Public Opinion on Colonial Affairs* (Social Survey, n.s. 119, June 1948), 5, 7, 10, 19, 23.
180. MO file 3046, pp. 11–18.

Chapter Eleven: **A Mongrel Library**

1. Richard Hoggart, in Goldman, *Breakthrough*, 95–103.
2. Hoggart, *Sort of Clowning*, 129–30, 134–35, 144. Richard Hoggart, *An Imagined Life* (London: Chatto & Windus, 1992), 89–98, 224–26, 240–42.
3. Hayden White, "Method and Ideology in Intellectual History: The Case of Henry Adams," in Dominick LaCapra and Steven L. Kaplan, eds., *Modern European Intellectual History: Reappraisals and New Perspectives* (Ithaca, NY: Cornell University Press, 1982), 307–8.
4. Burke, *Bloomsbury*, 312–13.
5. John Johnson, "How I Got On: Life Stories by the Labour MPs," *Pearson's Weekly* (10 May 1906): 787.
6. Steel, *Ditcher's Row*, 111.
7. Salmon, *Juvenile Literature*, 189–192. Patrick A. Dunae, "Penny Dreadfuls: Late Nineteenth-Century Boys' Literature and Crime," *Victorian Studies* 22 (1979): 133–50.
8. Okey, *Basketful of Memories*, 20–22.
9. J. H. Howard, *Winding Lanes* (Caernarvon: Calvinistic Methodist Printing Works, [1938]), 27–30.
10. Snell, *Men, Movements, and Myself*, 15.
11. Alfred Cox, *Among the Doctors* (London: Christopher Johnson, 1950), 17.
12. Smillie, *Life for Labour*, 15.
13. Frederick Willis, *101 Jubilee Road: A Book of London Yesterdays* (London: Phoenix House, 1948), 109–10.
14. Paton, *Proletarian Pilgrimage*, 45–46.
15. Frost, *Reminiscences*, 176–79, 256–61. Frost, *Forty Years' Recollections*, 77–95, 317–24.
16. Southgate, *That's the Way It Was*, 57–58.
17. Acorn, *One of the Multitude*, 49–50.
18. Blatchford, *Book About Books*, 140–52.
19. Blatchford, *Favourite Books*, 21–28.
20. Howard Spring, *In the Meantime* (London: Constable, 1942), 54.
21. Spring, *Heaven*, 93–94.
22. One man explained his choice of J. G. Brandon's *Death in Downing Street* in those terms: "Well, it's written snappy, you see. ... Modern writers may not be up to the standard of the old writers, Dickens, Thackeray and Scott, but they're snappy—they're quick

reading." As another said of a Nicholas Blake novel, "You don't have to have a lot of concentration to read these books." MO file 48, p. 20; see also file 2018, pp. 83–91.

23. Holt, *Japanese Parasol*, 110–17; Holt, *I Haven't Unpacked*, 46, 52; William Holt, *I Still Haven't Unpacked* (London: George G. Harrap, 1953), 13, 19–20.
24. Brierley, *Home Memories*, 32.
25. Stamper, *So Long Ago*, 162, 213–14.
26. Bourdieu, *Distinction*, 323–28.
27. [Freeman], *Equipment of the Workers*, 59.
28. Goring, untitled MS, p. 114.
29. Neil Bell, *My Writing Life* (London: Alvin Redman, 1955), 14–15.
30. Donnelly, *Yellow Rock*, 215.
31. George Smith, *The Autobiography of George Smith, LL.D. 1800–1868* (London: Dangerfield Printing Co., 1923), 15–16, 40.
32. Thomas Wood, "Methodism in Bingley Over 130 Years Ago," *Keighley News* (10 March 1956): 5, (24 March 1956): 9.
33. Ralph Whitlock, *A Family and a Village* (London: John Baker, 1969), 131–32.
34. Chaplin, *Tree with Rosy Apples*, 87.
35. Stapleton, *Threshold*, 230–31.
36. James Williams, *Give Me Yesterday* (Gwasg Gomer: J. D. Lewis & Sons, 1971), 26–27, 138–45.
37. Adams, *Social Atom*, 101.
38. Acorn, *One of the Multitude*, 49–50.
39. Rogers, *Labour, Life and Literature*, 11.
40. Davies, *North Country Bred*, 62.
41. Burton, *There Was a Young Man*, 95–97.
42. Wild, *Wild Oats*, 2, 10–12.
43. George Howell, draft autobiography, vol. B/b/4, pp. 3–5.
44. Muir, *Story and the Fable*, 83–91.
45. Cardus, *Second Innings*, 24–25, 48–71.
46. Todd, *Snakes and Ladders*, 107–109.
47. Derek Davies, in Goldman, *Breakthrough*, 29–32.
48. Charles Chaplin, *My Autobiography* (New York: Simon & Schuster, 1964), 48–49, 123, 134, 247–49, 441. David Robinson, *Chaplin: His Life and Art* (London: Collins, 1985), 235.
49. Blishen, *Right Soft Lot*, 164.
50. Winifred Foley, *A Child in the Forest* (London: British Broadcasting Corporation, 1974), 51–52.
51. Nellie Carbis, *Nellie Carbis Looks Back* (Kendal: Titus Wilson & Son, 1978), 30–31. Lily Need, "Struggling Manor," Keele University, p. 13. Newberry, *Bradford Mill Girl*, 37.
52. Winifred M. Renshaw, *An Ordinary Life: Memories of a Balby Childhood* (Doncaster: Doncaster Library Service, 1984), ch. 25.
53. Muriel Box, *Odd Woman Out* (London: Leslie Frewin, 1974), 42.
54. Ashby, *Ashby of Tysoe*, 242.
55. Burnham, *Dooms of Love*, 200–201, 212.
56. Pat Phoenix, *All My Burning Bridges* (London: Arlington, 1974), 19–20.
57. Wharton, *GI War Bride*, 81–82.
58. Lee, *Great Journey*, 17.
59. Lee, *Life with Nye*, 39.
60. Angela Rodaway, *A London Childhood* (London: B. T. Batsford, 1960), 82–83.

61. Kenney, *Memories of a Militant*, 1.
62. Jenkinson, *What Do Boys and Girls Read?*, 16, 174, 217.
63. Salmon, *Juvenile Literature*, 21–31.
64. Todd, *Snakes and Ladder*, 42–43.
65. "What Children Read," *Co-Partnership* (April 1911): 55.
66. Barbara Sicherman, "Sense and Sensibility: A Case Study of Women's Reading in Late-Victorian America," in Cathy N. Davidson, ed., *Reading in America* (Baltimore: Johns Hopkins University Press, 1989).
67. McAleer, *Popular Reading*, 197–99.
68. Orwell, "Boys' Weeklies," 471–72.
69. Mary Cadogan, *Frank Richards: The Chap Behind the Chums* (New York: Viking, 1988), 71–85.
70. Laqueur, *Religion and Respectability*, 209.
71. Michael Pickering, "White Skin, Black Masks: 'Nigger' Minstrelsy in Victorian England," in J. S. Bratton, ed., *Music Hall: Performance and Style* (Milton Keynes: Open University Press, 1986), 70–91. See also George F. Rehin, "Harlequin Jim Crow: Continuity and Convergence in Blackface Clowning," *Journal of Popular Culture* 9 (Winter 1975): 682–701.
72. Joseph Arch, *Joseph Arch: The Story of His Life* (London: Hutchinson, 1898), 29.
73. Mayhew, *London Labour*, 3:190–91.
74. Joseph Burgess, *A Potential Poet?* (Ilford: Burgess Publications, 1927), 72.
75. Philip S. Foner, *British Labor and the American Civil War* (New York and London: Holmes & Meier, 1981).
76. George Cooper, *The Story of George Cooper—Stockport's Last Town Crier 1824–1895* (n.p.: [1975]), 28.
77. Baggs, "Miners' Libraries," 363, 384.
78. Shaw, *When I Was a Child*, 65. Roger Langdon, *The Life of Roger Langdon* (London: Elliot Stock, 1909), 33–34. Hampson, "Reminiscences of 'Casey,'" 12.
79. Samuel Fielden, "Autobiography of Samuel Fielden," in *The Autobiographies of the Haymarket Martyrs*, ed. Philip S. Foner (New York: Humanities Press, 1969), 142.
80. Gallacher, *Rise Like Lions*, 90. Crawfurd, TS autobiography, p. 10.
81. Bess and Ralph Anstis, eds., *The Diary of a Working Man 1872–1873: Bill Williams in the Forest of Dean* (Stroud: Alan Sutton, 1994), entry for 18 December 1872, p. 85.
82. Anonymous, *Narrow Waters: The First Volume of the Life and Thoughts of a Common Man* (London: William Hodge, 1935), 67–68. For a similar reaction, see Foley, *Child in the Forest*, 181.
83. Bryson, *Look Back in Wonder*, 71.
84. George Clifton Hughes, "Shut the Mountain Gate," BUL, pp. 124–25.
85. Rolph, *Living Twice*, 12–13, 37–39.
86. Leslie Paul, *The Living Hedge* (London: Faber and Faber, 1946), 104–6.
87. William Lax, *Lax: His Book* (London: Epworth, 1937), 91–94.
88. Elton, *Ramsay MacDonald*, 29. See also Roberts, *Ragged Schooling*, 114; and James Spenser, *Limey Breaks In* (London: Longmans, Green & Co., 1934), 18–20.
89. Fagan, "Autobiography," pp. 18–19.
90. Bustin, "My Two Square Miles of London," pp. 74–75.
91. Coombes, *These Poor Hands*, 139–40.
92. Patrick McLoughlin, *The Johnson Street Bullies* (Bognor Regis: New Horizons, 1980), 118–21.
93. Battye, *Little Nut Tree*, 75.
94. Mayer, *British Cinemas*, 184.

95. Mayer, *Sociology of Film*, 248–49.
96. Douglas A. Lorimer, *Colour, Class and the Victorians: English Attitudes to the Negro in the Mid-Nineteenth Century* (Leicester: Leicester University Press, 1978), ch. 3. James D. Young, *Socialism and the English Working Class: A History of English Labour 1883–1939* (New York: Harvester Wheatsheaf, 1989), chs. 2, 6.
97. Waters, *Socialists and Popular Culture*, esp. ch. 6.
98. B. L. Coombes, *Miners Day* (Harmondsworth: Penguin, 1945), 40.
99. John Eldridge, Jenny Kitzinger, and Kevin Williams sum up some of these criticisms in *The Mass Media and Power in Modern Britain*, 155–59.
100. Thompson, *Lark Rise*, 252–53.
101. Beer, *Mrs. Beer's House*, 100–1, 104–15, 194–96.
102. Todd, *Snakes and Ladders*, 43–44, 48.
103. Michael R. Booth, *Theatre in the Victorian Age* (Cambridge: Cambridge University Press, 1991), 163–67.
104. Leslie Halward, *Let Me Tell You* (London: Michael Joseph, 1938), 79–80.
105. Mayer, *Sociology of Film*, 231, 234, 253–54.
106. Mayer, *British Cinemas*, 72. See also Mayer, *Sociology of Film*, 236.
107. Mayer, *British Cinemas*, 32–33.
108. Ibid., 116; Mayer, *Sociology of Film*, 184–85.
109. Mayer, *Sociology of Film*, 231. See also Mayer, *British Cinemas*, 81–82.
110. Mayer, *Sociology of Film*, 227, 235. Mayer, *British Cinemas*, 38.
111. Mayer, *Sociology of Film*, 259.
112. Mayer, *British Cinemas*, 27, 36, 52–53, 67.
113. Mayer, *Sociology of Film*, 225–26.
114. Ibid., 248–50; see also 257–58.
115. LeMahieu, *Culture for Democracy*, 119–20, 155–56.
116. Jacob Holkinson, "The Life of Jacob Holkinson, Tailor and Poet," *Saturday Evening Commonwealth* (Glasgow), (31 January 1857): 3.
117. Smith, *Curiosities of London Life*, 122.
118. Charles Manby Smith, *The Little World of London* (London: Arthur Hall, Virtue, 1857), 9–10.
119. Carter, *Memoirs*, 18–21, 26–28, 79–82, 145.

Chapter Twelve: **What Was Leonard Bast Really Like?**

1. The cartoon appeared in the 4 December 1883 issue, and is reproduced in Marsh, *Word Crimes*, 130.
2. Collyer, *Memories*, 23–24.
3. John Carey, *The Intellectuals and the Masses: Pride and Prejudice among the Literary Intelligentsia, 1880–1939* (London: Faber and Faber, 1992), chs. 1–2.
4. Mary Douglas and Baron Isherwood, *The World of Goods* (New York: Basic Books, 1979), 180–81.
5. Charles Knight, introduction to Carter, *Memoirs*, viii–ix.
6. Douglas and Isherwood, *Goods*, 76–80, 89.
7. Jack Goody, introduction to *Literacy in Traditional Societies* (Cambridge: Cambridge University Press, 1968), 11–20.
8. K. G. Ghurye, *Preservation of Learned Tradition in India* (Bombay: Popular Book Depot, 1950), 24–25.

9. Defoe, *Crusoe*, 216–17.
10. Lawrence Stone, "Literacy and Education in England 1640–1900," *Past and Present* 42 (February 1969): 73.
11. Gifford, *Memoir*, 7, 13–19.
12. Smith, *Autobiography*, 14.
13. Alan Richardson, *Literature, Education, and Romanticism: Reading as Social Practice, 1780–1832* (Cambridge: Cambridge University Press, 1994), 95–103, 124, 267–70.
14. Patrick Brantlinger, *The Reading Lesson: The Threat of Mass Literacy in Nineteenth-Century British Fiction* (Bloomington: Indiana University Press, 1998).
15. Craik, *Pursuit of Knowledge*, 2:3.
16. P. J. Keating, *The Working Classes in Victorian Fiction* (London: Routledge & Kegan Paul, 1971), 26–28.
17. Hugh Miller, "Literature of the People," in *Essays*, 3rd edn. (Edinburgh: William P. Nimmo, 1870), 291–99.
18. John Younger, *The Light of the Week* (London: Partridge & Oakley, 1849), v, xi.
19. Hardy, *Jude the Obscure*, 87, 116–21, 128–29.
20. Begbie, *Living Water*, 119.
21. A. L. Rowse, *A Cornish Childhood* (New York: Clarkson N. Potter, 1979), 208–9.
22. Pritchett, *Cab at the Door*, 107, 112–16.
23. Anne Tibble, *One Woman's Story* (London: Peter Owen, 1976), 17, 27–29, 66, 129.
24. Stamper, *So Long Ago*, 29–30, 42, 109–12, 152–54, 161–62, 169–71.
25. Willis, *Tom Mix*, 92–93, 110 152–53.
26. Virginia Woolf, "Introductory Letter," in *Life as We Have Known It*, xv, xxxviii–xxxix.
27. Mrs. Garrett, in *Life as We Have Known It*, 123–24.
28. Quentin Bell, *Virginia Woolf* (New York: Harcourt Brace Jovanovich, 1972), 2:205.
29. Leonard Woolf, *Growing: An Autobiography of the Years 1904 to 1911* (New York: Harcourt Brace Jovanovich, 1975), 63–66. For an even more contemptuous treatment of Board school graduates, see his short story "Pearls and Swine," reprinted in *A Bloomsbury Group Reader*, ed. S. P. Rosenbaum (Oxford and Cambridge, MA: Basil Blackwell, 1993), 34–36.
30. E. M. Forster, *Howards End* (London: Edward Arnold, 1973), ch. 6.
31. Ibid., 142.
32. Ibid., 320.
33. Ibid., 146.
34. Ibid., 336.
35. Forster to G. H. Ludolf, 16 July 1919, in *Selected Letters of E. M. Forster* (Cambridge, MA: Harvard University Press, 1983–85), 1:305–6.
36. Forster to Florence Barger, 10 November 1920, in *Selected Letters of E. M. Forster*, 1:319.
37. Nicola Beauman, *Morgan: A Biography of E. M. Forster* (London: Hodder & Stoughton, 1993), 345–46.
38. P. N. Furbank, *E. M. Forster: A Life* (New York: Harcourt Brace Jovanovich, 1977–78), 2:159.
39. Beauman, *Morgan*, 53.
40. Forster, *Howards End*, 47–48.
41. W. J. Brown, *So Far ...* (London: George Allen & Unwin, 1943), 27–28.
42. Armstrong, *Pilgrimage from Nenthead*, 156–64.
43. Haw, *Will Crooks*, 22–23, 176.
44. Brockway, *Socialism over Sixty Years*, 88–89.
45. George, *From Mill Boy to Minister*, 28–29.
46. Hodgkinson, *Sent to Coventry*, 4–5, 24.

47. Harry Brearley, *Knotted String: Autobiography of a Steel-Maker* (London: Longmans, Green, 1941), 50.

48. Dataller, "Yorkshire Lad," p. 29.

49. Rushton, *My Life*, frontispiece.

50. W. J. Brown, *I Meet America* (London: George Routledge & Sons, 1942), 51, 138.

51. Peter D. McDonald, *British Literary Culture and Publishing Practice 1880–1914* (Cambridge: Cambridge University Press, 1997), 99–100.

52. Brown, *So Far*, 43–46.

53. Ibid., 49–55.

54. Anonymous, *Narrow Waters*, 42, 61, 64–65, 79–80.

55. Pritchett, *Cab at the Door*, 193–95.

56. Joseph Toole, *Fighting through Life* (London: Rich & Cowan, 1935), 10, 48–50, 66–69, 85–86; ch. 6.

57. Cardus, *Autobiography*, 37–58.

58. Cardus, *Second Innings*, 127–36.

59. Thomas Burke, *The Real East End* (London: Constable, 1932), 7–13.

60. Leavis, *Fiction and the Reading Public*, 210.

61. William Lax, *Adventure in Poplar* (London: Epworth, 1933), 16.

62. Burke, *Out and About*, 124–33.

63. Pritchett, *Cab at the Door*, 184.

64. Lewis, *Soho Address*, 129.

65. Garratt, *Man in the Street*, 263–64, 274–76.

66. Rogers, *Labour, Life and Literature*, 43–46, 55–57, 142–45, 156; ch. 8.

67. William Margrie, *A Cockney's Pilgrimage in Search of Truth* (London: Watts & Co., 1927), 58–59.

68. Jackson, TS Autobiography, pp. 18–19.

69. Davies, North Country Bred, 83–89.

70. Bold, "Long and the Short of It" (1978), pp. 1, 14–16, 22–23, 36, 42–43.

71. Margaret Penn, *The Foolish Virgin* (London: Jonathan Cape, 1951).

72. Ring, *Up the Cockneys!*, foreword and pp. 32, 38, 41–42, 63–64, 127–31, 162.

73. Carey, *Intellectuals and Masses*, ch. 3.

74. Matthew Arnold, *Friendship's Garland*, in *Complete Prose Works*, 5:21–22.

75. Pritchett, *Cab at the Door*, 183–84.

76. Thomas Burke, *The Outer Circle: Rambles in Remote London* (London: George Allen & Unwin, 1921), 13–14.

77. Ibid., 59–64.

78. Richard Church, *Over the Bridge* (New York: E. P. Dutton, 1956), 18–19, 74, 198.

79. Ibid., 207–21, 229–31.

80. Richard Church, *The Golden Sovereign* (London: Heinemann, 1957), 9–10, 13–14, 27, 73, 91–92, 106–10, 124–25, 168–71, 187–94, 202–203, 232–34. Richard Church, *The Voyage Home* (London: Heinemann, 1964), 66–71, 80–81, 88, 166, 171, 209–11.

81. H. E. Bates, *The Vanished World* (London: Michael Joseph, 1969), 143–48.

82. G. Launders, "Reminiscences of Old Grimesthorpe" (1938), Sheffield Central Library, p. 22. John Miles Thomas, *Looking Back: A Childhood in Saint David's Eighty Years Ago* (Camarthen: privately published, 1977), 62.

83. Macadam, *Macadam Road*, 18–19, 24–28, 32–34, 87–88.

84. Forster, *Howards End*, 142.

85. Peter Keating, *The Haunted Study: A Social History of the English Novel, 1875–1914* (London: Secker & Warburg, 1989), 34.

86. W. J. Reader, *Professional Men: The Rise of the Professional Classes in Nineteenth-Century*

England (New York: Basic Books, 1966), 147, 211.

87. Forster, *Howards End*, 60.
88. Patterson, *Vagabondage*, 329–30, 351.
89. Thomas Burke, *Son of London* (London: Herbert Jenkins, 1946), 156–70.
90. Patrick MacGill, *Children of the Dead End* (London: Herbert Jenkins, 1914), 15–16, 136–40, 227–29, 271–73.
91. Thompson, *Lancashire for Me*, 26, 35.
92. Clough, *Public Eye*, 11–14.
93. Allen Clarke, "The 'Good Old Days' When Children Were Bred for the Factories," "Sad End to Works of Youthful Poet," "Early Endeavours to Join the Happy Slaves of the Press," "Drama, Romance, and the Moon of My Delight," "Flirting, Frolics, and Visions on Manhood's Threshold," *Liverpool Weekly Post* (21 April 1934): 2, (28 April 1934): 2, (16 June 1934): 2, (14 July 1934): 2, (21 July 1934): 2.
94. Bell, *Writing Life*, 25–26, 30–43, 253–54.
95. Coppard, *It's Me, O Lord!*, 39–40, 60–63, 66, 71–72, 84–85, 121–22, 131–32, 153–58, 161–69, 176, 185, 239.
96. Spring, *Heaven*, 11–12, 16, 23, 51.
97. Spring, *Meantime*, 129–31.
98. Spring, *Heaven*, 101–107.
99. Spring, *Meantime*, 133–36, 161–64.
100. Smith, *Bevan and South Wales*, 178, 190, 194. Foot, *Bevan*, 1:36–37, 56, 59–63, 89–90.
101. José Enrique Rodó, *Ariel*, trans. F. J. Stimson (Boston: Houghton Mifflin, 1922), 68–69, 112–13, 117.
102. John Campbell, *Aneurin Bevan and the Mirage of British Socialism* (New York: Norton, 1987), 63–71, 265.
103. Roger Dataller, *From a Pitman's Note Book* (New York: Dial Press, 1925), 12, 91–92, 131, 135–36.
104. Dataller, *Oxford into Coalfield*, 26, 35–36.
105. Ibid., 76.
106. Ibid., 197–200. Dataller, "Yorkshire Lad," pp. 133–34.
107. Dataller, "Self Expression in the Student," 254–56.
108. Roger Dataller, *The Plain Man and the Novel* (London: Thomas Nelson & Sons, 1940), 154–57, 170–71.
109. Joyce Piell Wexler, *Who Paid for Modernism?: Art, Money, and the Fiction of Conrad, Joyce, and Lawrence* (Fayetteville: University of Arkansas Press, 1997), esp. introduction, ch. 1, and p. 133.
110. Edward Short, *I Knew My Place* (London: Macdonald, 1983), 88–91.
111. Barclay, *Memoirs and Medleys*, 55–64, 69–74.
112. Muir, *Story and the Fable*, 119–24, 129–53, 166–67, 170–74, 180.
113. [Edward Moore], *We Moderns* (London: George Allen & Unwin, 1918), 156, 160–61, 172, 242, 246.
114. Willis, *Leonard and Virginia Woolf as Publishers*, 118–19, 137–38.
115. Paton, *Proletarian Pilgrimage*, 212–13.
116. Hugh MacDiarmid, *Lucky Poet: A Self-Study in Literature and Political Ideas* (London: Methuen, 1943), vi, xvii–xx, 4, 29, 39–44, 50, 76–78, 103–104, 137–38, 236–37, 349, 423. Alan Bold, *MacDiarmid* (London: John Murray, 1998), 46–50, 65, 144–47, 230, 238, 245, 252, 260–61, 266, 409–11.
117. For example, Ross McKibbin, *Classes and Cultures: England 1918–1951* (Oxford: Oxford University Press, 1998), 477–88. But for an exceptionally perceptive and sympathetic

treament of its American counterpart, see Joan Shelley Rubin, *The Making of Middlebrow Culture* (Chapel Hill: University of North Carolina Press, 1992).

118. In her *Collected Essays* (New York: Harcourt, Brace & World, 1967), 2:196–203.

119. For a treatment of cultural triage see David Grimsted, "Books and Culture: Canned, Canonized, and Neglected," *Proceedings of the American Antiquarian Society* 94 (1984): 297–335.

120. Patrick Brantlinger describes the fervent and pervasive intellectual hostility toward this stratum of culture in *Bread and Circuses: Theories of Mass Culture as Social Decay* (Ithaca, NY and London: Cornell University Press, 1983).

121. Garratt, *Man in the Street*, 291–92, 298–302.

122. Leavis, *Fiction and the Reading Public*, 85.

123. Geoffrey Crossick, "The Emergence of the Lower Middle Class in Britain: A Discussion," Hugh McLeod, "White Collar Values and the Role of Religion," and G. L. Anderson, "The Social Economy of Late-Victorian Clerks," in *The Lower Middle Class in Britain 1870–1914*, ed. Crossick (London: Croom Helm, 1977), 19, 35–37, 84, 113–33. See also Michael Savage, "Career Mobility and Class Formation: British Banking Workers and the Lower Middle Classes," in *Building European Society: Occupational Change and Social Mobility in Europe 1840–1940*, ed. Andrew Miles and David Vincent (Manchester: Manchester University Press, 1993), 196–216.

124. T. R. Gourvish, "The Standard of Living," in *The Edwardian Age: Conflict and Stability 1900–1914*, ed., Alan O'Day (London: Macmillan, 1979), 23–24.

125. Bell, *Virginia Woolf*, 2:39.

126. Richard H. Brodhead, *The School of Hawthorne* (New York: Oxford University Press, 1986), 5.

127. Ronald Schuchard, "T. S. Eliot as an Extension Lecturer, 1916–1919," *Review of English Studies* n. s. 25 (1974): 163–73, 292–304.

128. Cardus, *Second Innings*, 242.

129. Cardus, *Autobiography*, 16, 256–60.

130. Church, *Bridge*, 226–27.

131. Ezra Pound, "The New Sculpture," *Egoist* 1 (16 February 1914): 68.

132. Timothy Materer, "Make It Sell! Ezra Pound Advertises Modernism," and Leonard Diepeveen, "'I Can Have More Than Enough Power to Satisfy Me': T. S. Eliot's Construction of His Audience," in *Marketing Modernisms: Self-Promotion, Canonization, and Rereading*, ed. Kevin J. H. Dettmar and Stephen Watt (Ann Arbor: University of Michigan Press, 1996).

133. Michael H. Levenson, *A Genealogy of Modernism: A Study of English Literary Doctrine 1908–1922* (Cambridge: Cambridge University Press, 1984), 146–64.

134. Woolf, "Middlebrow," 202.

135. "The Third Programme," 3 February 1947, BBC R9/9/11/LR/47/161.

136. MO file 3105, p. 19. Another survey in the mid-1950s found that 35 percent of Third Programme listeners were working-class: see J. R. Williams, "Notes and Comments," *Highway* 48 (November 1956): 3–4.

137. Kate Whitehead, *The Third Programme: A Literary History* (Oxford: Clarendon Press: 1989), 14–18, 24–29, 48–62, ch. 11.

138. Bermant, *Coming Home*, 116–17.

139. Harold Rosenberg, "Everyman a Professional," in *The Tradition of the New* (New York: Horizon, 1959), 58–73.

140. Beauman, *Morgan*, 336.

Chapter Thirteen: **Down and Out in Bloomsbury**

1. Maurice Barrès, *Le Quartier Latin: Ces messieurs—ces dames* (Paris: C. Dalou, 1888), 13.
2. Jerrold Seigel, *Bohemian Paris* (New York: Viking, 1986), ch. 1.
3. Cameron, *Rustle of Spring*, 25, 122–27, 139, 156–62, 169, 180–83, 186–89, 247–61, 278–84.
4. Todd, *Snakes and Ladders*, 133–34, 139–42, 145–55.
5. Carter, *Memoirs*, 19. Laqueur, *Religion and Respectability*, 170–71.
6. Rodaway, *London Childhood*, 91–92, 96–98.
7. Ibid., 114, 128–29, 152–58.
8. Benney, *Low Company*, 86, 110–16, 122–28, 262–64, 272–74, 288–89, 297, 312–14.
9. Thompson, *Hyde Park Orator*, 123.
10. Michael Murphy explores the relationship between modernism and advertising in "'One Hundred Per Cent Bohemia': Pop Decadence and the Aestheticization of Commodity in the Rise of the Slicks," in *Marketing Modernisms*, ed. Dettmar and Watt, esp. pp. 85–86.
11. Ethel Mannin, *Young in the Twenties* (London: Hutchinson, 1971), 17.
12. J. E. Morpurgo, *Allen Lane: King Penguin* (London: Hutchinson, 1980), 56–57, 110, 132–34.
13. Mannin, *Confessions*, 14–15, 45–49.
14. Ibid., 230–32.
15. Mannin, *Twenties*, 101.
16. Andy Croft, "Ethel Mannin: The Red Rose of Love and the Red Flower of Liberty," in *Rediscovering Forgotten Radicals: British Women Writers, 1889–1939*, ed. Angela Ingram and Daphne Patai, (Chapel Hill: University of North Carolina Press, 1993), 205–25.
17. Mannin, *Confessions*, 73, 85, 90–92. Mannin, *Twenties*, 53, 55, 59.
18. Ethel Mannin, *Privileged Spectator* (London: Jarrolds, 1939), 72–73, 309–11, 321.
19. Frederick Willis, *A Book of London Yesterdays* (London: Phoenix House, 1960), 195–97.
20. Ibid., 179–81.
21. Douglas and Isherwood, *Goods*, 79, 95.
22. Dudley Barker, *G. K. Chesterton* (New York: Stein & Day, 1975), 71–76.
23. Willis, *London Yesterdays* (1960), 195.
24. Thomas Burke, *Nights in Town: A London Autobiography* (London: George Allen & Unwin, 1915), 253–54, 364–72.
25. Thomas Burke, *The London Spy* (New York: George H. Doran, 1922), ch. 11.
26. Burke, *Nights in Town*, 340–44.
27. Burke, *Real East End*, 5.
28. Burke, *Bloomsbury*, 39–47, 211–15.
29. Even George Scott, who won a scholarship to Oxford and achieved "affluence" in the 1950s, found himself crammed in a three-room flat with his wife and two children, writing on a washing machine in a kitchen laced with boiler fumes: "He has, after all, a room of his own." Scott, *Time and Place*, 220.
30. Goldman, *East End My Cradle*, chs. 22–24, 26, 28.
31. Pritchett, *Cab at the Door*, 14–16, 102–107, 111, 124–27, 195–96, 234.
32. Paul, *First Love*, 33, 51–55, 61–62.
33. No new edition of any work by Jefferies was published between 1910 and 1933. George Miller and Hugoe Matthews, *Richard Jefferies: A Bibliographical Study* (Aldershot: Scolar, 1993), sections B and C.
34. Paul, *First Love*, 38–39, 88, 94, 98–99.
35. The existence of such guerrilla scout troops is confirmed by Roberts, *A Ragged Schooling*, 94–95.

36. Leslie Paul, *Angry Young Man* (London: Faber and Faber, 1951), 50–60. See also Mark Drakeford, *Social Movements and Their Supporters: The Green Shirts in England* (Basingstoke: Macmillan, 1997), chs. 2–4.

37. Paul, *Living Hedge*, 155.

38. Paul, *First Love*, 63–73, 87. Paul, *Angry Young Man*, 62–74, 121–25.

39. John Springhall, *Youth, Empire and Society: British Youth Movements 1883–1940* (London: Croom Helm, 1977), ch. 7, 134.

40. Paul, *Angry Young Man*, 203–206, 292–93, 296.

41. Guy Hunter, "Vocation and Culture—A Suggestion," *Adult Eucation* 25 (Summer 1952): 13.

42. Barton, *Two Lamps in Our Street*, 83–84, 91, 125–31.

43. Lee, *Great Journey*, 96–97.

44. Bates, *Vanished World*, 156–57.

45. Ethel Mannin, *Brief Voices: A Writer's Story* (London: Hutchinson, 1959), 200.

46. Morrison, *Herbert Morrison*, 18–20, 24–29, 142–43.

47. Jack Dash, *Good Morning, Brothers!* (London: Lawrence & Wishart, 1969), 64–66, 78–79, 165.

48. Kops, *World is a Wedding*, 34–35, 92–93, 104, 107, 110–11, 114.

49. Ibid., 15, 29, 179–88.

50. "Norwegian Wood," in *The Beatles Lyrics Illustrated* (New York: Dell, 1975), 87.

51. Kops, *World is a Wedding*, 260.

52. Ibid., 232–35.

53. Aldous Huxley, "Selected Snobberies," in *Music at Night and Other Essays* (Freeport, NY: Books for Libraries Press, 1970), 197–202.

54. Bourdieu, *Distinction*, 84–85, 96.

55. Ibid., 229. Douglas and Isherwood, *Goods*, 198–203.

56. Frederick C. Wigby, *A Shilling, a Shutknife and a Piece of String* (Wymondham: Geo. R. Reeve, 1984), 120–24.

57. Martin Vander Weyer, "An Act of Creation," in *The World in 1999* (London: The Economist Publications, 1998), 68–69.

58. Glyn Hughes, *Millstone Grit* (Newton Abbot: Readers Union, 1975), 21–22, 100–101, 134–39.

59. Justin Lewis, *Art, Culture, and Enterprise: The Politics of Art and the Cultural Industries* (London and New York: Routledge, 1990), 14–20, 36–40, 77, 114–15.

60. This trend may be more advanced in the United States, where it was recently analyzed by David Brooks in *Bobos in Paradise: The New Upper Class and How They Got There* (New York: Simon & Schuster, 2000). Brooks is a sharp and perceptive journalist, and his conclusions deserve to be tested by more rigorous sociological methods.

Index